Building Trusted Data Platforms with Azure Databricks and GenAI

Second Edition

A Hands-On Guide to Creating Governed Data Products in a Lakehouse

Manoj Kukreja

<packt>

Building Trusted Data Platforms with Azure Databricks and GenAI

Second Edition

Portfolio Director: Sunith Shetty
Relationship Lead: Puneet Kaur
Project Manager: Shashank Desai and Aniket Shetty
Content Engineer: Saba Umme Salma
Technical Editor: Shweta Amale
Copy Editor: Saba Umme Salma
Indexer: Pratik Shirodkar
Proofreader: Saba Umme Salma
Production Designer: Prashant Ghare
Growth Lead: Varun Nair

First published: October 2021
Second edition: July 2026

Production reference: 1100726

Published by Packt Publishing Ltd.
Grosvenor House
11 St Paul's Square
Birmingham
B3 1RB, UK.

ISBN 978-1-80667-977-5
`www.packtpub.com`

To my greatest friend, Roopika —

May love and devotion continue to illuminate your journey,

just as your presence has illuminated mine.

To my children, Shagun, Saesha, and Chirag —

"Svadharme nidhanam śreyaḥ..."

The Bhagavad Gita reminds us that one's own path, walked with sincerity, is the truest strength.

Walk your paths with grace, letting each act of kindness become your purest karma.

And to those who have moved beyond this world —

May your eternal light remain with us,

in every breath, every step,

and every act of dharma we strive to uphold.

Foreword

I first met Manoj in my role as VP Development at Versa Systems Inc. (2000). We were engaged in navigating the complexities of developing and deploying intricate, secure, dependable, and adaptable data platforms and applications to support federal and regional government regulatory systems. Even in that era, it was immediately evident to me that Manoj embodied a unique combination of technical capacity with a persistent (one might say burning) curiosity that drove him to continue learning and exploring. Manoj stood out because he consistently turned complex, evolving technologies into secure, production-grade platforms in highly regulated environments.

In the intervening years, that same blend of intense curiosity and practical application mindset has led Manoj on a continuous journey of learning about and, more importantly, applying ever more rapidly evolving concepts and tools. As a consequence, his current expertise in Data Engineering, Data Governance, integration of AI, IT security, and provision of education (as both a teacher and author) is widely recognized.

This is why "Building Trusted Data Platforms with Azure Databricks and GenAI" is a vital addition to your bookshelf. It bridges the gap between just reading about and mastering underlying architectures. In this book, Manoj provides the reader with the practical, battle-tested insights required to build robust solutions. Following the proven methods in the book, you will be able to design, implement, and operate a trusted data platform that executives, auditors, and engineers can all rely on.

Whether you are a hands-on practitioner (data/analytics/ML engineers; data steward) or a leader shaping data strategy (heads or directors of data engineering, analytics, BI, data platforms, machine learning, AI), there is value here. Keep this book close to your workstation. You are unlikely to read it once and shelve it.

John Trainor

Owner and President,

Touchstone Technologies Inc.

Contributors

About the author

Manoj Kukreja is a Cloud Data Architect with deep expertise in data engineering, data governance, and modern cloud platforms. Over a career spanning enterprise strategy, large-scale architectures, governance frameworks, and ML/AI adoption, he has led transformative initiatives that enable organizations to build modern, trusted, secure, and scalable data ecosystems. Manoj is widely recognized for combining technical rigor with a strong foundation in information security, supported by industry certifications across AWS, Google Cloud, Azure, and CISSP. A long-time mentor and active contributor to the technology community, he brings a practitioner's clarity and a strategist's vision to the rapidly evolving world of data.

About the technical implementation expert

Mouli Saluja is a Data Engineer specializing in cloud-native data platforms on Microsoft Azure, with hands-on experience designing and deploying production-grade batch and streaming pipelines. Alongside her core engineering work, she actively explores the rapidly evolving GenAI landscape, including building voice-enabled agents as part of her freelance projects. Mouli is also an active researcher, with published work spanning Industry 5.0, biometric blood-group detection using fingerprint analysis, and Continual Learning in Artificial Neural Networks—her most recent research focusing on mitigating catastrophic forgetting in healthcare AI systems.

About the reviewers

Shruti Worlikar is a Senior Manager of Solutions Architecture at Amazon Web Services, leading a worldwide team of specialist architects focused on cloud analytics, data engineering, and AI/ML. She is the author of the Amazon Redshift Cookbook (Packt Publishing, 2021 & 2025). She has published peer-reviewed research in international journals on topics including real-time analytics, fraud detection, and healthcare monitoring systems. Shruti is an active speaker at industry conferences and has delivered keynotes at international academic conferences. She holds a leadership role with Women in Big Data, a global community for advancing women in data and AI.

Sivakumar Mahalingam is a Software Architect with over 15 years of experience in designing and delivering enterprise-scale data, analytics, and AI solutions. He has extensive expertise in data engineering, cloud platforms, data architecture, data governance, and modern AI technologies. Throughout his career, he has led the design and implementation of scalable data platforms, data lakes, and business intelligence solutions across multiple industries. Siva is passionate about emerging technologies, knowledge sharing, and helping organizations derive business value from data and AI. He holds multiple industry-recognized certifications in cloud, data, and analytics technologies.

Table of Contents

Chapter 3: Data Engineering on Microsoft Azure 53

Chapter 4: Designing Future Data Platforms 81

Chapter 12: Governing Data Products 611

Preface

The data landscape is undergoing a profound transformation. Organizations are no longer satisfied with simply collecting and storing information—they expect data platforms to be trusted, governed, intelligent, and capable of powering real-time decisions at scale. As cloud technologies mature and AI becomes deeply embedded in enterprise workflows, the need for a modern, reliable, and future-ready data foundation has never been greater. This book, Building Trusted Data Platforms with Azure Databricks and GenAI, is written to guide practitioners through that evolution.

Azure Databricks and the broader Databricks Lakehouse Platform sit at the center of this shift, offering a unified architecture that blends data engineering, analytics, governance, and AI into a single, collaborative environment. From Delta Lake's transactional reliability to the Medallion Architecture's elegant layering of Bronze, Silver, and Gold data, the platform provides the building blocks for scalable, high-quality data systems. Yet technology alone is not enough. Modern data platforms must also embrace data products, data contracts, and strong governance principles to ensure trust, accountability, and consistency across distributed teams.

Generative AI adds a new dimension to this journey. Tools like Claude Code and Genie Code are reshaping how engineers design, build, and optimize pipelines—accelerating development while introducing new considerations around validation, quality, and responsible use. GenAI can dramatically increase productivity, but it also requires thoughtful guardrails to prevent hallucinations, enforce correctness, and maintain architectural integrity. This book explores how to harness these capabilities effectively, blending automation with engineering discipline.

Throughout the chapters, you will learn how to design future-ready data platforms, implement Delta Lake best practices, enforce data quality and observability, and apply scalable governance frameworks. You will also see how GenAI can be integrated into the development lifecycle to streamline pipeline creation, documentation, and testing—without compromising trust.

My hope is that this book equips you with both the conceptual foundations and the practical patterns needed to build data platforms that are not only powerful, but dependable. Platforms that treat data as a product, uphold strong governance, and embrace the possibilities of AI responsibly. Platforms that earn trust—because trust is the true currency of modern data systems.

Welcome to the journey of building the next generation of intelligent, governed, and AI-augmented data platforms.

Who this book is for

For a book like "Building Trusted Data Platforms with Azure Databricks and GenAI," the audience spans several professional groups who are shaping, governing, or building modern data ecosystems. Here's a clear breakdown of who will benefit most:

- Data Engineers: Professionals designing and building pipelines, Delta Lake tables, and Medallion architectures on Azure Databricks.
- Data Architects & Cloud Architects: Those responsible for designing scalable, governed, future-ready data platforms and integrating GenAI into enterprise data ecosystems.
- Analytics Engineers & BI Developers: Practitioners who rely on high-quality, well-governed data products and need to understand upstream engineering and governance patterns.
- ML/AI Practitioners: Teams using Databricks for model training, feature engineering, and GenAI-augmented development workflows.

What this book covers

Chapter 1, The Story of Data Engineering and Analytics, introduces the foundational concepts of data engineering and guides the reader through the evolution of data analytics, the rise of cloud computing, and the growing role of data and AI in driving organic growth and enabling data monetization.

Chapter 2, Discovering Data Platforms, explains how modern data platforms address the rapidly expanding demands of today's analytical landscape. It introduces one of the most important principles in data engineering: separating storage from compute. Understanding this principle naturally leads the reader to the concept of building Lakehouse architectures.

Chapter 3, Data Engineering on Microsoft Azure, introduces readers to data engineering on the Microsoft Azure cloud platform. It familiarizes the reader with the key Azure tools and services that form the backbone of the Azure data engineering ecosystem.

Chapter 4, Designing Future Data Platforms, examines the defining characteristics of a modern data platform—one that embraces Lakehouse principles, is built on a cloud-native foundation, and upholds strong governance and security.

Chapter 5, Understanding Databricks, equips the reader with advanced knowledge of Apache Spark and Databricks Lakehouse Platform, building on the foundational concepts introduced earlier.

Chapter 6, Understanding Medallion Architecture and Delta Lake, introduces the Medallion Architecture and Delta Lake, providing readers with a clear understanding of their core concepts and features.

Chapter 7, Understanding Modern Data Pipelines, reinforces the point that modern data pipelines are becoming increasingly intelligent as generative AI reshapes how data is produced, transformed, and consumed.

Chapter 8, Data Ingestion Stage: Building the Landing Zone, takes the first practical steps in creating a fully operational data lakehouse. The journey starts with a deep dive into the landing zone—the foundational area where raw data is first collected.

Chapter 9, Building the Bronze Layer of the Medallion Architecture using Gen AI, takes the practical steps to build the structured bronze layer of the Lakehouse using Claude Code.

Chapter 10, Building the Silver Layer of the Medallion Architecture using Gen AI, continues to build the Lakehouse by focusing on the silver layer. This critical stage transforms raw, unrefined data into clean, reliable, and analytics-ready datasets.

Chapter 11, Building the Next-Gen Data Analytics Gold Layer, focuses on transforming curated data into high-value analytical assets. We begin by examining why data aggregation is essential, particularly for enabling performant analytics and business-friendly consumption.

Chapter 12, Governing Data Products, focuses on operationalizing governance practices that elevate data products to first-class organizational assets. This step goes beyond technical construction and examines how data products are owned, protected, certified, and sustained over time.

To get the most out of this book

- Follow the chapters in sequence to build a complete understanding of Azure Databricks, Delta Lake, and the Medallion Architecture.
- Practice hands-on by running the code samples directly in your Databricks workspace.
- Treat GenAI tools (Claude Code, Genie Code) as accelerators—use them to generate scaffolding, but always validate outputs.
- Compare GenAI-generated code with authoritative patterns and SQL files provided in the book's repository.
- Revisit chapters on data products, data contracts, governance, and observability as your platform matures.

- Experiment with variations of prompts to understand how GenAI behaves and how to control it effectively.
- Treat the book as both a learning path and a long-term reference for building trusted, scalable data platforms.

Download the example code files

This book includes a complete downloadable code bundle containing all the example projects and files used throughout the chapters. We recommend downloading the bundle so you can follow along smoothly and experiment with the examples.

Use the bundle as a practical starting point. Modify it, extend it, and apply what you learn by creating your own variations as you progress through the chapters.

Get the code bundle

If you bought the book directly from Packt:

1. Go to **packtpub.com**
2. Click your **profile picture** and select **Your Orders**
3. Find this book and click **Download Code**

If you bought this book from Amazon or any other channel partner:

1. Go to `packtpub.com/unlock` or scan the following QR code:
2. Search for this book
3. Sign up or log in to your free Packt account
4. Upload your proof of purchase and download the code bundle locally

Usage note: You're free to use and modify this code for personal learning and non-commercial projects.

Download the color images

Your purchase includes a color, DRM-free PDF copy of this book, ideal for viewing color images, screenshots, and diagrams. Refer to the *Free benefits with your book section* at the end of the *Preface* to unlock your PDF copy.

Conventions used

There are a number of text conventions used throughout this book.

`CodeInText`: Indicates code words in text, table names, folder names, filenames, file extensions, pathnames, URLs, and user input.

A block of code is set as follows:

```
RESOURCEGROUPNAME="training_rg"
LOCATION="canadacentral"
KEYVAULTNAME="electroniz-secret-kv"
```

Any command-line input or output is written as follows:

```
az keyvault create --location $LOCATION --name $KEYVAULTNAME --resource-group
$RESOURCEGROUPNAME
```

Bold: Indicates a new term, an important word, or words that you see on the screen. For instance, words in menus or dialog boxes appear in the text like this. For example: "Select **System info** from the **Administration** panel."

> Note
>
> Warnings or important notes appear like this.

> Tip
>
> Tips and tricks appear like this.

Get in touch

Feedback from our readers is always welcome.

General feedback: If you have questions about any aspect of this book or general feedback, please email us at customercare@packt.com and include the book's title in the subject line.

Errata: Although we have taken every care to ensure the accuracy of our content, mistakes do happen. If you have found a mistake in this book, we would be grateful if you could report it to us. Please visit `http://www.packt.com/submit-errata`, click **Submit Errata**, and fill in the form.

Piracy: If you come across any illegal copies of our works in any form on the internet, we would be grateful if you would provide us with the location address or website name. Please contact us at `copyright@packt.com` with a link to the material.

If you are interested in becoming an author and have expertise in a topic you would like to write or contribute to a book on, please visit .

Share your thoughts

Once you've read *Building Trusted Data Platforms with Azure Databricks and GenAI*, we'd love to hear your thoughts! Scan the QR code below to go straight to the Amazon review page for this book and share your feedback.

`https://packt.link/r/1806679779`

Your review is important to us and the tech community and will help us make sure we're delivering excellent quality content.

Free benefits with your book

This book includes free benefits designed to support your learning and help you apply what you learn effectively. Activate them now for instant access (see the *How to unlock* section for instructions).

Here's a quick overview of what you can instantly unlock with your purchase:

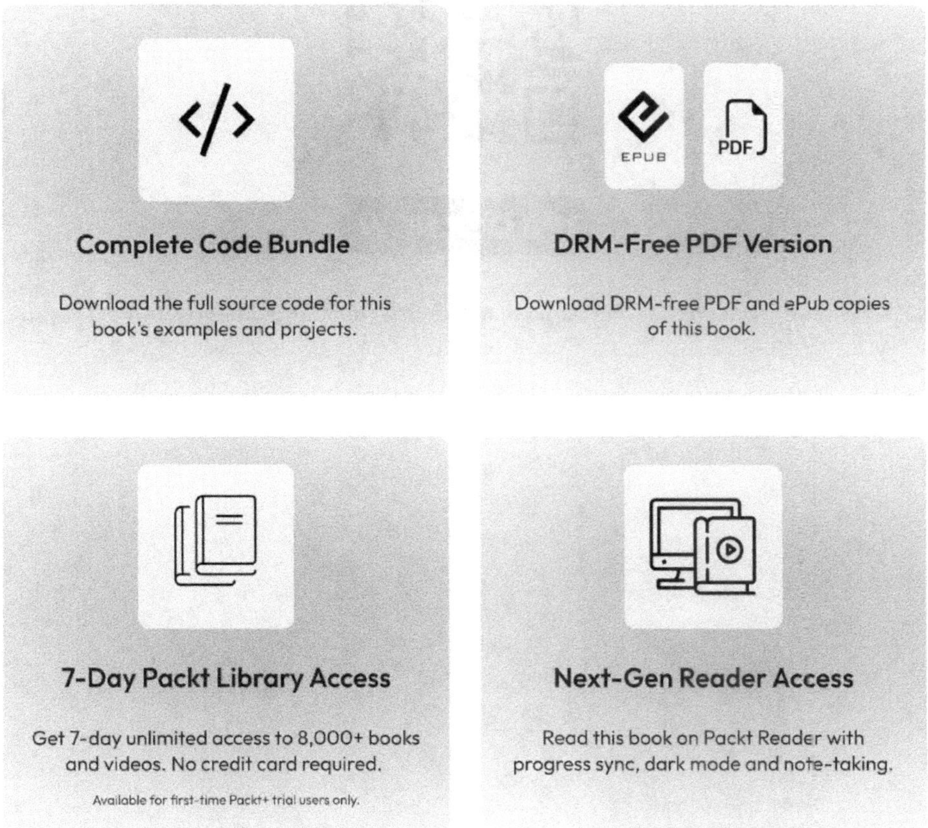

How to unlock

Scan the QR code (or go to `packtpub.com/unlock`). Search for this book by name, confirm the edition, and then follow the steps on the page.

UNLOCK NOW

Note: Have your invoice handy. Purchases made directly from the Packt website don't require an invoice.

1

The Story of Data Engineering and Analytics

Every byte of data has a story to tell. The real question is whether the story is being narrated accurately, securely, and efficiently. In the modern digital landscape, data embarks on a journey - from the moment it gets created to the point at which a user consumes it for their vast needs in the analytical world.

But what makes today's data journey so special and different from the past? After all, ETL is not a new concept. I remember collecting and transforming data since the time I joined the world of information technology just over 30 years ago. What has changed, however, is the scale, performance, and sophistication of data.

In this chapter, we will discuss some reasons why effective data engineering practices have a profound impact on data analytics, such as:

- The journey of data
- Exploring the evolution of data analytics
- The monetary power of data

The road to effective data analytics leads through effective data engineering.

> Note
>
> **Your purchase includes a free PDF copy + code bundle**
>
> Your purchase includes a DRM-free PDF copy of this book, the code bundle, and additional exclusive extras. See the *Free benefits with your book* section in the *Preface* to unlock them instantly and maximize your learning.

The journey of data

Data engineering is the vehicle that makes the journey of data possible, securely, durably, and timely. A data engineer is the driver of this vehicle, safely navigating around roadblocks along the way without compromising the safety of its passengers. Waiting at the end of the road are data analysts, data scientists, business intelligence engineers, and ML/AI engineers eager to receive this data and begin narrating the story of data. You can see this reflected in the following figure:

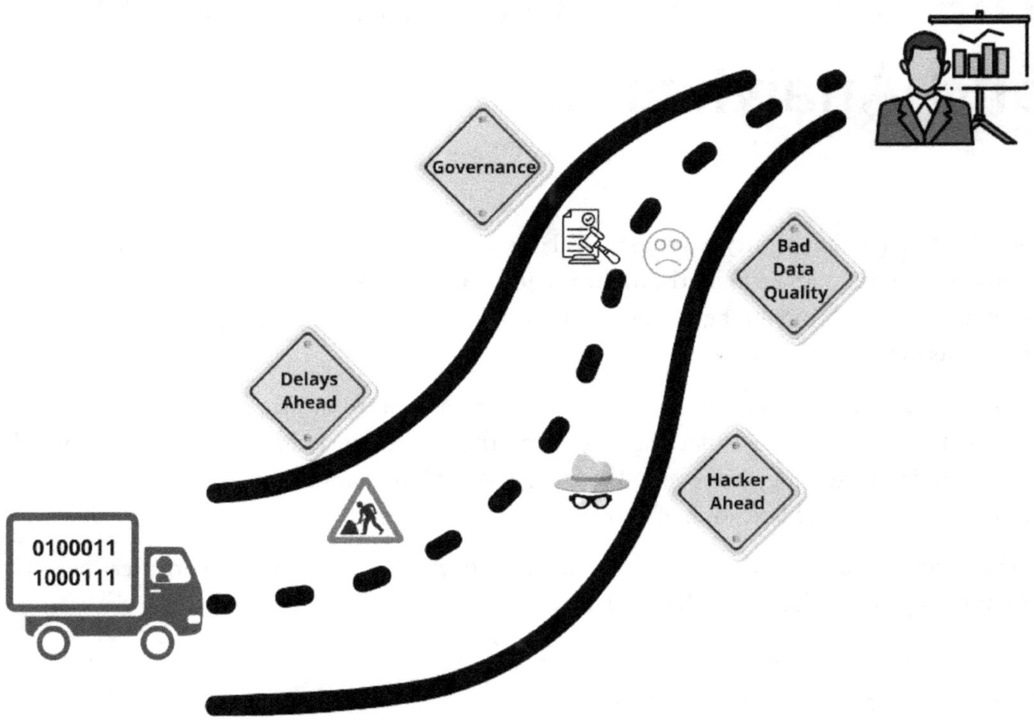

Figure 1.1: Data's journey to effective data analysis

Traditionally, the journey of data has centered around the typical **extraction**, **transformation**, and **loading** (**ETL**) process. Unfortunately, the traditional ETL process is no longer sufficient in today's data-driven era. Given the immense human dependence on data, there is a greater need than ever to streamline the data journey with cutting-edge architecture, advanced frameworks, and intelligent tools.

You may also be wondering why the journey of data is even required. Gone are the days when data sets were limited, computing power was scarce, and the scope of data analytics was very limited. We now live in a fast-paced world where decisions must be made at lightning speed, powered by data that is changing by the second. Let us explore how the evolution of data analytics has fundamentally transformed data engineering.

Exploring the evolution of data analytics

Data analytics has evolved over time, enabling us to do bigger and better. For many years, the focus of data analytics was limited to descriptive analysis, aimed at generating useful business insights from data in the form of reports. This type of analysis was useful to answer questions such as "*What happened?*". A hypothetical scenario would be that the company's sales sharply declined in the last quarter.

Over time, it became evident that several other indicators are available to determine *what happened,* but the real value lies in understanding *"why it happened"*. Core analytics has now shifted towards diagnostic analysis, focusing on identifying data anomalies to uncover the reasons. An example scenario would be the company's sales sharply declining in the last quarter because inventory levels dropped significantly due to floods at suppliers' manufacturing units. This form of analysis further enhances the decision support mechanisms for users. The decision support mechanisms for users are illustrated in the following figure:

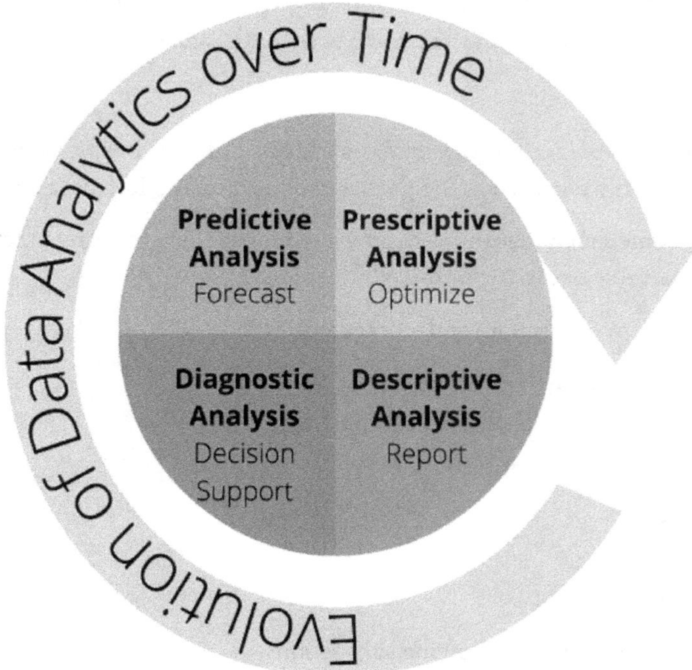

Figure 1.2: The evolution of data analytics

> **Note**
>
> Both descriptive and diagnostic analyses aim to influence the decision-making process using only factual data.

Since the dawn of time, it has been a core human desire to look beyond the present and forecast the future. If we can predict future outcomes, we can surely make a lot of better decisions, and so the era of predictive analysis dawned, where the focus revolves around "*What will happen in the future?*". Predictive analysis can be performed using **machine learning** (**ML**) algorithms—let the machine learn from existing and future data iteratively to identify patterns that enable accurate prediction of future trends.

Now that we are well-equipped to forecast future outcomes, it is essential to optimize the predictive analysis. Building on these results, the goal of prescriptive analysis is to recommend a set of actions to help meet business objectives.

> **Note**
>
> Unlike descriptive and diagnostic analyses, predictive and prescriptive analyses aim to influence the decision-making process, using both factual and statistical data.

But how can the dreams of modern-day analysis truly be fulfilled? Despite advancements, data engineering is commonly regarded as the primary support for modern data analytics needs.

The following are some major reasons as to why a strong data engineering practice is becoming an unignorable necessity for today's businesses:

- Core capabilities of compute and storage resources
- Availability of varying datasets
- The paradigm shift to distributed computing
- Adoption of cloud computing
- Data storytelling
- Compliance
- Widespread AI adoption

We'll explore each of these in the following subsections.

> Note
>
> Having a strong data engineering practice ensures that modern analytics needs are met in terms of durability, performance, and scalability.

Core capabilities of storage and compute resources

25 years ago, I had the opportunity to buy a Sun Solaris server—128 **megabytes** (**MB**) of **random-access memory** (**RAM**) and 2 **gigabytes** (**GB**) of storage—for close to $25K. The intended use of the server was to run a client/server application over an Oracle database in production. Given the high cost of storage and compute resources, I had to implement strict countermeasures to appropriately balance the demands of **online transaction processing** (**OLTP**) and **online analytical processing** (**OLAP**) for my users. One such limitation was the strict time windows imposed on running complex programs; otherwise, they would consume all available resources and significantly slow down other programs.

Today, you can buy a server with 64 GB RAM and several **terabytes** (**TB**) of storage at one-fifth the price. The extra power available can do wonders for us. Multiple storage and compute units can now be procured just for data analytics workloads. The extra available power enables users to run their workloads whenever and however they like. In fact, it is very common these days to run analytical workloads continuously using data streams, also known as **stream processing**.

The installation, management, and monitoring of multiple compute and storage units require a well-designed data pipeline, often achieved through data engineering practices.

Availability of varying datasets

A few years ago, the scope of data analytics was extremely limited. Performing data analytics simply meant reading data from databases and/or files, denormalizing the joins, and making it available for descriptive analysis. The structure of data was largely known and rarely varied over time.

We live in a different world now; not only do we produce more data, but the variety of data has increased over time. In addition to collecting the usual data from databases and files, it is common these days to collect data from social networking, website visits, infrastructure logs' media, and so on, as depicted in the following figure:

Figure 1.3: A variety of data increases the accuracy of data analytics

> **Note**
>
> More variety in data means data analysts have multiple dimensions to perform descriptive, diagnostic, predictive, or prescriptive analyses.

Naturally, the varying degrees of dataset quality introduce complexity into data collection and processing. On the flip side, it significantly affects decision-making accuracy and the ability to predict future trends. A well-designed data engineering practice can easily handle the complexity given.

The paradigm shift to distributed computing

The traditional data processing approach used over the last few years has been largely singular. To process data, you had to create a program that collected all required data for processing—typically from a database—followed by processing it in a single thread. This type of processing is also referred to as **data-to-code** processing. Unfortunately, there are several drawbacks to this approach, as outlined here:

- Since vast amounts of data travel to the code for processing, at times this causes heavy network congestion. Since a network is a shared resource, users who are currently active may start to complain about network slowness.

- Being a single-threaded operation means the execution time is directly proportional to the data. Therefore, the growth of data typically means the process will take longer to finish. This could significantly impact and/or delay the decision-making process, thereby rendering data analytics useless at times.
- Something as minor as a network glitch or machine failure requires the entire program cycle to be restarted, as illustrated in the following figure:

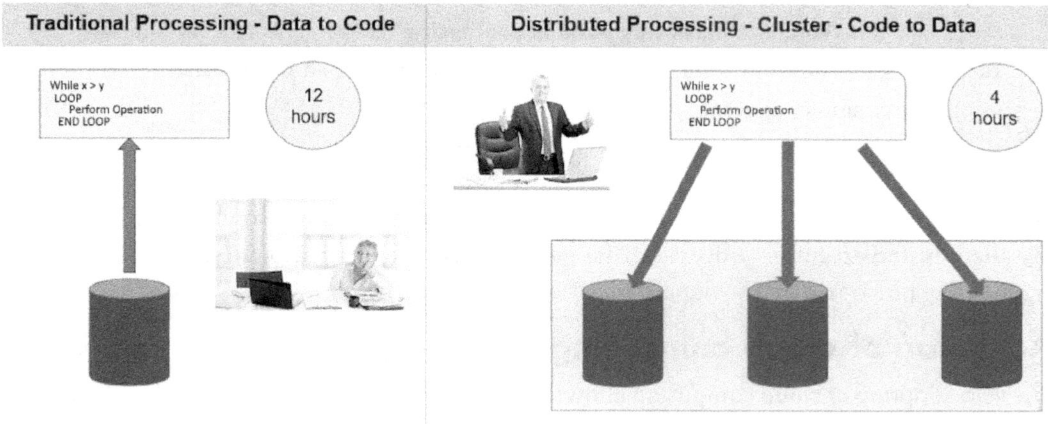

Figure 1.4: Rise of distributed computing

The distributed processing approach, which I refer to as the paradigm shift, largely addresses the previously stated problems. Instead of the traditional data-to-code route, the paradigm is reversed: code-to-data.

In a distributed processing approach, several resources work together as part of a cluster toward a common goal. In simple terms, this approach can be compared to a team model in which each team member takes on a portion of the load and executes it in parallel until completion. If a team member falls ill and is unable to complete their share of the workload, another team member is automatically assigned that portion.

Distributed processing has several advantages over the traditional processing approach, outlined as follows:

- The **code-to-data** paradigm shift ensures the network does not get clogged. The entire idea of distributed processing relies on the assumption that data is stored across multiple machines, also known as nodes. At the time of processing, only the code portion (usually a much smaller footprint than the actual data) is sent over to each node that stores the portion of the data being processed. This ensures that the processing happens locally on the node where the data is stored.

- Since several nodes are collectively participating in data processing, the overall completion time is drastically reduced.
- Program execution is immune to network and node failures. If a node fails, a portion of the work is assigned to another available node in the cluster.

> Note
>
> Distributed processing is implemented using well-known frameworks such as Hadoop, Spark, and Flink. Modern **massively parallel processing** (**MPP**)-style data warehouses such as Amazon Redshift, Azure Synapse, Google BigQuery, and Snowflake also implement a similar concept.

Since distributed processing is a multi-machine technology, it requires sophisticated design, installation, and execution processes. That makes it a compelling reason to establish good data engineering practices within your organization.

Adoption of cloud computing

The vast adoption of cloud computing allows organizations to abstract the complexities of managing their own data centers. Migrating their resources to the cloud offers faster deployments, greater flexibility, and access to a pricing model that, when used correctly, can yield significant cost savings.

In the previous section, we discussed distributed processing implemented as a cluster of multiple machines working together. For this reason, deploying a distributed processing cluster is expensive.

In the pre-cloud era of distributed processing, clusters were built with hardware deployed in on-premises data centers. Very careful planning was required before attempting to deploy a cluster (otherwise, the outcomes were less than desired). You might argue why such a level of planning is essential. Let me address this:

- Since the hardware needs to be deployed in a data center, you need to physically procure it. The real question is how many units you would procure, and that is precisely what makes this process so complex.
- Order more units than required, and you'll end up with unused resources, wasting money.
- Order fewer units than required, and you will have insufficient resources, job failures, and degraded performance.

To order the right number of machines, you begin by benchmarking the required data-processing jobs.

- The results from the benchmarking process are a good indicator of how many machines will be able to take on the load to finish the processing in the desired time. You now need to start the procurement process with the hardware vendors. Given the cycle of the procurement and shipping process, this could take weeks to months to complete.
- Once the hardware arrives at your door, you need to have a team of administrators ready who can hook up servers, install the operating system, configure networking and storage, and finally install the distributed processing cluster software—this requires a lot of steps and a lot of planning.

I hope you may now fully agree that the *careful planning* I spoke about earlier was perhaps an understatement. The complexity of on-premises deployments does not end after the initial server installation. You are still on the hook for regular software maintenance, hardware failures, upgrades, growth, warranties, and more.

This is precisely the reason why the idea of cloud adoption is being very well received. Having resources on the cloud shields an organization from many operational issues. Additionally, the cloud provides the flexibility to automate deployments, scale on demand, balance loads, and manage security.

> Note
>
> Many aspects of the cloud scale on demand, and the ability to offer low pricing for unused resources is a game-changer for many organizations. If used correctly, these features may save a significant amount of money. Having a well-designed cloud infrastructure can work wonders for an organization's data engineering, analytics, and AI practices.

Data storytelling

I started this chapter by stating: *Every byte of data has a story to tell.* Data storytelling is a new approach that helps non-technical people simplify the decision-making process through narrated data stories. Traditionally, decision-makers have relied heavily on visualizations such as bar charts, pie charts, and dashboards to gain useful business insights. These visualizations are typically created using the end results of data analytics. The problem is that not everyone views and understands data in the same way. Let me give you an example to illustrate this further.

Here is a BI engineer sharing stock information for the last quarter with senior management:

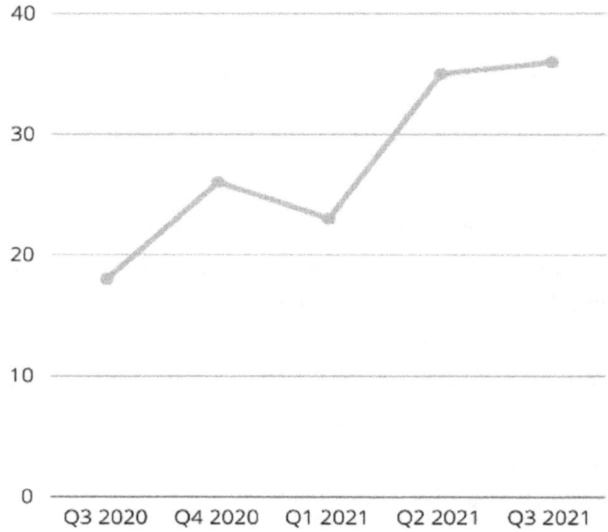

Figure 1.5: Visualizing data using simple graphics

And here is the same information being supplied in the form of data storytelling:

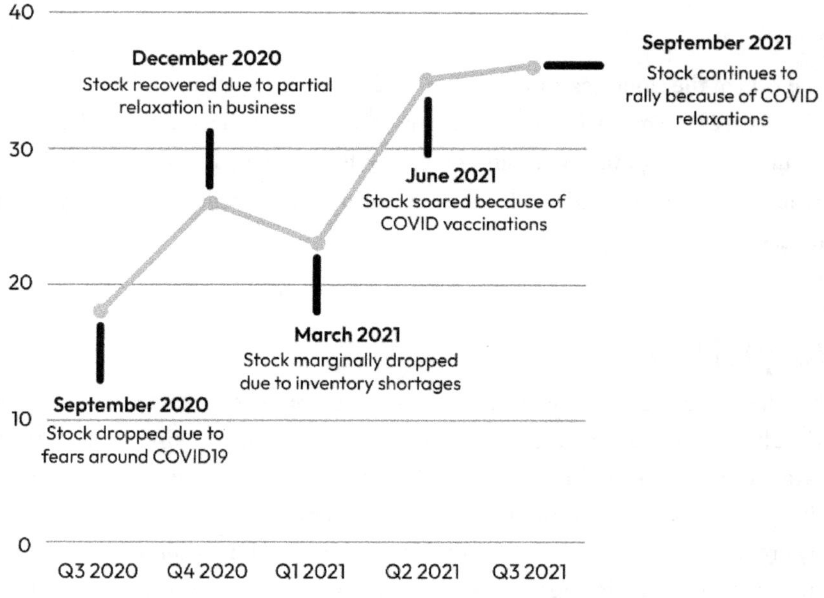

Figure 1.6: Storytelling approach to data visualization

> **Note**
>
> Visualizations communicate what happened; storytelling adds context, causality, and decisions. Data storytelling aims to communicate analytical insights to a layperson by presenting the data as a narrative in natural language. This does not mean that data storytelling is only a narrative. It is a combination of narrative data, associated data, and visualizations. Taken together, these create an interesting story—one everyone can understand.

As data-driven decision-making continues to grow, data storytelling is quickly becoming the standard for communicating key business insights to key stakeholders.

Compliance

In today's world, the power of data is undeniable. This power has enabled organizations to accelerate revenue growth by monetizing and marketing personal information—often in ways that blur the line between innovation and ethical responsibility. In some instances, data has been misused to the point that it has influenced human behavior and public opinion. Human principles are being challenged, underscoring the urgent need for responsible and transparent data practices.

In the past, regulations such as the **Health Insurance Portability and Accountability Act (HIPAA)** began emphasizing the importance of protecting **personally identifiable information** (**PII**). The landscape began to shift significantly in 2018 with the introduction of the European Union's **General Data Protection Regulation (GDPR).** GDPR not only rewrote the rulebook on ethical collection, storage, and use of personal data but also established strict enforcement mechanisms, including substantial fines and penalties for violations. More recently, the **California Consumer Privacy Act (CCPA)** introduced similar regulations aimed at curbing the over-collection, sale, and misuse of personal data.

In short, compliance is no longer a luxury—it has become an essential, non-negotiable requirement for any modern data-driven organization. A well-designed data engineering practice enforces compliance at every stage of the data lifecycle—spanning collection, transformation, and distribution.

Widespread AI Adoption

A new generation of workflows, commonly referred to as AI Agents, can automate complex tasks using independent reasoning and actions.

However, it is important to understand that the accuracy of AI agents' automated reasoning is directly proportional to the quality of the underlying data. Inconsistent, inaccurate, or incomplete data can easily skew the results for any AI agent, leading to flawed reasoning.

Paying attention to data quality is extremely important before venturing into the world of AI. A strong data engineering practice ensures that data is cleansed, reliable, and trustworthy, therefore laying the foundation for seamless and accurate AI adoption.

There's another benefit to acquiring and understanding data: *financial*. Let's look at the monetary power of data next.

The monetary power of data

Modern-day organizations are highly focused on accelerating revenue. Traditionally, organizations have focused on increasing sales to accelerate revenue... but is there a better approach?

Modern-day organizations at the forefront of technology have made this possible through **revenue diversification**. Here are some methods organizations use today, all made possible by the *power of data*.

Organic growth

During my early years in data engineering, I was part of several projects that went beyond the usual scope. On several of these projects, the goal was to increase revenue through traditional methods such as increasing sales, streamlining inventory, and targeted advertising. This meant collecting data from various sources, followed by employing the good old descriptive, diagnostic, predictive, or prescriptive analytics techniques.

But what can be done when the limits of sales and marketing have been exhausted? Where does revenue growth come from?

Some forward-thinking organizations realized that increasing sales is not the only way to diversify revenue. They began to realize that the real wealth of data accumulated over several years is largely untapped. Instead of focusing solely on sales growth, why not tap into data to find innovative ways to grow organically?

This innovative thinking led to the revenue diversification method known as **organic growth**. Subsequently, organizations started to use the power of data to their advantage in several ways. Let's look at several of them.

Customer retention

These days, machine learning engineers can easily create **predictive models** using existing data to assess whether certain customers may be at risk of terminating their service due to complaints or dissatisfaction. Based on this list, customer service can run targeted campaigns to retain these customers. By retaining a loyal customer, you not only make the customer happy but also protect your bottom line.

Fraud prevention

Banks and other institutions are now using data analytics to tackle **financial fraud**. Based on key financial metrics, they have built prediction models that can detect and prevent fraudulent transactions before they happen. These models are integrated into case management systems used to process credit card, mortgage, and loan applications.

Using the same technology, credit card clearinghouses continuously monitor live financial traffic and can flag and prevent fraudulent transactions before they occur. Detecting and preventing fraud goes a long way in preventing long-term losses.

Problem detection

I was part of an **Internet of Things** (**IoT**) project in which a company with several manufacturing plants in North America was collecting metrics from electronic sensors fitted to thousands of machinery components. The sensor metrics from all manufacturing plants were streamed to a common location for further analysis, as illustrated in the following diagram:

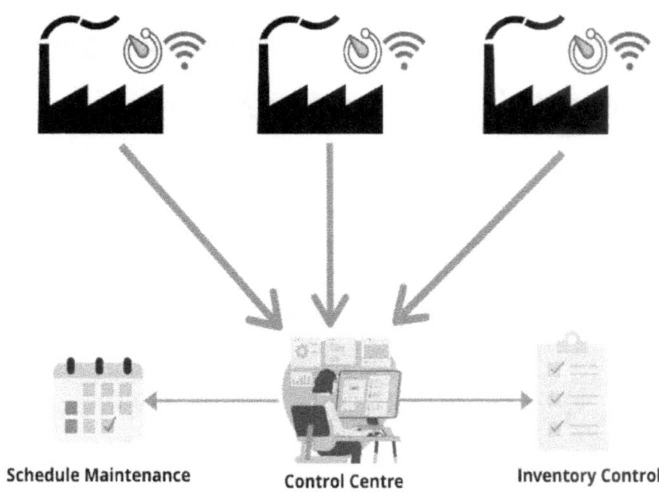

Figure 1.7: IoT is contributing to the major growth of data

These metrics help pinpoint whether certain consumable components, such as rubber belts, have reached or are nearing their **end-of-life** (**EOL**) cycle. Collecting these metrics is helpful to a company in several ways, including the following:

- The data indicates the machinery where the component has reached its EOL and needs to be replaced. Having this data on hand enables a company to schedule preventative maintenance on a machine before a component breaks (causing downtime and delays).
- The data from machinery where the component is nearing its EOL is important for inventory control of standby components. Before this system is in place, a company must procure inventory based on guesstimates. Buy too few, and you may experience delays; buy too many, and you waste money. At any given time, a data pipeline helps predict the inventory of standby components more accurately.

The combined power of IoT and data analytics is reshaping how companies make timely, intelligent decisions that prevent downtime, reduce delays, and streamline costs.

Data monetization

Innovative minds never stop or give up. They continually seek innovative methods to address their challenges, such as diversifying revenue. Organizations quickly realized that if the correct use of their data was so useful to themselves, then the same data could be useful to others as well.

As per Wikipedia, **data monetization** is the "*act of generating measurable economic benefits from available data sources*".

The following diagram depicts data monetization using **application programming interfaces** (**APIs**):

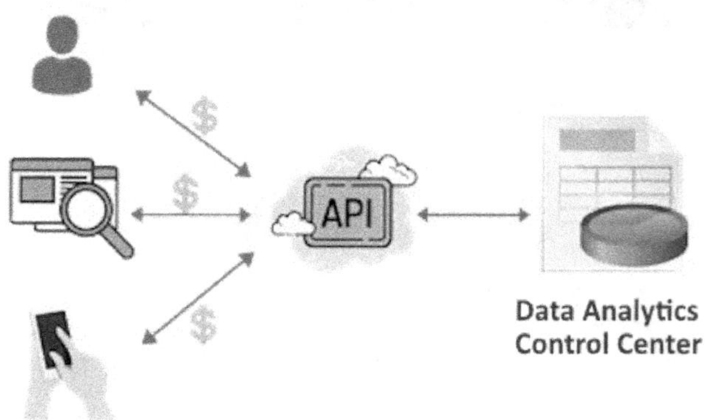

Figure 1.8: Monetizing data using APIs is the latest trend

In the latest trend, organizations are using data in ways that benefit not only themselves but also others. In a recent project in the healthcare industry, a company developed an innovative product that performs medical coding using **optical character recognition** (**OCR**) and **natural language processing** (**NLP**).

Before the project started, this company made sure we understood the real reason for the project—the data collected would not only be used internally but also distributed (for a fee) to others. Knowing the requirements beforehand helped us design an event-driven API frontend architecture for internal and external data distribution. On the backend, we built a complex data engineering pipeline using technologies such as Spark, Kubernetes, Docker, and microservices. This is how the pipeline was designed:

- Several microservices were designed on a self-serve model triggered by requests coming in from internal users as well as from the outside (public).
- For external distribution, the system was exposed to users with valid paid subscriptions only. Once the subscription was in place, several frontend APIs were exposed, enabling them to use the services on a per-request basis.
- Each microservice was able to interface with a backend analytics function that ended up performing descriptive and predictive analysis and supplying the results.

The power of data cannot be underestimated, but its monetary value cannot be realized until an organization has built a solid foundation that delivers the right data at the right time. Data engineering plays a vital role in achieving this objective.

Summary

In this chapter, we went through several scenarios that highlighted a couple of important points.

Firstly, data-driven analytics is a growing trend that will continue to expand. Data-driven analytics gives decision-makers the power to make key decisions and to back them up with valid reasons.

Secondly, data engineering is the backbone of all data analytics operations. None of the magic in data analytics could be performed without a well-designed, secure, scalable, highly available, and performance-tuned data repository—a **Lakehouse**.

In the next few chapters, we will discuss lakehouses in depth. We will start by highlighting the building blocks of effective data storage and computing. We will also look at some well-known architectural patterns that can help you create an effective lakehouse—one that handles analytical requirements across varying use cases.

Get this book's PDF version and more

Scan the QR code (or go to `packtpub.com/unlock`). Search for this book by name, confirm the edition, and then follow the steps on the page.

UNLOCK NOW

Note: Keep your invoice handy. Purchases made directly from Packt don't require an invoice.

2

Discovering Data Platforms

In the previous chapter, we discussed the immense power that data possesses, but with immense power comes increased responsibility. In the past, the key focus of organizations has been detecting trends in data to accelerate revenue. However, they have paid less attention to vulnerabilities caused by inconsistent data management and delivery.

In this chapter, we will discuss how data platforms can effectively deal with the ever-growing demands of today's analytical landscape. We will begin by introducing the concept of data platforms, then examine the importance of separating storage and compute for scalability. Finally, we will delve into data platform architectures to understand how they support carrying use cases in data analytics.

Introducing data platforms

Over the last few years, the markers for effective data engineering and data analytics have shifted. Up to now, organizational data has been dispersed over several internal systems (silos); each system performs analytics over its own dataset. Additionally, it has been difficult to interface with external datasets to extend the spectrum of analytic workloads. As a result, these organizations have had difficulty obtaining a unified view of their data and gaining global insights. A data platform is an integrated environment that collects, processes, stores, and manages data at scale to support data-driven operations within an organization.

In a world where organizations are seeking revenue diversification by fine-tuning existing processes and driving organic growth, a globally unified data repository has become a core necessity. Data platforms address this need by providing users with a unified view of data, enabling them to devise innovative techniques for the betterment of mankind.

The following diagram outlines the characteristics of a data platform:

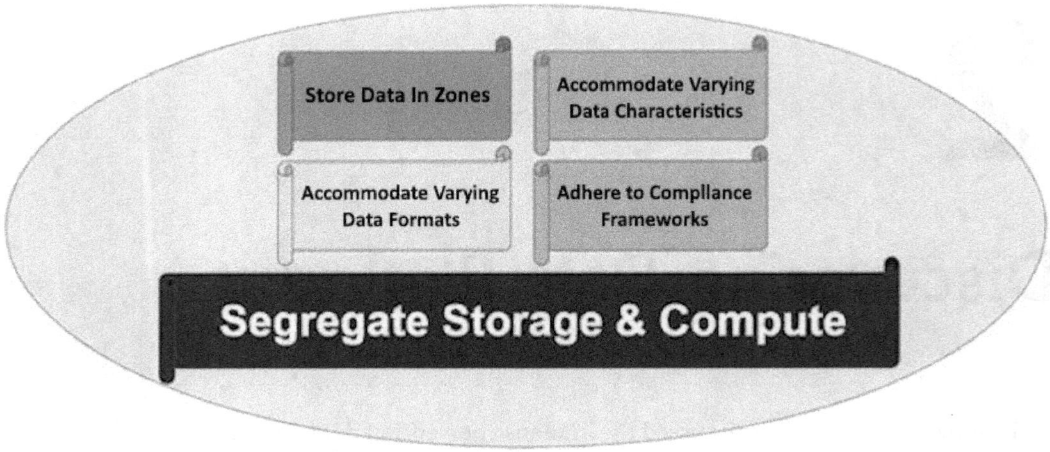

Figure 2.1: Characteristics of a data platform

You will find several varying definitions of a data platform on the internet. Instead of defining what a data platform is, let's focus on the benefits of having one for a modern-day organization.

We will also see how the storage and computation processes in a modern data platform differ from traditional data storage solutions such as databases and data warehouses.

> **Note**
>
> In the modern world, the typical **extract, transform, load** (**ETL**) process (collecting, transforming, and analyzing) is simply not enough. There are other aspects of the ETL process—such as security, orchestration, observability, and distribution—that need to be accounted for equally.

Exploring the benefits of a data platform

A data platform is an ecosystem of frameworks, technologies, services, and architectures all targeted towards a common goal. In addition to just being a simple repository, a data platform offers several benefits that make it stand out as a strong data management solution for modern data analytics needs.

Accommodating varying data formats

The most advertised benefit of a data platform is its ability to store **structured**, **semi-structured**, and **unstructured** data at scale. The increasing variety of data sources contributing to data analytics, machine learning, and artificial intelligence workloads has introduced a new challenge. Since there is no accepted standard for data exchange formats, it is pretty much up to the data provider to choose one for you. Some commonly used data exchange formats and their common uses are listed as follows:

- **Structured:** Database rows
- **Semi-structured**: **Comma-separated values** (**CSV**), **Extensible Markup Language** (**XML**), and **JavaScript Object Notation** (**JSON**).
- **Unstructured**: **Internet of Things** (**IoT**), logs, and emails

These can be better represented as follows:

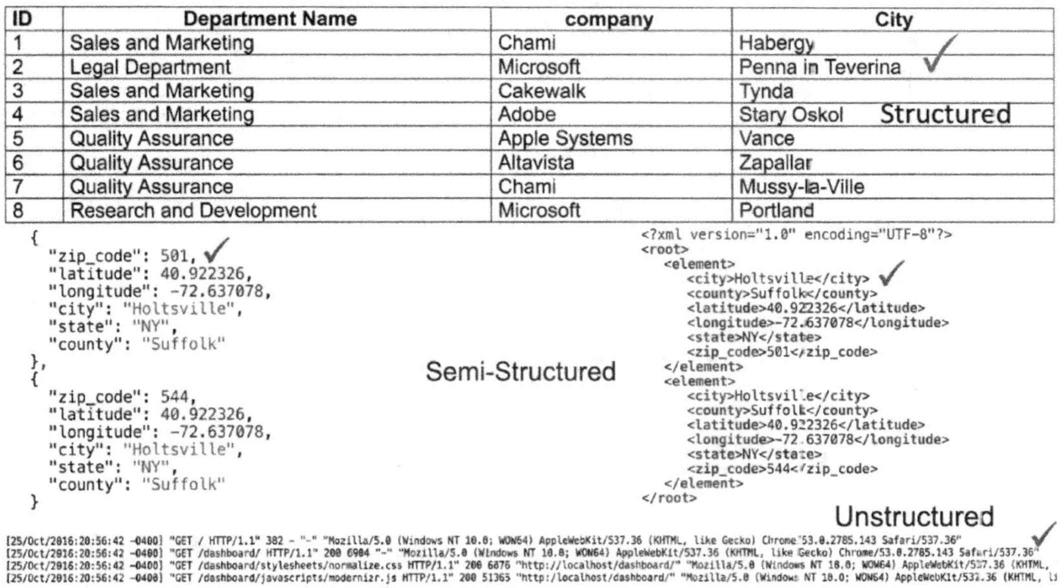

ID	Department Name	company	City
1	Sales and Marketing	Chami	Habergy
2	Legal Department	Microsoft	Penna in Teverina
3	Sales and Marketing	Cakewalk	Tynda
4	Sales and Marketing	Adobe	Stary Oskol
5	Quality Assurance	Apple Systems	Vance
6	Quality Assurance	Altavista	Zapallar
7	Quality Assurance	Chami	Mussy-la-Ville
8	Research and Development	Microsoft	Portland

```
{
  "zip_code": 501,
  "latitude": 40.922326,
  "longitude": -72.637078,
  "city": "Holtsville",
  "state": "NY",
  "county": "Suffolk"
},
{
  "zip_code": 544,
  "latitude": 40.922326,
  "longitude": -72.637078,
  "city": "Holtsville",
  "state": "NY",
  "county": "Suffolk"
}
```

```
<?xml version="1.0" encoding="UTF-8"?>
<root>
  <element>
    <city>Holtsville</city>
    <county>Suffolk</county>
    <latitude>40.922326</latitude>
    <longitude>-72.637078</longitude>
    <state>NY</state>
    <zip_code>501</zip_code>
  </element>
  <element>
    <city>Holtsville</city>
    <county>Suffolk</county>
    <latitude>40.922326</latitude>
    <longitude>-72.637078</longitude>
    <state>NY</state>
    <zip_code>544</zip_code>
  </element>
</root>
```

```
[25/Oct/2016:20:56:42 -0400] "GET / HTTP/1.1" 302 - "-" "Mozilla/5.0 (Windows NT 10.0; WOW64) AppleWebKit/537.36 (KHTML, like Gecko) Chrome/53.0.2785.143 Safari/537.36"
[25/Oct/2016:20:56:42 -0400] "GET /dashboard/ HTTP/1.1" 200 6904 "-" "Mozilla/5.0 (Windows NT 10.0; WOW64) AppleWebKit/537.36 (KHTML, like Gecko) Chrome/53.0.2785.143 Safari/537.36"
[25/Oct/2016:20:56:42 -0400] "GET /dashboard/stylesheets/normalize.css HTTP/1.1" 200 6876 "http://localhost/dashboard/" "Mozilla/5.0 (Windows NT 10.0; WOW64) AppleWebKit/537.36 (KHTML,
[25/Oct/2016:20:56:42 -0400] "GET /dashboard/javascripts/modernizr.js HTTP/1.1" 200 51365 "http:/localhost/dashboard/" "Mozilla/5.0 (Windows NT 10.0; WOW64) AppleWebKit/537.36 (KHTML, li
```


Figure 2.2: Support for varying formats in a data

> **Note**
>
> Data platforms do not differentiate data based on its structure, format, or size.

The **flexibility** of a data platform to store and process diverse data formats makes it a one-stop shop for data analytics operations, capable of handling a wide range of data sources in a single platform. Without a data platform in place, you would need to deal with silos of data, resulting in dispersed analytics without a unified view of data.

Storing data in zones

A data platform is a repository of data that stores data in various zones. Although there are no limits or rules for how many zones are ideally required, three zones are generally considered the best practice: **raw**, **curated**, and **aggregated**, as illustrated in the following diagram:

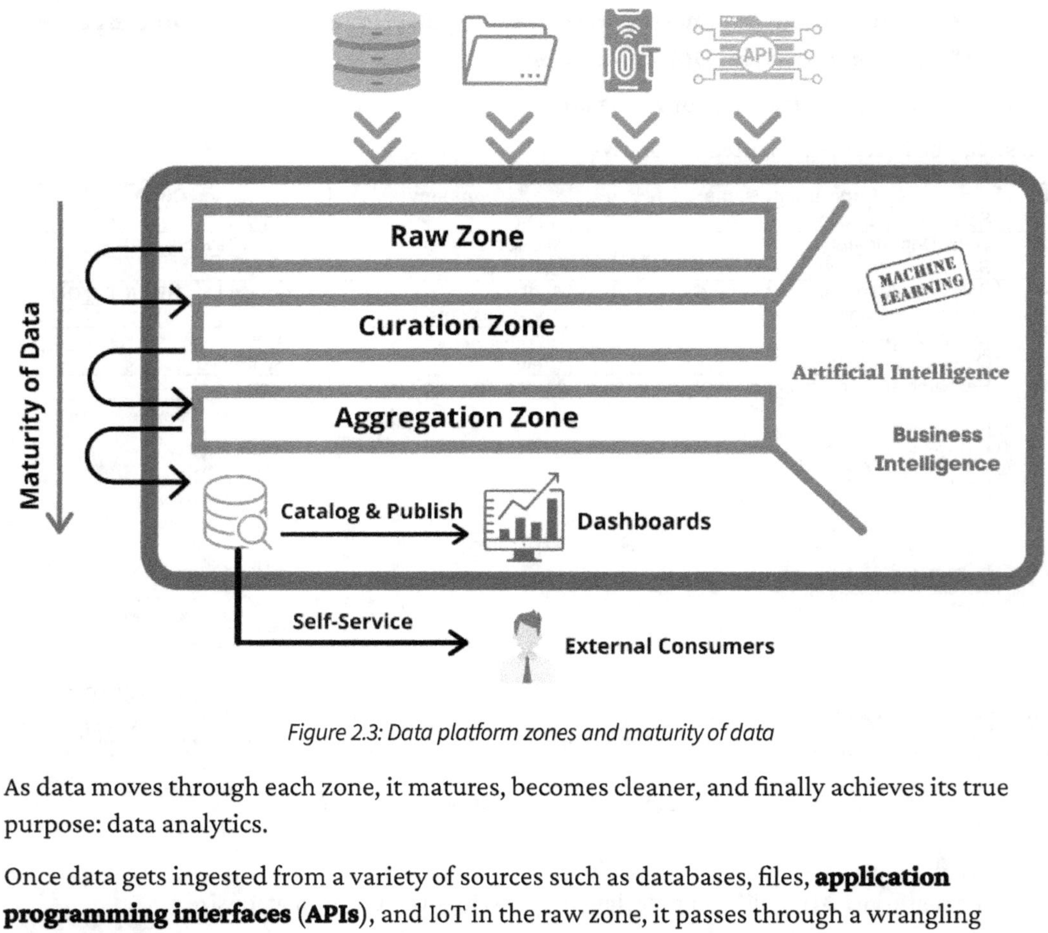

Figure 2.3: Data platform zones and maturity of data

As data moves through each zone, it matures, becomes cleaner, and finally achieves its true purpose: data analytics.

Once data gets ingested from a variety of sources such as databases, files, **application programming interfaces** (**APIs**), and IoT in the raw zone, it passes through a wrangling (cleaning) process to validate, standardize, and harmonize it-in short, bring all data to a common level in terms of format and organizational standards. After cleansing, data is saved to the curation zone.

The next phase of processing is done in a self-service model. Various sub-groups within the analytics group - such as data analysts, data scientists, **machine learning** (**ML**) engineers, and **artificial intelligence** (**AI**) engineers - start transforming data as per requirements.

> Note
>
> Each subgroup has different requirements and views data slightly differently from the others, but a data platform gives everyone the opportunity to use a unified dataset (in the curation zone) and reach different conclusions.

A typical set of transformation operations includes joining datasets, aggregating data, and modeling data. Finally, the results of the transformations are stored in the transformation/aggregation zone. Now, data is ready to make the final leg of its journey.

Once the data is in the transformation/aggregation zone, it needs to be properly cataloged and published. Very frequently, data gets published in a data warehouse where it can be queried by **business intelligence** (**BI**) engineers for creating visualizations - dashboarding, charting, and reporting. Alternatively, it may be queried by machine learning models for predictive modeling or by RAG frameworks to enhance the accuracy of **large language models** (**LLMs**). The data has now met its final purpose.

Accommodating varying data characteristics

Data platforms can support varying characteristics of data, outlined as follows:

- **Volume**: In the early days of big data, everyone was focused on dealing with the growing size of data. Due to the immense growth in data, the resource limits of databases and processing platforms were being pushed to the limit. It was at this time that **Hadoop** emerged as a distributed storage platform (Hadoop Distributed File System, or HDFS) and a distributed processing platform (MapReduce), capable of handling large-scale data processing.
- **Variety:** Once organizations started to use Hadoop, the need to store and process large data volumes started to slowly diminish. This was the phase when dealing with a wide variety of data—structured, semi-structured, and unstructured—became the top priority. The Hadoop framework was able to handle this quickly because it can store data in any format in HDFS, and MapReduce can read/write data using a variety of **serializers/deserializers** (**SerDes**).

- **Velocity**: The rise of modern data sources such as IoT, logs, and social networking has created the challenge of dealing with incoming data at high speeds. During this phase, the Hadoop framework began to fall short of effectively handling streaming data, and other frameworks such as Spark, Kafka, and Flink began to take its place. We still seem to be in this phase, where a lot of work is going into adopting frameworks that can accommodate both batch and streaming workloads.
- **Veracity**: As we continue to ingest, store, and process big data, a lot of organizations are getting concerned about the quality of data, asking: Is my data precise, out - of - date, or biased? While the other characteristics of data highlighted here are well defined, this one is a little more complex to handle. Organizations are seeking innovative methods to improve data quality at both the technical and operational levels.
- **Value**: Recently, organizations have started to put a measurable metric on a certain business outcome. Using this metric, the value of data can improve internal efficiency (streamlining processes, preventing fraud, etc.) and, in other cases, diversify revenue through data monetization.

> Note
>
> While a data platform is a globally accepted term/concept, it may be implemented using a range of tools, services, and frameworks. It can be created using on-premises hardware, but its true power is realized when a data platform is built in the cloud.

Adhering to compliance frameworks

It is becoming a standard practice to incorporate security in every layer of a data platform. It is safe to assume these days that a typical organization is likely to fall under at least one compliance framework or another, such as the **General Data Protection Regulation** (**GDPR**), **Health Insurance Portability and Accountability Act** (**HIPAA**), **Payment Card Industry** (**PCI**), or the **Sarbanes - Oxley Act** (**SOX**).

The three pillars of data security are depicted in the following figure:

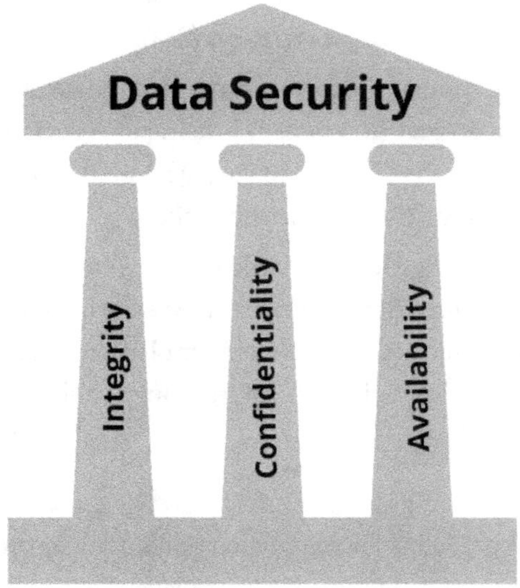

Figure 2.4: The three pillars of data security

For a brief period of my career, I focused heavily on data security audits. I still remember something one of the customers said jokingly over 15 years ago, as his words have resonated with me several times since. He held a sales report in his hand and said: "*There will come a time when people care less about the correctness of data but will care more that it was processed securely.*"

Quite honestly, the sentence did not make much sense to me at the time, but today, I can fully relate to it.

> **Note**
>
> For any organization that deals with data, security is no longer a luxury - it is a core requirement.

According to the CIA triad, the key pillars of security are confidentiality, integrity, and availability. Following these principles, security in a data platforms should be implemented in layers: the greater the number of layers, the more the protection. Data platforms can comply with the core requirements of most compliance frameworks using the following techniques to cover the key pillars of the CIA triad:

- **Perimeter security**: Access to data platform resources can be limited using a combination of site - to - site **virtual private networks** (**VPNs**), filtering **Internet Protocol** (**IP**) addresses, and blocking access to the internet.

- **Access control**: User access to the data platform can be controlled by a combination of **role-based access control** (**RBAC**), policies, **access control lists** (**ACLs**), **multi-factor authentication** (**MFA**), and **single-sign-on** (**SSO**).
- **Encryption**: A key method of protecting **data - in - motion** (traveling from one point to another) and **data-at-rest** (in storage) is using encryption. Encryption can be implemented not only at the file level in storage, but also on any **personally identifiable information** (**PII**) data within a file.
- **Authorization**: Extreme caution is desired during data distribution. The task becomes even more complex if data distribution includes external users. A data platform can comply with authorization requirements by implementing a **role-based access control** (**RBAC**) mechanism using a combination of table-, row-, and column-based security and data masking.

> Note
>
> The CIA triad is simply a guideline for an organization's security program. The strength of security is directly proportional to the number of layers implemented.

Next, we'll see how storage and compute can be segregated within a data platform.

Segregating storage and compute in a data platform

We saved the best for last. The ability of a data platform to segregate (decouple) the storage and compute layers is perhaps one of its most desirable features. But why is decoupling storage and computation such a big deal? To understand why, we should first understand the storage and compute layers.

Storage

The fundamental function of storage is to store data. Briefly, this is how storage has evolved over the last few years:

- **Direct - attached storage** (**DAS**): As the name suggests, a storage device (**hard disk drive/solid - state drive**, or **HDD/SSD**) is physically attached to the computer. This type of storage mostly exists in personal computers and laptops.

- **Network-attached storage** (**NAS**): Centralized storage using multiple hard drives connected as an array. NAS enables quick and easy data sharing between computers via standard Ethernet cables.
- **Storage area network** (**SAN**): High - performance shared storage using fiber - optic connectivity. A SAN enables fast data sharing between computers.
- **Cloud storage**: Cloud storage is a relatively recent addition to this list. In this case, storage physically exists on the cloud provider's servers. Cloud storage allows users to access it from anywhere and provides assurance that data is highly available and secure because multiple copies are maintained on the backend.

> Note
>
> Azure Blob Storage, Amazon **Simple Storage Service** (**S3**), and Google Cloud Storage are some of the best-known cloud storage solutions.

Block storage

All storage types in the preceding list (except cloud storage) are categorized as file or block storage. This means data is stored on the storage device in small blocks, usually 512 bytes. A group of contiguous blocks is deemed a file, and that is how humans relate to data.

Object storage

Cloud storage is categorized as . Object storage does not work like a traditional filesystem. Unlike block storage, every object contains the following:

- **Identifier (id)**: A **globally unique identifier** (**GUID**) for each object in storage
- **Data**: Stored as blobs all in one location (not broken into multiple blocks)
- **Metadata**: Data about the data, such as author, permissions, and timestamps

The differences between block and object storage are better illustrated as follows:

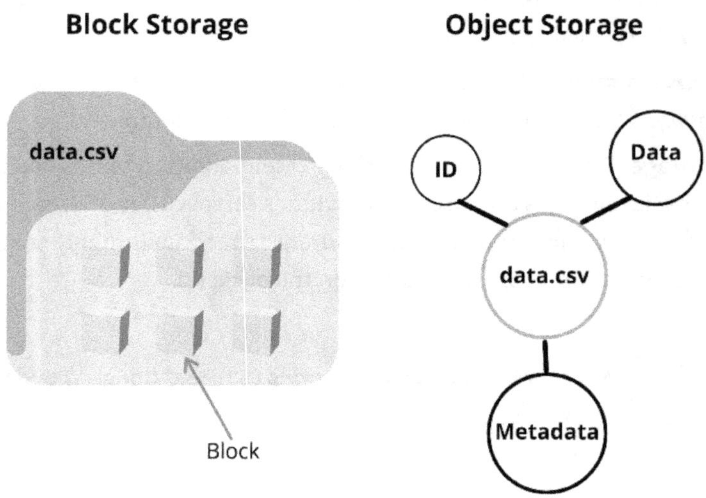

Figure 2.5: Block storage versus object storage

Object storage is quickly becoming the standard for data engineering and analytics operations due to certain key advantages, listed here:

- Object storage is highly scalable, meaning the storage can grow as per increasing data demands within an organization.
- You save money because there is no requirement to book storage capacity in advance.
- The feature of embedding metadata within the object facilitates data classification and analytics workloads.
- Data can easily be accessed via **HyperText Transfer Protocol** (**HTTP**) or APIs.
- Very suitable for storing large files, such as videos, audio, images, and data backups.
- Suitable for write-once, read-many-times scenarios such as data analytics.

However, there are a few drawbacks as well, as outlined here:

- The performance of object storage is slower compared to block storage, particularly for writing.
- Object stores don't support in-place append/update; updates typically create a new object/version. Suitable for workloads that require relatively static data.

> **Note**
>
> Since each change to an object amounts to deleting it and creating a new version, object storage is unsuitable for **online transaction processing** (**OLTP**) operations where data changes are very frequent. However, it is well-suited for **online analytical processing** (**OLAP**) operations because the data changes infrequently.

Compute

In the context of a data platform, compute is the ability to process (read and write) data for analytical operations such as wrangling, joining, and aggregating. In analytical computations, two resources are very critical for smooth operations, outlined as follows:

- **Central processing unit** (**CPU**): On any given computer, all calculations are performed in the CPU. The speed of the CPU is measured in clock speed—for example, 2.8 gigahertz. This means that this CPU can perform 2.8 billion computations per second. The greater the CPU speed, the more computational power. In the world of virtualization, this term is referred to as a **virtual CPU** (**vCPU**).
- **Random - access memory** (**RAM**): RAM stores active data that is required for any currently ongoing computations. This is done to prevent repeated read and write operations on hard drives, which are typically much slower (a 1:50 response time ratio) than RAM. Therefore, it is generally preferred to possess as much RAM as possible.

Containers

In analytical processing terms, resources are allocated to jobs in container units. The idea of a container was introduced in **Yet Another Resource Negotiator** (**YARN**), the distributed processing framework in Hadoop.

In simple terms, a container is a logical grouping of two key physical resources: a vCPU and RAM. Since YARN operates in a cluster, it maintains a total tally of RAM and vCPUs across the cluster.

During processing, YARN allocates containers based on the requirements of the job(s). If a cluster has enough resources to meet the job's demand, it starts immediately; otherwise, it puts the job in wait mode until resources free up. The differently-sized containers are depicted in the following screenshot:

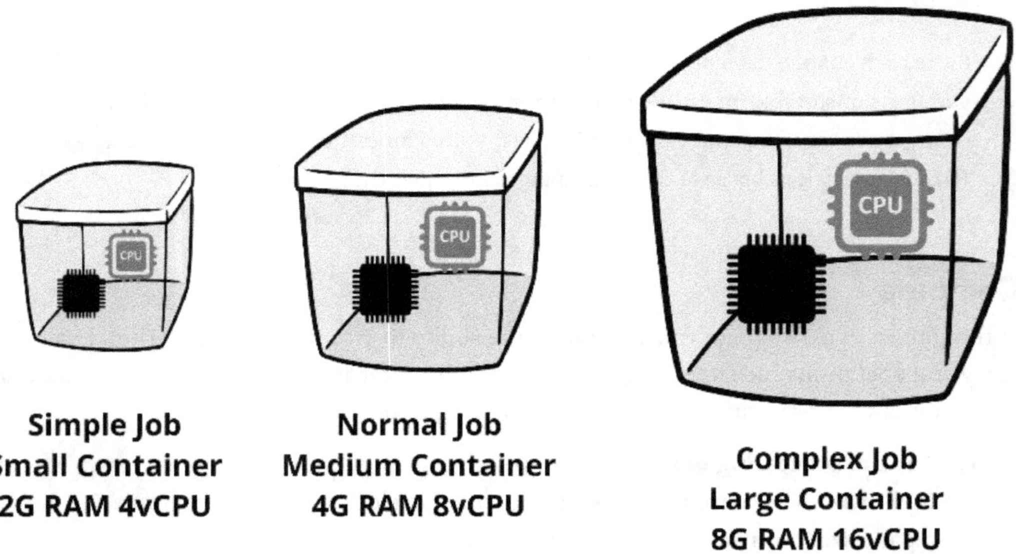

Figure 2.6: Varying container sizes

Modern-era distributed frameworks are extremely resource-hungry. Apache Spark and Apache Flink perform computations in memory, so at times, you need a lot of it. In the big data world, understanding how job resources are allocated and managed in a cluster goes a long way toward improving job completion times and overall performance.

> **Note**
>
> The balancing act of allocating the optimal resources to your jobs is a core skill every data engineer should master.

You might be wondering, "Why should I be bothered by all this? The cloud allows us to use practically endless amounts of resources anyway...". However, I assure you that I do have a point here, and a huge one...just wait for it.

Storage is cheap; compute is expensive

Here it is: *Storage is cheap, yet compute is expensive*. Now, what is that supposed to mean?

A few pages ago, I started this section by noting that a data platform's ability to segregate (decouple) the storage and compute layers is perhaps one of the most desirable features—particularly if an organization's infrastructure is in the cloud.

I am going to support this theory by doing a very high-level estimate on **Microsoft Azure**. Please note that the estimate I am presenting here is just an example to illustrate the preceding point.

The assumptions are as follows:

- **Storage**: 10 **terabytes** (**TB**) of hot-tier Data Lake Storage Gen2 in the East - US region
- **Compute**: Azure Synapse Analytics for 500 **data warehouse units** (**DWU**)/month in the East US region

We can use the Microsoft Azure calculator available at `https://azure.microsoft.com/en-ca/pricing/calculator/` to make this estimate, as shown in the following figure:

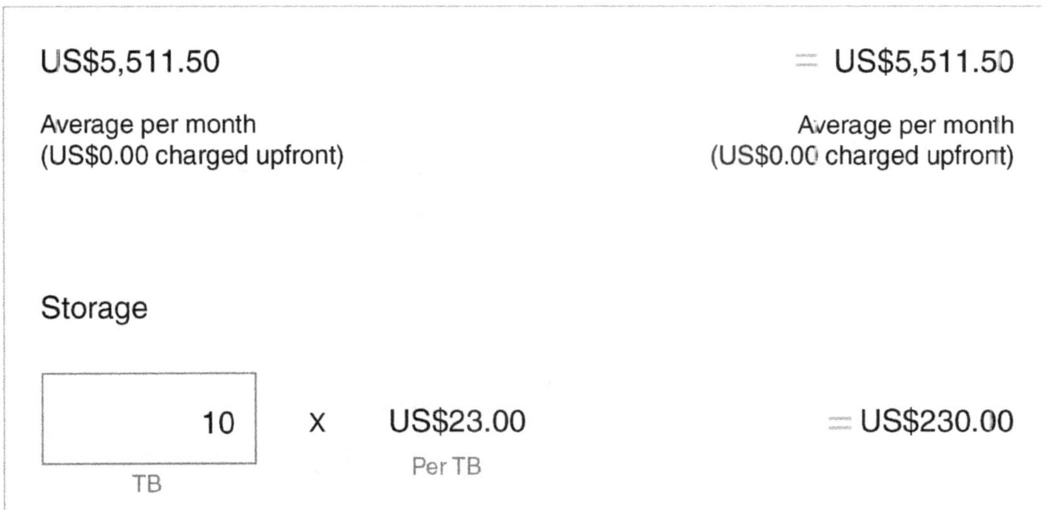

Figure 2.7: Comparison of storage and compute costs

I hope that proves the point I have been trying to make: Compute is more than 20 times as expensive as storage.

Now, let me ask you a question. Put yourself in the shoes of the data engineer. Which layer would you try to optimize the most to keep the costs in check? If your answer is *compute*, then I have managed to get my point across.

> **Note**
>
> As a data engineer, while choosing storage and compute resources, it is very important to keep cost optimization in mind. It is a rare skill to have, but it is something that your customers will thank you for the most.

In the pre-cloud era, big data platforms such as Hadoop were mostly installed on physical machines/**virtual machines (VMs)**. In this case, the storage layer was tightly coupled with the compute layer, as illustrated in the following diagram:

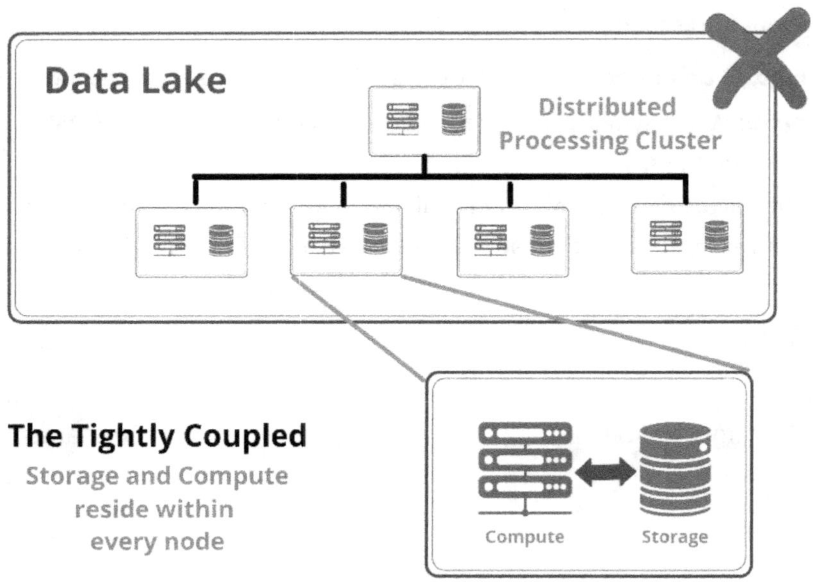

Figure 2.8: A tightly coupled data platform

There are a few drawbacks with this setup, outlined as follows:

- The required capacity for compute and storage needs to be **pre-purchased**. The purchased capacity is typically based on the requirements for the most complex job. Assuming the most complex job runs only for a fraction of the day, the unused capacity is underutilized for the rest of the day.
- You need the cluster to stay up 24/7 (whether you are actively using it or not). Costs to keep the cluster operational, such as air conditioning, real estate, electricity, and administrative costs, all add up.

In short, you are paying for something you are not using... and no one likes that.

In many respects, moving toward cloud computing has been a game-changer. Having a data platform in the cloud allows us to achieve something previously impossible: we can finally decouple storage and compute!

The following diagram shows a loosely coupled data platform:

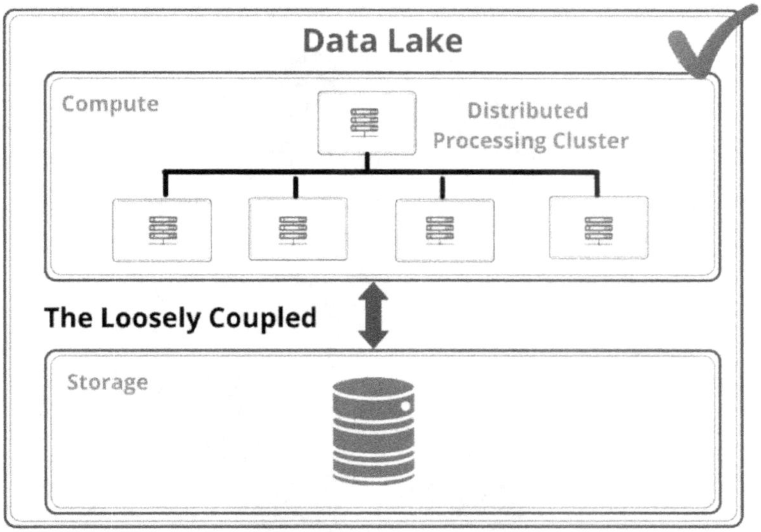

Figure 2.9: A loosely coupled data platform

Decoupling storage from compute offers several advantages, outlined as follows:

- With a loosely coupled data platform, the cheap (storage) layer is permanent, whereas the expensive (compute) layer is temporary. How does it work this way?
- Typically, during batch processing, computations are performed only for a brief period each day (usually just a few hours). Having your infrastructure in the cloud allows you to create a distributed processing cluster (Hadoop/Spark/Flink) every day, just before batch processing starts; all jobs are then run, and the cluster is finally deleted after all jobs finish.

Since the storage portion exists outside the compute cluster, there is no data loss if the cluster is destroyed. This process is depicted in the following figure:

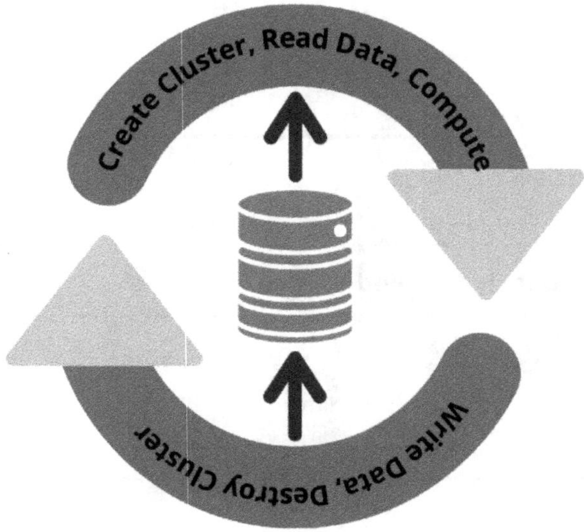

Figure 2.10: Preserving compute costs

By doing this, you ensure that compute costs are fully optimized... **You only pay for what you use**.

In *Chapter 1, The Story of Data Engineering and Analytics*, we discussed the journey of data and why a data engineering practice is becoming a core necessity for organizations serious about data analytics. The question is, how should they start this journey? In the next section, we will dive deep into the planning stages of creating a data platform, starting with an overview of well-known data platform architectures.

Discovering data platform architectures

Before we start the data platform creation journey, it is important to understand how we typically approach a journey in real life. Before going on a journey - a vacation, for instance - we often start by doing some preparations, such as these:

- **Plan**: Shortlist destinations that we want to visit during our trip.
- **Reserve**: Book the best airlines and hotels that fall within our budget.
- **Visit**: Hopefully, our preparations will make the trip both comfortable and secure.

Preparing for the journey of data platform creation is no different, as we can see here:

- **Plan**: Choose the correct data platform architecture that meets the objectives of the organization's analytical needs (**destination**).
- **Reserve**: Procure resources (computer and human) required to create a data within financial restrictions (**budget**).
- **Create**: Create the necessary infrastructure and data pipelines based on a chosen architecture that helps decision makers (**comfort**) and distributes as per individual clearances (**security**).

I hope it is evident from this comparison that without the correct choice of data platform architecture, all subsequent steps will fail to meet the organization's objectives.

A properly designed architecture should be capable of meeting the diverse needs of data storage and processing, including aggregating, joining, and querying—not only in batch mode but, more importantly, in streaming mode as well.

> **Note**
>
> In batch processing, analysis is performed on data collected and stored over a long period (typically a few hours), whereas in stream processing, analysis is performed as soon as data is collected. After processing, this data may or may not be permanently stored.

In this section, we will focus on four well-known data platform architectures that are very commonly used in the data world, listed as follows:

- Traditional data lake architecture
- Lambda architecture
- Kappa architecture
- Lakehouse architecture

Before we understand the various architecture types, we should know about a famous theorem applicable to distributed computing platforms.

The CAP theorem

In the era before distributed computing reached maturity, system scalability was increased by adding more hardware resources. This is likely done by adding more memory, disk, and CPU (or a combination of) to the pre-existing nodes. This type of scaling is commonly referred to as **vertical scalability**, as shown in *Figure 2.11*. But there are a couple of huge drawbacks with this type of scaling, as detailed here:

- Adding new hardware is limited to the maximum expandable in the node—for example, there are only a limited number of slots available on the motherboard for expanding memory.
- An existing node will eventually reach its expiration period and may need to be replaced entirely. Therefore, the cost of adding new hardware may not be justified.

In the modern era of computing, commonly referred to as **distributed computing**, system scalability is achieved laterally, as shown in *Figure 2.12*. This type of scaling is commonly referred to as **horizontal scalability**. It works on the principle of *just keep adding nodes.*

Vertical scalability can be depicted as follows:

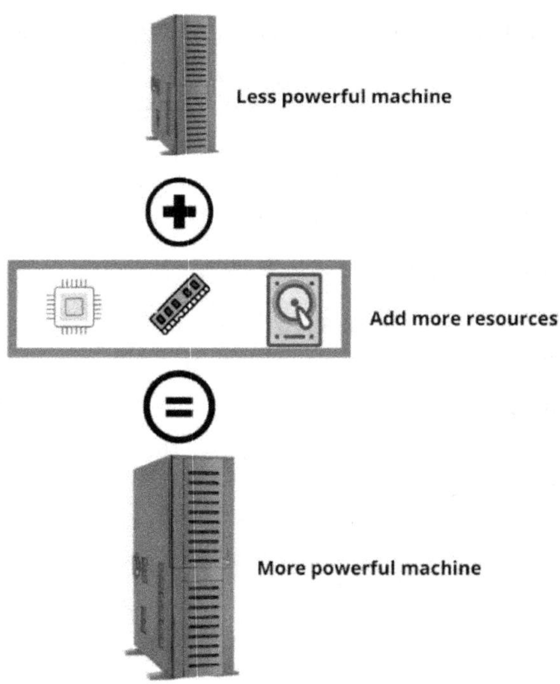

Figure 2.11: Vertical scalability

> **Note**
>
> Horizontal scaling is achieved not by adding hardware to existing nodes, but by adding new nodes when more power is required.

Horizontal scalability can be depicted as follows:

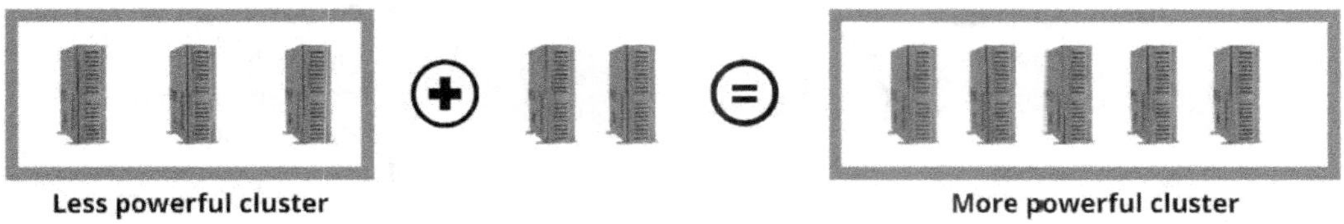

Figure 2.12: Horizontal scalability

The CAP theorem is based on three key characteristics of a distributed computing system, outlined as follows:

- **Consistency**: All nodes should contain the same data. This means that a write request should successfully propagate data to all other replicated nodes before it becomes available for read requests. In other words, a read request should receive the same data irrespective of which node served it.
- **Availability**: Users should be able to access the system even if a node goes down. This means they should always receive a success response to their read/write requests. However, this does not mean that the data read is necessarily the most recent.
- **Partition tolerance**: The system should be able to tolerate network delays and interruptions. This means that the data replication arrangement in the distributed system should be designed with network failures in mind. In Hadoop, this concept is implemented using rack awareness.

As per the CAP theorem, it is impossible for a distributed computing system to simultaneously provide all three guarantees at the same time. It can provide a maximum of two—you need to sacrifice the third. The concept is illustrated in the following figure:

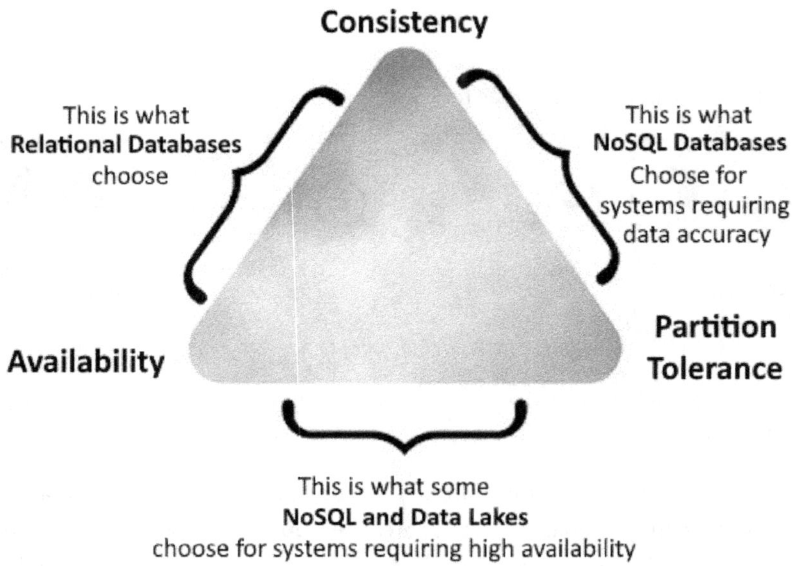

Figure 2.13: The CAP theorem

The CAP theorem is important to understand in the data platform world because it makes you aware of trade-offs that you may need to make in your case scenarios.

The trade-offs

As shown in *Figure 2.13*, for data platform operations, we usually opt for **availability** and **partition** (**AP**) tolerance and sacrifice consistency. This choice applies to most data analytics scenarios in which data accuracy can be sacrificed for the greater good. If the data is aggregated over a long period, a few inconsistent/incorrect values are unlikely to affect the overall correctness to a significant degree.

However, consider a case in IoT analytics where we are trying to monitor a room's temperature using sensors in the event of a fire. In this case, a missing or incorrect sensor reading could be catastrophic. Therefore, it may be advisable to choose **consistency** and **partition** (**CP**) tolerance for this situation. This is why using a NoSQL database is a better choice for mission-critical streaming analytics.

Traditional data lake architecture

Several years ago, Hadoop was the most popular engine for distributed data storage and processing systems - it was the phase of **batch processing**. Using Hadoop, a typical batch workflow functioned like this:

- **Orchestration**: Using preconfigured tools such as **Oozie** to invoke workflows (pipelines) that perform the following set of operations.
- **Batch collection**: Collecting and ingesting data every few hours. Initially, a 24-hour window was the norm, but as demand for real-time data grew, the windows began to shrink. Data collection was performed using a variety of Hadoop ecosystem tools, including **Sqoop** and **Flume**. The incoming data was stored in HDFS for further processing. Every time new data was collected, it was appended to the previous dataset, usually by creating a timestamp partition.
- **Batch processing**: Once the data had been saved to HDFS, processing was performed using the **MapReduce** engine (distributed processing framework). This was done using a variety of methods, such as writing programs in languages like **Java**, **Python**, or **Perl**, or using frameworks like **Pig** and **Hive**.

I must admit that in those times, my customers were simply thrilled that I managed to ingest and process their data from various sources in Hadoop, even though it came with high latency.

The following figure represents the state of `SALES` data 24 hours apart:

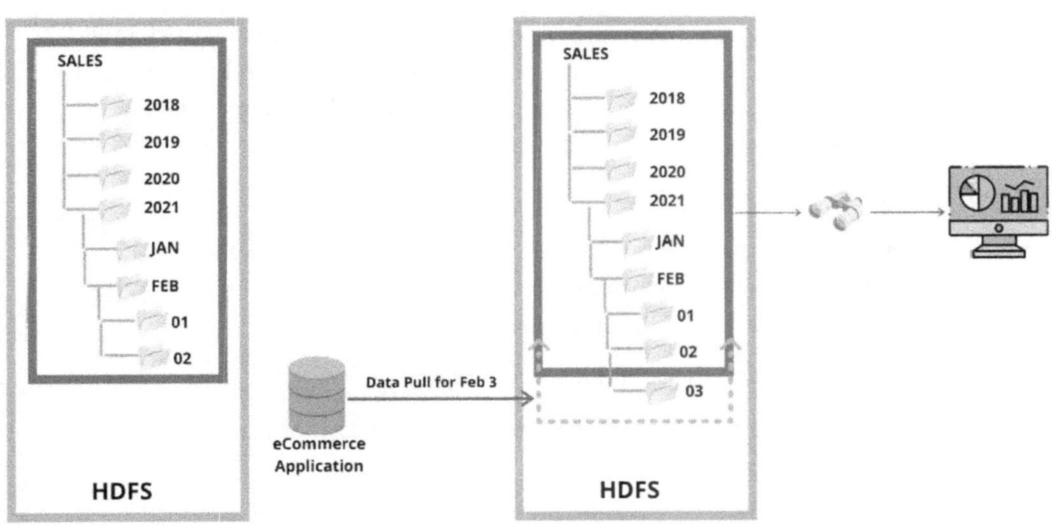

Figure 2.14: State of data 24 hours apart

Here are some insights:

- **Sales report created on February 2**: Includes all data from the start (2018) until February 2, 2021.
- **Sales report created on February 3**: Includes all data from the start (2018) until February 3, 2021.

Now, here is the problem with traditional architecture:

If the sales report is produced between the usual scheduled report generation times on February 2 and February 3, it will miss sales occurring on February 3. In other words, no matter when a report is generated during an interim period, it will always be partially inaccurate. To address this problem, we started bringing the batch window down to 12/8/4 hours, but no matter what, a fraction of the data would still be missing from the report.

As times changed, customers began requesting data analytics over near-real-time data, paving the way for a better architecture to address their growing demands.

> Note
>
> MapReduce's high-latency batch nature pushed the ecosystem toward newer engines, e.g., Spark for faster iterative processing and Flink/Storm for streaming.

Lambda architecture

Lambda architecture emerged to address the need for hybrid processing that can handle both batch and streaming data simultaneously. Lambda architecture was introduced by **Nathan Marz**, who created the famous real-time processing engine **Apache Storm**. Lambda architecture comprises three layers, detailed next.

Batch layer

The batch layer stores the master dataset. The master dataset includes all historical data collected since the collection process started. In the example we covered previously, the dataset shown in the screenshot is the **SALES** master dataset.

These are some of the characteristics of the master dataset:

- It is immutable. Immutability of data means that existing data cannot be changed, and new data can only be appended.
- It can be used by the serving layer to publish data.
- It can incrementally merge changed data on a regular basis.

You can see the file structure of the master dataset here:

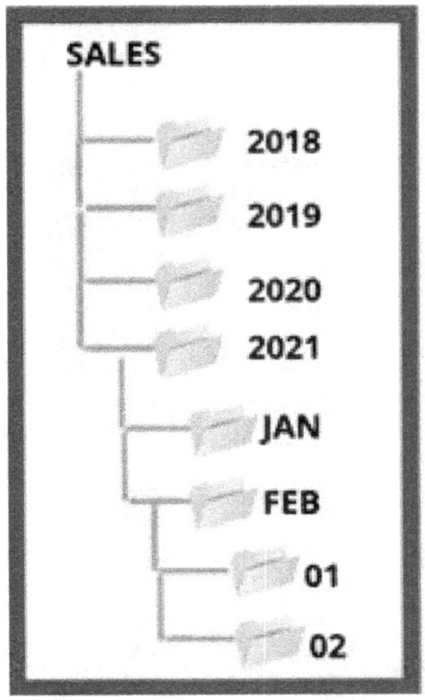

Figure 2.15: Master dataset

Let's now have a brief introduction to the term **change data capture**, or **CDC** in short. Successfully capturing and processing changing data over time has been one of the top three challenges I have faced in my career. We will dedicate a whole section to CDC in a future chapter.

A few well-known tools of the trade for creating the batch layer are Apache Hadoop, Apache Flink, and Apache Spark.

Serving layer

The serving layer makes the master data available to the query process using batch views. The batch views are often the results of precomputed aggregations. Because the data is largely precomputed, these views provide low-latency access for users.

The following screenshot shows a batch view that aggregates **SALES** by quarters. In this view, the aggregations of quarters in 2018 to 2020 will be accurate, because the data is not changing for those partitions anymore. However, data for **2021 > Q1** is still evolving and changing by the second due to the currently ongoing sales:

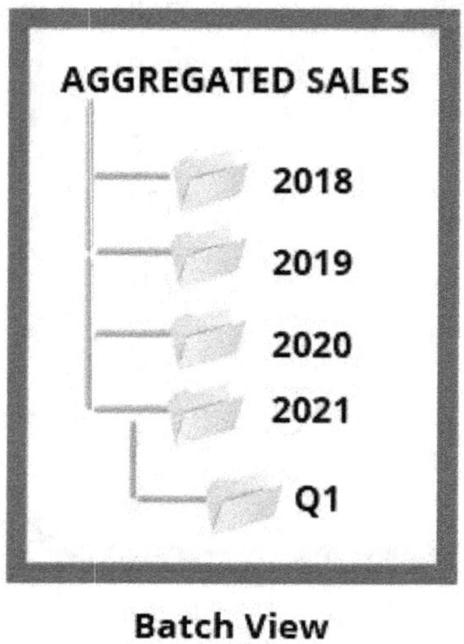

Figure 2.16: Aggregated batch view

Here is how we can achieve an accurate result for 2021 - Q1:

- 2021 - Q1 from batch view + Aggregate (February 3 SALES)
- The latter summation of data is missing, and this is where the speed layer will help us.
- The tools of the trade for the serving layer are Apache Hive and Presto.

Speed layer

The speed layer stores the most recent dataset (incremental) that has not yet been merged with batch views due to the latency of the merge process. This data is made available to the query process as real-time views, often created using stream processing. You can see a depiction of a real-time view here:

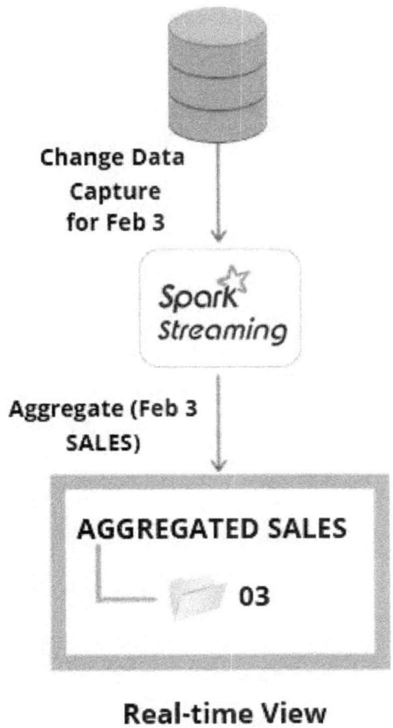

Figure 2.17: Aggregated real - time view

In traditional architecture, this is exactly the layer that could not be handled by Hadoop MapReduce; therefore, an advancement to newer frameworks was required.

The tools of the trade for the speed layer are Apache Spark Streaming, Apache Storm, and Apache Flink.

This is how everything comes together in Lambda architecture:

- Incremental data from the source is concurrently pushed to the batch and speed layers.
- The batch layer keeps accumulating the data over a certain period and refreshes the batch view after the period expires.

You can see the various layers of a Lambda architecture here:

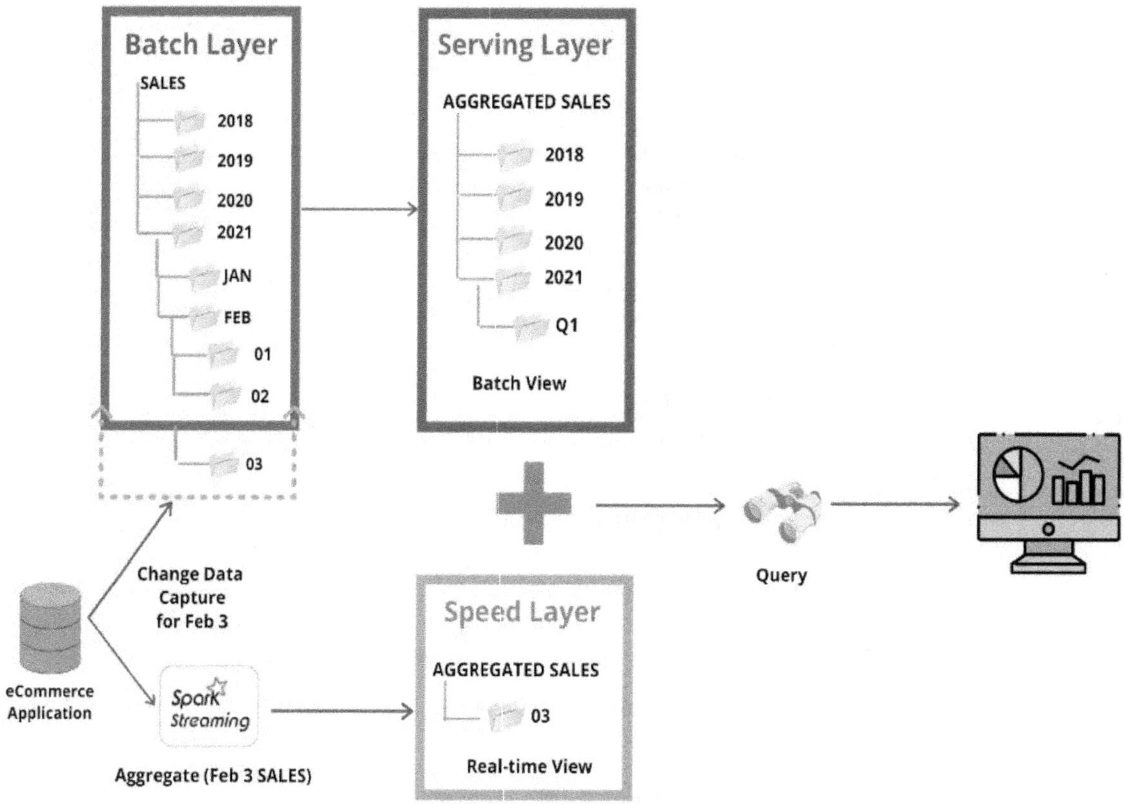

Figure 2.18: Various layers of a Lambda architecture

- Incremental data is pushed to the speed layer where it is aggregated in a streaming fashion as a real - time view.
- At query time, the results from the batch view are consolidated with the results from the real - time view to get the most recent and accurate figures.

Lambda architecture has several benefits, including low latency from precomputed views and high data accuracy from near-real-time access.

Here are some case scenarios where you might use the Lambda architecture with great success:

- **Access to near-real-time data**: There are scenarios in which the decision-making process is detrimentally impacted if access to the latest data is not available.
- **Large historical datasets**: There are situations in which the historical data is extremely large, so aggregations can take a long time to finish and cannot be performed frequently.

- **Dynamic nature of analytics (ad hoc)**: There are cases in which the case scenarios for data analytics are very dynamic and vary quite frequently. In this case, the batch and real-time views can be created or adjusted without affecting the underlying master data.

> Note
>
> A particular strength of the Lambda architecture is its ease of migration from traditional architectures. I have completed several of these migrations with great success.

Lambda architecture provides a nice balance of performance and data freshness. But in recent years, the requirements for streaming analytics have grown sharply. Use cases such as IoT monitoring and anomaly detection require a fast real-time analytics engine capable of supporting millions of incoming requests per second.

Despite all the advantages that Lambda architecture has, there are a few drawbacks, as outlined here:

- In a few cases, it is sometimes complex to implement due to the multiple layers. More layers also translate into higher costs for resources, administration, and monitoring.
- Each layer requires a different set of tools, services, and programming. Therefore, infrastructure and code management become a challenge.
- In some scenarios, implementing Lambda architecture may be an overkill due to the nature of the analytics.

Quite recently, a simpler architecture, the Kappa architecture, was introduced, often called the simplified version of the Lambda architecture.

Kappa architecture

The Kappa architecture was introduced in 2014 by **Jay Kreps**. This architecture eliminates the need for the batch layer altogether. Instead, all data is stored in a real-time layer that maintains an immutable stream of events in a stream-processing platform.

The major components of Kappa architecture are described in the following subsections.

Streaming layer

The streaming layer stores all raw data as sequential events (messages) sorted by creation timestamp. Since data is not stored on a regular filesystem, the chosen streaming platform should include built-in features such as **fault tolerance** (**FT**) and **high availability** (**HA**).

The tools of the trade for streaming layer storage are Apache Kafka, Azure Event Hubs, Amazon Kinesis, and Google Pub/Sub.

The stream-processing engine reads event data, performs required computations, and publishes the transformed data as views in the serving layer.

The tools of the trade for streaming - layer processing are Apache Spark Streaming, Apache Flink, and Kafka Streams.

Serving layer

The serving layer makes event data available to the query process using precomputed views. These views can be recomputed at regular intervals by relaunching the view build code.

The tools of the trade for serving layers are relational databases, data warehouses, cloud data warehouses, and cloud data storage.

Here is how the Kappa architecture functions:

- The stream - processing engine performs aggregations and publishes the results to the serving layer as precomputed views. As shown in *Figure 2.19*, at time *t*, the stream-processing code computes data from 2018 through the latest event in the sales topic.
- The computed data is published as the `AGGREGATED SALES` view, which is then queried for analysis.

You can see a diagram of the process here:

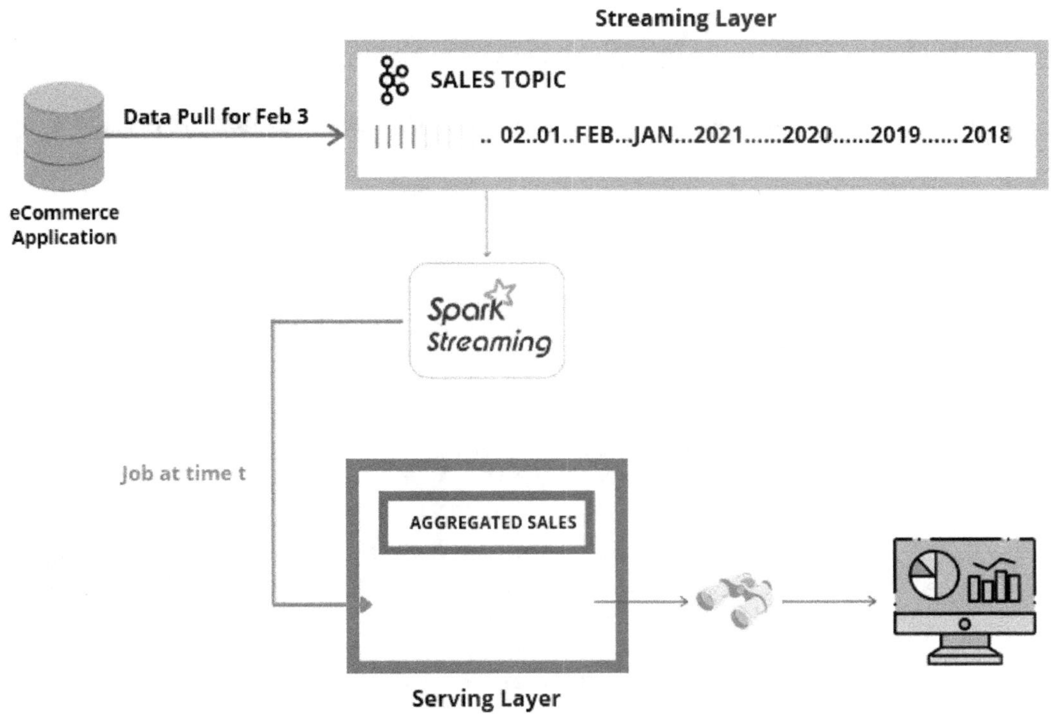

Figure 2.19: State of aggregate view at time t

At time **t + 1**, the stream-processing code recomputes data from 2018 through the most recent event in the sales topic. Notice that new events have been added to the queue since the last time the computations were performed. The recomputed data are published as follows:

- The previous version of the `AGGREGATED SALES` view is dropped.
- A new version of the `AGGREGATED SALES` view is computed to take its place.
- Queries are pointed to the recomputed view.

You can see a diagram of the process here:

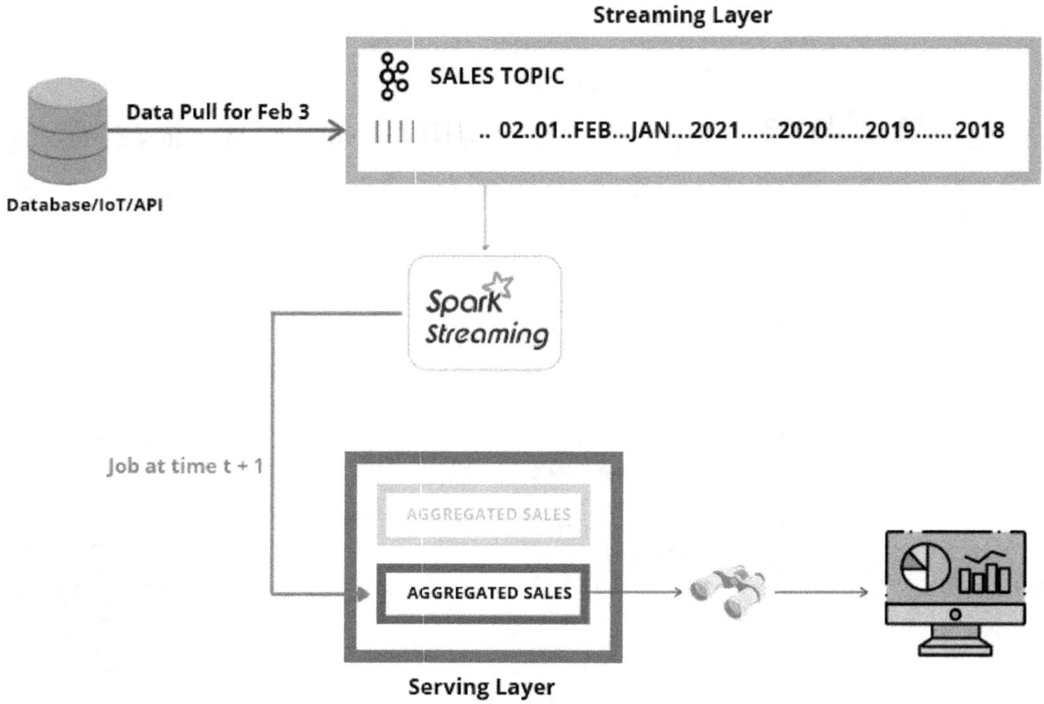

Figure 2.20: State of aggregate view at time t+1

Now that we understand how Kappa architecture generally functions, let's outline some of the pros and cons of it, as follows:

- The Kappa architecture works extremely well for use cases around IoT monitoring and real - time analytics with limited dependency on historical data.
- Unlike the Lambda architecture, a single code base is sufficient for data processing. This hugely simplifies infrastructure deployment and management requirements.
- Since Kappa stores all data in the streaming layer for larger datasets, typically in the TB range, the architecture becomes extremely expensive.

Let's compare the costs at a very high level, as follows:

- Storing 32 TB of data on Microsoft Azure Premium SSD Managed Disks will cost you roughly $4,194/month.
- Storing 32 TB of data on Microsoft Azure Blob storage will cost you just $682/month.

Many experts feel the Kappa architecture is a substitute for the Lambda architecture, although I see things a bit differently. I believe that each one of these architectures serves a different purpose. Here are some case scenarios where I have used the Kappa architecture with great success:

- **Real-time monitoring**: Monitoring of IoT sensors is a perfect use case for the Kappa architecture. In almost all monitoring cases, having access to historical data is not required.
- **Live dashboarding**: I am sure you have seen dashboards that visualize data in a live fashion. The visual is refreshed every few seconds based on incoming data.
- **Real-time ML**: Many companies are now exposing their ML models as microservices for use cases such as fraud detection.
- **Real-time data monetization**: We previously discussed data monetization as a means for revenue diversification. More and more companies are now exposing their data to external parties for real-time consumption.

> **Note**
>
> Before choosing any architecture, data engineers should carefully evaluate the strengths of each one based on customer requirements, the urgency of near-real-time analysis, and resource costs.

Both Lambda and Kappa are layered architectures - data is collected in the storage/streaming layer, processed, and finally published to a warehouse. Having used both architectures on several projects in the past, I can truthfully admit that implementing either one of them comes with a few challenges, such as the following:

- Keeping data fresh and up to date in each tier is difficult. Ever-changing data requires a carefully designed merge process.
- Infrastructure costs in both architectures can be steep at times.
- More layers mean more chances of failure. Dealing with failures is not only costly but also delays ongoing data analytics.
- If the data is being published externally for data monetization purposes, any failures or inaccuracies can cause revenue loss and customer dissatisfaction.

Some of the previously mentioned deficiencies in the Lambda and Kappa architectures have forced experts to rethink their approach.

Generally, in any data platform operation, we ingest data to storage, process it as per requirements, and finally publish the aggregated data to a warehouse so that it is available for analytics.

Recently, a new architecture has been rapidly gaining adoption, one that combines the power of a data lake and a data warehouse in one, as illustrated in the following diagram:

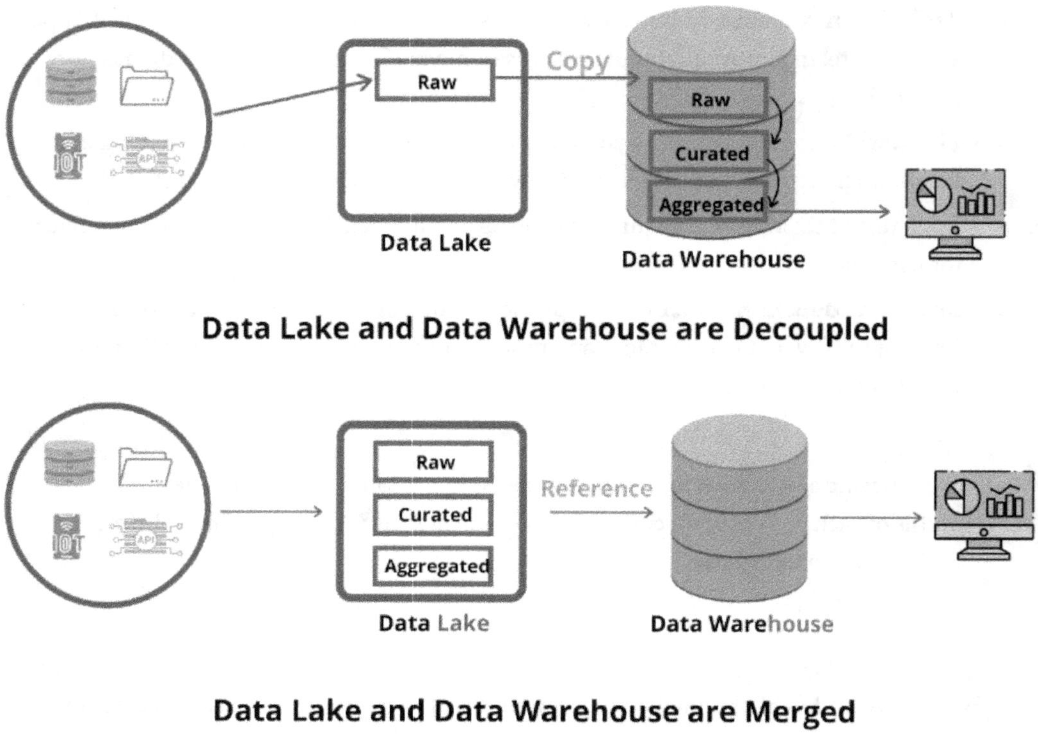

Figure 2.21: Rise of the Lakehouse architecture

In this section, we learned about the Kappa and Lambda architectures and the rise of the Lakehouse architecture.

Lakehouse architecture

Before we discuss Lakehouse architecture, it is important to understand what I call the power struggle between traditional and modern data processing systems.

The give-and-take struggle

There was a card game that I used to play when I was younger. In this game, to advance to the next level, you were required to sacrifice your best card.

Over many years in the data processing world, I have seen the same give-and-take struggle between the traditional method of data processing (databases/data warehouses) and the modern one (data lakes).

You can see this power struggle depicted in the following diagram:

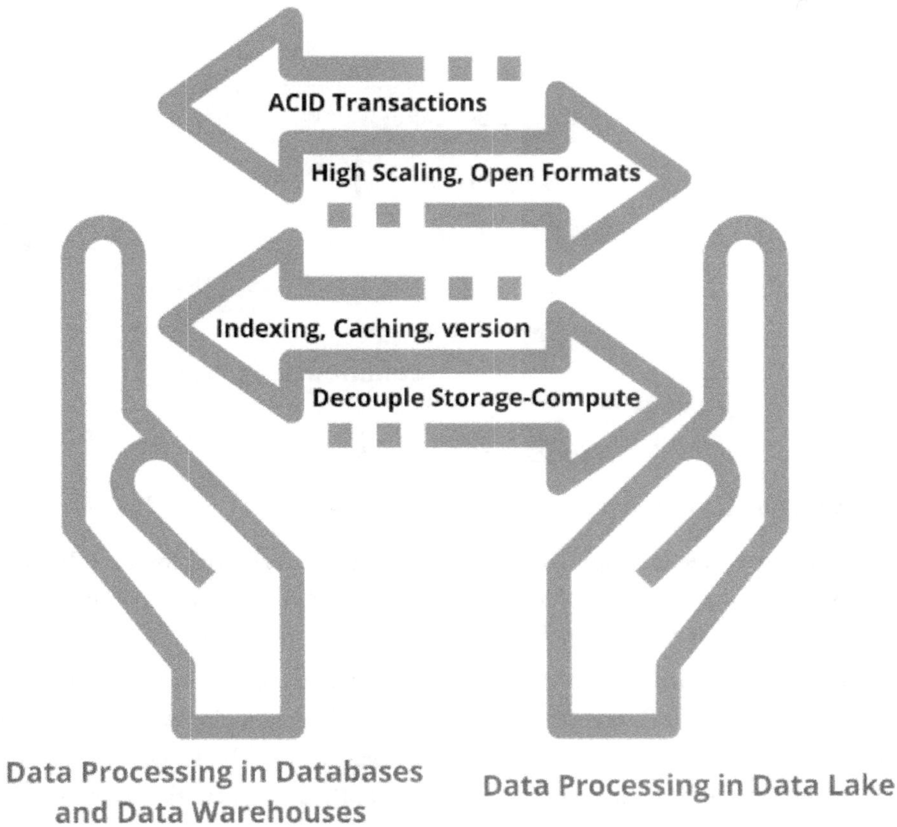

Figure 2.22: The power struggle

The decision to move toward modern data processing platforms has forced us to make some sacrifices; you gain some and you lose some. Let me highlight some of these give-and-take situations in which you must move from traditional to modern methods, as follows:

- Sacrifice durability and consistency features such as **atomicity**, **consistency**, **isolation**, and **durability** (**ACID**) transactions, but gain the ability to process on a highly scalable platform.
- Sacrifice performance features such as indexing and caching, but gain the ability to process data in multiple formats.
- Sacrifice security features such as versioning and auditing, but gain the ability to decouple storage and compute.

The Lakehouse architecture, as depicted in the following diagram, merges the low-cost storage with the **massively parallel processing** (**MPP**) power of a warehouse to serve the diverse and ever-evolving requirements of modern - era analytics:

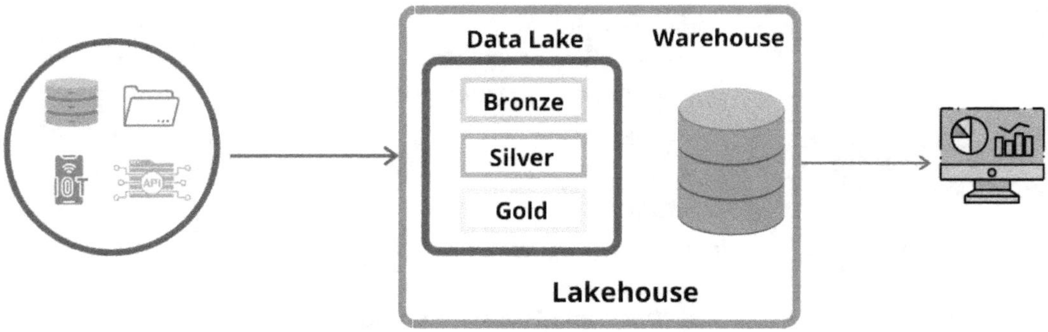

Figure 2.23: Lakehouse architecture

Here are a few important features of the Lakehouse architecture:

- **Supports low-cost storage**: The Lakehouse architecture carries forward the support for using low-cost storage. Data can be structured, semi-structured, or unstructured, and stored in open formats such as Parquet.
- **Supports ACID transactions**: Now, this one is big. An absence of transaction support significantly impacts data integrity and quality on the data platform. Over the years, dealing with duplicated and deleted data has been a huge challenge. In the early days, I remember going through a multi-step process in Hive to deal with this. A few years later, Spark took over, but the challenge stayed the same. But the struggle is finally over.... long live **Databricks Delta Lake**!

> **Note**
>
> Since its introduction, Delta Lake has proved to be a lifesaver for data engineers, not only to resolve the CDC challenge but also many other ones, such as schema evolution and time travel. The Lakehouse architecture assumes the use of an open-source storage engine, such as Delta Lake, for ACID transactions, metadata management, governance, and other features.

- **Metadata management**: The Lakehouse architecture offers strong metadata management features such as schema enforcement and evolution. Once again, the absence of such features in the past has forced us to perform similar checks using code.

- **Segregation of storage and compute**: The Lakehouse architecture preserves the idea of decoupling storage and compute for massive scalability and cost - saving.
- **Support for BI tools**: Lakehouse architecture supports connectivity to all major BI tools using standard **Java Database Connectivity** (**JDBC**)/**Open Database Connectivity** (**ODBC**) connectivity.
- **Native support for Structured Query Language (SQL)**: Users can easily utilize the power of the SQL language for performing analytics.

> **Note**
>
> In Azure, the Lakehouse architecture is implemented using either Databricks or Synapse Analytics. In addition to using SQL for performing analysis, both services additionally provide support for Apache Spark.

- **Supports streaming workloads**: The Lakehouse architecture supports real - time analytics and reporting using streaming data.

The tools of the trade for the Lakehouse architecture include Azure Synapse Analytics, Amazon Redshift Spectrum, Google BigQuery, and Snowflake.

These sections should explain how Lakehouse architecture provides a nice blend of traditional Lambda and Kappa architecture. The way I see it, Lakehouse architecture is the right recipe for creating a data - one that not only works but also provides the correct balance between **user experience** (**UX**), scalability, and cost.

Summary

In this chapter, we learned about a data platform and its various characteristics, such as multiple zones, the ability to deal with multiple formats, governance, and - most importantly - its ability to decouple storage and compute.

We also learned about four key data platform architectures: traditional, Lambda, Kappa, and Lakehouse. We analyzed each one based on its applicability to specific case scenarios, cost, and overall management.

In the next chapter, I will highlight various tools and services available in Microsoft Azure required to build a data platform using Lakehouse architecture.

Get this book's PDF version and more

Scan the QR code (or go to `packtpub.com/unlock`). Search for this book by name, confirm the edition, and then follow the steps on the page.

UNLOCK NOW

Note: Keep your invoice handy. Purchases made directly from Packt don't require an invoice.

3

Data Engineering on Microsoft Azure

In the previous chapter, we discussed how cloud adoption offers greater flexibility and faster deployments for data engineering and analytical workloads. A cloud platform is fundamental to successful data engineering practice, offering virtually unlimited storage and compute capabilities. Microsoft Azure stands out as a leading cloud service provider, delivering a comprehensive suite of IaaS, PaaS, and SaaS solutions for ingesting, processing, and distribution. In this chapter, we'll discuss the major tools and services in Microsoft Azure that may help us implement such a solution.

In this chapter, we will delve deeper into the wide range of Azure services that support data engineering and analytics.

Azure offers a comprehensive ecosystem designed to address a large range of data engineering and analytics use cases. In many scenarios, multiple services can be combined to deliver an optimal solution. By the end of this chapter, you will have a clear understanding of the Azure services for data engineering, along with practical guidelines on how to choose between them to maximize efficiency and business value.

In this chapter, we will cover the following topics:

- Azure self-managed data engineering services (IaaS)
- Azure-managed data engineering services (PaaS)
- Data-as-a-product Data engineering as a service (SaaS)

Introducing data engineering in Azure

In recent years, Microsoft Azure has added several powerful services to its arsenal that seamlessly collect, store, process, and publish data for both batch and streaming workloads. Gone are the days when choices for storage and compute are severely limited among cloud vendors. Previously, users were limited to the provided tools and services; now, you have a broader range of options.

Today, the cloud ecosystem looks very different from what it did previously. The growth of cloud services allows users to choose from a variety of storage, compute, and deployment options. For example, if I want to run a Spark program, I can choose from at least four options on **Microsoft Azure**. The real question is, if all four options are running **Apache Spark**, then why are these options even required?

> Note
>
> The array of options available in the cloud is not limited to compute; the same variety exists for data collection, infrastructure deployments, and pipeline orchestration services.

Here are some of the reasons why several options for performing similar kinds of operations in data engineering are available on Microsoft Azure:

- **Ease of use**: The ease of use of a service is a key factor in deciding which option to use. As a data engineer, you may code the entire **ETL** program yourself or opt for a service that can auto-generate and invoke the code for you after creating a visual workflow.
- **Data engineering team skills**: The skill level of the data engineering team plays a very important role in deciding which option to choose. Teams with skilled data engineers typically choose services for data workflows that require coding from scratch. Doing so gives engineers complete control over their programs and their dependencies.
- **The desired level of administration and monitoring**: Having a skilled data engineering team does not automatically mean that the same team will be involved in administering and monitoring the operations. The choice of service may need to be adjusted depending on who manages it in production.
- **Self-serve analytics**: Today, self-serve analytics is gaining momentum, empowering end users to take an active role in building ETL and ELT workflows. For this specific set of users, the ability to create a drag-and-drop workflow in a few clicks is extremely desirable.

> **Note**
>
> The idea of self-serve analytics is gaining popularity these days. Self-serve analytics enables fast-paced delivery of end-user analytical goals.

- **Generative AI**: **Generative AI** (**GenAI**) is reshaping the way users interact with data. The seamless integration of Microsoft CoPilot with data engineering and analytics tools such as Azure Synapse Analytics and Databricks accelerates development and collaboration among data teams.
- **Level of control that's desired over the infrastructure**: The level of control that's desired over the infrastructure is an important factor that impacts the choice of service. In some cases, the cloud-provided service may lack the desired functionality and may not permit changes to the underlying infrastructure. In this case, data engineers may want to choose a service that offers full control over the infrastructure.
- **Complete data isolation**: Some stringent compliance frameworks do not permit the use of multi-tenant services. In such cases, complete data isolation is mandatory, thus impacting which options are suitable.

> **Note**
>
> There is an ongoing debate around whether cloud services are truly compliant with well-known frameworks such as HIPAA. The multi-tenancy of cloud storage is a major roadblock to making that claim. It is fair to say that cloud storage supports compliance frameworks, but may not be fully compliant.

- **Prior familiarity with certain frameworks**: This is an extremely important factor for organizations migrating their analytics from on-premises to the cloud. Since they are already familiar with a particular tool or framework, they tend to choose the closest available option in the cloud.
- **Cost**: Finally, the cost of the service is a major factor that impacts the choice that should be made. Typically, the easier the usage and management of a particular service, the higher its cost. Therefore, before choosing a service, careful cost analysis is deemed necessary.

Note

As a data engineer, it is understandable to have a bias toward specific tools, languages, and frameworks. But once you leave, it becomes the customer's responsibility to manage this. Try to set your bias aside and provide the customer with a solution that uses technologies they feel comfortable with.

Performing data engineering in Microsoft Azure

Data engineering in Microsoft Azure can be performed using the following three options:

- Self-managed data engineering services (**IaaS**)
- Azure-managed data engineering services (**PaaS**)
- Data engineering as a service (**SaaS**)

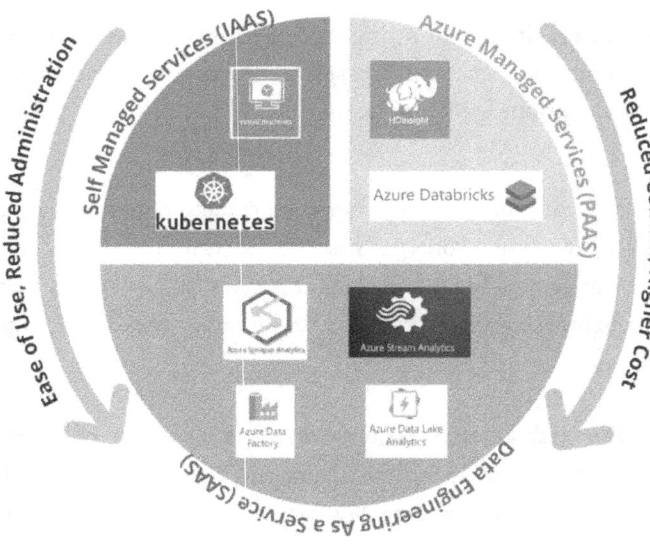

Figure 3.1: Data engineering option in Microsoft Azure

Self-managed data engineering services (IaaS)

In the early phases of data engineering, the use of well-known distributed frameworks such as Hadoop, Spark, and Kafka rose sharply. As a result, many organizations were deploying Hadoop/Spark/Kafka on on-premises infrastructures. Since Hadoop/Spark/Kafka are multi-node frameworks, installations were performed on physical and virtual machines hosted in either the organization's owned or co-located data centers.

Then came the period when the cloud began to become a reality, and organizations started moving their Hadoop/Spark/Kafka clusters to the cloud. In the very early stages of cloud evolution, using a self-managed service was perhaps the only option available for data engineering.

IaaS use case

Here are a few use cases where using an IaaS layer is warranted:

- An organization that has heavily customized Hadoop/Spark/Kafka clusters. This means they are tied to specific versions that are unavailable on the cloud PaaS equivalent service.
- The organization has developed its own libraries for data engineering and data science that can't easily be deployed on PaaS or SaaS offerings on the cloud.
- An organization where security regulations do not permit the use of multi-tenant cloud services. This forces them to use single-tenant dedicated cloud resources.
- An organization that cannot tolerate variability in the compute power of the use of shared services.

Let's look at how a typical Hadoop/Spark/Kafka deployment is performed using self-managed services that use the **Infrastructure as a Service** (**IaaS**) layer on Microsoft Azure.

Azure Virtual Machines (**Azure VMs**) allow you to create on-demand compute resources for data processing. The following list describes some of the features available using Azure VMs:

- Take the inventory of the on-premises Hadoop/Spark/Kafka nodes – the total number of nodes, aggregated CPU, and aggregated memory.
- Shortlist virtual machines on Microsoft Azure that offer similar aggregated CPU and memory as the on-premises inventory. This step requires careful planning and calculations. It is not necessary to procure the same number of nodes on Microsoft Azure, so long as the aggregated CPU and memory resources meet or exceed those of the on-premises deployment. In distributed computing, horizontal scalability of nodes is preferable. It is highly recommended to compare different classes of virtual machines on Microsoft Azure; in many cases, you may be able to procure smaller-class virtual machines that are cheaper than higher-class ones, both offering the same aggregated CPU and memory.
- Procure virtual machines on Microsoft Azure.
- Configure networking among nodes, open required firewall ports, and install operating system prerequisites.

- Install and configure Hadoop/Spark/Kafka and any other ecosystem tools, such as Sqoop, Oozie, Hive, and so on. These steps need to be performed on multiple nodes.
- Install and configure administration and monitoring software.

While IaaS provides greater granular control over the infrastructure, it often requires dedicated resources for ongoing management. Here are some pros and cons of self-managed services:

- Performing deployments using virtual machines provides the data engineer with complete freedom to choose any framework and any version and have complete control over its dependencies.
- It should be evident from the deployment process outlined previously that choosing self-managed services requires careful planning, design, and execution.
- Due to the wide variety of touchpoints, the data engineering team in charge of the deployment needs to be skilled in several areas, including cloud deployments, networking, administration, and monitoring. Note that these skills go above and beyond the usual expectations of a data engineering team, which typically involves pipeline development and data orchestration.
- Scaling a cluster using a self-managed service can become a challenge.

As we mentioned previously, deploying a Hadoop/Spark/Kafka cluster using self-managed services is not optional. However, there are ways you can minimize the effects of the limitations we have just discussed.

Hadoop/Spark/Kafka distributions

Deploying Hadoop/Spark/Kafka clusters using VMs involves multiple nodes. A simpler way to handle installing, upgrading, administering, and monitoring these clusters is to use distributions such as **Cloudera**, **Hortonworks**, and **MapR**. Each of these distributions includes software that enables minimal cluster provisioning. **Ambari** enables users to easily create, administer, and monitor a Hadoop cluster, whereas **Cloudera Manager** enables users to provision **Hadoop** and **Spark** clusters.

Infrastructure as Code

Infrastructure as Code (**IaC**) is a practice of deploying cloud resources, such as VMs, using configuration files. Using this practice, you may either create the entire infrastructure or modify it. Using IaC significantly reduces manual effort for recurring tasks while maintaining high consistency and accuracy. **Azure Resource Manager** (**ARM**) centralizes IaC deployments using resource templates.

Containerization

Containerization is the practice of abstracting application code from the underlying infrastructure. Using containerization provides several benefits, including isolation of the host environment, version control, and dependency management. This means the cluster nodes can now run in their own isolated environment called containers. These containers can be orchestrated using the well-known Kubernetes engine. **Azure Kubernetes Service** (**AKS**) allows you to easily deploy and manage containerized applications.

> Note
>
> In the cloud era, many organizations are adopting technologies that keep them cloud-agnostic. Who knows which vendor will drop their prices and when? Containerizing their applications keeps them open to moving between cloud vendors as desired.

Azure-managed data engineering services (PaaS)

Right after the big data wave gained momentum, cloud vendors such as Microsoft Azure began offering managed services to enable fast deployments and easy management. Before we go into the specifics of the services, let's focus on what an Azure-managed service that uses the **platform as a service** (**PaaS**) layer on Azure means:

- The resource is deployed with minimal configuration and user input.
- Azure takes care of monitoring the resource for downtime and recovers it automatically in case a failure is detected.
- Globally available.
- Well integrated with other Azure services.
- Automatically provides data redundancy.
- Contains built-in security mechanisms for data protection.

PaaS use case

Here are a couple of use cases where using the PaaS layer is warranted:

- An organization has on-premises Hadoop/Spark/Kafka clusters and quickly wants to migrate to the cloud.
- An organization has limited cloud-related skills, so they want to use services with low operational requirements.
- An organization where security regulations permit the use of multi-tenant cloud services and can tolerate variability in compute power.

The following are a few of the Azure-managed PaaS services.

Data storage services in Microsoft Azure

Azure Blob storage is an object storage solution that is highly optimized for storing large amounts of text and binary data. Azure Blob storage was built with a huge focus on scalability, high availability, and security. It stores data in three tiers: hot, cool, and archive. The hot tier is used for frequently accessed data, the cool tier for infrequently accessed data, and the archive tier for rarely accessed data. Depending on usage, you can choose between two performance tiers: standard and premium.

Data in Azure Blob storage is protected by several authentication mechanisms such as **Azure Active Directory**, shared keys, and **shared access signatures** (**SAS**). You can also protect your blobs using **role-based access control** (**RBAC**). You may turn versioning on for extra protection against accidental changes and deletions. This feature maintains the previous version of the blob in case you need to recover it.

Blobs in Azure Blob storage are automatically encrypted and redundant. Multiple copies of data are stored – three copies are stored within a single physical location by default, and several options exist for storing copies across zones and regions. For added security, Azure Blob Storage offers four redundancy options to suit your organization's business continuity requirements. The four redundancy options available are **Locally Redundant Storage** (**LRS**), **Zone-Redundant Storage** (**ZRS**), **Geo-Redundant Storage** (**GRS**), and **Read-Access Geo-Redundant Storage** (**RA-GRS**).

- **Storage account**: The storage account holds your data. A unique namespace for your account is allocated in Azure.
  An example namespace address is `https://mydataanalytics.blob.core.windows.net`.
- **Containers**: A container organizes a group of blobs. A container should have a valid DNS name such as `https://mydataanalytics.blob.core.windows.net/mydatacontainer`.
- **Blobs**: Actual data that is stored in the containers.

The following figure illustrates structured and organized data within Azure Blob Storage:

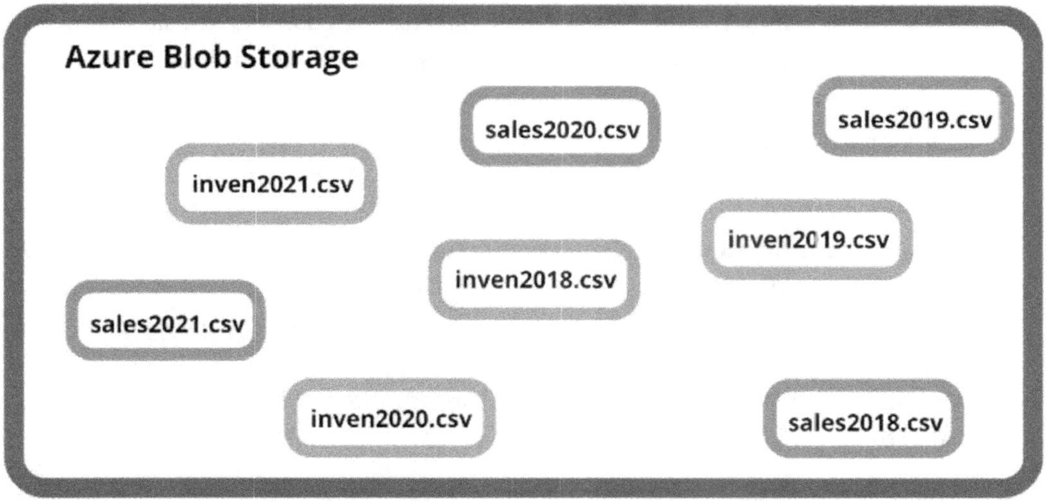

Figure 3.2: Storing blobs in Azure Blob storage

> **Note**
>
> A particular drawback of object storage is its slow search performance. In Azure Blob storage, you can speed up searches using index tags.

Azure Data Lake Storage Gen2

Azure Data Lake Storage (**ADLS**) has a significant edge over Azure Blob Storage in terms of suitability for analytical workloads. But before we proceed with the reasons why, let me make one clarification: Azure Data Lake Storage is a layer built on top of Azure Blob storage. Azure Data Lake Storage is compatible with Apache ecosystem tools such as Hadoop, Spark, and other distributed processing engines. It brings together all the great features offered by Azure Blob storage, plus more:

- **Hierarchical namespace**: Compared to Azure Blob storage, which has a flat namespace, Azure Data Lake Storage organizes blobs in a hierarchy of directories. This method of blob organization greatly enhances the performance of search operations.
- **Access control lists**: Azure Data Lake Storage supports the fine-grained security of blobs by using POSIX-style permissions.

> **Note**
>
> POSIX stands for Portable Operating System Interface. POSIX implements the file system permission model using **Access Control Lists** (**ACLs**). ACLs are a quick way to define **read**, **write**, and **execute** (**r-w-x**) permissions for users or user groups.

- **Designed for analytics**: Azure Data Lake Storage provides excellent support for major open-source platforms such as Hadoop, Spark, Flink, and many other distributed processing frameworks. Using the Azure Blob filesystem driver, the open-source platforms can easily access the object storage without the need for explicit code. The following figure illustrates hierarchical organization of blobs within Azure Data Lake Storage:

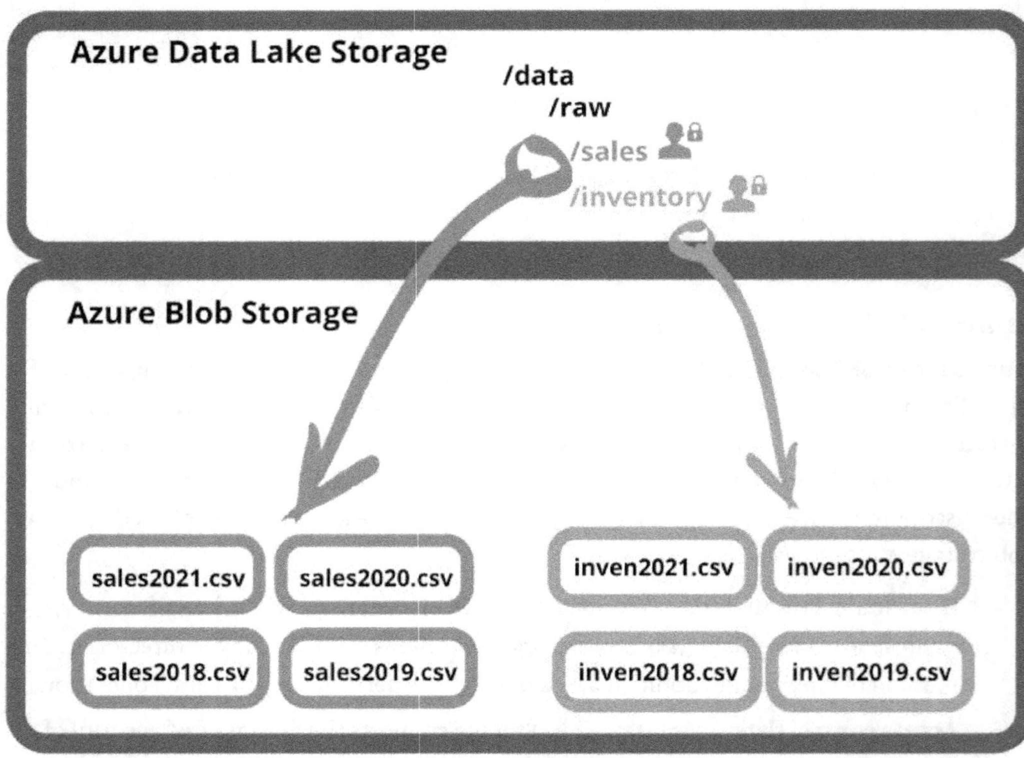

Figure 3.3: Storing blobs in a hierarchy in Azure Data Lake Storage

- **Tight integration with Azure services**: Azure Data Lake Storage integrates seamlessly with Azure services such as Azure Data Factory, Azure HDInsight, and Azure Stream Analytics.
- **Cost and performance**: The cost of Azure Data Lake Storage is very similar to Azure Blob storage. However, ADLS offers fast performance due to a hierarchical namespace and support for small and large files.

Azure Event Hubs

Azure Event Hubs is a real-time data streaming platform used for ingesting event data. The sources of the event data collected are usually application logs, clickstreams, and IoT data. Azure Event Hubs can be easily deployed with minimal configuration requirements.

You can use Azure Event Hubs for both batch and real-time processing. For batch processing, data from Event Hubs can be captured to Azure Blob Storage or Azure Data Lake Storage for later processing. For real-time processing, you may have to send data to Azure Stream Analytics, which could take further action based on events.

The figure below depicts the architectural differences between Azure Event Hubs single-tenancy and multi-tenancy models:

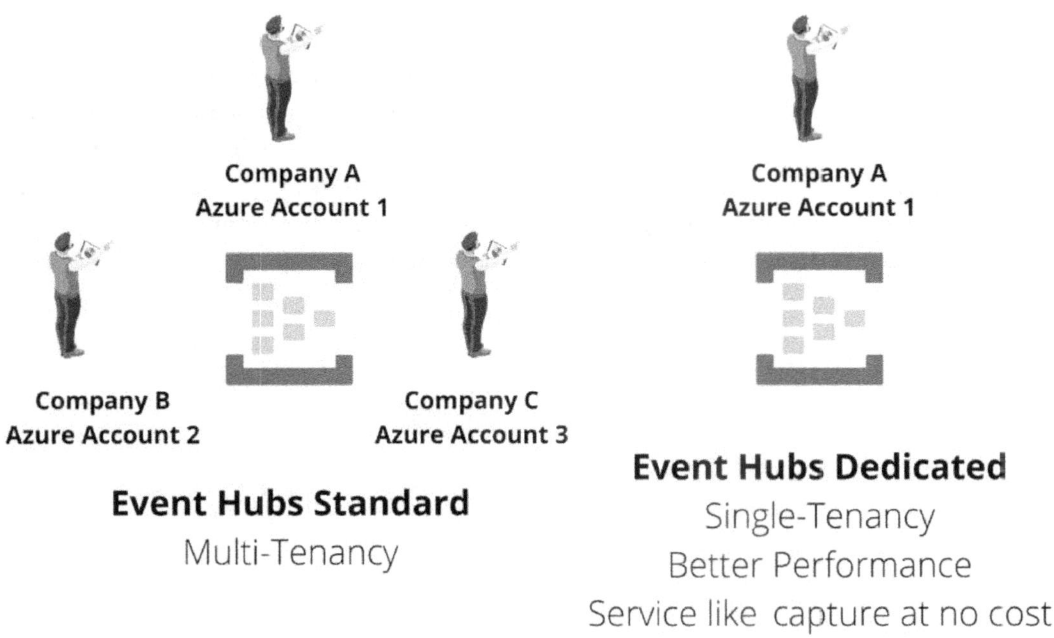

Figure 3.4: Multi-tenancy and single-tenancy in Azure Event Hubs

Data in Azure Event Hubs is not stored permanently. By default, the retention period is 1 day, but this can be increased to 7 days in the standard edition and 90 days in the dedicated edition.

Event data is stored in partitions – the higher the number of partitions, the higher the read and write throughput. The capacity of Azure Event Hubs is pre-purchased using throughput limits, once the throughput limit matches a write process (1 MB/1,000 events) or a read process (2 MB/4,096 events). The auto-inflate feature scales your throughput units based on peak demand. Azure Event Hubs replicates data within the primary data center with automated failure detection and recovery enabled. For extra protection, replication across availability zones can also be enabled.

Azure Cosmos DB

Azure Cosmos DB is a highly available, low-latency NoSQL-class database. As a managed service, Azure handles the usual administration challenges around installation, patching, and upgrades. Cosmos DB stores data on SSDs, and it is encrypted by default.

> Note
>
> **Solid-State Drive** (**SSD**) is a data storage device that uses flash memory chips to store data. Using the SSD backend, Azure Cosmos DB can offer high IOPS, low latency, and high durability.

Azure Cosmos DB is globally distributed, making it extremely suitable for applications requiring high responsiveness. Azure Cosmos DB is an automatic choice for applications that require low latency, such as telemetry, monitoring, and AI agents. In a globally distributed deployment, **Azure Traffic Manager** can route application requests to the closest Azure region without any code changes to your applications. This approach enables the application to deliver fast response times for both read and write operations.

The figure below depicts how traffic can be globally distributed in Azure Cosmos DB:

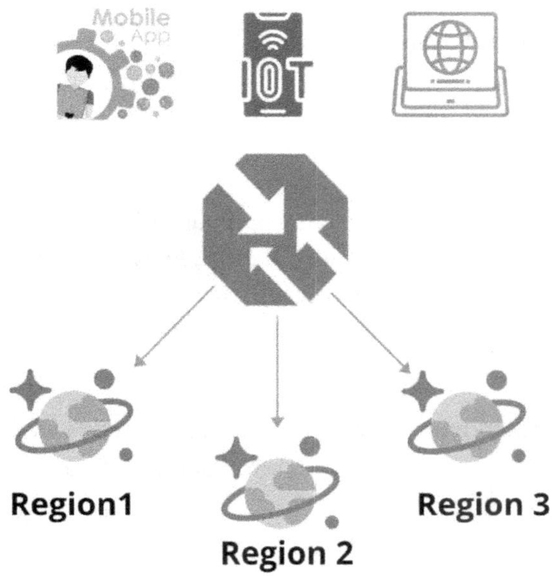

Figure 3.5: Global distribution with Azure Cosmos DB

Its schema-less architecture makes it simple to store semi-structured and unstructured data at a large scale. Here is what the resource model of Azure Cosmos DB looks like:

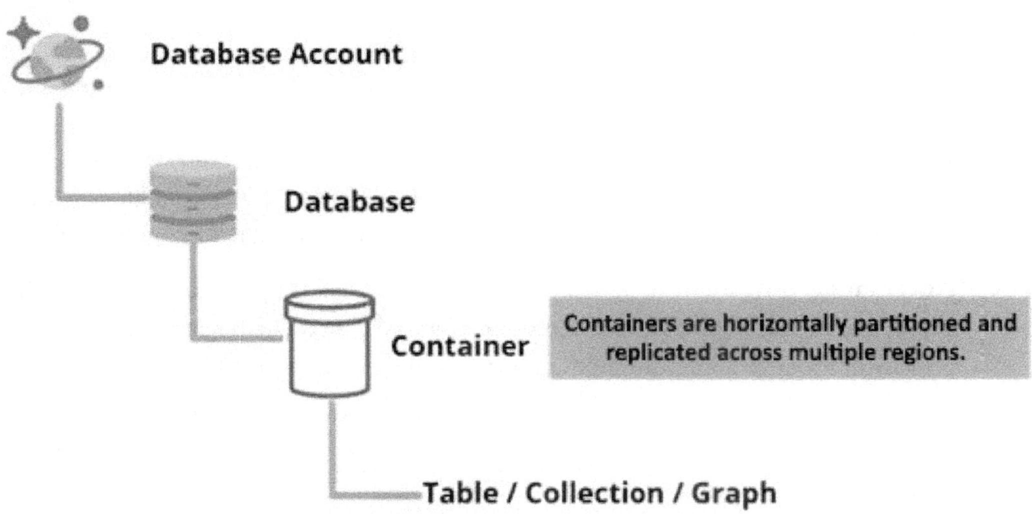

Figure 3.6: Azure Cosmos DB resource model

Under an Azure Cosmos DB account, you can create databases, containers, and items. Multiple APIs are supported in Azure Cosmos DB, and the API you choose impacts the item's type. Items store data in a container and have variable schemas based on the following mappings:

- **Table API and SQL API**: Table
- **Cassandra API**: Row
- **MongoDB API**: Document
- **Gremlin API**: Node

Partitioning is an important aspect of achieving optimal performance with Azure Cosmos DB. Based on a partition key, data is stored in subsets called **logical partitions**. Storing data in partitions significantly improves performance because all items in a logical partition share the same key value.

> Note
>
> Choosing the correct partition key is an extremely important skill for data engineers, as it can significantly affect your application's performance, both positively and negatively.

Data processing services in Microsoft Azure

Right after the big data wave began to gain momentum, cloud vendors began packaging popular open-source frameworks such as Hadoop, Spark, and Kafka and offering them as vendor-managed services. Let's look at a few Azure-managed data processing services.

Azure HDInsight

Azure HDInsight is a managed service for cloud distribution of Hadoop and its ecosystem. It embeds popular open-source frameworks such as Hadoop, Spark, Kafka, Hive, and Storm. Azure HDInsight allows you to spin up clusters with ease and greater efficiency. Azure HDInsight embeds the popular **Hortonworks Data Platform** (**HDP**). It has several benefits compared to self-managed Hadoop/Spark/Kafka clusters, as outlined in the following list:

- **Fully managed**: Azure HDInsight clusters are fully managed by Azure. This means the deployment cycle is seamless and highly accelerated. A new cluster can be spun up literally in a matter of minutes with minimal deployment steps.
- **Managed resources**: Azure HDInsight shields users from issues arising from underlying infrastructure problems. Underlying hardware and software components are monitored regularly and are self-healing.

- **Azure cloud-native security**: Azure HDInsight can leverage Azure cloud-native security services such as VNETs, transparent encryption, and **Azure Active Directory** integration for RBAC.
- **Azure cloud-native monitoring**: Azure HDInsight can leverage Azure cloud-native monitoring tools such as **Azure Monitor**.
- **Seamless integration with other Azure services**: Azure HDInsight can seamlessly integrate with Azure services such as Azure Data Lake Storage Gen 2, Azure Data Factory, Azure Cosmos DB, and Azure Synapse.
- **Decouples storage and compute**: Azure HDInsight truly segregates storage and compute by providing options to store data that's external to the cluster on services such as Azure Blob Storage and Azure Data Lake Storage Gen 2.
- **Auto-scalability**: Azure HDInsight can auto-scale nodes up and down based on preset triggers that are based on scheduled or, more likely, performance metrics.
- **Azure marketplace extensibility**: Azure HDInsight can use several marketplace extensions that can further extend its power and functionality.

While Azure HDInsight offers a convenient blend of Hadoop and Spark on a single platform, another service with native Spark capabilities has recently gained significant momentum.

Azure Databricks

Databricks is a company founded by the original creators of Apache Spark, Delta Lake, and MLflow. Databricks Spark can only be run on a cluster deployed in the cloud.

> Note
>
> **Databricks Community Edition** offers a free version that can be very useful if you are trying to learn about Spark. Here is the link: `https://login.databricks.com/signup`.

Azure Databricks is a data engineering and analytics platform for performing large-scale distributed computing on Microsoft Azure. Azure Databricks uses the Apache Spark framework for high-performance data processing. You may be wondering what makes the Azure Databricks version of Spark so special and widely recognized as the leader in distributed computing. Here are a few reasons why:

- **Medallion architecture**: Databricks **medallion architecture** is a data design pattern used to logically organize data in a lakehouse. The end goal of this architecture is to incrementally and progressively improve the structure and quality of data as it flows through each layer of the lakehouse: Bronze >> Silver >> Gold

- **Unified governance**: Azure Databricks enables a unified and consistent governance framework for assessing data assets residing either within Databricks or external sources.
- **Performance-enhanced runtime**: Azure Databricks has added several performance enhancements over the open-source version of Apache Spark. According to several benchmarks, Databricks Spark performs up to 8 times faster than the open-source version.
- **Collaborative environment**: Azure Databricks supports a collaborative environment between the data engineering, data analysis, and data science teams. Data engineers can easily share resources such as workspaces and jobs.
- **Interactive development**: Azure Databricks provides an **interactive development environment** (**IDE**) using notebooks. Data engineers can manage their code (notebooks) using popular source control tools such as GitHub and Bitbucket.
- **Decouples storage and compute**: Azure Databricks decouples storage from compute by storing data on Azure Blob Storage and Azure Data Lake Storage Gen2.
- **Seamless integration with other Azure services**: Azure Databricks can seamlessly integrate with other Azure services, including Azure Data Factory, Azure Event Hub, and Azure Synapse.
- **Active Directory integration**: Azure Databricks integrates well with Azure Active Directory.
- **Auto-scalability**: Azure Databricks supports autoscaling by adding or removing worker nodes based on workloads.
- **AI enablement**: Azure Databricks supports high-performance ML/AI computing required for deep learning using **graphics processing units** (**GPUs**).

Azure Databricks offers three broad-level services within its environment.

Data engineering

As a data engineering service, Azure Databricks offers end-to-end solutions for data ingestion, data transformation, and job scheduling. This service is primarily designed to support data engineers, data analysts, and ML/AI engineers in building scalable data pipelines.

Data warehousing

As a data warehousing service, Azure Databricks offers a highly scalable, high-performance analytics solution built on the lakehouse architecture. Powered by Databricks SQL, it can seamlessly integrate with established business intelligence services such as Power BI and Tableau. This service is targeted at data engineers and data analysts who are primarily interested in using SQL as the de facto language for performing data operations.

Machine learning and AI

Azure Databricks offers the Mosaic AI platform for creating ML/AI pipelines. Using **Mosaic AI**, you can build, train, and deploy machine learning models as well as create cutting-edge generative AI applications such as AI agents and **retrieval-augmented generation** (**RAG**).

While PaaS provides a robust platform for data engineers to build data platforms, some configuration may still be required to customize environments to meet specific needs. For organizations with limited technical expertise, a fully managed solution is often more desirable – one that eliminates the need for installation and configuration.

Data engineering as a service (SaaS)

In modern times, organizations want to be less burdened by maintaining infrastructure and more focused on what matters. This is the reason why the concept of offering **software as a service** (**SaaS**) has gained immense popularity. In a typical SaaS solution infrastructure, deployment, load balancing, high availability, and scalability are handled by the vendor. This gives their customers peace of mind when using the service, without having to worry about the underlying hardware or software.

SaaS use case

Here are a couple of use cases where using a SaaS layer is warranted:

- An organization that wants to focus on data engineering and analytics without going through the hassle of managing infrastructure or code.
- An organization where security regulations permit the use of multi-tenant cloud services and can tolerate variability in compute power.

Microsoft Azure offers several SaaS products via its pay-per-use model. Since the list of Azure-offered SaaS products is extensive, we will focus on those commonly used in data engineering and analytics.

Azure Data Factory

Azure Data Factory is a managed data integration and transformation service. You can use over 90 built-in connectors to collect data from a wide variety of data sources, including databases (relational and non-relational), APIs, file systems, and other SaaS applications.

Azure Data Factory is built to handle data integration workflows using the classical **Extract**, **Transform**, **Load** (**ETL**) approach or the modern **Extract**, **Load**, **Transform** (**ELT**) approach. An Azure Data Factory workflow is referred to as a **pipeline**.

A pipeline is a collection of activities that are units of work that perform actions on datasets. An activity uses a **linked service** to connect to external sources such as storage, databases, and clusters:

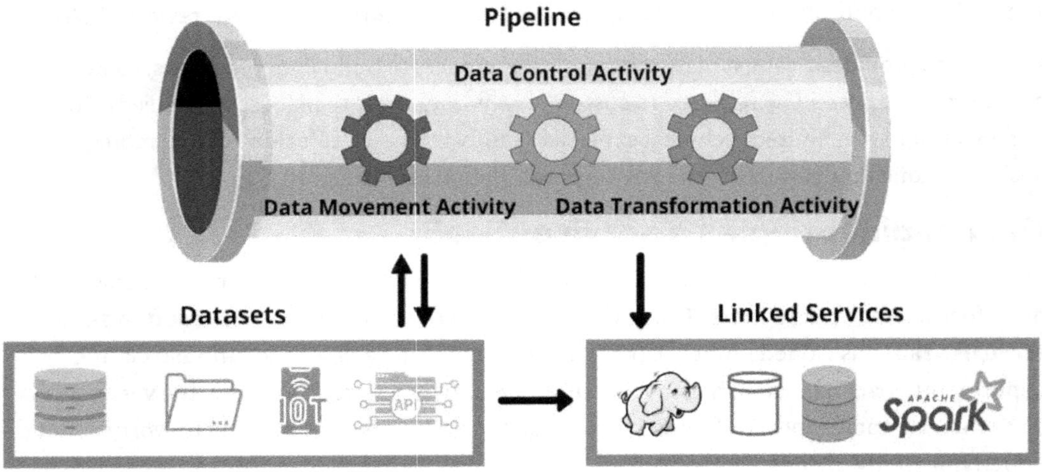

Figure 3.7: Interaction between the Azure Data Factory components

An activity in Azure Data Factory can be one of the following three types:

- **Data movement activity**: A data movement activity is used for copying data from a source data store to a sink data store. The data movement activity runs on an integration runtime, which serves as its compute environment. An integration runtime can be Azure-hosted (runs on Azure infrastructure), self-hosted (runs on customer infrastructure), or Azure-SSIS (runs on an Azure-managed SSIS cluster).
- **Data transformation activity**: A data transformation activity allows data engineers to build curation and transformation logic and execute it on a variety of computing environments, such as Azure HDInsight and Azure Databricks.
- **Control flow activity**: A control flow activity allows data engineers to build a data workflow using programmatic operations such as if-else, parameterization, and iterations.

Using Azure Data Factory, you can build, run, and monitor data-driven workflows without the need to write code. The following are the components of the Azure Data Factory service:

- **Ingest**: You can ingest data from over 90 data sources from on-premises, Azure cloud, or other cloud vendors.
- **Control flow**: You can generate code-free flows to control the execution of workflows using programmatic operations.
- **Data flow**: You can generate code-free transformations that execute in Spark or use pre-existing Spark clusters.
- **Schedule**: You can schedule pipelines using manual, event-based, or scheduled triggers.
- **Monitor**: You can view the pipeline's run history and create alerts/notifications.

Azure Data Factory replicates pipeline metadata across paired regions to protect against failures. It also implements RBAC for authoring, editing, and monitoring pipelines.

Azure Stream Analytics

Azure Stream Analytics is a fully managed real-time data analysis service. It is used to process high-velocity streaming data from data sources such as IoT sensors, logs, and social media. Here are some use case scenarios for Azure Stream Analytics:

- Real-time decision-making, such as fraud detection and predictive analysis
- IoT anomaly detection of IoT sensor data
- Monitoring infrastructure and application logs
- To facilitate dashboarding
- Invoking workflows based on conditions
- Identifying patterns and aggregating data across several data sources
- Alerting based on threshold values
- Performing sentiment analysis for social media posts

The figure below illustrates the core capabilities of Azure Stream Analytics:

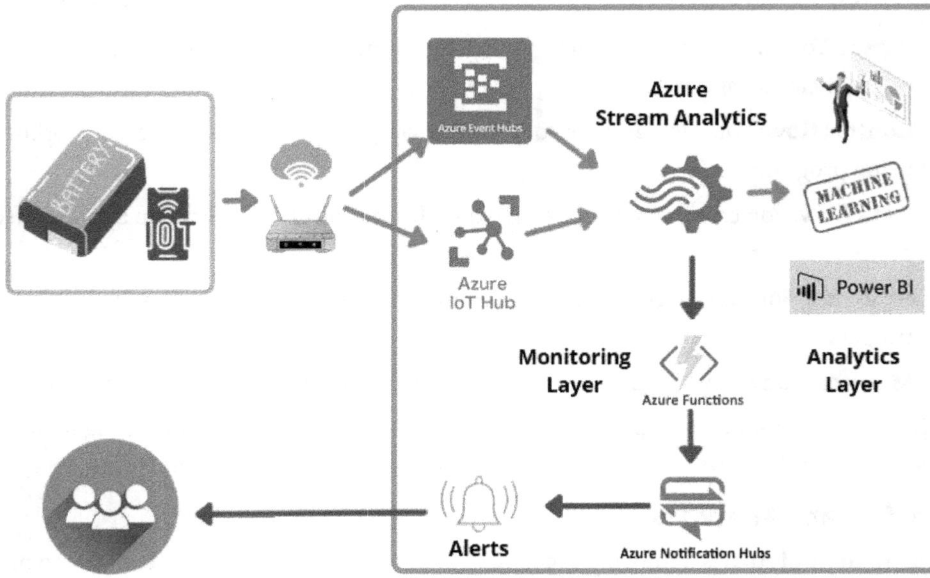

Figure 3.8: Core capabilities of Azure Stream Analytics

An Azure Stream Analytics job is set up with an input, a query, and an output. The job input can stream data from Azure Event Hubs, Azure IoT Hub, or Azure Blob storage.

The query engine is based on SQL and can be used in combination with JavaScript and C# user-defined functions to perform operations such as filtering, sorting, and aggregating. Finally, the output can be sent to several locations, including Power BI, Azure Synapse, and Azure Data Lake Storage.

During the input and output operations, there is a chance that the Azure Stream Analytics job will connect to sources outside your Azure VNET. This can be securely accomplished using private endpoints or by setting up trusted networking services.

By default, Azure Stream Analytics is a multi-tenant service. For extremely security-conscious organizations, there is another option called Azure Stream Analytics Cluster. Azure Stream Analytics Cluster operates in single-tenant mode, using isolated, dedicated hardware.

The capacity of an Azure Stream Analytics cluster is measured in **streaming units** (**SUs**). You may scale your SUs up and down based on traffic demands.

The following figure illustrates the various input sources and output destinations supported by Azure Stream Analytics:

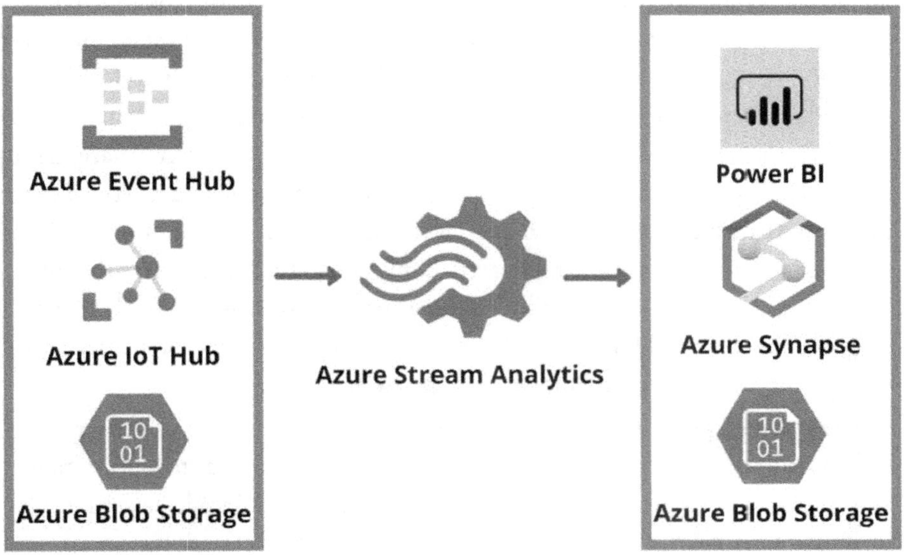

Figure 3.9: Input and output of Azure Stream Analytics

Since Azure Stream Analytics is a fully managed service, it has built-in recovery mechanisms for fault tolerance. It works on the principle of at least once delivery, so events are never lost in the event of failures. Azure Stream Analytics encrypts all incoming/outgoing communication and performs all computations in memory.

> **Note**
>
> The multi-tenancy nature of SaaS and PaaS may be a roadblock for highly regulated organizations due to compliance issues with shared infrastructure. Using a dedicated IaaS layer may be the only choice in those cases.

Azure Synapse Analytics

Azure Synapse Analytics is an enterprise-grade data engineering and analytics service. Synapse Analytics implements the lakehouse architecture by embedding a unique mixture of data processing services, as follows:

- **Synapse SQL**: This implements a SQL-based **massively parallel processing** (**MPP**) data warehouse. Synapse SQL employs a couple of models:

- **Dedicated SQL pool**: In the dedicated model, a set of resources is provisioned based on the chosen **data warehouse units** (**DWUs**). A dedicated SQL pool uses a node-based architecture for computations. At the lowest denomination, the DW100c (single-node cluster) stores 60 data distributions on a single node. At the highest denomination, the DW30000c (60-node cluster) stores a single data distribution per node. The performance and concurrency of queries increase linearly as more DWUs get added; however, the cost increases proportionally as well. Storage costs are charged separately based on usage. Compute nodes store tables in Azure Storage and use the **data movement service** (**DMS**) to run queries in parallel. Table distribution can be of three types: hash, round robin, and replicated. Compute and storage layers are fully decoupled. To save on costs, you can pause the compute layer, at which time the billing stops for the allocated DWUs. On the other hand, storage costs are incurred regardless of whether the compute layer is active or paused.
- **Serverless SQL pool**: In the serverless model, there is no need to provision resources or copy data to compute nodes. Instead, you can query data in Azure Blob storage using an external data source. Using this method, you can query data in several formats, including CSV, JSON, parquet, and delta. For files in parquet or delta format, you can automatically infer the schema. Querying data from Azure Cosmos DB is also supported using Azure Synapse Link. Serverless SQL pools automatically scale resources based on query demand. For faster execution, they utilize a **distributed query processing** (**DQP**) engine to split the query into multiple smaller queries. The cost of a serverless SQL pool is based on the data that's processed by queries.

> Note
>
> Dedicated and serverless pools follow different costing methods. While the dedicated pool is charged based on the number of DWUs, the serverless model is charged based on the amount of data processed. Generally, serverless pools will cost less than dedicated pools. But there may be cases involving large data scans, in which case you may be better off using a dedicated pool. It is highly recommended that the data engineer perform a benchmark test before choosing the appropriate pool.

- **Synapse Spark**: Synapse Spark implements the Apache Spark engine for distributed computing. This process involves creating a Spark pool in Azure Synapse. A Spark pool is simply a definition of the resource, including node size, autoscaling behavior, and the number of nodes. The actual Spark instance gets created when a job is submitted to the pool. To save on costs, you can use the **automatic pause** mechanism, which releases

Spark resources after a configurable idle period. Using a **Synapse Studio notebook**, a data engineer can manage data **wrangling**, **transformations**, and **visualizations**. Azure Synapse Analytics is compatible with the Delta Lake framework, which acts as the core storage component for implementing the lakehouse architecture.

> Note
>
> The ability of Azure Synapse to share table metadata across computational engines, namely serverless SQL pools and Spark pools, hugely simplifies data engineering tasks. The principle of cataloging data once and using it multiple times also establishes strong master data management strategies.

Data cataloging and sharing services in Microsoft Azure

Data catalogs and data-sharing services are redefining data distribution strategies for modern organizations. Data catalogs represent the trusted view of the data deemed worthy of consumption by internal and external users. Couple this with an easy and secure method of sharing data, and you are well on your way to providing your user base with a self-serve analytics platform. The following are two major services used in Azure for data cataloging:

Microsoft Purview

Microsoft Purview is a fully managed service that's used to discover, catalog, and consume data in a unified fashion. Microsoft Purview helps producers define a single source of truth for data that consumers may use in their downstream processes. It is important to understand that once the data source has been registered, only the metadata is stored in the data catalog; the actual data stays in its original location. Microsoft Purview does not give you access to the data itself; it simply helps users discover data sources and related information so they can gauge their utility for their own use.

> Note
>
> Microsoft Purview also supports features such as data classification and end-to-end data lineage, which are critical for data governance.

Microsoft Purview uses a data source registration tool to extract the following metadata information:

- Details of the data source's location.

- Schema, that is, the structure of the table.
- Data profile (object and columns); that is, the number of rows, whether it contains null values, the size of the table, and the last updated timestamps.

In addition to the discovered metadata, users can manually add their own metadata. Microsoft Purview supports a variety of data sources, including Azure Blob, Azure Synapse, Hive, MySQL, Oracle, and many more.

Unity Catalog

Unity Catalog is a unified governance solution for data and AI assets on Databricks, offering **centralized** access control, auditing, lineage, and data discovery capabilities. Unity Catalog provides fine-grained access control for tabular and unstructured data in multiple formats across multiple platforms, along with governance for AI assets such as machine learning models. It includes the tools you need to discover data, track usage, capture lineage, and monitor data quality. You may use Unity Catalog to manage metadata for both internal and external storage and data platforms. By leveraging a combination of native connectors and third-party integrations, Unity Catalog enables seamless access and interoperability between Databricks and external data sources and services.

Unity catalog represents a huge leap forward in data discoverability by offering tools that help users find the data they need. The Databricks Catalog Explorer tool provides a UI to explore and manage data, schemas (databases), tables, models, functions, and other AI assets. Using the catalog explorer, you can:

- **Find data assets**: View schema details, sample data
- Manage Unity Catalog objects: Create catalogs, create shares, and manage external locations
- **Create AI-generated comments**: Generate comments on data and AI objects, such as catalogs, tables, columns, volumes

In recent times, the term data collaboration has gained significant traction. Data collaboration is commonly implemented through data-sharing platforms that allow organizations to securely share data and AI assets with external entities – regardless of whether those entities use Azure. These are two major services for sharing data in Azure:

Azure Data Share

In *Chapter 1, The Story of Data Engineering and Analytics*, we had a section named "*The monetary power of data*". In that section, we discussed modern methods of revenue diversification, including data monetization through data sharing. An organization can realize this dream by using Azure Data Share or Delta Sharing using Azure Databricks. Azure Data Share facilitates the secure sharing of data with other parties, including customers and partners. Traditionally, securely sharing data via protocols such as SFTP or APIs has been very expensive. Using Azure Data Share, organizations can add datasets and invite customers/partners to safely access their shared data. Azure Data Share can be used in a couple of ways:

- **Snapshot-based sharing**: Once shared, data moves to the consumer's Azure subscription.
- **In-place sharing**: Once shared, a data link is created that can be accessed by the consumer.

Azure Data Share access is protected with managed identities using Azure Active Directory. In addition, data shares are protected by standard data-at-rest and data-in-motion mechanisms.

Delta Sharing

Delta sharing is the core of the Databricks data sharing platform. It enables you to share data and AI assets with users outside your organization, whether or not they use Databricks. Delta Sharing is also available as an open-source project that you can use to share Delta tables with other platforms. There are three ways to share data using delta sharing:

- **Databricks-to-Databricks sharing protocol**: Using this protocol, you can share data and AI assets from your Unity catalog-enabled workspace with other users who also have access to a Unity catalog-enabled Databricks workspace.
- **Databricks open sharing protocol**: Using this protocol, you can share tabular data that you manage in a Unity Catalog-enabled Azure Databricks workspace with users on any computing platform. This approach is very useful for sharing data with users who don't use Databricks or don't have access to a Unity Catalog-enabled Databricks workspace.
- **Customer-managed Delta sharing server**: This protocol is extremely useful for sharing data from any platform to any platform, whether Azure Databricks or not.

> Note
>
> For organizations migrating to the cloud, the sudden adoption of SaaS can seem quite far-fetched. Not everyone likes to lose control over the infrastructure and customizations.

Opening a free account with Microsoft Azure

In the upcoming chapters, we will use the services you just read about to build a data lakehouse. Therefore, it is time to open a free Azure account that gives you 12 months of free services, plus a one-time $200 credit for 30 days.

Please note that not all services are free; most are. To open a free account and browse through the free services, please visit the following link: `https://azure.microsoft.com/en-ca/free/`.

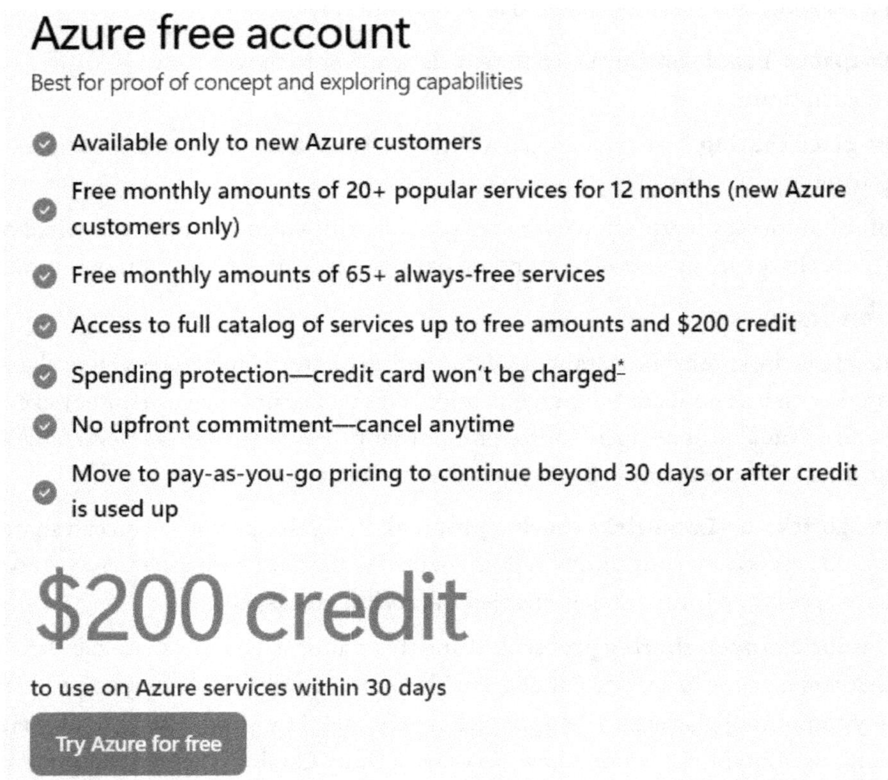

Figure 3.10: Azure free credit details

Here is some valuable advice:

- It is always a good idea to remove the compute resources once you've used them.
- You get 5 GB of **locally redundant data** (**LRS**) for free. There is no need to remove data that's stored during future exercises since we will not exceed this limit.
- While using the free services in Azure, please keep a strict eye on your billing using the following link: `https://portal.azure.com/#blade/Microsoft_Azure_Billing/BillingMenuBlade/Overview`.
- It is always a good idea to be extra cautious about billing. Azure allows you to create budgets so you do not exceed your budgeted amount. Azure will send you a notification if the set budget has been exceeded: `https://docs.microsoft.com/en-us/azure/cost-management-billing/costs/tutorial-acm-create-budgets`.

Summary

In this chapter, we learned about the IaaS, PaaS, and SaaS services in Azure that can help a data engineer build a lakehouse. We also discussed how cloud vendors offer many options for performing similar operations. It is up to the data engineer to choose the right service that provides the customer with benefits based on their usage patterns, in-house skills, and budget.

The modern-day data platforms are becoming increasingly sophisticated. Advanced data platforms are built to offer powerful analytical services, operational excellence, automation, and AI readiness. This enables organizations to extract timely, detailed data insights by combining publicly available data with their own internal data, thereby accelerating data-driven decision-making. In the next chapter, I will highlight a few important aspects of future data platforms that unify data engineering, analytics, AI, and governance under a single architecture.

Get this book's PDF version and more

4

Designing Future Data Platforms

In the previous chapter, we discussed how the various options available for data engineering on Microsoft Azure. We are slowly emerging from an era in which data platforms were designed primarily to support data-driven decision-making. Today, we are entering an era in which data platforms are becoming increasingly innovative, sophisticated, and autonomous. Rather than simply being passive data stores, future data platforms are becoming the central nervous systems for organizations by driving growth through user collaboration, process integration, and AI-driven automation.

In this chapter, we will begin by exploring the defining characteristics of a modern data platform – one that embraces the Lakehouse principles over a cloud-native foundation while ensuring strong governance and security. We will learn how master data management and the concept of data-as-a-product are transforming data democratization. Finally, we will delve into how the data mesh architecture is revolutionizing the landscape of organizational data delivery.

In this chapter, we will cover the following topics:

- Hallmarks of a future data platform
- Data mesh
- Data-as-a-product
- Federated Governance

Hallmarks of a future data platform

The evolution of future data platforms is a reimagining of data-driven decision-making. It's a reconceptualization of the *journey of data*—production, transformation, distribution, and consumption. Data platforms are quickly becoming corporate growth enablers, increasingly defining the core difference between organizational success and failure.

A well-designed future data platform represents a convergence of data-driven intelligence, modern data architecture, cutting-edge cloud-enabled services and frameworks, automation, and operational excellence. For these reasons, a modern data platform should be capable of supporting the following key traits:

- Use an easy-to-use, scalable base infrastructure (preferably using the cloud) to sustain critical loads with optimal performance.
- A data architecture that supports both batch and streaming workloads, adapts to varying data formats, and supports the ever-increasing demands of consumers.
- Deliver a certain level of trust to its users by delivering federated governance, high data quality, and certified data products.
- Facilitate a secure and seamless mechanism for distributing data across diverse internal domains and external entities.
- Leverage automation to streamline infrastructure and code deployments.
- Ensure health, visibility, and reliability of data using trustworthy data observability practices.
- Follow ethical AI standards by adhering to industry best practices.

The real question is: *what are the defining hallmarks of a truly futuristic and cutting-edge data platform?*

As illustrated in *Figure 4.1*, a next-generation, future-ready data platform that transcends traditional analytics to become the intelligent backbone of the organization should embody the following characteristics:

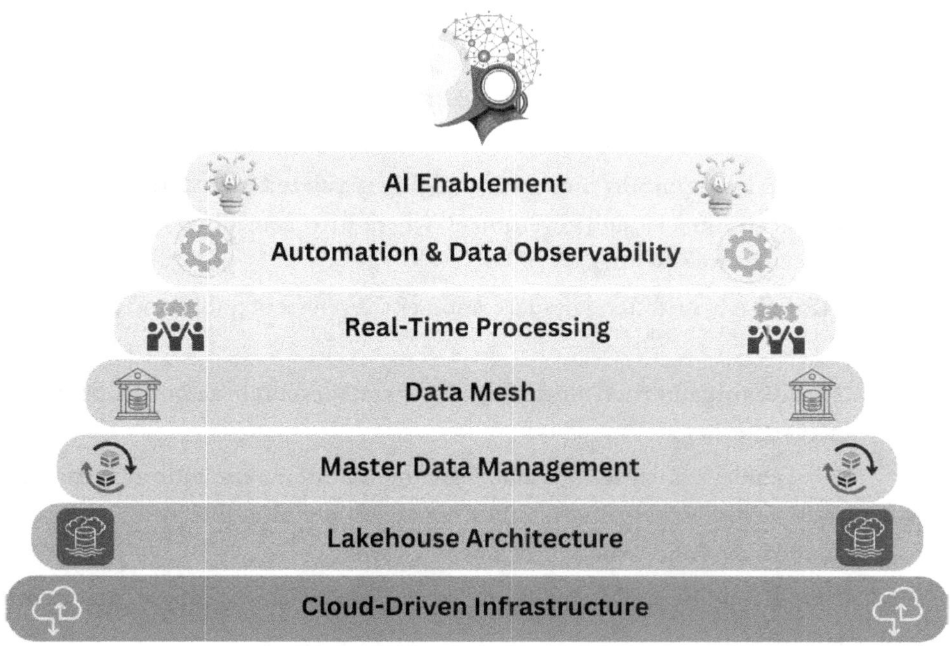

Figure 4.1: Hallmarks of a next-generation future data platform

As you can see, *Figure 4.1* is shown as a pyramid. Each block in the data platform strengthens the next until data transforms into actions. Together, these layers create a cohesive technology stack in which each layer serves as the foundation for the one above it. Missing a single layer weakens the structure, and the pyramid loses its balance. To understand how the pyramid achieves and maintains its balance, it is important that we explore each layer in greater detail to understand its role and contribution:

Cloud-driven infrastructure

The foundation of any building must not only be strong but also resilient to withstand unforeseen events such as earthquakes and floods. The same stands true for the infrastructure of a future-ready data platform. Cloud-driven infrastructures can be deployed in four specific ways:

1. **Public Cloud**: In this model, the compute resources, including hardware and software, are the property of the cloud provider.
    - Compute resources are **shared** across multiple customers within the provider's infrastructure.
    - Consumption follows a **pay-as-you-go** model, allowing customers to use resources on demand and pay only for what they consume.

2. **Private Cloud**: A private cloud infrastructure is a dedicated model, also known as the "*single tenant*" model.
    - Compute resources are isolated and **dedicated** to a single organization, even when hosted by a cloud provider.
    - This model is typically preferred by **highly regulated industries** such as healthcare, finance, and government, where strict control, compliance, and data protection are essential.
3. **Hybrid Cloud**: A hybrid cloud model combines the power of public and private clouds in one.
    - It enables organizations to deploy and operate resources across **on-premises infrastructure** and the cloud.
    - This approach is especially valuable for organizations **transitioning to the cloud** or those with workloads that must remain on-premises due to security, compliance, or licensing constraints.
4. **Multi-Cloud**: A multi-cloud deployment model leverages two or more cloud providers simultaneously.
    - It enables organizations to select the most suitable or cost-effective services across vendors based on workload needs, though egress costs and data governance may present a challenge.
    - Distributing workloads across multiple providers, multi-cloud architectures offer greater resilience and support stronger business continuity.
    - Although adoption is still emerging, multi-cloud strategies are expected to grow, as organizations seek flexibility, vendor neutrality, and improved risk mitigation.

> **Note**
>
> You are very likely to encounter the hybrid cloud model in the data engineering world. Many organizations continue to store their databases and file systems in on-premises infrastructures. Data from these sources is often ingested into cloud-based data lakehouses for analytics.

As the foundational layer, cloud-driven infrastructure provides several benefits:

Resilience of cloud services

Services on the cloud are **fault-tolerant**. They have been designed to recover gracefully from failures, ensuring zero to minimal downtime and minimizing interruptions. Almost all components in the cloud data center, ranging from networks to storage and compute services, are distributed across multiple availability zones within a given region.

As illustrated in *Figure 4.2*, in case of failure, services are seamlessly designed to shift from an unhealthy resource to a healthy one. This ensures high availability and resilience for applications deployed on the cloud.

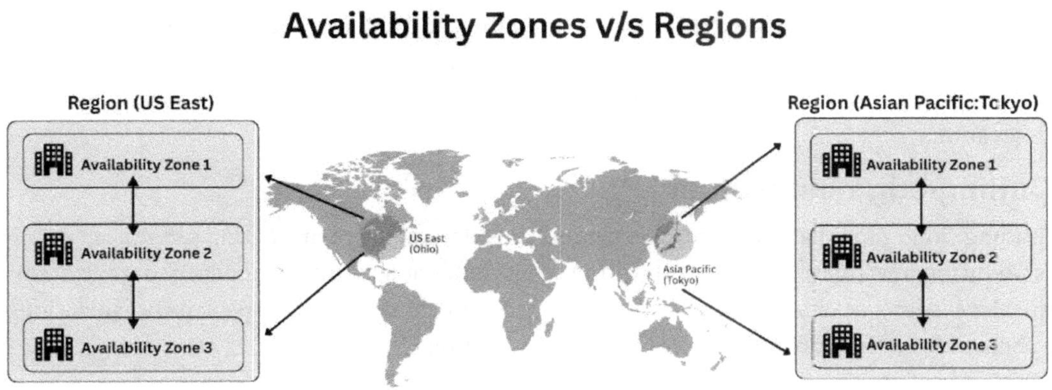

Figure 4.2: Cloud global infrastructure – regions and availability zones

Faster ramp-up time

In the digital era, time not only transforms into money but also into a competitive advantage. Using on-demand infrastructure and pre-built services significantly reduces ramp-up times and accelerates deployment cycles. Using cloud-driven infrastructure, data teams can deploy pipelines in hours rather than weeks or months. It is common for cloud providers to offer preconfigured templates and stacks for common workloads. This eliminates the need for repetitive manual configurations when replicating environments, thereby shortening the overall deployment cycle. Additionally, deployments become largely consistent, error-free, and automated. In short, faster ramp-up, faster time-to-market, and increased agility.

Cost Control

In the pre-cloud era, improving system performance and/or high availability meant administrators needed to procure additional hardware, software, and network components to extend the infrastructure's capabilities. This automatically meant a steep increase in costs covering not only hardware and software but also server racks, redundant internet lines, and sometimes real estate.

Having your infrastructure in the cloud solves this problem by redefining how resources are provisioned – they can be created on demand when required and, most importantly, released when no longer in use. This allows organizations to optimize system performance by scaling capacity up or down, ensuring precise control. Scaling capacity not only ensures high availability and consistent performance but also keeps costs in check.

Data security and governance

In the world we live in, the power of data cannot be challenged. This power has helped several companies accelerate their revenue by monetizing and marketing personal data in ways that cross boundaries of ethical use. Cloud providers go to great lengths to ensure their services and operations comply with the latest security, regulatory, and industry standards. They go through regular certifications and audits to demonstrate their compliance. Having taken the compliance burden off their shoulders, organizations can grow faster by accelerating their innovation.

Cutting-edge innovation

Leading cloud providers constantly innovate, either enhancing their existing services or introducing new ones. Constant innovation often comes at a high cost; not every organization may have deep pockets to sustain it. Leveraging the cloud infrastructure permits organizations to benefit from this cutting-edge innovation at a fraction of the cost.

Global outreach

Cloud providers operate data centers spanning across geographic regions, enabling organizations to function seamlessly on a global scale. In the modern era, the global workspace has become a standard operating model for many organizations. Leveraging cloud infrastructure enables seamless access to data and collaboration across the globe, ensuring uninterrupted productivity for their workforce. Organizational employees can connect to centralized data systems across time zones. It allows remote workers access to critical systems while maintaining data locality, governance, and compliance standards.

Based on the points highlighted above, it is needless to stress the fact that the foundation of a future-ready data platform needs to be built on a cloud-driven infrastructure. Having this in mind, let's move to the next building block of the future data platform.

Lakehouse architecture

We introduced the lakehouse architecture in *Chapter 2, Discovering Data Platforms,* of this book. The lakehouse architecture provides a nice blend of a data lake and a data warehouse. While preserving the strong characteristics of a data lake - such as support for varying formats, large volumes, and a variety of data at scale - and the features of a data warehouse, including structured datasets and SQL support, the lakehouse architecture unifies them.

The greatest strength of the lakehouse architecture is that it promotes a no-copy data platform, therefore promoting the **single-source-of-truth** approach. As illustrated in *Figure 4.3*, this means data from varying sources can be safely ingested, cleansed, and aggregated in a data lake without the need to copy it into a data warehouse for querying purposes. This prevents creating unnecessary copies of data and preserves the idea of a single source of truth layer in the data platform.

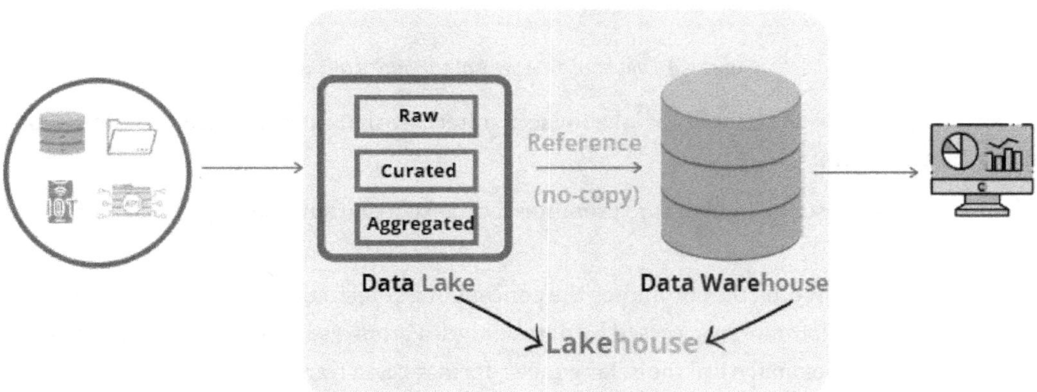

Figure 4.3: Lakehouse – A blend of data lake and data warehouse

Lakehouse architecture is most suited for a future data platform. The data lakehouse becomes the central storage for all types of organizational data – both batch and streaming. The ability of the lakehouse architecture to store data in a cost-effective storage layer and process it on demand when needed makes it extremely cost-efficient for modern data management and analytics.

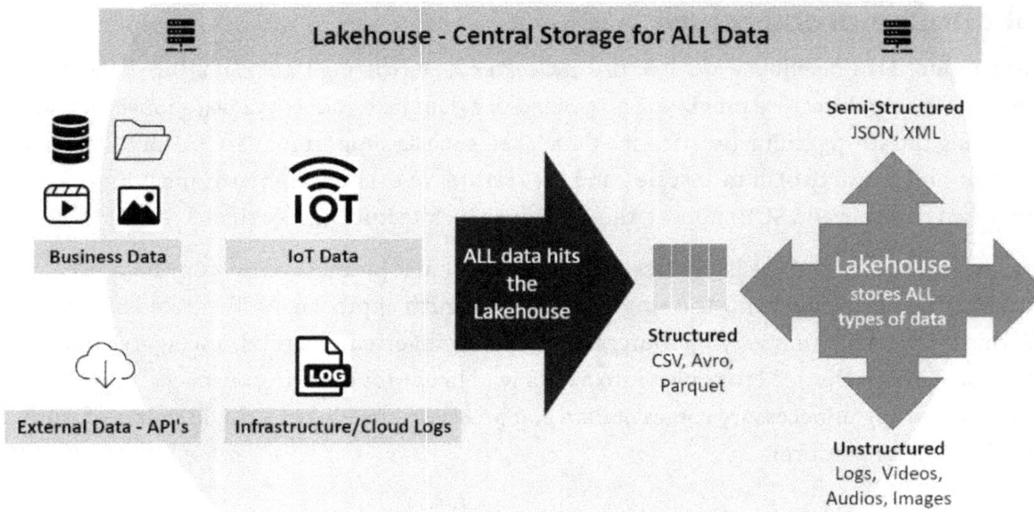

Figure 4.4: Lakehouse – A central storage of all data

Here are some of the core benefits of lakehouse architecture that make it a strong hallmark of a future data platform:

- The no-copy data architecture promotes a clear segregation of storage and compute layers.
- Lakehouse architecture promotes the concept of a single-source-of-truth data layer that can be commonly accessed by data analytics groups such as BI, ML, and AI using their choice of analytical tools, languages, formats, and frameworks.
- Stores data in an open format such as Delta or Iceberg with strong support for ACID transactions. Delta or Iceberg formats provide strong metadata management, schema enforcement, and schema evolution.
- Prevent a single vendor lock-in, attributed to the fact that the underlying data is stored in an open format, which can be either copied or easily accessed by other vendors.

Support for the lakehouse architecture paves the way for the next hallmark of a future-ready data platform. The lakehouse architecture's ability to ingest data from multiple sources introduces a unique challenge: data duplication. Now let's examine how **Master Data Management (MDM)**, a key building block of a future data platform, addresses this unique challenge.

Master data management

We learned previously that a data lakehouse is likely to ingest data from multiple data sources. Although this flexibility forms the foundation for building a centralized data platform, it also introduces unique challenges for data entities, including duplication, inconsistency, and accuracy issues.

> **Note**
>
> A data entity refers to a distinct person or object that corresponds to a real-world item. Examples of data entities include customers, employees, and suppliers.

Before we dive deeper into the data entity issues, let's understand the general categories of data in a data platform:

- **Master Data**: Master data refers to the core information that is essential for running a business. It includes key entities such as individuals, places, and things that the organization relies on. Master data is critical to business operations because it forms the foundation for running transactions.
- **Transactional Data**: Transactional data represents the operational events of the business. These are typical day-to-day events, such as buying/selling products, shipping products, and processing returns and exchanges.
- **Reference Data**: Reference data is standardized information that is referenced by business transactions. Examples include order statuses (`NEW`, `RETURN`, `SHIPPED`), zip/postal codes, country codes, state codes, and airline codes.

While transactional and reference data can be uniquely identified through their identifiers, master data is much harder to uniquely distinguish. It is hard to envision this without examples, so let's look at a scenario that illustrates this:

- Entity 1: John Doe, who lives at 123 Main St., Queens, NY
- Entity 1: J Doe, who lives at 123 Main St., Queens, New York
- The attributes for name and address closely resemble those of entity 1 and entity 2, so most likely they belong to the same entity. We just discovered a duplicate record. Now here are a few problems:
- If entity 1 and entity 2 are duplicates, how should we handle this when managing master data? After all, there can only be one John Doe.
- When this entity makes a purchase, which master data record should be linked to this transaction - entity 1 or entity 2?
- In the future, if the organization runs a marketing email campaign, which email address should be used - entity 1 or entity 2?

Figure 4.5 shows the duplicate entities arising from multiple data source ingestion.

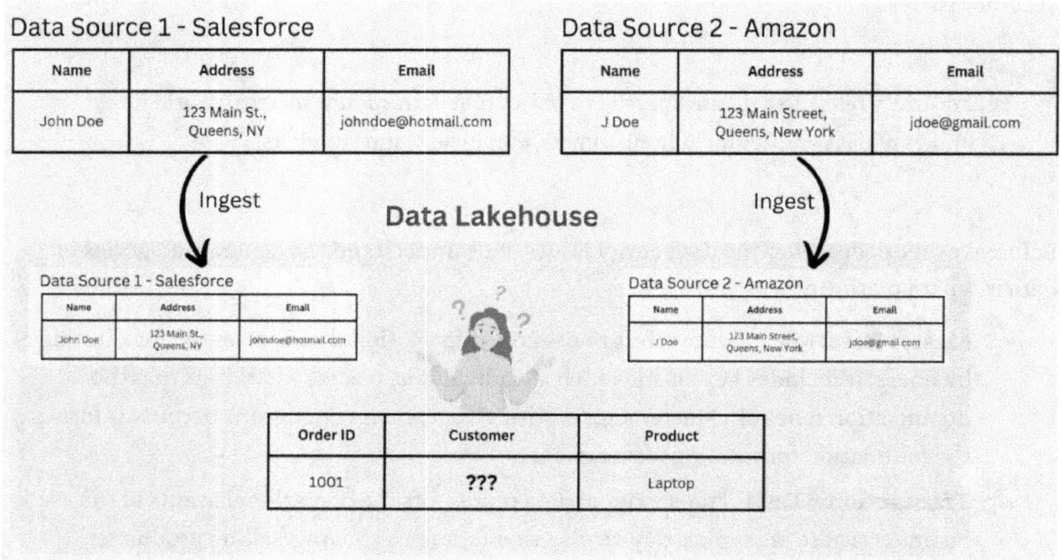

Figure 4.5: Single entity from two distinct data sources

It seems that we have a lot of unanswered questions. This is exactly why the discipline of **Master Data Management (MDM)** is gaining popularity in future data platforms. MDM ensures that the organizational master data is as accurate and consistent as possible. The purpose of master data management is to *consolidate, deduplicate,* and *refine* data to create *a single source of truth* (*SSOT*) - the "golden record".

The following are some core components of MDM:

- **Entity matching and deduplication:** A key component of MDM is matching, linking, and deduplicating entities from varying datasets where unique identifiers are missing. This can be accomplished using libraries such as **Splink**, a Python package designed for probabilistic record linkage and entity resolution. Splink is a Python library that provides a machine-learning–driven, unsupervised record-linkage engine capable of processing millions of records. It automatically identifies and links similar records using advanced fuzzy-matching techniques. Databricks comes built-in with Databricks **Automated Record Connector** (**ARC**), a Databricks solution accelerator that enables simple, automated, scalable probabilistic data deduplication and linking. Databricks ARC uses Splink to find near duplicates in the input data.
- **Master data model:** Master data model defines the structure of the master entity. This is done by selecting attributes from similar entities across multiple datasets and consolidating them into a unified structure for the golden record.

- **Survivorship rules**: A fundamental aspect of MDM that specifies the rules used to determine which entity's attributes *wins* when they get merged into a single golden record.
- **Governance and workflow**: Establish policies and automated processes to manage golden record approval and maintain audit trails.
- **Reverse integration:** Specifies the target systems and methods to distribute the golden record back to the original source systems.

With the golden record established, the scenario now appears as shown in *Figure 4.6* below.

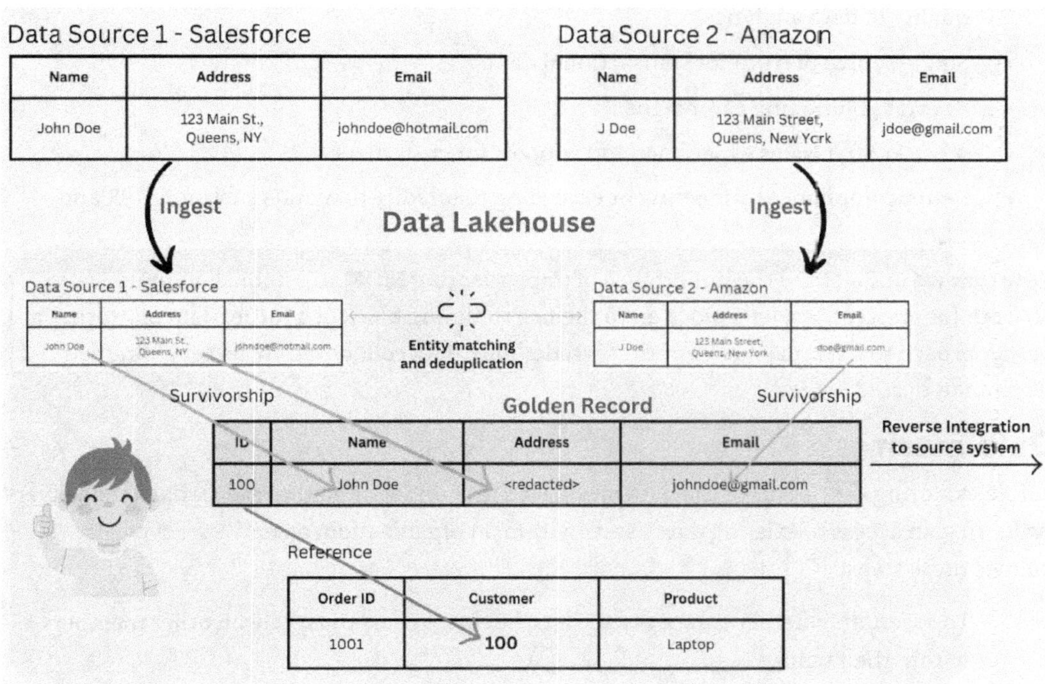

Figure 4.6: Creating the golden record – entity matching and deduplication

The MDM scenario demonstrates the creation of the golden record:

- Entity 1 and entity 2 were *deduplicated* and *merged* into a single golden record.
- *Survivorship rules* determined which attributes were retained in the *master data model.*
- The address attribute was *redacted* in the golden record to comply with *governance* policies.
- A new record identifier (ID) attribute was added to the *master data model* for the golden record.

- This golden record now serves as the single-source-of-truth for all future transactions related to this entity. Notice how the ID attribute from the golden record is *referenced* in the orders table.
- Finally, *reverse integration* distributes the golden record back to the source systems.

Creating a golden record provides significant benefits to organizations, including supporting their customer 360º initiatives. The following is a list of some core benefits of implementing MDM:

- Maintaining a golden record ensures accuracy, improved efficiency, and better overall quality of data analytics.
- Single source of truth for transactional data.
- Accurate marketing campaigns.
- A better after-sales experience and support for customers.
- Better compliance by meeting or exceeding regulatory demands such as GDPR and CCPA.

Now that we understand the importance of implementing MDM to establish a single-source-of-truth for master data, let's move on to the next building block of a future data platform - a new approach to data management that is redefining data collaboration and enabling self-serve analytics.

Data mesh

Before exploring the details of the data mesh, let's first understand the traditional data delivery cycle. To gain access to existing data assets within an organization, an end-user typically follows these steps:

1. To ascertain whether a data asset exists, business users must rely on other members within their team.
2. After identifying a data asset, users were left to make their own judgment regarding its trustworthiness.
3. To gain access to the data asset - often without clear instructions - the business user submits a request to a data manager or a data engineer.
4. The data manager/engineer sends approval to the IT administrator.
5. The IT administrator grants the request.
6. The business user finally receives access to the data asset – most likely with a lack of proper documentation.

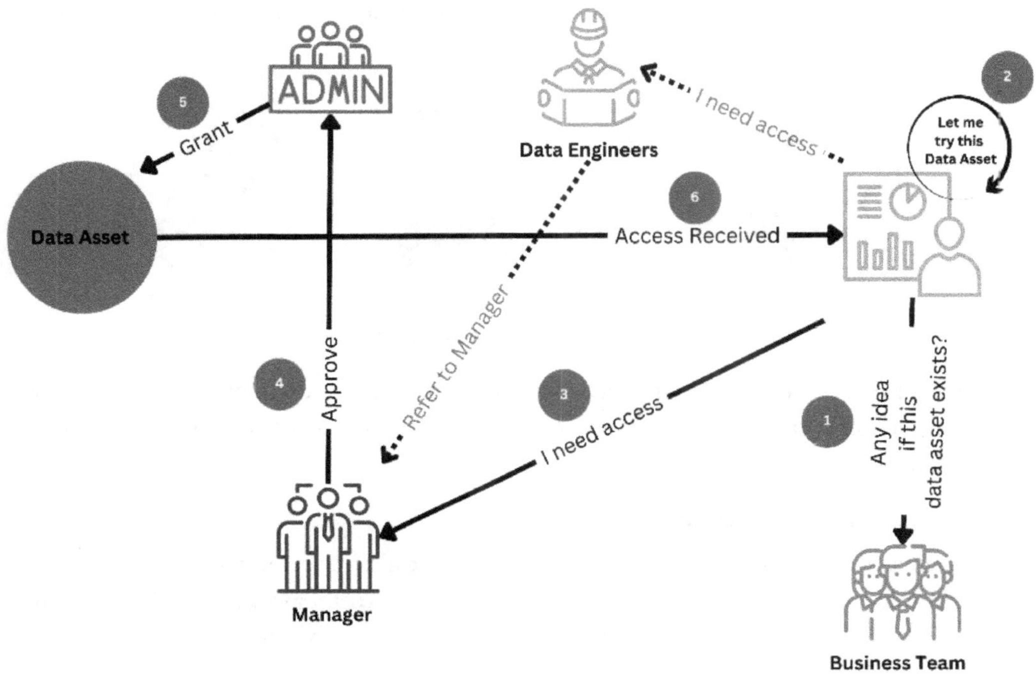

Figure 4.7: Traditional data delivery cycle

As shown in *Figure 4.7* above, on the surface, the above process may seem simple and straightforward, but it suffers from several deficiencies as outlined below:

- **Delayed data access**: Timely access to data is one of the foremost requirements for effective decision-making. Depending on the workload of data engineers and IT administrators, the traditional process may result in delayed data delivery.
- **Data quality issues**: Data engineers may be skilled at ingesting and transforming data; however, they often overlook many data quality issues due to limited business domain knowledge. As a result, business users may discover several quality issues. Rendering it untrustworthy for use.
- **Lack of data governance**: The data asset may be shared with unauthorized users, potentially exposing personal data (PII) or classified data.

The following figure highlights several well-recognized deficiencies inherent in the traditional data delivery cycle:

Figure 4.8: Deficiencies of the traditional data delivery cycle

The shortcomings of the traditional data delivery approach clearly demonstrate the need for a better method - one that uses convergence to eliminate delays and accelerates access without compromising security or data privacy.

Convergence in data delivery

With reference to the data delivery approach, convergence aims at bringing diverse data systems, formats, and sources under a common framework – **unification**. Convergence fosters interoperability, streamlining the flow of data from producers to consumers.

The following figure highlights several well-recognized deficiencies inherent in the traditional data delivery cycle:

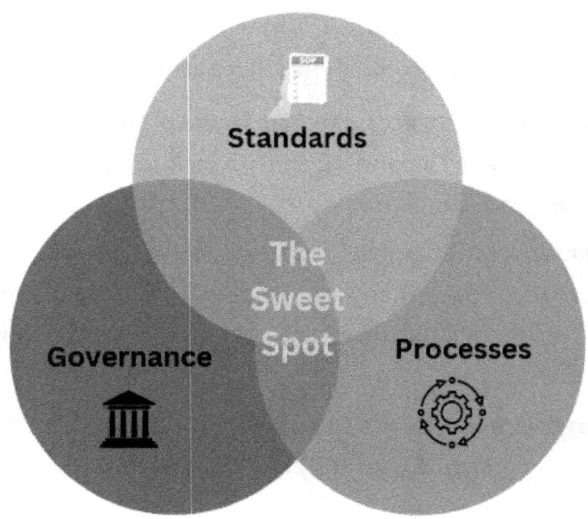

Figure 4.9: Finding the sweet spot in data delivery

As depicted in the image above, convergence aims to find the sweet spot among standards, processes, and governance in the data delivery cycle. What does finding the sweet spot require?

- **Converging Standards**: Data delivery platform should follow common standards related to data formats, data models, compute frameworks, protocols and storage services.
- **Converging Processes**: All data delivery processes related to ingestion, transformations, and distribution should adhere to standardized patterns.
- **Converging Governance**: Implement a unified framework that should be employed for compliance tracking, data quality assurance, and validation of data contracts.

When it comes to finding the sweet spot in convergence, data mesh is the most practical option. Data mesh is an architectural paradigm designed to democratize data by removing data silos, simplifying discoverability, and centralizing governance.

Before diving into the data mesh concepts, it is crucial to distinguish between two often-confused ideas - **data that is easily available** versus **data that is easily accessible** – they are not the same. It's true that organizations have been storing data for years across various platforms, including databases, warehouses, file systems, and data lakes. This data often resides in silos and lacks proper documentation- yet technically it is *available*, assuming you know where to look. The challenge is that available data doesn't automatically mean it is readily usable for consumption. The data may be in a format that is unsuitable for high-volume processing, lack consistency, or rely on non-standard connectivity protocols. In contrast, *accessible* data carries an entirely different meaning. Highly accessible data is reliable, easily discoverable, consistent, and distributed using standard protocols and interfaces.

Future data platforms should emphasize making data truly accessible rather than merely available – and that's exactly what the data mesh architecture is designed to achieve. The goal of the data mesh architecture is to *decentralize* data ownership and promote a *federated* governance model.

Now that is a mouthful, so let's elaborate. The image below shows the four foundational principles of the data mesh architecture:

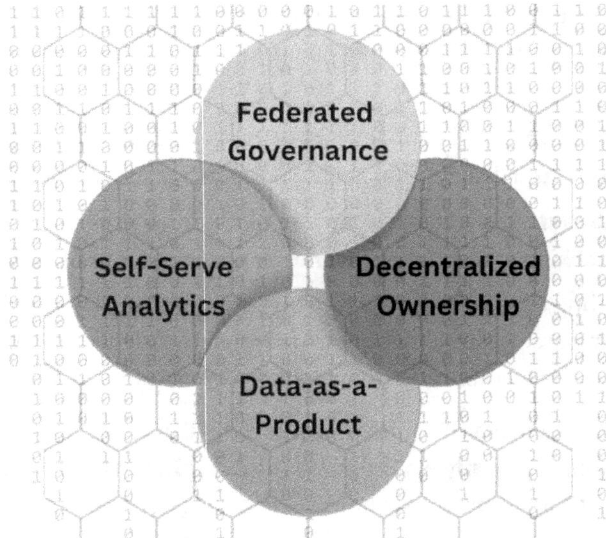

Figure 4.10: Foundational principles of the data mesh architecture

Let's take a closer look at each of the four core principles in detail:

Data-as-a-product

Data-as-a-product is a modern approach to data management in which data is treated as a product. The *data-as-a-product* concept redefines ownership by clearly outlining who creates data assets, who is responsible for improving data quality, and how they are distributed to end consumers. *Figure 4.11* below illustrates several common issues associated with traditional data-asset delivery.

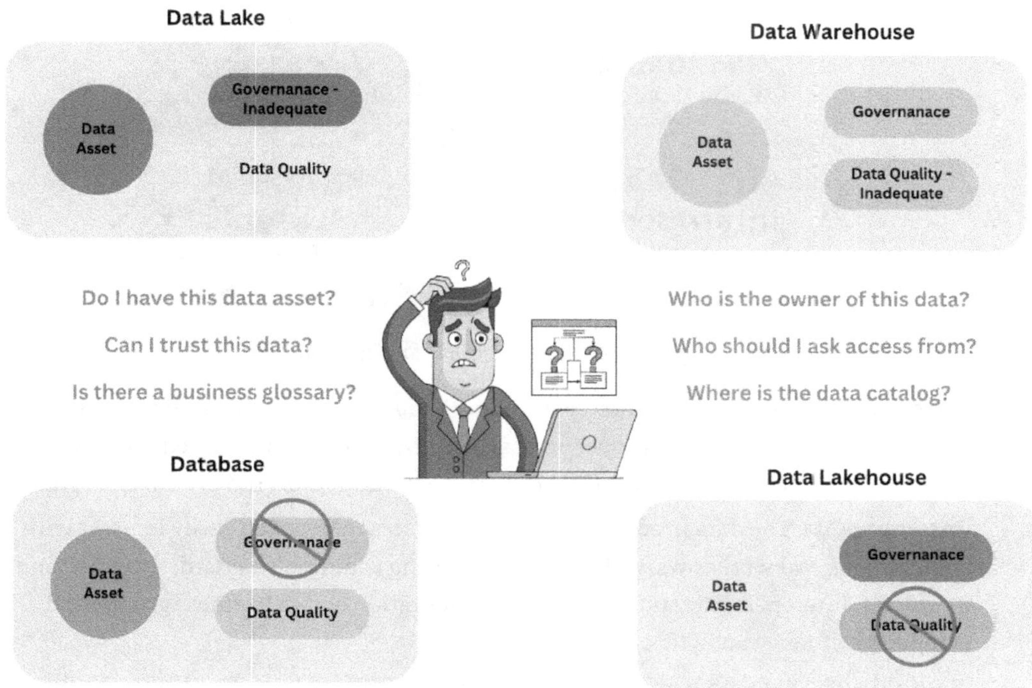

Figure 4.11: Problems associated with traditional data assets

By shifting away from the traditional model that places the entire burden of data management on data producers (such as data engineers), the new approach establishes clear accountability for teams that produce, maintain, and share data across the organizations or with external partners. The new approach promotes a major shift towards *self-serve analytics* that **democratizes** data, enabling faster and more accurate insights.

The real question is how data-as-a-product addresses these issues. Let's find out. To be referred to as a **data product**, data must follow the **FAIR** principle:

- **Findable**: Data products should be easily *discoverable*. This can be achieved by adding metadata to the data product – owner, a unique identifier, a clear description, source information, schema details, tags, and business glossary terms. As shown in *Figure 4.12* below, these attributes serve as a roadmap that guides users to the appropriate data product when they search for a term.

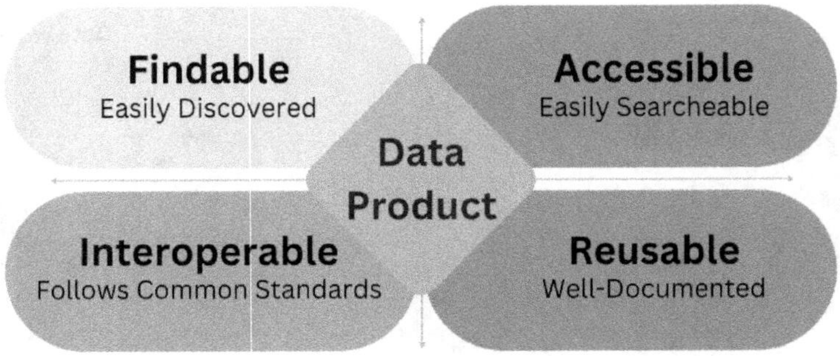

Figure 4.12: The FAIR principle for data products

- **Accessible**: Users who are granted permission should be able to easily access the data product seamlessly through proper access controls. Users can be granted access via programmatic access (such as Python or Java), SQL endpoints (JDBC/ODBC), or APIs.
- **Interoperable**: The data product should be in a state where it can easily interact with applications and workflows. It should be built using common standards, formats, and protocols. Interoperability promotes data collaboration across business groups and supports self-serve analytics.
- **Reusable**: The data product should have a well-documented usage policy, a clearly defined data contract, and adhere to key governance standards. These measures help build user trust in the data product, which indirectly promotes its overall usability.

In essence, the FAIR principles ensure that data products are high-quality assets that foster trust and can be easily analyzed or integrated into data pipelines for further enhancement. At this point, it's beneficial to understand how a data product is created, including the collaborative process that drives its development. We will begin by understanding key terminologies and understanding the team structure involved in creating a data product.

A data product is a reusable data asset designed to deliver value across many use cases. Unfortunately, most organizations operate with a use-case-centric mindset, in which each initiative ingests, transforms, and aggregates independently to meet its specific needs. This siloed practice often results in data duplication, increased storage, computing, and operational costs, and inconsistent datasets.

Figure 4.13 illustrates the way activities are organized according to specific use cases:

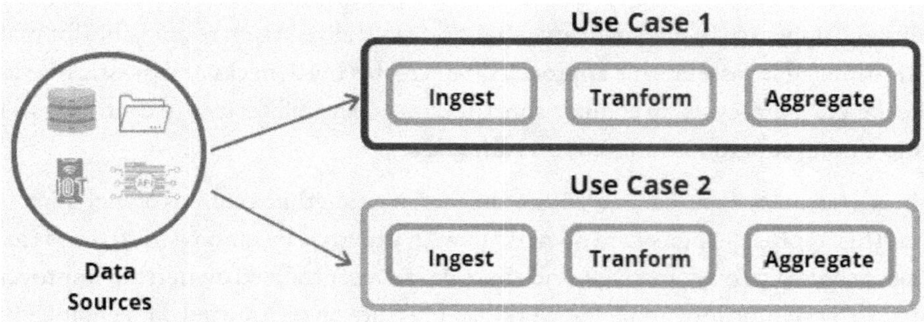

Figure 4.13: The use case-centric mindset for creating data assets

In contrast, adopting a data product approach ensures data consistency and drastically reduces storage, compute, and operational costs by promoting **reusability**. As shown in *Figure 4.14* below, the benefits of adopting a data product strategy are achieved by carefully planning organizational data requirements, creating standardized data assets referred to as data products, and reusing them across multiple use cases.

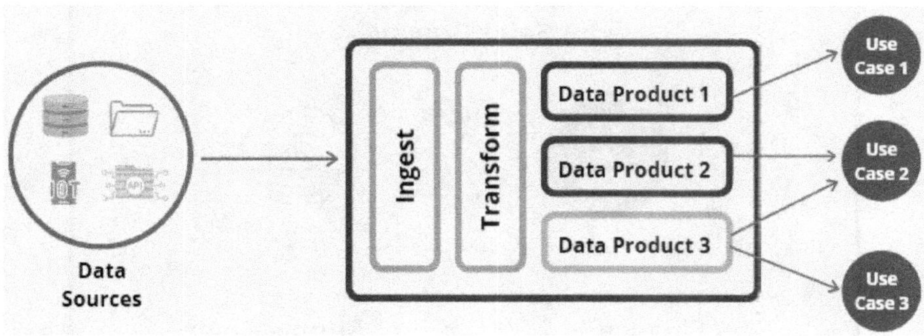

Figure 4.14: The data product mindset promoting reusability

The data product mindset leverages pre-built, business-driven, trusted, and governed data assets to deliver faster, more efficient, and accurate data insights.

> **Note**
>
> Implementing a data-as-a-product approach may require higher upfront investment, but it consistently delivers superior ROI over time.

Now that we have a good grasp on the data-as-a-product approach. It's time to dive into the next principle of the data mesh.

Decentralized ownership

The traditional approach to data delivery relies on a centralized team responsible for managing all organizational data assets. This approach often creates bottlenecks and drastically slows down the data delivery cycle. In comparison, the data mesh architecture decentralizes data ownership among subgroups referred to as **domains**.

A domain is a business-focused area within the organization that assumes ownership of its own data. This approach aligns data ownership with expertise by empowering those closest to the business context to own, manage, and share data. Decentralized ownership improves the delivery cycle by significantly reducing workload pressure on centralized data engineering teams, as domains actively participate in managing and delivering data products to consumers. As shown in the figure below, the collaboration in decentralized ownership not only accelerates data delivery but also fosters a culture of shared responsibility within an organization.

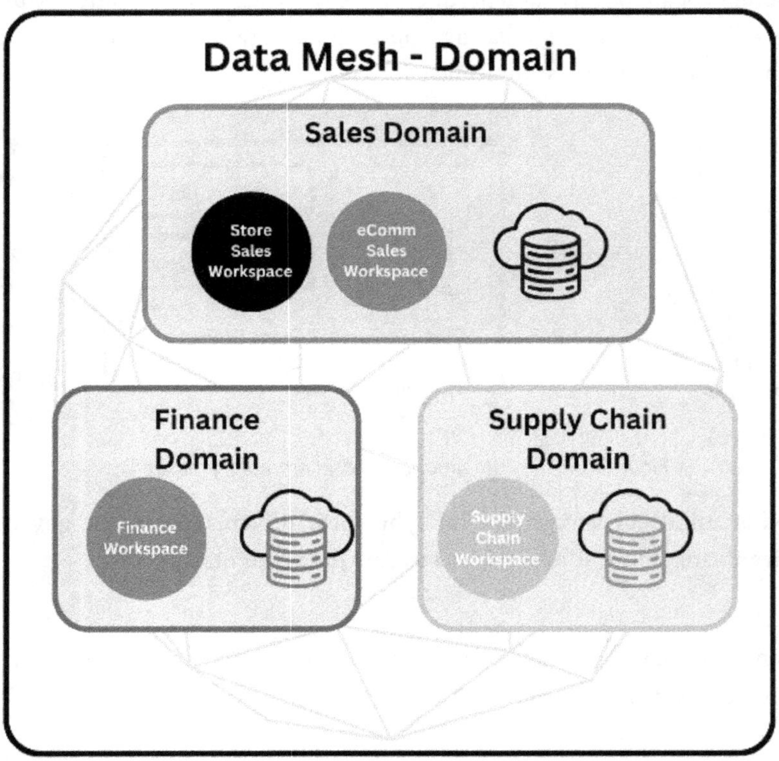

Figure 4.15: Sample representation of decentralized domains managing their own data

So, how does the team structure look in a decentralized ownership model? The centralized team in the traditional data delivery model is replaced by cross-functional teams organized around expertise. The teams usually include the following:

> **Note**
>
> The shift in accountability from data engineering teams to domain owners may not be universally welcomed within organizations. Strong executive support and a clear articulation of benefits can significantly ease resistance.

Domain experts

As discussed earlier, a **domain** is a logical grouping of business functions within an organization, such as Finance, Sales, or HR. When it comes to data products, a *domain* can be a consumer, a producer, or both. A data product is owned by a domain that retains full ownership and overall accountability for its data quality, maintenance, distribution, and governance. *Figure 4.16* below illustrates a sample domain structure within an organization.

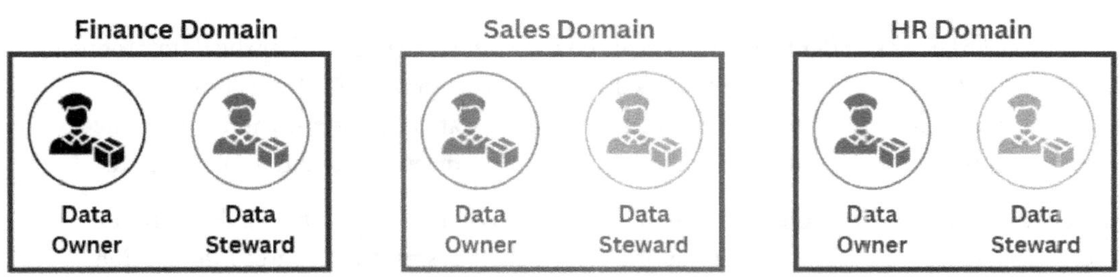

Figure 4.16: Domains and data product ownerships

A *data owner* is an entity within a particular domain responsible for the overall vision and roadmap of the data product. They help define product features and data contracts, and ensure that the data product meets user requirements as well as organizational and regulatory requirements.

As shown in *Figure 4.17* below, because data owners are subject-matter experts, they are best positioned to define data quality rules and establish data privacy rules. A data owner plays a key role in controlling access to the data product. They manage access requests from other domain members, either approving or denying their requests.

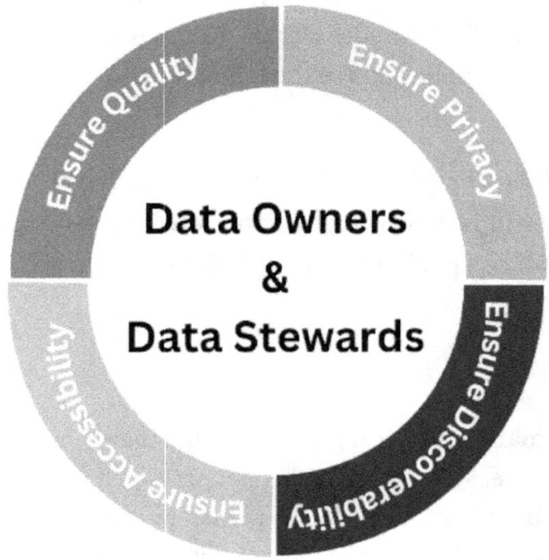

Figure 4.17: Role of data owners and data stewards

A *data steward* works under the guidance of the data owner to ensure that the data product complies with the usability requirements and governance standards. Data stewards collaborate closely with data experts to ensure that all data quality rules and governance requirements defined by data owners are accurately communicated and implemented.

Data stewards play a key role in enhancing data discoverability by entering data product metadata in form of a *data contract* that includes a clear description, source information, schema details, tags, and business glossary terms. Since a data contract is an integral component of a well-defined data product, it's essential that we examine it in greater detail.

Data experts

In the context of data products, data experts are a team comprised of data architects, data engineers, data modelers, and data scientists. Each expert contributes to the data product lifecycle in their unique way. A data architect designs the overall blueprint of the data product to align it with organizational standards for infrastructure, cloud services, and frameworks. Data modelers define the logical and physical structure of data for optimum usage and performance. Data engineers are responsible for building and maintaining data pipelines that drive the flow of data.

Guided by instructions from data architects, data modelers, and data stewards, they handle data ingestion, implement core transformations, enforce data quality rules, and create final aggregations for consumption.

Figure 4.18 below shows a sample team of data experts within an organization.

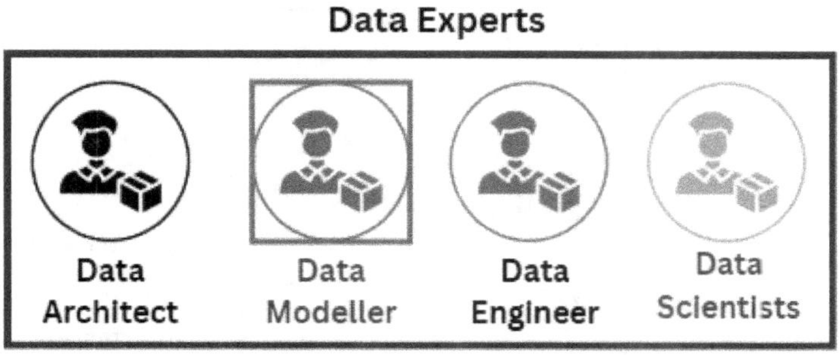

Figure 4.18: Team of data experts

Finally, data scientists leverage curated data for advanced analytics, predictive modeling, and intelligent agents. Data experts often serve as data custodians, the technical guardians of an organization's data assets.

Data contract

A *data contract* is a key element of a data product that establishes clear expectations for how it should be used. With reference to *Table 4.1*, the data contract serves as a bridge between producers and consumers, outlining essential information, usage instructions, and guidelines for critical aspects of the data product. Data contracts include key formation such as structure, data quality validations, data governance policies, service-level objectives, and established standards for discovery and consuming data products.

A data contract is a formally written agreement drafted in a data format such as YAML, that can easily be understood by computers. The following is a sample data contract that is exchanged between the producer and consumer of a data product. A data contract includes data assets from a variety of sources – databases, data warehouses, data lakes, and data lakehouses.

The following are key components of a data contract.

Component	**Sub- Components**	**Description**
domain		Business group that owns the data product.

Component	Sub- Components	Description

data-product	`id`
	`name`
	`version`
	`type`
	`description`
	`purpose`
	`environment`
	`tags`
		Metadata that describes the data product. This information plays a key role in the findability of the data product.

ownership	`owner` `steward`	Metadata regarding the data product owner and the data product steward. This establishes the point of contact for consumers for any questions or clarifications they may have.
privacy	`contains-pii` `secured-using`	Metadata that signals whether the data product contains sensitive data and the technique used to mask it. This information goes a long way in enforcing established governance guidelines. This hugely promotes the reusability of the data product.

Component	Sub- Components	Description

connection	`protocol`
	`connection_type`
	`schema`
	`table-name`
	`requirements`
	`url`
		Metadata regarding the connectivity details of the data product. This information goes a long way in establishing accessibility and interoperability details of the data product.

service-level-objective	`critical`
	`freshness`
	`availability`
	`resolution-time`
		Metadata regarding the uptime expectations and data delays. It defines clear SLAs for resolution in case there is a delay or issue.

identity	`primary-key-columns` `foreign-key-columns`	Metadata regarding the primary key constraints and relationships with other data products.

columns	`data_type`
	`description`
	`unique`
	`data-quality_rules`
		Metadata regarding the schema of the data product. Information includes the structure and constraints of the data product and key data quality checks that were performed on the data product at creation time.

Table 4.1: Critical components of a data contract

Clear guidelines and transparency in data contracts create trust among consumers, fostering confidence in using the data product. Data contracts not only enhance data governance by defining clear accountability but also standardize data usage across the organization.

So, what exactly is a contract? It is a written or spoken agreement between two parties – in this context, a data producer and a consumer. But if a contract exists, how is it **enforced** or **validated**? Let's find out in the next section.

Contract validation

Contract validation ensures that the data product complies with all contract-defined rules related to quality, availability, consistency, and compliance. The validation may occur in several phases of the data journey – at ingestion, during transformations, or during consumption. From the accountability standpoint, data contract validation is a collaborative effort between data producers, domain owners, and data consumers.

The data producers' (typically the data engineering team) responsibilities include choosing the most appropriate data format, defining schemas, and implementing data quality checks. Domain owners (typically data owners and stewards) are responsible for defining data quality rules, validating checks, maintaining contracts, and providing feedback to data producers in the event of violations. Once data is available, consumers may still uncover inconsistencies or new requirements that slipped through the cracks during initial validation.

Figure 4.19 illustrates a typical data contract validation process.

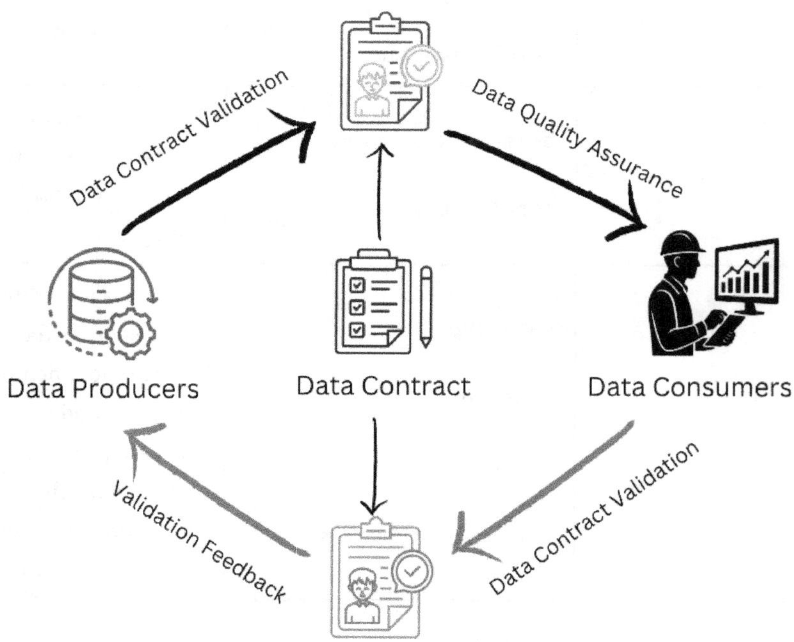

Figure 4.19: Data contract validation process

Technically, data contract validation may happen in one of the following two methods:

1. **Manual validation**: Data quality rules and constraints defined in the data contract can be validated manually using custom programs after the data transformation phase. This validation is typically performed on batches of data at scheduled intervals - such as daily, weekly, or monthly.
2. **Automated validation**: In this scenario, data quality rules and constraints embedded in the data contract are validated automatically, either using custom programs integrated within data pipelines or, even better, via real-time streaming checks. Recently, Databricks introduced a new feature built within its lakeflow declarative pipelines service known as *expectations*. This capability allows you to apply and monitor quality constraints on data as it flows through pipelines continuously.

We will learn about the expectations feature of Databricks in greater detail in *Chapter 6, Understanding Medallion Architecture and Delta Lake*, of this book.

Data consumers

Data product consumers include team members within the same domain as the product, as well as users from other domains. Increasingly, data is also shared externally, meaning consumers may include partners, suppliers and other third-party stakeholders. For organizations with a *data marketplace*, consumers include largely unknown public entities that require access to your data products through a secure sharing platform.

With the decentralized ownership concept under our belt, let's move on to the next principle of the data mesh.

Self-Serve Analytics

In today's organizations, business teams are under immense pressure to create data-driven insights. However, generating these insights is highly dependent on data experts who must first ingest, transform, and aggregate data from various sources. As the demand for data analytics continues to surge, centralized data engineering teams are facing unprecedented workload pressures. This dependency creates significant bottlenecks, which limit strategic decision-making and hamper overall growth.

Organizations strive for faster decision-making; therefore, something needs to change. Data mesh architecture enables self-serve analytics by empowering business domains with analytical tools and access to data. This approach allows them to explore data, build dashboards, and generate insights independently, thereby reducing dependency on data engineering teams. The challenge is that business users lack technical expertise. To overcome this, modern data engineering tools are building low-code/no-code services that can perform data exploration, generate insights, build data pipelines, generate SQL and Python code without any technical knowledge. Using the power of conversational AI, business users can ask questions in natural language and generate instant insights.

Enabling self-serve analytics requires careful planning and execution. It requires the right blend of technology, governance, and process transformation. It should be clear that high-quality data products are fundamental for self-serve analytics. Creation, distribution, and consumption of data products depend on well-defined processes. Let's explore which processes are essential to enable self-serve analytics within an organization.

Data product creation process

The data product creation process begins with a discovery phase performed by domain experts – the data owner and the data steward. Together, they identify key features, data quality standards, and privacy rules that the data product must address. During the process, they may consult with other stakeholders within their domain to align key objectives and outcomes. Once these features and rules are finalized, they are communicated to the team of data experts so that they can start building the data product.

Figure 4.20 below illustrates a typical data product creation process. Following the discovery phase, data experts implement the data product blueprint by ensuring compliance with organizational standards, designing data models, ingesting source data, developing data pipelines, and creating final aggregations for consumption. Once the data product is delivered, the ownership transitions back to the domain experts. At this stage, data stewards enhance the product metadata to improve data discoverability. They populate the data contract with details such as descriptions, source information, schemas, tags, and business glossary terms.

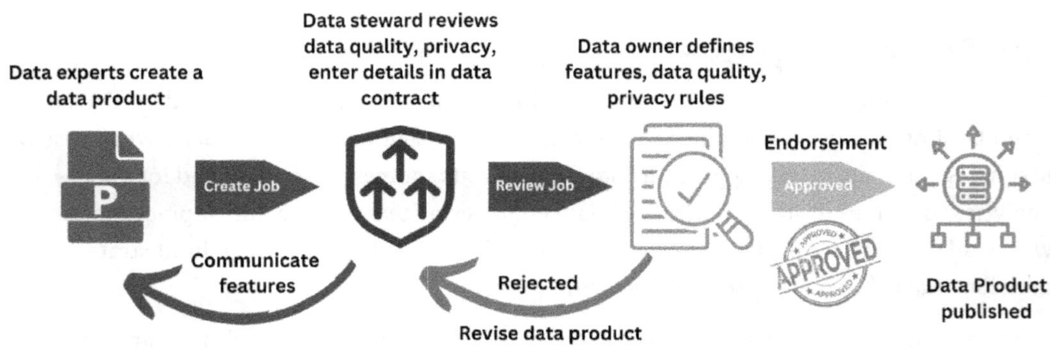

Figure 4.20: Data product creation process

This process included a built-in feedback loop between the data steward and the data owner. After completing the metadata updates, the data steward submits an approval request to the data owner. The data owner then conducts a thorough review before granting a final sign-off.

The final step of the data product creation process is data owner endorsement. Endorsement is a formal approval process that certifies a data product as accurate, secure, and ready for use. Endorsement ensures consumers can find high-quality, trustworthy content. Endorsed items are identified with a badge/governed tag, and depending on the badge/governed type, some data products receive higher precedence during searches.

Figure 4.21: Endorsement badges/governed tags

Data product distribution process

The data product distribution process begins when a consumer searches for keywords. These searches are typically executed through user-friendly interfaces or programmatically using APIs. Both methods leverage metadata stored in data contracts, tags, and business glossary terms to drive accurate results.

For example, the following image shows a sample search performed by the consumer on Databricks UI.

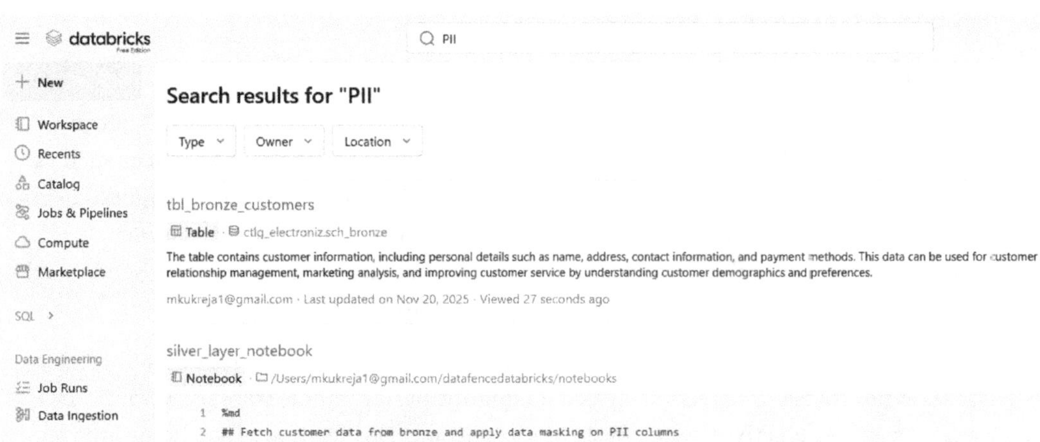

Figure 4.22: Sample search for data product

The data product distribution process is depicted in *Figure 4.23*. The consumer carefully reviews the metadata associated with each result to determine which data product best aligns with their analytical requirements. Once the selection is finalized, they proceed to subscribe to the chosen data product. At this point, an access request for the selected data product is automatically generated and sent to the data owner for approval. The consumer may require a clear and valid justification for requesting access to the data product.

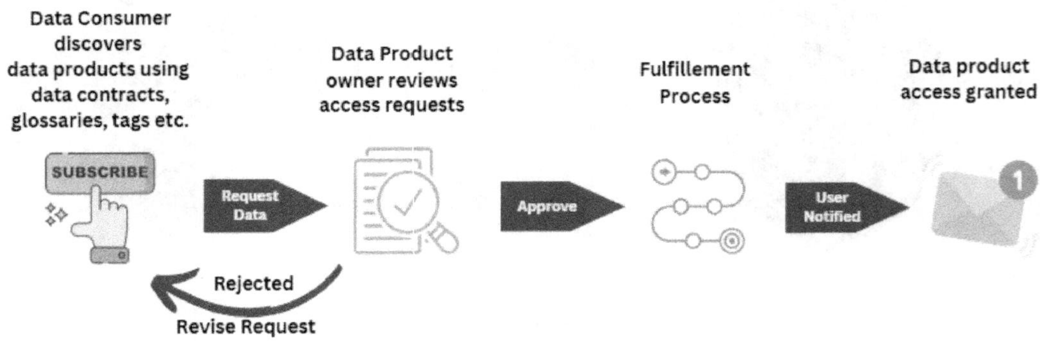

Figure 4.23: Data product distribution process

The data owner reviews the access request and decides whether to approve or reject it. In some cases, they may require additional details before granting approval. Once the request is approved, the fulfillment process begins to enable access to the data product. The process typically operates in the background, provisioning the permissions and grants needed to ensure seamless access to the data product. Once completed, the data consumer is notified regarding the approval of their request. They can then access the data product for analysis, ad hoc reporting, or other decision-making activities.

Data product consumption process

The data consumer begins by reviewing the data contract for connection details. Typically, consumers leverage dashboarding and other business intelligence tools and services such as Power BI, Tableau, or Looker. Access to these tools and services can be easily configured using common ODBC/JDBC protocols or APIs. Using the connectivity details, the consumer establishes a connection to the data product. From here onwards, this connection serves as the foundation of all future analytics activities for this data product.

As shown in *Figure 4.24* below, the consumption process includes a continuous feedback loop to the data owner covering aspects such as data quality, performance, stability, uptime, and adherence to service objectives stated in the data contract. This feedback loop helps improve the data product over time, ensuring it continues to meet organizational and domain needs.

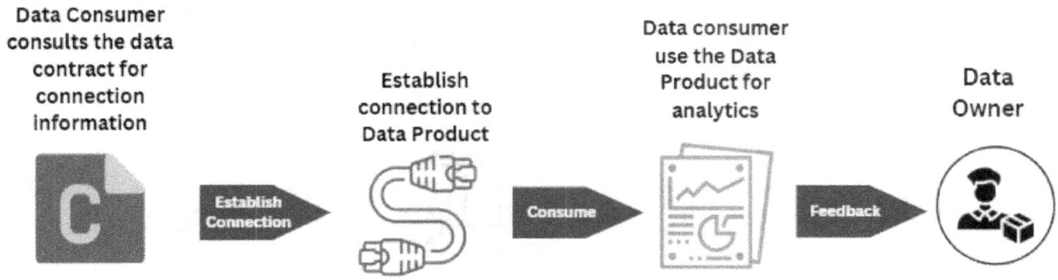

Figure 4.24: Data product consumption process

Having explored the concept of self-serve analytics, we will next focus on the last principle of the data mesh.

Federated Governance

Let's refer to *Figure 4.9: Finding the sweet spot in data delivery*, where we highlighted that, in the data delivery cycle, convergence focuses on finding the sweet spot among standards, processes, and governance. In earlier sections, we examined how various standards and processes support the three core principles of the data mesh: decentralized ownership, data-as-a-product, and self-serve analytics. Now we shift our focus to the final principle – **federated governance**.

Before we delve into federated governance, it's important to first define what data governance entails. Data governance encompasses a set of principles, policies, processes, and technologies that ensure an organization remains secure and compliant with regulatory requirements. Historically, governance models have been either **centralized** or **decentralized**. While centralized models follow a one-size-fits-all approach, decentralized models often lack consistency across business domains. **Federated governance** takes a hybrid approach – with a central governance authority and *decentralized* execution.

Federated governance is all about striking the right balance - a **central body** sets global standards and guardrails while providing oversight, and each domain has the freedom to implement policies and processes in its own way. Due to its scalable nature, the federated governance model fits perfectly for large, globally distributed organizations that want to balance control with autonomy.

Figure 4.25 clearly depicts how federated governance promotes central-authority policy formulation and local-domain execution within a domain.

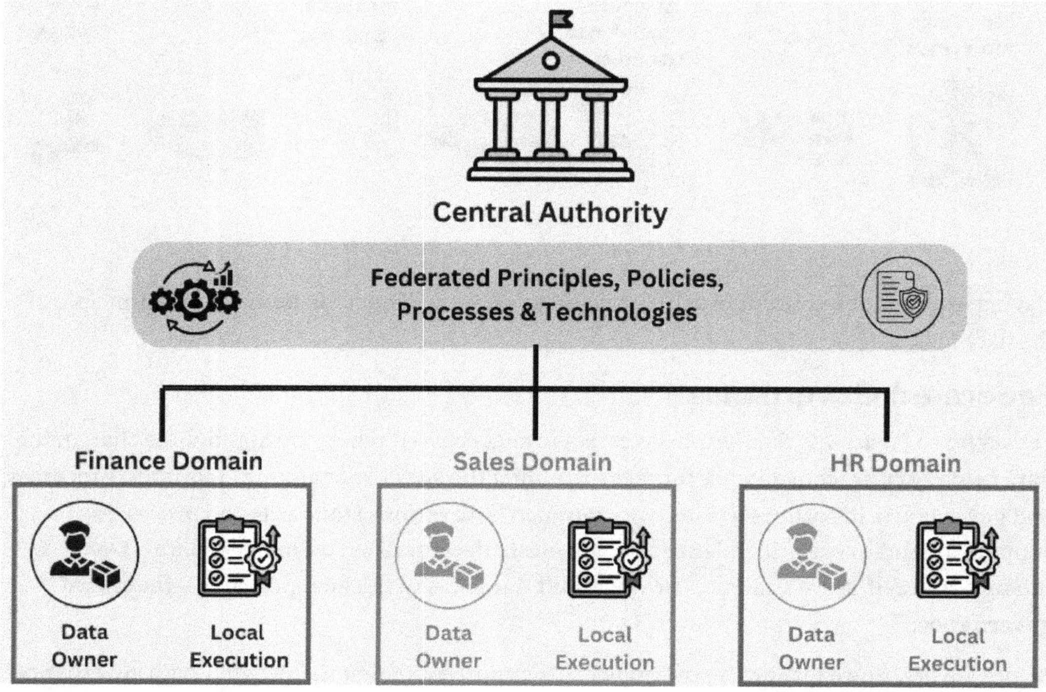

Figure 4.25: Federated governance – central authority with local execution

Role of the central authority

In federated governance, the central authority serves as the guiding body, establishing and enforcing mandatory policies and standards for the entire organization. The central authority fosters stronger collaboration with domains, ensures unified compliance, and greater oversight and control. The central authority is responsible for the following key roles:

- **Define global standards and policies**: The definition of global standards and policies is the most critical responsibility of the central authority. This includes selecting the data governance frameworks, establishing data classification standards, and setting guidelines for data ingestion, processing, and integration. It also involves defining standards for data masking and encryption, specifying data exchange and storage formats, and choosing platform technology.

- **Ensure regulatory compliance**: Identify all applicable regulations for the organization. Once the regulations are determined, map their rules and regulations to security policies.
- **Set guardrails for local autonomy of domains**: Define which policies and standards can be customized locally by the domains, and which ones remain mandatory across the organization.
- **Perform audits and oversight**: The central authority performs regular audits of domains to verify compliance with established policies and standards.

The role of federated governance in ensuring compliance and control is critical. We will learn more about these roles in *Chapter 12, Governance of Data Products*, of this book. Now let's move on to the next building block of a future data platform – an approach that is revolutionizing data processing with minimal latency.

Real-time processing

Decision-making has undergone a major transformation in recent years, with an increasing demand for faster, **real-time** data processing to support timely insights. The speed and agility of data processing have become essential to a business's competitive edge. Although speed and agility remain the primary drivers for real-time processing, there is another equally important factor in play. As discussed in *Chapter 2, Discovering Data Platforms* of this book, we examined the CAP theorem and the operational constraints it imposes on data platforms. Over the past decade, distributed data platforms have chosen **AP** (**availability** and **partition** tolerance) over **consistency**. This trend is primarily driven by the sacrifice of data quality in favor of faster data processing. While minor delays in data consistency may have minimal impact in the short-term, their compounding effect over several years can severely undermine business analytics. Real-time processing helps prevent data drift by ensuring accurate, consistent data, even if it means slightly reducing availability.

The primary goal of real-time data processing is to enable continuous data ingestion and computations, often referred to as streaming ingestion and stream processing. Let's explore how this works:

- **Streaming ingestion**: Streaming ingestion is a continuous process of capturing changing datasets from data sources such as databases, IoT sensors, and APIs. Streaming ingestion can be performed using a variety of open-source, cloud-based, and proprietary software solutions such as AWS DMS, Debezium, and Databricks Lakeflow Connect. These tools continuously monitor data changes – often using **change data capture** (**CDC**) - and promptly deliver updates to streaming platforms.

- **Streaming platforms**: Streaming platforms store continuously flowing data as *events*. However, this storage is **temporary**; the data is retained for a configurable time, allowing streaming processing to catch up. In essence, streaming platforms serve as an intermediary buffer between the data producers (streaming ingestion) and the data consumers (stream processing). Streaming platforms are built to store events in a distributed and fault-tolerant manner, enabling them to handle high throughputs with minimal latency. *Figure 4.26* shows some of the most widely used streaming platforms, including Apache Kafka, Amazon Kinesis, Azure Event Hubs, and Google Pub/Sub.

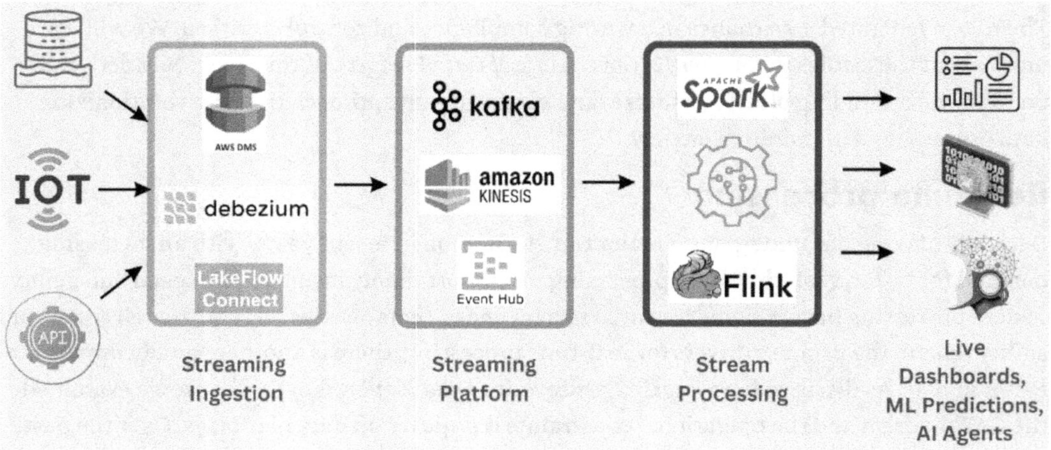

Figure 4.26: Streaming ingestion and stream processing

- **Stream processing**: Stream processing is the practice of analyzing data in real-time. When connected to streaming platforms, popular frameworks like Apache Spark and Apache Flink can process micro-batches of data at very short intervals. Databricks provides **Lakeflow Declarative Pipelines** (**LDP**), enabling data engineers to perform stream processing using SQL or Python, while automatically merging data incrementally into structures such as materialized views. As an added benefit, top, LDP enables continuous data quality monitoring as it moves through the pipelines. Data stored in materialized views can be easily accessed by modern dashboarding software and ML/AI applications.

We will learn about Databricks Lakeflow Declarative Pipelines in greater detail in *Chapter 6, Understanding Medallion Architecture and Delta Lake*, of this book.

> **Note**
>
> Integrating real-time stream processing and AI agents marks a significant leap forward in the enablement of autonomous, context-aware decision making.

Future data platforms deliver instant data insights through real-time analytics, helping organizations improve customer retention, detect fraud early, and prevent potential hazards. Coordinating all these processes requires intelligent platform operations. Let's dive into how automation and data observability are redefining data platform operations.

Automation and data observability

Future data platforms must achieve operational excellence to ensure they are fast, reliable, consistent, trustworthy, and dependable. Achieving this requires leveraging automation to streamline workflows, simplify cloud infrastructure deployments, and accelerate product delivery.

Automation

As the demand for data analytics continues to surge, skilled data engineers are becoming increasingly scarce and costly. With the growing number and complexity of data pipelines and the rise of real-time analytics, organizations are embracing innovative strategies to maximize efficiency and justify high investments in resources and computing - ultimately doing more with less. Organizations are increasingly adopting automated infrastructure provisioning to accelerate cloud deployments. At the same time, the increasing demand to develop, manage, and deploy large-scale codebases is pushing the limits of modern data engineering teams. Let's explore these automation concepts in greater detail below:

Infrastructure as code

Infrastructure as code (**IaC**) is the practice of deploying and managing infrastructure components through source code. By adopting IaC, system administration teams – commonly known as DevOps - are no longer constrained by manual processes and documented actions. Instead, they can execute automated, repeatable deployments using configuration files, ensuring consistency and scalability across environments.

Figure 4.27 shows several key benefits of using Infrastructure as Code (IaC):

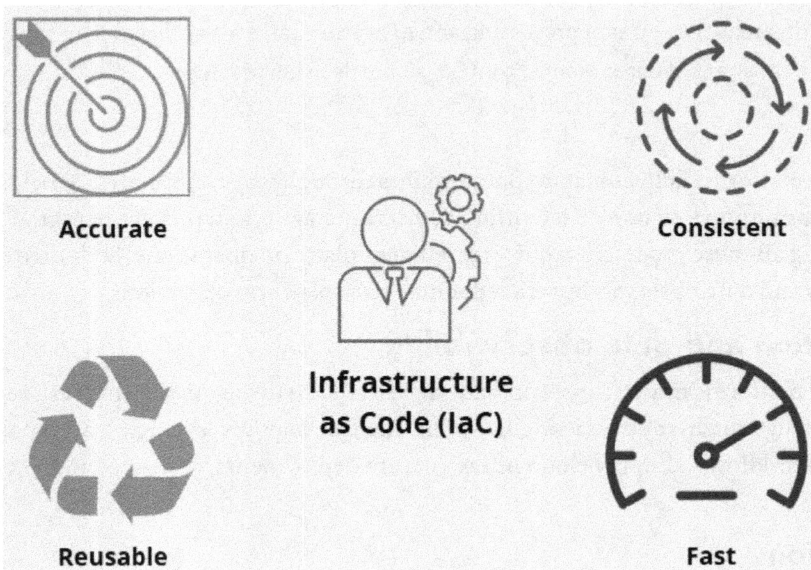

Figure 4.27: Benefits of using IaC

Infrastructure deployed through infrastructure as code is accurate, consistent, reusable, and fast. DevOps teams create, manage, and control infrastructure configuration files much like application developers handle code. This approach follows established protocols for bug fixing, testing, and code promotions, ensuring reliability and repeatability. A variety of IaC tools - both open source and commercial - are available, including Ansible, Terraform, Chef, and Puppet.

For infrastructure provisioning in the cloud, **Azure Resource Manager** (**ARM**) or Bicep serves as Azure's native solution, enabling organizations to standardize deployments for uniformity, security, and performance. IaC tools leverage templates to implement infrastructure as code. Once created, these templates are stored in the enterprise code repository, just like other application code. An IaC template is essentially a JSON or YAML file that contains resource configuration. ARM templates use a declarative syntax, allowing you to deploy multiple Azure resources in a single template. At deployment time, ARM automatically sequences the operations in the correct order and fires them either sequentially or in parallel. IaC not only accelerates infrastructure deployment, but it is also frequently integrated with CI/CD, enabling automated testing and continuous delivery.

Continuous integration and deployment (CI/CD)

As the new era of analytics unfolds, the demand for data engineers – and the volume of code they produce – continues to rise. Fortunately, an emerging trend is helping ease this burden.

Continuous integration and deployment (CI/CD) is a set of practices designed to accelerate code delivery through small, incremental changes, enabling faster and more reliable development cycles.

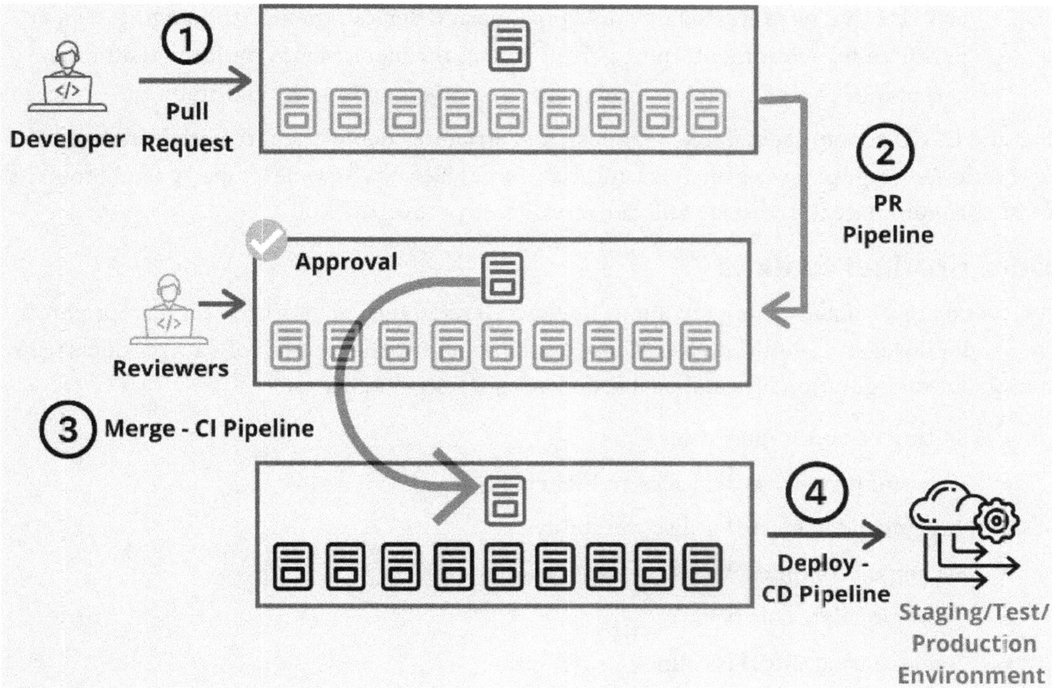

Figure 4.28: Data flow in CI/CD pipelines

This is how a typical CI/CD pipeline works to automate code delivery:

1. **Create a branch**: Developers author and unit test their code within their respective branches. Each branch typically implements a new feature of fixing a recently discovered bug.
2. **Create a pull request (PR pipeline)**: After completing work on a new feature or bug fix, the developer creates a pull request to merge code into the main branch. This triggers the **Pull Request (PR) pipeline** that checks dependencies and runs unit tests. If any test fails, the code is returned to the developer for fixes, and the pipeline proceeds to the review and approval stage.
3. **Merge code into environments (CI pipeline)**: Once the team completes the code review and approves the changes, the code is merged into the main branch. This triggers the **Continuous Integration (CI) pipeline**, which runs the same tests as the

PR pipeline along with additional integration tests to ensure the new changes work seamlessly with the existing codebase.

4. **Deploy code (CD pipeline)**: The **Continuous Deployment (CD) pipeline** retrieves the artifacts that were created by the CI pipeline and deploys them to the staging, test, or production environment. During deployment, the pipeline may perform additional acceptance checks in each environment to ensure functionality and stability.

IaC and CI/CD enable dependable, seamless, and error-free deployment of both infrastructure and code. Leveraging these principles, futuristic organizations have developed custom toolkits to further automate the creation and delivery of data products.

Data product toolkits

By leveraging automation, organizations have accelerated the delivery cycle for data products by developing custom-built toolkits. These toolkits simplify the creation of data products using templated configuration files and enable end-to-end functionality for:

- Setting up code repositories
- Provisioning new workspaces and schemas
- Tagging data objects for discoverability
- Setting up compute clusters
- Validating data contracts
- Orchestrating CI/CD pipelines

This holistic approach not only shortens delivery cycles but also maintains a high degree of consistency and automation. By using toolkits, organizations have found an effective way to enforce best practices and manage the data product lifecycle by providing a structured framework for consistent development and deployment. Shifting from automation, let's turn our attention to another concept that is transforming how we approach data reliability.

Data observability

Reliability in future data platforms is no longer optional - it depends on having a comprehensive view of the data ecosystem. **Data observability** provides the visibility needed to ensure that the platform is operating correctly, at peak performance, and is cost-efficient. This visibility is achieved by accessing the health of data products through a blend of real-time monitoring and periodic data checks. Using proactive health checks, data observability helps organizations reduce downtimes, optimize resources, and increase operational efficiency. Data observability bases the health of data on five key parameters:

1. **Timeliness**: Is the data arriving according to the service-level objective as defined in the data contract?

2. **Completeness**: Is the data complete and fully delivered within the specified limits outlined in the data contract?
3. **Schema compliance**: Does the data conform to the agreed-upon schema as promised in the data contract?
4. **Consistent volumes**: Is the volume of data delivered consistent over time?
5. **Lineage**: Is the data lineage being accurately tracked from upstream to downstream?

Future data platforms are designed for agility, with their health continuously monitored across the five critical dimensions outlined above. Future data platforms closely monitor emerging patterns and automatically trigger corrective actions when patterns or conditions are detected in the changing data. This holistic approach ensures reliability, performance, and trust in every stage of the data lifecycle. We will learn about data observability in greater detail in *Chapter 11, Building the Next-Gen Data Analytics Gold Layer*, of this book. With this in mind, we are nearing the final building block of a future-ready data platform – one that is transforming how machines progressively gain intelligence, enabling them to perform tasks that were once the sole domain of humans.

AI enablement

Future data platforms are evolving into intelligent ecosystems – capable of reasoning, decision-making, and acting like humans. Beyond simply storing data, future data platforms continuously learn evolving trends, enabling it to optimize and automatically take corrective actions. Using Generative AI, new data instances can be created based on previously learned probability distribution - the possibilities are endless.

Below are some ways in which AI is reshaping modern data analytics:

Exploring data using natural language

Interacting with data using natural language is democratizing data access and unlocking new opportunities for self-serve analytics. Self-serve analytics reduces the burden of data management teams by empowering domain users to run queries and generate reports independently. Services like Databricks Genie empower business domains to interact with their data using natural language. Through Genie spaces, domain experts can seamlessly translate business questions into analytical queries and generate visualizations to interpret operational data – all without writing a single line of code.

Code generation

Data engineers often face the challenge of managing large, complex codebases while racing against tight deadlines for bug fixes and new data products, pushing them to their limits. AI enablement solves this problem by acting as a code assistant for data engineers. In Databricks, the Databricks Assistant is natively integrated into each code-editing environment. Whether you are working in Notebooks or SQL editor, it can generate SQL queries, Python scripts, or Spark code through a conversational interface. Such code generation services significantly accelerate development by creating boilerplate code and providing a solid starting point for data engineers. Databricks Assistant can review existing code, detect potential issues, and recommend fixes.

Domain specific chatbots

Future data platforms are leveraging **Retrieval Augmented Generation (RAG)** to combine traditional sources – such as databases, data warehouses, data lakes, or lakehouses - with the power of generative **large language models** (**LLMs**). This approach bridges the gap between static knowledge & dynamic information. By using domain-specific chatbots, business units can help customers get answers to data-driven questions on proprietary information.

Embedding in SQL

Future-ready SQL platforms like Databricks SQL come with built-in GenAI capabilities for ad hoc operations, powered by state-of-the-art LLMs optimized for data-related tasks. With SQL AI Functions, you can apply AI directly on data – performing tasks such as text translation or sentiment analysis.

> Note
>
> As GenAI becomes increasingly integrated into corporate systems, AI governance is emerging as a critical priority. How can organizations ensure responsible use of AI while safeguarding data privacy and ethical usage?

This section provides an introduction to how AI is transforming modern data analytics. In *Chapter 10, Building the Silver Layer of the Medallion Architecture using Gen AI*, we will explore the impact of generative AI on data analytics in much greater detail.

Summary

In this chapter, we examined the hallmarks of a future-ready data platform. We began with a strong foundation of a cloud-enabled platform designed to support a data lakehouse capable of handling large volumes of data in diverse formats. From there, we explored the importance of establishing a single-source-of-truth layer through a golden record. We also discussed the convergence in data delivery by data mesh architecture – creating data products, decentralizing data ownership, and promoting federated governance. Additionally, we highlighted the roles of data owners and data experts, as well as the value of adopting data contracts for data distribution. We looked at how real-time analytics, automation, and data observability are enhancing data platform operations. Finally, we discussed how AI enablement is redefining how modern data platforms are utilized.

Together, these elements form the blueprint for future-ready data platforms—systems that are not only well-governed, resilient, and intelligent, but also adaptable to continuous change. They enable organizations to operate with confidence in an environment defined by rapid data growth, evolving regulatory expectations, and accelerating advances in AI.

Get this book's PDF version and more

Scan the QR code (or go to `packtpub.com/unlock`). Search for this book by name, confirm the edition, and then follow the steps on the page.

UNLOCK NOW

Note: Keep your invoice handy. Purchases made directly from Packt don't require an invoice.

5

Understanding Databricks

In *Chapter 4, Designing Future Data Platforms*, we explored the foundational elements of future data platforms, emphasizing that modern data analytics is advancing towards a highly innovative paradigm, with autonomy and observability at its core. Building such platforms requires data engineers to leverage robust tools, services, and frameworks. Modern data engineering demands a robust environment capable of handling massive, rapidly evolving datasets while also supporting advanced use cases such as machine learning and artificial intelligence.

In this chapter, we will explore **Databricks** - a cloud-based platform for data engineering, machine learning, and artificial intelligence built on Apache Spark. Databricks provides a unified environment that fosters collaboration among data engineers, data scientists, and ML/AI engineers.

We'll begin by defining what a harmonized data platform is and how Databricks' capabilities enable it. Then we'll take a deeper look at how Databricks manages storage and compute, and how the Unity Catalog provides an efficient governance layer across both. Finally, we'll explore how Databricks approaches data sharing, security, and billing.

In this chapter, we will cover the following topics:

- Understanding Databricks
- Databricks architecture
- Databricks capabilities
- Unity Catalog
- Data sharing

Introduction to Databricks

Databricks is a US-based enterprise software company founded in 2013 by the creators of **Apache Spark**. It offers a cloud-based platform for data engineering, data analytics, machine learning, and artificial intelligence, hosted on AWS, Azure, or Google Cloud. Databricks has been a partner with Microsoft Azure since 2016, delivering Azure Databricks, a service that offers native integration with other Azure services, including Active Directory, Azure SQL Data Warehouse, and Power BI.

In June 2025, Databricks and Azure announced a multi-year extension of their strategic partnership, reaffirming their shared commitment to unlocking the power of data. Databricks sets itself apart from its competitors by making **unification** a cornerstone of its strategy.

Unified data platform

Databricks is an intelligent, **unified data analytics platform** for building and managing enterprise-grade data solutions. But what does "unified" really mean - and why does it matter? Data analytics often requires a mix of specialized skills, handles a wide array of workloads, and works with data sets scattered across multiple sources. Achieving a high-quality product requires a data platform that fosters collaborative innovation while ensuring strong data governance. A unified data analytics platform brings every aspect of data together in the following ways:

Harmonized data platform

In *Chapter 2, Discovering Data Platforms*, we explored the ongoing challenge of choosing between traditional data processing approaches - such as databases and data warehouses - and modern alternatives like data lakes. We also examined some trade-offs associated with data lakes, such as the lack of ACID compliance, indexing, and versioning. Databricks combines the power of a data lake and a data warehouse in a single, integrated platform. Leveraging its medallion architecture, which we will discuss in greater detail in the next chapter, enables the creation of an ACID-compliant single source of truth, eliminating the need for data duplication across a data lake and the data warehouse.

Unified governance

With its built-in **Unity Catalog**, Databricks ensures consistent data discovery, access control, quality control, and compliance across all business domains. Unified governance extends beyond internal data assets to include external data sources, without requiring their migration into Databricks. The unified data discovery process equips end users with essential business context, enabling more accurate and efficient utilization of data.

Figure 5.1 illustrates the key harmonization capabilities enabled by the Unity Catalog.

Figure 5.1: Aspects of a unified data analytics platform

Collaborative development

Databricks provides a **collaborative** environment for data professionals - data engineers, data scientists, analysts, ML/AI engineers, domain experts – data owners and data stewards – and data consumers, forming what we call a **data community**. Databricks enables the data community to collaborate in a shared environment. The shared environment empowers community members with diverse perspectives to brainstorm, share ideas, and innovate to develop data products and solutions. When this data community works together, the chances of delivering data products that align with business objectives increase significantly. By leveraging version-controlled code repositories, they can build workflows using interactive notebooks and SQL queries. A collaborative development approach streamlines workflow development and accelerates the delivery of insights to stakeholders.

Integrated analytics workloads

By providing an integrated environment, Databricks removes the need for multiple tools to handle different analytical workloads. Databricks offers core capabilities spanning data engineering, data science, machine learning, and artificial intelligence. These core capabilities empower data teams to ingest, transform, model, distribute, and collaborate – all within a single, unified platform. Let's now explore the Databricks architecture to understand how these concepts connect and reinforce one another.

Databricks architecture

In *Chapter 2, Discovering Data Platforms*, we learned about data lakes, the central repository of all types of data. Although data lakes have been widely adopted for data analytics, they come with several inherent limitations, including the following:

- They need a separate data warehouse to support BI and ad-hoc queries.
- Lack of transactional support.
- Challenges in data governance.
- High data storage requirements.
- Duplication of data across multiple copies.
- Significant challenges in sharing data internally and externally.

Lakehouse architecture combines the benefits of data lakes and data warehouses. Using the Delta framework and the Unity Catalog at its core, Databricks implements the lakehouse architecture by continuously merging data as it transitions from staging to aggregation. These foundational principles underpin Databricks' approach to building a Lakehouse:

- Eliminate data silos through a no-copy storage approach.
- Segregate storage from compute to flexibility and scalability.
- Distribute data as products rather than isolated data assets.
- Enable self-service to democratize data access.
- Implement a federated governance model.
- Support open data formats and interoperable interfaces.
- Leverage on-demand scalability to optimize costs and enhance efficiency.

Later in the chapter, we will explore the Delta framework and Unity Catalog in detail, including how they address the limitations of the traditional data lake. Now, let's understand the mechanics of Databricks in action.

Operating model

A **Databricks account** is the top-level entity for managing Databricks across an organization. Databricks deployments are cloud-native and can be hosted on any major cloud platform – AWS, Azure, or GCP. The following functions are managed at the account level:

- **Identity and access management**: Includes **single sign-on** (**SSO**) configurations and the administration of users, groups, and service principals.
- **Unity Catalog management**: Covers metastore creation and linking metastore to workspaces.

- **Workspace management**: Manage workspaces across multiple cloud regions.
- **Billing, compliance, and policy enforcement**: Handle financial operations, regulatory compliance, and governance policies.

The **Unity Catalog metastore** is the top-level component of the Databricks data governance framework. It stores metadata for data assets – catalogs, schemas, tables, views, volumes, lineages, and models. Each metastore is **region-specific**, meaning it can only exist in one cloud region. A Databricks account can have multiple metastores, provided each resides in a different cloud region.

A Databricks account can host multiple workspaces – an environment where data and domain experts collaborate to build ETL pipelines, train ML models, develop AI agents, and perform interactive exploration. The workspace serves as an **interactive development environment (IDE)** that your team can use to access Databricks' assets. Each workspace can be linked to only one metastore, but a single metastore can be shared across multiple workspaces.

> **Note**
>
> When creating a workspace, the auto-assignment feature can automatically associate it with a designated metastore.

Databricks operates across two distinct layers: the control plane and the compute plane.

Control plane

The Databricks control plane comprises services hosted and managed by Databricks that handle back-end functions for coordinating and orchestrating your account. These services work behind the scenes to ensure your Databricks environment operates smoothly. Below is the list of services that operate within the control plane:

- **Authentication and authorization mechanisms**: Covers user and API authentication through SSO and **OAUTH** protocols. Also includes **Role-Based Access Control (RBAC)** for managing permissions across users, groups, and service principals.
- **Unity catalog and workspace management**: Encompasses workspace administration tasks such as creating, updating, and deleting workspaces, configuring workspace settings, defining cluster policies, and managing compute resources. Additionally, includes catalog operations for managing schemas, tables, views, models, volumes, and functions.
- **Cluster and job orchestration**: Involves managing cluster lifecycle operations such as creation, termination, autoscaling, enforcing cluster policies, and orchestrating workflow tasks through dependency chaining.

- **User interface**: Covers management of the Databricks UI, including workspace navigation, notebooks, SQL editor, Catalog Explorer, and monitoring tools for jobs and clusters.
- **Billing, auditing, and monitoring**: Includes services for tracking account costs and usage, maintaining detailed logs for compliance purposes, and monitoring overall system health and performance.

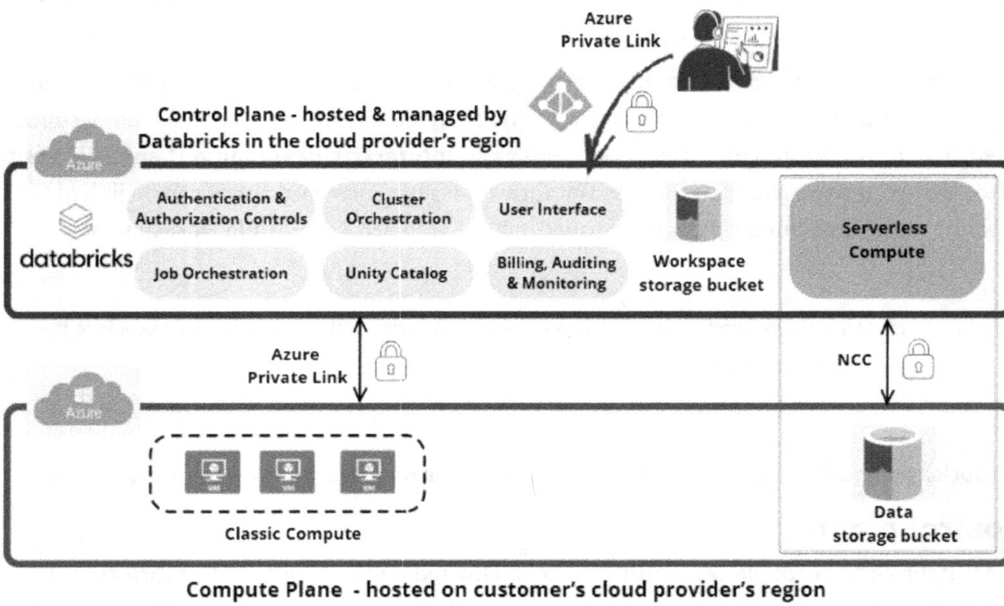

Figure 5.2: Databricks control and compute planes

Compute plane

The Databricks compute plane resides entirely within your own cloud account and serves as an execution layer for processing your analytical data. Because it operates in your own cloud environment, you retain full control over network configurations, security policies, and data residency requirements. This plane ensures that your sensitive data never leaves your cloud account while still benefiting from the orchestration and management capabilities of the Databricks control plane. Below is the list of services that operate within the compute plane:

- **Data computing**: Provides the core infrastructure for executing workloads. It hosts the Apache Spark distributed computing framework, machine learning libraries, and the Photon engine for high-performance query execution. This layer also includes the compute resources required to run Spark jobs efficiently.

- **Managing read/write operations from storage**: Handles read and write operations across storage layers such as Amazon S3, Azure Data Lake Storage Gen 2, and Google Cloud Storage.
- **Cluster lifecycle management**: Executes cluster creation, termination, and autoscaling based on instructions from the control plane.

> Note
>
> Whenever possible, Databricks places the control plane and compute plane in the same cloud region. This approach minimizes latency, avoids cross-region data transfer costs, and simplifies compliance by ensuring all data remains within the same cloud region.

There are two types of compute planes:

- **Classic compute plane**: The classic compute plane consists of resources deployed within your cloud account and operating inside your virtual network. This infrastructure includes **virtual machines** (**VMs**) for running workloads, cloud storage buckets for analytical data and workspace metadata, as well as services such as secrets manager, key management servers, and networking services required to support secure and efficient communications with the control plane.
- **Serverless compute plane**: The serverless compute plane is managed entirely by Databricks, eliminating the need for deployment of virtual machines or underlying networking. To maintain a high level of security and compliance, Databricks provisions the serverless resources within the same region as your workspace's network boundary. The compute capacity automatically scales up or down based on workload demand. For cost efficiency, you are billed only for the compute consumed, with no idle cluster overhead.

Deployment options

A common point of confusion during deployment is whether to use a single Databricks account for multiple environments—such as development, testing, and production—or to create separate accounts for each environment.

The image below illustrates the various Databricks deployment scenarios that can be considered.

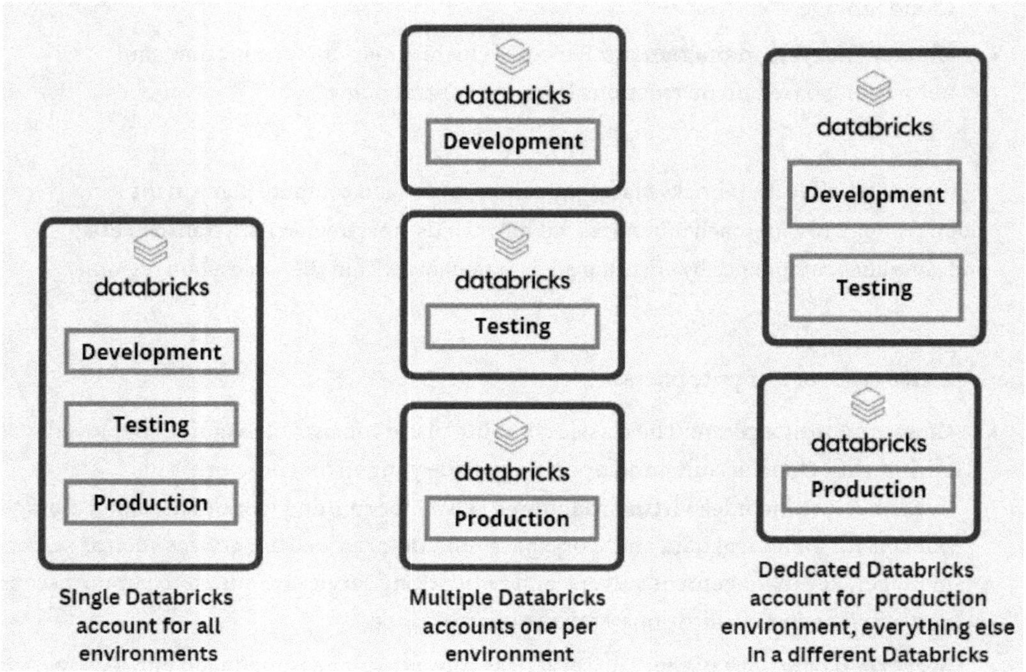

Figure 5.3: Databricks account deployment scenarios

This architectural decision must be approached thoughtfully to ensure Databricks is configured for true enterprise-scale operation. The following sections examine each deployment scenario in greater depth.

- **Single Databricks account for all environments**: Using a single Databricks account across all environments centralizes authentication and authorization controls. This approach simplifies deployment and reduces administration overheads. You can achieve logical isolation by setting up a dedicated workspace for each environment, with a separate Unity catalog and storage, workspace-level network isolation, secrets, and cluster control policies. From the billing perspective, you receive a single invoice, but allocating costs across environments can be challenging. A single Databricks account is ideal for organizations operating within the same cloud region for all environments, seeking simplified governance tracking and shared guardrails.

The image below illustrates the optimal configuration of workspaces and Unity catalogs for the single Databricks account setup.

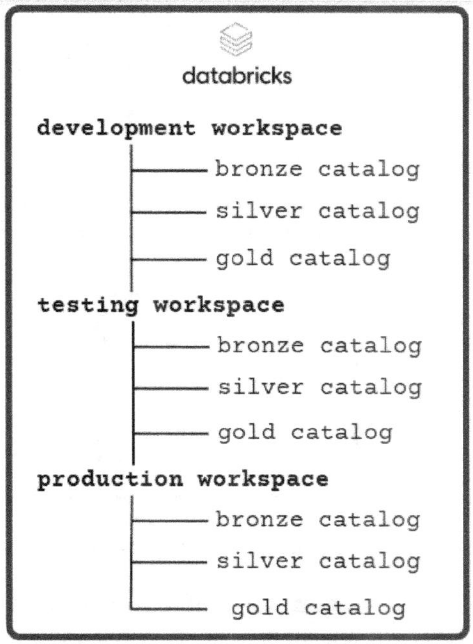

Figure 5.4: Single Databricks account workspace and Unity Catalog configuration

> **Note**
>
> To ensure best practices, establish a clear software delivery process for deploying code across environments. Leveraging Databricks Repos and a robust CI/CD pipeline significantly streamlines and strengthens this workflow.

- **Multiple Databricks accounts, one per environment**: Using multiple Databricks accounts achieves a complete workspace, Unity Catalog, storage, and network isolation. Unlike the single Databricks account approach, authentication controls need to be configured separately for each account. You receive multiple invoices, so a clear financial segregation can be achieved. The deployment and administrative costs in this model are slightly higher than a single-account approach. In some ways, complete separation enforces strict regulatory isolation, but it may be harder to track lineage across accounts. The image below illustrates the optimal configuration of workspaces and Unity Catalogs for multiple Databricks accounts setup.

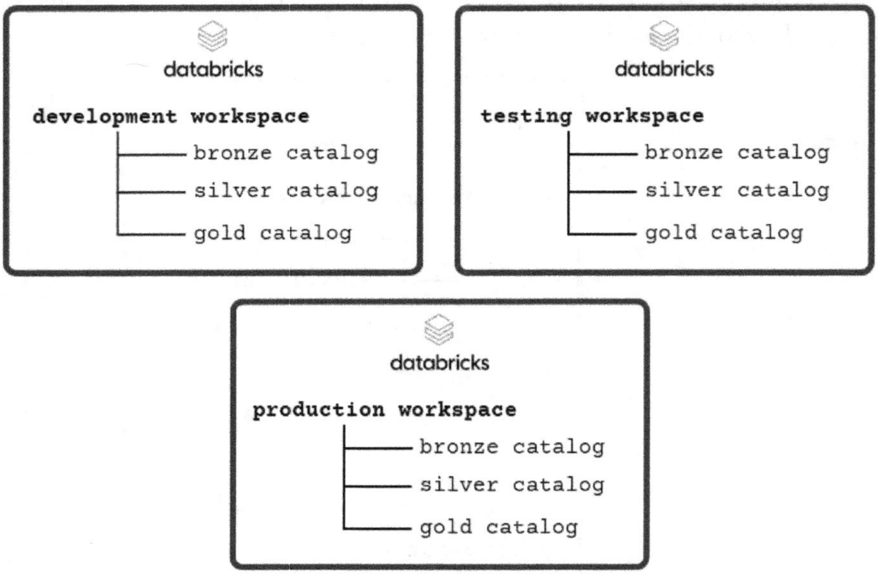

Figure 5.5: Multiple Databricks accounts workspace and Unity catalog configuration

- **Dedicated Databricks account for production, shared for development and testing**: In this setup, a dedicated Databricks account is used exclusively for production, while a shared account supports development and testing. This approach ensures that the production environment remains completely isolated – both physically and logically. All other environments are deployed within a shared Databricks account, where they are logically isolated from one another. You receive two invoices with clear financial segregation for production use. In this model, deployment and administrative costs are higher than in a single-account approach but remain significantly lower than in a multiple-account setup.

The image below illustrates the configuration of workspaces and Unity Catalogs for this setup:

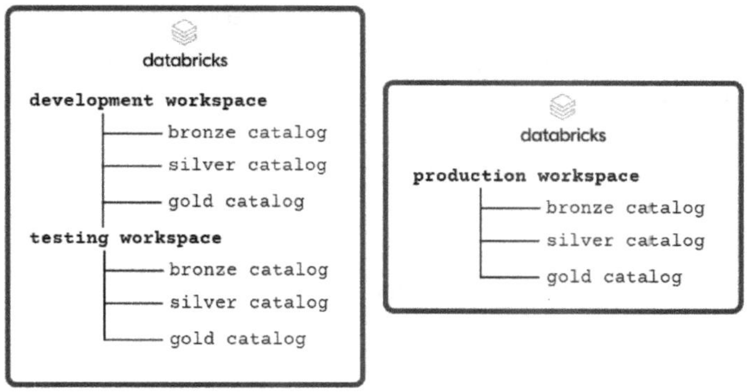

Figure 5.6: Hybrid Databricks accounts workspace and Unity Catalog configuration

Note

One limitation of using multiple Databricks accounts is the lack of resource sharing. To mitigate this, it is crucial to closely monitor resource utilization and perform regular tuning.

Workspaces

Databricks workspace is the user environment to manage your data, code artifacts and compute resources.

Workspace overview

Each account can include multiple workspaces – collaboration environments designed for building and running data pipelines, developing machine learning models, creating AI agents, and performing interactive data exploration. The workspace user interface is designed for data engineers and ML/AI engineers to easily navigate and interact with essential components, including:

- **Data Engineering services:** Job run history and data ingestion
- **SQL services:** SQL editor, Genie, alerts, and dashboards
- **AL/ML services:** Agents, Playground, experiments, models, and features
- **Core workspace tools:** Workspace browser, Unity Catalog objects, jobs and pipelines, compute resources, and marketplace

Workspace access

Each Databricks workspace is deployed within a single cloud provider region. To manage workspace assets, you can use **Workspace UI**, the **Databricks CLI**, or **Workspace APIs**. The workspace browser can be used to perform actions on the services above, including notebooks, queries, dashboards, and model experiments. Databricks now supports unique URLs for each workspace, following the format below:

```
adb-<workspace-id>.<random-number>.azuredatabricks.net
```

This is how the Databricks workspace UI looks:

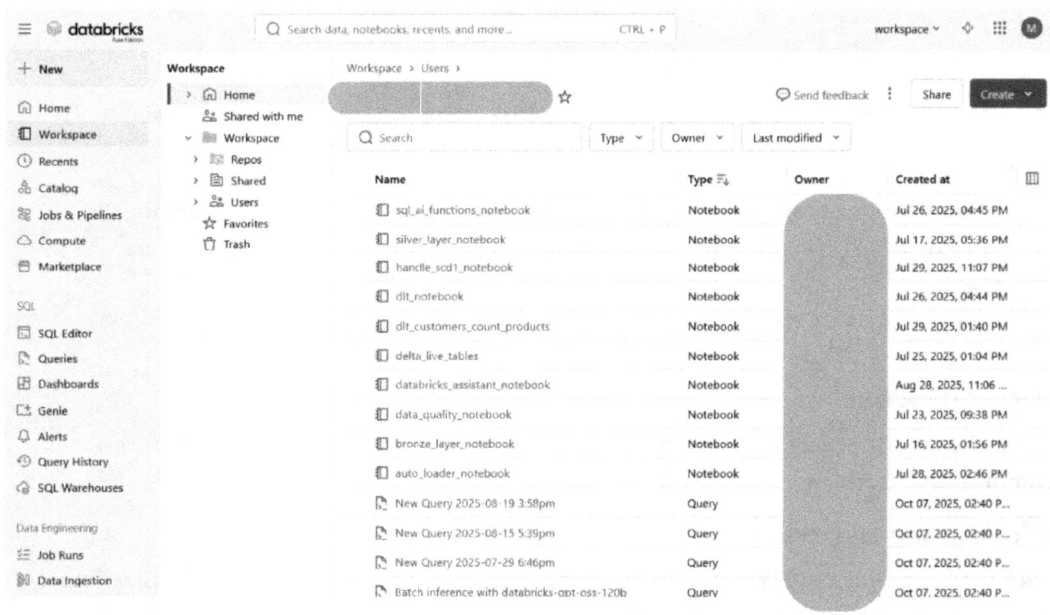

Figure 5.7: Databricks workspace UI

Workspace repositories

Workspace Repos let you connect your workspace to a Git provider such as GitHub, Azure DevOps, or Bitbucket. Once linked, the repository appears under *Workspace → Repos* as a folder that stays synchronized with the selected Git branch. The Workspace UI makes it easy to share objects with your team, enabling seamless collaboration across your organization. The shared objects appear under *Workspace → Shared* folder. Each user has a personal home folder under *Workspace → Users*, where they store their code artifacts.

> **Note**
>
> Although a single Databricks account can host multiple workspaces, Azure recommends a soft limit of 20-50 workspaces per account to ensure optimal performance and simplify management.

Domain-driven Workspace deployment

As previously discussed, choosing between a single workspace or multiple workspaces within a Databricks account is a critical architectural decision. This decision typically depends on factors such as isolation needs, resource contention, and governance requirements. In today's data landscape, an additional factor has emerged that significantly influences this choice. In *Chapter 4, Designing Future Data Platforms,* we explored the data-as-a-product approach to data management, where data is treated as a product. We had also discussed domains as logical groupings within an organization that owns the data product and retains full ownership and overall accountability for its data quality, maintenance, distribution, and governance.

A **domain-driven** data platform can leverage Databricks workspaces aligned with individual data products, as shown in the figure below.

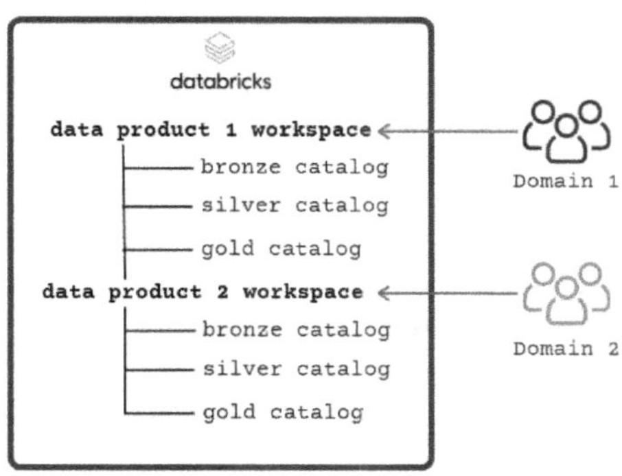

Figure 5.8: Dedicated workspace for each data product

> **Note**
>
> For a robust governance audit, it's essential to regularly review users and groups with access to Databricks objects. While broader access may be acceptable in development or testing environments, access in production should be restricted to a select few. As best practice, enforce the principle of the least privilege access model when configuring ACLs.

Having a dedicated workspace for each data product ensures strong business domain isolation, minimizes resource contention, and enables independent billing. However, this approach can complicate the configuration of appropriate ACLs for domain users. Careful planning with each domain team is essential to establish clear guidelines for processes, resource tagging, and software delivery practices.

Assigning a dedicated workspace to each data product can become difficult to manage if the organization owns many products. An alternative approach is to create workspaces that isolate business domains. For example, as shown in the image below, there are three workspaces owned by the Supply, HR, and Finance domains.

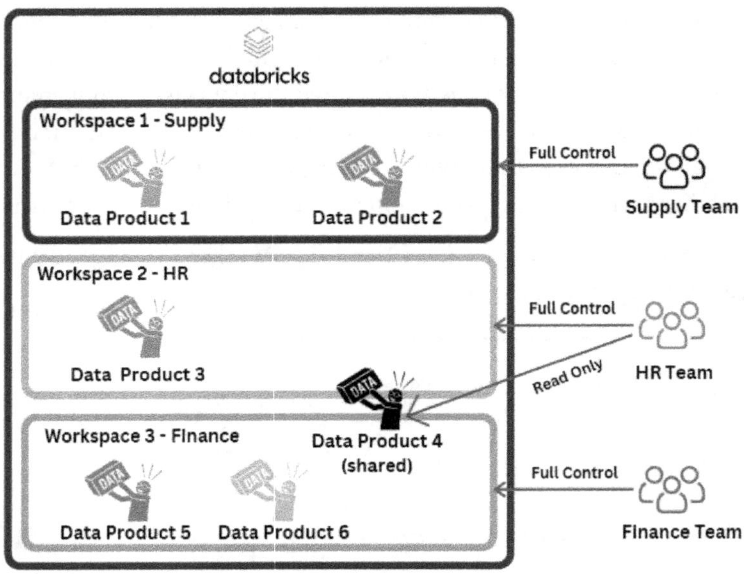

Figure 5.9: Isolating workspaces by business domains

Each domain manages its own set of data products, except for Data Product 4, which is owned and maintained by Finance but shared with the HR domain. Business domain teams maintain full ownership of their data products but may be granted read-only access to products shared by other domains.

This workspace structure simplifies resource sharing across domains and is rapidly becoming the standard approach. While Databricks workspaces are primarily designed for data engineers and ML/AI practitioners, they may not fully meet the needs of less-technical users. To bridge this gap, Databricks has recently introduced a new product experience tailored specifically for data analysts and business stakeholders.

Databricks One

Databricks One is built for non-technical users for exploring data and AI without needing to understand clusters, notebooks, queries, or models. Its intuitive UI provides an easy entry point into organizational data products, dashboards, Databricks Genie Spaces, and custom-built Databrick Apps.

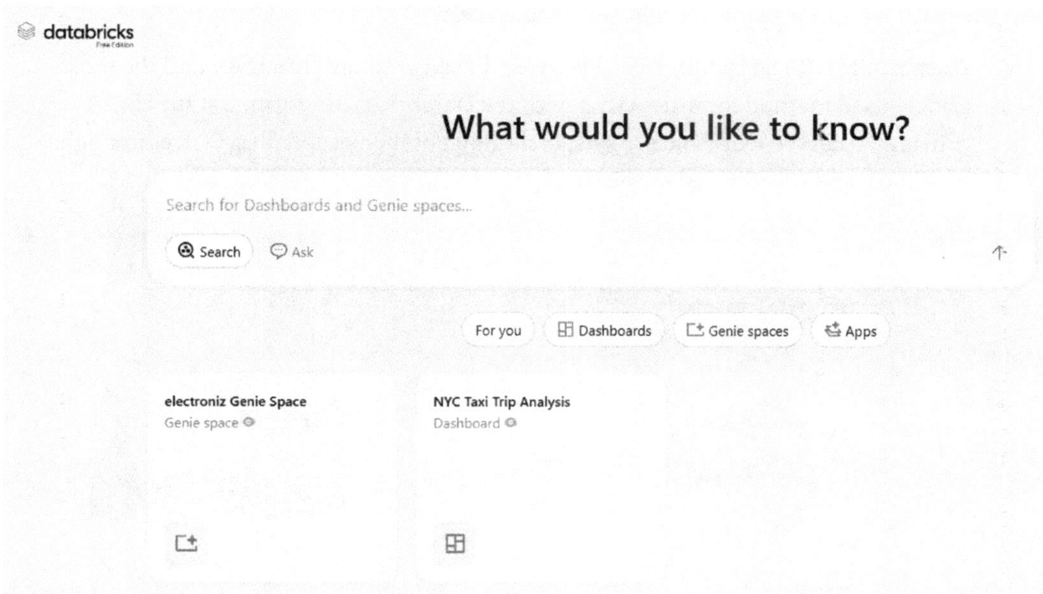

Figure 5.10: Databricks One UI

Databricks One closes the gap between technical and non-technical users by allowing non-technical users to interact with data through conversational AI. To access the Databricks One UI, users must have the Consumer access entitlement. It can be accessed using a dedicated URL in the following format:

```
https://<WORKSPACE_URL>/one?o=<WORKSPACE_ID>
```

> **Note**
>
> In Databricks, entitlements define the permissions that control what actions a user or group can perform within a workspace.

Now that we've explored how Databricks provides access for both technical and non-technical users, let's explore the various ways they can access Databricks.

Interfaces

The primary purpose of any interface is to boost efficiency, reduce complexity, and enhance its users' overall productivity. Databricks offers a convenient and user-friendly way to interact with the platform assets using the following interfaces:

- **Databricks UI**: The Databricks UI is a web-based graphical interface and the most widely used method for interacting with the Databricks platform. Databricks UI provides access to workspace assets, including notebooks and files, SQL editor, jobs, pipelines, and AI-powered services.

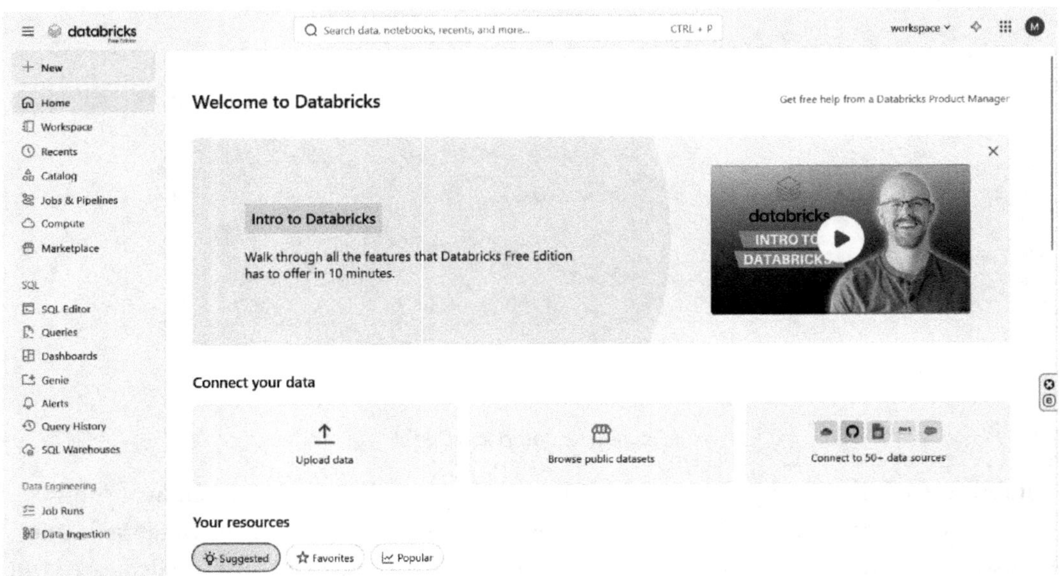

Figure 5.11: Databricks UI interface

- **Databricks REST API:** The Databricks REST API provides a programmatic interface for interacting with both account-level and workspace-level resources. Its primary purpose is to support automation - such as creating clusters, jobs, and pipelines; managing permissions; and integrating Databricks with CI/CD workflows. The following example demonstrates how to use the Databricks REST API to list clusters in a Databricks workspace.

```
curl --request GET "https://<databricks-instance>/api/2.0/clusters/list" \
--header "Authorization: Bearer <DATABRICKS_TOKEN>"
```

- **Databricks SQL REST API:** The Databricks SQL REST API is a dedicated interface for SQL-specific operations. Its primary purpose is to automate the management of SQL objects such as queries, alerts, and dashboards. The following example demonstrates how to use the Databricks SQL REST API to execute SQL against a Databricks SQL Warehouse.

```
curl -X POST -H "Authorization: Bearer $DATABRICKS_TOKEN" \
-H "Content-Type: application/json" \
-d '{
  "statement": "SELECT * FROM table LIMIT 100;",
  "warehouse_id": "$DATABRICKS_SQL_WAREHOUSE_ID"
}' \
https://$DATABRICKS_HOST/api/2.0/sql/statements
```

- **Databricks CLI**: Built on top of Databricks REST APIs, Databricks CLI is a command-line interface that enables you to interact with the Databricks platform from your local terminal or automation scripts.

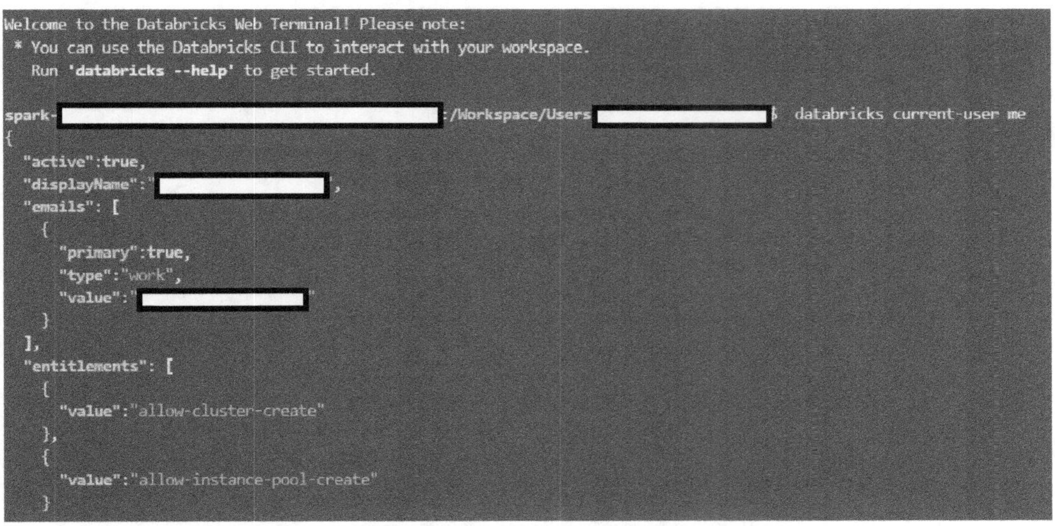

Figure 5.12: Databricks CLI interface

Databricks interfaces are built to support a diverse set of user personas—including data engineers, analysts, business users, administrators, and ML/AI practitioners. However, these interfaces are only effective when paired with well-defined access mechanisms. Next, let's explore how access is configured within Databricks.

Authentication and authorization

Authentication verifies the identity of authorized entities before granting them access to Databricks resources, services, the user interface, or data. Databricks defines authorized entities as identities, the fundamental building blocks for managing authentication and access control across accounts and workspaces. There are three types of identities available for authentication and authorization control:

- **Users:** An entity identified by an email address that signs in using their email, SSO, or external accounts such as **Google Sign-in**, **Microsoft Entra ID** to access the **user interface** (**UI**), APIs, and data.
- **Groups:** A collection of users organized for simplified permission management. Groups can be assigned specific entitlements and workspace roles.
- **Service Principals:** A non-human identity primarily used for running unattended jobs, **infrastructure-as-code** (**IaC**) automation, and CI/CD pipelines. Service principals cannot sign in to the Workspace UI.

Databricks employs a unified login framework that delivers a consistent authentication experience across all Databricks products, including workspaces, the account console, Databricks One, and APIs.

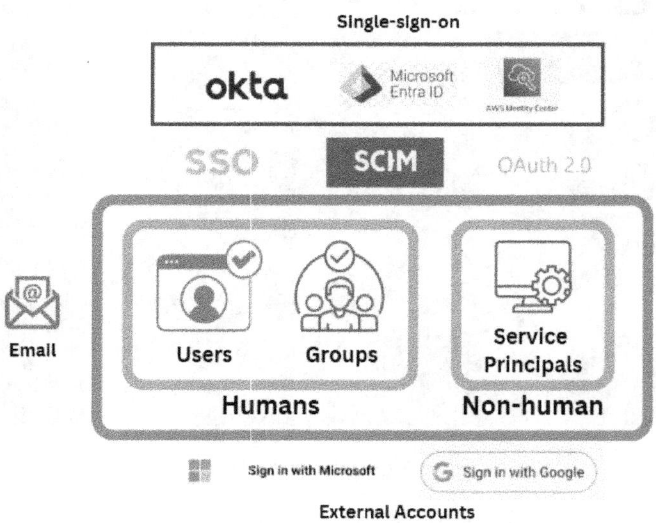

Figure 5.13: Authentication of Databricks identities

Databricks identities may be authenticated through the following methods:

- **Single-sign-on (SSO):** Users, groups, or service principals can authenticate to Databricks using SSO. Databricks supports a wide range of identity providers, including **Okta**, **Microsoft Entra ID**, **OneLogin**, and **AWS IAM Identity Center**, provided the identity provider supports **SAML 2.0** or **OpenID Connect** (**OIDC**). SSO is the preferred authentication approach for Databricks. With SSO, all authentication is managed by your identity provider, eliminating the need to create or maintain local user accounts within Databricks.
- **Identity Syncing from identity providers:** You can synchronize users and groups from the identity provider into Databricks. Databricks recommends using **System for Cross-domain Identity Management** (**SCIM**) to automatically synchronize identities.

> Note
>
> SCIM is an open standard that enables automated provisioning and lifecycle management of user identities. It supports the full lifecycle of creating, updating, and deprovisioning identities across platforms such as Databricks.

- **OAuth for service principals:** For service principal authentication, Databricks recommends following the OAuth token approach. Using this approach, the identity provider issues and manages **OAuth tokens**, which are then used across workflows, Databricks CLI, Databricks API integrations, Terraform deployments, and CI/CD pipelines.
- **Email**: Users may authenticate to Databricks using their email address. Upon initiating the login process, a one-time passcode is delivered to the user's email. The user is then required to retrieve this passcode and enter it on the login page to verify their identity.

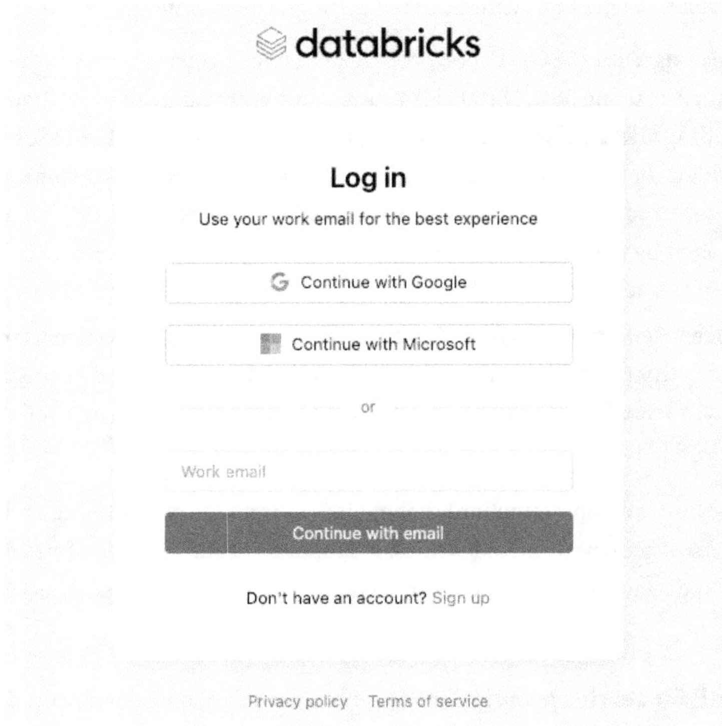

Figure 5.14: Authentication using email and external accounts

- **External accounts**: Users may authenticate to Databricks using Google or Microsoft accounts. Using external identity accounts streamlines access management by allowing users to sign in with the same credentials they already use across other organizational services.

After successfully verifying the user's identity through one of the authentication methods described above, the next step is to configure access controls to protect Databricks objects. Databricks uses a layered approach for role assignment. Using this model, roles are applied to identities in distinct tiers, ensuring a structured and consistent approach to access control.

> **Note**
>
> In Databricks, access control is configured at three levels: account, workspace, and data.

The following diagram illustrates how access control of identities is managed through delegated administration:

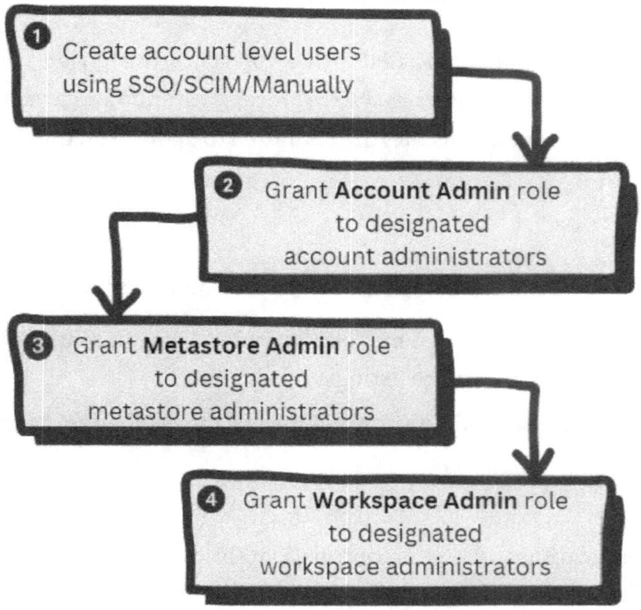

Figure 5.15: Access control through delegated administration

1. **Identity management:** The process starts by manually creating or syncing users from the identity provider using SSO or SCIM.
2. **Account-level access control**: In the next phase, a select group of users is designated as account administrators. These administrators hold the highest level of privileges, allowing them to create workspaces, manage groups, assign workspace administrators, and configure billing settings. Account-level access control is enabled via RBAC.
3. **Metastore-level access control**: After account administrators are established, a designated group of users is assigned as metastore administrators. This role carries elevated privileges and is responsible for managing the Unity Catalog. Like account-level access, metastore-level access control is enforced through RBAC.
4. **Workspace-level access control**: In the final step, a workspace administrator is assigned to each workspace. Their privileges are limited to managing objects, compute permissions, jobs, and pipelines within their specific workspace. Workspace-level access control is enforced through **Access Control Lists** (**ACLs**).

> **Note**
>
> An ACL is a set of permissions associated with a workspace, cluster, job, table, or experiment. It specifies which users or system processes are allowed to access these objects and defines the operations they are permitted to perform on the associated data assets.

Optionally, users may be assigned additional roles based on organizational requirements:

- **Marketplace access control**: A marketplace administrator manages the provider profile and creates marketplace listings.
- **Billing access control**: A billing administrator can view budgets and administer budget policies.

Entitlements

In addition to authentication and access controls, Databricks allows you to define how users interact with the platform. This is accomplished by defining entitlements at the workspace level. Each entitlement grants a specific set of features to the user or the service principal.

> **Note**
>
> Entitlements are available only with the Databricks Premium plan. To work within a workspace, a user must be granted at least one entitlement.

Following is the list of entitlements available in Databricks:

- **Access entitlements**: Access entitlement defines which Databricks capabilities the user can access within a workspace. The following three types of access entitlements can be assigned to users:
- **Consumer access**: Designed for business users, this entitlement grants read-only access to Databricks, including the ability to view dashboards, Genie spaces, and Databricks Apps.
- **Databricks SQL access**: Designed for power users, this entitlement grants access to Databricks SQL features such as queries, SQL warehouse, and dashboards.
- **Workspace access**: Designed for developers, this entitlement grants access to workspace features including notebooks, jobs, and pipelines.

- **Compute entitlements**: These entitlements allow users or service principals to provision compute resources for data processing within a workspace. The following two types of compute entitlements may be assigned:
- **Allow unrestricted cluster creation**: Grants the principal the ability to create clusters without any policy restrictions. Because this may bypass governance and cost control, it should be assigned only after careful consideration.
- **Allow pool creation**: This enables the group principals to create instance pools.

Entitlements are designed to prevent unauthorized users and service principals from accessing certain features, while also helping to manage and control costs. From here on, we shift our focus to some key data management features of Databricks.

Databricks capabilities

The Databricks platform is unique in that it combines the capabilities of data engineering, machine learning, artificial intelligence, and data analytics within a single unified environment.

Data engineering

Databricks provides a unified Lakehouse platform to support the full spectrum of data engineering workloads. From batch and streaming pipelines to procedural and declarative models, Databricks offers comprehensive capabilities to meet diverse data engineering needs.

For data engineering purposes, Lakeflow Connect, Lakeflow Jobs, and Lakeflow SDP operate together as an integrated data-movement stack. Lakeflow Connect ingests data from operational systems into the lakehouse, Lakeflow Jobs orchestrates and automates the processing and transformation of that data, and Lakeflow SDP extends these capabilities to continuous, real-time pipelines. Collectively, they provide a unified framework for ingesting, transforming, and delivering both batch and streaming data.

The following are some important data engineering capabilities of Databricks described in greater detail:

Lakeflow Connect

Lakeflow Connect is a fully managed ingestion solution that simplifies the development of reliable data pipelines while significantly reducing maintenance overhead. It boosts performance by leveraging incremental loading for both reads and writes and provides unified governance through Unity Catalog, coordinated execution using Lakeflow Jobs, and comprehensive monitoring across all ingestion workflows. Built on the open Databricks Data Intelligence Platform, it offers the flexibility to integrate third-party tools, making it easy to adapt to your current environment and future architectural needs.

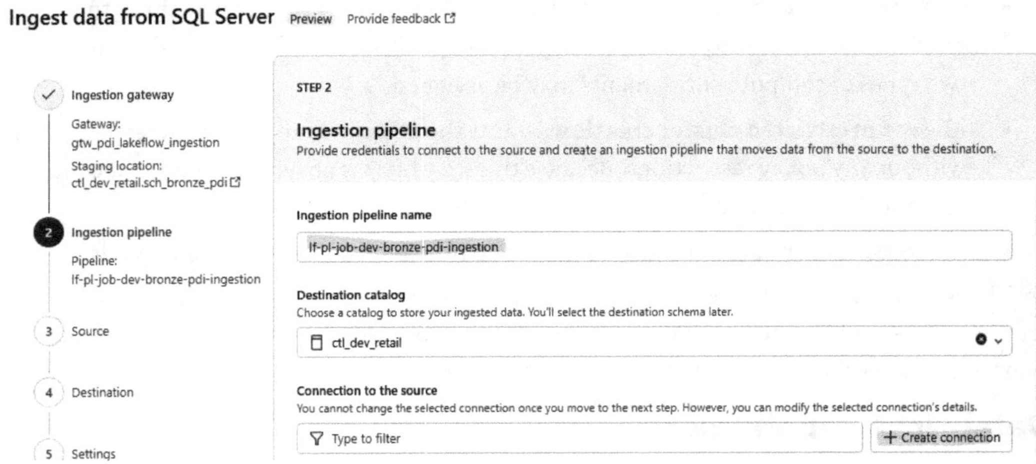

Figure 5.16: Ingest data from SQL Server using Lakeflow connect

The platform includes streamlined, high-efficiency connectors that make it easy to pull data from a wide variety of sources, including:

- Local file systems
- Major enterprise systems such as Google Analytics and ServiceNow
- Relational and operational databases
- Cloud storage providers
- Message-uses

Built on the open Databricks Data Intelligence Platform, Lakeflow Connect offers the flexibility to integrate third-party tools, making it easy to adapt to your current environment and future architectural needs.

Procedural processing

Procedural processing involves executing logic in a strict, step-by-step sequence, with operations implemented through functions and procedures. Historically, large-scale data processing has relied heavily on this procedural style, and it remains the dominant programming approach in much of data analytics today. Databricks enables procedural programming through Apache Spark, Python, SQL, and Scala. Databricks notebooks serve as the primary method of writing procedural logic.

Notebooks

Data and ML/AI engineers rely on notebooks to build data pipelines and develop machine learning models. A notebook functions as an **interactive development environment** (**IDE**), enabling users to construct data workflows, train models, and visualize results. Notebooks support multiple programming languages—including Python, Scala, SQL, and R—allowing engineers to choose the best tool for their specific task.

Notebooks default to Python as the primary language. However, you can change the language on a per-cell basis by using **magic commands**, such as `%sql` to run SQL statements or `%scala` to execute Scala code. After connecting a notebook to a cluster and running its commands, the notebook preserves both its execution state and the output generated in each cell. You can also share your notebooks to enable a truly collaborative development experience. The collaborators can review the code and provide feedback using the built-in **Comments** feature.

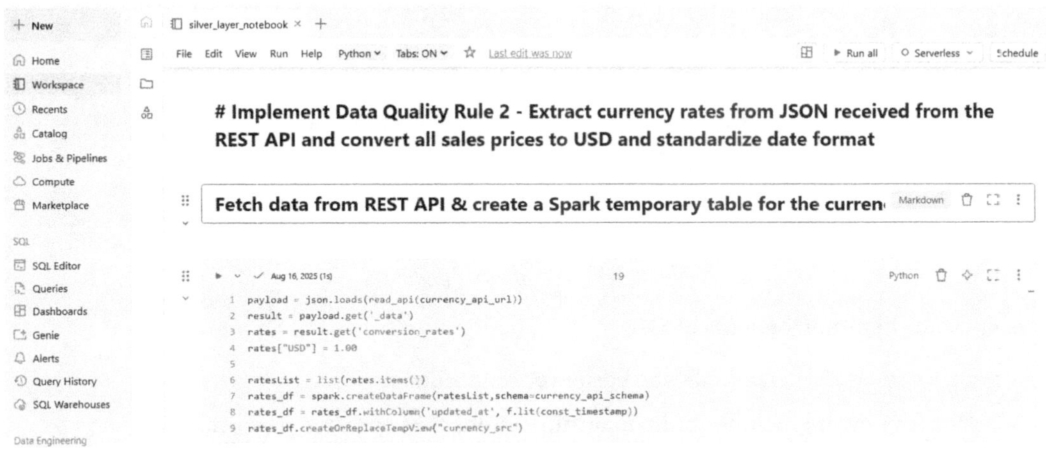

Figure 5.17: Databricks notebook

Databricks notebooks allow you to create and run procedural code within individual cells. Each cell can contain instructions written in Python, Scala, SQL, or R. Cells can also be formatted as **Markdown**, in which case the content is treated as documentation rather than executable code. With notebooks, you can not only build new code but also troubleshoot issues and leverage GenAI to generate ready-to-use code snippets. In the modern era, programming paradigms are shifting from procedural to declarative approaches. Let's explore how Databricks supports and enables this transition.

Lakeflow Spark Declarative Pipelines

In declarative programming, you focus on defining *what* outcome you want rather than *how* to achieve it. The declarative framework interprets this desired outcome and automatically translates it into the underlying logic required to produce it. Some of the most common examples of declarative programming include SQL, REGEX, YAML, and **Terraform**.

Databricks recently introduced the **Lakeflow Spark Declarative Pipelines** (**SDP**) framework to develop data pipelines, extending the Apache Spark declarative framework.

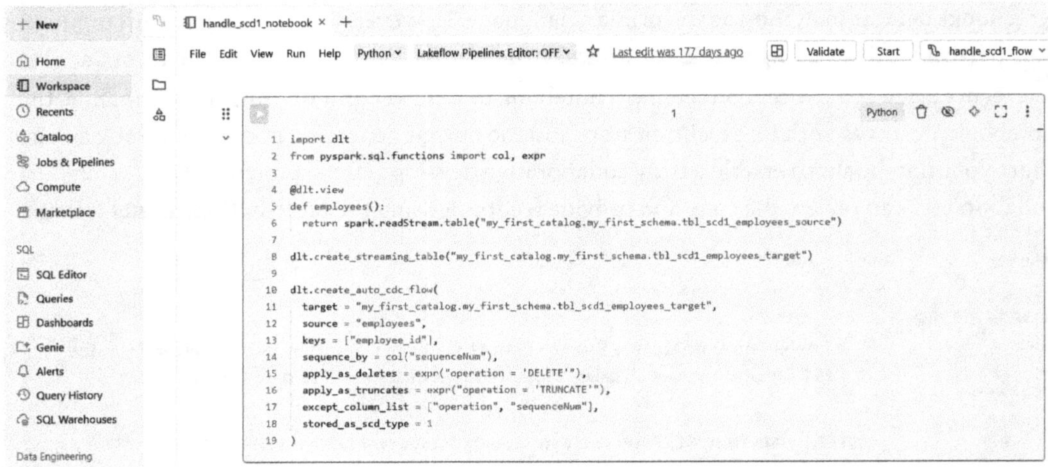

Figure 5.18: Example SDP pipeline

Here are some common benefits of SDP:

- SDP code is more readable and easier to comprehend.
- The framework includes built-in optimizations that enhance performance automatically.
- Reduced complexity makes SDP pipelines simpler to maintain over time.
- SDP provides native orchestration with support for parallel execution.

Lakeflow Jobs

After development and testing are complete, the next step is to orchestrate the workload using workflows. **Lakeflow Jobs** enables workflow automation in Databricks by allowing teams to orchestrate multiple data processing tasks within a single, unified workflow. It supports scheduling and optimization of recurring workloads while efficiently handling complex task dependencies. Lakeflow Jobs can be triggered manually, scheduled to run at specific intervals, or initiated through event-based mechanisms.

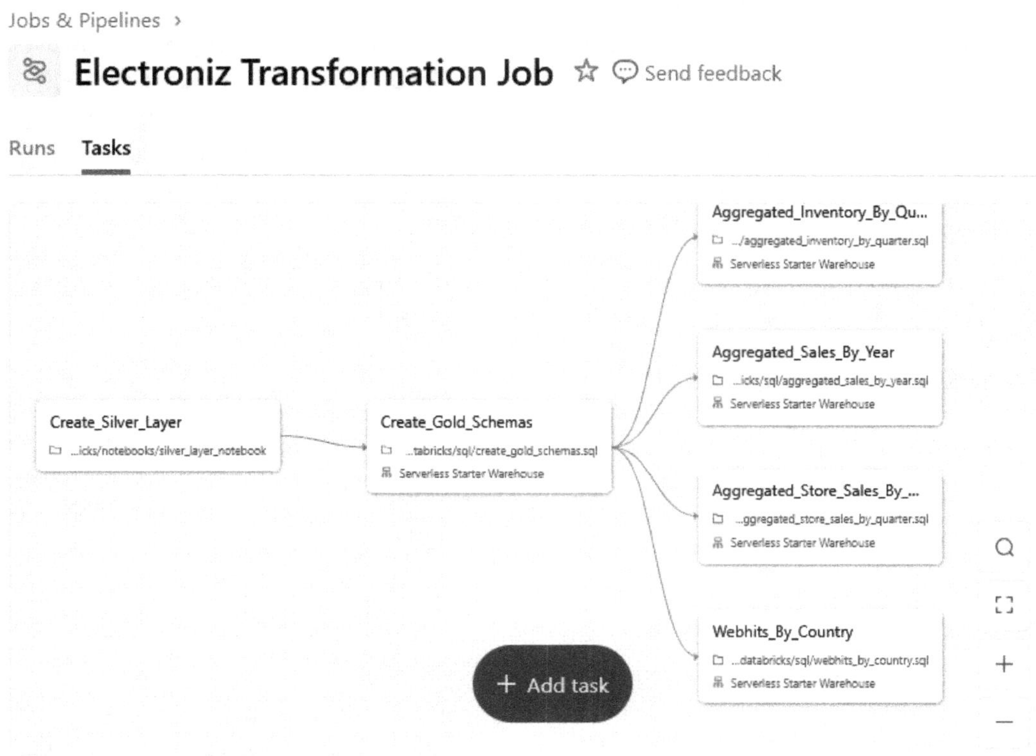

Figure 5.19: Example Lakeflow Job

In the upcoming chapters, we will explore notebooks, Lakeflow **Spark Declarative Pipelines** (**SDP**), and Lakeflow Jobs in greater depth through hands-on, practical examples. For now, let's turn our attention to the next capability, which introduces a more relational way of working with data.

Data warehousing

In *Chapter 2, Discovering Data Platforms*, we learned how the Lakehouse architecture unifies the scalable storage of a data lake with the **massively parallel processing** (**MPP**) capabilities of a data warehouse. Data warehousing in a Lakehouse context allows users to query files stored in low-cost data lake storage using SQL - without needing to copy or move the data into a separate warehouse system. Databricks delivers a high-performance data warehousing solution with robust governance, enabled through its deep integration with Unity Catalog.

Databricks SQL Warehouse

Databricks SQL Warehouse is a scalable, high-concurrency SQL execution engine designed for analytics on the Databricks Lakehouse. Fully managed by Databricks, it provides a secure, governed environment for querying data via Unity Catalog. SQL Warehouses support large volumes of concurrent queries and power a broad range of use cases, including BI tools such as Power BI and Tableau, Databricks dashboards, ad hoc exploratory SQL workloads, and third-party applications that connect via JDBC or ODBC.

There are three types of SQL warehouses, each differentiated by its performance capabilities. The following image illustrates a sample workflow in Lakeflow Jobs:

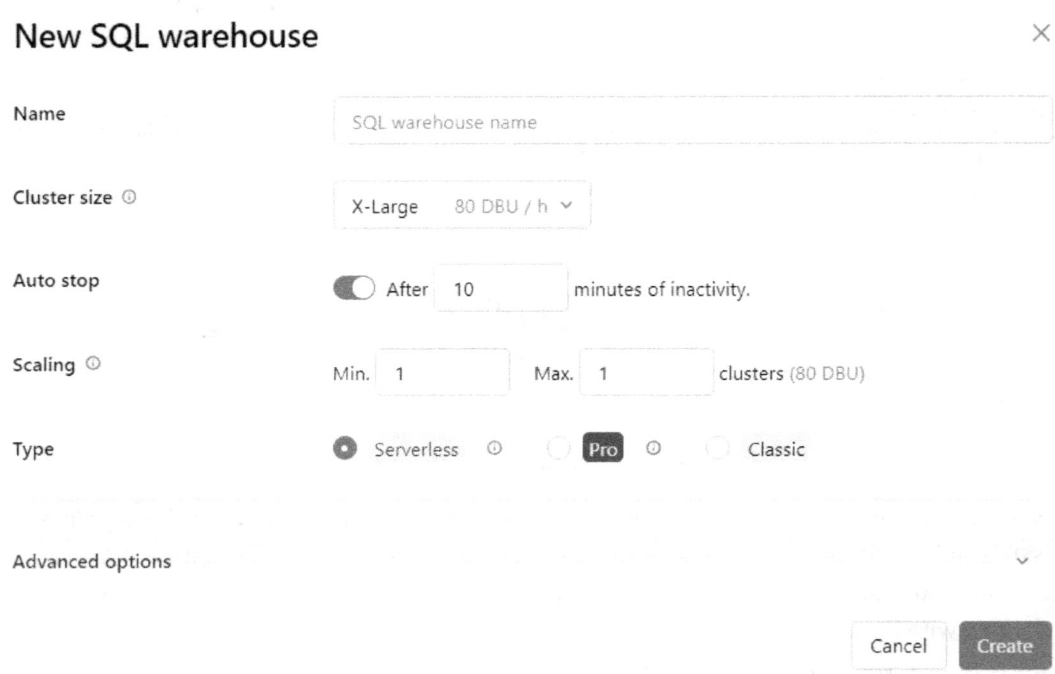

Figure 5.20: Databricks SQL Warehouse compute

Before exploring these types in detail, it is important to understand the key performance features that influence the choice of the SQL warehouse compute.

- **Intelligent workload management:** IWM uses AI-driven predictions to execute SQL queries efficiently. IWM predicts the amount of compute resources required for each running query. This allows the engine to stagger SQL executions and perform auto-scaling when necessary.

- **Predictive IO:** Predictive IO accelerates SQL performance by optimizing underlying data scan operations.
- **Photon:** Databricks photon is a vectorized query engine which means it executes data operations in efficient batches rather than row by row. Photon offers significant performance for SQL joins and aggregations. Photon is deeply optimized for Parquet and Delta formats, enabling faster insert, update, and merge operations.

Serverless SQL Warehouse

The serverless SQL warehouse supports all the performance features described above. It delivers the fastest startup times and provides highly efficient query processing with intelligent, automatic resource utilization.

Pro SQL Warehouse

The Pro SQL warehouse deploys its compute infrastructure within your organization's cloud account and supports only the Photon and Predictive IO performance features. This warehouse type is particularly beneficial in scenarios that require data federation, such as integrating with on-premises data stores or connecting to cloud services like event hubs or streaming platforms.

Classic SQL Warehouse

The Classic SQL warehouse supports only the Photon performance feature. Like the Pro SQL warehouse, its compute infrastructure runs within your organization's cloud account. As a result, its overall performance is lower than that of the Pro or Serverless SQL warehouse types.

Databricks SQL Warehouse helps eliminate data duplication by enabling direct SQL-based querying of data stored in the lake. We now move on to the next Databricks capability that unifies data engineering with ML/AI workloads.

Machine learning and artificial intelligence

Databricks offers an integrated platform for machine learning and artificial intelligence solutions. By integrating data engineering capabilities with ML workflows and end-to-end AI model lifecycle management, the platform delivers greater unification. With Databricks, ML engineers can build and train models, then deploy them as RESTful endpoints with built-in usage tracking and monitoring. Using services such as AI Playground, Agent Bricks, and the Mosaic AI Agent framework, AI engineers can work with **Large Language Models** (**LLMs**) to build Generative AI applications and **Retrieval-Augmented Generation** (**RAG**) solutions.

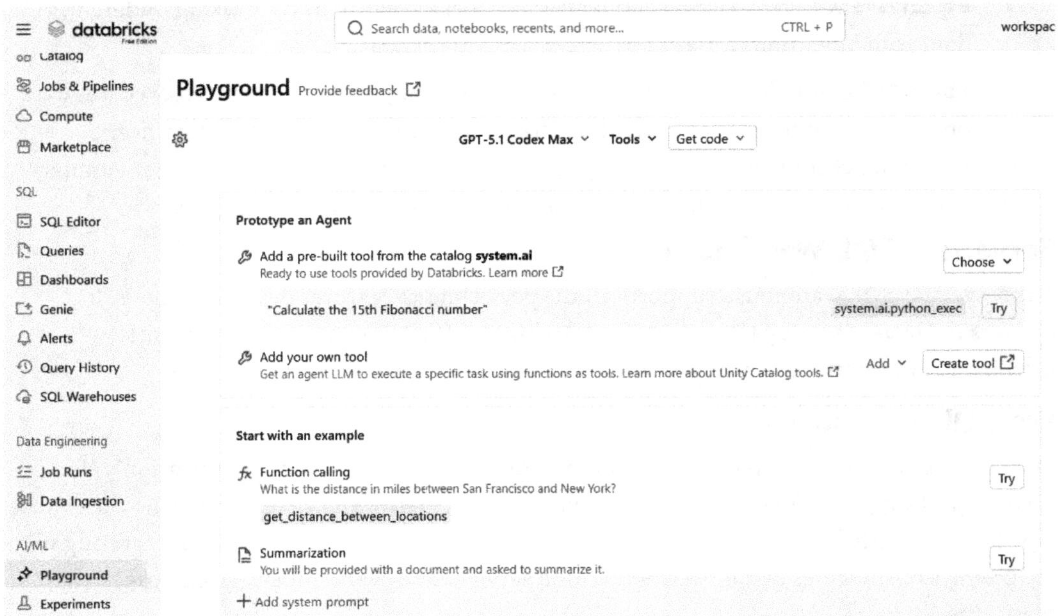

Figure 5.21: Databricks GenAI services

We will explore several Databricks AI services in greater detail later in this book. For now, let's turn our attention to the final Databricks capability - visualizing and presenting results.

Business intelligence

In the first chapter of this book, *The Story of Data Engineering and Analytics*, we introduced the idea that "*every byte of data has a story to tell*". Data storytelling helps translate complex data into meaningful narratives, enabling non-technical audiences to make informed decisions more easily. Databricks BI enables organizations to tell the story of data through built-in dashboards and seamless integration with external BI tools such as Power BI, Tableau, and Looker. With the AI/BI tool, non-technical users can easily create sophisticated dashboards by interacting with data through conversational AI. Once created, dashboards can be shared with both internal and external users, enabling broad access to insights without requiring direct access to underlying data.

Databricks AI/BI is fully integrated with Unity Catalog, ensuring alignment with enterprise data-sharing and governance policies. Built-in data lineage and usage tracking provide data owners with full visibility into how data is accessed and used across the platform.

The image below shows the UI of the Databricks Playground, offered as part of the Databricks AI Services suite:

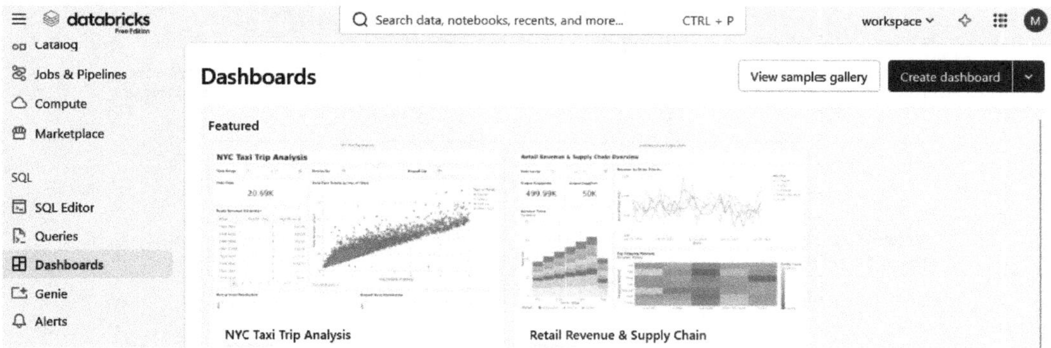

Figure 5.22: Databricks BI services

With that foundation in place, we now turn our attention to the storage and data management mechanisms Databricks uses behind the scenes.

Storage

In *Chapter 2, Discovering Data Platforms*, we explored the distinctions between object storage and block storage, and examined how each storage type is best suited for different real-world use cases. Although object storage is recognized for its high resilience, scalability, and lower cost, block storage delivers far better performance.

> **Note**
>
> With its unlimited scalability, object storage is ideal for massive organizational datasets, while block storage excels at providing fast access to temporary files.

The following figure illustrates how Databricks uses both object storage and block storage to manage data, whether for long-term retention or temporary use.

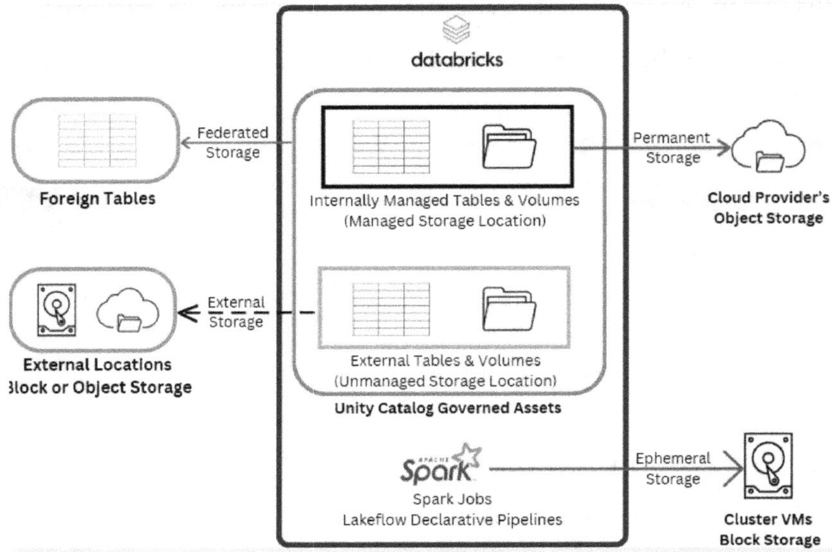

Figure 5.23: Data storage locations in Databricks

Data storage locations in Databricks fall into the following categories:

- **Unity Catalog managed storage location:** Unity Catalog managed storage is the cloud provider's object storage location that Unity Catalog automatically uses to store managed tables and volumes. Typically, this location holds the organization's analytical data used for decision-making.

> **Note**
>
> Databricks supports the object storage services of all major cloud providers—Azure ADLS, Amazon S3, and Google Cloud Storage—as backends for both managed and unmanaged Unity Catalog data.

- **Unity Catalog unmanaged storage location:** A Unity Catalog unmanaged storage location is an external location used to reference external tables and volumes. The underlying data remains external, either in cloud storage or on-premises, and Databricks accesses it via storage credentials configured within Unity Catalog.

- **Federated location:** Federated locations are registered in Unity Catalog as read-only, as they belong to external data systems not governed by Databricks. Both the data and its metadata are fully managed by the external system.
- **Ephemeral location:** Distributed computing frameworks like Spark generate numerous temporary files during job execution, particularly during shuffle and sort operations, and these files are needed only for the duration of the job. However, because shuffle and sort operations demand high performance, it is best to use block storage for this purpose. For this reason, Databricks uses the local disks on Spark cluster VMs to store temporary data.

> Note
>
> Previously, Databricks allowed you to use the **Databricks File System** (**DBFS**) abstraction layer to access cloud storage as a simplified, Unix-like file system. This capability has since been deprecated in favor of Unity Catalog volumes.

Having seen how Databricks organizes data across object and block storage, let's now focus on how this data is processed for analytical purposes.

Compute

In the data engineering domain, the term "compute" refers to the underlying power that drives ingestion, curation, and aggregation workloads. In *Chapter 2, Discovering Data Platforms*, we explained that compute power is largely determined by two key factors: the number of processing units and the amount of available memory. Higher CPU speed and greater memory will result in faster, more efficient computation. Databricks provides flexible compute options that you can tailor to your data engineering, data analytics, and ML/AI workloads.

Classic compute clusters

Classic compute refers to user-managed clusters, which means the user is responsible for cluster lifecycle management – including provisioning, capacity planning, scaling, and administering them. There are three types of classic compute clusters:

All-purpose compute clusters

The all-purpose cluster is useful for interactive and exploratory workloads, such as running notebooks and SQL queries for ad hoc data analysis.

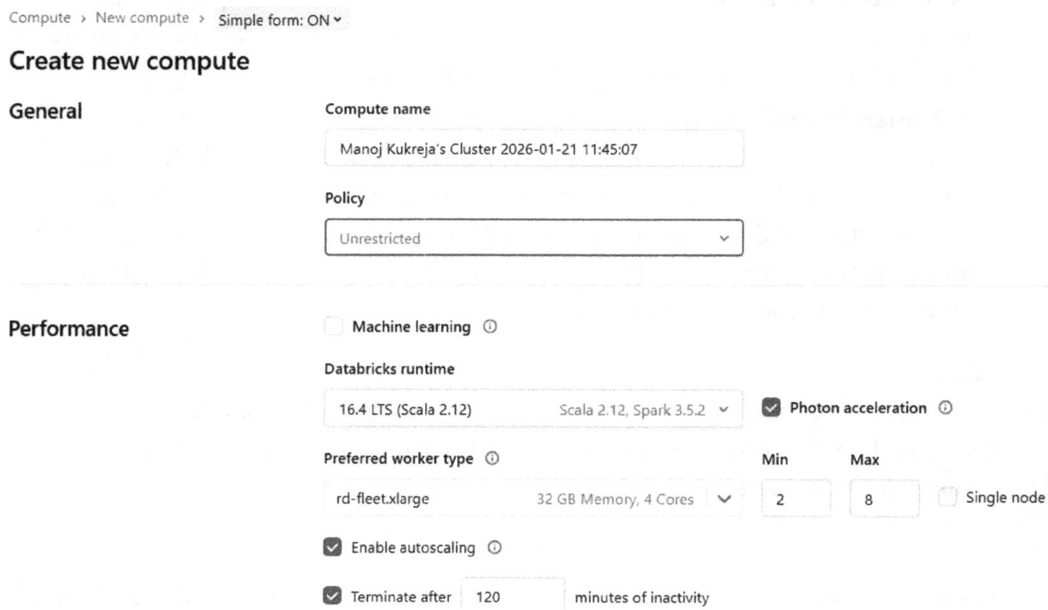

Figure 5.24: Databricks all-purpose compute cluster

These all-purpose clusters are primarily used during the development and testing phases for debugging.

Job compute clusters

The job compute clusters are purpose-built for running unattended workflows. Job clusters are **ephemeral** - automatically provisioned at the start of each job run and terminated after their completion. Job clusters are well-suited for production environments, delivering automation and cost efficiency.

Pipeline compute clusters

Pipeline compute is dedicated exclusively to Lakeflow Declarative Pipelines, with most cluster attributes fully managed and enforced by the pipeline runtime. As a result, users cannot modify the compute configuration, ensuring a strict consistency of the pipeline's execution model.

Classic compute clusters can be created in the following modes:

- **Standard:** Allows multi-user usage, promotes collaboration, and cost efficiency.
- **Dedicated:** The cluster is assigned to a single user or group.

The following image illustrates the UI of how an All-purpose cluster is created in Databricks

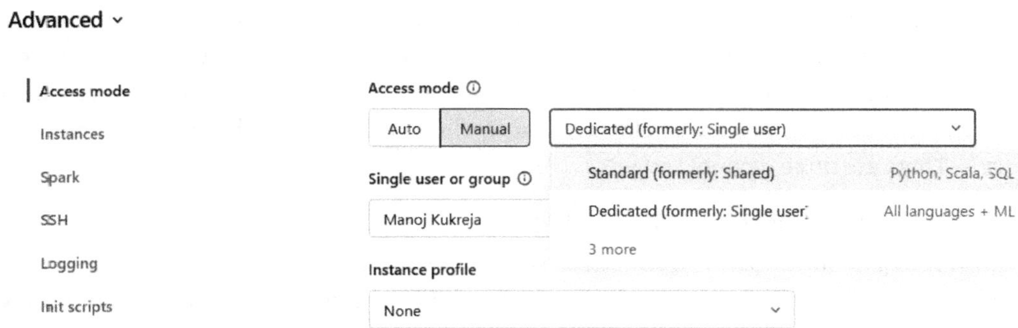

Figure 5.25: Classic compute cluster modes

Now that we understand how Databricks provisions compute clusters, it's important to recognize that this process involves creating multiple worker-node VMs within your cloud provider account. The number of worker nodes is specified during cluster configuration. In practice, the provisioning process can be slow, often requiring 15 to 30 minutes to complete. For critical workloads, this delay may be unacceptable. To address this challenge, Databricks recommends using **Instance Pools**.

When enabled, a pool pre-provisions a set of virtual machines and keeps them running as idle instances until a cluster requires them. Because these VMs are already in a ready state, cluster startup times are significantly reduced. After the job completes, the instances are returned to the instance pool, making them immediately available for reuse by other clusters.

> **Note**
>
> Databricks instance pools provide more predictable cluster startup times and accelerate job execution by maintaining pre-warmed compute capacity. However, they may be less cost-efficient for workloads with highly variable demand, since you continue paying for the underlying VMs even when they're idle and not attached to an active cluster.

By now, it should be evident that classic compute clusters require manual configuration and continuous operational administration. The next category of compute clusters is designed to eliminate these burdens.

Serverless compute

Serverless compute is fully managed by Databricks, which requires no cluster configuration or user-managed infrastructure. Databricks handles the underlying infrastructure provisioning, seamless auto-scaling, and optimizations. By having these operational burdens removed, data engineers can focus entirely on developing data pipelines, building dashboards, and training models. There are three types of serverless compute:

Serverless compute for notebooks

When working in notebooks, you can attach serverless compute to run your data processing workloads. Because serverless compute provisions resources automatically, it attaches quickly and provides near-instant execution, allowing you to begin processing data with minimal startup delay.

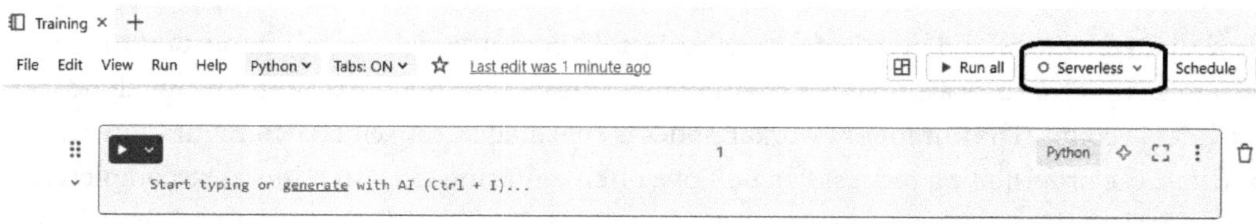

Figure 5.26: Attaching serverless compute for notebooks

> **Note**
>
> There is a common misconception that serverless compute eliminates the need for virtual machines and is always the most cost-effective option. Serverless simply abstracts infrastructure management from the consumer, removing the need to provision or maintain the underlying cluster. While serverless can reduce administrative overhead and lower costs for simple, unpredictable, or short-lived workloads, it is not universally the cheapest choice and must be evaluated in the context of workload patterns and performance requirements.

Serverless compute for Jobs

Serverless compute for Jobs can run Lakeflow workloads without deploying any infrastructure.

Figure 5.27: Serverless compute for jobs

Serverless pipelines

Serverless compute for jobs allows Lakeflow Declarative Pipelines to run entirely without provisioning or managing any underlying infrastructure. Resource allocation and auto-scaling are handled by Databricks.

Figure 5.28: Serverless compute for pipelines

> **Note**
>
> Although most Spark APIs are supported, certain features—such as DataFrame caching and persistence—are not available when using serverless compute.

SQL Warehouse compute

The primary purpose of a SQL warehouse is to support data exploration and analytics through SQL. Users can query Unity Catalog–governed objects, run interactive or scheduled SQL queries, and download results for further analysis. As discussed earlier, you can choose among Serverless, Pro, and Classic warehouse types based on the required performance, scalability, and operational characteristics.

At the beginning of this chapter, we introduced Databricks as an intelligent, unified data analytics platform built to support enterprise-grade data solutions. We will now explore how Databricks governs and manages harmonized data assets across the organization.

> **Note**
>
> The Auto Stop feature in Databricks SQL Warehouse automatically shuts down a warehouse after it has been idle for a specified duration. This prevents unnecessary compute charges from accumulating during inactive periods.

Unity Catalog

Through Unity Catalog, Databricks provides a central layer for uniform data discovery, centralized access control, data quality oversight, and regulatory compliance across all business areas.

The image illustrates the difference between Databricks deployments with and without Unity Catalog, using two business domains—Finance and Supply—as examples.

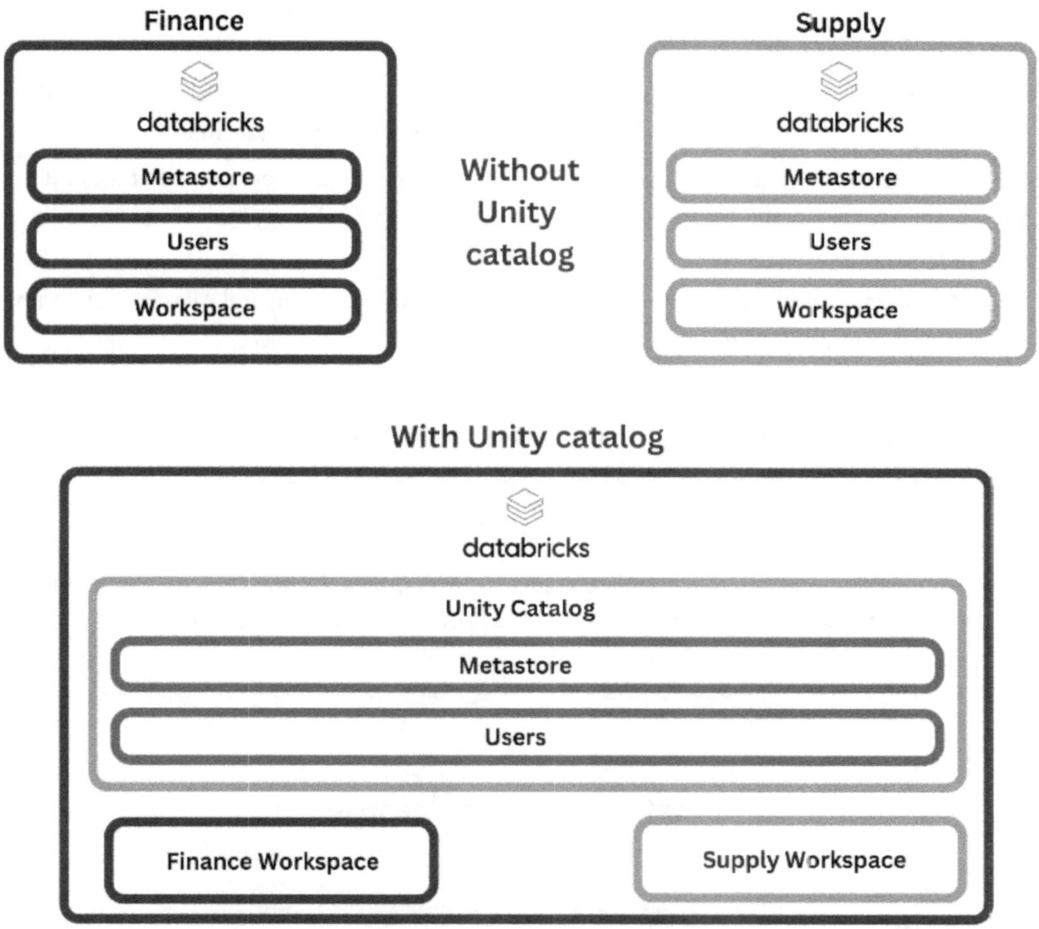

Figure 5.29: Depiction of workspaces with or without Unity Catalog

In a Databricks deployment without Unity Catalog, there is no centralized governance layer. As a result, each workspace maintains its own metastore, user management, and compute resources, leading to duplication and fragmented controls. In contrast, a deployment with Unity Catalog provides a centralized metastore and unified access control, enabling secure collaboration and consistent governance of data and compute across multiple business domains. In addition, Unity Catalog includes built-in auditing and data lineage capabilities, as well as a well-defined data discovery layer.

Metastore

A **metastore** is a centralized repository that stores metadata for an organization's data and AI assets. Every Databricks workspace must be associated with a metastore to manage metadata related to data structure, discovery, access control, security, and auditing. The Unity Catalog stores the following categories of metadata:

- **Data structure metadata**: Information about data assets such as tables, views, and volumes, including table schemas, column data types, and data formats.
- **Governance metadata**: Details related to data ownership, access permissions, and governance policies for Databricks principals, along with lineage tracking and audit history.
- **ML/AI metadata**: Metadata associated with machine learning and AI assets, including models, features, and other AI artifacts.

Note

The metastore stores metadata only and is hosted within the Databricks control plane, while the organization's actual data is stored in its cloud provider accounts.

A metastore can be attached to multiple Databricks workspaces to continuously track data flows across notebooks, SQL queries, tables, and downstream consumers.

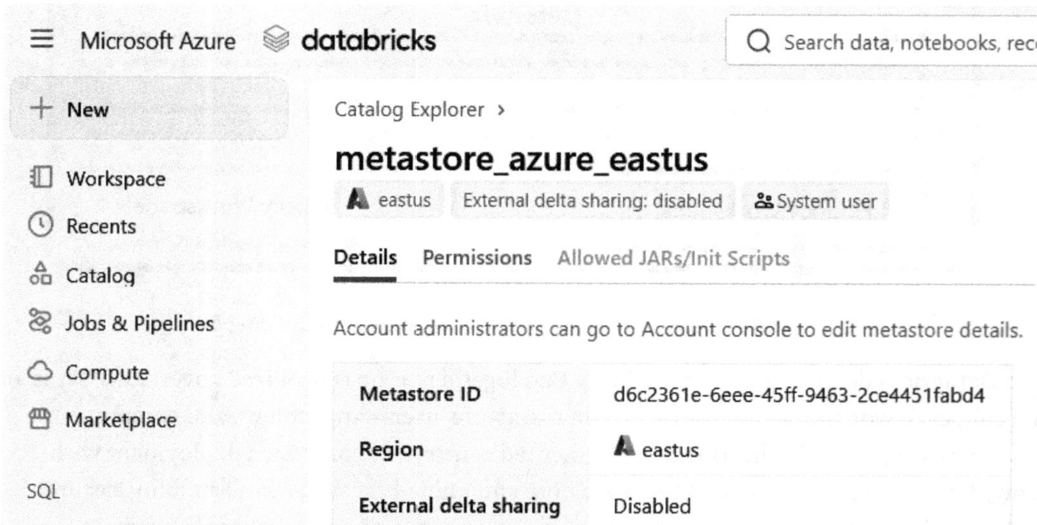

Figure 5.30: Databricks Metastore ID

Each metastore is assigned a **globally unique identifier** that serves as the top-level container for data governance. This metastore ID is required during infrastructure automation to configure tools such as Databricks REST APIs and Terraform.

Object model

An object model is a **conceptual** representation of how data, entities, and their relationships are structured within a data platform. It describes metastore objects, the types of data they contain, and how those objects relate to one another.

In Databricks, metastore organizes data using a **three-level namespace** hierarchy, which is used across the Databricks account to uniquely identify objects.

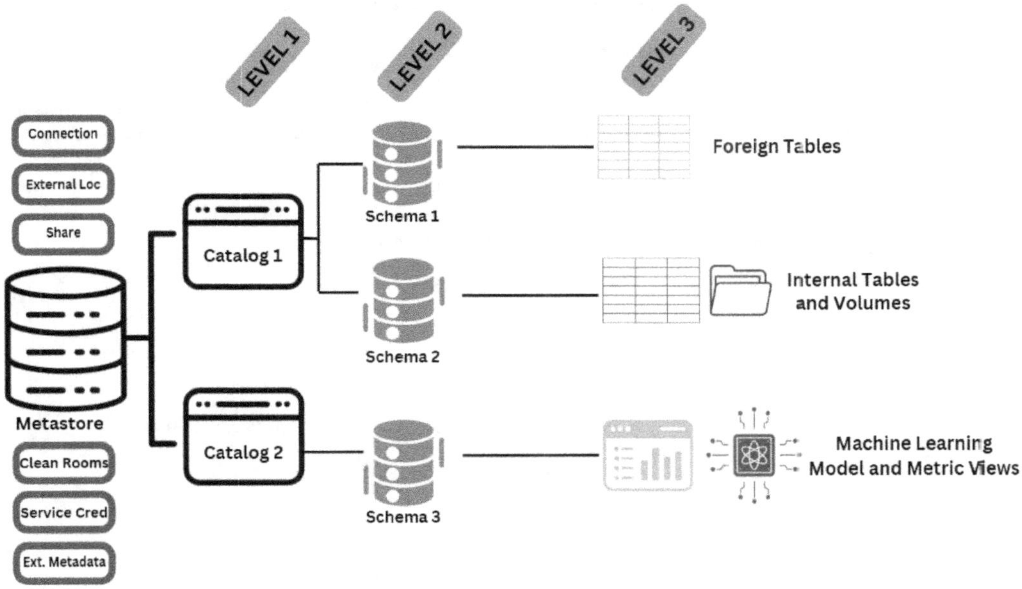

Figure 5.31: Metastore object model

Catalogs

A **catalog** serves as the highest-level, searchable collection that organizes data assets. Catalogs are typically aligned with business domains and are named after the teams or functions responsible for producing and sharing data products. The diagram below shows the catalog overview UI within Databricks:

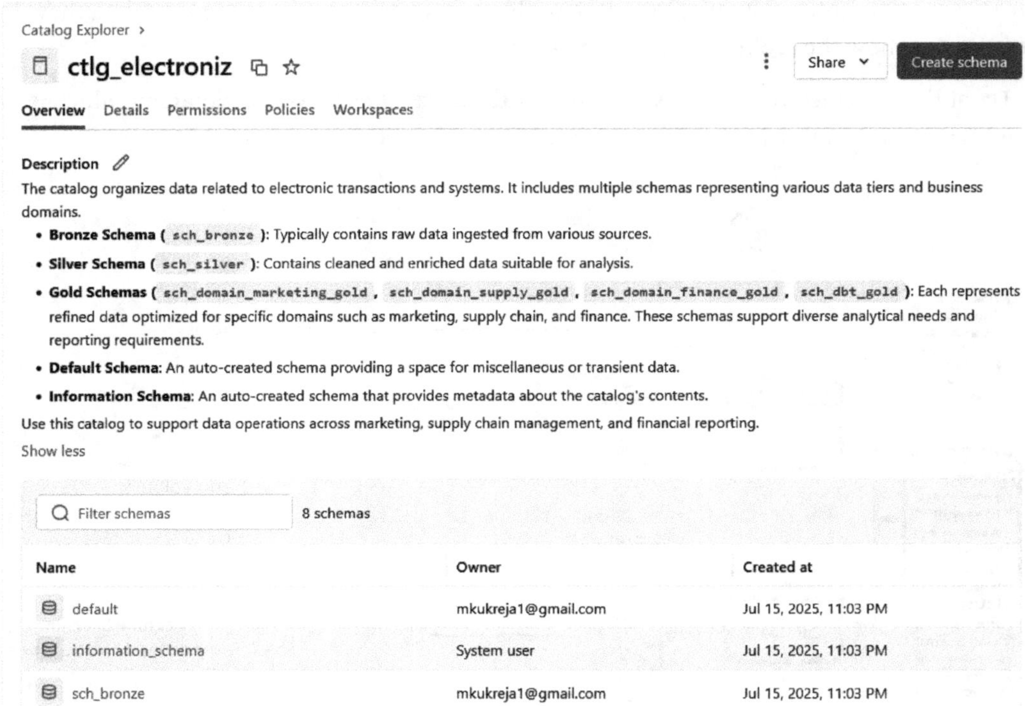

Figure 5.32: Databricks catalogs

Catalogs organize data assets into schemas, and permissions can be assigned at the catalog level. Granting permissions at the catalog level provides unrestricted access to all schemas and objects within the catalog and should generally be avoided. Catalogs can be shared with workspaces within the same Databricks account or externally using Delta sharing.

Schemas

Schemas represent the second level in the metastore namespace hierarchy and serve as logical containers for organizing tables, views, functions, volumes, and models. Schemas are referenced as `catalog.schema` in the Unity Catalog namespace.

The diagram below shows the schema overview UI within Databricks:

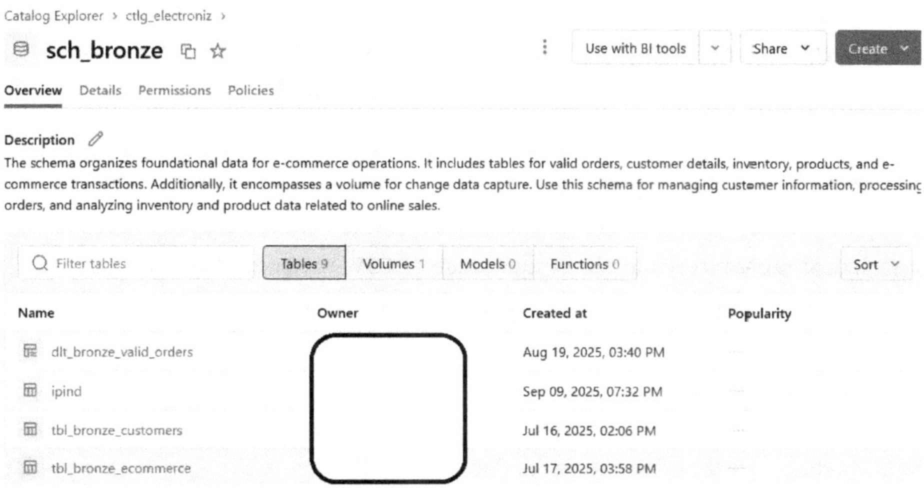

Figure 5.33: Databricks schemas

Permissions can be applied at the **schema level** to restrict access to sensitive or unwanted datasets. Schemas are commonly used to logically separate data based on processing stages, such as **raw**, **curated**, and **aggregated** datasets.

Schemas are categorized into the following types:

- **Managed schema**: This is the default schema type in which Databricks manages both the storage and metadata of the contained objects. When an object is deleted from a managed schema, both its data and metadata are permanently removed.
- **Unmanaged schema**: Also known as an external schema, this type of schema acts as a reference to data stored in external locations such as cloud object storage or external databases. Unmanaged schemas persist only metadata; dropping the schema or its objects removes the metadata from Databricks but leaves the underlying data intact at its original location. External schemas are especially useful during data migrations or when referencing infrequently accessed datasets.

Data objects

Data objects are controlled resources that encapsulate data and AI assets within the Databricks environment. These objects are managed and secured through Unity Catalog and are organized within the metastore namespace. They are centrally governed and protected using Unity Catalog and are structured within the metastore namespace at the third level. Databricks stores the following types of data objects:

Tables

A table is a structured collection of data organized into rows and columns. Databricks stores data using **open formats**, with **Delta Lake** being the default. Tables are referenced as `catalog.schema.table` in the three-level Unity Catalog namespace.

- **Managed tables** store data in Delta format by default, with the option to use the **Iceberg** format. The underlying data for a managed table is stored in object storage within the organization's cloud provider account.
- **External tables** store data in formats such as **CSV**, **Parquet**, **ORC**, or **JSON**, with the underlying data hosted in object storage or external provider databases.

Views

A **view** is a virtual data object that does not physically store data. Instead, it represents a saved SQL query, abstracting and hiding the underlying query logic to simplify data access. A view is a virtual data construct that does not store data physically. Instead, it represents a predefined SQL query that abstracts complex logic and simplifies data access for consumers. Views are referenced as `catalog.schema.view` in the three-level Unity Catalog namespace. Databricks supports three types of views:

- **Standard views:** Standard views evaluate queries at runtime and retrieve data directly from the underlying tables. They are commonly used to encapsulate complex transformations, apply row and column-level security, filter irrelevant records, and conceal sensitive information.
- **Materialized views:** Materialized views persist the results of a query rather than recalculating them each time. They automatically refresh when the source data changes and are typically used to improve query performance, especially for frequently accessed aggregated datasets.
- **Metric views:** Metric views define reusable business metrics and **key performance indicators** (**KPIs**) that can be shared across dashboards and analytical queries. They are particularly valuable when multiple teams rely on consistent definitions for the same business metrics. A metric view is typically written in YAML.

Volumes

Databricks Volumes are storage areas within Unity Catalog that let you organize and manage files. Volumes support all formats of data, including structured, semi-structured, and unstructured - such as images, PDF and Word files, logs, audio, video, JSON, CSV, Parquet, and ML training files. Volumes are referenced as `catalog.schema.volume` in the three-level Unity Catalog namespace.

The diagram below shows the volume overview UI within Databricks:

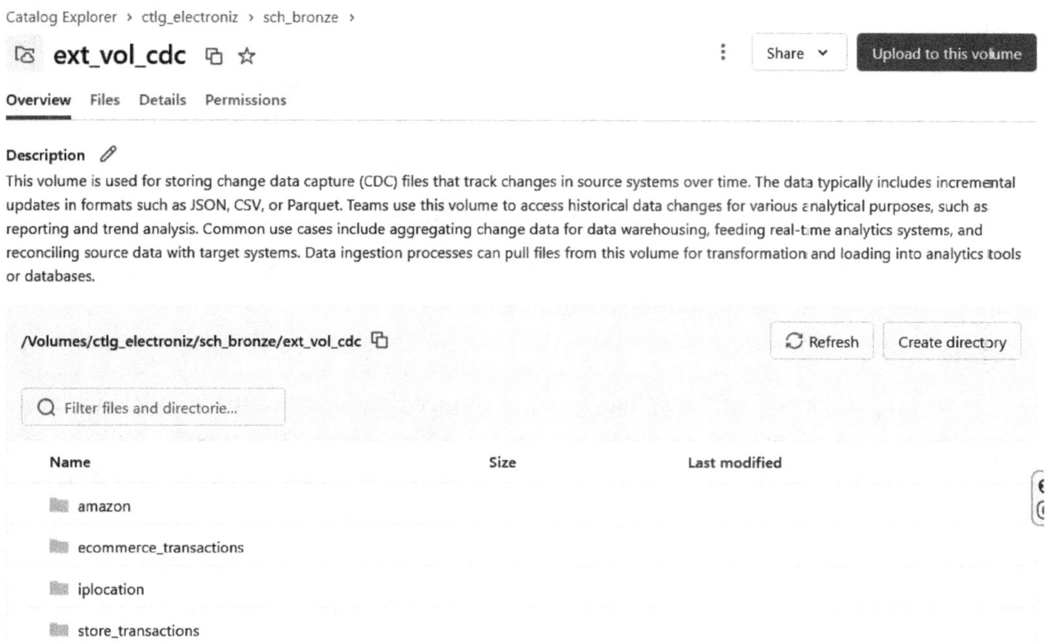

Figure 5.34: Databricks volumes

- **Managed volumes** are storage locations administered entirely by Databricks, making them well-suited for internal or platform-managed tasks.
- **External volumes** point to data kept in external cloud storage services, with Databricks maintaining just the metadata about these resources.

The rise of ML and AI workloads has led to extensive use of volumes for storing a wide range of data artifacts that support Generative AI and Agentic AI applications.

Functions

User-defined functions (**UDFs**) are reusable logic that return a single scalar value. They can be invoked in notebooks, SQL queries, and machine-learning workflows. Functions are commonly used to encapsulate complex logic and improve reusability in data transformations. Functions are referenced as `catalog.schema.function` in the three-level Unity Catalog namespace.

The image below displays sample UDF code within Databricks:

11:05 AM (1s) 14: Create a column masking function

```
CREATE OR REPLACE FUNCTION my_first_catalog.my_first_schema.format_club(Club STRING)
  RETURNS STRING
  RETURN regexp_replace(Club, '[^a-zA-Z0-9]', ' ')
```

Figure 5.35: Databricks UDF

You may create a function using either SQL or Python, register them in the Unity Catalog, and securely reuse it across the computing environments.

Models

Models are ML/AI-trained artifacts that represent trained datasets. A trained model includes the model binaries, associated metadata, version history, and evaluation metrics. Unity Catalog also tracks feature lineage and training lineage to provide complete traceability over the model's lifecycle. Models are referenced as `catalog.schema.model` in the three-level Unity Catalog namespace.

Not every object in Databricks stores data; some simple complement data objects by storing configurations necessary for operations on the data platform.

Non-data objects

Databricks non-data objects support data engineering, machine learning, and AI workflows by encapsulating configurations and metadata needed for operations such as accessing external storage locations, managing storage credentials, and connecting to cloud storage platforms, including Azure, AWS, and Google Cloud.

> **Note**
>
> Storage credentials and connections should always be configured in accordance with the principle of least privilege. The users and service principals assigned to them should be granted only the minimal permissions required to access the relevant data.

Databricks Connections enable secure, governed access to external data systems—such as Oracle, Amazon Redshift, Microsoft SQL Server, MySQL, and Google BigQuery—through Unity Catalog, eliminating the need to embed credentials directly in notebooks or clusters.

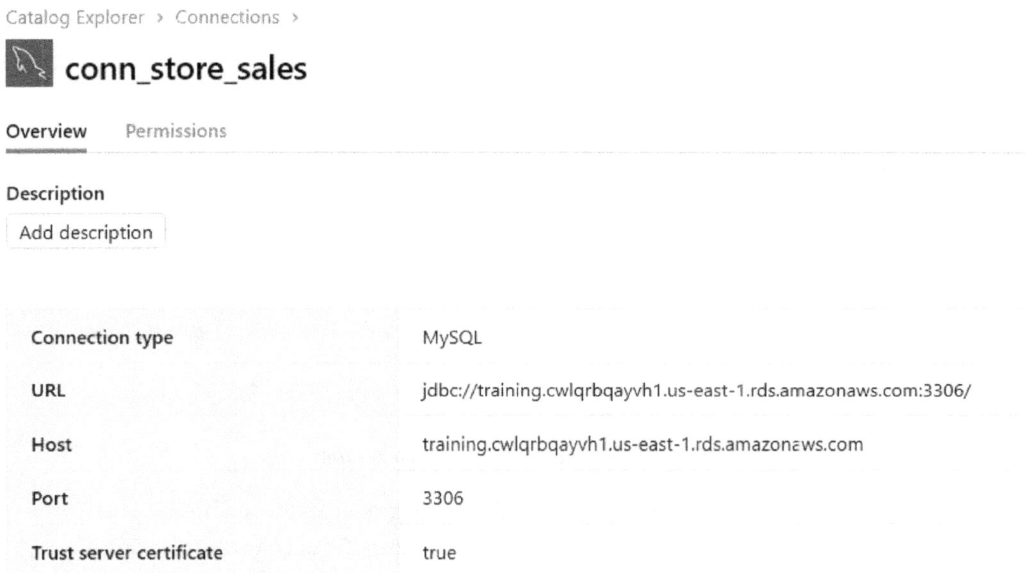

Figure 5.36: Databricks connection to MySQL database

A **storage credential** provides the authentication and authorization needed to access an external location. These credentials can be linked to both human and non-human managed identities, such as those configured in Microsoft Entra ID. Storage credentials can be associated with human as well as non-human identities - often referred to as service principals or managed identities. Storage credentials reduce the reliance on hard-coded secrets and strengthen the overall security posture when connecting to external data sources.

The image below displays sample credential within Databricks:

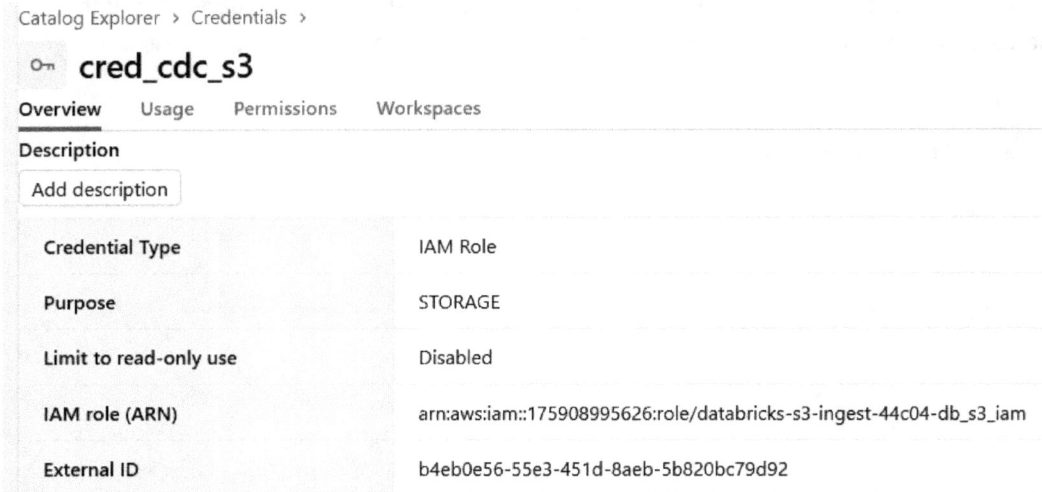

Figure 5.37: Databricks storage credentials

A Databricks external location uses its associated storage credential to authorize access to a designated storage path in cloud environments such as Azure Data Lake Storage Gen 2, Amazon S3, and Google Cloud Storage. External locations are managed within the Unity Catalog governance layer, ensuring consistent enforcement of security and access policies across all connected data sources.

The image below displays a sample external location that points to an S3 path within Databricks:

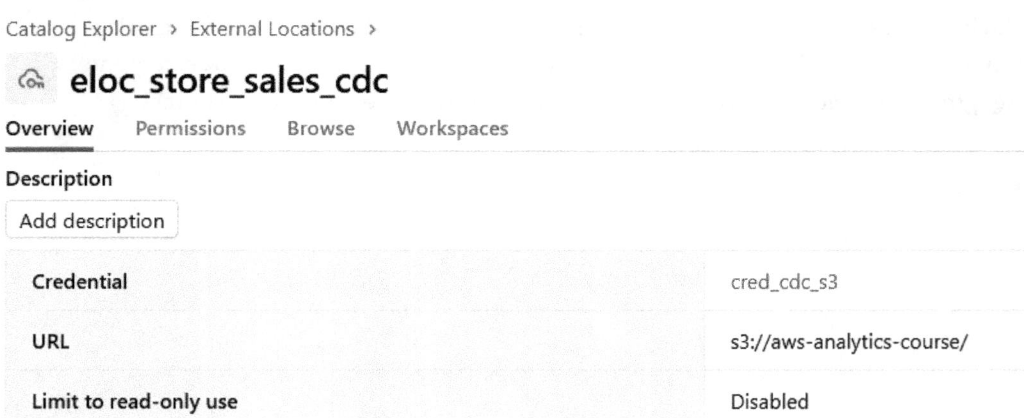

Figure 5.38: Databricks external locations

A defining hallmark of a modern data platform is the ability to query both internal and external data sources from a single, unified interface. Let's explore the Databricks services that make this possible.

Lakehouse Federation

Databricks Federation creates a virtual query layer over external data systems, allowing you to access and query data without moving or ingesting it into Databricks. This enables real-time access to datasets while providing a unified way to query external databases, data warehouses, data lakes, and Lakehouses.

The image below displays sample credential within Databricks:

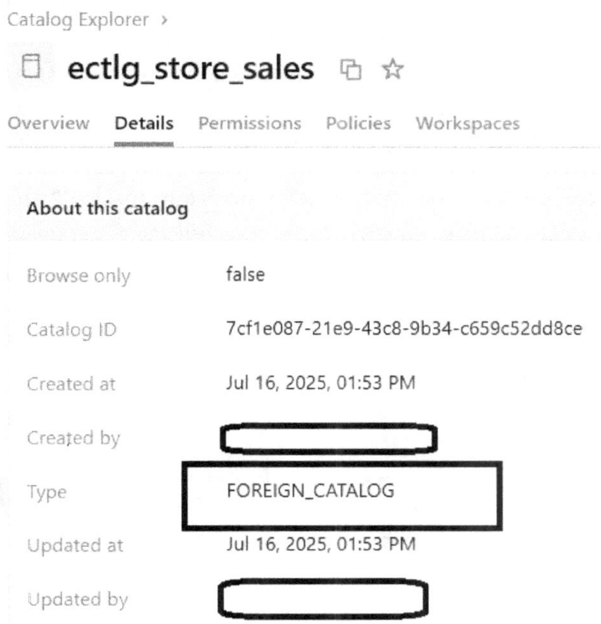

Figure 5.39: Databricks federation

Behind the scenes, Databricks leverages external locations, connections, and storage credentials to securely retrieve data from external sources or foreign catalogs. For faster performance, Databricks implements pushdown query processing for certain data operations at the source system, such as filtering, grouping, and aggregating results. Databricks federation is gaining popularity among organizations with hybrid data platforms, data mesh implementations, ad hoc data explorations, and gradual migrations.

> **Note**
>
> Data federation comes with certain limitations. Performance can vary due to network latency and the scalability constraints of the underlying source system.

Privilege management

A **securable object** is a Unity Catalog asset stored in the metastore to which permissions can be assigned for a user, service principal, or group. These objects follow a hierarchical structure, where authorization settings cascade downward through the hierarchy. At the top of this structure is the catalog, which serves as the highest-level container. Granting privileges at the catalog or schema level automatically applies those permissions to all existing and future objects beneath them. This inheritance model ensures consistent and streamlined access control across the entire data environment. Databricks account admins, workspace admins, and metastore admins have escalated permissions to manage Unity Catalog.

Each Unity Catalog object has an assigned owner, who is automatically granted full privileges on that object. Owners can delegate any privileges they hold to other users, service principals, or groups. They can also transfer ownership of the object to another user when needed.

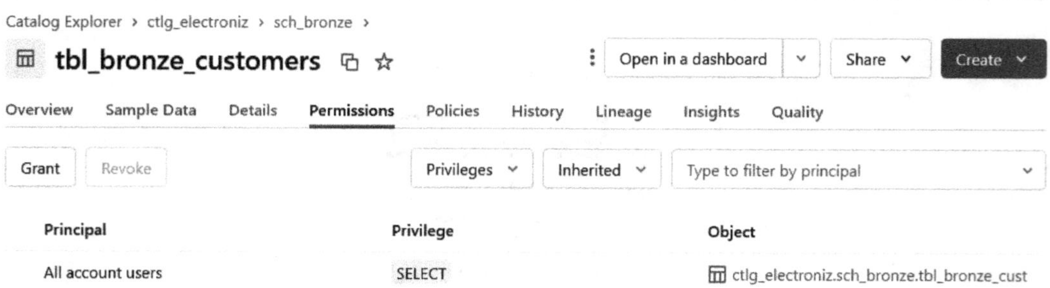

Figure 5.40: Privilege management

Governed tags

Governed tags are defined at the account level and can be applied to various objects. They help enforce organizational standards by using **tag policies** that control allowable values and ensure consistent governance across the environment.

The image below shows an example of a governed tag, where the *email* column in a table has been classified as **Personal Identifiable Information** (**PII**).

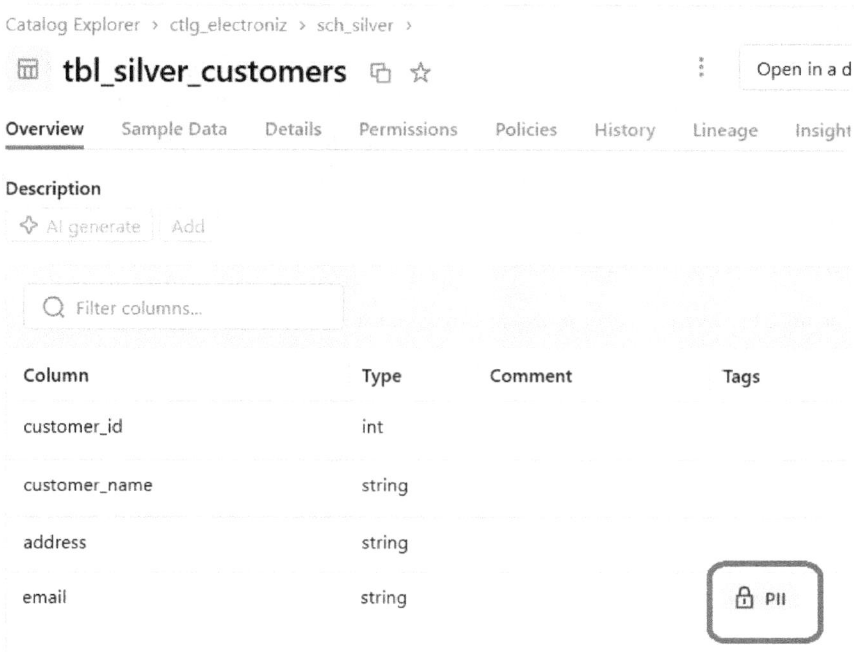

Figure 5.41: Databricks governed tags

Governed tags support a wide range of use cases, including:

- **Discoverability and trust:** Governed tags improve the discoverability of data assets by enabling consumers to easily search for data products based on standardized metadata. By tagging data products as *certified* or *deprecated*, organizations can clearly signal their trustworthiness and lifecycle status, helping consumers identify reliable and up-to-date products.
- **Resource cost attribution:** Tags such as *environment* or *project* help organizations accurately track and allocate costs (chargebacks) to specific business domains.
- **Automation:** Tagged objects can be efficiently identified for automated workflows related to deprecation or archiving.
- **Data classification:** Governed tags make it easy to label and identify sensitive data, including PII.
- **Attribute-Based Access Control (ABAC):** Tags can be used to filter rows and columns based on classification attributes, enabling fine-grained access control.

A critical aspect of modern data governance is the ability of future data platforms to trace data from its origin through to its destination. Let's explore how Databricks addresses this capability.

Data lineage

Data lineage captures the full lifecycle of data—from its origin and ingestion to the transformations it undergoes and its destination. Clear lineage builds consumer trust, supports compliance requirements, and enables effective impact analysis when upstream or downstream jobs are affected by schema changes or modifications to transformation logic.

The image below illustrates data lineage, showing how data flows, transforms, and evolves across different stages of the pipeline.

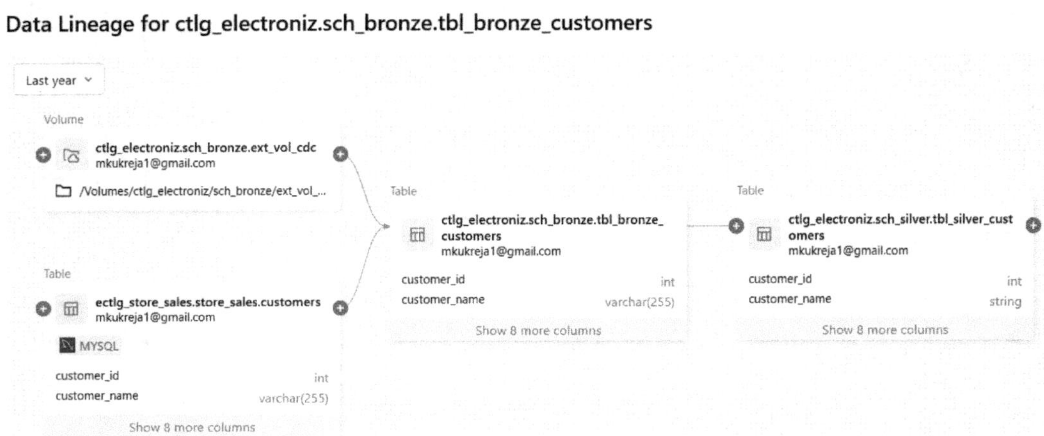

Figure 5.42: Databricks lineage tracking

Databricks automatically captures lineage for notebooks, jobs, and queries, and presents it in an intuitive, visual format within the Catalog Explorer UI. Lineage information is retained for up to one year. While we moved through these data governance concepts relatively quickly, rest assured that we will explore them in much greater depth in *Chapter 12, Governing of Data Products*, later in this book.

Now that we understand how Unity Catalog enforces governance across all layers of the data platform, we can shift our focus to how metastore enables advanced data-sharing capabilities in Databricks, including Delta Sharing, the Databricks Marketplace, and Clean Rooms.

Data sharing

In *Chapter 1, The Story of Data Engineering and Analytics,* we explored the power of data and how it enables organizations to unlock new revenue streams through data monetization. However, this vision cannot be fully realized without the ability to share data beyond organizational boundaries. Historically, companies have relied on a variety of data-sharing approaches, including email, SFTP, APIs, cloud storage, and even physical hard drives. While these approaches can be effective, many of them operate outside centralized controls and often bypass established organizational governance and security policies. Databricks enables secure data sharing while fully respecting the organizational governance boundaries. With Databricks sharing capabilities, data can be made accessible to:

- Internal and external users
- Internal and external applications
- External organizations

Here are a few methods used by Databricks to share data:

Delta Sharing

Delta Sharing is the foundation of the Databricks data sharing platform. It enables you to securely share data and AI assets stored in Databricks with users outside your organization, regardless of whether they use Databricks.

Delta Sharing is also available as an open-source project, allowing organizations to share Delta tables across different platforms and ecosystems.

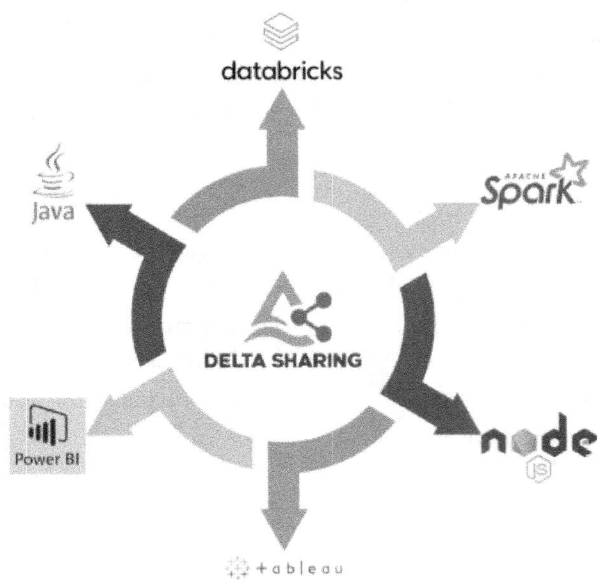

Figure 5.43: Databricks Delta Sharing

There are three ways to share data using Delta Sharing.

1. **Databricks-to-Databricks sharing protocol:** This option allows you to share data and AI assets from a Unity Catalog–enabled Databricks workspace with users who also have access to a Unity Catalog–enabled Databricks workspace. It leverages the Delta Sharing server built directly into Databricks. Tight integration with Unity Catalog simplifies configuration, strengthens governance for both data providers and recipients, and delivers improved performance.
2. **Databricks open sharing protocol:** This option allows you to share tabular data managed in a Unity Catalog–enabled Databricks workspace with users on any computing platform. It leverages the built-in Delta Sharing server in Databricks, making it ideal for organizations that manage data through Unity Catalog. This approach is especially useful for sharing data with users who do not use Databricks or who lack access to a Unity Catalog–enabled Databricks workspace.
3. **Customer-managed Delta Sharing server:** This method lets you share from any platform to any platform, whether it is Databricks or not. In this case, a separate installation of the delta sharing server is required.

Delta sharing provides consumers with near real-time access to data without the need for replication. Its open protocol simplifies secure data sharing across multiple cloud platforms. Databricks also provides a data marketplace that enables data sharing and collaboration between organizations.

Data Marketplace

The **Databricks Marketplace** serves as an open exchange for data products, enabling organizations to easily discover, publish, and consume trusted data and AI assets. It extends the Databricks ecosystem through Partner Connect integrations, allowing seamless interoperability with third-party tools, platforms, and data services. Databricks Marketplace is built on Delta Sharing, providing secure, governed mechanisms to distribute data products without copying or moving data.

The following diagram illustrates the user interface of the Databricks Marketplace:

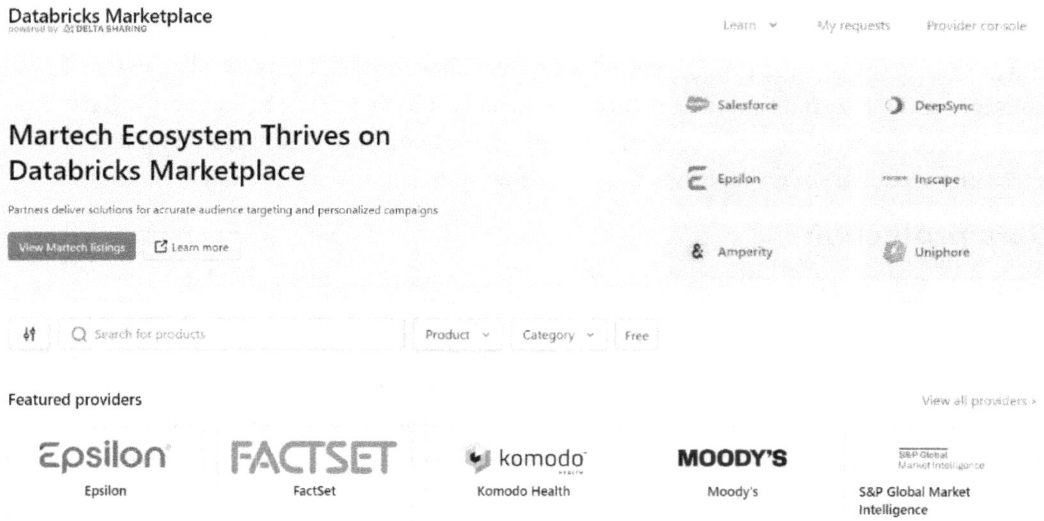

Figure 5.44: Databricks marketplace

Marketplace offerings include a wide range of assets such as datasets, notebooks, and machine learning or generative AI models. Although most are structured, the marketplace also supports non-tabular unstructured data through Databricks volumes.

In today's digital landscape, trust has taken on a new meaning, shaped by data, technology, and interconnected systems. How do you share data with parties you don't fully trust? This is where Databricks Clean Rooms come into play.

Clean rooms

Databricks Clean Rooms operate on a zero-trust collaboration model. In this model, all participants—including the clean room creator—are granted the same level of permissions. No individual has implicit authority over others. The Clean Rooms architecture is intentionally designed to prevent both unauthorized code execution and unintended data exposure. Security is enforced through explicit collaboration controls that require collective agreement. Before any notebook can be executed, it must be reviewed and approved by all collaborators. Even if a user uploads their own notebook, execution is blocked until the remaining participants provide approval. The primary benefit of this approach is that it enables multiple parties to perform analytics on sensitive information without revealing the underlying data. Privacy and security are fundamental to modern data platforms. Let's now explore how Databricks addresses these critical requirements.

Security

The Databricks security model primarily centers on the shared responsibility model, **Identity and Access Management** (**IAM**), centralized governance through Unity Catalog, network isolation, and secure data sharing. Security is a broad topic, and many of these areas have already been covered in detail in earlier sections of this book or will be explored further in upcoming sections. For now, we will focus on a few additional security-related topics.

Data protection

The purpose of data protection is to ensure that information remains unreadable even if unauthorized users gain access to the underlying infrastructure. This is why cloud service providers depend on encryption to maintain the privacy and security of sensitive data. Within an encryption framework, responsibility is shared between the cloud provider and the customer, both of whom must implement encryption correctly as part of a comprehensive security strategy. Azure Data Lake Storage Gen2 secures data at rest by encrypting all data stored within a storage account.

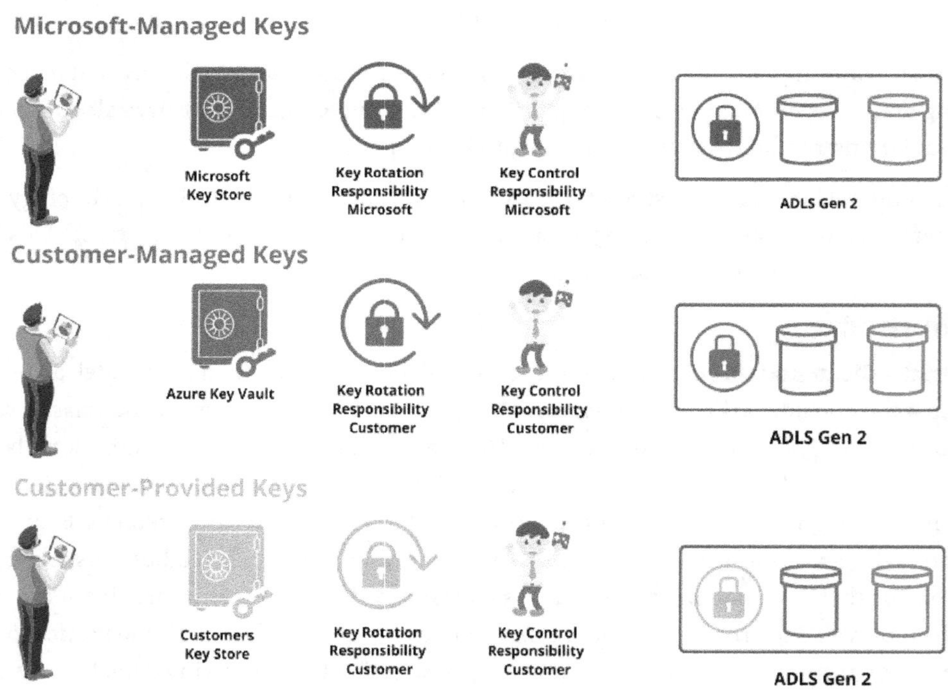

Figure 5.45: Azure Data Lake Storage Gen2 encryption management

By default, data in ADLS Gen2 is secured using **Microsoft-managed encryption** (**MMK**). With this approach, data is encrypted automatically and transparently, without requiring customers to manage key creation, rotation, protection, or ongoing maintenance.

For organizations that need greater control over how encryption keys are handled, ADLS Gen2 also supports the following encryption methods:

- **Customer Managed Keys (CMK):** Customers maintain full ownership of the encryption keys, including key rotation and management. These keys are stored and managed separately using services such as Azure Key Vault.
- **Customer Provided Keys (CPK):** Customers supply the encryption key for each data operation and remain fully responsible for key storage and rotation. Keys can be managed outside of Azure, such as in an on-premises or external key management system.

These options allow customers to meet stricter security, compliance, or regulatory requirements while maintaining full protection of their data at rest. Securing data at rest is essential, but it is equally critical to protect the credentials—such as passwords, passphrases, and authentication keys—that enable a data platform to load and offload data.

Secrets manager

Databricks Secrets Manager is a service for storing and handling sensitive values aka secrets that can be used to connect to external systems for data ingestion and data export.

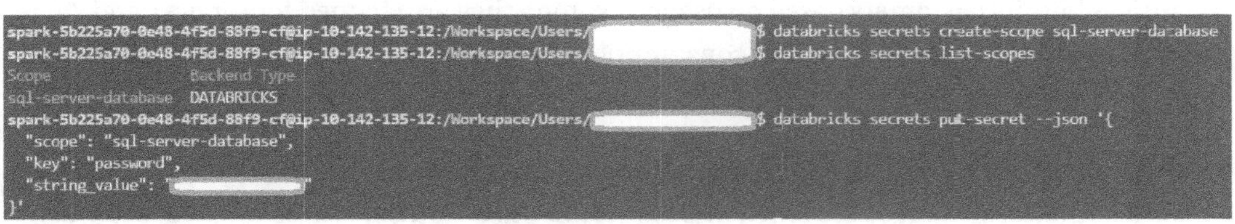

Figure 5.46: Databricks secrets manager

Secrets are stored within secret scopes, which are maintained in an encrypted database owned and managed by Databricks. Access permissions are assigned to Databricks principals at the secret scope level. At runtime, secrets can be securely retrieved from notebooks and Databricks SQL using built-in functions, eliminating the need to hard-code sensitive information in programs. Just as Databricks Secrets Manager isolates and protects sensitive values during storage and retrieval, Databricks also provides additional technologies to ensure Spark workloads execute in their own isolated, secure environments.

Process Isolation

By default, Apache Spark components such as drivers and executors run on shared compute infrastructure. Multiple processes therefore operate on the same underlying hardware, which can introduce the risk of unintended data exposure if isolation is not properly enforced. **Databricks Lakeguard** enforces strong code and process isolation, enabling multiple Spark processes to safely share underlying hardware without compromising data or process boundaries.

> **Note**
>
> Spark's isolation security risks arise from shared-node clusters and unrestricted user code execution, which can expose data, disrupt workloads, or enable cross-tenant interference if not properly governed. These risks are significantly reduced for an organization that uses dedicated clusters.

This is not the end of our discussion on Databricks security. Many of these concepts, along with additional security topics, will be revisited and expanded upon throughout this book. For now, we shift our focus to a subject that data engineers often overlook—but one that consistently ranks as a top priority for senior leadership: **billing**.

Billing

Databricks bills its customers based on usage, meaning they are charged for services and compute resources according to their consumption. In practice, the customers typically receive two separate bills:

Databricks platform costs

Databricks platform charges are billed in **Databricks Units** (**DBUs**). These costs reflect usage based on workload type, such as all-purpose, Jobs, or ML/AI workloads. Each workload type has its own DBU pricing rate. You may refer to the following link for the most current and up-to-date pricing information: `https://azure.microsoft.com/en-us/pricing/details/databricks/`.

The **Pay As You Go** pricing has two distinct tiers: **Standard** and **Premium**. The Standard tier is designed for development and testing workloads in less-regulated environments. In contrast, the Premium tier is intended for production use cases that require stricter regulatory controls, enhanced collaboration capabilities, and centralized governance. You can use the Unity Catalog only in the Premium tier, and enabling the Photon Engine for performance increases the DBU count.

Customers who are willing to commit for 1, 2, or 3 years can purchase **Databricks Commit Units (DBCU)**, which offer discounted pricing compared to the standard pay-as-you-go model. Refer to the image below, which shows a sample bill broken down by workspace. As a customer, you can view a detailed cost breakdown, including DBU usage and the corresponding dollar amounts.

Pay As You Go

Azure Databricks bills* you for virtual machines (VMs) provisioned in clusters and Databricks Units (DBUs) based on the VM instance selected. A DBU is billed on a per-second usage. The DBU consumption depends on the size and type of instance running Azure Databricks. Feature availability may vary information please review our documentation.

Workload	Standard Tier Prices	Premium Tier Prices
Interactive Serverless Compute***	-	$1/DBU-hour
All-Purpose Compute**	$0.40/DBU-hour	$0.55/DBU-hour
Automated Serverless Compute***	-	$0.47/DBU-hour
Jobs Compute**	$0.15/DBU-hour	$0.30/DBU-hour
Jobs Light Compute	$0.07/DBU-hour	$0.22/DBU-hour

Figure 5.47: Sample Databricks bill broken by workspace

Cloud infrastructure costs

In addition to Databricks platform charges, customers are also responsible for the costs associated with the underlying cloud infrastructure. These charges include cloud resources such as virtual machines, object storage, key management services, data transfer fees, NAT gateways, and the hourly usage of private endpoints. In practice, Databricks follows a pay-per-use pricing model, where compute consumption represents the largest portion of overall cost, far exceeding storage expenses. The following image shows a high-level overview of the most common cost components reflected in the Databricks and cloud provider bills.

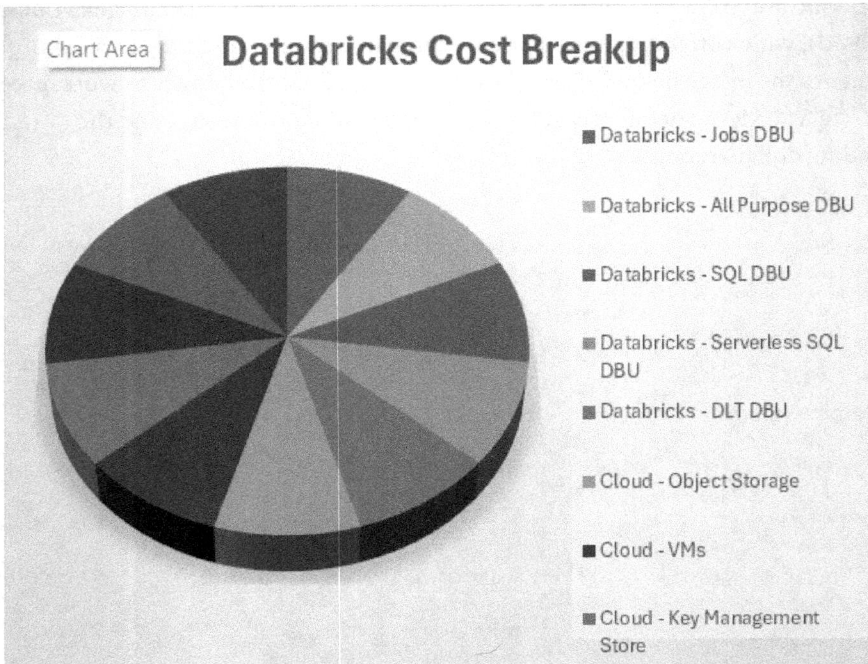

Figure 5.48: Databricks cost breakup

Summary

In this chapter, we explored the key elements that shape the design, architecture, and governance of a Databricks-powered data platform. We began with the concept of a harmonized data platform, demonstrating how organizations can integrate disparate data sources, eliminate silos, and establish a unified, scalable foundation for analytics, machine learning, and data-driven decision-making.

We then examined how Databricks' core components—including compute, storage, and workspaces—interact to form a resilient, cloud-optimized architecture that supports diverse workloads across the data and AI lifecycle. This provided readers with a strong understanding of the platform's underlying structure and operational principles.

Understanding the various aspects of a Databricks-powered data platform is essential because it determines how effectively the platform scales, operates, and delivers trusted data across the enterprise. A well-designed architecture ensures that storage, compute, security, and data-movement patterns are aligned with business needs and optimized for performance.

Next, we turned our attention to Unity Catalog, the central governance framework within Databricks. Here, readers learned how Unity Catalog brings together permissions, lineage, data classification, governed tags, and **Attribute-Based Access Control** (**ABAC**), ensuring consistent governance across all data assets and workspaces.

To address operational considerations, the chapter also covered Databricks billing, explaining how compute usage, jobs, clusters, and storage contribute to overall cost. Finally, we discussed advanced data-sharing capabilities enabled by Unity Catalog and metastore, including Delta Sharing, the Databricks Marketplace, and secure Clean Rooms. Together, these topics prepare the reader to confidently navigate and apply Databricks concepts in the chapters that follow.

Get this book's PDF version and more

Get this book's PDF version and more

6

Understanding Medallion Architecture and Delta Lake

In the previous chapter, we examined the Databricks Unified Data Platform and its role in enabling future-ready data architectures built on the Lakehouse paradigm. A core principle of the Lakehouse approach is its ability to continuously ingest data from diverse sources, progressively enhance its quality through well-defined transformation stages, and finally organize these stages using what it calls the Medallion Architecture.

A key pillar of a modern Lakehouse is its use of open data formats, which provide flexibility, portability, and long-term resilience for data assets. These formats are strengthened by **atomicity**, **consistency**, **isolation**, **durability** (**ACID**) transaction support, allowing Lakehouses to deliver the dependability typically associated with data warehouses—while still benefiting from the scalable, cost-efficient storage foundation of data lakes.

Together, ACID-enabled open formats and the Medallion Architecture create the core of a robust, interoperable, and future-ready Lakehouse environment. This combination equips organizations to design data platforms that can evolve alongside changing analytics, AI, and governance requirements.

This chapter covers the following topics:

- Medallion architecture
- Understanding Spark
- Understanding Delta Lake

Medallion architecture

Databricks structures data using the Medallion Architecture—a term they originally introduced, using *bronze*, *silver*, and *gold* layers as symbolic references to medal tiers. This naturally raises the question: why are the layers compared to medals in the first place? The explanation centers on the progression of data quality and refinement. Each layer represents a step in data refinement: Raw data in Bronze, standardized and cleansed data in Silver, and analytics-ready, aggregated datasets in Gold. This structured progression ensures that data quality increases systematically as it moves closer to business consumption.

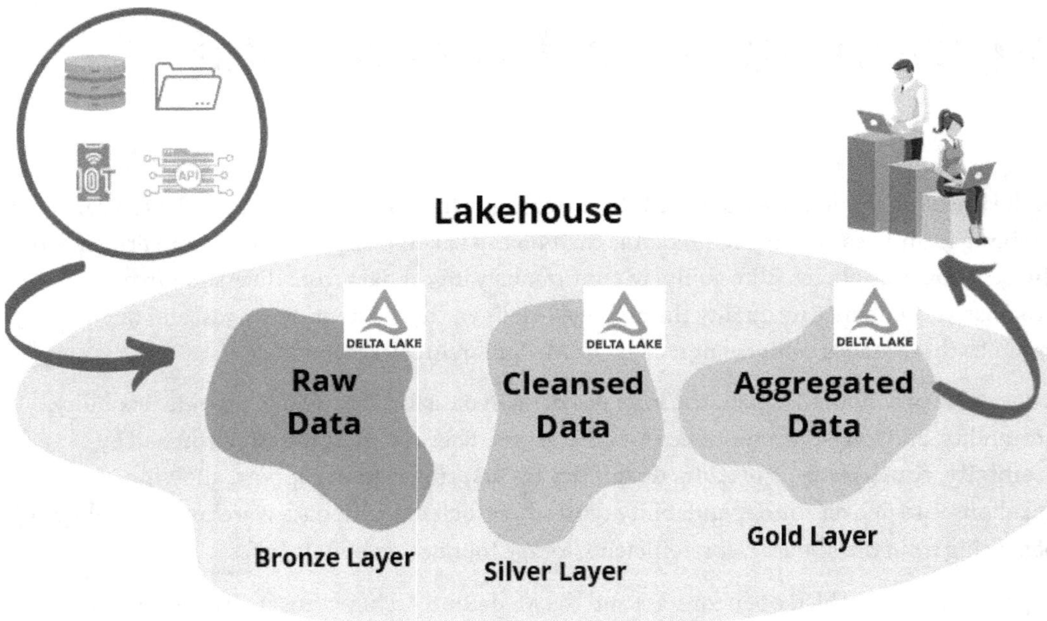

Figure 6.1: Data maturity in a Lakehouse

According to Kimball, *The notion of time pervades every corner of the data platform.* He proposed the data warehousing methodology, where data moves through three key layers: **Staging**, **Integration**, and **Presentation**. They each serve a distinct purpose in preparing data for analytics. At its core, modern analytics is the continuous consolidation of data that evolves over time. With every passing moment, data platforms must adhere to a disciplined lifecycle—from collection to consumption—ensuring that data becomes increasingly mature, reliable, and ready for analytical use. Data maturity is a measure of quality, feature readiness, support for open formats, and governance. The medallion architecture organizes data into three successive layers, each representing an increasing level of cleanliness, structure, and usability.

Bronze layer

The **bronze layer** in the Medallion architecture serves as the foundational landing zone for all ingested data. At this stage, data is stored exactly as it arrives from the source systems, without any cleaning, standardization, or transformations. The structure and quality are fully preserved, ensuring a copy of data that matches its source system. Data stored in the bronze layer typically exhibits the following characteristics:

- **Unclean and non-standardized**: Because the data is captured in its raw form, it often contains inconsistencies, errors, missing values, and irregular formatting. As a result, it is not suitable for analytical workloads or business consumption in this state.
- **Multi-format and multi-type**: The bronze layer can contain structured, semi-structured, and unstructured data, ranging from text types such as CSV, XML, or JSON files to binary files such as images, logs, or binary blobs.
- **Immutable**: Once written, data in the bronze layer is never edited. If the upstream source changes or resends corrected values, these updates are stored as additional records, ensuring a complete historical view.
- **Retained indefinitely**: Bronze-layer data is generally stored forever as long-term reference material. Because modern cloud storage is inexpensive, retaining raw data poses little concern, though older or less critical data may be archived periodically to reduce costs.

Maintaining data in its native, unaltered form provides several important advantages:

- **Reprocessing and replay**: In cases where the downstream silver or gold layers need to be corrected—perhaps due to new requirements or coding errors—pipelines can be re-executed from the original raw data. This allows teams to rebuild refined datasets without re-extracting from source systems.
- **Flexibility for new use cases**: As business needs evolve, having access to the original, unmodified data enables engineers to develop new processing logic, derive additional insights, or support novel analytical workloads.
- **Auditability and lineage**: A complete, untouched copy of the source data is invaluable for compliance, validation, and traceability. It forms the authoritative reference point for understanding how data changed as it progressed through the silver and gold layers.

Having established the raw data foundation in the bronze layer, we now transition to the silver layer, where quality and consistency are introduced.

Silver layer

Data curation refers to the combined processes of cleaning, sanitizing, standardizing, and deduplicating data. In the Lakehouse framework, the **silver layer**—often called the *refinement layer*—is where this curated data is stored. When data reaches this stage, it has been cleansed, conformed, and enriched, providing data analysts, data scientists, and machine learning engineers with high confidence in its quality and reliability. Key activities in the silver layer include:

- **Deduplication**: Duplicate records can arise for many reasons. Changes in source systems—such as updates to customer addresses, phone numbers, or order status (including purchases and returns)—often generate multiple versions of the same record. Managing these evolving changes, commonly handled through **Change Data Capture** (**CDC**), becomes difficult when duplicates appear. Additional duplicates may be introduced through process retries, system errors, or late-arriving events.

customer_id	email	customer_name	address	city	updated_at
501	Phasellus.vitae@vitae.co.uk	Prescott Barnes	960-5386 Vel, Road	Pangnirtung	2021-04-28T17:56:10.520+0000

customer_id	email	customer_name	address	city	updated_at
501	Phasellus.vitae@vitae.co.uk	Prescott Barnes Jr.	960-5386 Vel, Road	Pangnirtung	2021-04-28T18:25:40.927+0000

Figure 6.2: Duplicate records arising due to a name change in the source system

  Deduplication is therefore essential to ensure that downstream analytics remain accurate, reliable, and free of inconsistencies as data continually evolves.

- **Correct type casting**: Many data sources store values using incorrect data types—for example, dates often appear as plain strings. During the curation process, type casting ensures that all fields are converted to their appropriate data types, so that the information stored in the silver layer is accurate, consistent, and ready for reliable downstream use.
- **Fixing inconsistent data**: Data inconsistencies often occur when the same information appears differently across multiple datasets. For example, I might be listed as "John Doe" in one system and "J Doe" in another. Resolving these discrepancies can be particularly challenging, as it often requires probabilistic data matching to determine whether two slightly different values refer to the same entity.

Data Source 1

Person ID	Name	Address	Email	BirthDate
1	John Doe	123 Main Street, Queens, NY	johndoe@hotmail.com	01/01/1970
2	J Doe	123 Main Street, NY		

Data Source 2

ID	Name	Address	Email	BirthDate
2000	John Doe	562 Union Street, Brooklyn, NY	jdoe@hotmail.com	07/01/1970

Data Source 3

PID	Name	Address	Email	BirthDate
101	John Doe	123 M Street, Queens, NY	jdoe@yahoo.com	

Figure 6.3: Inconsistent representations of the same entity across three different source systems

- **Standardization**: Data arriving in the bronze layer is often not in an interoperable state, especially due to geographic or system-specific differences. For example, one source system might store first and last names in separate fields, while another combines them into a single field. Similarly, some countries—such as the United States—use the MM/DD/YYYY date format, whereas many others follow DD/MM/YYYY.

Figure 6.4: Non-standard date entries originating from two separate ordering systems

As a result, a significant portion of the curation effort focuses on standardizing timestamps, currencies, and measurement units so that data is consistent and comparable across all downstream processes.

- **Fix uniformity**: Non-uniform data often appears in the bronze layer due to variations across different datasets. These differences can stem from factors such as the use of abbreviated versus non-abbreviated values or inconsistent formatting conventions.

Figure 6.5: Non-uniform country values from two separate systems

- **Fixing orphaned, missing, or lookup records**: It's common for data arriving in the bronze layer to fail lookup validations, include null values, or break referential integrity rules. The purpose of data curation is to resolve these issues so that only clean, reliable, and well-structured data moves into the silver layer. Below are some common types of data quality issues:

a. **Type Validity**: Columns must use the correct data type, such as integer, date, or float.

b. **Value Ranges**: Column values should fall within an acceptable or expected range.

c. **Uniqueness**: Certain columns are required to contain unique values with no duplicates.

d. **Relational Integrity**: Records must not be "orphans"; foreign key values should always correspond to existing entries in the parent table.

- **Redact Personally Identifiable Information (PII)**: Regulations such as the **General Data Protection Regulation** (**GDPR**) and the **California Consumer Privacy Act** (**CCPA**) impose significant penalties when data privacy is compromised. To comply with these requirements, PII must be properly protected before it is exposed to end users. In the silver and gold layers, PII is masked or transformed using techniques such as anonymization and pseudonymization to ensure that sensitive information remains secure while still enabling analytical use.

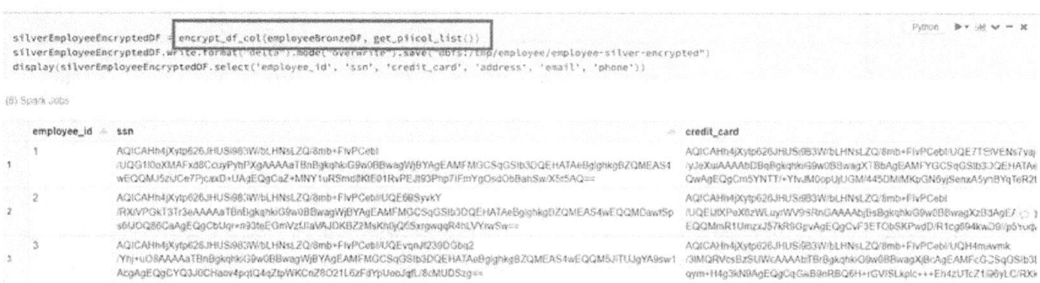

Figure 6.6: Redacting PII

- **Handle Slowly Changing Dimensions (SCD)**: In dimensional modeling, dimensions hold descriptive attributes, and when those attributes evolve, SCD techniques determine whether older values should be overwritten or preserved as historical records. Modern analytics and AI/ML workloads increasingly rely on this historical perspective, making it essential for the silver layer to maintain a complete record of how data changes over time.

ID	name	address	phone	startdate	enddate	status
1	Julie Rich	Ap #255-3031 Dui Avenue, Billings, USA	1-528-884-4331	2017-05-12		Current
2	Eden Byrd	Ap #476-7527 Aenean Road, Harrisburg, USA	1-375-910-8385	2020-04-19		Current
3	Magee Cash	**P.O. Box 333, 5820 Vel Avenue, New Haven, USA**	1-853-137-7417	**2019-02-22**		**Current**

Change of Address

ID	name	address	phone	startdate	enddate	status
1	Julie Rich	Ap #255-3031 Dui Avenue, Billings, USA	1-528-884-4331	2017-05-12		Current
2	Eden Byrd	Ap #476-7527 Aenean Road, Harrisburg, USA	1-375-910-8385	2020-04-19		Current
3	Magee Cash	P.O. Box 333, 5820 Vel Avenue, New Haven, USA	1-853-137-7417	2019-02-22	**2022-03-24**	**Expired**
3	Magee Cash	**687 Magnis Rd., New Haven, USA**	1-853-137-7417	**2022-03-24**		**Current**

Figure 6.7: Handling Slowly Changing Dimensions (SCD)

The goal of data curation is to ensure that only clean, reliable, and well-structured data is stored in the silver layer. This curated data then serves as the trustworthy foundation for all downstream aggregations and transformations performed in the gold layer.

After achieving consistency and quality in the silver layer, the data advances to the gold layer for modeling, aggregation, and domain-specific enrichment.

Gold layer

The gold layer is built using the cleansed, secure, and trusted data curated in the silver layer. Information stored at this stage is considered fully consumption-ready, making it suitable for reporting, dashboarding, machine learning models, and AI-driven workflows. In the gold layer, data is typically aggregated, enriched, and optimized for specific analytical or business use cases, providing end users with fast, reliable access to high-value insights.

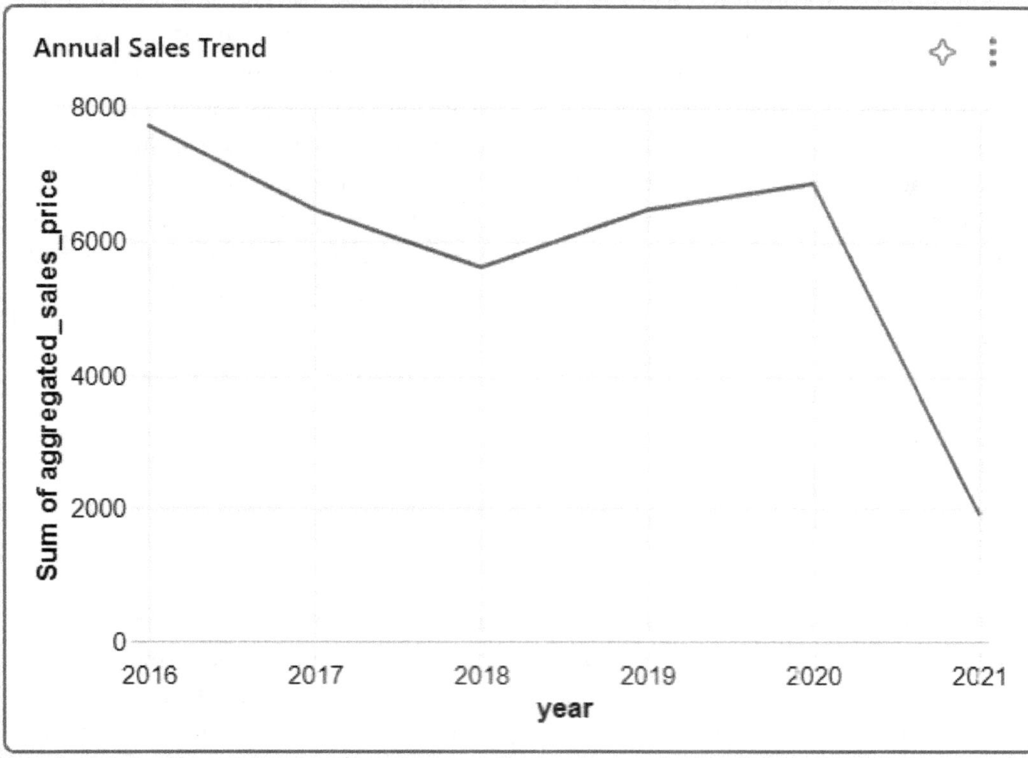

Figure 6.8: High-maturity analytics- ready data in the gold layer

In *Chapter 1, The Story of Data Engineering and Analytics*, we began with the idea that *"Every byte of data has a story to tell. The real question is whether the story is being narrated accurately, securely, and efficiently."* The Medallion Architecture embodies this principle by guiding data through a structured journey—transforming it from a raw, untrusted state into fully business-ready information. Taken together, the Medallion Architecture ensures that by the time data reaches end users, its story is not only accurate but also secure, consistent, and ready to drive meaningful impact across the business. But there is one framework that truly transforms the Lakehouse by delivering the reliability and consistency it needs: Delta Lake.

Understanding Spark

In the data lake era, Apache Spark—originally developed at UC Berkeley's AMPLab—became the de facto standard for large-scale data processing. In addition to its impressive performance, Spark provided a unified engine capable of handling both batch and streaming workloads with ease. The project was later donated to the Apache Software Foundation, where it continues to be maintained as an open-source, cluster-based processing framework.

Building on the momentum and widespread adoption of Apache Spark, its original creators founded Databricks to deliver a commercial, enterprise-grade platform built around the technology. Their vision was to simplify large-scale data processing by offering a fully managed environment that seamlessly integrates Spark with complementary capabilities in data engineering, data science, machine learning, and analytics. Databricks continues to contribute advancements back to the open-source Spark project, while also expanding the platform through its own innovations. The Databricks Runtime—the engine that underpins the Databricks platform—includes additional performance optimizations, integrations, and proprietary features that enhance and extend the core functionality of Apache Spark.

Spark supports a wide range of workloads, including:

- Batch Processing
- Data Science
- Machine Learning
- Continuous Applications - Streaming
- Artificial Intelligence

Spark's execution model is grounded in several core principles, including in-memory computation, immutability, persistence, and lazy evaluation. Together, these principles enable Spark to optimize end-to-end workflows through intelligent planning, resulting in a resilient, efficient, and highly performant data processing engine. The following sections explore each principle in greater depth.

In-memory computations

The primary driver of Spark's performance is storing intermediate results in distributed memory (RAM) rather than stable storage (disk). This memory-centric approach is key to Spark often outperforming older Hadoop MapReduce systems. Spark abstracts data through its in-memory distributed data constructs known as **Resilient Distributed Datasets** (**RDDs**).

Here's a clear explanation for RDDs:

- **Resilient**: As computations run, Spark maintains detailed lineage information for each RDD. If data stored in memory is lost, maybe due to a node failure, Spark can quickly reconstruct any lost partitions by replaying the sequence of transformations that originally produced them.
- **Distributed**: Each RDD is composed of multiple partitions, and these partitions are distributed across different nodes in the Spark cluster.
- **Flexible Dataset Source**: RDDs can be created from external files or generated programmatically within Spark.

Partitioning

Spark is a **distributed computing framework**, and RDD partitions serve as the fundamental units of distributed processing. An RDD is composed of multiple **partitions** spread across different nodes in the Spark cluster. Each partition is processed independently as a separate task, so increasing the number of partitions can improve parallelism and overall computation speed. Effective partitioning ensures that work is evenly distributed among workers while reducing unnecessary data shuffles, thereby minimizing network overhead and improving performance.

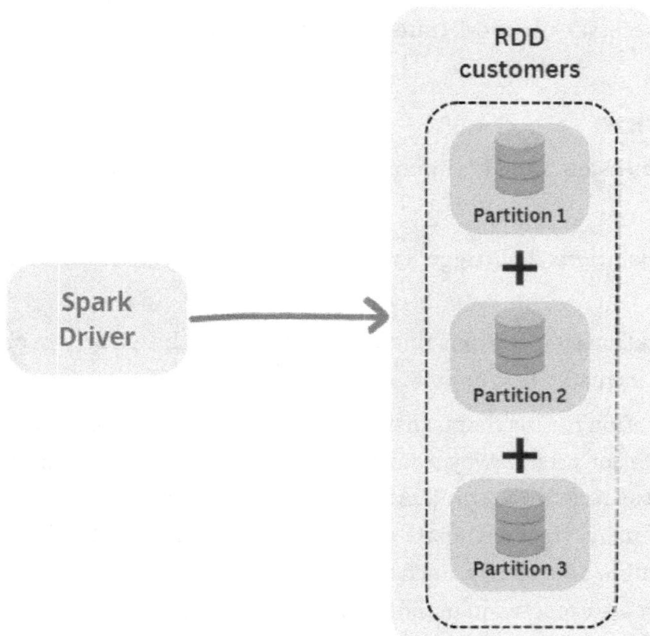

Figure 6.9: RDD partitions

After understanding how Spark partitions data for parallelism, the next principle to consider is immutability, which governs how datasets are created and maintained.

Immutable

RDDs are immutable; once created, their data cannot be modified. This immutability is intentional, as it allows Spark to maintain **consistency** across RDD partitions and reliably track lineage. Any transformation applied to an RDD produces a new RDD rather than altering the original one.

Persistence

Spark allows RDDs to be persisted by caching them in memory or storing them on disk. This capability is especially valuable when the same data is used across multiple operations. By persisting RDDs, Spark avoids repeated computations and eliminates unnecessary disk reads during iterative or repeated workloads, resulting in significantly improved performance.

Location Stickiness

During execution, Spark attempts to schedule tasks on nodes that already contain the relevant data—a behavior known as **data locality**. This approach keeps computation close to the data and minimizes unnecessary network transfers, improving performance and reducing cluster overhead.

Lazy evaluation

Before exploring lazy evaluation, it's important to understand the two types of RDD operations in Spark:

- **Actions**: Operations that trigger computations and return a result, such as count, sum, or collect.
- **Transformations**: Operations that define a new RDD based on one or more existing RDDs, such as map, filter, or join.

In Spark, lazy evaluation means that transformations are not executed immediately. Instead of performing computations right away, Spark logs each transformation into a logical execution plan called a **Directed Acyclic Graph** (**DAG**)—a core component of Spark's execution model. When an action is finally triggered, Spark analyzes the DAG and divides it into stages, which are separated by shuffle boundaries. Each stage is then broken down into tasks, typically one per partition, which are executed in parallel across the cluster.

> Note
>
> The concept of DAGs is not limited to Spark; it is also used in workflow orchestrators like Airflow, Prefect, and Dagster.

Earlier, we learned that RDDs serve as Spark's low-level, distributed abstraction layer. While RDDs provide fine-grained control over data and the transformations applied to it, they offer limited support for structured data and schema management. To overcome these limitations, Spark introduced a more optimized and higher-level abstraction.

DataFrames

A **DataFrame** represents data as a relational table with a well-defined schema, making it easier to work with structured information. Built on top of the Spark SQL engine, DataFrames provide a more SQL-friendly interface and benefit from advanced query optimizations powered by the Catalyst optimizer and Tungsten.

> Note
>
> Tungsten is a high-performance execution engine introduced in Apache Spark to significantly improve the memory efficiency and CPU performance of DataFrame operations.

Unlike RDDs, which execute functions at the element level, DataFrames achieve greater memory and execution efficiency through Tungsten's optimized in-memory storage and code generation. Because of these optimizations, DataFrames are particularly effective when handling structured and semi-structured data, offering both ease of use and high performance.

✓ Just now (<1s)

```
curated_cust_df.printSchema()
```

```
root
 |-- customer_id: integer (nullable = false)
 |-- customer_name: string (nullable = true)
 |-- city: string (nullable = true)
 |-- postalcode: string (nullable = true)
 |-- updated_at: timestamp (nullable = false)
 |-- email: string (nullable = true)
 |-- country: string (nullable = true)
 |-- phone: string (nullable = true)
 |-- credit_card: string (nullable = true)
 |-- address: string (nullable = true)
```

Figure 6.10: Well-defined schema of a DataFrame

DataFrames are especially useful because they provide built-in functions for common data transformations, such as reading CSV, JSON, Parquet, and Avro files, as well as operations like grouping, filtering, and aggregating data. As a result, most data engineers rely on DataFrames when authoring Spark applications.

Spark SQL

Spark SQL is designed to work with data using SQL queries, allowing Spark to represent information in familiar relational concepts such as tables, rows, and columns. The following are a few key advantages of using Spark SQL:

- **Integrated Processing**: Spark SQL enables you to seamlessly combine SQL queries with regular Spark code. This tight integration makes it easier to execute SQL queries alongside advanced analytical operations within the same application.
- **Unified Data Access**: Spark SQL provides a single interface for loading and querying data from a wide range of sources. This unified access layer simplifies working across different storage systems and data types.

```
curated_cust_df.createOrReplaceTempView("customers")
spark.sql("SELECT * FROM customers").display()
```

	customer_id	customer_name	city	postalcode	updated_at
1	1	Ariel Hale	College	98362	2026-02-02T17:22:00.000+00
2	2	Aubrey Norris	Coldstream	D10 5JV	2026-02-02T17:22:00.000+00
3	3	Bruno Hebert	Llangollen	CE2 4WW	2026-02-02T17:22:00.000+00
4	4	Ira Lucas	Shreveport	67365	2026-02-02T17:22:00.000+00
5	5	Hannah Ferrell	Watson Lake	C6Y 7M3	2026-02-02T17:22:00.000+00

Figure 6.11: Spark SQL relation concepts

Earlier, we noted that traditional data lakes lack essential processing capabilities—such as ACID transactions, indexing, and versioning—which can undermine the reliability, quality, and overall performance of the data they store. According to the ACID principles, the concept of *isolation* states that "*the intermediate state of a transaction should never be visible to other transactions.*" This principle underlies nearly all modern relational databases. Unfortunately, most traditional big data frameworks, including Spark, do not adhere to this principle. Even small updates—such as merging a few CDC records from source systems—often require recomputing the entire batch, therefore refreshing the entire dataset rather than updating only the modified records. This leads to longer processing times, wasted compute resources, and higher costs.

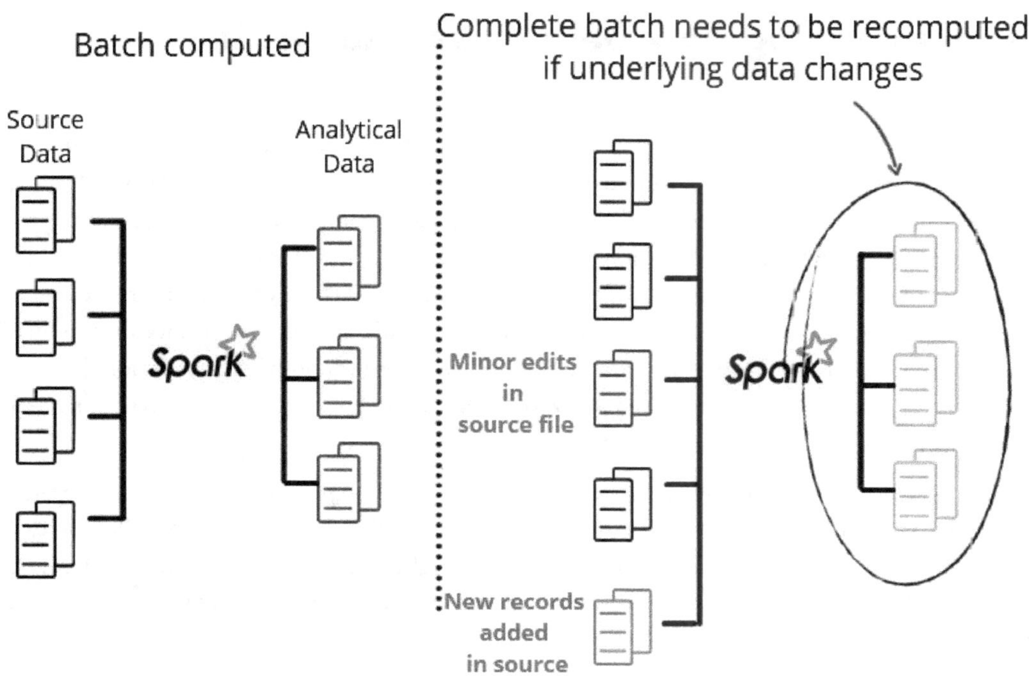

Figure 6.12: Spark requires the entire batch to be recomputed even for minor edits to the source

While Spark excels at large-scale data processing, it was not originally designed with full transactional guarantees. As a result, Spark lacks several essential principles of transaction management:

- **No data locking during writes**: Spark does not lock existing data when performing write or overwrite operations. This can briefly expose downstream readers to data that is temporarily unavailable or partially overwritten.
- **Risk of data inconsistency during overwrites**: During the re-computation period, downstream consumers may receive inconsistent or partially updated data. If Spark deletes old data during an overwrite operation and the subsequent write fails, the dataset may be left incomplete or inconsistent.
- **No protection against concurrent writes**: Spark does not prevent multiple processes or jobs from writing to the same location simultaneously, which can result in corrupted files, conflicting updates, or unpredictable outcomes.

These inconsistencies can adversely affect data products, underscoring the need for a more robust framework that supports incremental processing to deliver consistent, atomic, low-latency updates.

Understanding how Delta Lake enables the Lakehouse

In *Chapter 2, Discovering Storage and Compute Data Lake Architectures*, we discussed the give-and-take between traditional warehouse systems and data lakes. Over the past several years, many organizations have modernized their data engineering and analytics ecosystems by shifting from traditional data warehouses to data lakes. This transition has provided significant flexibility—allowing storage and computation of virtually any data format at massive scale. However, these benefits have come with trade-offs, the most notable of which is reduced data reliability. Unlike data warehouses, data lakes lack built-in transactional guarantees. This gap created the need for **Delta Lake**, an open-source storage layer designed to bring ACID transactions and reliability to data lakes.

Following Delta Lake's introduction, industry experts began exploring ways to combine the reliability and transactional strength of data warehouses with the scalability and flexibility of data lakes. This unified architecture became known as the **lakehouse**. The combined strengths of a data lake and a data warehouse create a uniquely powerful architecture with the following advantages:

- Enables analysis across all data types—structured, semi-structured, and unstructured.
- Maintains the benefits of low-cost storage and on-demand compute scalability.
- Supports a wide range of use cases, including analytics, data science, machine learning, and artificial intelligence.
- Ensures data quality through robust techniques such as curation, standardization, and deduplication.
- Provides secure, compliant mechanisms for storing, accessing, and sharing data.

The bronze layer captures raw, continuously ingested data from various sources in their native formats, while the silver layer consolidates this data and stores it in the Delta format. Because it integrates and standardizes data from all sources, the silver layer is often regarded as the **Single Source of Truth** (**SSOT**).

The Single Source of Truth (SSOT)

The silver layer within the medallion architecture represents a dependable, trusted, and well-governed version of the data—one that end-consumers can confidently use for all analytics, reporting, and machine learning needs. Its reliability is achieved through a blend of rigorous standardization practices, robust security controls, and comprehensive data-quality checks and remediation processes, all reinforced by the transactional consistency and schema enforcement provided by the Delta framework.

The Silver layer serves as the Single Source of Truth because it offers:

- **Robust data quality management**: It centralizes all rules for refining, cleansing, and harmonizing data.
- **Uniform consumption**: Every downstream application, report, model, and AI application relies on the same standardized dataset.
- **Robustness**: Delta Lake's ACID transactions ensure data integrity, preventing errors or inconsistencies.
- **Reuse**: All analytics use cases built using the same silver layer.

Note

In data warehouse terms, ACID is the short form for atomicity, consistency, isolation, and durability of data. These properties are intended to make database transactions accurate, reliable, and permanent.

By now, it should be evident that the Delta Lake framework plays a central role in establishing the SSOT layer. Let's take a closer look at how it achieves this.

Understanding Delta Lake

The **Delta Lake framework** functions as a storage layer on top of Apache Spark's distributed computing engine.

Delta Lake adds several key features to Spark by supporting the following capabilities:

- **ACID transactions**: When working with systems such as databases, data warehouses, and lakehouse platforms, ACID principles provide the foundation for reliable **transaction management**.

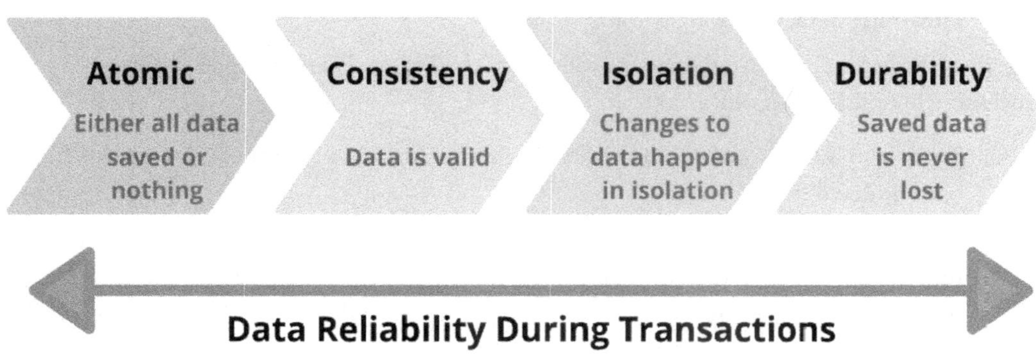

Figure 6.13: ACID properties in Delta Lake

These guarantees ensure that transactions remain safe and consistent even during system failures or periods of high user activity. ACID offers four guarantees as follows:

- **Atomicity**: Each transaction either completes fully or has no effect at all, preventing data from being left in a partial or incomplete state.
- **Consistency**: Every transaction must adhere to defined business rules and referential constraints, ensuring the data never ends up in an invalid or contradictory state.
- **Isolation**: Concurrent transactions operate under isolation rules that prevent them from interfering with one another, eliminating issues such as reading uncommitted or "dirty" data. Delta Lake provides **Serializable** and **WriteSerializable** isolation to guarantee consistent reads and conflict-free writes.
- **Durability**: Once a transaction is committed, its results are permanently stored and remain intact even in the event of unexpected system crashes.
- **Schema evolution**: Delta Lake manages schema changes seamlessly over time by allowing structured modifications to occur directly on existing tables. Instead of requiring full table rebuilds, it supports evolving schemas—adding or adjusting fields—while maintaining data integrity and consistency.
- **Time-travel**: Delta Lake maintains a complete history of data changes through its transactional log, enabling automatic versioning of every write operation. This versioning makes it possible to query or restore earlier snapshots of the data, supporting rollback, troubleshooting, and auditability with ease.
- **High optimization**: Delta Lake automatically compacts small files and applies optimizations such as data pruning and Z-ordering to improve query performance and overall storage efficiency.
- **Unified batch and streaming data merge**: Delta Lake supports merging data as part of CDC workflows, enabling seamless upserts and updates for both batch and streaming datasets.

Together, these capabilities enhance the reliability, quality, and performance of data processing in Spark. With Delta Lake:

- There is no need to recompute entire batches when only a subset of CDC records has been added or modified.
- At runtime, the engine identifies only the files that contain updated data, loads them into memory, and writes the results into new, optimized files, ensuring efficient incremental processing.

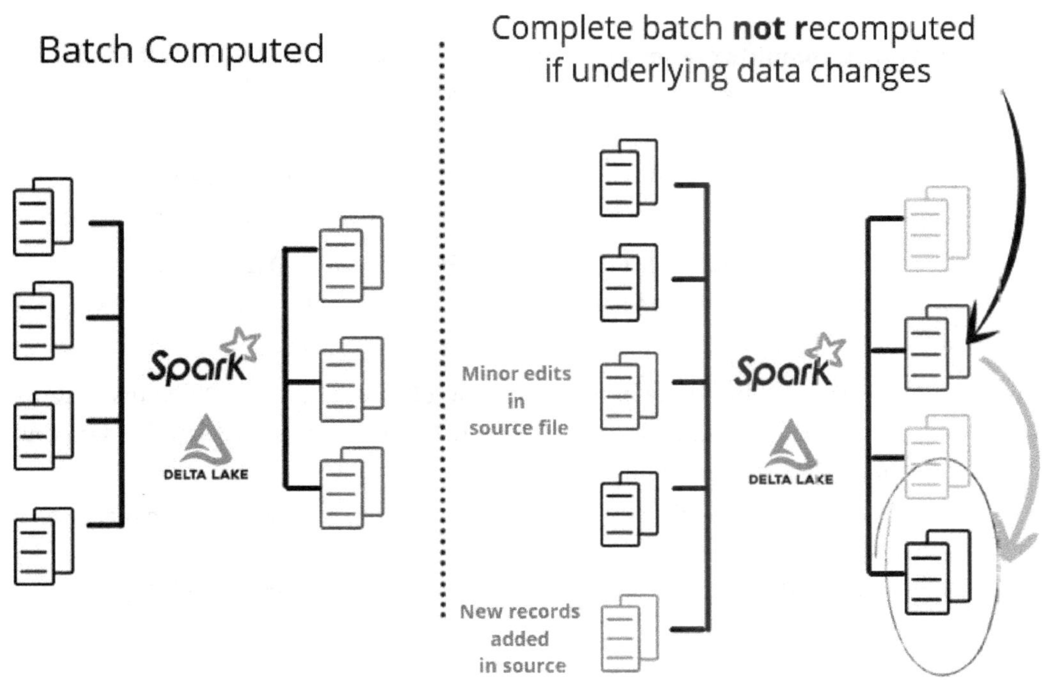

Figure 6.14: Delta Lake does not require the entire batch to be recomputed for minor edits to the source

We are going to learn about some key features of Delta Lake through a series of live examples. Let's get started by preparing the environment for this exercise.

Preparing Azure resources

Before we deep dive into the workings of Delta Lake, we need to spin up a few Azure resources as follows. Let's start by opening an Azure account.

Opening a free account with Microsoft Azure

In the upcoming chapters, we will use several Azure services you've just learned about to build a data lake following the lakehouse architecture. To begin hands-on work, you'll need access to an Azure environment. Microsoft offers a free Azure account that includes a one-time USD $200 credit valid for 30 days. Please keep in mind that while many services are free or fall under the free tier, not all of them are.

To create your free account and explore the available free services, visit the following link: `https://azure.microsoft.com/en-ca/free/`.

Here is some helpful guidance:

- **Shut down compute resources when you're done using them.** Compute services often incur the highest costs, so it's a best practice to deallocate or remove them as soon as they are no longer needed.
- Azure has two types of free services – **Always free** and **12 months free**. See the complete list at: `https://azure.microsoft.com/en-ca/pricing/free-services/`.
- For extra protection, enable **Multi-Factor Authentication** (**MFA**) for your Azure account. More details can be found here: `https://learn.microsoft.com/en-us/entra/identity/authentication/concept-mfa-howitworks`.
- You receive 5 GB of **locally redundant storage** (**LRS**) at no cost for 12 months. Because our exercises will remain well within this limit, there is no need to delete the data you store throughout the upcoming chapters.
- Monitor your billing closely while using Azure's free services. Even though many services offer a free tier, it's important to monitor your usage. You can track your charges at: `https://portal.azure.com/#blade/Microsoft_Azure_Billing/BillingMenuBlade/Overview`.
- Set budgets to avoid unexpected costs. Azure allows you to configure spending budgets and receive alerts if your usage exceeds the threshold you define. You can learn how to set up budgets here: `https://docs.microsoft.com/en-us/azure/cost-management-billing/costs/tutorial-acm-create-budgets`.

Now that we've successfully created the free Azure account, we can move on to enabling the Azure Databricks service.

Provision Azure Databricks

To work with Delta Lake commands, you'll need to provision an Azure Databricks workspace.

1. Log in to the Azure free tier account, using the URL: `https://portal.azure.com/`.
2. In the Azure portal, navigate to the **Home** screen, then use the search bar at the top to search for *Databricks*.
3. Click on **Azure Databricks.**
4. Click on **Create**.
5. For Azure subscription, select **Free Tier or Paid Subscription**.

6. For the Resource group, click on **Create new**. For the name of the resource group, enter *temporary_rg*. Click **OK**.
7. For Workspace name, enter **delta-lake-training**.
8. For Region, enter **Canada Central**. Alternatively, you can choose any region closer to you.
9. For Pricing tier, choose **Trial** or **Premium**.
10. For Workspace type, choose **Hybrid**.
11. Click **Review + create.**
12. After validation, click on **Create**.
    Azure will provision a new Azure Databricks account for you, once completed it will display a success message as below:

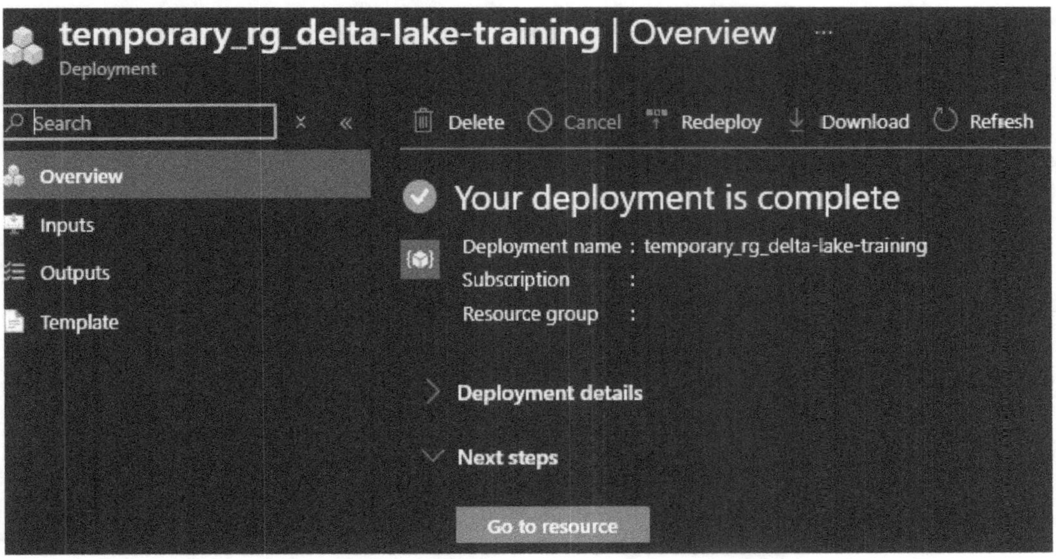

Figure 6.15: Azure Databricks deployment successful message

13. Click on **Go to resource**. The Azure Databricks account will look like this.

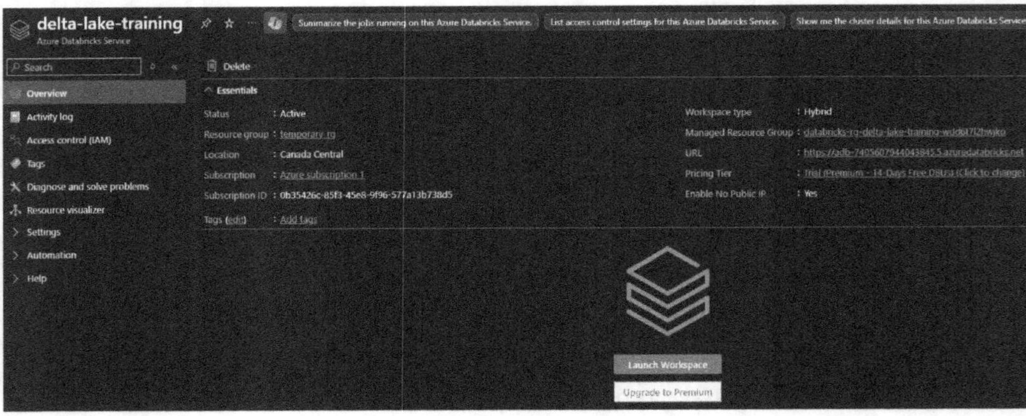

Figure 6.16: Azure Databricks account

14. Click on **Launch workspace**. This will open the Azure Databricks workspace.

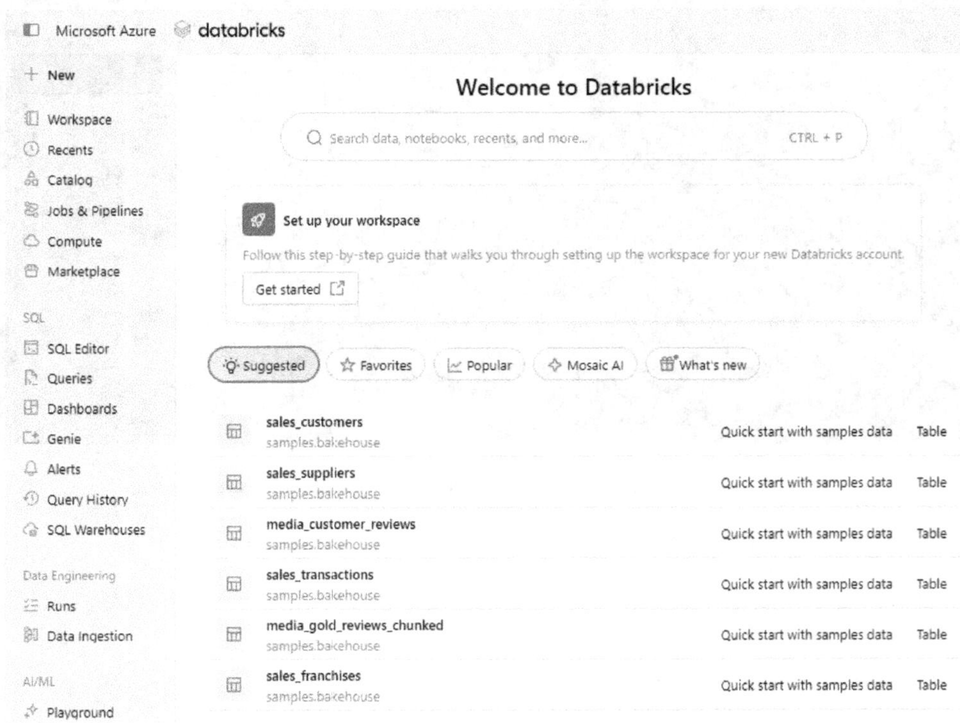

Figure 6.17: Azure Databricks workspace

Having completed the configuration of Azure Databricks, we now turn our attention to setting up **Azure Data Lake Storage** (**ADLS**) as the platform's foundational storage layer.

Provision Azure Data Lake Storage (ADLS)

To save data in Delta format, we will use a temporary ADLS account for this exercise.

1. In the Azure portal, navigate to the **Home** screen
2. Then, use the search bar at the top to search for *Storage Accounts*. Click on **Storage accounts**.
3. Click **Create**.
4. For Azure subscription, select **Free Tier or Paid Subscription**.
5. For Resource group, choose **temporary_rg**. Click **OK**.
6. For Storage account name**,** enter **templearningdelta**. Please note that Azure storage accounts have globally unique names, so you may need to change the name if it is already taken.
7. For Preferred storage type, choose **Azure Blob Storage or Azure Data Lake Storage Gen 2**.
8. For Redundancy, choose **Locally-redundant-storage (LRS)**.
9. Click on **Next**.
10. Check the box **Enable hierarchical namespace**.
11. Click on **Review + create**.
12. After validation, click on **Create**.

13. Azure will provision a new storage account for you, once completed it will display a success message as below:

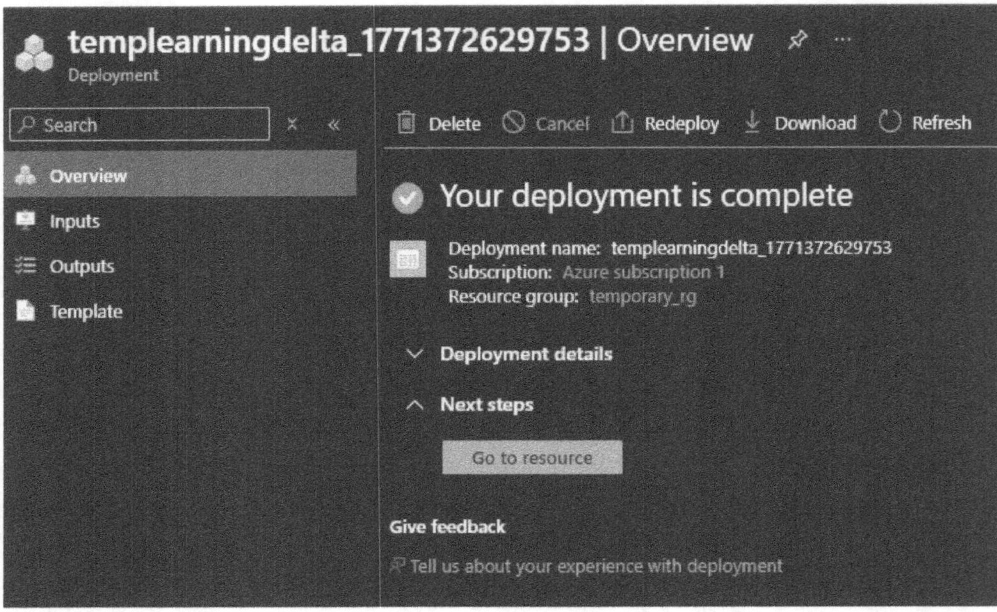

Figure 6.18: Storage account deployment successful message

14. Click on **Go to resource**.

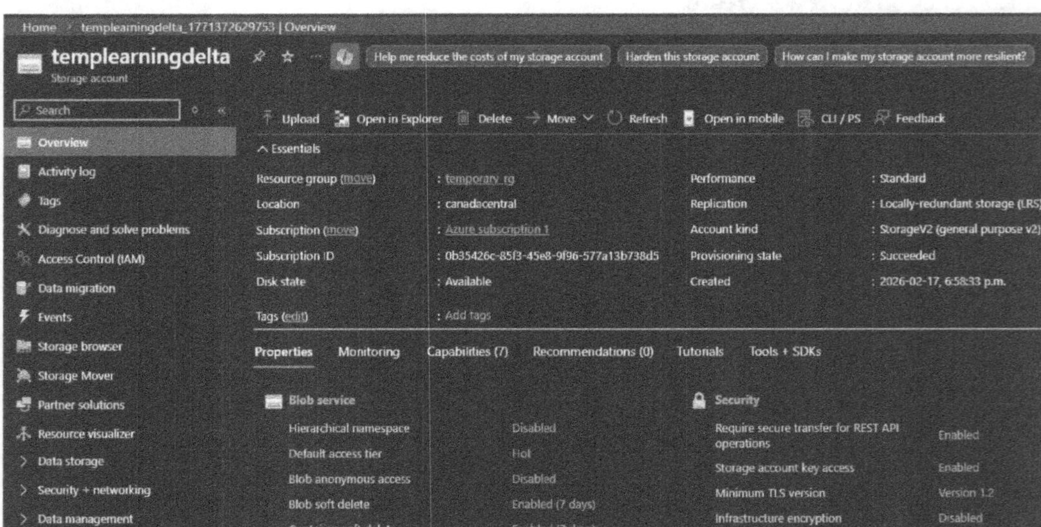

Figure 6.19: Newly created storage account

15. Now let's create a container that will store Delta Lake data. Using the menu on the left, click on **Storage browser**. Using the panel on the right, click on **Blob containers**.
16. Click on **Add container**.
17. For name, enter **delta**. Click on **Create**.

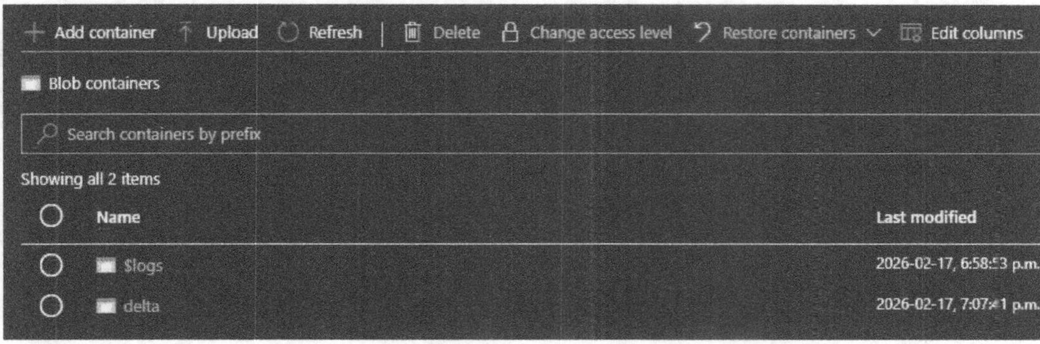

Figure 6.20: Newly created blob container

Azure Databricks must have access to Azure Blob Storage at runtime. It requires grants to the following roles:

a. Storage Blob Data Contributor
b. Storage Account Contributor
c. `EventGridEventSubscription` Contributor
d. Storage Queue Data Contributor

18. Assign this role to your user by clicking on the **Identity Access control (IAM)** menu on the left. Click on Add role assignment. Under Job function roles, search for **Storage blob data contributor**.
19. Click on **Storage Blob Data Contributor**. Click **Next**.
20. Click on **Managed Identity**, followed by **Select members**.
21. In the *Select managed identities* window for Managed Identity, choose **Access Connector for Databricks**.

22. Now choose **unity-catalog-access-connector**. Click on **Select**.

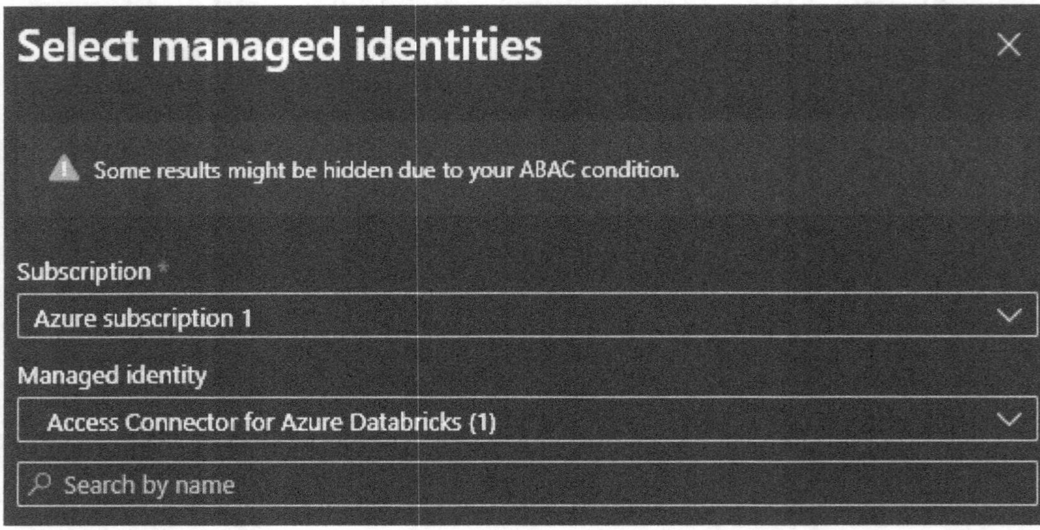

Figure 6.21: Add Databricks role to ADLS

23. Click on **Review + assign**.
24. Using the method above, grant the other three roles to **unity-catalog-access-connector**.
25. To check the access for the managed identity, click on **Check access**. The newly assigned role assignment should be visible for Access Connector for Databricks.

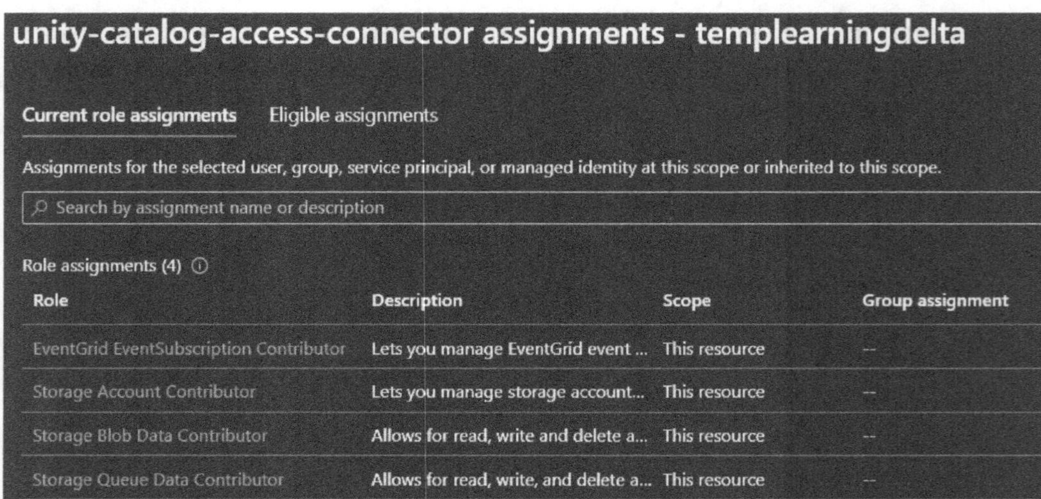

Figure 6.22: Roles required for Databricks access to ADLS

> **Note**
>
> The Access Connector for Azure Databricks is an Azure resource that provides a proxy identity for Databricks. It enables Azure Databricks to authenticate to other Azure services—such as Azure Data Lake Storage Gen2 or Azure Key Vault.

With the access connector now authorized to interact with ADLS, the next step is to establish how Databricks will securely reference and use that storage. This begins with creating storage credentials and external locations in Unity Catalog, which formalize the connection between the platform and your data lake while enforcing consistent governance and access controls.

Creating storage credentials and an external location in Databricks

Reference to *Chapter 5, Understanding Databricks*, a storage credential defines the permissions required for Databricks to authenticate and access data stored outside the platform. These credentials can be tied to both user identities and service-based identities, including those managed through Microsoft Entra ID.

When you configure a Databricks external location, it relies on the assigned storage credential to verify and authorize access to a specific cloud storage path—whether that's Azure Data Lake Storage Gen2, Amazon S3, or Google Cloud Storage.

All external locations are governed through Unity Catalog, which centralizes security, permissions, and oversight. This ensures that the same access rules and governance policies apply consistently across every connected storage system.

When working with ADLS Gen2, every notebook you create must be linked to a storage credential and an external location to access data securely. Let's walk through how these components are set up.

1. Before we create a Databricks credential, we will need the **Access connector ID**. On the Azure portal, search for **unity-catalog-access-connector**. Locate and take note of the **Resource ID**. It will be required in subsequent steps.

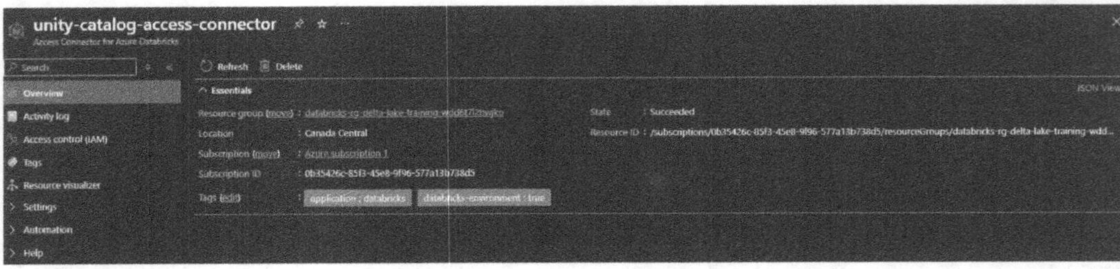

Figure 6.23: Locating the access connector ID

2. Navigate back to the Databricks workspace. Using the menu on the left, click on **Catalog**. Click on **Manage**; it has a gear icon.
3. Select **Credentials**.

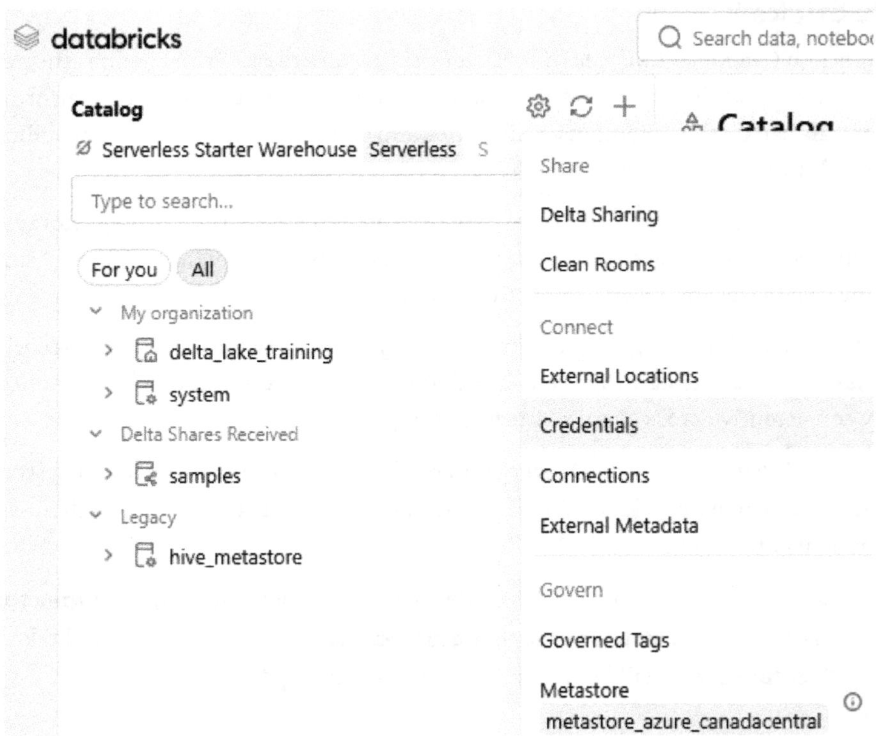

Figure 6.24: Managing Databricks credentials

4. On the next screen, click on **Create credential**.
5. Choose **Storage Credential**.
6. For Credential type, choose **Azure Managed Identity**.

7. For Credential name, enter **delta_credential**.
8. For Access connector ID, paste the *Resource ID* of the unity-catalog-access-connector retrieved previously.

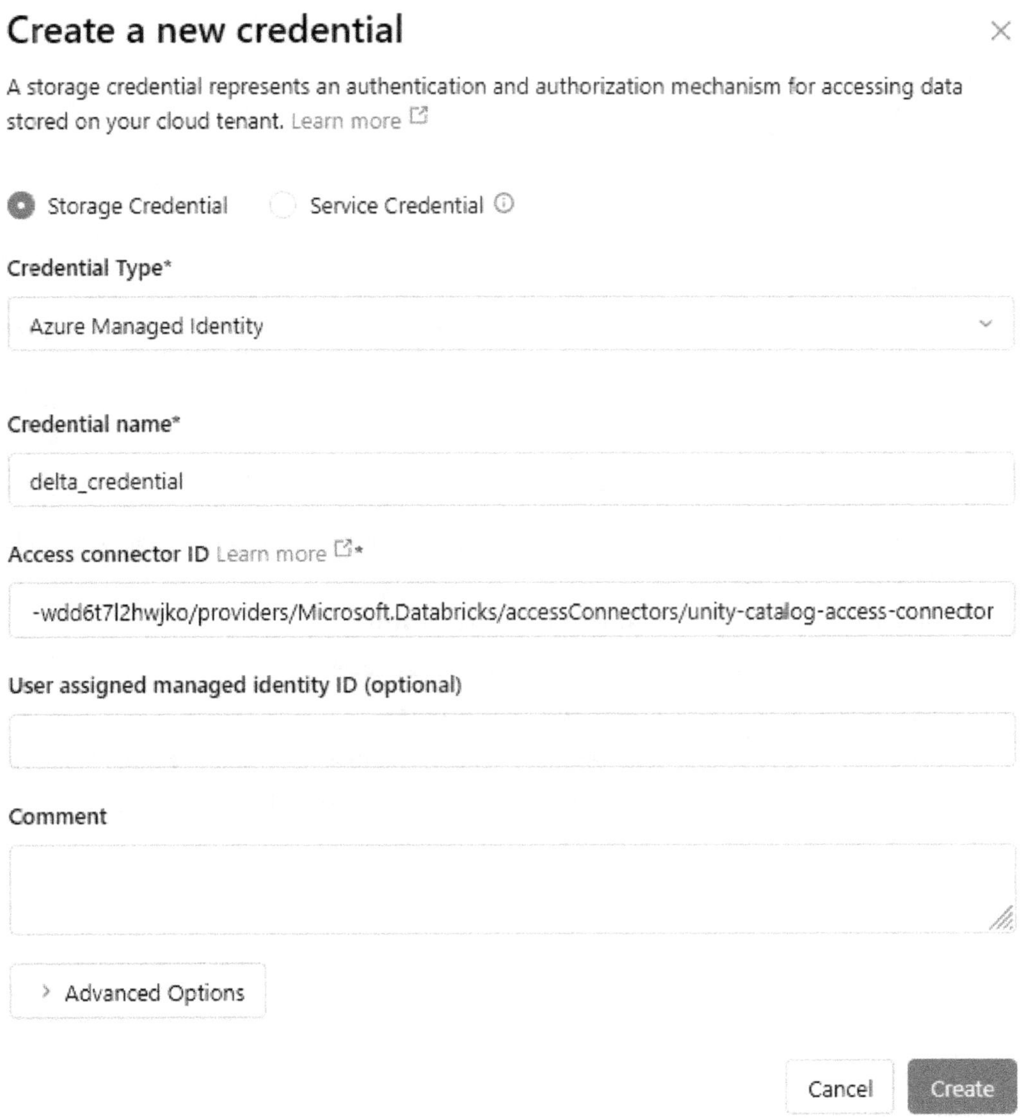

Figure 6.25: Creating a new storage credential

9. Click on **Create**.

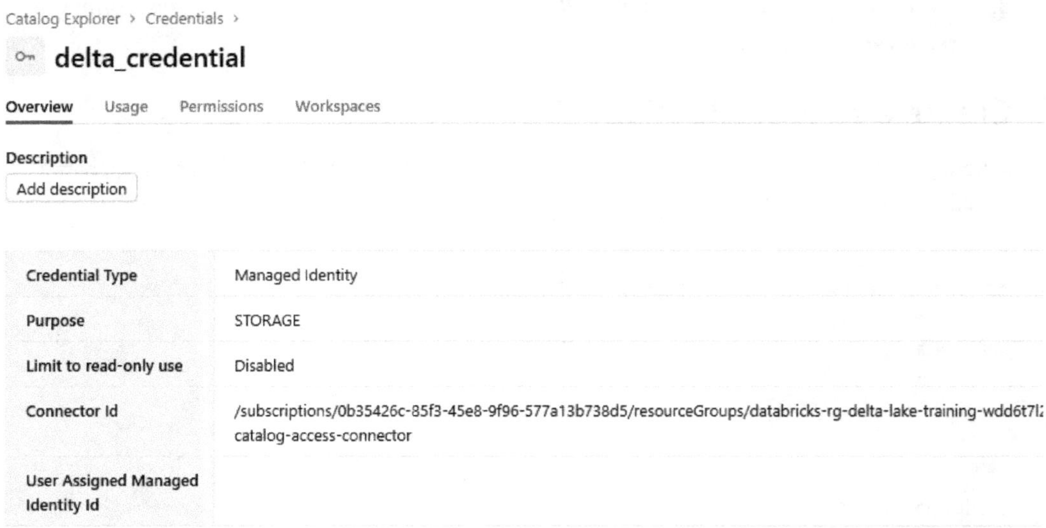

Figure 6.26: Confirmation of new storage credential

10. Using the menu on the left, click on **Catalog**. Click on **Manage**; it has a gear icon. Select **External Locations**.
11. On the next screen, click on **Create external location**.
12. For External location name, enter **delta_external_location**.
13. For Storage type, choose **Azure Data Lake Storage**.
14. For URL, enter **abfss://delta@templearningdelta.dfs.core.windows.net/**. Make sure you replace the Azure Data Lake Storage bucket that was created previously.

15. For Storage credential, choose **delta_credential**.

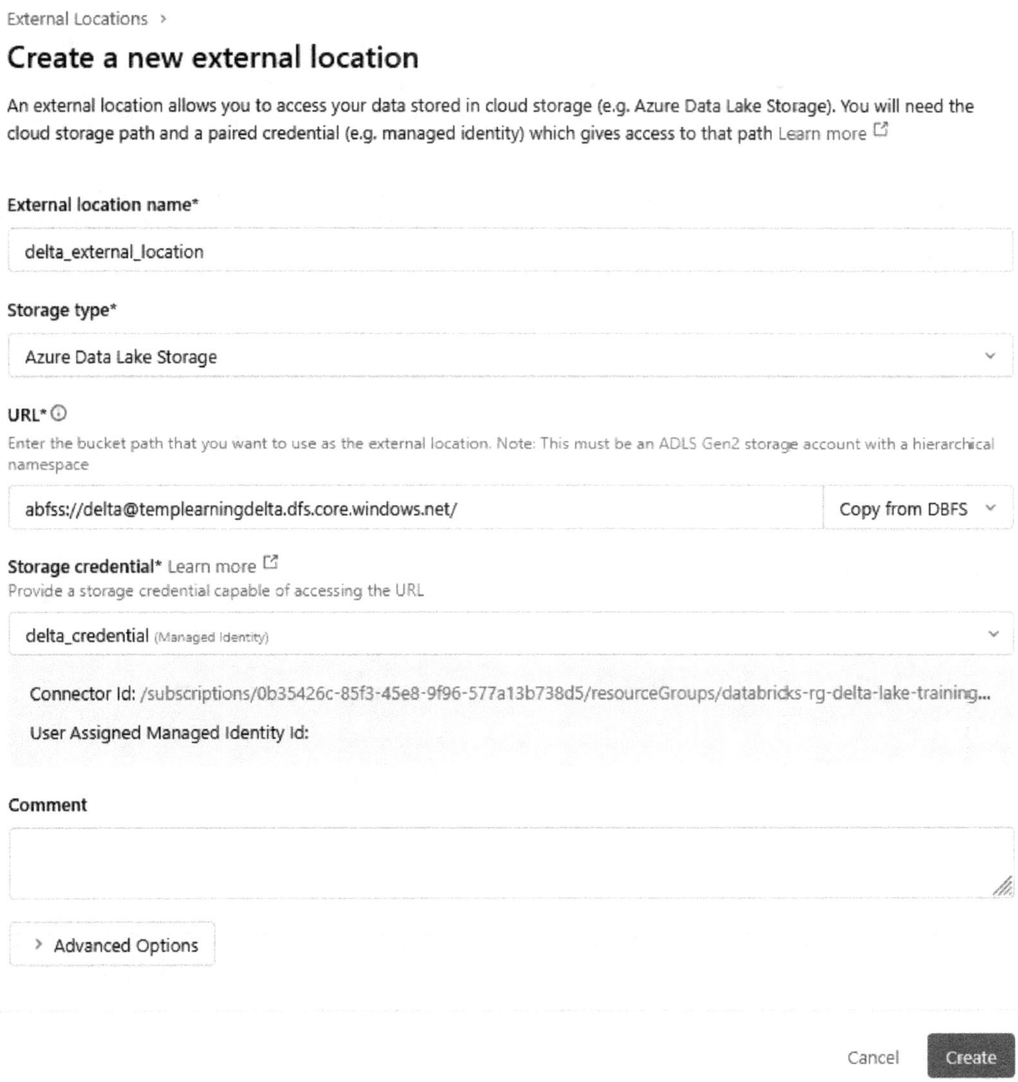

Figure 6.27: Creating a new external location

16. Click on **Create**.

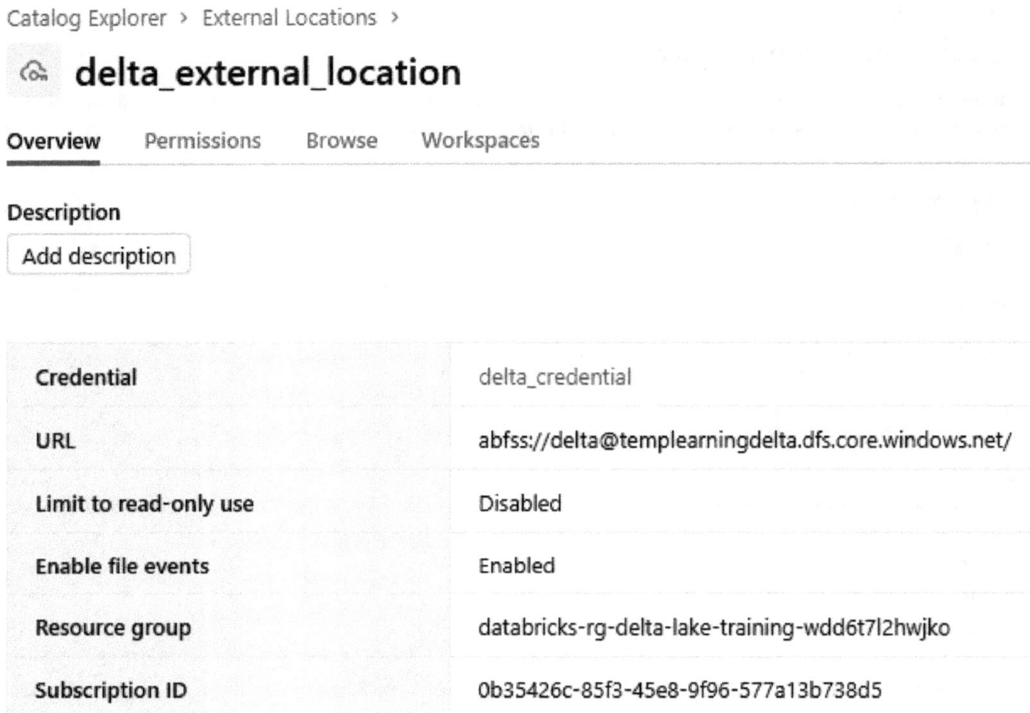

Figure 6.28: Confirmation of new external location

We now have the necessary resource to start running the notebook.

Running the notebook

To continue, we'll need a notebook to serve as our workspace for writing and executing code throughout this exercise. Notebooks provide a browser-based environment where you can run PySpark commands, explore data, and build visual outputs.

Prepare code repository

1. Throughout this book, we will use the *Packt Git course repository*. Git folders can integrate with Git repositories such as GitHub and Bitbucket.
2. On the Databricks workspace, click on **Workspace**, then click on **Repos**. Towards the right, click on **Create Git folder**.
3. For Git repository URL, enter: **https://github.com/PacktPublishing/Data-Engineering-with-Apache-Spark-Databricks-and-Lakehouse-Second-Edition.git**.
4. For the Git provider, choose **GitHub**.
5. For Git folder name, enter **book_code_repository**.

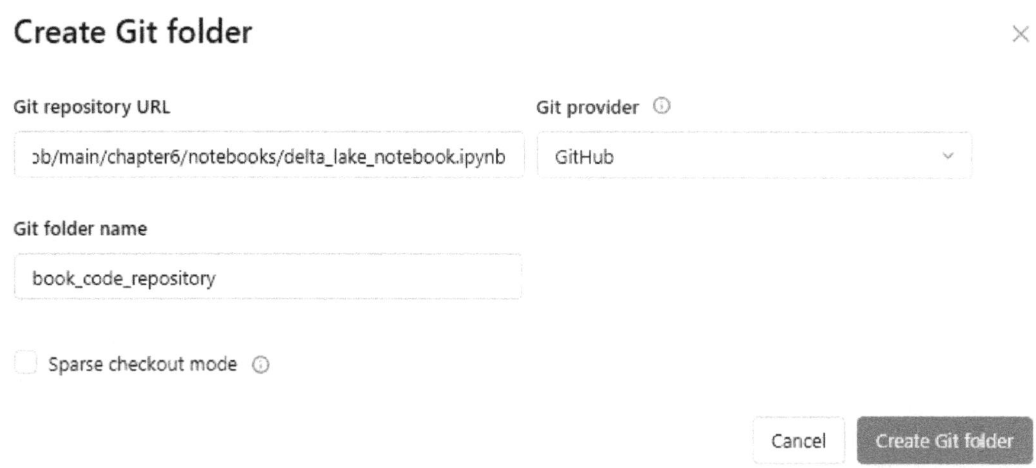

Figure 6.29: Create a git folder

6. Press **Create Git folder**.
7. To run the Delta Lake practice notebook, navigate to **book_code_repository > chapter6 > notebooks > delta_lake_notebook**.

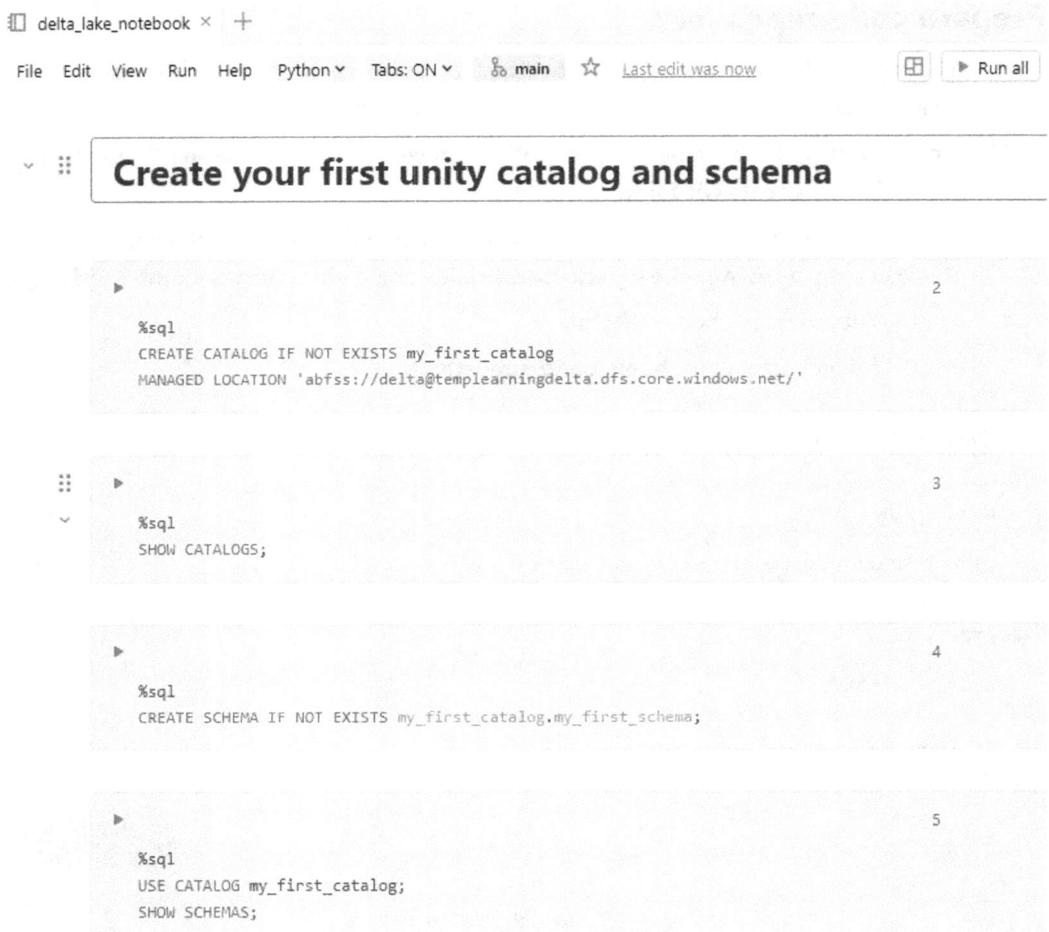

Figure 6.30: delta_lake_notebook ready for use

Databricks notebooks require compute to run, meaning they must be attached to an active cluster or a serverless compute resource before any code can be executed.

Prepare Spark compute cluster

1. The notebook requires a Spark compute cluster. Click on **Connect**.
2. In the **Attach to an existing compute resource** window, for **Compute type**, choose **General compute**.
3. Click on **Create new resource**.
4. For Name, enter **Delta Lake Practice Cluster**.

5. For Instance Type, choose **Standard_DS3_v2**. If this instance type is unavailable in your Azure region, you can select the next higher-class instance as an alternative.
6. Uncheck the **Machine Learning** checkbox.

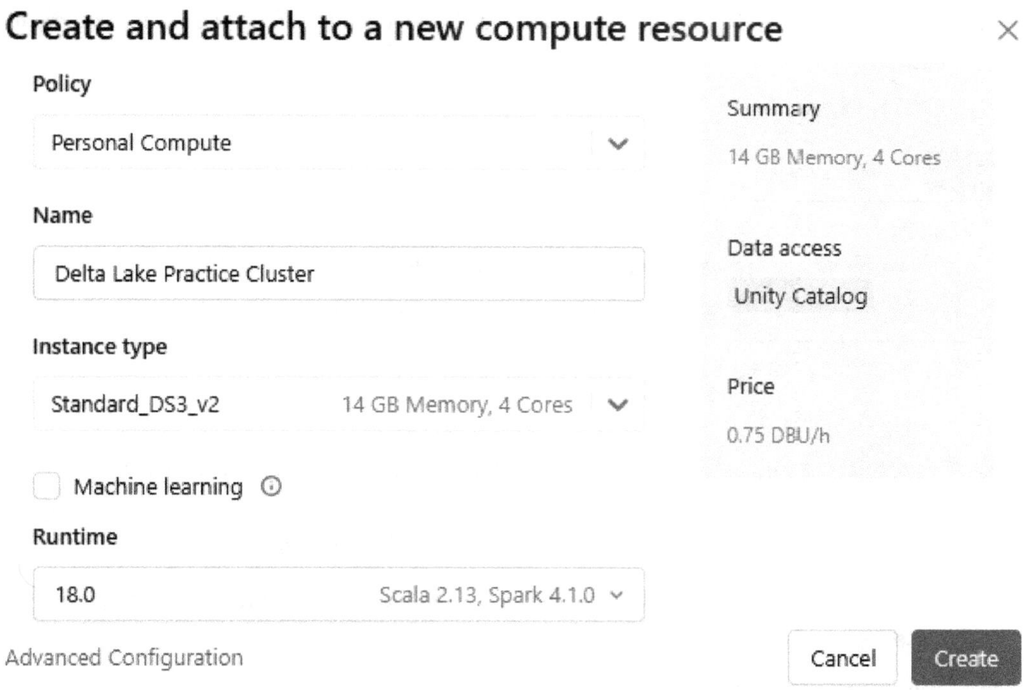

Figure 6.31: Create a new compute cluster

7. Click on **Create**. Wait for a few minutes for the cluster to be provisioned.
8. If you are new to using notebooks, it is highly recommended to visit the following link to get used to some common notebook commands: `https://docs.microsoft.com/en-us/azure/databricks/notebooks/notebooks-use`.

We are ready to execute the code. Focus your attention on the first section of the notebook marked "**Create your first catalog and schema**". This section will create a new Unity Catalog in a managed location.

> **Note**
>
> While running the notebook, you'll notice a direct one-to-one correspondence between the Markdown cells and the section headings. This structure is intentional and helps you easily match each part of the narrative explanation with the code or configuration steps that follow.

With the cluster now available, we can proceed to execute the notebook cells, starting with configuring Unity Catalog.

Create your first Unity Catalog and schema

1. Modify the Azure Storage account name in the first cell to reflect the values you created earlier.
2. Click on **Run**.

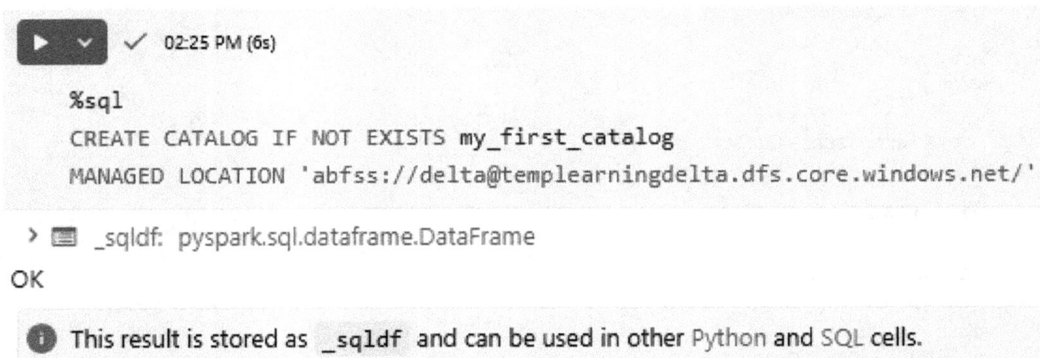

Figure 6.32: Create a new Unity Catalog

3. Open a new Databricks workspace tab, using the menu on the left by clicking on **Catalog**.
4. Notice the newly created Unity Catalog.

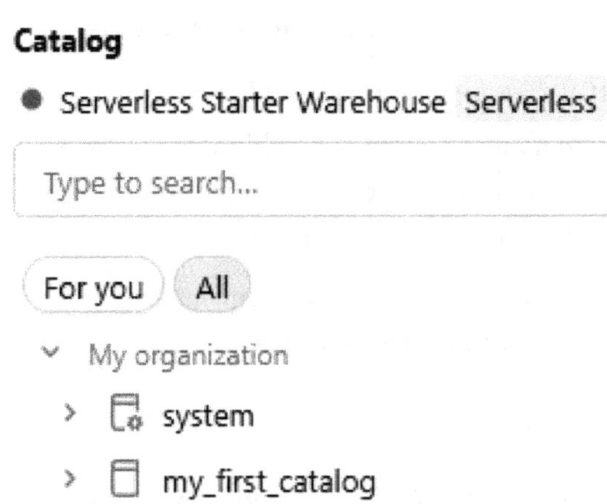

Figure 6.33: Check the newly create Unity catalog

5. Navigate back to the notebook and run the other three cells. The instructions will create a new schema under the newly created catalog.

Figure 6.34: Create a new schema under the newly created Unity Catalog

The Unity Catalog items are now in place, and we're ready to attach the required Python and Spark libraries to support our data engineering workflows.

Import PySpark libraries and DataFrame functions

1. Run the next cell. The first line imports the public classes and functions for Delta Lake in PySpark. The second and third lines import statements commonly used in PySpark to define schemas and use built-in DataFrame functions.

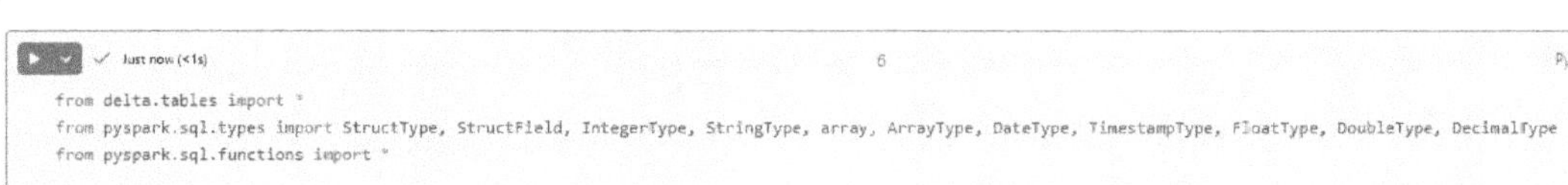

Figure 6.35: Import python libraries

In the next section of the notebook, we generate sample employee data using a list of Python dictionaries.

Create a Pyspark Dataframe

In a typical production environment, the data used to build a DataFrame is sourced from secure, centralized systems—such as databases, data warehouses, APIs, or file-based ingestion pipelines—rather than being manually created within the notebook. With that context in place, the following sequence outlines the steps involved in creating the PySpark DataFrame.

- Create in-memory employee data as a list of Python dictionaries.
- Defines an explicit schema for that data (column names + types).
- Build a Spark DataFrame using the data and schema.
- Converts the `hire_date` column from a string to an actual `DateType`.
- Prints the schema and displays the DataFrame.

Here's how you can do it:

1. Run this cell.

9: Cell 7

```
employee_data = [
    {"emp_id": 1, "emp_name": "John Sean", "dept_id": 101, "salary": 60000.00, "hire_date": "2025-01-15"},
    {"emp_id": 2, "emp_name": "Alice Cooper", "dept_id": 102, "salary": 75000.00, "hire_date": "2025-03-20"},
    {"emp_id": 3, "emp_name": "Bob K.", "dept_id": 101, "salary": 50000.00, "hire_date": "2025-07-10"},
    {"emp_id": 4, "emp_name": "David Harbour", "dept_id": 103, "salary": 82000.00, "hire_date": "2026-02-05"},
    {"emp_id": 5, "emp_name": "Emma Norton", "dept_id": 102, "salary": 67000.00, "hire_date": "2026-01-25"},
    {"emp_id": 6, "emp_name": "Frank Jeff", "dept_id": 103, "salary": 70000.00, "hire_date": "2025-04-15"},
    {"emp_id": 7, "emp_name": "Grace Morgan", "dept_id": 104, "salary": 55000.00, "hire_date": "2026-01-09"},
    {"emp_id": 8, "emp_name": "Henry J. Knott", "dept_id": 104, "salary": 60000.00, "hire_date": "2025-06-03"},
    {"emp_id": 9, "emp_name": "Ivy Lee", "dept_id": 101, "salary": 72000.00, "hire_date": "2025-09-18"},
    {"emp_id": 10, "emp_name": "Jack White", "dept_id": 103, "salary": 65000.00, "hire_date": "2026-02-08"},
]

schema = StructType([
    StructField("emp_id", IntegerType(), True),
    StructField("emp_name", StringType(), True),
    StructField("dept_id", IntegerType(), True),
    StructField("salary", DoubleType(), True),
    StructField("hire_date", StringType(), True)
])

df_employees = spark.createDataFrame(employee_data, schema=schema)

df_employees = df_employees.withColumn("hire_date", to_date("hire_date"))

df_employees.printSchema()
df_employees.show()
```

Figure 6.36: Create a new dataframe that stores employee records

2. Check the output of this cell. It displays the schema and the `dataframe` content.

```
root
 |-- emp_id: integer (nullable = true)
 |-- emp_name: string (nullable = true)
 |-- dept_id: integer (nullable = true)
 |-- salary: double (nullable = true)
 |-- hire_date: date (nullable = true)

+------+-------------+-------+-------+----------+
|emp_id|     emp_name|dept_id| salary| hire_date|
+------+-------------+-------+-------+----------+
|     1|    John Sean|    101|60000.0|2025-01-15|
|     2| Alice Cooper|    102|75000.0|2025-03-20|
|     3|       Bob K.|    101|50000.0|2025-07-10|
|     4|David Harbour|    103|82000.0|2026-02-05|
|     5|  Emma Norton|    102|67000.0|2026-01-25|
|     6|   Frank Jeff|    103|70000.0|2025-04-15|
|     7| Grace Morgan|    104|55000.0|2026-01-09|
|     8|Henry J. Knott|    104|60000.0|2025-06-03|
|     9|      Ivy Lee|    101|72000.0|2025-09-18|
|    10|   Jack White|    103|65000.0|2026-02-08|
+------+-------------+-------+-------+----------+
```

Figure 6.37: Data for the new dataframe that stores employee records

> **Note**
>
> `StructType` lets you explicitly define your DataFrame's schema, giving you full control over data types and structure. However, manually defining schemas becomes less practical when working with a large number of DataFrames.

In the next three cells, we create a new Delta-managed table in Databricks using the employee DataFrame defined earlier.

Create a Delta table and apply partitioning to optimize query performance

1. The `DataFrameWriter` API writes the data in Delta format into a table called `employees`. The write mode is configured as `append`, meaning new records are added without overwriting existing data. This write pattern is typical for bronze-layer ingestion pipelines, where raw data is continuously collected in an immutable fashion.
2. Run the next three cells.

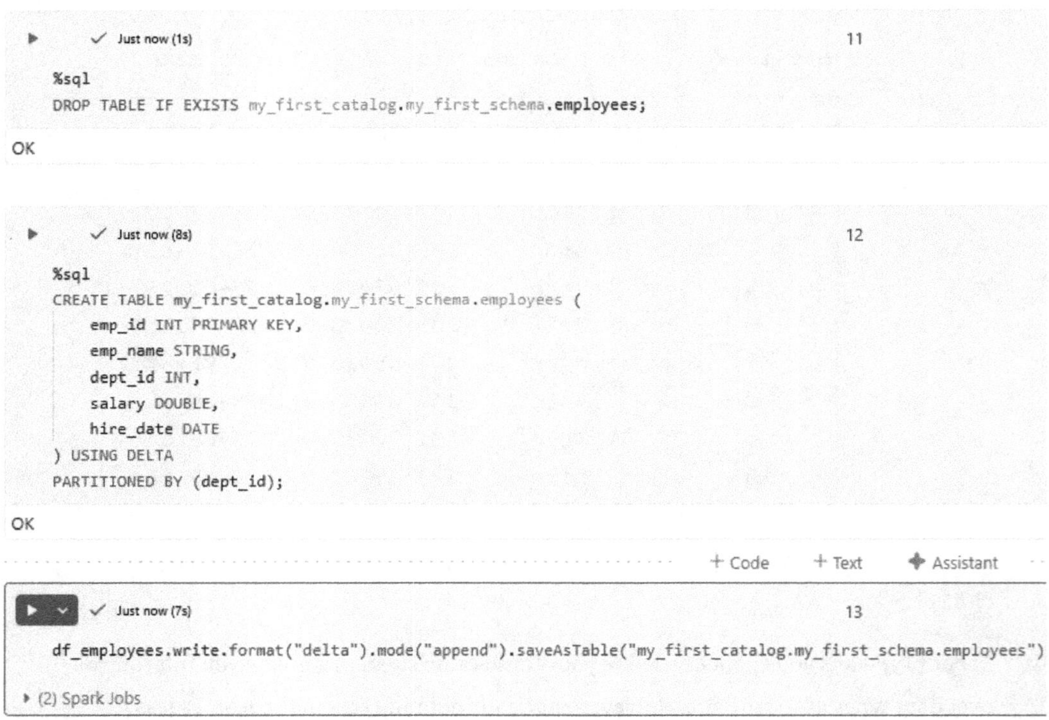

Figure 6.38: Creating a new managed delta table

3. Spark automatically stores the data of the Delta table inside the default metastore location. Let's go back to the Azure Storage account and check the delta files. On the Azure portal, navigate to **Home** > **templearningdelta** > **delta**. Click on **__unitystorage** > **catalogs**. Inside this folder, you will find a directory whose ID will match the `my_first_catalog` ID in the Unity catalog.

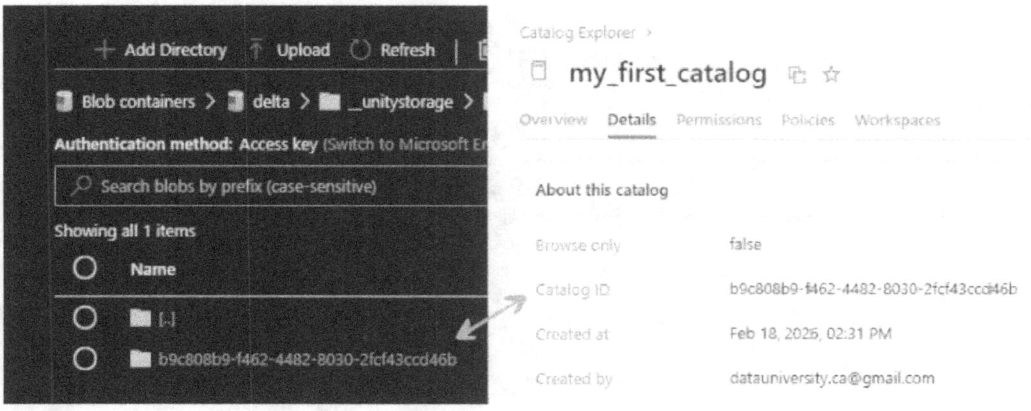

Figure 6.39: Unity Catalog ID in storage location vs. Unity Catalog

4. On the Azure portal, click on the **<catalog_id> > tables**.
5. Like the catalog, the ID in this folder should correspond to the `employees` table in the Unity Catalog.

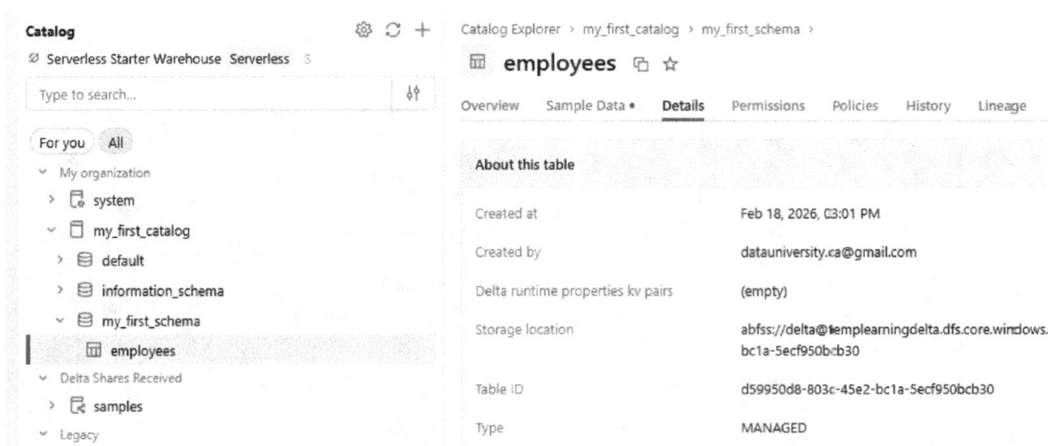

Figure 6.40: Corresponding table ID in the Unity Catalog

6. Click on the **<table_id>**. This folder contains a partitioned folder structure for the `employees` table.

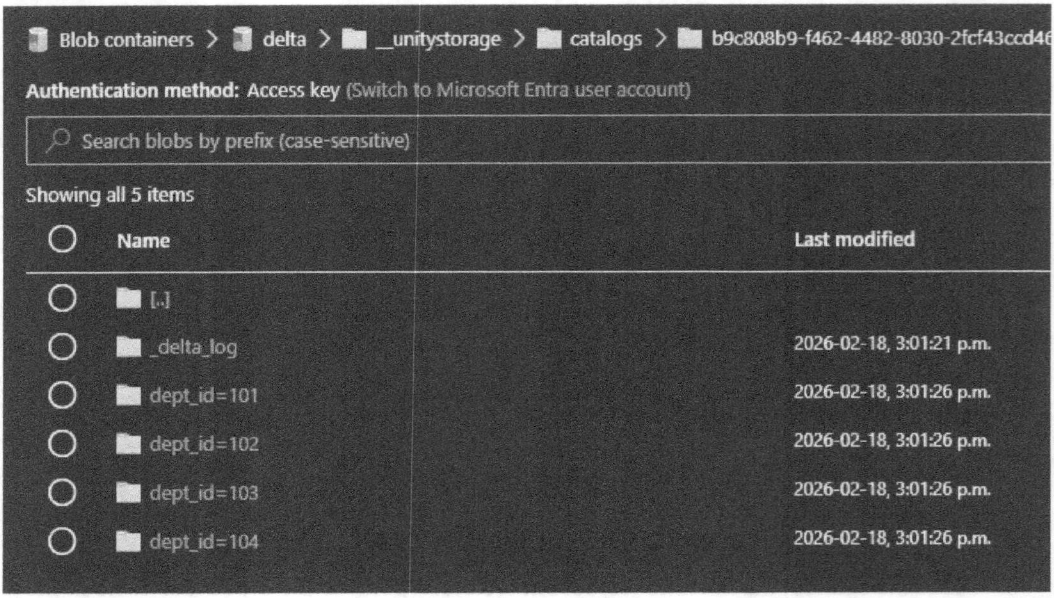

Figure 6.41: Partitioned delta table

7. Click on any partitioned folder. The partitioned folder contains the data for that partition in parquet format.

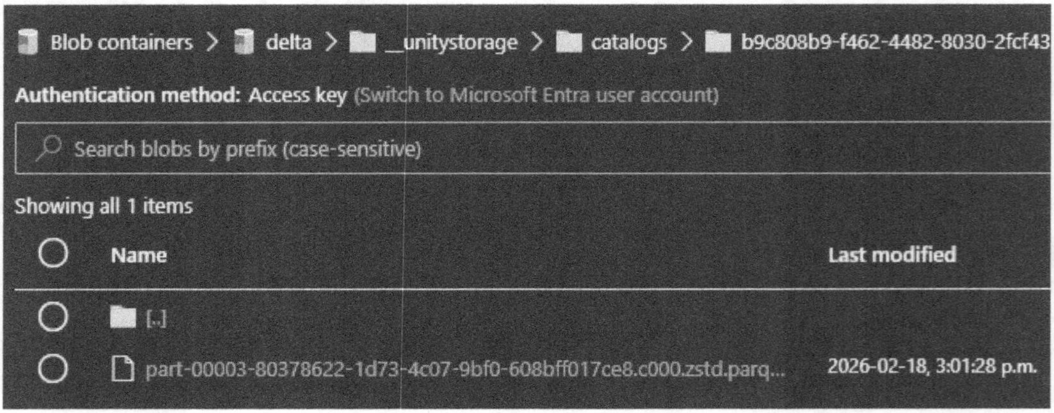

Figure 6.42: Contents of the partitioned folder

Partitioning plays an important role in optimizing query performance by enabling Spark to avoid scanning unnecessary data. Using a technique called partition pruning, Spark reads only the partitions that match the query filters, rather than scanning the entire table directory. These filters—known as **predicates**—are the conditions in your

WHERE clause that Spark evaluates to determine which partitions can be skipped entirely.

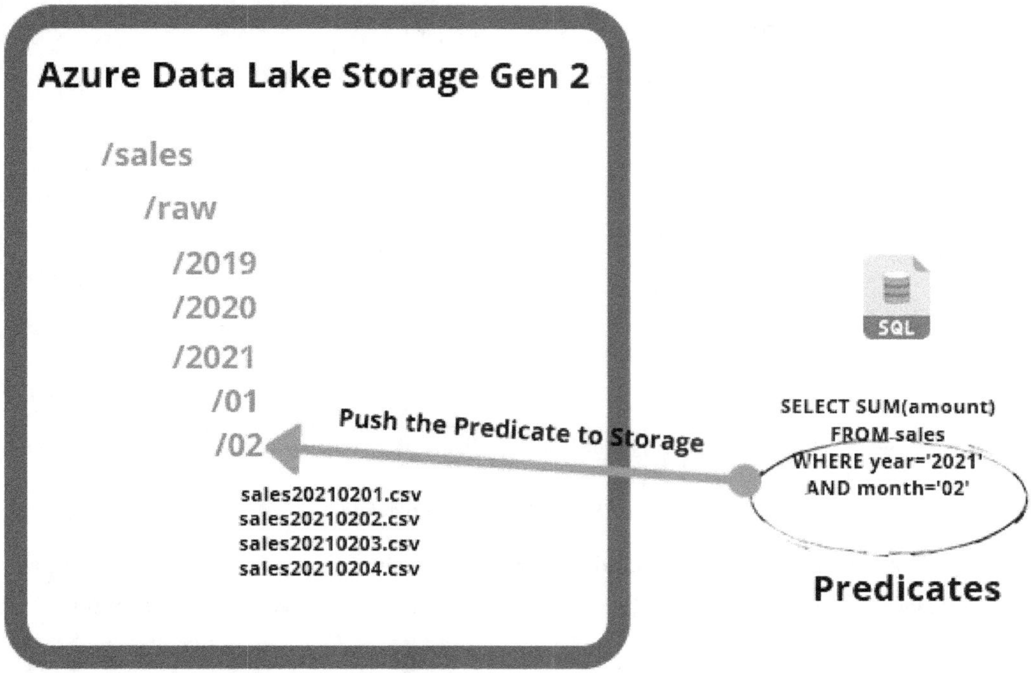

Figure 6.43: Spark partition pruning

> **Note**
>
> Partitioned Delta tables improve performance and efficiency by organizing data into directory-based segments according to commonly filtered columns.

With the partitioned Delta table created, we can now inspect its contents.

Check the Delta table data and details

1. Run the next two cells. The first cell simply shows you the contents of the newly created Delta table.

Figure 6.44: Delta table data

The `DESCRIBE DETAIL` command shows the metadata about a Delta table. It's a quick way to see its properties, such as location, size, number of files, and partitioning details.

2. Run the next cell.

Figure 6.45: Delta table details

Now let's check the version history of the newly created Delta table.

Check Delta history

1. Run the following cell.

Figure 6.46: Delta table history

2. Delta table history always begins with version 0. Each operation—such as an insert, update, or delete—creates exactly one new table version and records the details of what changed in that commit.
3. It would be interesting to check how this history corresponds to what was written in Azure storage.
4. Go back to the Azure Storage account and click on **_delta_log** folder. This directory, within every Delta table, stores JSON and checkpoint files that describe every change ever made to the table.

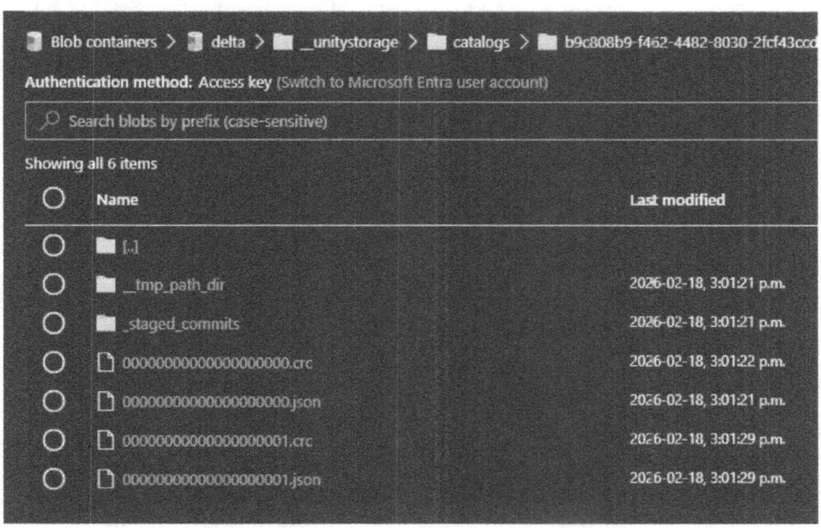

Figure 6.47: Contents of the _delta_log folder

5. On the storage side, the delta transaction history is stored in JSON and checkpoint files inside the `_delta_log` directory of the table. Each JSON file corresponds to one version of the Delta table and records exactly what changed in that commit. Notice in the

image above that there are two JSON files - `00000000000000000000.json` and `00000000000000000001.json`. They correspond to the following two versions in the delta log history.

> **Note**
>
> Delta Lake stores its table-level metadata in JSON transaction log files, beginning with `00000000000000000000.json`. This initial file contains the foundational metadata that aligns with the information returned when running the `DESCRIBEDETAIL` command in the notebook.

We can now turn our attention to the generated column feature in Delta Lake, which is especially useful for defining calculated columns that are automatically maintained by the system.

Create a Delta table with a generated column

Delta Lake allows you to define generated columns—fields whose values are automatically derived from an expression that references other columns in the table.

1. Run the next two cells. You'll see the `hire_year` column, which is generated from the `hire_date` value. Keep in mind that this column is calculated during data insertion and does not originate from the source data.

Just now (2s) 20

```
%sql
CREATE TABLE my_first_catalog.my_first_schema.employees_gen (
    emp_id INT,
    emp_name STRING,
    dept_id INT,
    salary DOUBLE,
    hire_date DATE,
    hire_year INT GENERATED ALWAYS AS (YEAR(hire_date))
) USING DELTA
PARTITIONED BY (dept_id);
```

> _sqldf: pyspark.sql.dataframe.DataFrame

OK

This result is stored as `_sqldf` and can be used in other Python and SQL cells.

Just now (2s) 21

```
df_employees.write.format("delta").mode("append").saveAsTable("my_first_catalog.my_first_schema.employees_gen")
```

Figure 6.48: Delta table with generated column

> **Note**
>
> The generated columns capability in Delta ta DML operations is fully supported on Delta tables, allowing you to insert, update, delete, and merge data with ACID reliability. This is especially useful in the silver and gold layers of the medallion architecture, where transformed data is required.

2. Run the next cell. Check the data that has been calculated in the `hire_year` column.

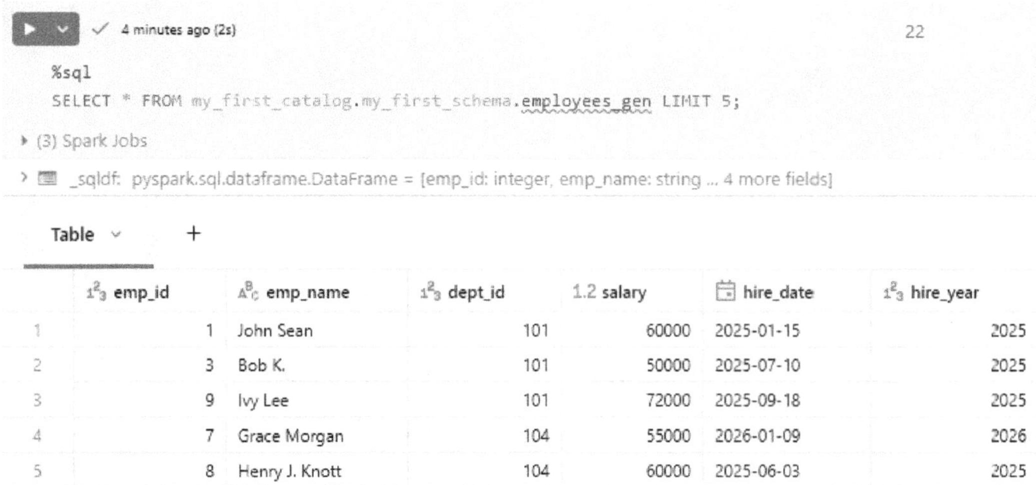

Figure 6.49: Data in the Delta table with a generated column

Data naturally evolves over time, and Delta Lake is designed to handle that change gracefully. Let's learn how Delta Lake handles DML operations.

Perform DML operations in the Delta table

As discussed previously, Delta Lake brings full ACID transactional capabilities to your Lakehouse, so you can run standard SQL data manipulation commands—`INSERT`, `UPDATE`, `DELETE`, and `MERGE`—directly against Delta tables with reliability and consistency. Each DML statement produces a new table version that captures the exact change in the transaction log.

Perform DML operations in the Delta table - INSERT

1. Run the next cell to insert a new record in the Delta table.

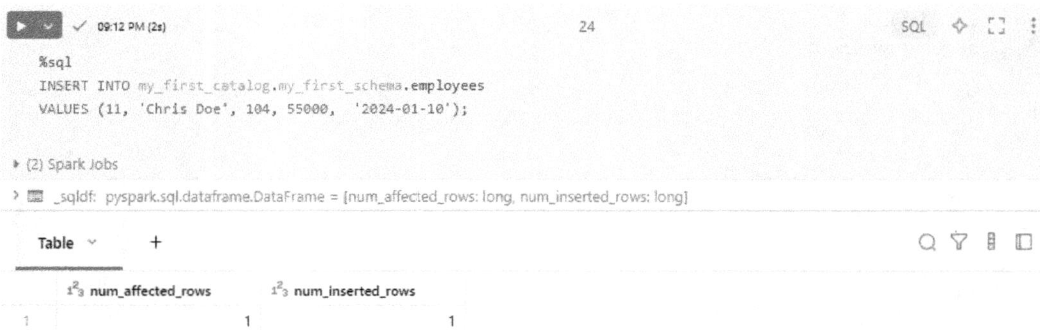

Figure 6.50: Insert a new record in the Delta table

2. The insert operation creates a new version in Delta table history.

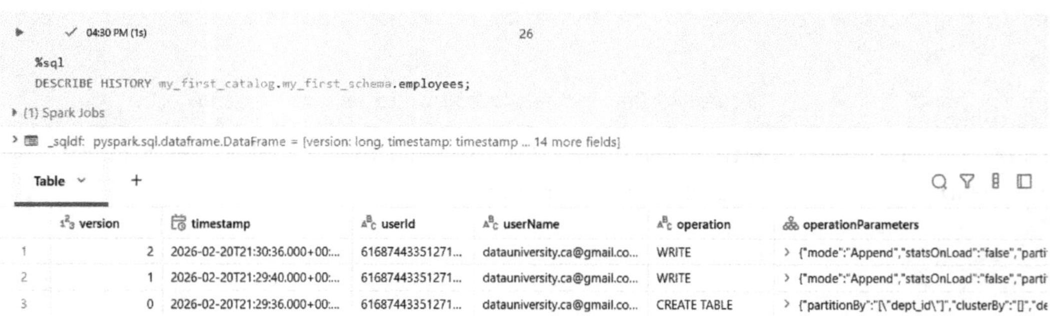

Figure 6.51: Delta table history after an insert operation

We now check how the Delta table reacts to an update.

Perform DML operations in the Delta table – UPDATE

Next, we'll perform an update operation—with a slight twist. This time, we'll also include user-defined metadata in the form of table comments to capture additional context about the change.

1. Run the next cell. The insert operation creates a new version in the Delta table history.

✓ Just now (<1s)

```
spark.conf.set(
    "spark.databricks.delta.commitInfo.userMetadata",
    "This row was updated because of a salary change of the employee."
)
```

Figure 6.52: Record userMetaData for a Delta table

2. Run the next two cells. A couple of things to note here. The update operation creates a new version in Delta table history.

Table

	version	timestamp	userId	userName	operation	operationParameters
1	3	2026-02-20T21:31:13.00...	61687443351271...	datauniversity.ca@gmail.c...	UPDATE	> {"predicate":"["(emp_id#3828 = 5)"]"}
2	2	2026-02-20T21:30:36.00...	61687443351271...	datauniversity.ca@gmail.c...	WRITE	> {"mode":"Append","statsOnLoad":"false","parti.
3	1	2026-02-20T21:29:40.00...	61687443351271...	datauniversity.ca@gmail.c...	WRITE	> {"mode":"Append","statsOnLoad":"false","parti.
0	0	2026-02-20T21:29:36.00...	61687443351271...	datauniversity.ca@gmail.c...	CREATE TABLE	> {"partitionBy": "[\"dept_id\"]", "clusterBy":"[]", "d

Figure 6.53: Delta table history after an update operation

3. Scroll towards the right on the history output panel. Notice that the `userMetadata` has been recorded for this transaction.

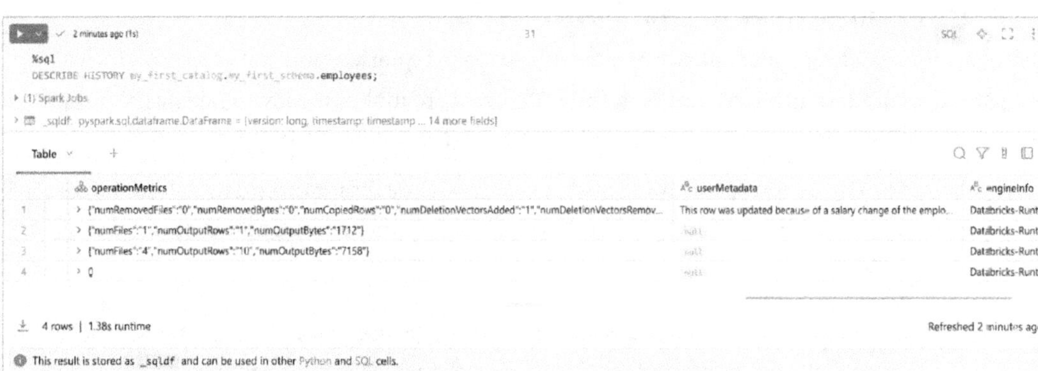

Figure 6.54: userMetaData recorded in the history of the update transaction

Including `userMetadata` is especially valuable during audits, as it helps document the reason behind each change. We now check how the Delta table reacts to deletes.

Perform DML operations in the Delta table – DELETE

1. Run the next three cells. The delete operation creates a new version in the Delta table history.

Figure 6.55: Delta table history after a delete operation

2. You may have noticed the latest history of the table has advanced twice. There is a new version with the `OPTIMIZE` operation. There is a reason for this. When autoOptimize is set to TRUE, Delta will automatically compact files after your transaction, creating an extra commit that appears as an `OPTIMIZE` after the `DELETE`.

> **Note**
>
> In many big data environments, repeated write activity often leads to a buildup of small files—a challenge known as the small-file problem. Delta Lake's Auto Optimize feature helps alleviate this by intelligently controlling file sizes both at write time and through background compaction. Generally, it is recommended that you OPTIMIZE right after a large batch load.

A standout capability of Delta Lake is its time travel support, which allows you to query and restore earlier versions of a table.

Perform time-travel in the Delta table

Using options such as `versionAsOf` or timestamp-based queries, you can access historical snapshots created at different points in time. This feature makes it easy to revisit prior data states—ideal for debugging, auditing, and recovering from unintended changes.

1. Imagine the operator had an "oops" moment—they didn't intend to delete that record. Based on the table history, the version right before the delete operation is `version 3`.

> **Note**
>
> Delta Lake's time-travel capability naturally provides data lineage, an essential component for audits and regulatory compliance. This built-in lineage allows

> teams to trace how data has changed over time, making it invaluable for identifying and investigating data anomalies.

2. Run the next cell to view the previous snapshot and confirm the deleted record. Note the use of `VERSION AS OF` in the SQL below. You may need to edit the version number as per your history data above.

✓ Just now (2s) 37

```
%%sql
SELECT * FROM my_first_catalog.my_first_schema.employees VERSION AS OF 3 WHERE emp_id=5;
```

▸ (3) Spark Jobs

> _sqldf: pyspark.sql.dataframe.DataFrame = [emp_id: integer, emp_name: string ... 3 more fields]

Table +

	emp_id	emp_name	dept_id	salary	hire_date
1	5	Emma Norton	102	90000	2026-01-25

Figure 6.56: Delta table time-travel using version number

3. Run the next cell. You can time-travel using a timestamp instead of a version number. Note the use of `TIMESTAMP AS OF` in the SQL below. You may need to edit the timestamp as per your history data above.

✓ Just now (2s) 38

```
%%sql
SELECT * FROM my_first_catalog.my_first_schema.employees TIMESTAMP AS OF '2026-02-22
```

▸ (3) Spark Jobs

> _sqldf: pyspark.sql.dataframe.DataFrame = [emp_id: integer, emp_name: string ... 3 more fields]

Table +

	emp_id	emp_name	dept_id	salary	hire_date
1	5	Emma Norton	102	90000	2026-01-25

Figure 6.57: Delta table time-travel using timestamp

4. The operator can breathe a sigh of relief—Delta tables can be restored to any earlier version. Run the next cell to return the table to the state it was in before the record was accidentally deleted.

✓ 1 minute ago (60s) 39

```
%sql
RESTORE TABLE my_first_catalog.my_first_schema.employees TO VERSION AS OF 3;
SELECT * FROM my_first_catalog.my_first_schema.employees WHERE emp_id=5;
```

▸ (18) Spark Jobs

› _sqldf: pyspark.sql.dataframe.DataFrame = [emp_id: integer, emp_name: string ... 3 more fields]

Table

	emp_id	emp_name	dept_id	salary	hire_date
1	5	Emma Norton	102	90000	2026-01-25

Figure 6.58: Delta table time-travel using timestamp

5. The record is back. Run the next cell. The restore operation creates a new version in Delta table history.

✓ Just now (2s) 40

```
%sql
DESCRIBE HISTORY my_first_catalog.my_first_schema.employees;
```

▸ (1) Spark Jobs

› _sqldf: pyspark.sql.dataframe.DataFrame = [version: long, timestamp: timestamp ... 14 more fields]

Table

	version	timestamp	userId	userName	operation	operationParameters
1	6	2026-02-20T21:40:55.000+00:...	61687443351271...	datauniversity.ca@gmail.co...	RESTORE	› {"version":"3","timestamp":null}
2	5	2026-02-20T21:31:24.000+00:...	61687443351271...	datauniversity.ca@gmail.co...	OPTIMIZE	› {"predicate":"[\"('dept_id <=> cast(102 as int))\
3	4	2026-02-20T21:31:23.000+00:...	61687443351271...	datauniversity.ca@gmail.co...	DELETE	› {"predicate":"[\"(emp_id#4678 = 5)\"]"}
4	3	2026-02-20T21:31:13.000+00:...	61687443351271...	datauniversity.ca@gmail.co...	UPDATE	› {"predicate":"[\"(emp_id#3828 = 5)\"]"}
5	2	2026-02-20T21:30:36.000+00:...	61687443351271...	datauniversity.ca@gmail.co...	WRITE	› {"mode":"Append","statsOnLoad":"false","partit
6	1	2026-02-20T21:29:40.000+00:...	61687443351271...	datauniversity.ca@gmail.co...	WRITE	› {"mode":"Append","statsOnLoad":"false","partit
7	0	2026-02-20T21:29:36.000+00:...	61687443351271...	datauniversity.ca@gmail.co...	CREATE TABLE	› {"partitionBy":"[\"dept_id\"]","clusterBy":"[]","de

Figure 6.59: Delta table history after the restore process

Delta Lake's time travel restore feature provides a robust, built-in safeguard against accidental data deletions, allowing teams to revert to earlier versions of tables with ease. This capability also enables engineers to recreate historical reports exactly as they appeared at any point in time, ensuring consistent and reliable results across the organization.

Up to this point, we've executed DML operations as individual statements. In real production workloads, however, DML is typically applied in batches. Let's now explore how Delta Lake handles batch-based CDC using the MERGE operation.

Perform the CDC merge in the Delta table

Delta Lake supports **upserts** through the MERGE operation, allowing new records to be seamlessly appended to existing data in a table. This approach is essential in the Lakehouse architecture, where incremental data is frequently ingested and merged into established Delta tables. Each time fresh data arrives, the MERGE process updates existing rows or inserts new ones as needed, helping maintain a consistent and reliable single source of truth in the silver layer of the lakehouse.

1. To illustrate an upsert operation, assume we've just ingested three CDC records from the source: two records (`emp_id` = 2 and `emp_id` = 11) already exist in the `Employees` table, and one new record (`emp_id` = 12). Run the next cell to create a PySpark dataframe of the CDC records. Run the next cell.

Just now (1s) 42

```
employees_cdc_data = [
    {"emp_id": 2, "emp_name": "Alice Cooper", "dept_id": 102, "salary": 80000.00, "hire_date": "2025-03-20"},
    {"emp_id": 11, "emp_name": "Jack Mathew", "dept_id": 104, "salary": 50000.00, "hire_date": "2026-02-10"},
    {"emp_id": 12, "emp_name": "Kristen Johnson", "dept_id": 103, "salary": 45000.00, "hire_date": "2025-02-10"}
]

df_employees_cdc = spark.createDataFrame(employee_cdc_data, schema)
df_employees_cdc = df_employees_cdc.withColumn("hire_date", to_date("hire_date"))
display(df_employees_cdc)
df_employees_cdc.createOrReplaceTempView("cdc_employees")
```

(2) Spark Jobs

df_employees_cdc: pyspark.sql.dataframe.DataFrame = [emp_id: integer, emp_name: string ... 3 more fields]

Table +

	emp_id	emp_name	dept_id	salary	hire_date
1	2	Alice Cooper	102	80000	2025-03-20
2	11	Jack Mathew	104	50000	2026-02-10
3	12	Kristen Johnson	103	45000	2025-02-10

Figure 6.60: CDC records received from ingested data

2. Before we perform the upsert, let us check the current state of a record (`emp_id` = 2) of the `Employees` table.

```
%sql
SELECT * FROM my_first_catalog.my_first_schema.employees WHERE emp_id=2;
```

▸ (2) Spark Jobs

> _sqldf: pyspark.sql.dataframe.DataFrame = [emp_id: integer, emp_name: string ... 3 more fields]

	emp_id	emp_name	dept_id	salary	hire_date
1	2	Alice Cooper	102	75000	2025-03-20

Figure 6.61: Checking the state of the record before upsert operation

3. Run the next cell to check the count of the `Employees` table.

```
%sql
SELECT count(*) FROM my_first_catalog.my_first_schema.employees;
```

▸ (2) Spark Jobs

> _sqldf: pyspark.sql.dataframe.DataFrame = [count(1): long]

	count(1)
1	11

Figure 6.62: Checking the count of records before the upsert operation.

4. Run the next cell. Notice the upsert operation has updated two existing records and inserted a new one.

5 minutes ago (9s) 45

```sql
%sql
MERGE INTO my_first_catalog.my_first_schema.employees
USING cdc_employees
ON cdc_employees.emp_id = my_first_catalog.my_first_schema.employees.emp_id
WHEN MATCHED THEN
  UPDATE SET *
WHEN NOT MATCHED THEN
  INSERT *
```

(10) Spark Jobs

_sqldf: pyspark.sql.dataframe.DataFrame = [num_affected_rows: long, num_updated_rows: long ... 2 more fields]

Table

	num_affected_rows	num_updated_rows	num_deleted_rows	num_inserted_rows
1	3	2	0	1

Figure 6.63: Delta Lake merge process

5. Run the next cell. Check the state of the merged records.

Just now (2s) 46

```sql
%sql
SELECT * FROM my_first_catalog.my_first_schema.employees WHERE emp_id=2
UNION
SELECT * FROM my_first_catalog.my_first_schema.employees WHERE emp_id=11
UNION
SELECT * FROM my_first_catalog.my_first_schema.employees WHERE emp_id=12;
```

(2) Spark Jobs

_sqldf: pyspark.sql.dataframe.DataFrame = [emp_id: integer, emp_name: string ... 3 more fields]

Table

	emp_id	emp_name	dept_id	salary	hire_date
1	2	Alice Cooper	102	80000	2025-03-20
2	11	Jack Mathew	104	50000	2026-02-10
3	12	Kristen Johnson	103	45000	2025-02-10

Figure 6.64: State of the records before the upsert operation.

6. Run the next cell. The merge operation creates a new version in the Delta table history.

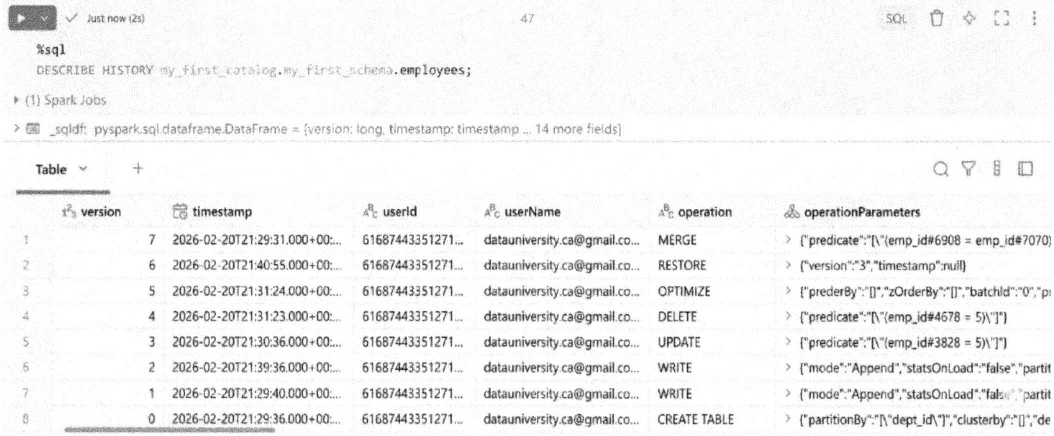

Figure 6.65: Delta table history after the merge process

We just performed a Delta Lake `MERGE`, assuming that the schema of the target Delta table and the incoming CDC data are perfectly aligned. In practice, that's not always the case. Schema drift—such as new columns, missing fields, or unexpected data types—can occur in upstream systems, and Delta Lake provides mechanisms to handle these changes safely and predictably. Let's find out how Delta Lake handles schema drifts.

Perform CDC merge in the Delta table with schema evolution

As businesses grow, requirements shift, and new data sources emerge, so schemas change. In modern data platforms, there is a constant pressure to adapt to schema evolution. As data systems grow and new functionality is introduced, structural changes to data are unavoidable. In other words, schema evolution is guaranteed. Because of this, the ability to seamlessly adapt to evolving schemas becomes a critical requirement for modern data pipelines.

Typically, development begins with well-defined base schemas for tables early in the project. However, by the time pipelines reach production, it's highly likely that the schema of at least one incoming file or table has changed—sometimes subtly, sometimes significantly.

1. Run the next cell. One fine day, the data source sends you data with an extra column named `birth_date`. Fortunately, Delta Lake not only protects your data through strict schema validation but also enables automatic schema evolution, without requiring table versioning or rewriting historical records with placeholder fields.

```python
cdc_data1 = [
    {"emp_id": 13, "emp_name": "Jane Marry", "dept_id": 102, "salary": 85000.00, "hire_date": "2025-02-22", "birth_date": "1968-02-12"},
    {"emp_id": 14, "emp_name": "Andrew Anderson", "dept_id": 103, "salary": 55000.00, "hire_date": "2026-02-11", "birth_date":
    "1971-06-02"},
    {"emp_id": 15, "emp_name": "Carl Degz", "dept_id": 102, "salary": 75000.00, "hire_date": "2026-02-11", "birth_date": "1976-12-11"}
]

df_employees_cdc1 = spark.createDataFrame(cdc_data1)
df_employees_cdc1 = df_employees_cdc1.withColumn("hire_date", to_date("hire_date"))
df_employees_cdc1.show()
df_employees_cdc1.printSchema()
df_employees_cdc1.createOrReplaceTempView("cdc_employees_1")
```

```
▸ (2) Spark Jobs
> df_employees_cdc1: pyspark.sql.dataframe.DataFrame = [birth_date: string, dept_id: long ... 4 more fields]

+----------+-------+------+---------------+----------+-------+
|birth_date|dept_id|emp_id|       emp_name| hire_date| salary|
+----------+-------+------+---------------+----------+-------+
|1968-02-12|    102|    13|     Jane Marry|2025-02-22|85000.0|
|1971-06-02|    103|    14|Andrew Anderson|2026-02-11|55000.0|
|1976-12-11|    102|    15|      Carl Degz|2026-02-11|75000.0|
+----------+-------+------+---------------+----------+-------+
```

Figure 6.66: Data arrives with a modified schema

2. When new data arrives, Delta Lake automatically compares its schema to the existing table schema. If differences are found, Delta Lake raises an exception by default to prevent silent corruption. However, you can override this behavior and allow Delta Lake to merge the new schema seamlessly into the existing table—again, without the need to rewrite prior data. Run the next cell. Notice the use of **WITH SCHEMA EVOLUTION** option.

```sql
%sql
MERGE WITH SCHEMA EVOLUTION INTO my_first_catalog.my_first_schema.employees
USING cdc_employees_1
ON cdc_employees_1.emp_id = my_first_catalog.my_first_schema.employees.emp_id
WHEN MATCHED THEN
  UPDATE SET *
WHEN NOT MATCHED THEN
  INSERT *
```

▸ (7) Spark Jobs

> _sqldf: pyspark.sql.dataframe.DataFrame = [num_affected_rows: long, num_updated_rows: long ... 2 more fields]

	num_affected_rows	num_updated_rows	num_deleted_rows	num_inserted_rows
1	3	3	0	0

Figure 6.67: Delta Lake merge with schema evolution

3. Run the next cell. Notice how Delta Lake was able to evolve the schema by adding the new `birth_date` column at the end of the `Employees` table.

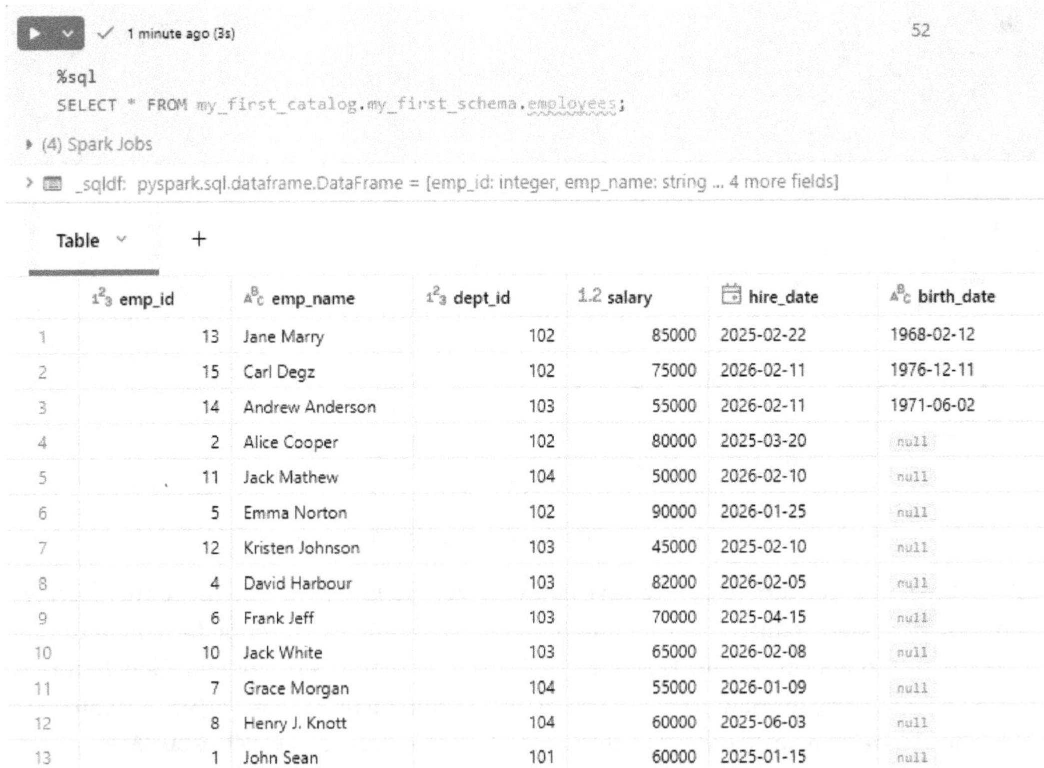

1 minute ago (3s) 52

```
%sql
SELECT * FROM my_first_catalog.my_first_schema.employees;
```

(4) Spark Jobs

_sqldf: pyspark.sql.dataframe.DataFrame = [emp_id: integer, emp_name: string ... 4 more fields]

Table

	emp_id	emp_name	dept_id	salary	hire_date	birth_date
1	13	Jane Marry	102	85000	2025-02-22	1968-02-12
2	15	Carl Degz	102	75000	2026-02-11	1976-12-11
3	14	Andrew Anderson	103	55000	2026-02-11	1971-06-02
4	2	Alice Cooper	102	80000	2025-03-20	null
5	11	Jack Mathew	104	50000	2026-02-10	null
6	5	Emma Norton	102	90000	2026-01-25	null
7	12	Kristen Johnson	103	45000	2025-02-10	null
8	4	David Harbour	103	82000	2026-02-05	null
9	6	Frank Jeff	103	70000	2025-04-15	null
10	10	Jack White	103	65000	2026-02-08	null
11	7	Grace Morgan	104	55000	2026-01-09	null
12	8	Henry J. Knott	104	60000	2025-06-03	null
13	1	John Sean	101	60000	2025-01-15	null

Figure 6.68: Delta Lake table after schema evolution

> **Note**
>
> Before using the evolve schema option, ensure the stakeholders fully understand and agree with the chosen strategy for handling schema evolution. Changing this approach after the solution is in production can be extremely disruptive—and potentially very costly.

Explicitly modify the schema of the Delta table

In addition to using the **WITH SCHEMA EVOLUTION** option, you can modify the table structure explicitly as data requirements change.

1. Run the next two cells. This operation adds a new column named `phone`. Notice that the column appears immediately after `emp_name`, following the order specified in the SQL statement.

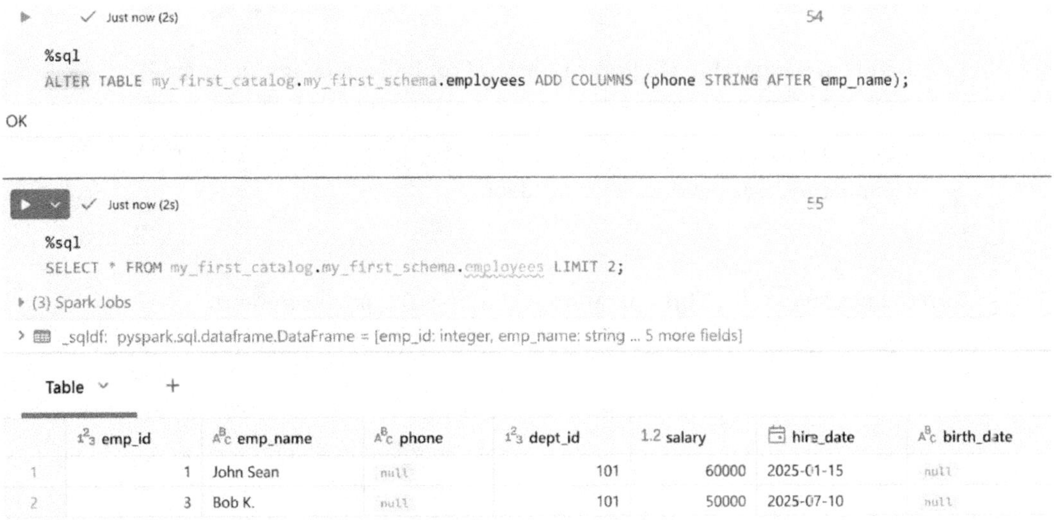

Figure 6.69: Adding a new column in a Delta table

2. Run the next two cells. This operation will rename the phone column to `cell_phone`.

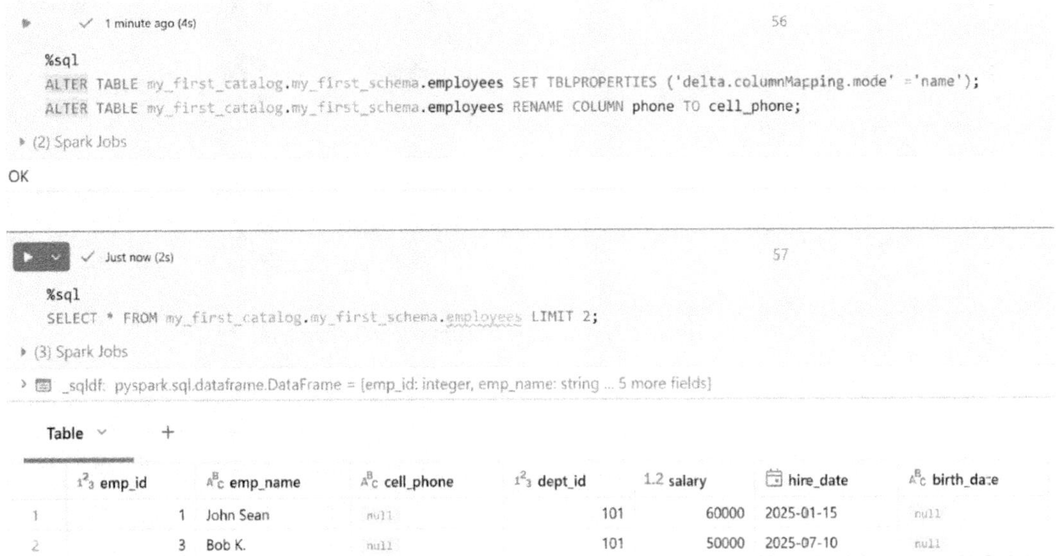

Figure 6.70: Renaming a column in a Delta table

> **Note**
>
> Delta Lake maintains a logical-to-physical column mapping in its metadata, and setting `TBLPROPERTIES ('delta.columnMapping.mode' = 'name')` enables name-based column tracking so you can safely rename or reorder columns without rewriting existing data.

3. Run the next two cells. This operation will drop `cell_phone` column.

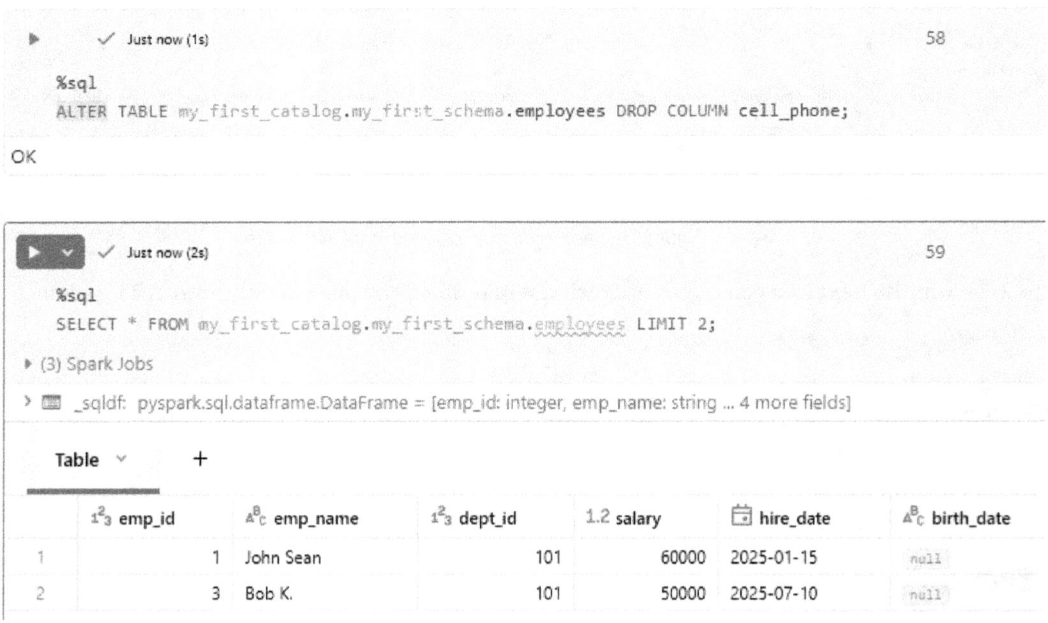

Figure 6.71: Dropping a column to a Delta table

Use the replaceWhere feature in Delta Lake

The `replaceWhere` option in Delta Lake enables atomic, targeted overwrites by replacing only the rows or partitions that satisfy a specified predicate. Being atomic means that even if one row fails to update, the table remains unchanged. Recall the earlier scenario where the CDC merge operation introduced a new column named `birth_date`. As shown below, this left the table in an inconsistent state because all existing rows had their `birth_date` values set to null.

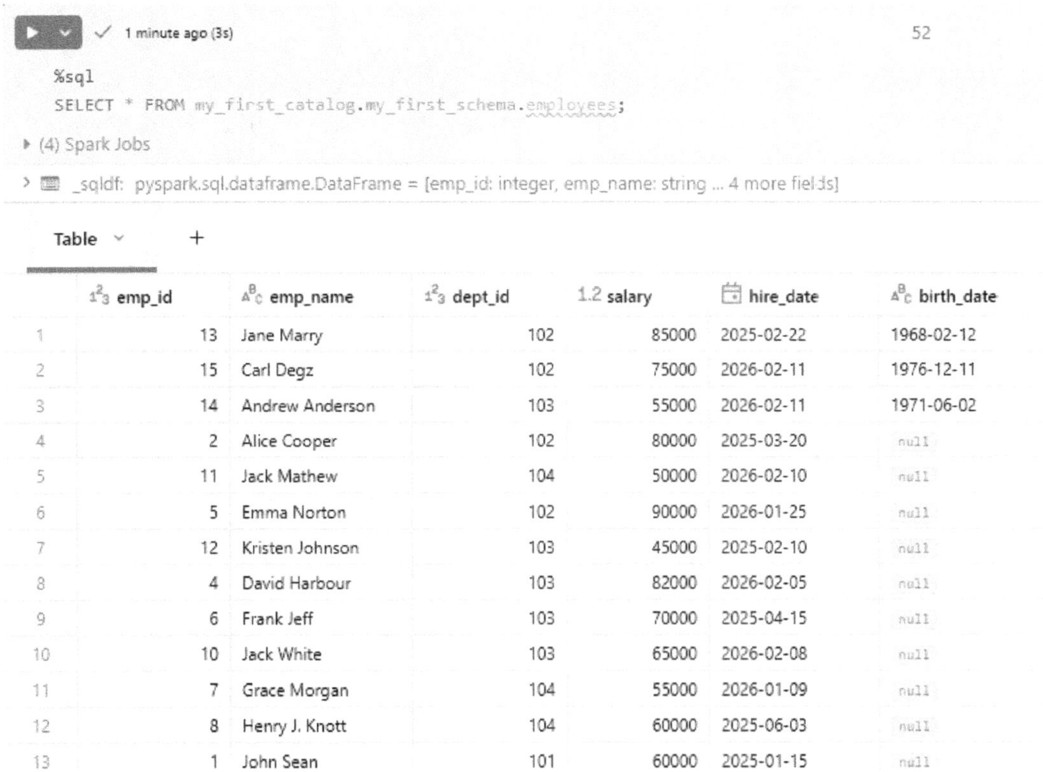


```
%sql
SELECT * FROM my_first_catalog.my_first_schema.employees;
```

	emp_id	emp_name	dept_id	salary	hire_date	birth_date
1	13	Jane Marry	102	85000	2025-02-22	1968-02-12
2	15	Carl Degz	102	75000	2026-02-11	1976-12-11
3	14	Andrew Anderson	103	55000	2026-02-11	1971-06-02
4	2	Alice Cooper	102	80000	2025-03-20	null
5	11	Jack Mathew	104	50000	2026-02-10	null
6	5	Emma Norton	102	90000	2026-01-25	null
7	12	Kristen Johnson	103	45000	2025-02-10	null
8	4	David Harbour	103	82000	2026-02-05	null
9	6	Frank Jeff	103	70000	2025-04-15	null
10	10	Jack White	103	65000	2026-02-08	null
11	7	Grace Morgan	104	55000	2026-01-09	null
12	8	Henry J. Knott	104	60000	2025-06-03	null
13	1	John Sean	101	60000	2025-01-15	null

Figure 6.72: Checking the birth_date records that have null values

1. Run the next two cells. The first cell declares a Dataframe to filter the records where `birth_date` column has a NULL value. In the next cell it overwrites the records with the value of "Unknown".

✓ 04:58 PM (<1s) 61

```
replace_data = (
    spark.table("my_first_catalog.my_first_schema.employees")
        .filter("birth_date IS NULL")
        .withColumn("birth_date", lit("unknown"))
)
```

replace_data: pyspark.sql.dataframe.DataFrame = [emp_id: integer, emp_name: string ... 4 more fields]

✓ 1 minute ago (5s) 62

```
spark.conf.set("spark.databricks.delta.replaceWhere.constraintCheck.enabled", False)
(replace_data.write
  .mode("overwrite")
  .option("replaceWhere", "birth_date IS NULL")
  .saveAsTable("my_first_catalog.my_first_schema.employees")
)
```

Figure 6.73: Replacing the birth_date records to 'unknown'

2. Run the next cell. Note that the change in `birth_date` column.

```
%sql
SELECT * FROM my_first_catalog.my_first_schema.employees;
```

▸ (4) Spark Jobs

▸ _sqldf: pyspark.sql.dataframe.DataFrame = [emp_id: integer, emp_name: string ... 4 more fields]

Table

	emp_id	emp_name	dept_id	salary	hire_date	birth_date
1	13	Jane Marry	102	85000	2025-02-22	1968-02-12
2	15	Carl Degz	102	75000	2026-02-11	1976-12-11
3	14	Andrew Anderson	103	55000	2026-02-11	1971-06-02
4	12	Kristen Johnson	103	45000	2025-02-10	unknown
5	4	David Harbour	103	82000	2026-02-05	unknown
6	6	Frank Jeff	103	70000	2025-04-15	unknown
7	10	Jack White	103	65000	2026-02-08	unknown
8	11	Jack Mathew	104	50000	2026-02-10	unknown
9	7	Grace Morgan	104	55000	2026-01-09	unknown
10	8	Henry J. Knott	104	60000	2025-06-03	unknown
11	2	Alice Cooper	102	80000	2025-03-20	unknown
12	5	Emma Norton	102	90000	2026-01-25	unknown
13	1	John Sean	101	60000	2025-01-15	unknown
14	3	Bob K.	101	50000	2025-07-10	unknown
15	9	Ivy Lee	101	72000	2025-09-18	unknown

Figure 6.74: birth_date records after replacement

Set up constraints in the Delta Table

Delta tables support built-in mechanisms that enforce data correctness whenever new records are written. These controls act as safeguards to ensure only valid, high-quality data is stored. Delta Lake provides several types of integrity rules, such as preventing nulls in required columns, validating values with custom conditions, and using automatically computed fields to maintain consistency. Together, these features help protect your table from bad or inconsistent data during ingestion or updates.

Set up a NOT NULL constraint in the Delta Table

A `NOT NULL` constraint ensures that the column cannot contain NULL values.

1. Run the next cell. This cell creates a `NOT NULL` constraint on the `emp_id` column.

Figure 6.75: Create a not null constraint on a Delta table

2. Run the next cell. Once the `NOT NULL` constraint is in effect, the insert operation fails because it attempts to insert a NULL value into `emp_id`, demonstrating that the constraint is correctly enforced.

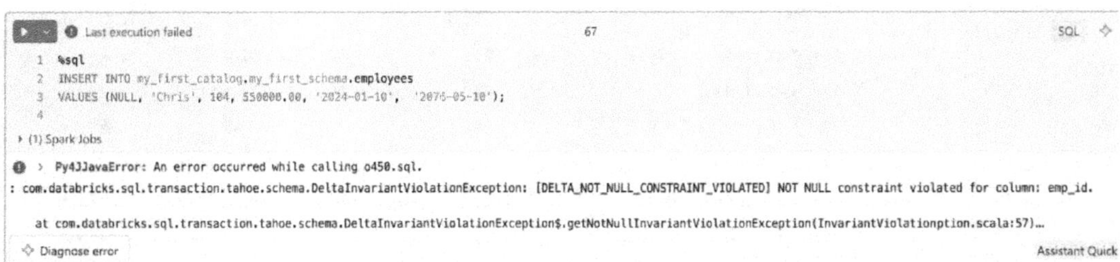

Figure 6.76: Insert command failure for a row that contains a null value for emp_id

Now we check how Delta tables react to a `CHECK` constraint.

Set up a CHECK constraint in the Delta Table

A `CHECK` constraint ensures that a column's values meet specific conditions, such as falling within an approved set of values or a defined range.

1. Run the next cell. This cell creates a `CHECK` constraint on the `hire_date` column to ensure it falls within a specified date range.

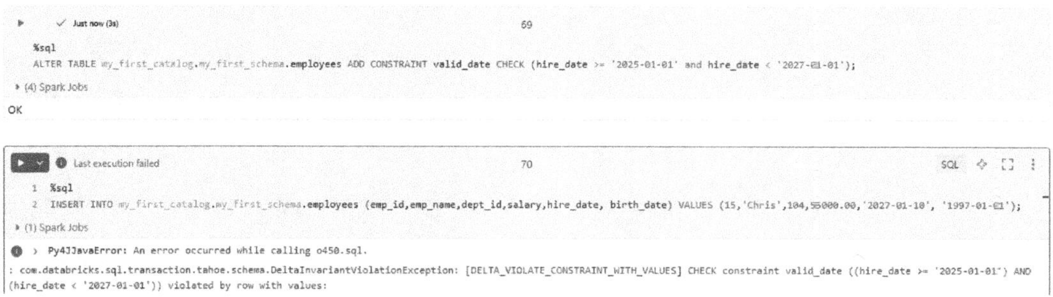

Figure 6.77: Create a check constraint on a Delta table

2. Run the next cell. After adding the `CHECK` constraint, the following insert operation fails because it attempts to insert a `hire_date` outside the acceptable date range, demonstrating that the constraint is correctly enforced.

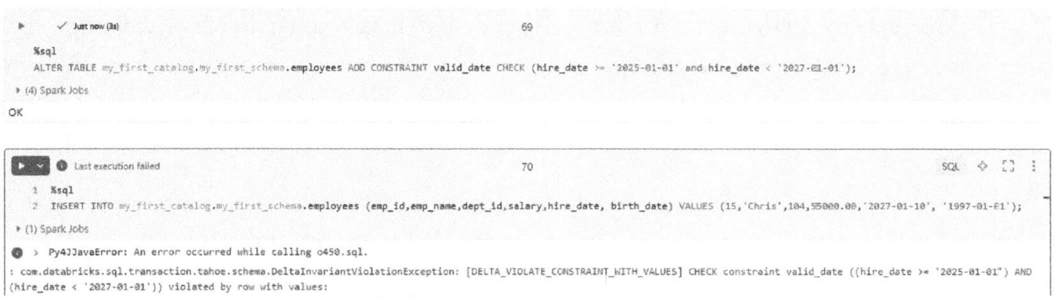

Figure 6.78: Insert command failure due to a hire_date value outside the check-constraint range.

Next, we'll examine how Delta tables respond to `FOREIGN KEY` constraints. This feature is particularly interesting because the behavior differs from that of traditional relational databases, offering a modified lakehouse-oriented approach to referential integrity.

Set up a foreign key constraint in the Delta table

A `FOREIGN KEY` constraint ensures a value in one table corresponds to an existing value in another table, thereby establishing a parent-child relationship between them.

1. Run the next two cells. Because a foreign key constraint requires a parent table, we'll create that table first before adding the `FOREIGN KEY`. Notice that the `dept_id` column is defined as the `PRIMARYKEY`, and we've also inserted a few sample rows into this table to support the upcoming constraint check.

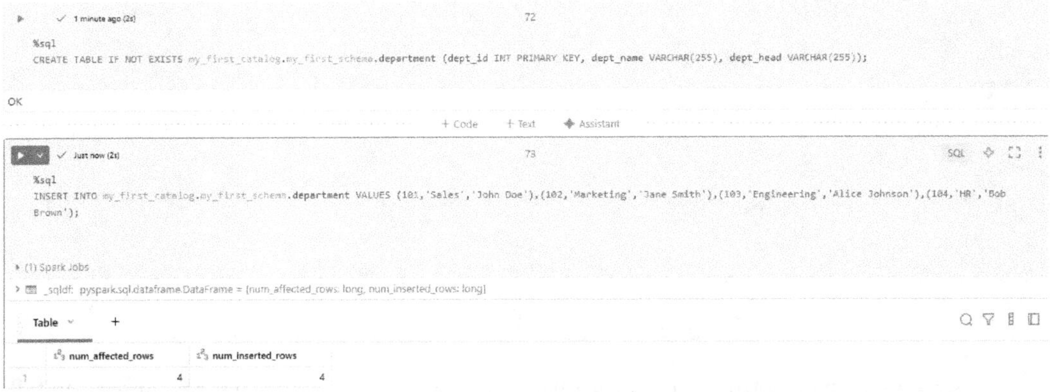

Figure 6.79: Create a parent table with a primary key constraint on the Delta table

2. Run the next cell. This operation creates a new foreign key constraint on the `Employee` table, specifying that `dept_id` is the dependent field that must match an existing `dept_id` value in the `Department` table.

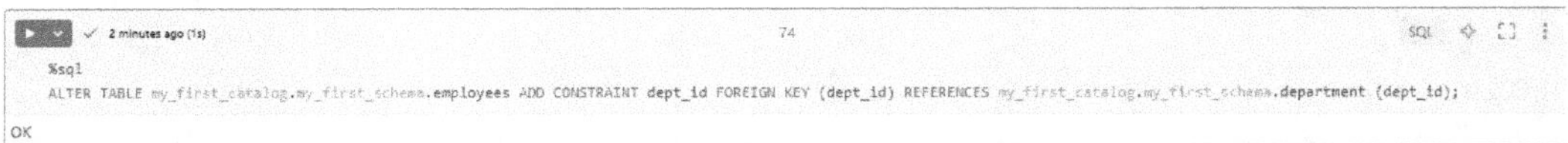

Figure 6.80: Alter table to create a foreign key constraint on the Delta table

3. Run the next cell. This statement inserts a new row into the `Employees` table using a `dept_id` that does not exist in the `Department` table. Interestingly, Delta Lake does **not** report a constraint violation in this case.

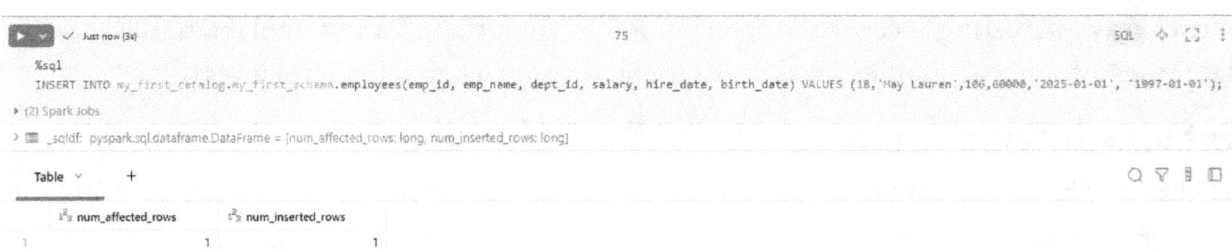

Figure 6.81: Foreign key constraint in a Delta table is not enforceable

> **Note**
>
> The reason is that Delta tables do *not* enforce foreign key constraints the way traditional relational databases do. If that's the case, then why is this feature available at all? Having the foreign key constraint simply serves as semantic metadata for documentation, data governance, lineage tracking, and query optimization.

Modern data platforms commonly handle massive volumes of information. When managing large datasets in Delta Lake, a major challenge is maintaining consistently high query performance. Without ongoing tuning and optimization, query operations can gradually become slower and less efficient.

Improve Delta table performance

To help maintain strong performance, several optimization techniques can be applied to Delta tables, including the following:

Partitioning the Delta table

Previously, we explored partitioning as a common method to organize large datasets into more manageable segments, helping queries scan only the relevant portions of data rather than the entire table-a technique known as data skipping. This technique reduces the amount of data read during query execution and can significantly improve performance for workloads that filter on partitioned columns.

While partitioning is effective in many scenarios, it can significantly reduce performance if a table is over-partitioned or if the wrong columns are chosen for partitioning.

Optimize the Delta table

The basic OPTIMIZE feature in Delta Lake reduces the number of files by merging many small files into larger ones, thereby improving read speed and reducing metadata overhead.

1. Run the next cell. Note that you may either run the `OPTIMIZE` command manually or use the `autoOptimize` feature, which performs the optimization automatically. As a best practice, Delta tables should be optimized weekly to maintain performance and storage efficiency.

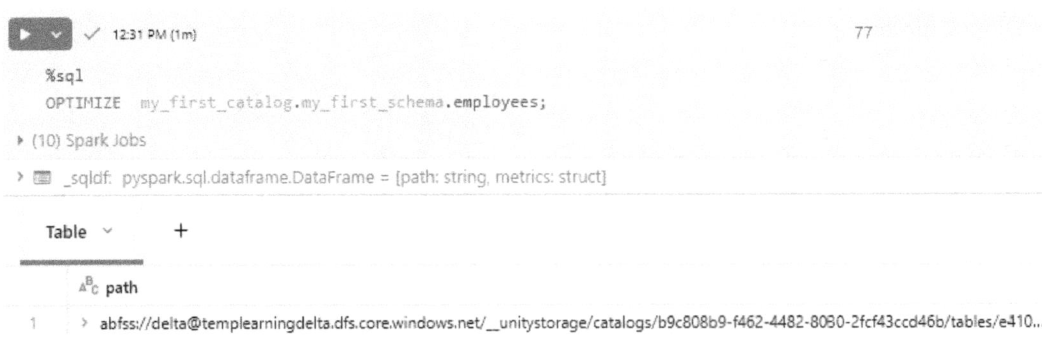

Figure 6.82: Running OPTIMIZE on the Delta table

Beyond using `OPTIMIZE`, several additional techniques can further improve the performance of Delta tables.

Optimize using Z-ordering in the Delta table

Z-ordering organizes data within files by **grouping** values from columns commonly used in filters, without increasing the number of partitions. Generally suitable for a large table, Z-ordering enhances data skipping and helps maintain efficient, well-sized files. Z-ordering improves Delta Lake performance by reorganizing data, so queries scan fewer files as follows:

- **Row Ordering**: Within each file, the data is rearranged using a Z-order curve, which effectively maps values from multiple columns into a single sequence so that related records remain close together.
- **File Optimization**: During this process, files are rewritten so that rows with similar characteristics are grouped, reducing the amount of data that needs to be scanned during queries.
- **Improved Data Locality**: Because related entries (such as those sharing the same city and date) are positioned near one another on disk, the system performs less I/O, resulting in faster query execution.

> Note
>
> In Delta tables, performance can also be improved by using numeric types instead of strings, storing dates in efficient native formats, and keeping frequently filtered attributes out of deeply nested structures.

The following infographic shows the difference between querying a Delta table with and without Z-ordering.

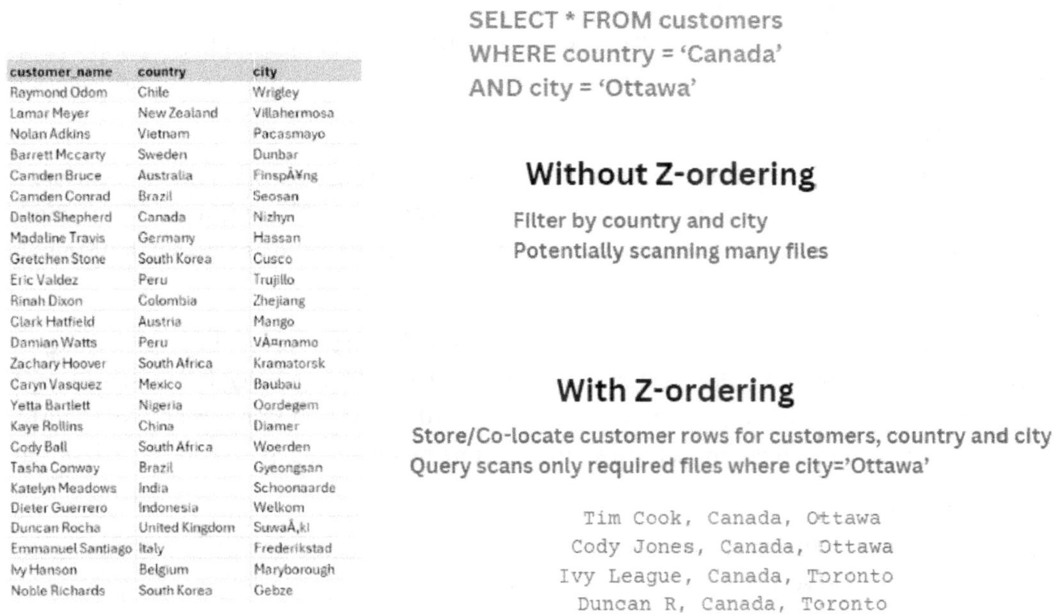

Figure 6.83: Improve performance using Z-ordering

> **Note**
>
> Z-ordering can only be applied to non-partitioned data columns, as its purpose is to optimize the layout of data within partitions, not the partitions themselves.

1. Run next cell. Note that the SQL applies Z-ordering on `emp_name` and `hire_date` columns.

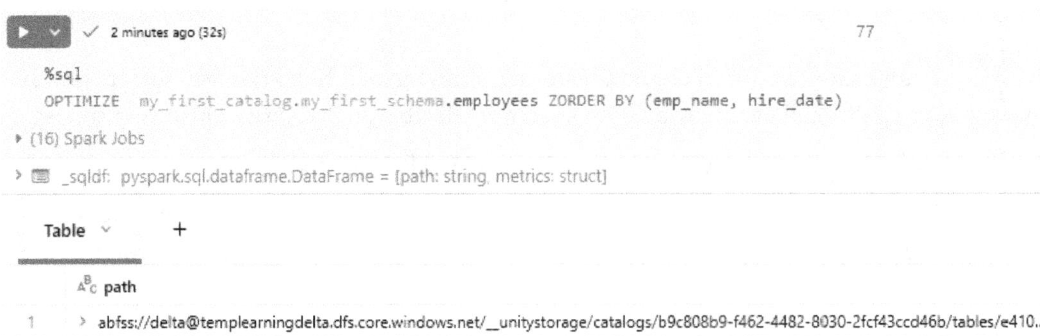

Figure 6.84: Z-ordering on Delta table

The above scenario is precisely where Z-ordering becomes highly effective—it restructures the underlying data so that commonly filtered values are grouped together, leading to faster lookups and improved overall query performance.

Optimize writes

Optimized writes help structure data files more efficiently during writes, resulting in better file sizing and faster read performance on Delta tables. You can control the output file size using the `targetFileSize` configuration, and it's generally recommended to use sizes in multiples of 128 MB—common choices include 128 MB, 256 MB, and 512 MB.

These optimizations are especially valuable for partitioned tables because they significantly reduce the number of small files created in each partition. Producing fewer, larger files is far more efficient than generating many small ones. The trade-off is that writes may take slightly longer, as data must be reorganized and shuffled before being written in the optimized format.

Run Analyzer

The Delta Analyzer calculates and refreshes statistical information about a table. These statistics give the query optimizer better insight into the data, allowing it to generate more efficient execution plans, improve join strategies, enhance filter pushdown, and support more effective data pruning, all of which contribute to faster query performance. Updated statistics are especially valuable for BI or interactive workloads, where accurate metadata leads to more efficient planning, better pruning, and faster, more predictable query performance.

> **Note**
>
> It's advisable to refresh table statistics after significant updates—such as large data ingestions, running OPTIMIZE, or applying schema changes—because each of these actions modifies the underlying data layout or structure, and updated statistics enable the optimizer to generate more efficient query plans.

Recently, Delta Lake introduced Liquid Clustering, a next-generation approach to data layout that replaces traditional partitioning with a far more flexible and adaptive clustering strategy.

Optimize using Liquid Clustering in the Delta table

Although both basic optimization and Z-ordering are effective in most cases, Databricks now recommends using Liquid Clustering as a replacement for partitioning and Z-ordering.

Although partitioning and Z-ordering are effective in many scenarios, they can still lead to issues such as:

- Uneven data distribution can occur across partitions, reducing parallelism and query efficiency.
- Higher maintenance overhead may arise if repartitioning or restructuring becomes necessary.
- Suboptimal column choices for partitioning or Z-ordering can lead to high cardinality and poor query performance.
- Z-ordering requires regular reprocessing, which increases compute costs over time.

> **Note**
>
> Data skipping is an optimization technique that enables the query engine to bypass scanning files that are known not to contain data relevant to the query conditions.

Liquid Clustering offers cutting-edge data layout optimization for Delta tables by automatically organizing Delta table data around clustered columns, delivering Z-order-quality performance without **rigid partitions** or heavy maintenance. Liquid Clustering adaptively adjusts the data layout based on real query behavior and changing data patterns. It's important to recognize that Z-Ordering is a point-in-time optimization, whereas Liquid Clustering provides a more flexible and continuously maintained data layout. Migrating from Z-Ordering is straightforward—simply stop running Z-ORDER and enable Liquid Clustering. The only additional consideration is a one-time cost to reorganize existing data when Liquid Clustering is first activated.

In the example below, liquid clustering automatically adapts to the distribution of country values in the dataset. Countries with a large volume of records are assigned dedicated clusters to prevent them from overwhelming smaller groups and to keep data well-balanced. Meanwhile, countries with fewer rows are intelligently grouped into shared clusters, ensuring the storage layout remains efficient and avoids unnecessary fragmentation.

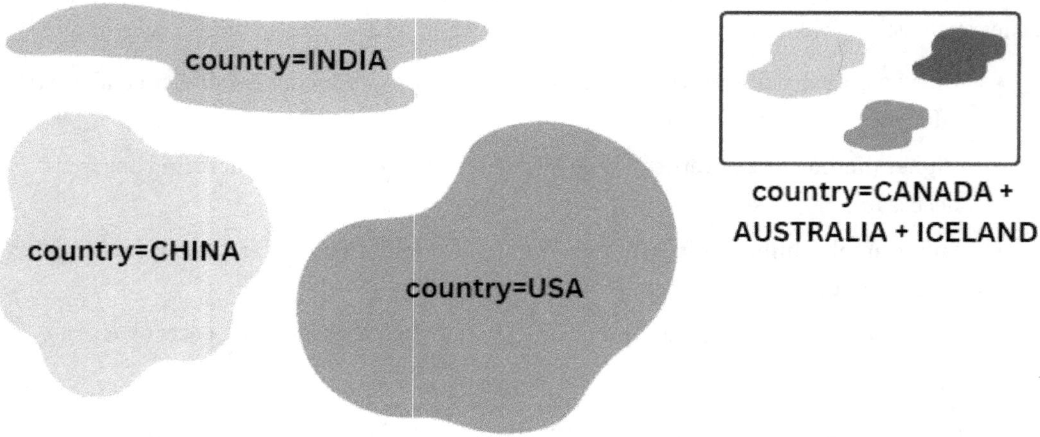

Figure 6.85: Liquid clustering by country

In liquid clustering, Delta distributes rows across cluster ranges rather than folder partitions. These ranges adjust over time—hence *liquid*. This adaptive behavior helps maintain optimal query performance regardless of how skewed or uneven the data distribution becomes over time.

We will now enable liquid clustering on a new Delta table.

1. Run next cell. This operation will create a new table, `employees_clustered`, with clustered columns, `dept_id` and `hire_date`.

Just now (6s)

```
df_employees.write \
  .format("delta") \
  .clusterBy("dept_id", "hire_date") \
  .saveAsTable("my_first_catalog.my_first_schema.employees_clustered")
```

(5) Spark Jobs

Figure 6.86: Create a Delta table with liquid clustering

2. Run the next cell. Check out the clustering columns.

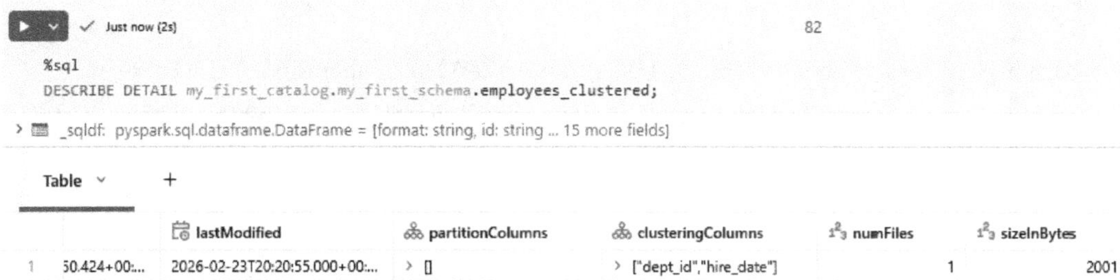

Figure 6.87: Check the clustering columns in the Delta table

While Z-Ordering and Liquid Clustering are effective techniques for improving Delta table performance, additional methods for reclaiming unused storage space can further enhance efficiency.

Regularly clean old Delta files

The `VACUUM` operation in Delta Lake removes old, unreferenced files from storage to free up space and keep the table clean. Over time, updates, deletes, and merges can create stale data files; `VACUUM` permanently deletes them once they are no longer needed for version history. By cleaning up this leftover data, `VACUUM` helps reduce storage costs and can improve overall query performance. However, retaining older versions always involves a trade-off: shorter retention periods reduce your recovery window and increase the risk of data loss, while longer retention periods consume more storage and can gradually degrade performance.

1. Run the next cell. This operation will run a `VACUUM` of the Delta table.

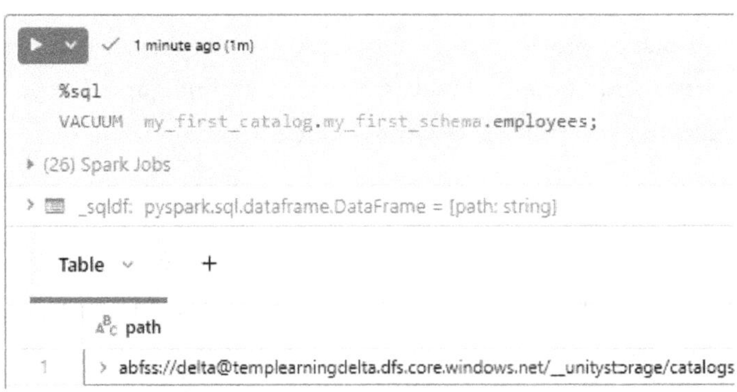

Figure 6.88: Run VACUUM on Delta table

> **Note**
>
> Although it's best practice to run `VACUUM` after each `OPTIMIZE` operation, Delta Lake still applies a default retention period of 7 days, meaning stale files are removed only after a week.

Now that we've covered how `VACUUM` interacts with retention and time travel, we can shift our focus to isolation levels. While `VACUUM` governs how long historical data remains available, isolation levels determine how concurrent reads and writes behave, ensuring transactional consistency in Delta Lake.

Isolation levels in the Delta table

In Delta Lake, a table's isolation level determines how strongly a transaction is protected from changes made by other transactions running concurrently. Delta Lake supports two isolation levels:

- **WriteSerializable (default)**: This lighter isolation level requires only write operations to behave as though they run sequentially. Read operations may occur concurrently as long as they do not conflict with ongoing writes.
- **Serializable**: This is the strictest isolation level, ensuring that both read and write operations occur as if they were executed one after another in a single, **sequential** order.

> **Note**
>
> Serializable isolation provides the strongest consistency but can slow performance and limit concurrency. `WriteSerializable` offers better throughput but provides weaker read isolation and may still lead to write conflicts in certain scenarios.

Let's understand the isolation level using the examples below:

1. Run the next cell. The isolation level for each transaction can be queried from the table's history.

Figure 6.89: Check the isolation level of transactions in the Delta table

2. Although the default isolation level for delta tables is `WriteSerializable`, it can be changed as desired. We can set the isolation level for the employees table to `Serializable`.

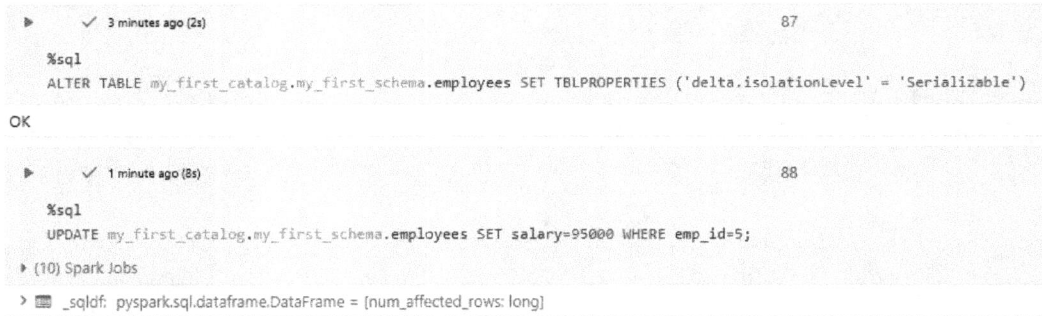

Figure 6.90: Run a transaction with a Serializable isolation level

3. Notice below that the `UPDATE` statement was run using the `Serializable` isolation level.

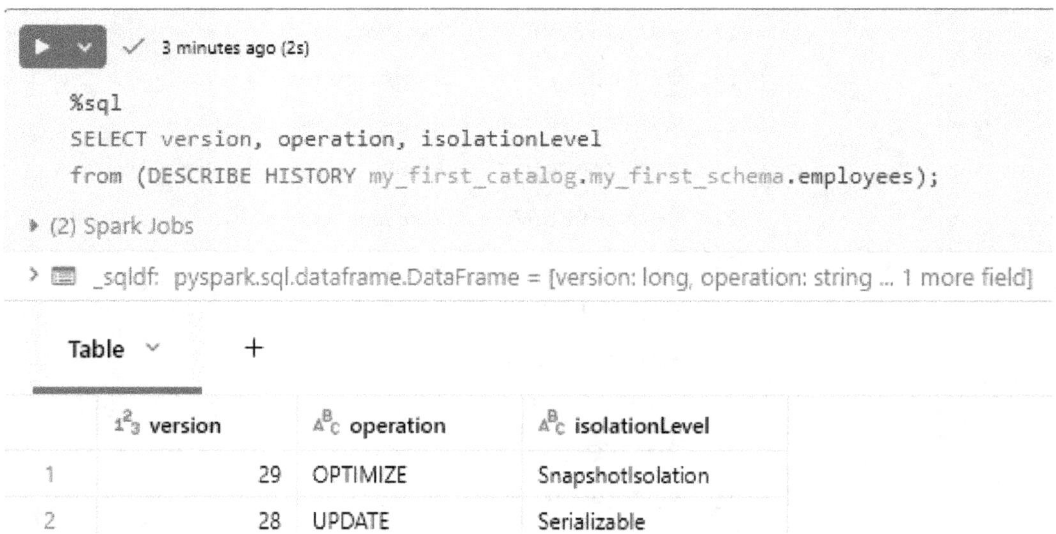

Figure 6.91: Check the isolation level of the transaction

With isolation levels established, we can now turn our attention to concurrency. Isolation defines the guarantees each transaction receives, while concurrency determines how multiple transactions interact in practice—especially when they read, write, or update the same Delta table simultaneously.

Understanding concurrency control in the Delta table

By this point, we should have a solid grasp of how Delta Lake ensures ACID compliance through its transaction log. So far, all actions in our examples have been performed by a single user, but real-world environments often involve multiple users reading from and writing to the same Delta table simultaneously. Delta Lake's concurrency control mechanisms are designed to handle exactly these situations, ensuring consistency and reliability even under heavy multi-user workloads.

Delta Lake uses optimistic concurrency control to manage situations where multiple users or jobs read and write to the same table at the same time. Instead of locking data, Delta Lake allows operations to proceed in parallel and then uses the transaction log to detect conflicts.

If a write operation conflicts with another concurrent transaction, Delta Lake retries or fails the operation to maintain ACID guarantees and ensure data consistency.

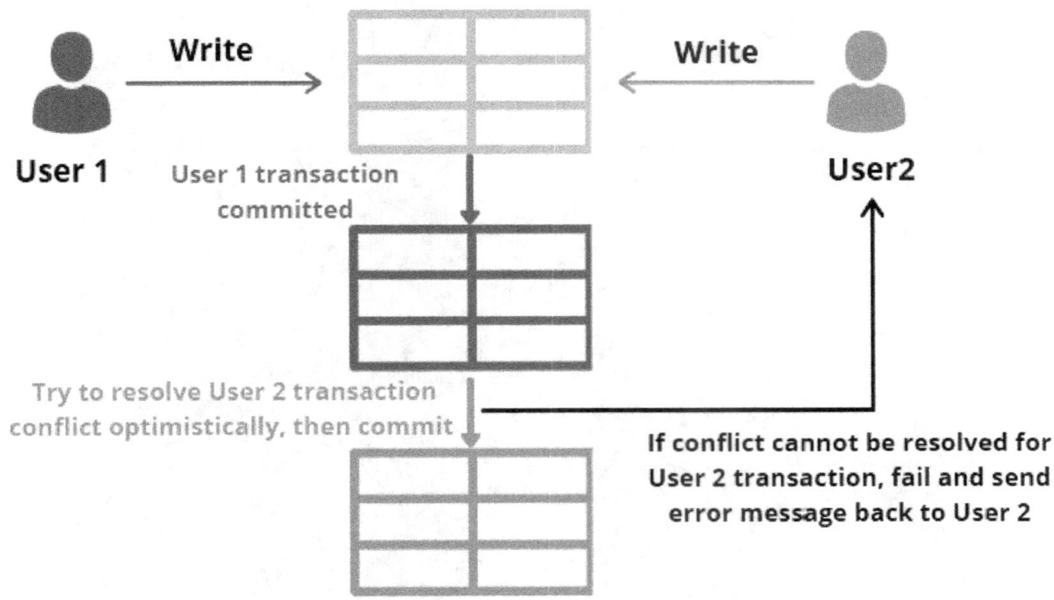

Figure 6.92: Concurrency control in Delta table

- Imagine User 1 and User 2 both try to write to the same Delta table at the same time.
- Delta Lake first notes the table's version before any changes are made.
- User 1's write goes through and is committed successfully.
- User 2's write does not immediately fail. Instead, Delta Lake checks whether User 2's changes conflict with the data that User 1 already committed.
    a. If no conflicts are found, User 2's write is also committed.
    b. If there *is* a conflict, Delta Lake rejects the write and sends an error back to User 2.

This behavior is known as **optimistic concurrency control**.

Understanding deletion vectors in the Delta table

Deletion vectors (DVs) enable rows to be deleted, updated, or merged without rewriting entire Parquet files. Rather than modifying the underlying files, Delta simply flags the affected rows as removed using a compact bitmap structure.

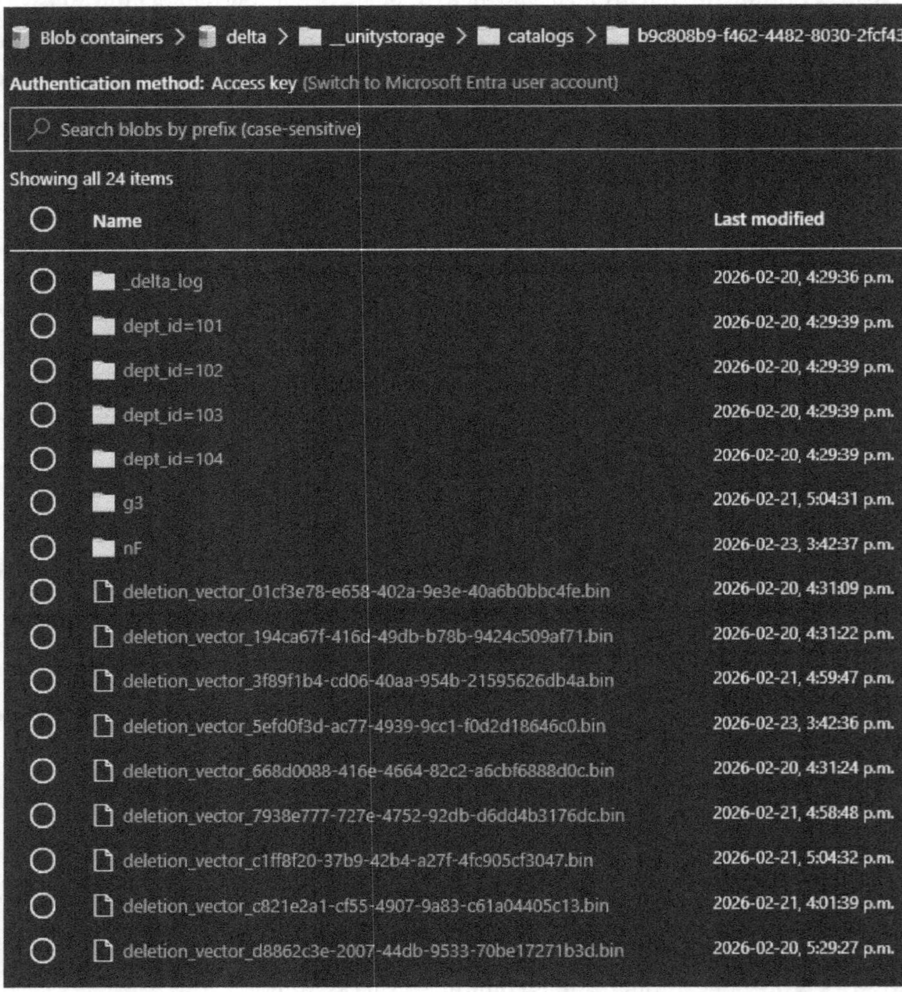

Figure 6.93: Deletion vectors in the Delta table

Deletion vectors significantly improve the efficiency of Delta Lake operations by avoiding costly file rewrites. Instead of rewriting entire Parquet files when a single row is deleted or updated, Delta Lake uses deletion vectors to mark affected rows in lightweight metadata, allowing operations like `DELETE`, `UPDATE`, and `MERGE` to complete much faster because only metadata is written rather than the full data files. This approach also reduces I/O and storage costs, since only small bitmap files are created and Delta's query engine simply skips the marked rows at read time, filtering them out based on the deletion vector entries.

> **Note**
>
> Deletion vectors are particularly beneficial for large datasets that undergo frequent modifications—for example, tables requiring GDPR-related deletions, **Slowly Changing Dimension Type 2** (**SCD2**) updates, or high-volume streaming inserts.

In this section, Delta Lake enhances data reliability and performance by bringing ACID transactions, schema enforcement, and versioned data management to lakehouse storage. Using the transaction log, Delta ensures consistent reads and writes, even when multiple users access the same table concurrently. We also examined how Delta supports optimistic concurrency control, allowing parallel operations while still preventing conflicting writes. From a performance perspective, we learned that techniques such as partitioning, Z-ordering, file compaction (OPTIMIZE), and data skipping help speed up queries by efficiently organizing data. We also discussed the limitations of these methods—such as uneven data distribution and maintenance overhead—and how newer features like Liquid Clustering offer more adaptive data layout optimization.

Additionally, we looked at `VACUUM` for removing stale files and **Deletion Vectors** (**DVs**) to enable efficient updates and deletes without rewriting entire Parquet files, making Delta better suited for large, frequently changing datasets.

Together, these features create a scalable, consistent, and performant foundation for managing big data workloads in the lakehouse.

Summary

In this chapter, we explored the medallion architecture and gained a deeper understanding of how Spark works, leading to an appreciation of Delta Lake as the core engine behind the modern lakehouse design. Delta Lake truly enables the lakehouse by providing ACID transactions, open standards, and strong reliability guarantees. We examined several of its key capabilities—such as ACID compliance, schema enforcement, and transaction logging—and then applied those concepts through hands-on exercises that demonstrated common table operations and how Delta Lake manages data isolation and concurrency.

Delta Lake serves as the foundation of modern lakehouses. Its ACID transactions, schema enforcement, and advanced storage optimizations enable the construction of robust analytical platforms that support both batch and streaming workloads. This architectural strength directly enables Medallion Architecture. Delta Lake provides the transactional backbone, performance optimizations, and governance features that make each Medallion layer dependable, scalable, and production-ready.

Delta Lake serves as the foundation of modern lakehouses by unifying warehouse-grade reliability with the scalability of data lakes, and this strength directly enables the Medallion architecture. Performance optimizations like Z-Ordering and Liquid Clustering deliver fast, predictable analytics at scale. Across all layers, VACUUM helps manage storage by removing unreferenced files while preserving time travel within the configured retention window. Together, these capabilities make Delta Lake not just a storage format but the transactional, optimization, and governance backbone that allows Medallion-structured lakehouses to operate with consistency, performance, and enterprise-grade resilience.

We will use Delta tables extensively in the upcoming chapters, particularly when we build the bronze, silver, and gold layers. For now, we move to *Chapter 7, Understanding Modern Data Pipelines*, where we will explore how data pipelines are structured and why their design requires thoughtful, deliberate planning. We will also introduce the Electroniz Lakehouse data platform, which will serve as our hands-on, real-world project throughout the rest of the book.

Get this book's PDF version and more

Scan the QR code (or go to `packtpub.com/unlock`). Search for this book by name, confirm the edition, and then follow the steps on the page.

UNLOCK NOW

Note: Keep your invoice handy. Purchases made directly from Packt don't require an invoice.

7

Understanding Modern Data Pipelines

In the previous chapter, we explored Apache Spark and the Delta Lake framework in depth. Gaining a solid understanding of Spark's distributed computing capabilities—combined with Delta Lake's transactional engine—is essential for improving the reliability and overall quality of data processing.

As a data engineer, designing a data pipeline requires careful and deliberate planning. This chapter outlines the key phases involved in building a data pipeline and highlights the recommended actions and considerations for each stage. Thoughtful planning ultimately leads to smoother execution and more reliable outcomes. Rather than focusing solely on tools or technology, we will break down the pipeline lifecycle—from initial planning and data discovery to orchestration, monitoring, and optimization—so you can appreciate not just how to build a pipeline but also *why* each step matters.

Toward the end of the chapter, we will introduce the sample **Electroniz Lakehouse data platform** project, which will serve as our hands-on, real-world project throughout the remainder of the book. This platform will be constructed incrementally in later chapters, allowing you to see how individual concepts and techniques fit together to form a cohesive, production-grade data solution.

In this chapter, we will cover the following topics:

- Exploring data pipelines
- Understanding the data pipeline creation process
- Electroniz data platform project

Exploring Data Pipelines

In *Chapter 1, The Story of Data Engineering and Analytics,* we explored the journey of data and compared data engineering to the vehicle that transports data through sharp turns, obstacles, and unpredictable conditions—ensuring it reaches its destination securely and on time. If data engineering is the vehicle, then the **data pipeline** is the underlying **engine** that **powers** the journey. Like any engine, a data pipeline is composed of multiple specialized components, each performing a distinct operation. When these parts operate in harmony, they propel the entire system forward and ensure the data reaches its intended destination efficiently and reliably.

In simple terms, a **data pipeline** is the engine that moves data through the stages of **collection**, **curation**, and **aggregation** until it reaches its final analytics destination.

> Note
>
> We live in an era defined by abundant choices. It is the data engineer's responsibility to select the most suitable tool or service for each task, ensuring that every action in the pipeline is executed as efficiently and effectively as possible.

Components of a data pipeline

A **data pipeline** is a collection of components. Each component of a data pipeline performs a specialized operation that contributes to the overall success of the data's journey. While data engineers often devote considerable attention to designing and developing the pipeline itself, the **operational aspects** are frequently overlooked. Although building the individual components is essential, it is equally important to consider how these components will be **assembled, deployed, orchestrated, and monitored** over time. To deepen our understanding of data pipelines, let us now examine their core components in detail.

Data source

Data sources are data systems where raw data originates before it is collected and stored in data platforms.

These sources continuously produce real-time data, which can then be processed, analyzed, and used to support business decisions. Common types of data sources include:

- Databases and data warehouses.
- Files, such as spreadsheets, text files, or logs.

- **Application Programming Interfaces** (**APIs**) that provide programmatic access to data.
- Sensor data generated by **Internet of Things** (**IoT**) devices.
- Social media platforms and other **Software-as-a-Service** (**SaaS**) applications.

Data ingestion

A typical data pipeline begins by ingesting data from one or more data sources. Over time, data engineers have used both push and pull methods to perform this ingestion. Depending on the characteristics of the data source, they may select either batch ingestion or streaming ingestion.

The complexity of ingestion is closely tied to whether the data is **static** or **dynamic**. Ingesting data from static sources is generally straightforward. The true challenges in data engineering arise when working with dynamic data sources that change frequently at the source. In these cases, data engineers must apply effective **Change Data Capture** (**CDC**) techniques to ingest data incrementally and ensure that updates are captured accurately and efficiently.

Data ingestion systems typically employ a few techniques for loading incremental data. We will study them in the following sections.

Watermark technique

A **watermark** represents the reference point up to which data has been successfully ingested from a source system. During the next cycle, the system extracts only records in which the watermark value exceeds the stored watermark value, enabling efficient detection of inserts, updates, and deletes. In most scenarios, a **timestamp** column or an **identity-based** primary key is the optimal choice for defining this watermark. An effective watermarking approach requires the source systems to maintain fields such as `created_timestamp`, `updated_timestamp`, and `deleted_timestamp`. Without these columns, it becomes difficult to reliably track incremental inserts, updates, and deletes during data ingestion. Have a look at the following figure:

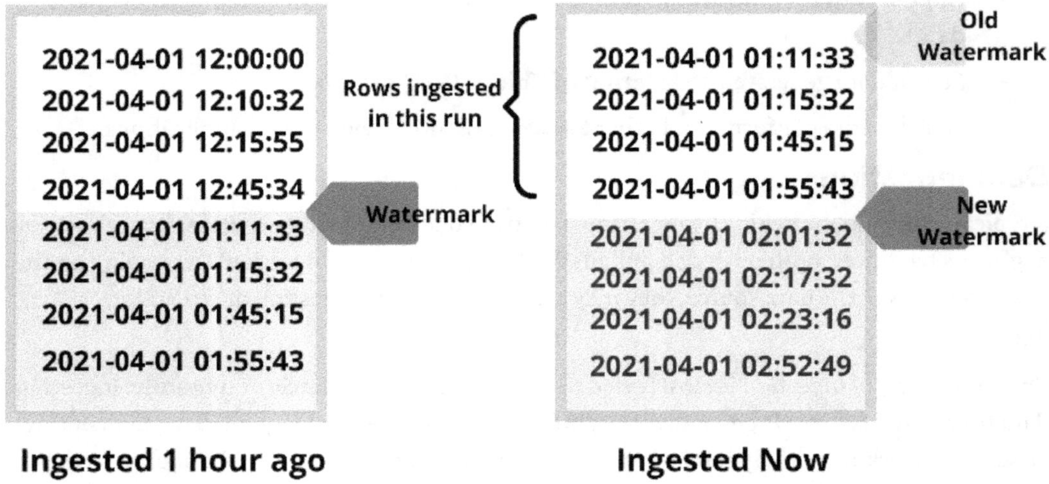

Figure 7.1: Watermark technique of data ingestion

In practice, introducing new columns to track inserts, updates, and deletes for watermarking can become an operational challenge. This is because the schemas of source databases and data warehouses are often long-established and may have been in place for years, making structural changes disruptive or difficult to implement. If modifying the data source is not allowed, data engineers can still implement effective incremental ingestion by enabling **Change Data Capture** (**CDC**). Let's see what that is.

Change Data Capture (CDC)

Change Data Capture (CDC) is a technique used to detect and record real-time inserts, updates, and deletes occurring in a live database or data warehouse. By capturing **row-level changes** as they happen, CDC enables downstream systems to process incremental updates efficiently without repeatedly scanning entire tables. This approach supports near real-time data replication, streaming analytics, and synchronized data pipelines while minimizing load on the source system. CDC can be performed primarily using the two techniques, Log-based CDC and change tracking. Let's learn about these two next.

Log-based CDC

Log-based CDC uses the database's native transaction log to detect changes. Although the concept is the same across platforms, the transaction log is referred to by different names depending on the database engine. As depicted in the image below, MySQL uses **binlogs**, Oracle uses **redo logs**, and SQL Server uses the **transaction log**:

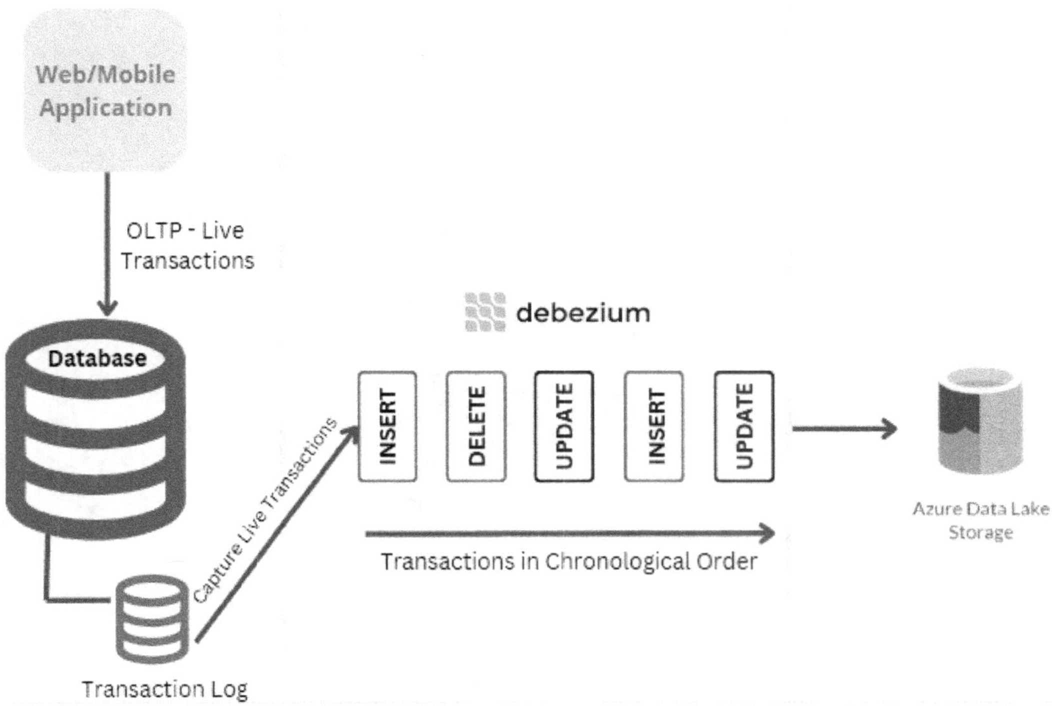

Figure 7.2: Log-based CDC technique

> **Note**
>
> While many tools can read CDC events directly from database transaction logs, Debezium stands out as a robust and widely adopted open-source option.

The following is a sample update event. Notice how the event is marked as `op=u` and consists of both `before` and `after` row values. Events for insert are marked as `op=i` and deletes as `op=d`.

```
"schema": {...},
"payload": {
  "before": {
    "id": 50001,
    "first_name": "Manoj",
    "last_name": "Kukreja",
    "email": "manoj@hotmail.com"
  },
  "after": {
"id": 50001,
    "first_name": "Manoj",
    "last_name": "Kukreja",
    "email": "manoj@gmail.com"
  },
  "source": {
    "name": "3.4.1.Final",
    "name": "dbserver1",
    "server_id": 54678,
    "ts_sec": 1486501486,
    "gtid": null,
    "file": "mysql-bin.000007",
    "pos": 364,
    "row": 0,
    "snapshot": null,
    "thread": 3,
    "db": "sales",
    "table": "customers"
  },
  "op": "u",
  "ts_ms": 1486501486308,
```

Figure 7.3: Sample change event for an updated row

Change Tracking

Change Tracking is a SQL Server feature that identifies which rows in a table have changed since the last synchronization. These changes are recorded in an internal structure that can be queried using the `CHANGETABLE` function. Because it does not store the row's previous and current values, Change Tracking is considered a lightweight mechanism. Instead of providing before-and-after states, it simply flags that a row has changed and relies on downstream processes to read the latest data from the base table.

In general, log-based CDC provides the most complete and reliable change-data-capture solution. However, it typically requires database administrators at the source system to enable and configure the necessary logging features, which may introduce operational or security considerations.

Data transformation

Before ingested data can be used effectively, it must undergo a series of refinement steps, including curation, standardization, declassification, deduplication, and ultimately aggregation. Collectively, these activities are known as **data transformation**. In essence, data transformation elevates raw data to a level where it becomes clean, consistent, and readily consumable for analytical and business operations.

Depending on the use case, data transformation can range from straightforward to highly complex. Its complexity is driven by several factors, including:

- The number of data sources involved in the pipeline.
- The volume, velocity, and variety of incoming data.
- The complexity of business rules required for cleaning, declassification, validation, and aggregation.
- The frequency of ingestion, including CDC operations, and how often transformations may be applied.
- Data governance and compliance requirements, such as lineage, traceability, masking, and retention policies.
- Dashboard freshness expectations, which dictate how quickly transformed data must be available for reporting and analytics.

Transformed data progressively matures as it moves from one layer to the next until it reaches its final resting place.

Data destination

Data destinations are the locations where the results of data transformations are stored. These destinations may correspond to different layers of the medallion architecture, with each layer designed to support a specific level of data refinement and consumption. Data destinations typically fall into two categories:

- **Intermediate Destinations**: These destinations store **partially** processed or intermediate transformation outputs.
  - In traditional architectures, these are known as the raw or curation layers where initial cleansing, standardization, and integration occur.
  - In Lakehouse architectures, this includes the bronze and silver layers, which hold raw ingested data and refined, enriched datasets, respectively.
- **Final Destinations**: These destinations store the fully processed, business-ready outputs of the transformation process.
  - In traditional data architectures, this corresponds to the transformation or presentation layer.
  - In Lakehouse architectures, this aligns with the gold layer, where aggregated, curated, and analytics-ready datasets are stored.

Data orchestration

Data orchestration automates the entire data pipeline by unifying workflow management, scheduling, and monitoring into a single, integrated framework. It coordinates every step involved in ingesting, transforming, and managing data across the platform, ensuring processes run reliably, efficiently, and in the correct sequence. This orchestration layer brings consistency and control to complex data ecosystems. The core components of data orchestration include the following:

- Workflow actions
- Workflow scheduling
- Workflow monitoring

Let us understand each of these in the following sections.

Workflows

A **workflow** is a structured unit of work composed of a sequence of actions executed in a defined order. Workflows are designed to run a series of actions in an automated manner, typically triggered manually, by a predefined schedule, or by specific events.

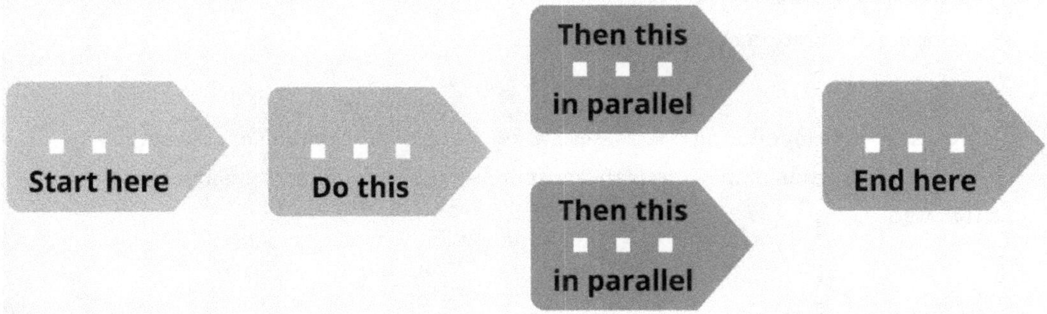

Figure 7.4: Series of actions in a workflow

Workflow actions

Much like the interconnected components of a physical engine, a workflow relies on a sequence of well-designed **actions** to perform its work. Each action carries out a specific task —whether executed once or repeatedly—and contributes to the overall objective of delivering clean, reliable, and ready-to-use data.

A data engineer is responsible for **organizing** these actions into a well-structured sequence of steps that efficiently meet analytics needs. This ordered sequence of tasks is collectively known as a **workflow**. A typical workflow consists of the following types of actions:

Input and output actions

These actions handle data movement into and out of the system. They include:

- Ingesting data from various data sources.
- Writing processed or transformed data to designated destinations.

Transformation Actions

These actions perform the operations needed to refine, clean, standardize, and enrich data. They may include:

- Data cleaning and validation.
- Business rule application.
- Aggregation, enrichment, and formatting.
- Object tagging.

Control Actions

These actions orchestrate the workflow's logical flow. They manage:

- Action chaining (defining execution order).
- Forking and joining branches of execution.

- Conditional logic and decision-making.
- Looping or iteration over sets of tasks.

> **Note**
>
> In a data pipeline monitoring system, several key metrics are essential for assessing performance and reliability. Among the most important are latency, throughput, and error rates.

Workflow Scheduling

Workflow scheduling determines when each task in the workflow is triggered. Workflows are typically instantiated using the following three methods:

- **Manually**: Manually triggering a workflow is the simplest form of invocation. It can be started from the control panel, command-line tools, or through APIs. For example, data engineers may run a job manually while performing unit tests or when a scheduled run fails, and a one-time execution is required. This approach is best suited for development, testing, or ad-hoc executions.
- **Scheduled**: In this approach, the workflow is triggered by a **scheduler**. The scheduler may be operating system–based, part of an orchestration platform, or built directly into the ETL tool. This is the most common method for running jobs in production environments. Depending on business requirements, jobs can be scheduled to run daily, hourly, or at any frequency needed to ensure timely data refreshes.
- **Event-based**: There are situations where schedule-based invocations are not effective —particularly when a job depends on external factors such as the availability of data or the completion of another workflow. In many cases, a job cannot run until upstream data ingestion has finished, and because the timing of that process can vary, an event-based trigger is often a better choice.

It is common for curation jobs to be initiated via event-based mechanisms immediately after an ingestion job completes successfully. Likewise, an aggregation pipeline is typically triggered only after the curation process has finished.

Workflow Monitoring

Once a pipeline is triggered, each action within it must be closely monitored. Monitoring should be configured to capture and store the execution state of every action in each pipeline run, typically as logs. If any action fails, the operational team should be notified immediately so corrective measures can be taken. Monitoring data pipelines provides several key benefits:

- **Establishes overall pipeline health**: Monitoring allows development and operation support teams to quickly determine whether a pipeline run has succeeded or failed.
- **Tracks total runtime for each pipeline**: Understanding the execution time is essential for evaluating **Service-Level Agreement (SLA)** breaches.
- **Identifies performance bottlenecks**: Detailed logs and metrics highlight slow-running tasks or steps, enabling data engineers to optimize code, resource allocation, and system configuration.

> Note
>
> Understanding what each component of a data pipeline does in isolation—and how it contributes to the pipeline's overall success—empowers a data engineer to conceptualize, design, and develop pipelines more efficiently and with greater confidence.

In the following sections, we will walk through the various phases involved in creating a data pipeline. Alongside the conceptual overview of each phase, we will outline recommended tasks and actions to consider during implementation. Together, these guidelines offer a solid foundation that readers can continue to refine and expand as they gain experience through real-world projects.

Data pipeline types

You may recall from *Chapter 5, Understanding Databricks, that* we discussed both **procedural** and **declarative** processing. While procedural processing is an **imperative** technique that focuses on a step-by-step sequence of operations, it explicitly defines *how* a task should be performed. In contrast, declarative processing emphasizes *what* outcome you want to achieve, without prescribing the exact sequence of steps required to get there.

In the context of **data pipelines**, both paradigms can be used effectively. Modern data engineering platforms—including Databricks—support a blend of both styles. This flexibility empowers teams to choose the most appropriate approach depending on pipeline complexity, performance requirements, governance considerations, and organizational preferences.

Imperative pipelines

Imperative pipelines explicitly define *how* data should flow and the precise **step-by-step operations** that must occur. They follow a **procedural programming model**, where the developer specifies detailed instructions that the system must execute in a fixed order. This approach offers granular control over the logic and execution path, making it well-suited for scenarios that require custom transformations, conditional branching, or tightly managed workflow behavior.

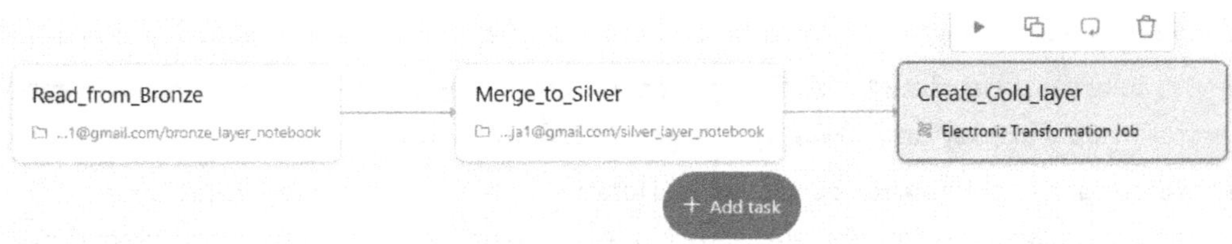

Figure 7.5: Sample imperative pipeline

In imperative pipelines, the data engineer has full control over task sequencing, resource usage, and error handling. Imperative pipelines are especially well-suited for workflows that require loops, dynamic branching, conditional logic, or integration with external services and APIs. Their flexibility and precision allow data engineers to craft highly tailored workflows that may not be easily expressed through higher-level declarative abstractions.

Declarative pipelines

Declarative pipelines, on the other hand, allow you to define data transformations at a higher level of abstraction, enabling engines like Spark or SQL to optimize execution automatically. You simply define the desired outcome, and the framework determines the plan and selects the most effective path to execute it.

```
import dlt

@dlt.table
def dlt_customers_count_products():
  facts = spark.readStream.table("my_first_catalog.my_first_schema.dlt_transactions")
  dims = spark.read.table("my_first_catalog.my_first_schema.dlt_customers")

  return (
    facts.join(dims, on="customer_id", how="inner").groupBy("customer_id").count()
  )
```

Figure 7.6: Sample declarative pipeline

Declarative pipelines automatically manage execution order and parallelism, ensuring tasks run in the correct sequence without the need for explicit control logic. As a result, the amount of code required is significantly reduced compared to imperative approaches.

Understanding the data pipeline creation process

In analytics-driven organizations, it is common to maintain multiple data pipelines, each designed to support a different use case. Often, these use cases are owned by separate business domains and rely on common datasets. In such environments, it is essential to carefully plan and design pipeline operations to uncover efficiencies and eliminate redundant work. Data pipelines are typically developed in phases, and in the following sections, we will explore each phase in detail.

Before diving into the details, the following diagram is essential in showing how each phase builds on the previous one. The key takeaway is that when a data engineer carefully follows the recommended actions for each phase, the effort required in subsequent phases is greatly reduced—and the likelihood of a successful outcome increases significantly.

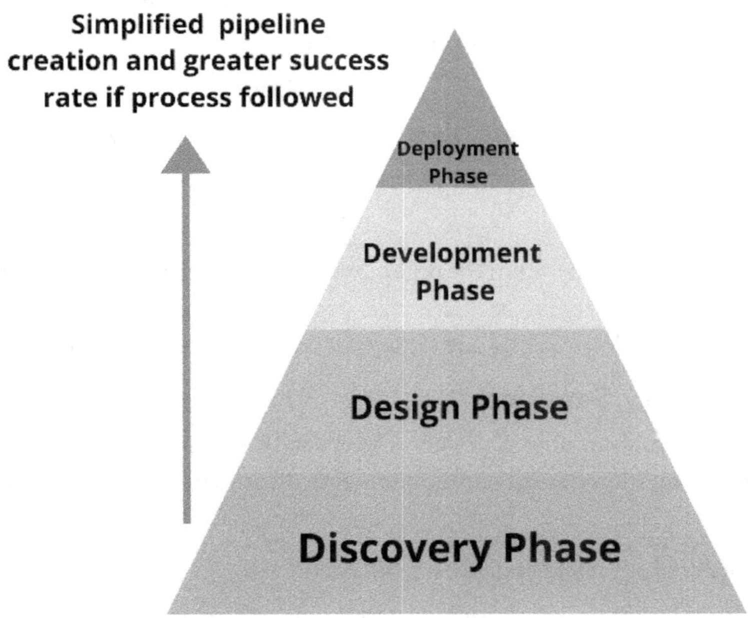

Figure 7.7: Various phases of data pipeline creation

Let us explore the steps that can help a data engineer kick-start the pipeline design process.

Discovery Phase

The creation of a data pipeline should begin with a discovery phase. This stage helps the data engineer understand the team, identify key stakeholders, refine use cases, and—most importantly—surface potential roadblocks or gaps that could jeopardize the project's success.

Identify the product owner

The **product owner** is accountable for the project's overall success and serves as the primary decision-maker. They should have direct access to senior management to align on goals and communicate project progress. The product owner is typically a senior leader within the business domain who brings several years of domain-specific experience. They must be able to answer—or obtain answers to—key questions such as:

- Current and future connectivity requirements for cloud integration.
- Security and compliance regulations that the organization must adhere to.
- Any required **service level agreements** (**SLAs**).
- End-user locations (on-premises, remote, or hybrid).
- The desired level of automation for infrastructure and code deployment.
- Whether the deployment should be vendor-agnostic.

Shortlist use cases

Engage each business domain within the organization to identify and document its specific use cases. Assign a dedicated owner to each use case—someone who will act as the knowledge champion and have decision-making authority over data access and requirements.

Conduct Discovery Sessions

The data engineer should conduct discovery sessions with each sub-group to gather comprehensive information about their requirements. These sessions should capture details such as:

- Use case description and end goals.
- Data source locations, connectivity details, and any anticipated challenges (e.g., MFA requirements, token renewals, firewall restrictions).
- Datasets involved, such as tables, files, or APIs, along with data types and schema information.
- Frequency of schema changes and expected impact.
- Estimated data volume for both historical loads and incremental updates.
- Approximate size of incremental data to plan ingestion and processing capacity.

- Acceptable data latency between OLTP and OLAP systems (e.g., minutes, hourly, daily, or near real-time).
- Information about data consumers such as data analysts, data scientists, or application teams.
- Whether the use case is new or already exists.
    a. If it exists, request access to the current ETL code, as well as any dashboards or reports that rely on it.
    b. If it is new, request a written specification detailing required joins, aggregations, filters, and business rules.
- PII considerations, whether personally identifiable information must be masked and using why technique.
- Data classification rules that govern handling and storage.
- Security requirements, including table, row, and column-level access controls.
- Encryption needs, including whether cloud-provider keys or customer-managed keys will be used.
- Current technical skill sets within the team and their willingness to adopt modern frameworks (e.g., Spark).
- Any planned data science, ad-hoc analysis, or advanced analytics activities that may impact data design or processing needs.

I understand this requirement-gathering process may seem time-consuming, but the effort is worthwhile. The more thoroughly you prepare up front, the smoother the design, development, and deployment phases will be. I strongly recommend making it standard practice to address the items listed above before beginning any data lake initiative. As you gain experience, you can continue to expand and refine this checklist.

The key deliverables of the discovery phase should include:

- A detailed understanding document (one per use case) that summarizes all information collected during the discovery process.
- A consolidated list of gaps, risks, and roadblocks, each with an assigned owner responsible for resolution.

The understanding document should be reviewed and approved by the product owner before moving to the next phase. It is acceptable to proceed even if some gaps or roadblocks remain unresolved, as long as there is a clear agreement to address these issues before pipeline development begins.

Note

Discovery serves as both a foundation and a forward-looking guide. It enables early identification of gaps, weaknesses, and risks that could affect the project. By surfacing these issues upfront, data engineers can resolve them before they become costly or disruptive later in the lifecycle.

Design Phase

Now that the discovery phase is complete, it is time to design the data pipeline. The information gathered during discovery should serve as the foundation for the design process. When designing the pipeline, the data engineer should address considerations such as:

Shortlist Common Datasets

Gather all use case documents from the discovery phase and identify the datasets that appear repeatedly across multiple use cases. This step is critical and deserves careful attention. Recognizing common datasets across sub-groups promotes data reusability and supports strong **master data management** (**MDM**) practices.

The figure below illustrates a multi-pipeline design approach in which each previously identified use case is implemented as an independent pipeline with no shared dependencies. While this may appear straightforward, it often results in the same dataset being ingested multiple times across different pipelines.

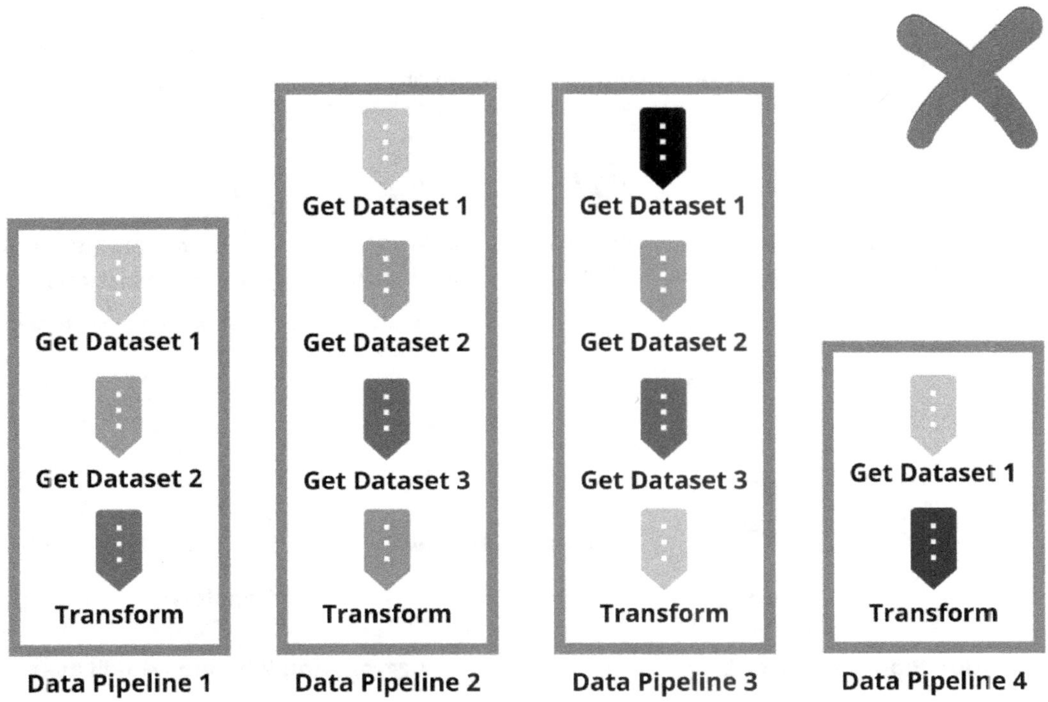

Figure 7.8: The multi-pipeline design approach on the lines of use cases

This duplication leads to unnecessary consumption of storage and compute resources, ultimately increasing operational costs for the organization. For example, ingesting 5 GB of duplicate data across five pipelines can unnecessarily consume up to 25 GB of storage, increasing both storage usage and costs. For these reasons, the multi-pipeline design approach is not recommended.

Design Pipeline using Parent-Child Approach Common Datasets

You may recall from *Chapter 1, The Story of Data Engineering and Analytics*, that *"storage is cheap, yet compute is expensive."* This is an opportunity to apply that principle. By investing a bit more effort during the design phase, the data engineer can deliver a solution that adheres to best practices, promotes reusability, and reduces both compute usage and overall cost.

Notice in the image below how all ingestion datasets have been consolidated into a parent ingestion pipeline, while each previously identified use case has been implemented as its own child pipeline. This structure offers several advantages over maintaining multiple independent pipelines and is strongly recommended:

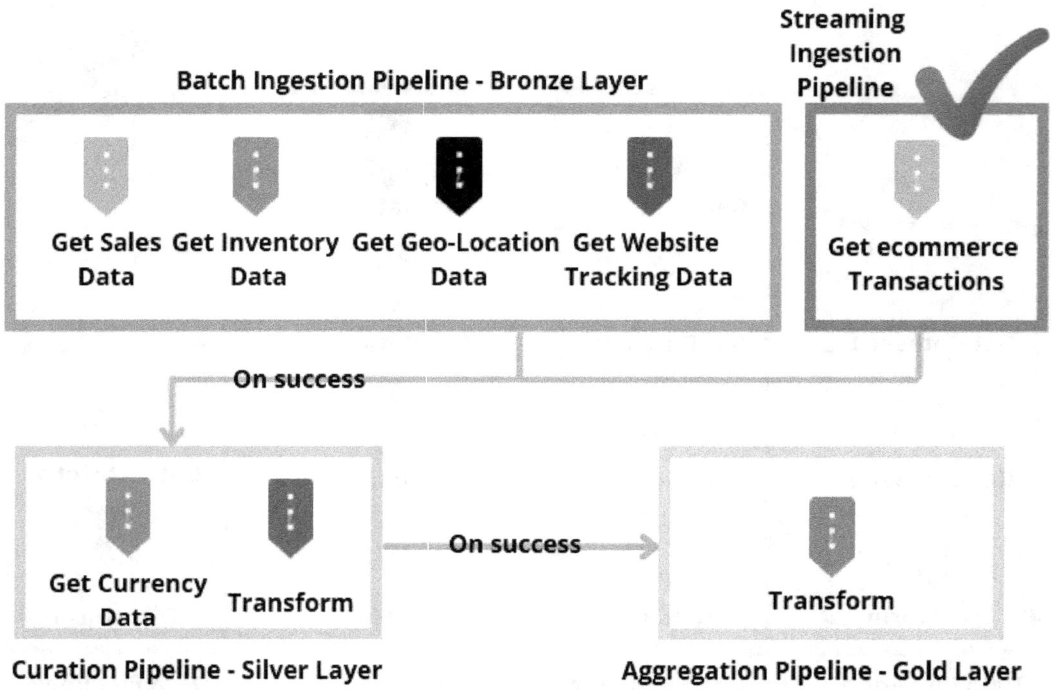

Figure 7.9: The parent-child approach of pipeline design

The parent–child pipeline design offers several key benefits:

- Each dataset is ingested only once, and all child pipelines can reuse it.
- Reduces both storage and compute costs by eliminating redundant processing.
- Improves execution control by allowing the parent pipeline to enforce dependencies and manage when child pipelines run.

> **Note**
>
> The parent–child pipeline structure provides a useful example for choosing appropriate invocation mechanisms. In most cases, the parent pipeline should be scheduled, while the child pipelines should run on event triggers—executing only after the parent pipeline completes successfully.

Design Cloud Architecture

Based on the approved discovery documents, the data engineer should create a diagram illustrating the cloud resources required to build the data pipeline. This diagram should include components such as networking, connections to on-premises and external systems, storage services, compute resources, and orchestration tools.

Design Automation and Monitoring

Based on the desired level of automation, the data engineer should design CI/CD pipelines to handle both infrastructure provisioning and code deployment in the cloud. In addition, the data engineer should define the monitoring and notification mechanisms required to track pipeline performance and ensure timely alerts for any failures or anomalies.

Costing

Once the high-level design is complete, the data engineer should prepare rough cost estimates for the required cloud resources, including:

- **Development Environment Costs**: Estimate the monthly cost of cloud resources for development and testing environments. Keep in mind that storage and compute requirements are typically lower than those in production, so resources should be sized accordingly to avoid unnecessary expense.
- **Production Environment Costs**: Estimate the monthly cost of cloud resources for the production environment. This estimate should account for additional expenses associated with auto scaling during periods of peak demand.

Note

When preparing cost estimates, the data engineer should thoroughly research how pricing varies between on-demand and reserved resources. Significant savings can often be achieved by reserving resources for one or more years rather than relying solely on on-demand consumption.

The key deliverables of the design phase are a comprehensive document that summarizes the following key elements:

- Cloud architecture overview.
- Detailed descriptions of the parent and child pipelines.
- How the pipeline design meets key compliance and security requirements.
- Approaches for handling incremental data, CDC, data latency, and schema evolution.
- Methods for publishing the final data to end-users.
- Notification processes for informing end-users about pipeline execution status.
- Development strategy, including programming languages, tools, and environments.
- Cloud service model selection (IaaS, PaaS, or SaaS).

- Deployment strategy for infrastructure and code through CI/CD pipelines.
- Monitoring and observability strategy for production pipelines.
- Cost estimates for all cloud resources.

Once the design is complete, the data engineer should submit the design document to the client and schedule walkthrough sessions. These sessions should be held with each sub-group involved in the discovery phase, as well as with the IT team responsible for deploying and managing the pipelines.

The design document must be thoroughly reviewed and formally approved by the product owner before moving on to the next stage.

> **Note**
>
> Building confidence with the IT team through walkthrough sessions is essential. Since they will ultimately be responsible for deploying and managing the pipelines, their alignment and support for the proposed design are critical to the project's success.

Development Phase

If you've reached this stage, it likely means the product owner has formally approved the design document. Congratulations! With most of the preparatory work now complete, it's time to move into the development phase, which will follow the steps outlined below:

- Start with the parent pipeline, as it forms the foundation for all subsequent work.
- Test connectivity to each data source and become familiar with the data formats and schemas.
- Determine how incremental data will be delivered from each source system.
- Define a strategy for merging incremental data into the data lake.
- Develop approaches to handle schema evolution within the data lake.
- Plan the intermediate and final storage locations that will be used throughout the pipeline.
- Build the parent pipeline, ensuring that it is robust and designed for long-term scalability.
- Apply strong data security practices at every stage of development.
- After completing the parent pipeline, begin work on the child pipelines.
- For each child pipeline, design transformations to minimize repeated compute operations and maximize dataset reuse.

Unit testing phase

Once the pipeline development is complete, the data engineer and product owner should validate small, testable components—such as ingestion processes, transformations, functions, SQL models, and logic blocks—individually to ensure each behaves as expected. After this validation, the data engineer should prepare and submit a formal unit testing document that confirms successful data ingestion, verifies correct data types, validates data-quality expectations, and confirms the accuracy of aggregations.

> Note
>
> Multiple frameworks support unit testing in data pipelines, with popular options including pytest and unittest for code-based pipelines, dbt tests for SQL models, and Great Expectations for data quality validation.

Deployment Phase

Assuming an agile development methodology, newly developed data pipeline code is continuously merged into a shared source control repository and deployed across multiple environments—typically development, testing, and production. Because this process may occur dozens or even hundreds of times during a project, it is essential that deployments be automated, repeatable, and reliable. Manual deployments not only slow down delivery but also introduce inconsistency, errors, and operational risk.

This is exactly where modern software delivery, built on **Continuous Integration** and **Continuous Delivery** (**CI/CD**), becomes indispensable. CI/CD provides a framework and toolset that automates the movement of code from development to production, ensuring that each increment of work is integrated, validated, tested, and deployed seamlessly. Traditionally, the creation and management of CI/CD pipelines have been the responsibility of dedicated DevOps teams. However, as the industry evolves, data engineers are increasingly expected—often required—to develop these capabilities as part of their role.

> Note
>
> DevOps, derived from the words Development and Operations, is a set of practices designed to accelerate software delivery by unifying teams, automating workflows, and leveraging shared tools and best practices.

The core principle of modern software delivery is straightforward: **develop, test, and integrate small increments of code frequently**. Through the practice of **Continuous Integration (CI)**, developers are encouraged to make small, manageable code changes, merge them into the main branch, and validate them using automated tests. This approach provides rapid feedback on how new changes interact with existing components, allowing teams to detect issues early and reducing the complexity of troubleshooting.

Once the code has passed all integration checks, **Continuous Deployment (CD)** automates pushing these validated changes to testing or production environments. This ensures that updates are deployed consistently and reliably, while giving developers immediate insight into how their code behaves in real-world environments.

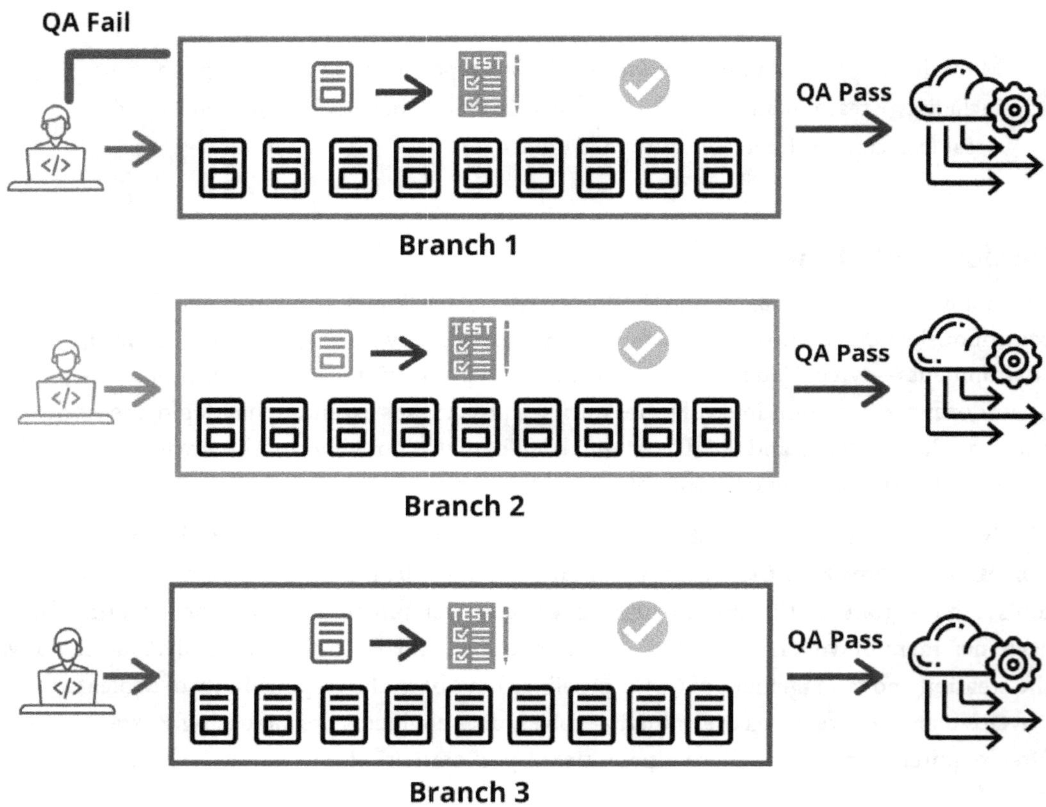

Figure 7.10: Modern software delivery cycle using CI/CD

There are several DevOps tools available for implementing CI/CD pipelines, including **Jenkins**, **GitLab CI/CD**, and **CircleCI** and **Azure DevOps**, Azure's native SaaS platform, provides modern development teams with robust capabilities for planning, collaboration, and seamless code delivery.

> **Note**
>
> Implementing CI/CD is more about changing team culture than adopting new tools. Securing buy-in from the development team and senior management is essential before beginning the rollout. Implementing CI/CD may encounter cultural resistance, especially from teams accustomed to manual deployments or those who are uneasy about automated changes being pushed into production.

Monitoring phase

Enabling and monitoring the pipeline involves turning on the production workflow and continuously tracking its performance, run status, and overall health. Effective monitoring helps detect failures, delays, or anomalies early, enabling the data engineer to respond promptly and maintain reliable data flow. Pipeline monitoring is built into Databricks, providing native visibility into the health, performance, and reliability of data pipelines without requiring external tooling. Some common examples of pipeline failures include unusually long runtimes, resource exhaustion, and interruptions caused by data source connection issues. During the initial days of production, it is advisable for the data engineer to be part of the pipeline's notification group, as their deep understanding of the logic and design allows them to identify subtle issues that others may overlook. Once the pipeline stabilizes, ongoing monitoring responsibilities can be transitioned to the operations team.

Documentation phase

The final deliverable of this phase is the **runbook**, which provides guidance for handling operational and administrative tasks, including:

- Running CI/CD pipelines
- Monitoring data pipelines
- Responding to failures and restarting pipelines after errors
- Updating or modifying pipeline schedules
- Disabling pipelines when necessary

Electroniz data platform

Up to this point, we have explored the theoretical foundations of data engineering in depth. Theory helps us understand the *why* behind modern data systems—why pipelines fail, why architecture choices matter, why clean data is essential, and why automation and governance are non-negotiable in mature organizations. But theory alone is not enough. Data engineering is a highly practical discipline, and the real learning begins when we move from the conceptual to the hands-on.

Now, we shift our focus to the practical realities of how everything comes together. In the upcoming chapters, we will walk step-by-step through the process of building a fully functional Lakehouse. Instead of abstract examples, we will immerse ourselves in a realistic project scenario that mirrors the challenges, conversations, and decisions a data engineer faces in the real world.

To make the experience authentic, we will assume the role of a newly hired data engineer at **Electroniz**—a leading big-box retailer specializing in consumer electronics. Electroniz operates hundreds of stores and has a rapidly expanding e-commerce business, generating massive amounts of transactional, inventory, and behavioral data every day. Like many modern retailers, Electroniz is at an inflection point: the industry is evolving, customer expectations are shifting, and competitors are aggressively leveraging data to gain an advantage. Recognizing this, the company's leadership has committed to modernizing its data engineering and analytics capabilities. Their goal is to streamline internal operations, enable better decision-making, improve customer experiences, and unlock new revenue opportunities through advanced analytics, machine learning, and AI-driven insights.

Data platform requirements

On your very first day, the CTO personally welcomes you and outlines the company's vision for the future. Instead of lengthy documents or high-level speeches, he hands you a single diagram —a blueprint representing the strategic direction for Electroniz's future data platform. The diagram highlights how raw data from stores, suppliers, e-commerce systems, currency conversion, and product reviews will flow into a centralized Lakehouse environment, where it will be transformed into high-quality datasets ready for analytics, BI dashboards, and machine learning applications.

This vision sets the stage for your journey. During the next few chapters, you will be responsible for:

- Assessing the business requirements
- Designing the data architecture
- Defining data products strategy
- Designing and implementing ingestion pipelines
- Ensuring data quality, security, and governance
- Building curation and aggregation pipelines
- Deploying pipelines into a production-ready Lakehouse
- Making data platform ready for self-serve analytics and AI-driven insights
- Implementing data observability

The following image illustrates how data flows from various source systems into the future Electroniz data platform built on Databricks.

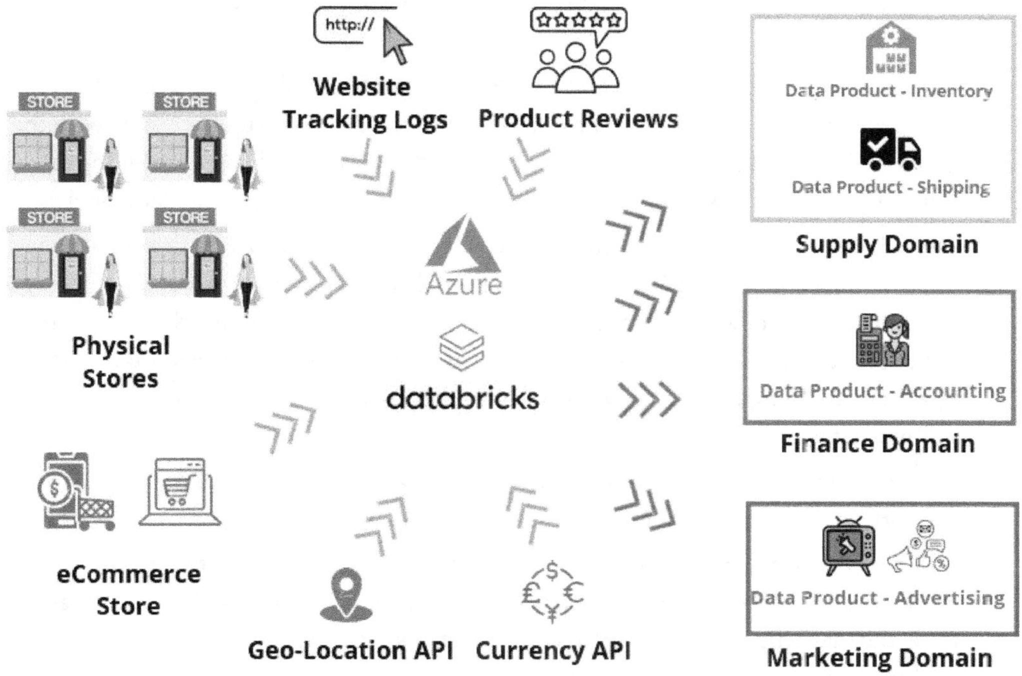

Figure 7.11: Electroniz future data platform capabilities

The CTO also shared several high-level details to help you kick-start your work. These insights paint a picture of Electroniz's current operational landscape, its challenges, and the expectations for the new data platform:

- Electroniz operates a large retail footprint, selling consumer electronics through dozens of brick-and-mortar stores across the United States, as well as a rapidly growing e-commerce website. Online orders can be shipped not only within the U.S. but also to Canada, Europe, and Asia.
- Shipping and logistics are outsourced to major third-party carriers such as DHL, Purolator, and UPS. Each vendor provides its own tracking systems, delivery timelines, and data formats—adding complexity to the integration process.
- The current analytics platform relies on an on-premises SQL Server database. Over time, performance limitations, storage constraints, and a lack of scalability have made it increasingly difficult to support advanced analytics and real-time reporting.

- Electroniz wants to use sales data to optimize multiple business functions, including inventory management, shipping performance, accounting workflows, and targeted advertising. The company sees data as the backbone of operational efficiency and future growth.
- Compliance is a major concern. As a retailer that handles credit card transactions and sells products in California and the European Union, Electroniz must comply with the GDPR and the CCPA. This means all sensitive customer information—including PII—must be properly masked, encrypted, and secured at every stage of the data pipeline.
- The existing ETL process runs only once per day, which creates a significant 24-hour lag. This delay has resulted in several operational issues, especially around inventory and fulfillment. For example, customers have purchased items online that were already out of stock, but the website remained unaware because the data was outdated. This has led to shipping delays, backorders, cancellations, and ultimately a noticeable decline in customer satisfaction—and sales.
- The company's vision is to move toward a near-real-time analytics platform capable of supporting fast decision-making and improving customer experience.
- Electroniz also aims to use intelligent analytics to optimize its advertising and marketing budget. By analyzing customer behavior and website traffic in near real time, the marketing team hopes to reduce wasted spend and target customers more effectively across different regions and channels.

Building on the requirements outlined above, and assuming the discovery and design phases have been completed, the following represents the proposed blueprint for Electroniz's future-state data platform. This blueprint reflects the insights gathered through stakeholder interviews, current-state assessments, capability gap analyses, and architectural design workshops.

> **Note**
>
> While you are waiting for final approvals from the customer regarding design and architecture documents, it is a good use of time to set up code repositories, test cloud connectivity, and set up development environments.

Data platform blueprint

The Electroniz data platform will evolve into a modern, scalable, and resilient data ecosystem designed to support advanced analytics, optimize operational efficiency, and enable sustainable long-term business growth. The data platform blueprint serves as a comprehensive, high-level plan that outlines the future-state architecture—including storage layers, data product patterns, governance foundations, and the design of data ingestion and transformation pipelines. A well-drafted data platform blueprint ensures a unified vision across all business domains, IT, and data teams, a scalable architecture, and strong data governance. It provides a modular architecture capable of supporting diverse analytics and operational workloads, as well as future growth.

To establish this blueprint, we begin by defining the reference architecture that will guide how all components of the Electroniz data platform fit together.

Reference architecture

The **reference architecture** diagram provides a conceptual map of how Databricks fits within a modern Azure-based data architecture. It outlines how data flows from ingestion services, such as Azure Data Factory and Event Hubs, into a scalable storage foundation, such as Azure Data Lake Storage Gen2. It illustrates how Azure Databricks acts as the primary compute and transformation engine—leveraging Apache Spark, Delta Lake, and Unity Catalog to support advanced analytics workloads. Have a look at the following diagram:

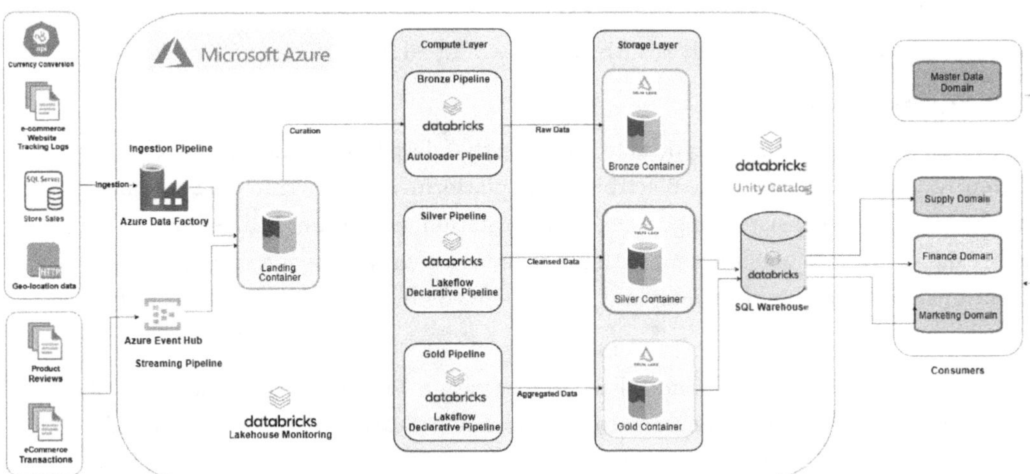

Figure 7.12: Electroniz reference architecture diagram

The reference architecture diagram provides a holistic, future-state view of the platform, helping teams understand how each Azure service interacts with Databricks to deliver a unified, high-performance, and fully governed data and AI ecosystem.

Data storage design

Selecting and designing the appropriate storage layers is critical for ensuring performance, scalability, and reliability across all analytics workloads. In alignment with the reference architecture, the Electroniz data platform will implement a multi-zone data lake structure within Azure Data Lake Storage Gen2. The required storage layers include:

- **Landing zone**: Azure Data Lake Storage Gen 2
- **Bronze layer**: Azure Data Lake Storage Gen 2
- **Silver layer**: Azure Data Lake Storage Gen 2
- **Gold layer**: Azure Data Lake Storage Gen 2

This layered approach supports progressive data refinement, governance, and optimized consumption patterns.

Data compute design

All notebooks and SQL workloads within the Electroniz Data Platform will leverage Databricks Serverless Compute. This compute model provides fully managed, on-demand execution environments that automatically scale based on workload requirements.

Data pipeline design

The design of data pipelines is central to ensuring that data flows reliably, securely, and efficiently across all layers of the Electroniz data platform. A well-architected pipeline framework enables consistent ingestion, transformation, validation, and delivery of high-quality data products. In alignment with the reference architecture and storage layer definitions, the following principles and components define the future-state data pipeline design.

This pipeline design includes standardized orchestration with Azure Data Factory, scalable processing with Lakeflow **Spark Declarative Pipelines** (**SCP**) and Delta Lake, embedded governance with Unity Catalog, and integrated data quality checks at each stage of the pipeline.

The following diagram outlines the pipelines that form the foundation of Electroniz's future-state data pipeline design, ensuring that all data entering the platform is properly ingested, curated, transformed, validated, and published as trusted data products.

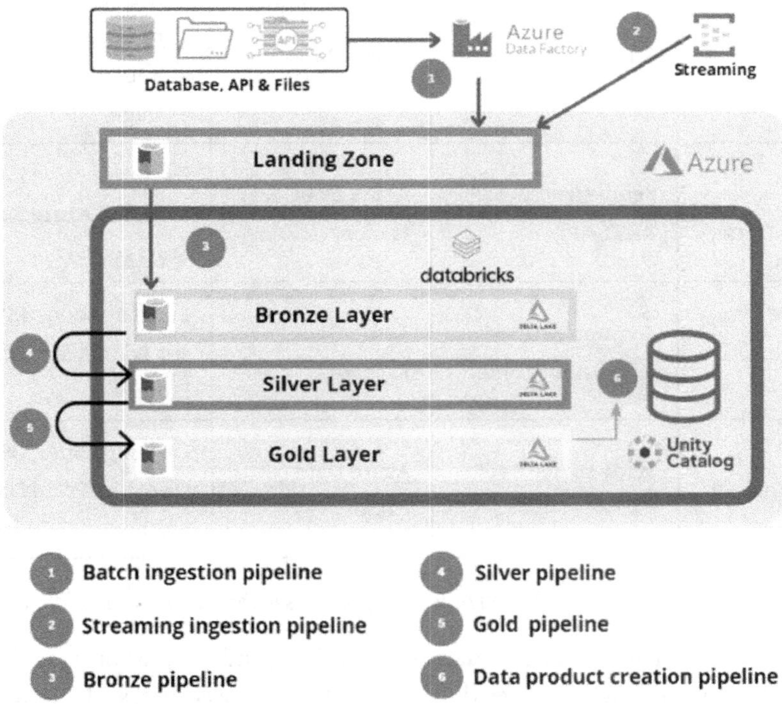

Figure 7.13: Electroniz data pipeline design

Batch ingestion pipeline

The **batch ingestion pipeline** serves as the entry point to the Electroniz data platform, enabling the secure, reliable, and scalable movement of data from source systems into the Landing Zone of Azure Data Lake Storage Gen2. A well-designed ingestion layer ensures that data arrives in its raw form with full fidelity, appropriate metadata, and the necessary controls to support downstream transformation and governance. The data ingestion pipeline will be developed using **Azure Data Factory (ADF)** as the primary orchestration and integration service. ADF manages the end-to-end ingestion process, including source connectivity, scheduling, dependency control, data movement, and error handling. ADF is designed as a robust ingestion mechanism that ensures data arrives in its raw form with full fidelity, enriched with appropriate metadata, and governed by the necessary controls to support downstream transformation and governance. It manages the entire ingestion lifecycle—including source connectivity, scheduling, dependency management, data movement, and error handling.

Data Source	Data Source Type	Data Collection Mechanism	Data Destination
Store Sales Database	Structured: Azure SQL Database	Azure Data Factory	Landing zone - CSV files stored in Azure Data Lake Storage
Currency Conversion Data	Semi-structured: REST API	Azure Data Factory	Landing zone - JSON files stored in Azure Data Lake Storage
e-commerce Website Tracking Logs	Semi-structured: Azure Bob Storage	Azure Data Factory	Landing zone - JSON files stored in Azure Data Lake Storage
Geo-location data	Semi-structured: HTTP	Azure Data Factory	Landing zone - CSV files stored in Azure Data Lake Storage

Table 7.1: Information regarding batch data sources in the Electroniz data project

By leveraging ADF's native connectors, managed identities, and integration capabilities with Azure Data Lake Storage Gen2, the ingestion layer will provide a secure, scalable, and highly reliable mechanism for onboarding raw data into the platform.

Streaming ingestion pipeline

The **streaming ingestion pipeline** enables Electroniz to process data continuously and in near real-time. Unlike batch pipelines, which run at scheduled intervals, the streaming pipeline ingests and processes data as soon as it arrives. The following data sources will be ingested using the streaming approach:

Data Source	Data Source Type	Data Collection Mechanism	Data Destination
Product Reviews	Unstructured: Files on S3	Azure Event Hubs	Landing zone - Text files stored in Azure Data Lake Storage

Data Source	Data Source Type	Data Collection Mechanism	Data Destination
e-commerce Transactions	Structured: Event streaming	Azure Event Hubs	Landing zone – AVRO files stored in Azure Data Lake Storage

Table 7.2: Information regarding streaming data sources in the Electroniz data project

Bronze pipeline

The **bronze pipeline** is the first processing layer in the Electroniz data platform's medallion architecture. Its primary role is to ingest raw data from the Landing Zone and convert it into structured, **append-only** Delta Lake tables while maintaining the full fidelity of the source data. This layer forms the foundational dataset on which all subsequent cleansing, transformation, and data product development activities rely.

The pipeline will be implemented in **Databricks notebooks** using **Auto Loader**, which enables efficient, incremental ingestion by automatically detecting and processing new files as they land in ADLS.

Silver pipeline

The **silver pipeline** is the second processing layer in Electroniz's medallion architecture. It refines the raw, append-only bronze data into clean, conformed, and analytics-ready Delta Lake tables. This layer focuses on applying data quality rules, standardizing formats, resolving schema inconsistencies, handling missing or invalid values, deduplication, and performing the necessary transformations to create a trusted, enriched dataset suitable for downstream modeling and data product development.

The silver pipeline will be built in **Databricks notebooks**, leveraging **Lakeflow Spark Declarative Pipelines (SCP)** to efficiently transform bronze data into curated data in a streaming fashion.

Gold pipeline

The **gold pipeline** represents the final and most refined layer of Electroniz's medallion architecture. It transforms the curated, high-quality silver datasets into **business-ready,** purpose-built data models that directly support analytics, reporting, data science, and operational use cases. Gold datasets are optimized for performance, usability, and consumption across BI tools and downstream systems. They serve as authoritative sources for dashboards, machine-learning features, and enterprise decision-making.

The gold pipeline will be implemented in **Databricks notebooks**, leveraging **Lakeflow Spark Declarative Pipelines (SCP)** to efficiently transform silver data into aggregated data in a streaming fashion.

Data product creation pipeline

The **data product creation pipeline** is the final stage of Electroniz's end-to-end data lifecycle and is built on top of the gold layer. Its purpose is to transform curated, business-ready datasets into **consumable data products** tailored to specific analytical, operational, or domain-driven needs. These products are designed with clear owners, defined SLAs, and measurable quality standards to ensure they deliver consistent value to their consumers.

The data product creation pipeline will be implemented using an open-source command-line tool called datacontract. It natively supports the **Open Data Contract Standard (ODCS)** for validating data contracts and executing quality tests.

Data product strategy

The data product strategy defines how Electroniz will design, build, manage, and deliver high-value, reusable, and business-aligned data assets across the organization. This strategy establishes the standards, domain ownership model, and data assets that guide the creation and maintenance of data products across the Electroniz data platform.

From the producer's standpoint, each data product represents a curated, business-ready dataset designed to support analytical, operational, and reporting needs across the organization. Each data product will be built through a structured, multi-layer pipeline: **Landing → Bronze → Silver → Gold → Data Product.** Data products will be governed by a rigorous data contract that guarantees producers deliver high-quality, well-managed data, while providing consumers with clear guidance on how to use that data safely and consistently across both analytical and operational workflows.

Consumers will be able to validate the data contract downstream, allowing them to review and confirm that it accurately reflects their expectations and usage requirements.

Governance

Governance is a top priority at Electroniz. The future data platform will reinforce governance standards as follows:

- PII data will be fully masked, tokenized, or redacted in the silver layer in accordance with governance policies, ensuring that no sensitive information propagates beyond tightly controlled transformation stages.
- Because the Bronze layer contains raw, unredacted source data, it will remain strictly restricted and will never be published or made accessible to any consumer-facing systems.

- Access to all datasets in Unity Catalog will be managed through Electroniz's **Role-Based Access Control** (**RBAC**) model, ensuring that only authorized users and service principals can interact with data according to their defined privileges.
- Column-level, row-level, and dynamic masking policies will be applied where appropriate to ensure sensitive attributes are protected.
- Unity Catalog lineage, audit logging, and access monitoring will provide full traceability of how data—especially PII—flows, transforms, and is consumed across the platform.
- Data contract validation will ensure compliance with Electroniz governance rules.
- Environment-based isolation and governed promotion workflows will ensure that data and metadata move through dev, test, and prod environments in a controlled and auditable manner.
- Monitoring and alerting will proactively notify data stewards if bad quality data appears in non-approved zones or violates governance policies.
- All data will be encrypted at rest or in motion.

Deployment Strategy

In line with industry best practices, the deployment of the Electroniz Lakehouse will be carried out via a CI/CD process. At a high level, the CI/CD process will operate as follows: Developers begin by authoring and unit testing their Data Factory pipelines in their individual feature branches. Once development is complete, they submit a pull request, enabling the team to review and validate the changes. After the code has been examined and approved, the feature branch is merged into the main branch.

When a deployment is required, the updated main branch is promoted to the **User Acceptance Testing** (**UAT**) environment for further validation. Upon successful verification and testing in UAT, the same release is deployed to the production environment, ensuring a controlled and reliable progression from development to live operations.

Observability

Observability within the Electroniz Data Platform will provide end-to-end visibility into the health, performance, and reliability of all data pipelines, data products, and platform components. We will use a combination of Databricks Jobs and Databricks Monitoring to track operational metrics, pipeline execution behavior, data quality, and platform-level performance.

Over the past few days, we've made substantial progress, and it's clear that the project is moving in the right direction. At this stage, we will assume that Electroniz has completed its review of all submitted design and architecture documents. According to the product owner, Electroniz is fully satisfied with the proposed design and architecture for the lakehouse and is eager to proceed to the next phase of the implementation. With their approval in place, we are now ready to formally commence the development cycle.

The journey of data has **started**.... We have some serious work ahead of us, so let us get started.

Summary

In this chapter, we explored the complete **data pipeline lifecycle**, from discovery to design, development, testing, deployment, and operations. One of the most important lessons to carry forward is that the discovery and design phases are far more critical than the development itself. Writing code may feel like the core of a data engineer's role, but without a solid understanding of business requirements, data sources, compliance expectations, and architectural constraints, even the best-written code can lead to systems that are costly, inefficient, or misaligned with organizational needs.

The discovery phase lays the foundation by clarifying *what* needs to be built and *why*. The design phase then transforms that understanding into a structured, scalable, and maintainable blueprint for implementing the solution. When these two phases are done thoroughly, development becomes faster, cleaner, and significantly less error-prone. Conversely, skipping or rushing these steps often leads to rework, frustration, and wasted resources.

As you move into the next chapter, where we shift from theory to hands-on implementation, we begin to architect and build the Electroniz Lakehouse environment from the ground up.

Get this book's PDF version and more

Scan the QR code (or go to `packtpub.com/unlock`). Search for this book by name, confirm the edition, and then follow the steps on the page.

UNLOCK NOW

Note: Keep your invoice handy. Purchases made directly from Packt don't require an invoice.

8

Data Ingestion Stage: Building the Landing Zone

In the previous chapters, we explored key aspects of data pipelines and their importance in constructing and managing modern data systems. With this theoretical foundation established, you now have the context needed to shift from understanding how lakehouses function to building one. This transition marks an important milestone because hands-on implementation is where conceptual knowledge becomes practical and begins to resemble real-world data engineering practices.

In this chapter, we begin the first practical steps in creating a fully operational data lakehouse. Our journey starts with a deep dive into the **landing zone**—the foundational area where raw data is first collected. We will begin by gathering data in the landing zone, which is intentionally designed to maintain data in its original, unaltered state while supporting future transformation and enrichment.

At the start, we will focus on establishing the data sources that feed the lakehouse. This includes connecting to the systems where data originates—such as operational databases, APIs, files, or streaming platforms—and configuring these connections to ensure consistent, reliable, and repeatable ingestion.

Next, we will set up the destinations within the lakehouse environment. This involves defining how and where data will be stored, determining appropriate formats and schemas, and establishing structures that support scalability, performance, and governance as the data volume grows.

With both sources and destinations configured, we will then construct the ingestion pipelines that move data into the landing zone. These pipelines form the operational core of the lakehouse, managing orchestration, data movement, error handling, and performance optimization.

Finally, we will validate these ingestion pipelines through thorough testing. This step is essential as it confirms their reliability, accuracy, and resilience when handling real-world data scenarios—both predictable and exceptional—before we build more advanced transformations and business logic in later chapters.

This chapter will cover the following topics:

- Need for a landing zone
- Preparing data sources
- Building the ingestion pipelines

Technical requirements

This chapter assumes the following technical prerequisites:

- An active Azure free account. You may recall that we created this account in *Chapter 3, Data Engineering on Microsoft Azure.*
- Access to the Packt Publishing GitHub repository to download the code samples and datasets used throughout this chapter. To access the repository, follow the steps in the "Download the example code files" section of the *Preface*.

Need for a landing zone

The landing zone of a lakehouse stores raw data exactly as it arrives from source systems, preserving its original shape, structure, and format without any transformations applied. The following are a few advantages of storing data in its native format:

- **Used for raw file drops**: The landing zone stores raw files exactly as delivered (CSV, JSON, logs, images, PDFs, etc.).
- **Re-playable**: If analysts or engineers detect issues in transformation logic, the bronze, silver, and gold layers can be rebuilt from scratch because the original, unaltered data is always available.
- **Easily repurposed**: As new business requirements emerge, the same raw data can be used to generate new transformations without requiring re-ingestion.

- **Support for multiple formats and types**: The landing zone can house **structured**, **semi-structured**, and **unstructured** data, including both text-based and binary assets.
- **Supports audit and lineage**: Keeping data in its native state ensures full traceability, which is essential for validating accuracy and maintaining compliance.
- **Clear separation from the lakehouse**: A landing zone creates a distinct boundary between incoming data and the lakehouse environment.

> Note
>
> Some may view the landing zone as an unnecessary use of resources, but it offers several important benefits, including pre-processing and file validation, as well as a controlled area for files delivered by external sources.

In modern lakehouse architectures, the landing zone is often optional, as many ingestion frameworks can now land raw data directly in the bronze layer without an intermediate storage step.

High-level plan to build the landing zone

In a typical project, the landing zone is built by identifying the right data sources. Once the sources are known, teams typically validate access and connectivity, ensuring credentials, networking, and security configurations are all in place. Only after these foundational steps are complete do engineers begin implementing the ingestion pipelines that will land raw data into the landing zone.

However, in our training scenario, we face a unique challenge: there is no existing data to work with. Since this is a controlled learning environment, we will simulate the early stages of a project. To do this effectively, we will generate our own sample datasets that mimic real-world structures and behaviors. These demo datasets will allow us to practice every stage of the ingestion workflow—from source discovery to pipeline deployment, and finally unit testing.

Before we begin preparing the data sources, let's review the section of the Electroniz architecture diagram in *Figure 8.1* that we'll be building in this chapter. The red-outlined area in the following figure shows the components we will be building in this chapter.

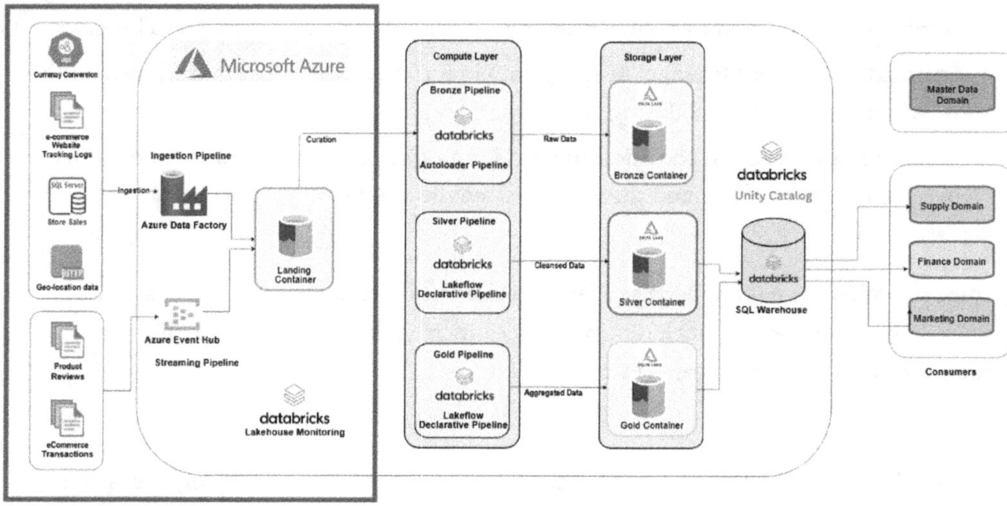

Figure 8.1: Portion of the Electroniz architecture that will be built in this chapter

Both the batch and streaming pipelines will be developed in this chapter. Before we begin, please take a moment to review the data sources, their collection mechanisms, and their intended destinations.

Batch ingestion pipeline

The batch ingestion pipeline sources data from the following systems. Azure Data Factory serves as the ingestion mechanism, orchestrating data collection and landing it in Azure Data Lake Storage for downstream processing.

Data Source	Data Source Type	Data Collection Mechanism	Data Destination
Store Sales Database	Structured: Azure SQL Database	Azure Data Factory	Landing zone - CSV files stored in Azure Data Lake Storage
Currency Conversion Data	Semi-structured: REST API	Azure Data Factory	Landing zone - JSON files stored in Azure Data Lake Storage

Data Source	Data Source Type	Data Collection Mechanism	Data Destination
e-commerce Website Tracking Logs	Semi-structured: Azure Blob Storage	Azure Data Factory	Landing zone - JSON files stored in Azure Data Lake Storage
Geo-location data	Semi-structured: HTTP	Azure Data Factory	Landing zone - CSV files stored in Azure Data Lake Storage

Table 8.1: Data sources for the batch ingestion pipeline

To reflect the diversity of real-world environments, the examples intentionally span multiple systems—including databases, blob storage, and APIs—and multiple file formats such as CSV and JSON.

Streaming ingestion pipeline

The streaming ingestion pipeline sources data from the following systems. In this case, Azure Event Hubs serves as the real-time collection layer, streaming events into Azure Data Lake Storage where they are landed for downstream processing.

Data Source	Data Source Type	Data Collection Mechanism	Data Destination
Product Reviews	Unstructured: Event Streaming	Azure Event Hubs	Landing zone – AVRO files stored in Azure Data Lake Storage
e-commerce Transactions	Structured: Event streaming	Azure Event Hubs	Landing zone – AVRO files stored in Azure Data Lake Storage

Table 8.2: Data sources for the streaming ingestion pipeline

To reflect the diversity of real-world environments, the examples intentionally incorporate both unstructured and semi-structured data formats. With that foundation in place, let's begin preparing the data sources for the batch and streaming pipelines.

Preparing data sources

We will begin by provisioning a set of Azure resources that form the foundational infrastructure for our data ingestion process. These resources provide the necessary data sources, storage, security, compute, and orchestration capabilities required to reliably move data from various sources into the Electroniz data platform.

It's important to note that in real customer projects, data sources usually already exist. However, it can often take considerable time and effort for data engineers to gain access to them, as they may need to navigate multiple technical, security, and approval processes before connectivity is fully established. The key is to start access requests as early as possible; otherwise, delays can significantly impact the project timeline. We start by creating an Azure SQL database for the Electroniz store sales data.

Electroniz store sales database

The store sales data is an Azure SQL database. We'll start preparing source data using the following steps:

1. Log in to the Azure free-tier account using the URL `https://portal.azure.com/`.

   > **Note**
   >
   > A quick reminder: The Azure free-tier account provides you with USD $200 in credits, which expire 30 days after activation. Try to complete the Electroniz project within that 30-day window to make the most of your free resources.

2. Create a new Azure SQL database, browse to: `https://portal.azure.com/#create/Microsoft.AzureSQL`

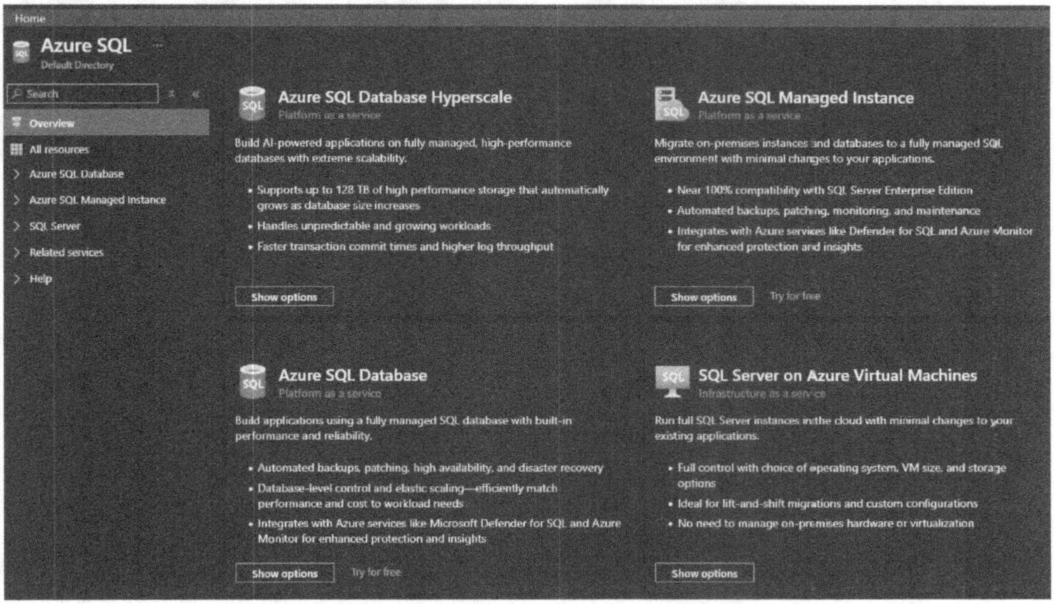

Figure 8.2: Deploy Azure SQL database

3. Click on **Azure SQL Database** > **SQL databases** > **Create** > **SQL database (Free offer)**. A new window will open as follows:

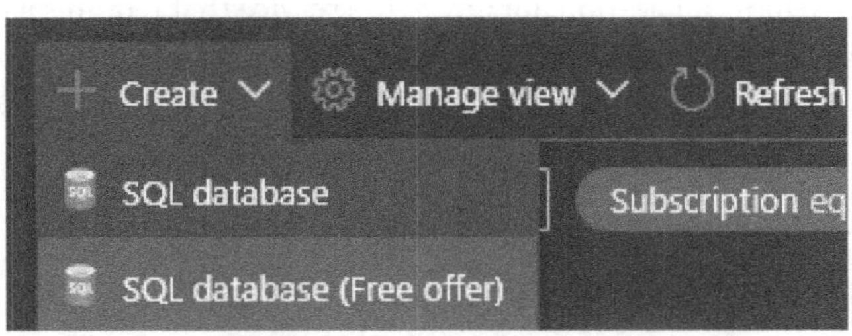

Figure 8.3: Azure database options

4. At the top of the screen, you should see the following option to create a Serverless SQL Database. Click on **Advanced configuration**.

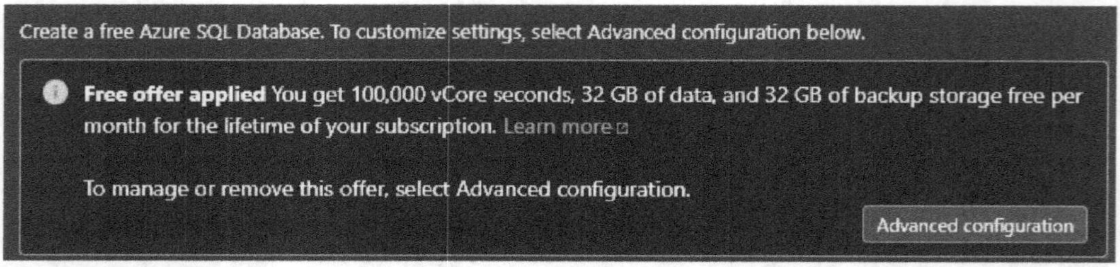

Figure 8.4: Enable a Serverless SQL Database offer

5. For Subscription, choose the **Free Tier** or **Paid subscription**.
6. For Resource group, click on **Create new**. For the resource group name, enter **training_rg**. Click **OK**.
7. For Database name, enter **salesdb**.
8. For Server, click on **Create new**. A new Create SQL Database window will open.
9. For Server name, you need to enter a globally unique name that is available.

> **Note**
>
> Some Azure services such as Azure SQL, storage accounts, and even hubs must have globally unique names because they expose a DNS endpoint for connections.

Here's a helpful suggestion: for any Azure service that requires a globally unique name, consider adding a small, unique suffix to the resource name. For example, if the instructions ask you to create a resource named `salesdb`, you might instead use `salesdb101` or any similar variation to ensure uniqueness.

10. For Server name, enter a globally unique name. If the name is available, you will see a message like this confirming your choice is available.

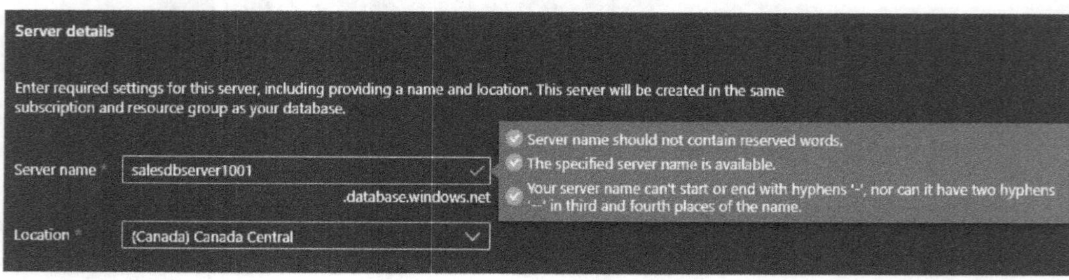

Figure 8.5: Entering a globally unique server name

Some Azure subscriptions can't deploy SQL servers in certain regions, even when those regions are normally available, due to errors such as "Your subscription does not have access to create a server in the selected region". Try switching to a different region in case you encounter this issue.

11. Choose the location closest to you.
12. For Authentication method, choose **Use both SQL and Microsoft Entra authentication**.
13. For Server admin login, enter **salesadmin**.
14. In Password and Confirm Password, enter a password as per the policy and remember it for future steps.
15. Click **OK**. You will navigate back to the **Create SQL Database** window.
16. Click on **Next**.
17. In Networking, for Connectivity method, choose **Public endpoint**.
18. For Allow Azure services and resources to access this server, choose **Yes**.
19. For Add current client IP address, select **Yes**.
20. Leave the rest of the settings as default.
21. Click on **Review + Create**.
22. Azure will validate the settings and enable the **Create** button.
23. Click on **Create**. The Azure SQL database is now being deployed.

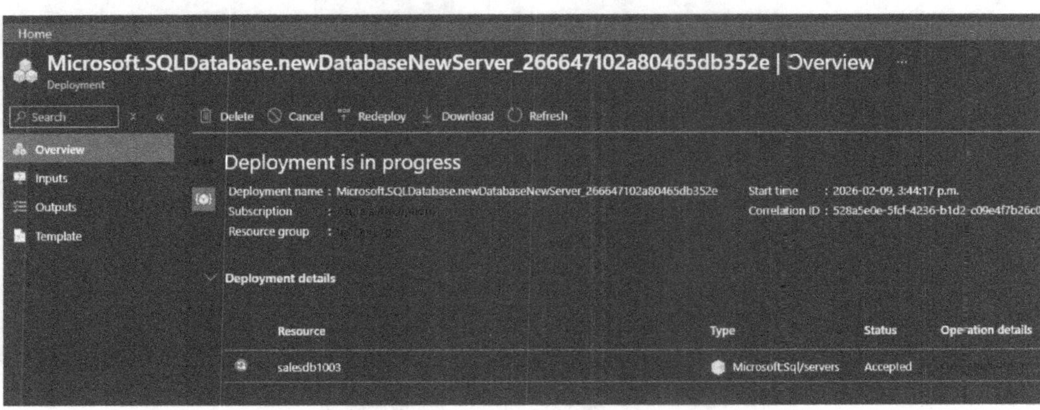

Figure 8.6: Azure SQL deployment in progress

24. Once the deployment is complete, you should see a **Go to resource** button.

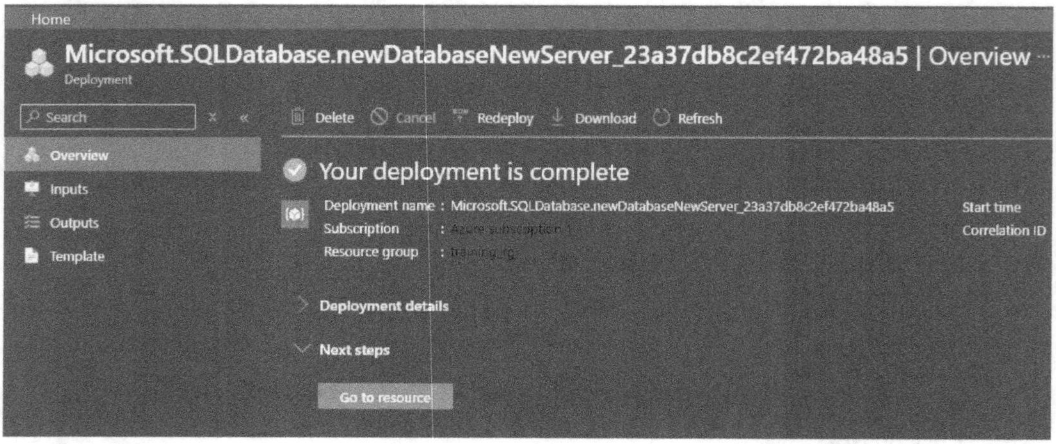

Figure 8.7: Azure SQL deployment completed

The "Your deployment is complete" message signals that the Azure SQL database has been created successfully.

25. Click on **Go to resource**. Navigate to the Azure SQL control panel for *salesdb*.

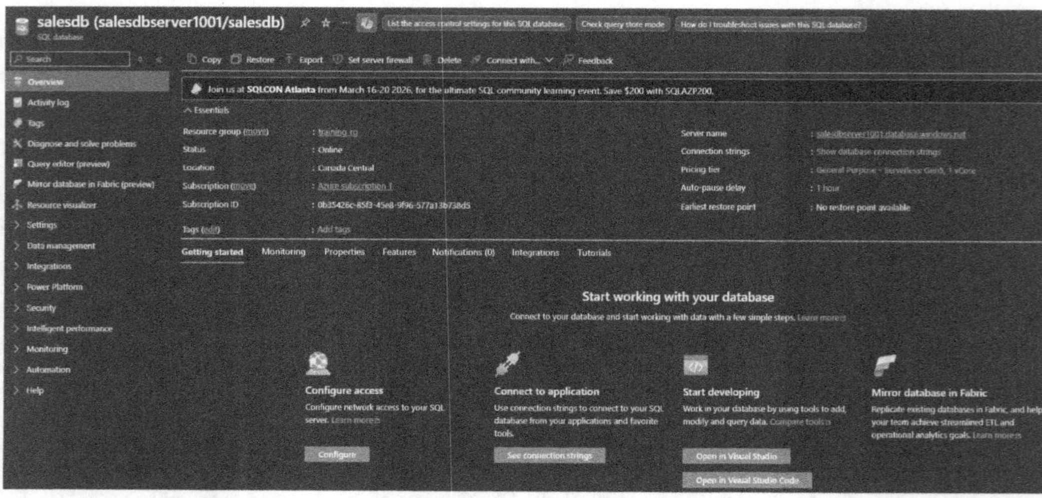

Figure 8.8: Azure SQL control panel

26. To connect to the newly created Azure SQL database, using the menu on the left, click on Query Editor.
27. Using SQL Server authentication, log in with your username *salesadmin* and the password created previously.

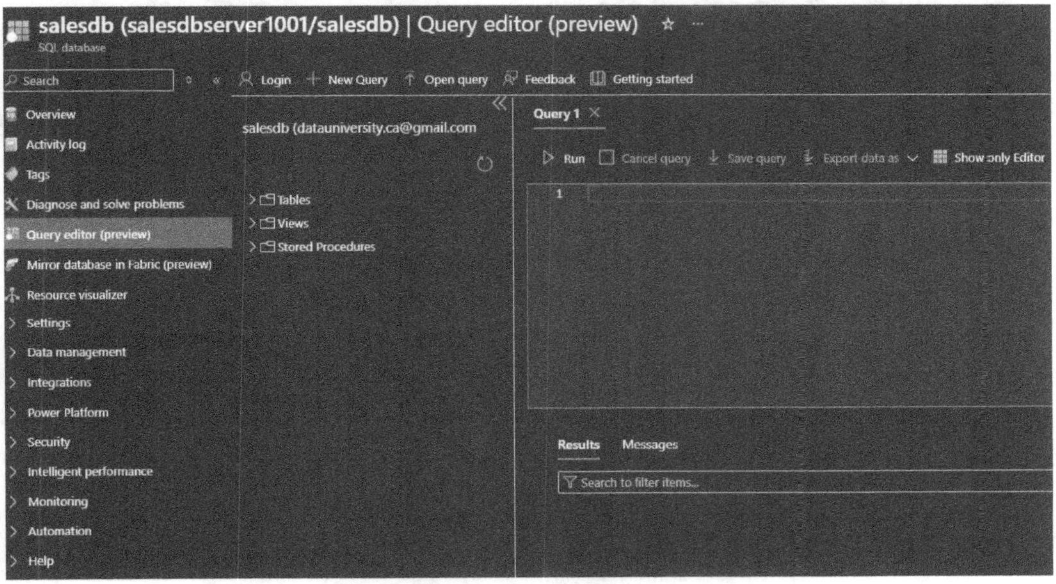

Figure 8.9: Azure SQL query editor

28. We are ready to create new tables and insert data into the *salesdb* database. Throughout this book, we will use the Packt Publishing Git course repository to download code samples and datasets. This repository is publicly available here: `https://github.com/PacktPublishing/Data-Engineering-with-Apache-Spark-Databricks-and-Lakehouse-Second-Edition`.

    Copy the contents of the following file from the course Git repository: `https://github.com/PacktPublishing/Data-Engineering-with-Apache-Spark-Databricks-and-Lakehouse-Second-Edition/blob/main/chapter8/sql/storedb_history.sql`.

    The contents of the *storedb_history.sql* file are a SQL script that will create new tables and insert data into them. It contains historical data for 3000 Electroniz customers and their 2500 orders.

29. Click on **New Query** and paste the SQL script inside the Query editor window.

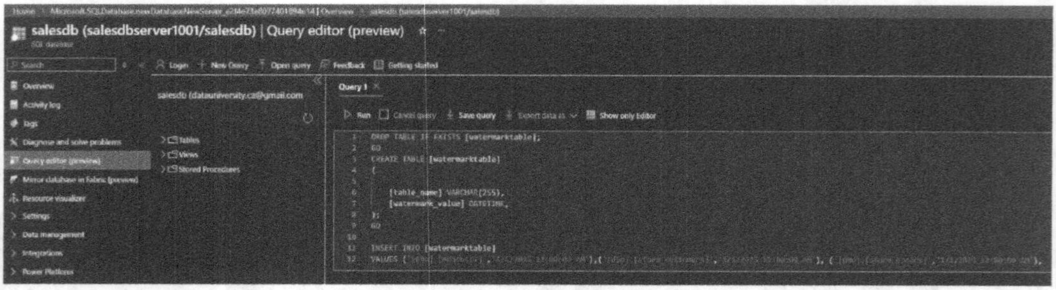

Figure 8.10: Creating new tables in salesdb

30. Click on **Run**. Watch out for logs in the **Messages** panel. If the SQL script ran successfully, you should see a *Query succeeded* message as below:

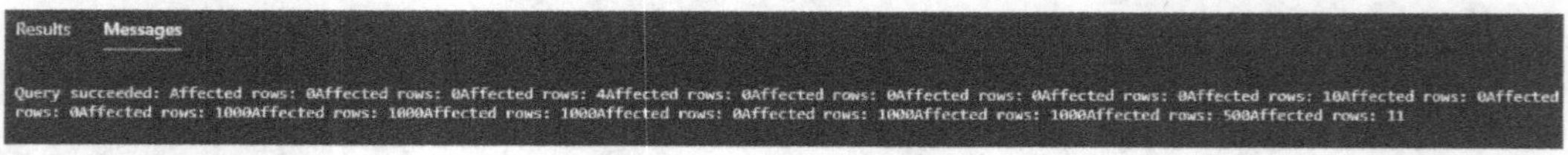

Figure 8.11: Successful query execution message

31. To the left of the query window, click on a small arrow beside Tables.

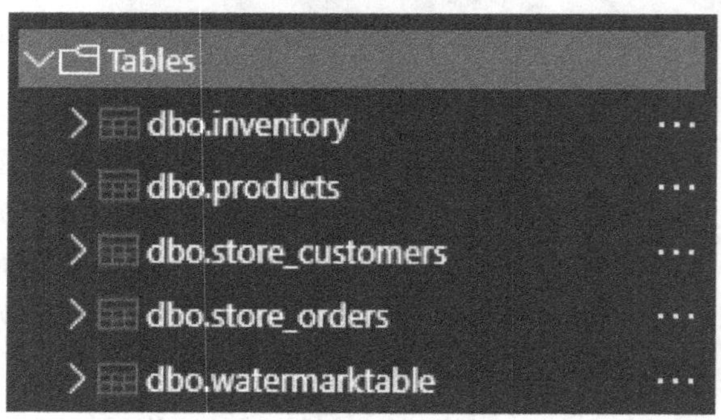

Figure 8.12: Electroniz stores database tables

32. Click on the three dots beside *dbo.store_customers* and click on **Select Top 1000 Rows**.

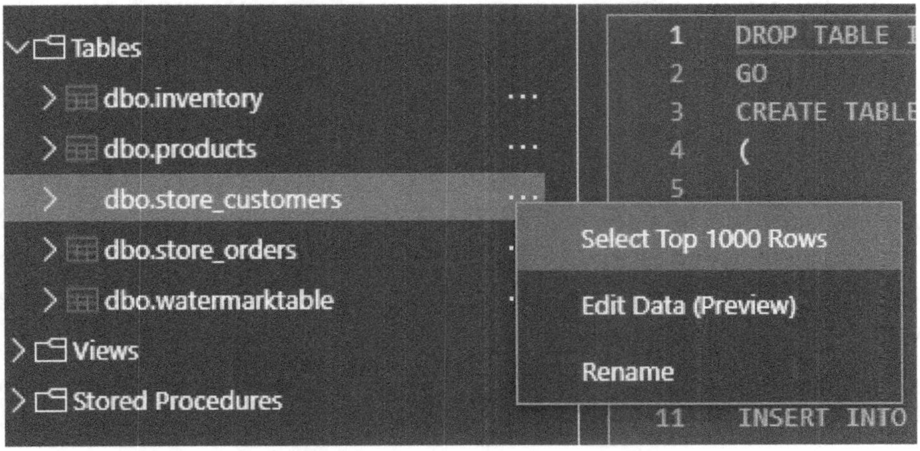

Figure 8.13: Checking for data in dbo.store_customers table

33. You should be able to see the data for the *dbo.store_customers* table.

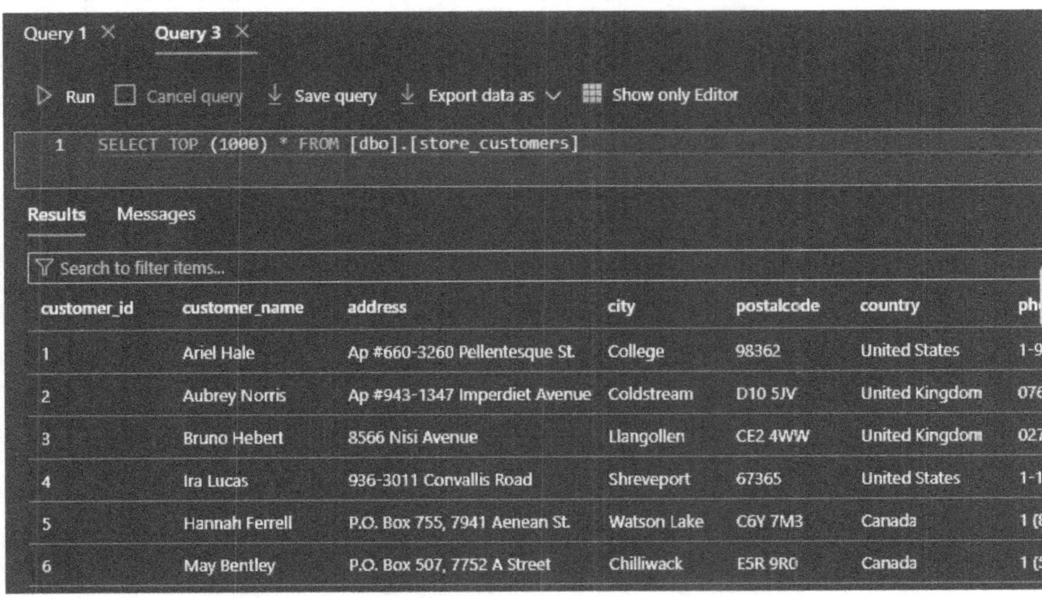

Figure 8.14: Data in dbo.store_customers table

With the data prepared in the store sales database, you're ready to move forward. The next step is to create a new Azure Data Factory instance, which will serve as the ingestion and orchestration engine for the batch pipeline.

Azure Data Factory

The batch ingestion pipeline will be implemented using **Azure Data Factory** (**ADF**) as the core service for orchestration and integration. Leveraging its native connectors, ADF will oversee the entire ingestion workflow—handling source connectivity, scheduling, dependency management, data transfer, and error mitigation throughout the process. We will begin by creating an ADF instance:

1. In the Azure portal, use the search bar at the top to look for **Data factories.** From the results, select *Data factories (V2)* to proceed.
2. Click on **Create data factory (V2)**.
3. For Resource group, enter **training_rg**.
4. For Name, enter **electronizlakehouse-df** or any other available value. Azure Data Factory requires a globally unique name, so choose one that is not already in use across the Azure ecosystem. After creation, be sure to reference the selected Data Factory name consistently throughout the remaining instructions.
5. For Region, enter **Canada Central**.
6. For Version, choose **V2**.
7. Click on **Review + Create**.
8. After you get a "Validation passed" message, click on **Create**. Data Factory deployment will start.
9. Once the Data Factory deployment has been completed, click on **Go to resource**.

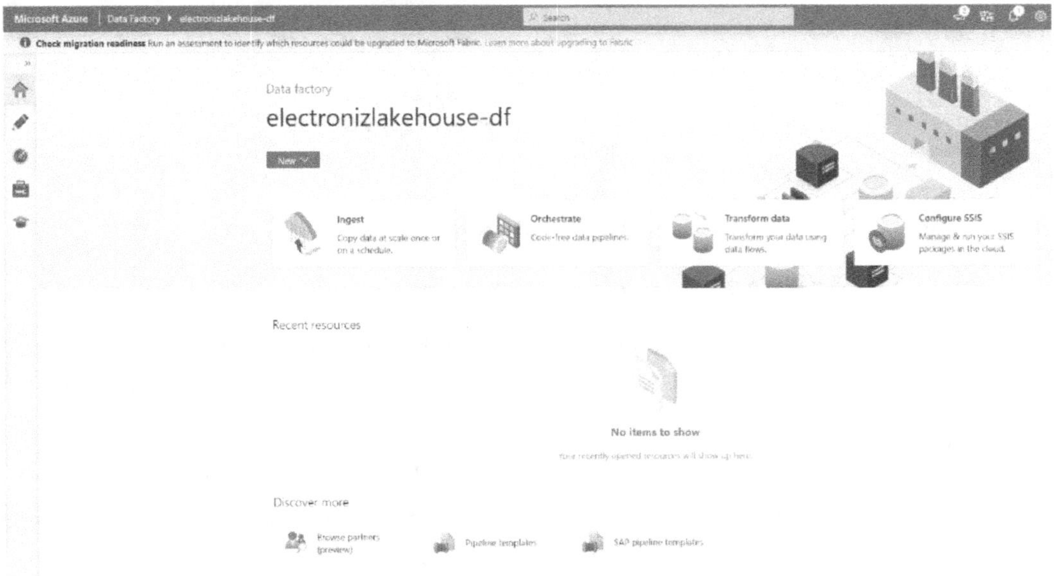

Figure 8.15: Data Factory control panel

The deployment of the new Azure Data Factory instance is now complete. Next, you will subscribe to a currency-conversion API, which will serve as one of the data sources for the batch ingestion pipeline.

Currency conversion API

During the development of the batch ingestion pipeline, one step will involve connecting to a REST API to retrieve currency conversion data from the internet. Figure 8.16 below illustrates how Azure Data Factory integrates securely with external APIs by retrieving credentials from Azure Key Vault rather than embedding secrets directly in pipelines. In this pattern, the API key is stored as a secret in Key Vault, and ADF accesses it through a managed identity. The linked service for the API is then configured to reference the Key Vault secret at runtime, ensuring that authentication is handled securely and centrally without exposing sensitive information in code or configuration.

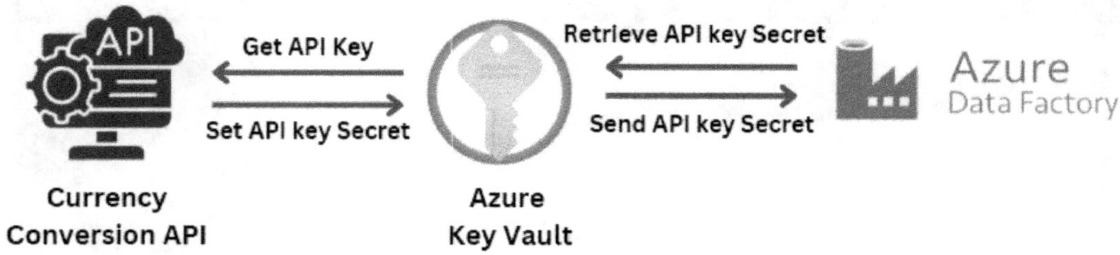

Figure 8.16: Currency conversion API key stored in Azure Key Vault

To support this, we will first register for an API key and store it securely in Azure Key Vault. Azure Data Factory will then reference this key when the batch ingestion pipeline is created and executed.

1. Open a new browser window and navigate to `https://exchangeratesapi.io/`.
2. This site offers a free and user-friendly REST API for retrieving currency exchange rate data, but it does come with a usage limit. Fortunately, our pipeline is expected to make far fewer than 100 requests, so this restriction should not pose any issues for our needs.

Figure 8.17: Exchange Rate API limitation

3. Click on **Get API Key** and choose the **free** subscription plan, fill in personal details, and how you wish to use the API key. The site requires you to verify your email address.

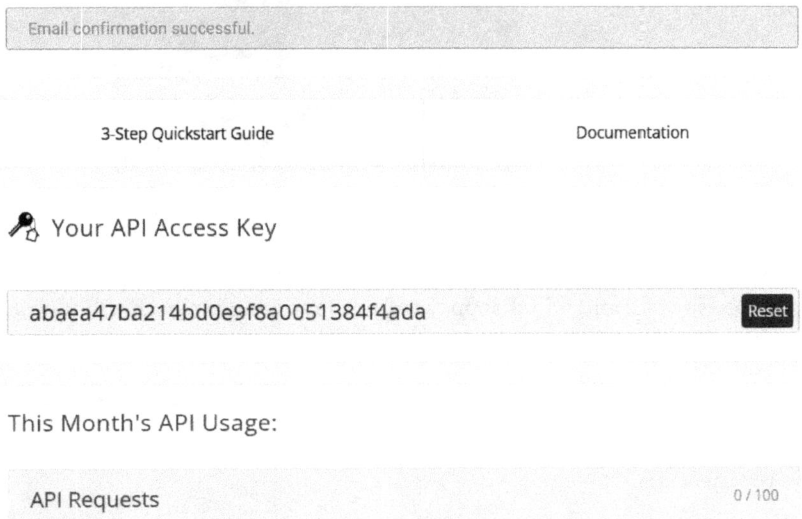

Figure 8.18: Exchange Rate API key

Once the verification is complete, your API key will be displayed on the screen as shown below. Take note of the API key; you will need it in the subsequent steps.

> **Note**
>
> Storing credentials — such as passwords, API keys, tokens, certificates, or connection strings — directly in Spark notebooks, Python scripts, or local files creates a high-risk security vulnerability. Instead, these sensitive values should be stored in secure services like Azure Key Vault.

4. Create a new **Azure Key Vault** for storing the Currency API key.
5. We will use Azure Cloud Shell to run the commands required to create the Azure Key Vault. If you are new to Azure Cloud Shell, you may find it helpful to review the following overview before proceeding: `https://learn.microsoft.com/en-ca/azure/cloud-shell/overview`

6. Open **Azure Cloud Shell** using the Cloud Shell icon that is available from the top right menu of the Azure portal.

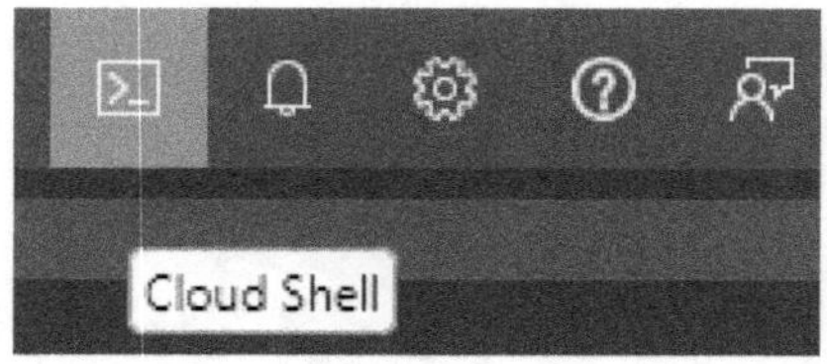

Figure 8.19: Cloud shell icon on Azure portal

7. Click on **Bash**. We want to persist command files for future use; otherwise, files are session-specific and will disappear after the session is closed. Click on **Apply**.

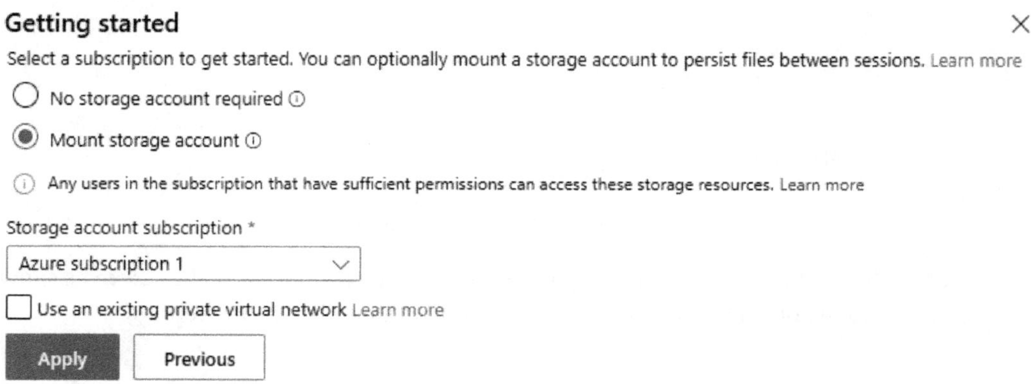

Figure 8.20: Mounting storage for persisting shell scripts

8. You will be presented with a mount storage option. Choose the middle option and click **Next**.

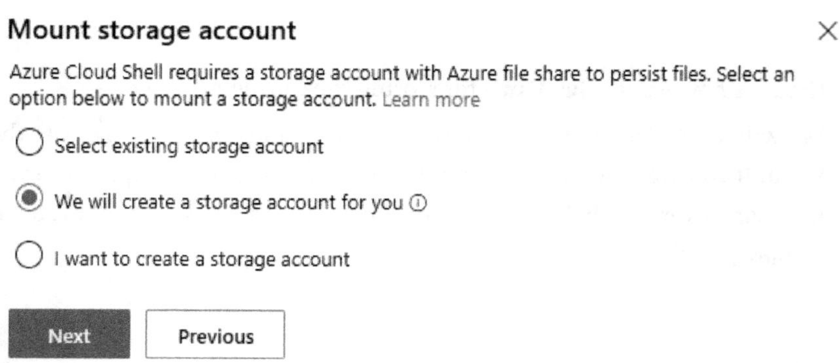

Figure 8.21: Create storage account for persisting shell scripts

9. You will be presented with the following Cloud Shell screen.

Figure 8.22: Azure Cloud Shell ready for operation

The figure above shows the Cloud Shell interface. When provisioning Azure resources, data engineers should avoid relying solely on the Azure portal and instead develop proficiency with command-line tools such as the Azure CLI. Scripted and command-line workflows are typically faster, more consistent, and far less error-prone than manual, point-and-click operations in the portal.

10. Clone the Packt Publishing GitHub repository on Azure Cloud Shell. Paste the commands below into Azure Cloud Shell.

```
git clone https://github.com/PacktPublishing/Data-Engineering-with-Apache-
Spark-Databricks-and-Lakehouse-Second-Edition
```

The above command will create a folder named "Data-Engineering-with-Apache-Spark-Databricks-and-Lakehouse-Second-Edition" on Azure Cloud Shell.

11. Paste the commands below into Azure Cloud Shell. You can run the commands by copying and pasting them into Azure Cloud Shell one at a time, or execute the entire block as a single batch.

```
RESOURCEGROUPNAME="training_rg"
LOCATION="canadacentral"
KEYVAULTNAME="electroniz-secret-kv"
az config set extension.use_dynamic_install=yes_without_prompt
az keyvault create --location $LOCATION --name $KEYVAULTNAME --resource-
group $RESOURCEGROUPNAME
```

12. If the previous commands have completed successfully, return to the Azure portal and navigate to **Home** > **All resources** > **electroniz-secret-kv**. You should now see the newly created Azure Key Vault.

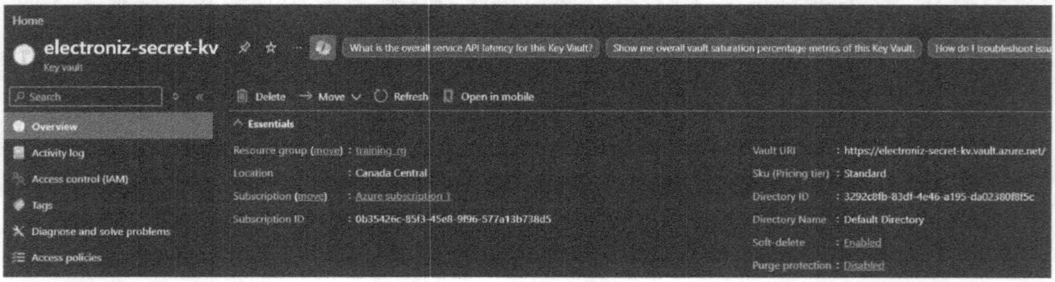

Figure 8.23: Electroniz Key Vault

13. Azure administrators must have *Key Vault administrator* role to create secrets. Assign this role to your user by clicking on the **Access control (IAM)** menu on the left. Click on **Add role assignment**. Under **Job function roles**, search for **Key Vault Administrator**.

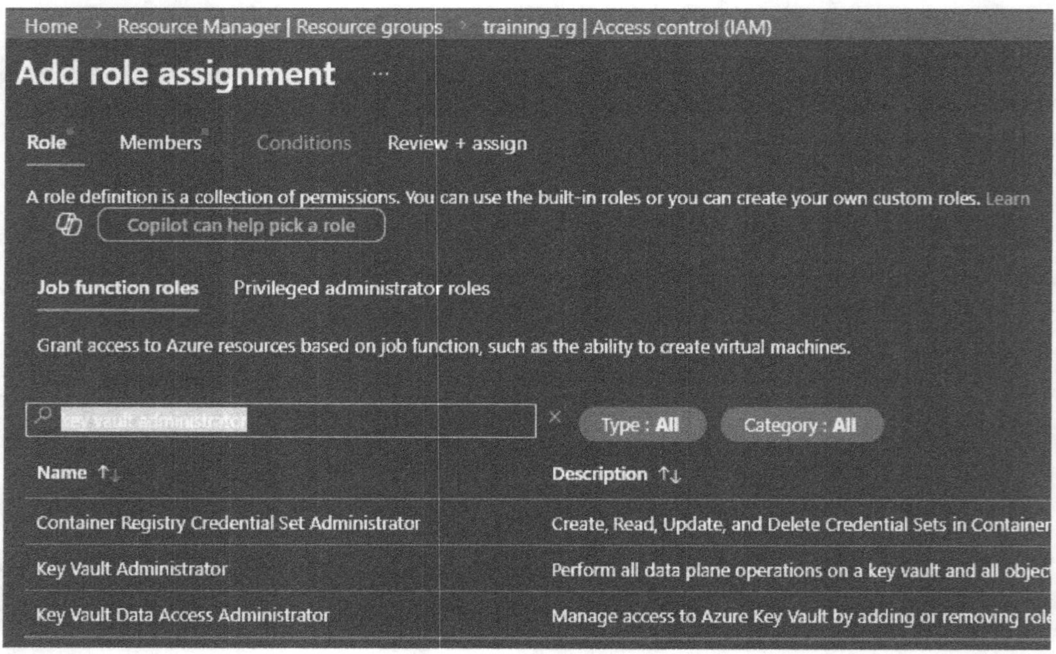

Figure 8.24: Azure key vault administrator role

14. Click on **Key Vault Administrator**.
15. Click **Next**.
16. Click on **Select members**.
17. In the Select members panel, choose your own email ID, the one that you use to log in to Azure. Press **Select**.

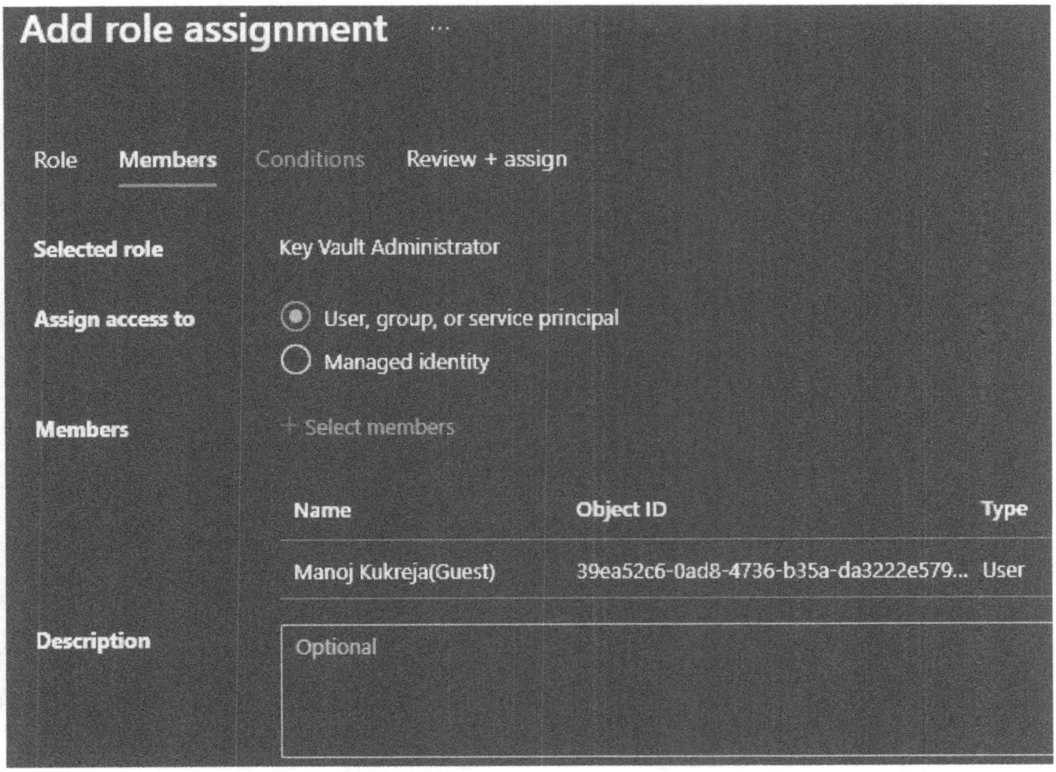

Figure 8.25: Choose member for key vault administrator role

18. Click on **Review + assign**.
19. Azure Data Factory must have the Key Vault Secrets User role to access secrets at runtime. Assign this role to your user by clicking on the **Access control (IAM)** menu on the left. Click on **Add role assignment**. Under **Job function roles**, search for **Key Vault Secrets User**.

20. Click on **Key Vault Secrets User**. Click **Next**.
21. Click on **Managed Identity** followed by **Select members**.
22. In the Select managed identities window for Managed Identity, choose **Data factory (V2)**.
23. Choose **electronizlakehouse-df** (the name may be different in your case). Click on **Select**.

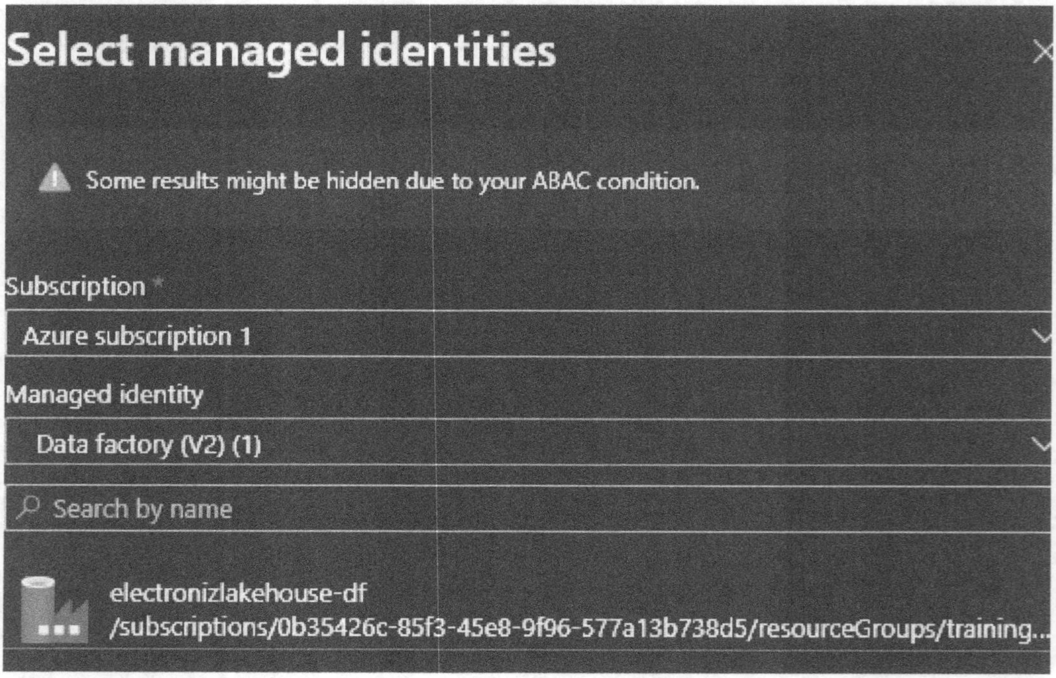

Figure 8.26: Adding role to managed identity

24. Click on **Review + assign**.

25. To check the role got assigned, click on **View my access**. The newly assigned role assignment should be visible as follows:

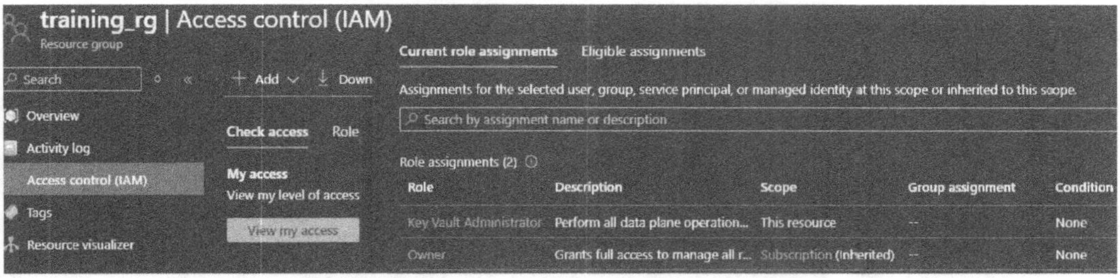

Figure 8.27: Confirmation of key vault administrator role

26. To check the access for managed identity, click on **Check access**.

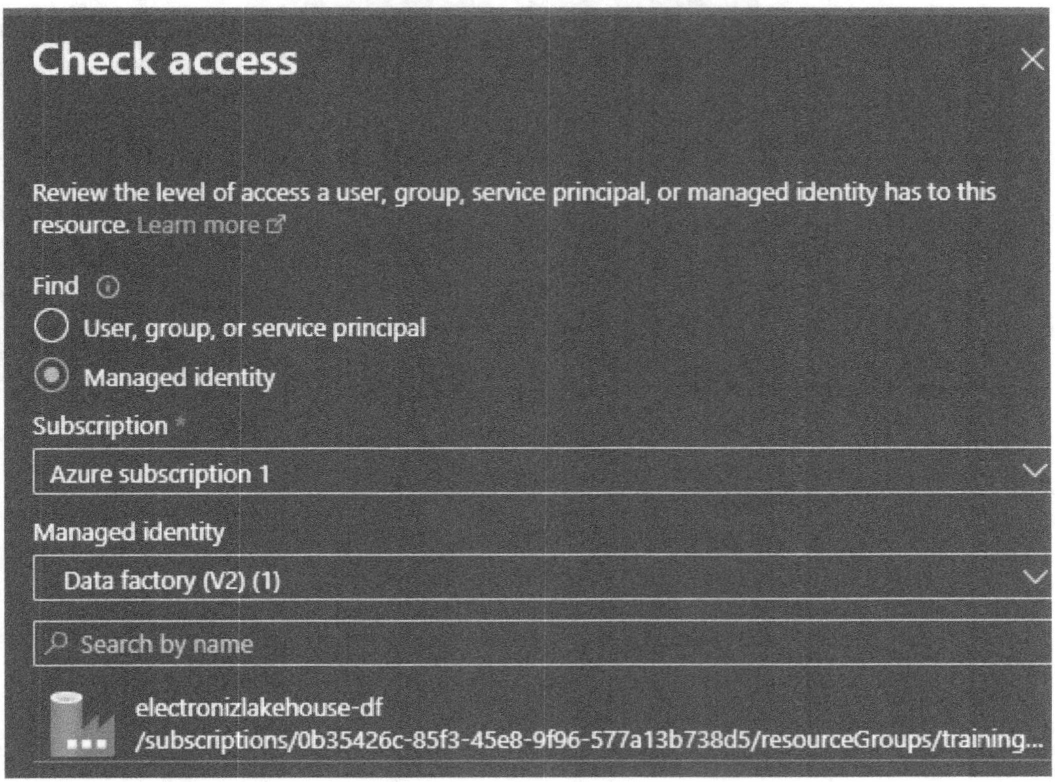

Figure 8.28: Confirmation of key vault secrets user role to managed identity

The figure above shows the Data Factory (V2) managed identity access for the newly created Key Vault.

27. Next, we will create a new secret in Key Vault. Using the left menu, click on **Objects** > **Secrets**.

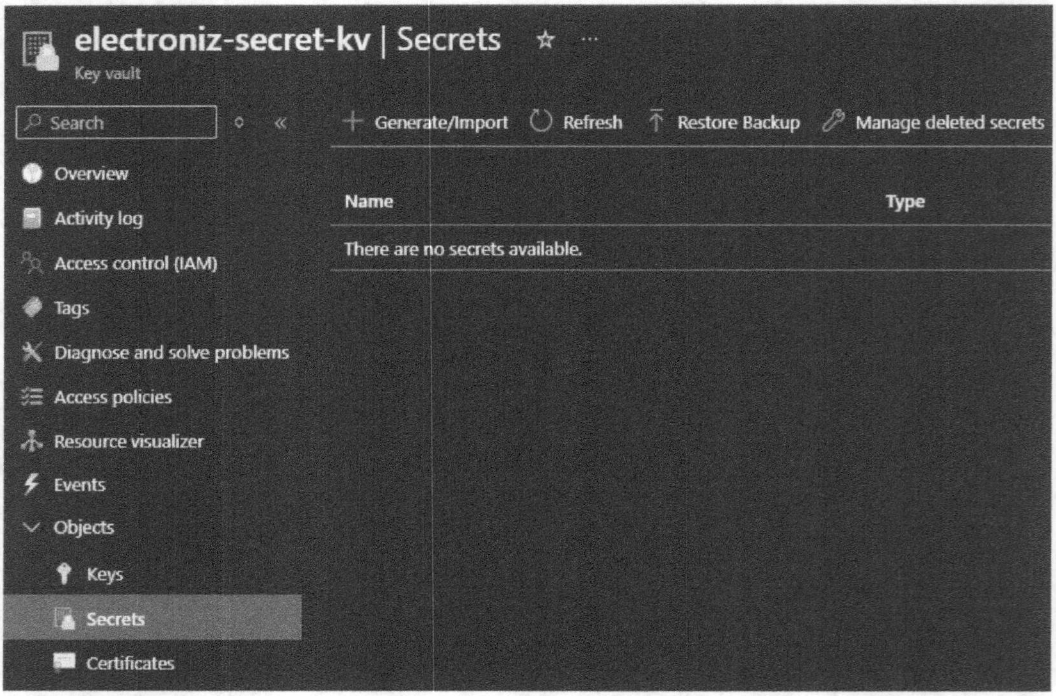

Figure 8.29: Create a new secret

28. Click on **Generate/Import**.
29. For Name, enter **CURRAPIKEY**.

30. For Secret Value, enter the Exchange Rate API key noted above. Leave the rest as default values, Click on **Create**.

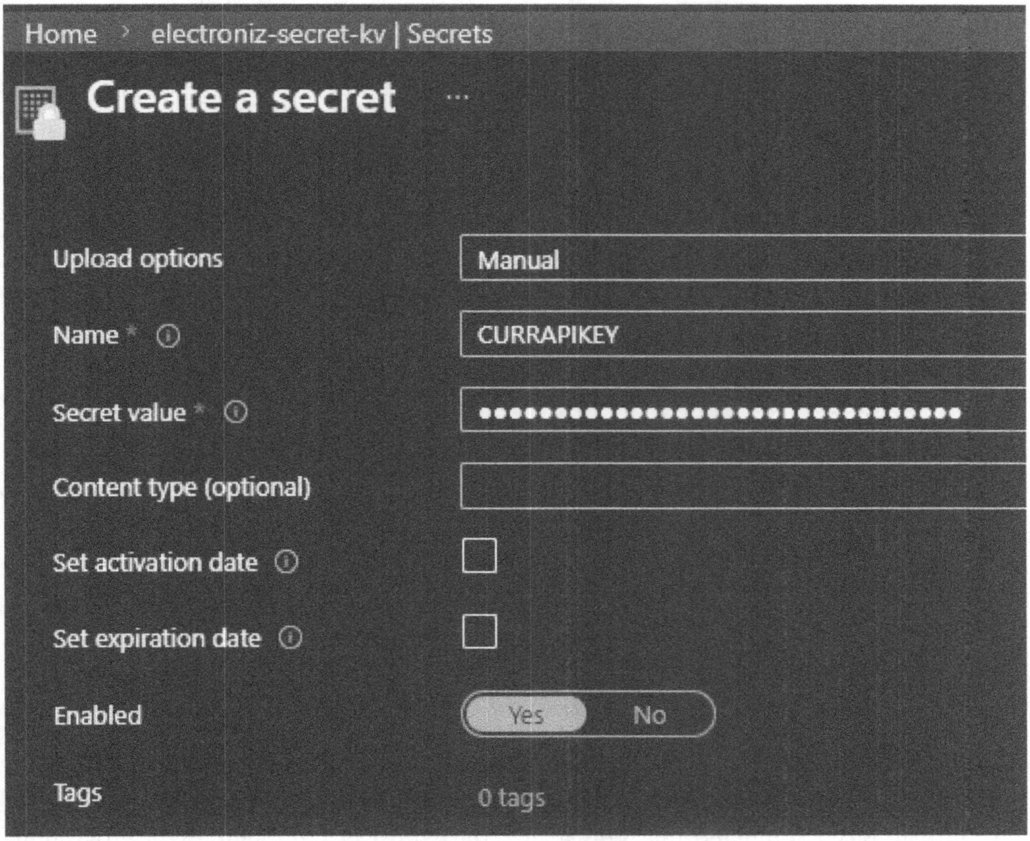

Figure 8.30: New secret for Exchange Rate API key

Secrets in Azure Key Vault are stored as fully encrypted blobs and are decrypted only when requested by an application or service explicitly authorized to access them.

With Azure Key Vault configured and the API secret securely stored, we can now focus on provisioning the platform components required for streaming data collection.

Electroniz e-commerce transactions

Electroniz e-commerce platform uses Azure Event Hubs to stream transactions and product reviews, with all incoming events continuously ingested into the landing zone of Azure Data Lake Storage Gen2. The figure below illustrates the flow of streaming data within the Electroniz e-commerce platform.

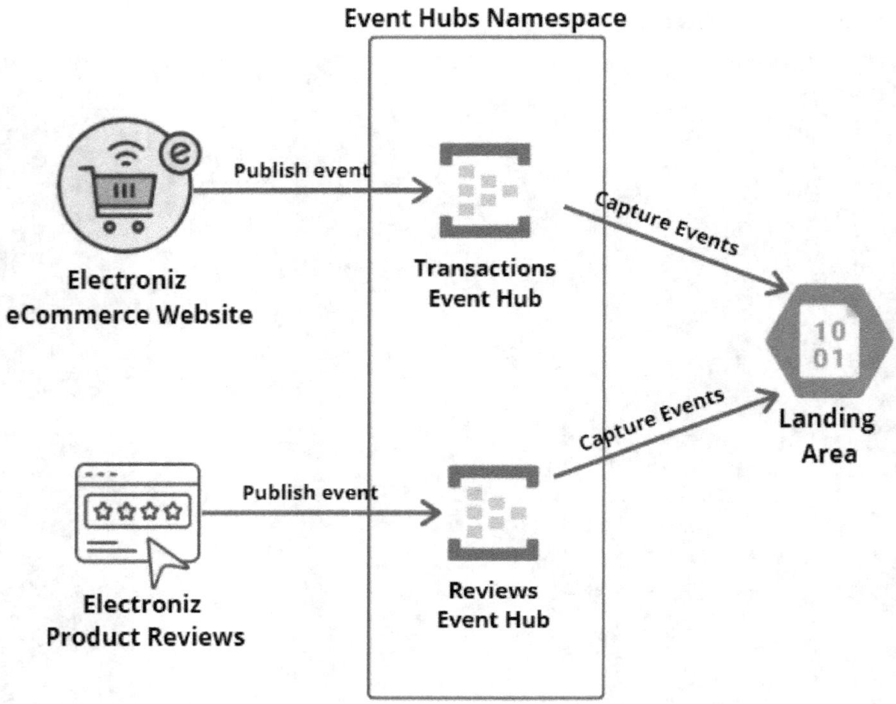

Figure 8.31: Electroniz e-commerce platform

Not all cloud resources are created through the portal or graphical **user interface (UI)**. Many organizations rely on automation—using **Infrastructure as Code (IaC)** tools such as Terraform or Bicep, command-line tools such as the Azure CLI, or programmatic provisioning via APIs. Now, let's walk through creating an Azure Event Hubs instance using command-line tools:

1. Now, let's create an Event Hubs namespace to stream ecommerce transactions and product reviews for the Electroniz project. Feel free to edit the **LOCATION** to the nearest region you prefer. Paste the commands below into Azure Cloud Shell. You can execute them one at a time or run the whole block together.

```
RESOURCEGROUPNAME="training_rg"
LOCATION="canadacentral"
EVENTHUB_NAMESPACE="electroniz-ecommerce-ns"
az eventhubs namespace create \
--name $EVENTHUB_NAMESPACE \
--resource-group $RESOURCEGROUPNAME \
```

```
--location $LOCATION \
--sku Standard \
--tags owner="data engineering" project=lakehouse environment=development
domain=marketing
```

An Event Hubs namespace is essentially a container or logical grouping for one or more Event Hubs within Azure. Notice that the Event Hubs namespace is assigned a DNS-integrated network endpoint for sending or receiving events.

> **Note**
>
> Azure Event Hubs and Kafka are similar data streaming platforms. Both support high throughput, partition-based scalability, and real-time ingestion of large volumes of events, making them well-suited for building modern streaming and event-driven architectures.

2. If the previous commands have completed successfully, return to the Azure portal and navigate to **Home** > **All resources** > **electroniz-ecommerce-ns**. You should now see the newly created Event Hubs namespace.

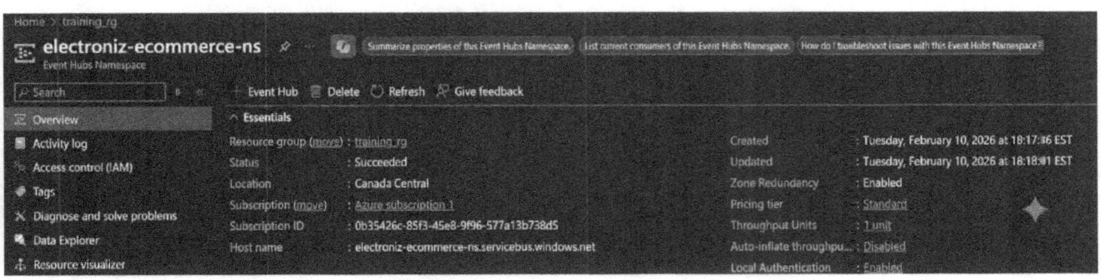

Figure 8.32: Azure Event Hubs namespace

3. To capture live event data, we need a streaming entity, known as an *Event Hub*, inside the namespace. Paste the commands below into Azure Cloud Shell. You can execute them one at a time or run the whole block together.

```
EVENTHUB_NAME_TRANSACTIONS="transactions"
EVENTHUB_NAME_REVIEWS="reviews"
az eventhubs eventhub create \
--resource-group $RESOURCEGROUPNAME \
--namespace-name $EVENTHUB_NAMESPACE \
--name $EVENTHUB_NAME_TRANSACTIONS \
--partition-count 2
```

```
az eventhubs eventhub create \
--resource-group $RESOURCEGROUPNAME \
--namespace-name $EVENTHUB_NAMESPACE \
--name $EVENTHUB_NAME_REVIEWS \
--partition-count 2
```

Event Hub receives incoming data, stores it temporarily, and makes it available for consumption. Since our scenario involves two event types—transactions and reviews—we will create two separate Event Hubs to handle each stream independently.

> **Note**
>
> Notice the use of the tags option when creating the Event Hub. In addition to supporting governance and resource organization, tags enable you to categorize cloud assets, making it easier to track and allocate cloud spending across different business domains.

4. On the Azure portal, navigate to **Home** > **All resources** > **electroniz-ecommerce-ns**, click on **Entities** > **Event Hubs**.
5. Notice that two Event Hubs have been created, each configured with two partitions.

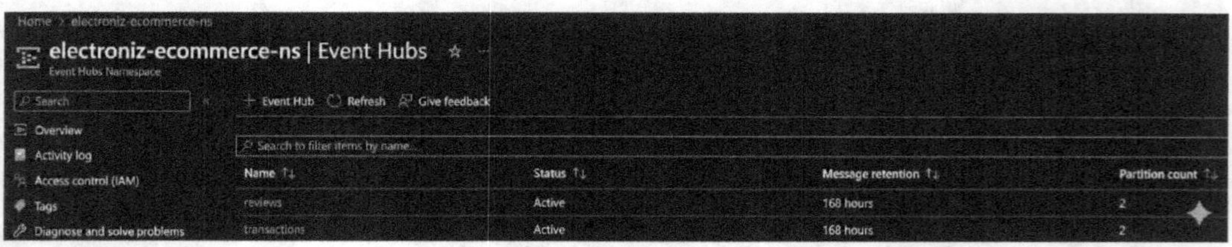

Figure 8.33: Azure Event Hubs

Event Hub partitions act as parallel data streams within an Event Hub. Increasing the number of partitions enables higher ingestion and consumption throughput.

> **Note**
>
> Azure Event Hubs guarantee event ordering only within a single partition, not across partitions. You need one consumer per partition to read events in parallel, because each consumer reads from one partition at a time to maintain ordering and independently track offsets.

Now that the Electroniz streaming infrastructure is in place and ready to receive event traffic, we can proceed with creating a new data source—one that will store files related to website tracking.

Electroniz website tracking logs

Website tracking logs are records generated by web servers that capture detailed information about user interactions with a site. These logs are critical for understanding traffic patterns, diagnosing issues, and identifying the countries users are visiting from. *Figure 8.33* illustrates how website activity logs from the Electroniz platform are continuously streamed and written to Azure Blob Storage.

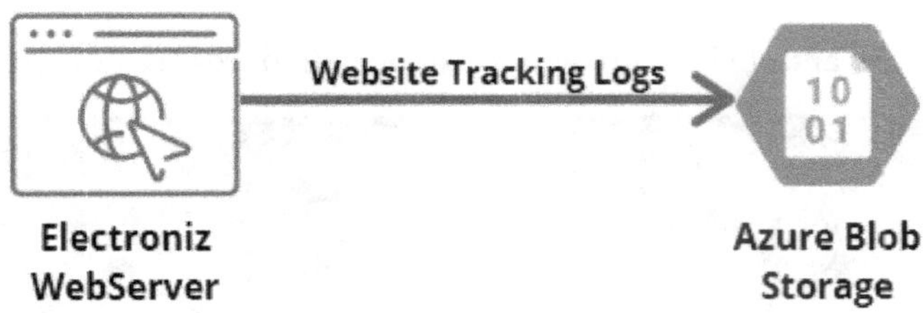

Figure 8.34: Electroniz website tracking logs continuously pushed to Azure Blob Storage

Website tracking logs are typically streamed or periodically uploaded to object storage services, making them easily accessible for analytics platforms to process. Let's now prepare the necessary infrastructure to support this data transfer:

1. Create the Azure Blob Storage account for the Electroniz website tracking logs and upload a sample tracking file. Note that Azure Storage Accounts have globally unique names, so in the next set of commands choose a **LOGSTORAGEACCOUNTNAME** that is not already in use across the Azure ecosystem. Adjust the **LOGSTORAGEACCOUNTNAME** and **LOCATION** before running the commands below. After creation, be sure to reference the selected Azure Storage Account name consistently throughout the remaining instructions.
2. Paste the commands below into Azure Cloud Shell. You can execute them one at a time or run the whole block together.

```
LOGSTORAGEACCOUNTNAME="websitetracking"
LOGSCONTAINER="tracking-logs"
RESOURCEGROUPNAME="training_rg"
LOCATION="canadacentral"

az storage account create \
--name $LOGSTORAGEACCOUNTNAME \
```

```
--resource-group $RESOURCEGROUPNAME \
--kind StorageV2 \
--location $LOCATION \
--sku Standard_LRS \
--tags owner=data engineering project=lakehouse environment=development

KEY=`az storage account keys list -g $RESOURCEGROUPNAME -n
$LOGSTORAGEACCOUNTNAME | jq .[0].value`
```

Now that the Azure Storage Account has been created, we can proceed with creating a container within it.

3. Paste the commands below into Azure Cloud Shell to create a new container.

```
az storage container create \
-n $LOGSCONTAINER \
--account-name $LOGSTORAGEACCOUNTNAME \
--account-key $KEY
```

An Azure Blob container is a logical storage unit that is used to organize and store blobs

4. Upload a sample website tracking log file to Azure Blob Storage. This log file should already be available in your Azure Cloud Shell environment from the previously cloned Packt GitHub repository.

```
az storage blob upload \
--container-name $LOGSCONTAINER \
--account-name $LOGSTORAGEACCOUNTNAME \
--name electroniz_access_log_1.json \
--file ~/Data-Engineering-with-Apache-Spark-Databricks-and-Lakehouse-
Second-Edition/chapter8/data/electroniz_access_log_1.log
```

5. For Azure Data Factory to collect data from **LOGSCONTAINER** at runtime, it must have the *Storage Blob Data Contributor* role assigned to it. Assign this role to your user by clicking on the **Access control (IAM)** menu on the left. Click on **Add role assignment**. Under **Job function roles**, search for **Storage blob data contributor**.
6. Click on **Storage Blob Data Contributor**. Click **Next**.
7. Click on **Managed Identity,** followed by **Select members**.

8. In the Select managed identities window for Managed Identity, choose **Data factory (V2)**.
9. Choose **electronizlakehouse-df** (the name may be different in your case). Click on **Select**.
10. Click on **Review + assign**.
11. To check the access for the managed identity, click on **Check access**. The newly assigned role assignment should be visible for **Data Factory (V2)**.

We have now successfully created the data sources for the Electroniz store sales database, e-commerce transactions, and website tracking logs. Next, we will configure the landing bucket that will serve as the data destination.

Preparing data destination

Once the batch and streaming ingestion pipelines are triggered, they extract data from the defined source systems and load it into the landing container within the Azure Data Lake Storage Gen2 account. This landing zone serves as the raw data destination, capturing source data in its original form before any cleansing, transformation, or enrichment occurs.

1. Create the Azure Blob Storage account for the landing area. Once again, Azure Storage Accounts have globally unique names, so choose a **STORAGEACCOUNTNAME** that is not already in use across the Azure ecosystem. Adjust the **STORAGEACCOUNTNAME** and **LOCATION** before running the commands below. After creation, be sure to reference the selected Azure Storage Account name consistently throughout the remaining instructions.
2. Paste the commands below into Azure Cloud Shell. You can execute them one at a time or run the whole block together.

```
STORAGEACCOUNTNAME="electronizlanding"
RESOURCEGROUPNAME="training_rg"
LOCATION="canadacentral"
az storage account create \
--name $STORAGEACCOUNTNAME \
--resource-group $RESOURCEGROUPNAME \
--kind StorageV2 \
--location $LOCATION \
--hns true \
--sku Standard_LRS \
--tags owner=data engineering project=lakehouse environment=development
```

3. To confirm the storage account was created, go back to the Azure portal and navigate to Home > **All resources** > **electronizlanding**.

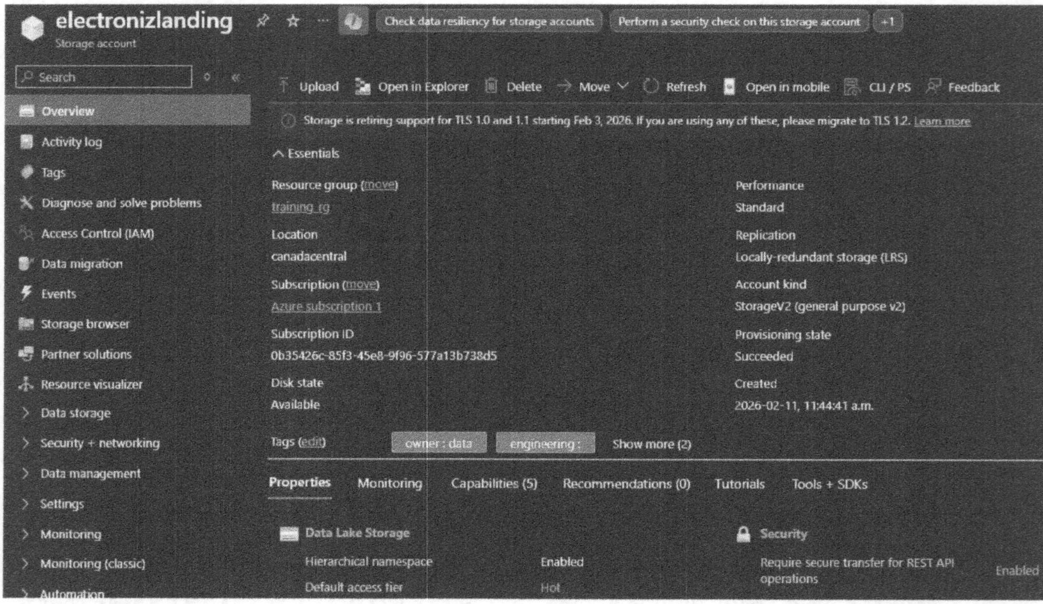

Figure 8.35: Electroniz landing area storage account

Notice the use of the `--hns true` option when creating the storage account. This enables hierarchical namespace support, allowing files to be organized in a traditional folder-style structure. Enabling this feature significantly improves both manageability and performance.

4. Azure Data Factory must have the **Storage Blob Data Contributor** role to access ADLS at runtime. Assign this role to your user by clicking on the **Access control (IAM)** menu on the left. Click on **Add role assignment**. Under **Job function roles,** search for **Storage blob data contributor**.
5. Click on **Storage Blob Data Contributor**. Click **Next**.
6. Click on **Managed Identity**, followed by **Select members**.
7. In the Select managed identities window for Managed Identity, choose **Data factory (V2)**.

8. Choose **electronizlakehouse-df** (the name may be different in your case). Click on **Select**.
9. Click on **Review + assign**.
10. To check the access for managed identity, click on **Check access**. The newly assigned role assignment should be visible for **Data Factory (V2)**.
11. Azure Data Lake Storage will store data in blobs. In Azure Data Lake Storage, blobs are organized in a filesystem hierarchy. To enable the hierarchy, we need to create a namespace for the landing layer. Paste the commands below into Azure Cloud Shell. You can execute them one at a time or run the whole block together.

```
STORAGEACCOUNTNAME="electronizlanding"
NAMESPACE="raw"
az storage fs create \
-n $NAMESPACE \
--account-name $STORAGEACCOUNTNAME \
--metadata project=lakehouse environment=development layer=landing \
--only-show-errors
```

At this point, we have successfully prepared the data sources and data destinations for the Electroniz Lakehouse landing zone. In the next section, we will begin building the ingestion pipeline to fetch data from sources and store it in destinations.

Building the ingestion pipelines

Electroniz ingestion pipelines securely transfer data from a wide range of sources into the landing area, ensuring that raw information is consistently captured, protected, and ready for downstream processing. These pipelines accommodate both batch and streaming workloads, reliably ingesting data from databases, APIs, and real-time event streams.

Batch ingestion pipeline

With reference to the Electronic pipeline architecture discussed in *Chapter 7, Understanding Modern Data Pipelines*, the section we will focus on here corresponds to the highlighted component shown in the following figure.

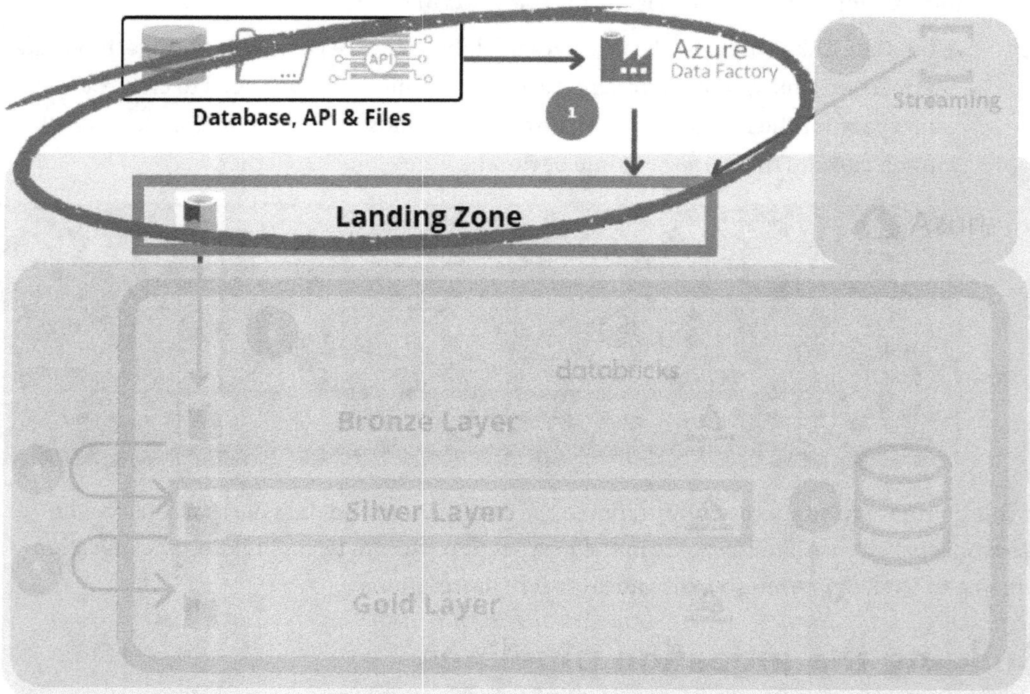

Figure 8.36: Electroniz batch ingestion pipeline

It's time to build the batch ingestion pipeline. To do that, we'll navigate to the Azure Data Factory instance we previously created.

Creating linked services

Azure Data Factory linked services act as connection configurations, defining the details ADF needs to connect securely to external data sources or compute resources.

Creating source linked service

A linked service that maps to source data as its origin is known as a source linked service.

Azure SQL linked service for store sales database

The following steps will create an Azure SQL linked service for ingesting SQL Server data.

1. On the Azure portal, navigate to **Home** > **All resources** > **electronizlakehouse-df**.
2. Click on **Launch Studio**.

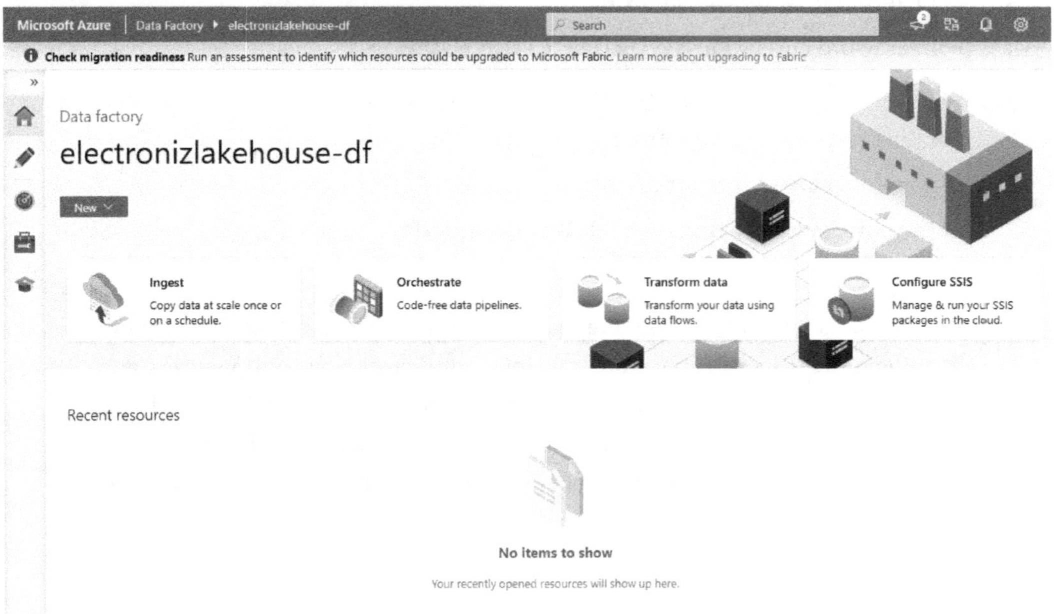

Figure 8.37: Electroniz Data Factory control panel

3. Using the panel on the left, click on **Manage**. Our first step in Azure Data Factory is to create the required linked services for the source system.
4. To create the source linked service, select **Create linked service**. In the *New linked service* window, choose the *Azure SQL Database* icon and click **Continue**. This should open a new configuration window titled **New linked service**.
5. For Name, enter **salesdb_source_service**.
6. For Connect via integration runtime*, enter **AutoResolveIntegrationRuntime**.
7. For Version, choose **2.0**.
8. For Account selection method, choose **From Azure subscription**.

9. For Azure subscription, select **Free Tier** or **Paid Subscription**.
10. For Server name, choose **salesdbserver1001** (the name may vary in your case).
11. For Database name, choose **salesdb** (the name may vary in your case).
12. For Authentication type, choose **SQL authentication**.
13. For Username, enter **salesadmin**.
14. For Password enter **<PASSWORD SET PREVIOUSLY>**.
15. Check the **Always encrypted box**.
16. For Encrypt, choose **Mandatory**.
17. Check the **Trust server certificate** box.
18. At the bottom of the window, click **Test Connection**.

> **Note**
>
> Azure Data Factory offers more than 90 built-in connectors that enable data engineers to ingest, move, and transform data across cloud, on-premises, and SaaS platforms. These connectors support a wide range of pipeline activities—including Copy operations, Mapping Data Flows, Lookups, and Metadata extraction—making it easier to integrate diverse data sources into modern data engineering workflows.

19. After the successful connection message is displayed, click on **Create**.

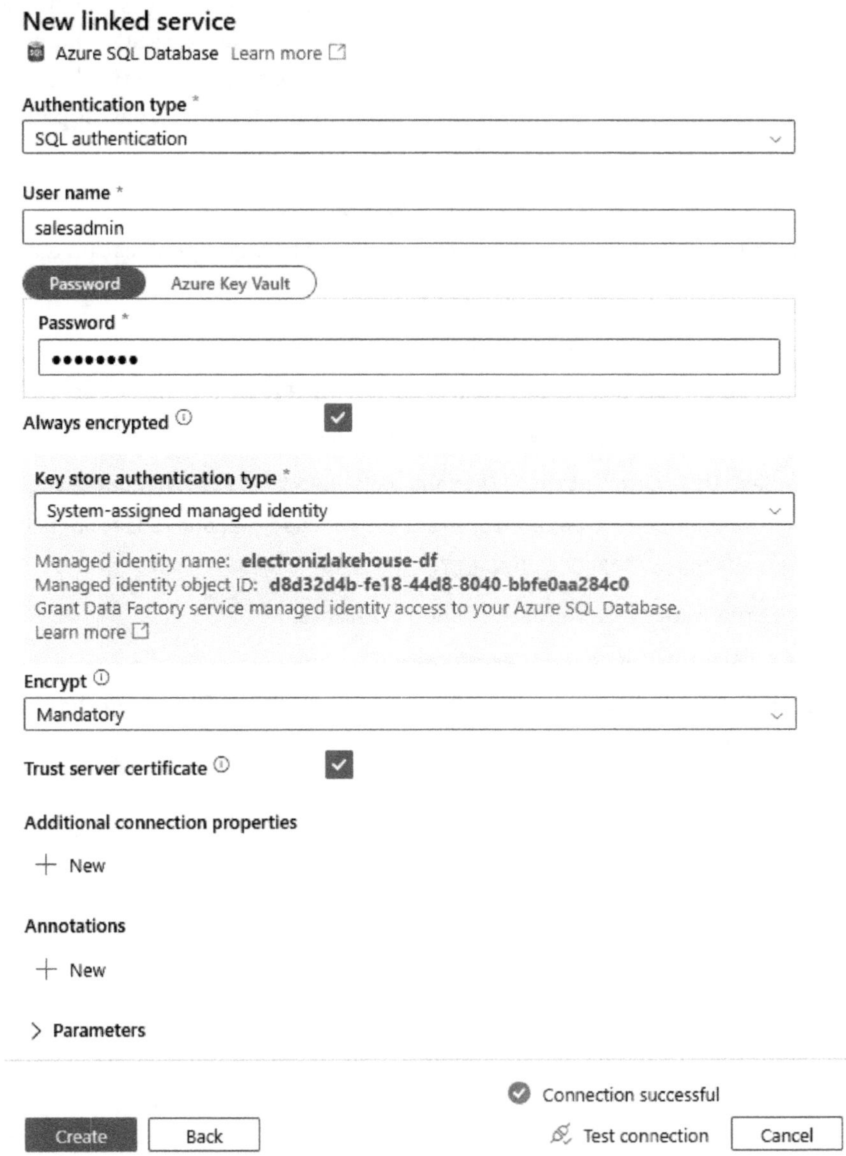

Figure 8.38: Testing the linked service for store sale database

If a connection error occurs while testing the linked service, first verify that all configuration settings are correct. Also ensure that the Azure SQL Database is active and running. Databases on free or serverless tiers may automatically pause during periods of inactivity, preventing new connections. If the database is paused, resume it from the Azure Portal before retrying the connection.

HTTP linked service for geo-location data

The following steps will create an HTTP-linked service to ingest geolocation data.

1. Using the panel on the left, click on **Manage**.
2. To create the destination linked service, select **New**.
3. In the **New linked service** window, search for **HTTP** and click **Continue**.
4. For Name, enter **geolocation_source_service**
5. For Base URL, enter: `https://github.com/PacktPublishing/Data-Engineering-with-Apache-Spark-Databricks-and-Lakehouse-Second-Edition/blob/main/chapter8/data/IP2LOCATION-LITE-DB1.CSV`
6. For Server certificate validation, choose **Enable**.
7. For Authentication, choose **Anonymous**.
8. Click on **Test connection**. If the "Connection successful" message has been received, click **Create**.

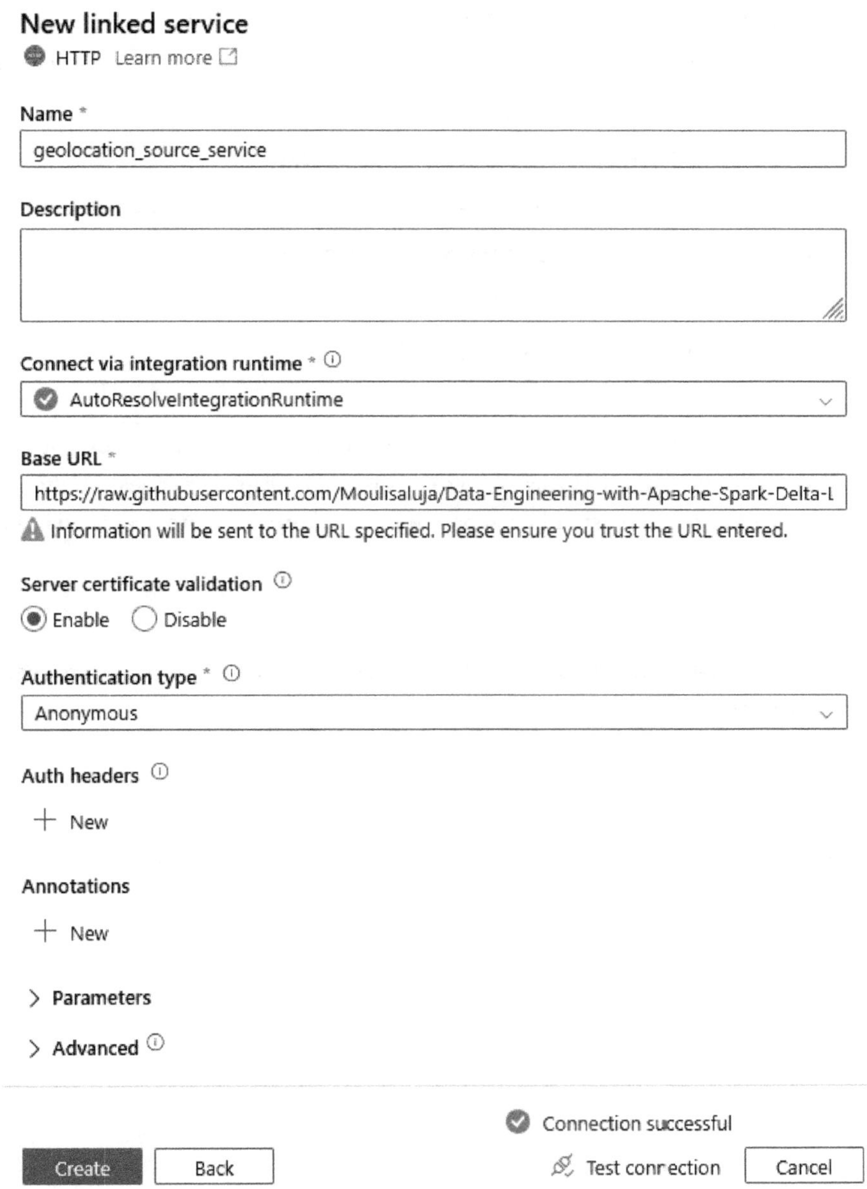

Figure 8.39: Testing the linked service for geo-location

REST linked service for currency conversion data

The following steps will create a REST-based linked service to ingest currency conversion data.

1. Using the panel on the left, click on **Manage**.
2. To create the destination linked service, select **New**.
3. In the New linked service window, search for **REST** and click **Continue**.
4. For Name, enter **currency_conversion_source_service**.
5. For Base URL, enter `https://api.exchangeratesapi.io/v1`.
6. For Authentication, choose **Anonymous**.

> **Note**
>
> In Azure Data Factory, when a single linked service is shared across multiple datasets, a failure in that service can disrupt multiple pipelines simultaneously. To reduce the blast radius, separate critical workloads into dedicated linked services.

7. Click on **Test connection**. If the "Connection successful" message has been received, click **Create**.

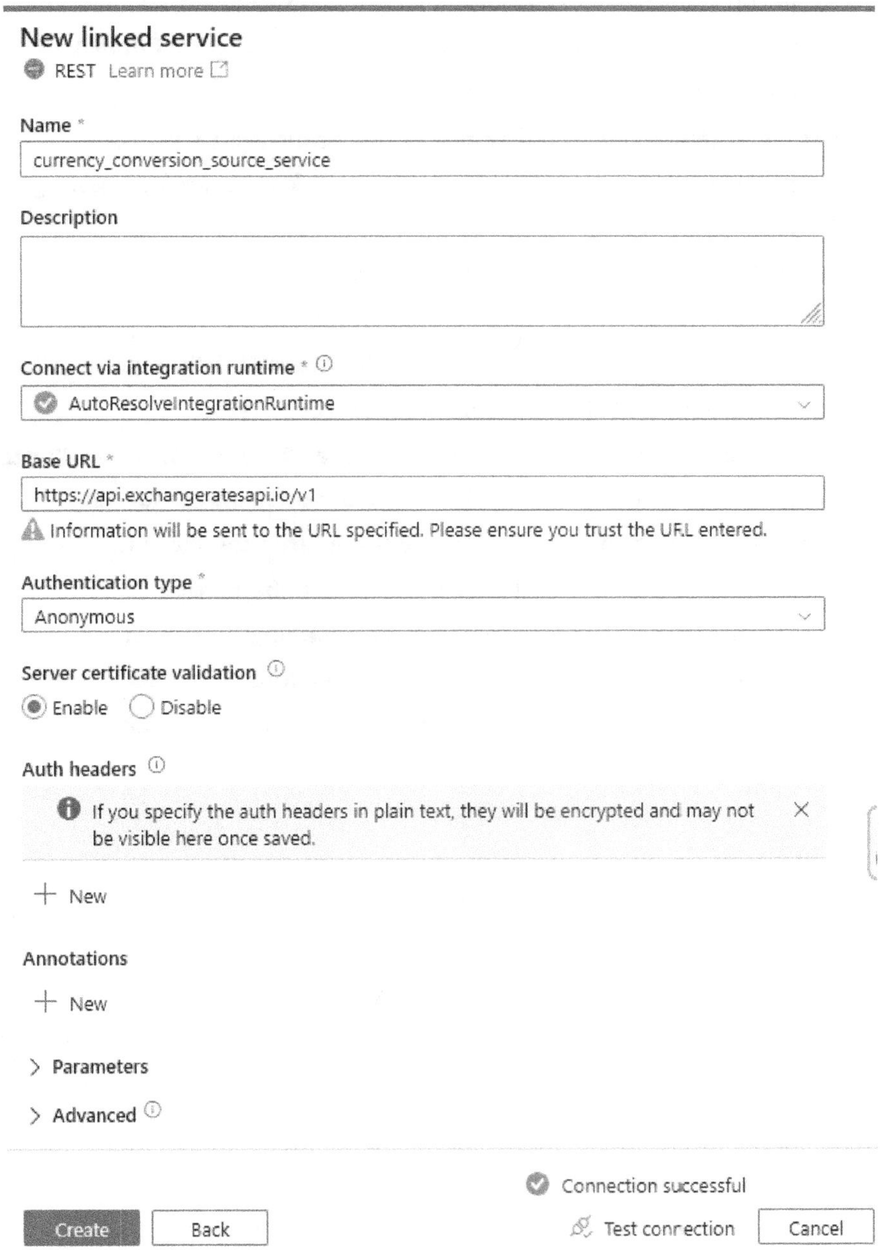

Figure 8.40: Testing the linked service for currency conversion

8. At the top of the Linked service window, click on **Validate All**.
9. If you get a message *"Your factory has been validated"*, click on **Publish all**.
10. On the *Publish All* window, click on **Publish**.

Azure Blob linked service for website tracking logs

The following steps will create an Azure Blob Storage linked service for ingesting website tracking logs.

1. Using the panel on the left, click on **Manage**.
2. To create the destination linked service, select **New**.
3. In the New linked service window, search for **Azure Blob Storage** and click **Continue**.
4. For Name, enter **website_tracking_logs_source_service.**
5. For Connect via integration runtime*, enter **AutoResolveIntegrationRuntime**.
6. For Authentication type, choose **System-assigned managed identity**.
7. For Account selection method, choose **From Azure subscription**.
8. For Azure subscription, select **Free Tier** or **Paid Subscription**.
9. For Storage account name, choose **websitetracking** (the name may vary in your case).
10. At the bottom of the window, click **Test Connection**.
11. After the "*Connection successful*" message is displayed, click on **Create**.

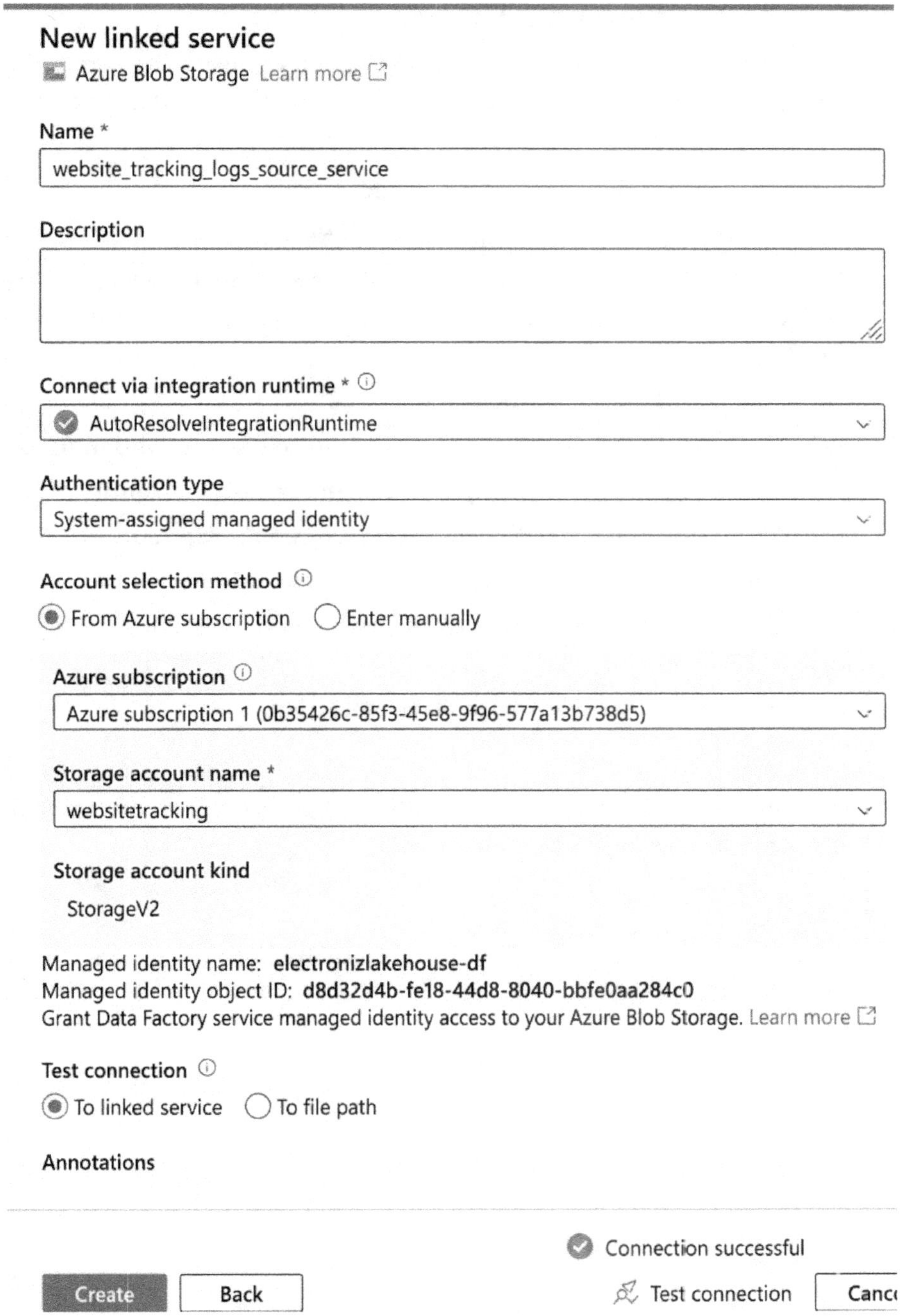

Figure 8.41: Testing the linked service for website tracking logs

Creating destination linked service

A linked service that connects to the system where it writes or loads data is known as a **destination linked service**. The following steps will create an Azure Data Lake Storage linked service for storing data in the landing zone.

1. Using the panel on the left, click on **Manage**.
2. To create the destination linked service, select **New**.
3. In the New linked service window, choose the **Azure Data Lake Storage Gen2** icon and click **Continue**. This should open a new configuration window titled **New linked service**.
4. For Name, enter **landing_destination_service**.
5. For Connect via integration runtime*, enter **AutoResolveIntegrationRuntime**.
6. For Authentication type, choose **System-assigned managed identity**.
7. For Account selection method, choose **From Azure subscription**.
8. For Azure subscription, select **Free Tier** or **Paid Subscription**.
9. For Storage account name, choose **electronizlanding** (the name may vary in your case).
10. At the bottom of the window, click **Test Connection**.

    > **Note**
    >
    > The ADF Monitor captures pipeline and activity run details; these logs persist in Azure for ongoing tracking and analysis.

11. After the "*Connection successful*" message is displayed, click on **Create**.

Figure 8.42: Destination linked service configurations and testing the connection

12. At the top of the Linked Service window, click on **Validate All**.
13. If you get a message *Your factory has been validated,* click on **Publish all**.
14. On the *Publish All* window, click on **Publish**.
15. If everything was configured correctly, your linked service should now appear as shown below:

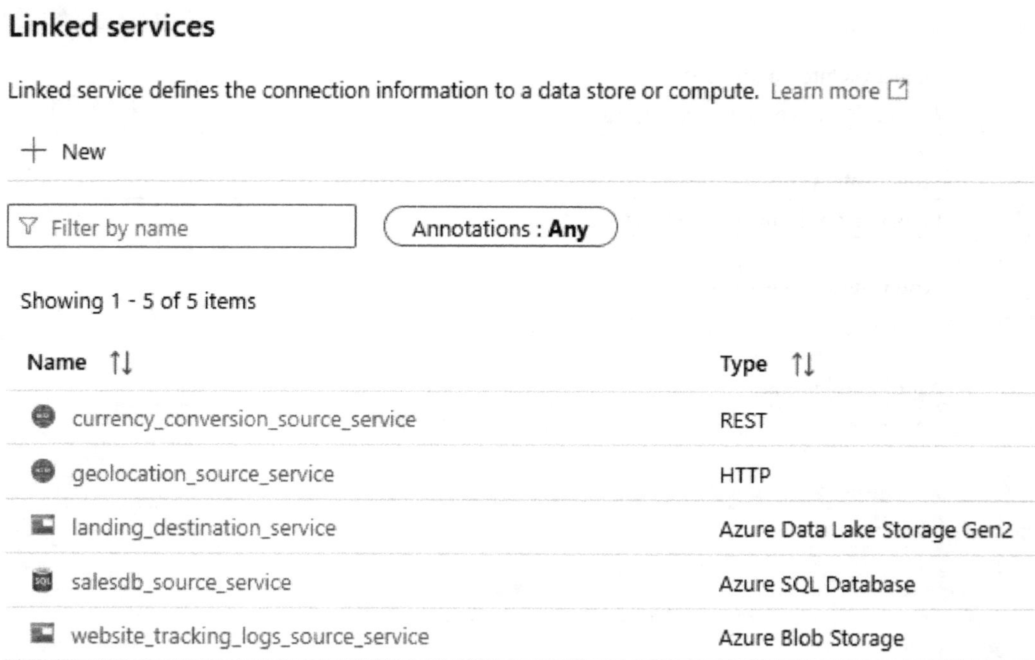

Figure 8.43: Linked services for source and destination

Now that the source and destination linked services are configured, we can begin building the actual batch ingestion pipeline.

Creating the batch ingestion pipeline

Creating a pipeline in ADF requires using the **Author** workspace, where you create and edit pipelines, build dataflows, configure linked services, create datasets, manage triggers, and debug and publish your changes. Let's follow the steps below to create the batch ingestion pipeline.

1. On the Azure portal, navigate to **Home** > **All resources** > **electronizlakehouse-df.**
2. Click on **Launch Studio**.
3. Using the menu on the left, select **Author**.
4. In the Factory Resources panel, hover over **Pipelines**, click the three dots that appear, and choose **New pipeline**.
5. In the Properties panel, input the following:
6. For Name, enter **electroniz_batch_ingestion_pipeline**.
7. For Description, enter **This pipeline will ingest data from the store sales database, currency conversion, geo-location, and ecommerce website tracking**.
8. In the Activities panel, search for **Web**. Now, drag the Web activity to the panel on the right.
9. For Name, enter **Get Currency API Secret**.
10. Click on **Settings**.
11. For the URL, retrieve the vault *URI* from the Azure Key Vault secret that we created previously. You can find this by navigating to **Home** > **All resources** > **electroniz-secret-kv** > **Objects** > **CURRAPIEY**. You can adjust resource navigation based on the name of your Key Vault.

12. Select the entry in the current version. Copy the value of the **Secret Identifier**.

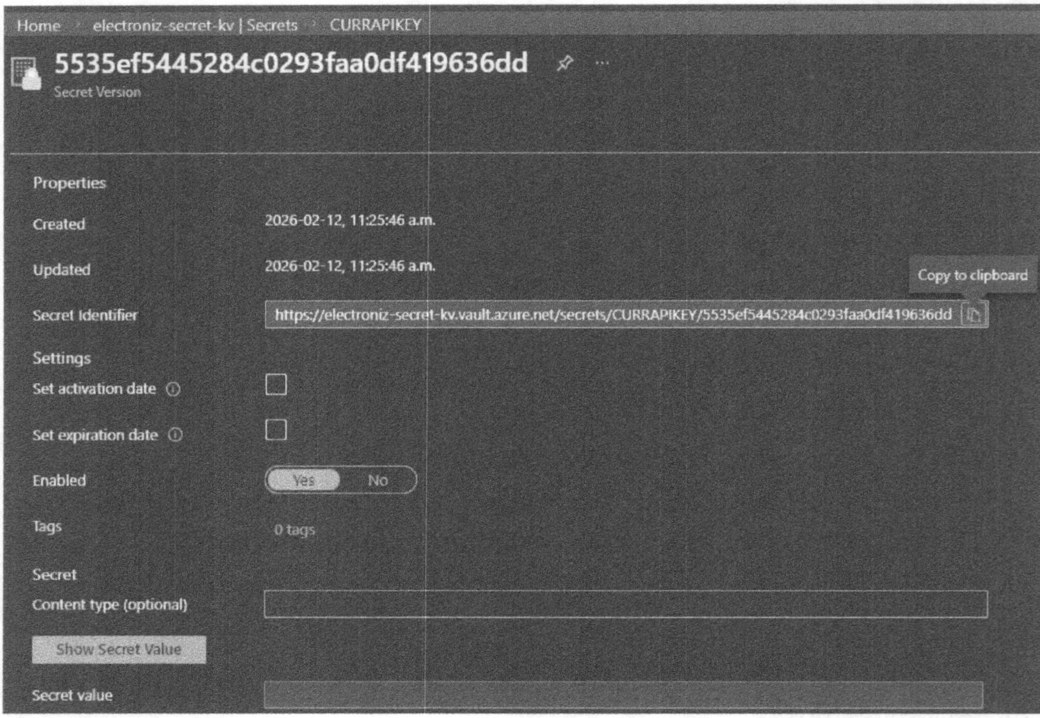

Figure 8.44: Retrieving secret URI

13. Append this to the end of the URI:*?api-version=7.0*, as follows: `https://electroniz-secret-kv.vault.azure.net/secrets/CURRAPIKEY/5535ef5445284c0293faa0df419636dd?api-version=7.0`. Please note that the name of the Key Vault in your URI will be different in your case.
14. For Method, choose **GET**.
15. For Authentication, choose **System-Assigned Managed Identity**.
16. For Resource, enter `https://vault.azure.net`.

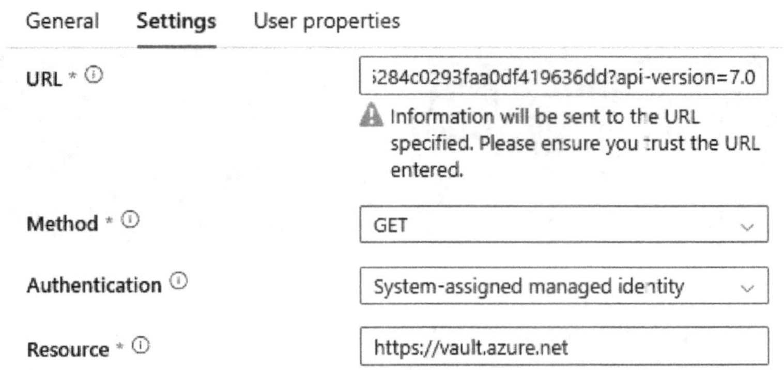

Figure 8.45: Web activity settings

Now we move on to creation of geo-location data activities.

Configure geo-location data activities

The steps below will create the activities needed to ingest the geo-location data.

1. In the **Activities** panel, search for **Copy data**. Now, drag the **Copy data** activity to the panel on the right.
2. For Name, enter **Get Geo-location mapping data**.
3. Click on **Source** tab. For Source dataset, click on **New**.
4. In the New dataset window, search for *HTTP*. Click **Continue**.
5. For Select format, click on **DelimitedText**. Click **Continue**.
6. In the Set properties window, for Name, enter **GeoDelimitedTextSource**.
7. For Linked service, choose **geolocation_source_service**.
8. Uncheck **First row as header**.
9. Click **OK**.
10. Now click on **Sink** tab. For Sink dataset, click on **New**.
11. In the new dataset pane, click on **Azure Data Lake Storage Gen2**. Click on **Continue**.
12. Click on **DelimitedText**. Press **Continue**.
13. In the Set properties window, for Name, enter **GeoDelimitedTextSink**.
14. For Linked service, choose **landing_destination_service**.
15. For File path, enter **raw** in the first box.
16. Click **OK**.
17. Now click on the **Open** icon next to Sink dataset.

18. For **Directory,** enter:

```
geolocation/year=@{formatDateTime(utcnow(),'yyyy')}/
month=@{formatDateTime(utcnow(),'MM')}/
date=@{formatDateTime(utcnow(),'dd')}/
hour=@{formatDateTime(utcnow(),'HH')}/
hour=@{formatDateTime(utcnow(),'mm')}/min=@{formatDateTime(utcnow(),'mm')}
```

> **Note**
>
> Azure Data Factory uses the Dynamic Content expression language to build parameterized, flexible, and metadata-driven pipelines that adapt to different inputs, environments, and runtime conditions.

19. For File name enter **@concat(dataset().FileTime,'.',dataset().FileExt)**.
20. Click on **Parameters** tab.
21. Click on **Add New**. For Name, enter **FileExt**, Type enter **String**, Value enter **csv**
22. Click on **Add New**.
23. For Name, enter **FileTime**, Type enter **String**, Value enter **@pipeline().TriggerTime**
24. Under Factory Resources, click on **electroniz_batch_ingestion_pipeline**.
25. Chain the two activities together by dragging the arrow from **Get Secret** to **Get Geo-location mapping data**. Make sure you connect the On Success outcome, marked by a checked box, as illustrated in the following figure.

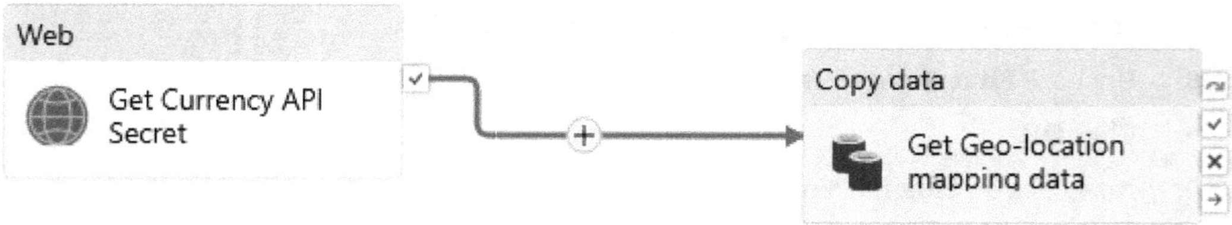

Figure 8.46: Chaining Get Currency API secret and Get Geo-location mapping data

26. At the top of the window, click on **Validate All.**
27. If you get a message *"Your factory has been validated"*, click on **Publish all**.
28. On the *Publish All* window, click on **Publish**.

Now that we've completed the ingestion of the geo-location data, let's move on to the next data source on our list - store sales data.

Configure store sales data activities

The steps below will create the activities needed to ingest the store sales data.

1. In the Activities panel, search for **Lookup**. Now, drag the **Lookup** activity to the panel on the right.
2. Under the General tab, for Name, enter **Find SalesDB Tables**.
3. Click on the **Settings** tab. In Source dataset, click on **New**.
4. In the New dataset panel, click on **Azure SQL Database**.
5. Click on **Continue**.
6. In the Set properties panel, for Name, enter **SalesDBSource**
7. For Linked service, choose **salesdb_source_service**.
8. Click on **OK**. You should now be back in the Settings tab of **Find SalesDB Tables**.
9. Uncheck the box **First rows only.**
10. For Use query, choose **Query**.
11. For Query enter

```
SELECT QUOTENAME(table_schema)+'.'+QUOTENAME(table_name) AS Table_Name
FROM information_Schema.tables WHERE table_name not in ('watermarktable',
'database_firewall_rules')
```

12. Notice that the preceding dynamic select statement generates a list of tables that will be ingested inside the lakehouse. If you want to exclude some tables from the list, you can use the *NOT IN* clause.

> **Note**
>
> Running SQL statements from Azure Data Factory can be prone to SQL injection if you concatenate user-supplied values into queries; use parameterized queries or stored procedures with validated inputs to mitigate the risk.

13. After the settings above, the **Settings** tab looks like this:

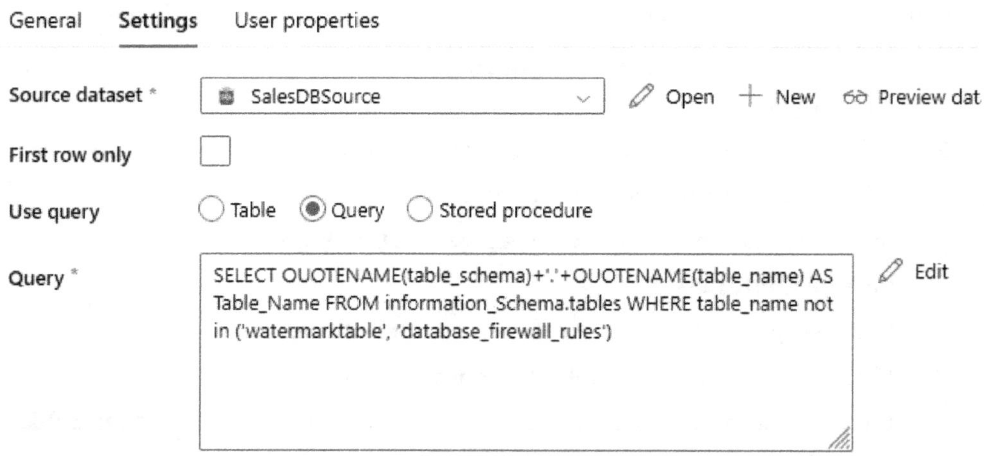

Figure 8.47: Settings configuration for Find SalesDB tables

14. Chain the activities together by dragging the arrow from *Get Geo-location mapping* to *Find SalesDB Tables*. Make sure you are connecting the *On Success* outcome.
15. Now that we have the list of tables that need to be ingested from the database, we will loop through each one to copy its data.
16. In the Activities panel, search for **ForEach**. Now, drag the **ForEach** activity to the panel on the right-hand side. The ForEach activity will iterate over the list of tables returned by the Find SalesDB Tables activity.
17. In the General tab of the ForEach activity, for Name, enter **For Each SalesDB Table**.
18. Click on the **Settings** tab.
19. For Items enter **@activity('Find SalesDB Tables').output.value**.
20. Notice the use of **@activity**. At runtime, each activity returns a JSON response that includes elements such as output and status. You can reference values from this response using the **@activity** syntax. In this example, we are retrieving the output of the **Find SalesDB Tables** activity, which returns the list of tables produced by the preceding SQL query.
21. Next, chain the activities together by dragging the arrow from **Find SalesDB Tables** to **For Each SalesDB Table**. Make sure you are connecting the **On Success** outcome. Chaining ensures that the output of one activity is passed as the input to the next activity.

The pipeline should now appear as shown below.

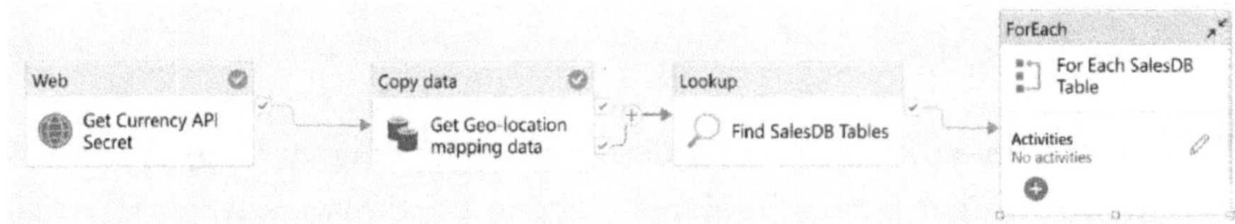

Figure 8.48: Chaining Find SalesDB Tables and For Each SalesDB Table

Now that we have identified the tables and set up the iterative loop, we can proceed to configure the activities that will copy data from the source. For each iteration, it will perform the following operations:

- Retrieve the **previous** watermark
- Generate a **new** watermark
- Ingest data from the table using the **range** between the old and new watermarks
- Update the control table with the new watermark

22. Click on the pencil icon in the Activities section of *For Each SalesDB Table*. In the Activities panel, search for **Lookup**. Now, drag the **Lookup** activity to the panel on the right-hand side.
23. For Name, enter **Lookup Old Watermark**.
24. Click on **Settings**. For the **Source** dataset, choose **SalesDBSource**.
25. For Use Query, choose **Query**.
26. For Query, enter:

```
SELECT * FROM [dbo].[watermarktable] AS WatermarkValue WHERE
table_name='@{item().Table_Name}'
```

27. Notice that the dynamic `SELECT` statement retrieves the watermark of the table being ingested from the previous iteration of the ingestion run.
28. In the Activities panel, search for **Lookup**. Now, drag the **Lookup** activity to the panel on the right-hand side. Place it just below **Lookup Old Watermark**.
29. For Name, enter **Lookup New Watermark**
30. Click on **Settings**. For the Source dataset, choose **SalesDBSource**.
31. For Use Query, choose **Query**

32. For Query, enter:

```
SELECT MAX(updated_at) as NewWatermarkvalue FROM @{item().Table_Name}
```

33. In the Activities panel, search for **Copy data**. Now, drag the **Copy data** activity to the panel on the right-hand side. Place it right next to the two watermark activities.
34. For Name, enter **Copy Table Data**.
35. Click on **Source**. For the Source dataset, choose **SalesDBSource**.
36. For Use Query, choose **Query.**
37. For Query, enter

```
SELECT * FROM @{item().Table_Name} WHERE updated_at > '@{activity('Lookup
Old Watermark').output.firstRow. watermark_value}'
```

38. Notice this SQL is selecting records that are greater than the old watermark of the table being ingested. We have chosen *updated_at* as the watermark column.
39. Click on **Sink**. A sink is a destination to which the output of the preceding SQL will be stored.
40. In the Sink dataset, click on **New**. Then in the Azure tab, click on **Azure Data Lake Storage Gen2**. Click on **Continue**.
41. In Select Format, click on **DelimitedText**. Then, click on **Continue**.
42. In the Set properties pane, for Name, enter **SalesDelimitedTextSink**.
43. For Linked service, choose **landing_destination_service**.
44. In File path, for Filesystem enter **raw**.
45. Uncheck **First row as header**. Click **OK**.
46. Next to the Sink dataset, click on **Open**. For Directory, enter:

```
sales/@{activity('Lookup Old Watermark').output.firstRow.table_name}/
year=@{formatDateTime(utcnow(),'yyyy')}/
month=@{formatDateTime(utcnow(),'MM')}/
day=@{formatDateTime(utcnow(),'dd')}/hour=@{formatDateTime(utcnow(),'HH')}/
min=@{formatDateTime(utcnow(),'mm')}
```

47. Notice that we are storing the output in a date-partitioned folder. For File enter:

```
@concat(dataset().FileTime,'.',dataset().FileExt)
```

48. Click on **Parameters**. Then, add the following parameters:

Name: `FileExt`	Type: `String`	Default Value: `csv`
Name: `FileTime`	Type: `String`	Default Value: `@pipeline().TriggerTime`

Table 8.3: Pipeline Parameters for File Extension and Trigger Time Configuration

49. Under Factory Resources, click on **electroniz_batch_ingestion_pipeline**.
50. Chain the two activities together by dragging the arrow from **Lookup Old Watermark to Copy Table Data**. Also, from **Lookup New Watermark to Copy Table Data**. Make sure you are connecting the **On Success** outcome, which is marked by a checked box, as illustrated in the following figure.

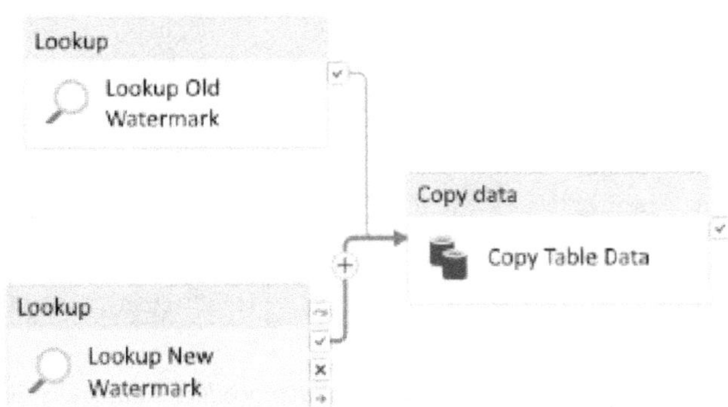

Figure 8.49: Chaining activities together

We're progressing well so far. Next, we'll create an activity that updates the control table with the new watermark.

1. In the Activities panel, search for **Stored procedure**. Now, drag the **Stored procedure** activity to the panel on the right-hand side.
2. For Name, enter **Update Watermark**
3. Click on **Settings**. For Linked Service, choose **salesdb_source_service**
4. For Stored procedure name, choose **[dbo].[usp_write_watermark]**. Be patient—if the database has entered sleep mode, it may take a moment to wake up.
5. Underneath the **Stored procedure parameters**, add two new parameters. Click on **New**.
   a. **Name**: `LastModifiedtime`

b. **Type**: `Datetime`

c. **Value**: `@{activity('Lookup New Watermark').output.firstRow.NewWatermarkvalue}`

6. Click on **New** one more time.

    a. **Name**: `TableName`

    b. **Type**: `String`

    c. **Value**: `@{activity('Lookup Old Watermark').output.firstRow.table_name}`

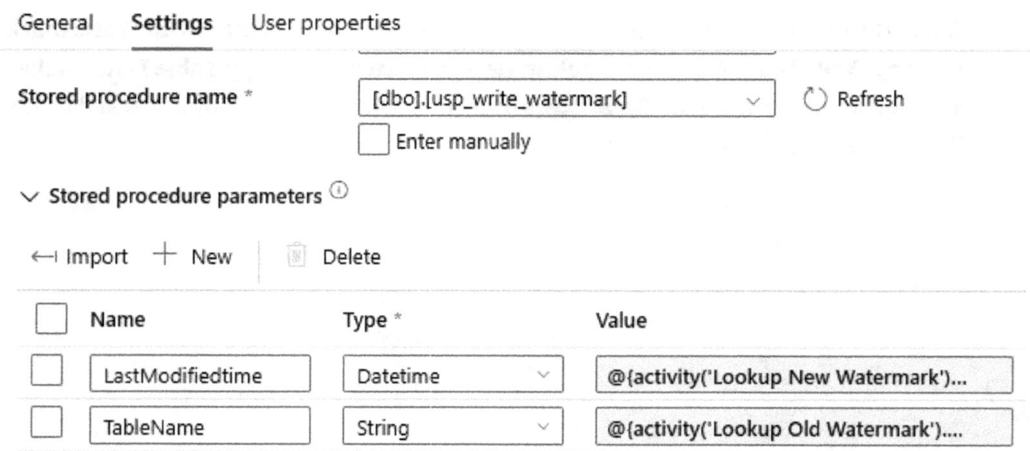

Figure 8.50: Stored procedure parameters

7. Chain the two activities together by dragging the arrow from **Copy Table Data** to **Update Watermark**. Make sure you connect the **On Success** outcome, marked by a checked box, as illustrated in the following figure.

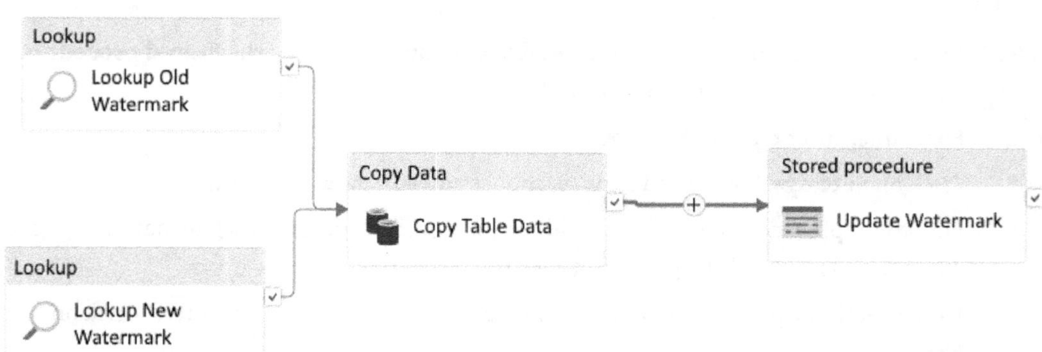

Figure 8.51: Chaining Copy Table Data to Update Watermark

8. Under Factory Resources, click on **electroniz_batch_ingestion_pipeline**.
9. We have now completed the batch ingestion pipeline for the store sales data. The pipeline should look like this:

Figure 8.52: Batch ingestion pipeline for the store sales data

10. At the top of the window, click on **Validate All**.
11. If you get a message *"Your factory has been validated"*, click on **Publish all**.
12. On the *Publish All* window, click on **Publish**.

Now that we've completed the ingestion of the store sales data, let's move on to the next data source on our list - currency conversion data.

Configure currency conversion data activities

The steps below will create the activities needed to ingest the currency conversion data:

1. In the Activities panel, search for **Copy Data**. Now, drag the **Copy Data** activity to the panel on the right.
2. For Name, enter **Get Currency Conversion File**.
3. Click on **Source** tab. For Source dataset, click on **New**.
4. In the New dataset window, search for **REST**. Click **Continue**.
5. In Set properties for Name, enter **CurrencyConversionJSONSource**.
6. For Linked service, choose **currency_conversion_source_service**. Click **OK**.
7. Next to the Source dataset, click on **Open**.
8. For Relative URL enter

```
@concat('/latest?access_key=', activity('Get Currency API
Secret').output.value)
```

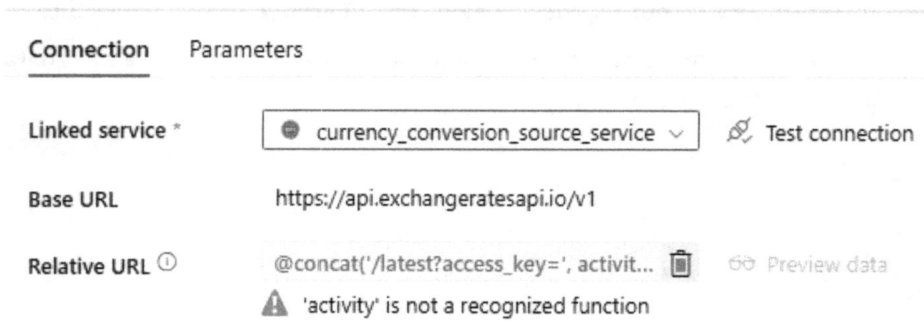

Figure 8.53: Editing the relative URL

Although the figure shows an error for reasons not fully understood, it is safe to proceed with these settings.

9. Now click on **Sink** tab. For Sink dataset, click on **New**.
10. In the new dataset pane, click on **Azure Data Lake Storage Gen2**. Click on **Continue**.
11. Click on **JSON**. Press **Continue**.
12. In the Set properties window, for Name, enter **CurrencyConversionJSONSink**
13. For Linked service, choose **landing_destination_service**.
14. For File path, enter **raw** in the first box.
15. Click **OK**.
16. Now click on the **Open** icon next to Sink dataset.
17. For Directory, enter

```
currency_conversion/year=@{formatDateTime(utcnow(),'yyyy')}/
month=@{formatDateTime(utcnow(),'MM')}/
day=@{formatDateTime(utcnow(),'dd')}/hour=@{formatDateTime(utcnow(),'HH')}/
min=@{formatDateTime(utcnow(),'mm')}
```

18. For File name enter:

```
@concat(dataset().FileTime,'.',dataset().FileExt)
```

19. Click on **Parameters** tab.
20. Click on **Add New**.
    a. For Name, enter `FileExt`.

b. For Type, enter `String`.

c. For Value, enter `csv`.

21. Click on **Parameters**. Then, add the following parameters:

Name: `FileExt`	Type: `String`	Default Value: `json`
Name: `FileTime`	Type: `String`	Default Value: `@pipeline().TriggerTime`

Table 8.4: Pipeline Parameters for JSON File Extension and Trigger Time Configuration

22. Under Factory Resources, click on **electroniz_batch_ingestion_pipeline**.
23. Chain the two activities together by dragging the arrow from **For Each SalesDB Table** to **Currency Conversion File**. Make sure you are connecting the **On Success** outcome, which is marked by a checked box, as illustrated in the figure below.

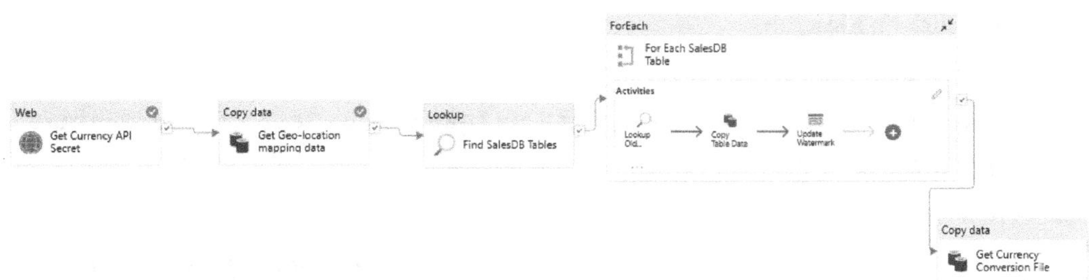

Figure 8.54: Batch ingestion pipeline with currency conversion activities

24. At the top of the window, click on **Validate All**.
25. If you get a message *"Your factory has been validated"*, click on **Publish all**.
26. On the *Publish All* window, click on **Publish**.

We're nearing the finish line—only one last component of the batch ingestion pipeline remains: e-commerce website tracking logs.

Configure e-commerce website tracking logs data activities

The steps below will create the activities needed to ingest the e-commerce website tracking logs.

1. In the Activities panel, search for **Copy Data**. Now, drag the **Copy Data** activity to the panel on the right.
2. For Name, enter **Copy Website Tracking Logs**

3. Click on **Source** tab.
4. For Source dataset, click on **New**.
5. In the New dataset window, search for **Azure Blob Storage**.
6. Click **Continue**.
7. For Select Format, choose **JSON**.
8. Click **Continue**.
9. In Set properties for Name, enter **WebsiteTrackingLogsJSONSource**.
10. For Linked service, choose **website_tracking_logs_source_service**. Click **OK**.
11. Now click on the **Open** icon next to **Source** dataset.
12. For Container, enter **tracking-logs**.
13. Click on **electroniz_batch_ingestion_pipeline** tab.
14. In the Source tab, for File path type, choose **Prefix**.
15. For Prefix, enter **electroniz_access**
16. Now click on **Sink** tab.
17. For Sink dataset, click on **New**.
18. In the new dataset pane, click on **Azure Data Lake Storage Gen2**. Click on **Continue**.
19. Click on **JSON**.
20. Press **Continue**.
21. In the Set properties window, for Name, enter **WebsiteTrackingLogsJSONSink**
22. For Linked service, choose **landing_destination_service**.
23. For File path, enter **raw** in the first box.
24. Click **OK**.
25. Now click on the **Open** icon next to Sink dataset.
26. For Directory, enter

```
ecommerce_logs/year=@{formatDateTime(utcnow(),'yyyy')}/
month=@{formatDateTime(utcnow(),'MM')}/
day=@{formatDateTime(utcnow(),'dd')}/hour=@{formatDateTime(utcnow(),'HH')}/
min=@{formatDateTime(utcnow(),'mm')}
```

27. In the Activities panel, search for **Delete**.
28. Now, drag the **Delete** to activity the panel on the right.
29. For Name, enter **Delete Website Tracking Logs**.

30. Click on **Source**.
31. For Dataset, choose **WebsiteTrackingLogsJSONSource**.
32. For File path type, choose File path in dataset.
33. Click on **Logging settings**.
34. Uncheck **Enable logging**.
35. Under Factory Resources, click on **electroniz_batch_ingestion_pipeline**.
36. Chain the two activities together by dragging the arrow from **Get Currency Conversion File** to **Copy Website Tracking Logs**.
37. Also chain **Copy Website Tracking Logs** to **Delete Website Tracking Logs**. Make sure you are connecting the *On Success* outcome, which is marked by a checked box.
    The final state of the Electroniz batch ingestion pipeline should look like this.

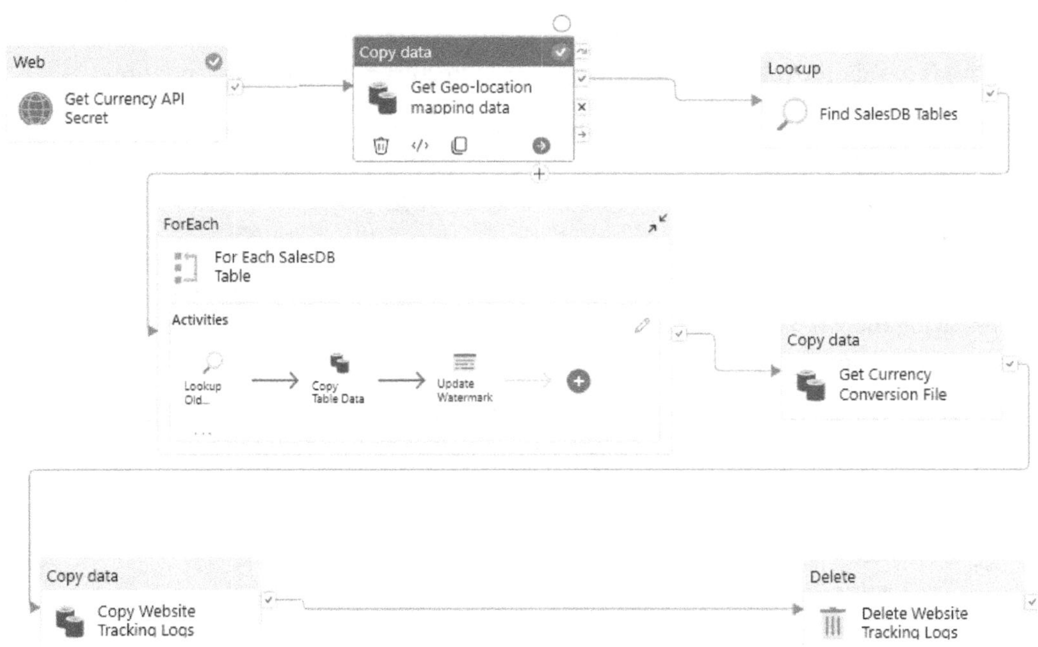

Figure 8.55: Electroniz batch ingestion pipeline with all activities

38. At the top of the window, click on **Validate All**.
39. If you get a message *"Your factory has been validated"*, click on **Publish all**.
40. On the *Publish All* window, click on **Publish**.

All done! Now it's time to verify that the newly created Electroniz batch ingestion pipeline is functioning correctly. Proceed with the next steps to unit test the pipeline.

Unit testing the batch ingestion pipeline

We are now ready to test the `electroniz_batch_ingestion_pipeline`. As you may recall, Electroniz requires a near–real-time view of data within their platform. Ensuring that the ingestion pipeline processes new records quickly and consistently is therefore critical to meeting their business requirements.

> **Note**
>
> Unit testing a data pipeline is the practice of validating the smallest independently testable components of your pipeline using controlled inputs and expected outputs.

In a production environment, this pipeline will be configured to run automatically on a recurring schedule, allowing new data from the sales system to flow into the lakehouse with minimal delay. While that automated trigger will be implemented later, our immediate objective is to validate that the pipeline performs correctly under manual execution.

To achieve this, we will invoke the pipeline several times using manual triggering, observing how it ingests, processes, and lands data across multiple runs. This will help us confirm that the logic behaves as expected, handles incremental loads properly, and produces consistent results each time it is triggered.

During pipeline execution, you may encounter various issues—this is expected, as identifying and resolving them is a core objective of unit testing. Below are some common issues you might run into, along with recommended solutions.

- When copying content like this, it is safer to first copy it to Notepad, make sure the content below appears in one line (not wrapped):

  ```
  geolocation/year=@{formatDateTime(utcnow(),'yyyy')}/
  month=@{formatDateTime(utcnow(),'MM')}/
  date=@{formatDateTime(utcnow(),'dd')}/
  hour=@{formatDateTime(utcnow(),'HH')}/
  hour=@{formatDateTime(utcnow(),'mm')}/min=@{formatDateTime(utcnow(),'mm')}
  ```

- Having an unnecessary extra line after the expression will give an error.

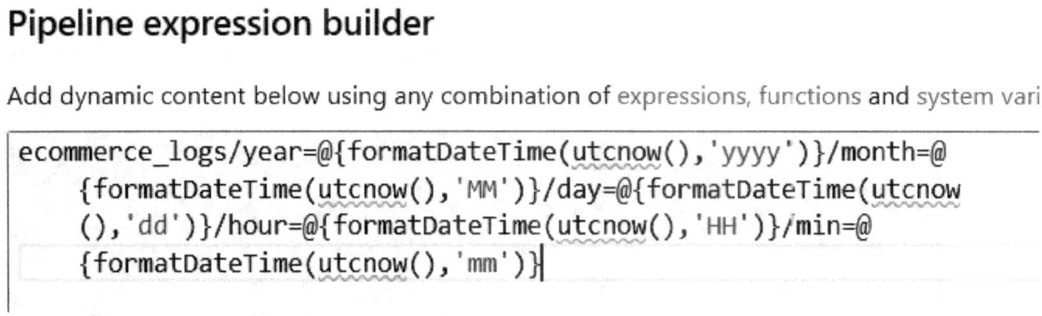

Figure 8.56: Errors due to extra line in expression builder

- Inadvertently including spaces within a variable name can cause errors.

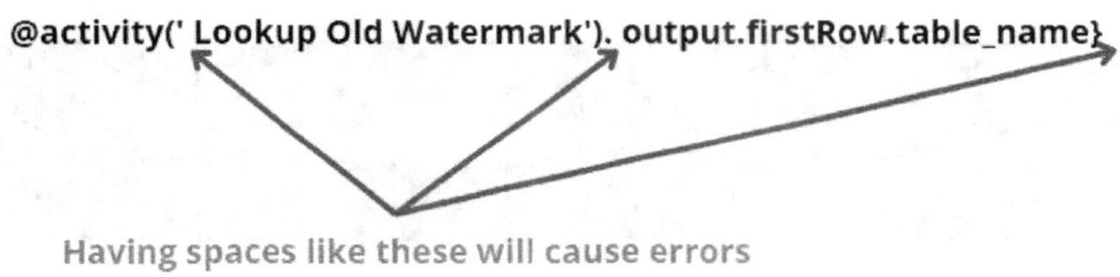

Figure 8.57: Errors due to space characters

- Activity names are case-sensitive.

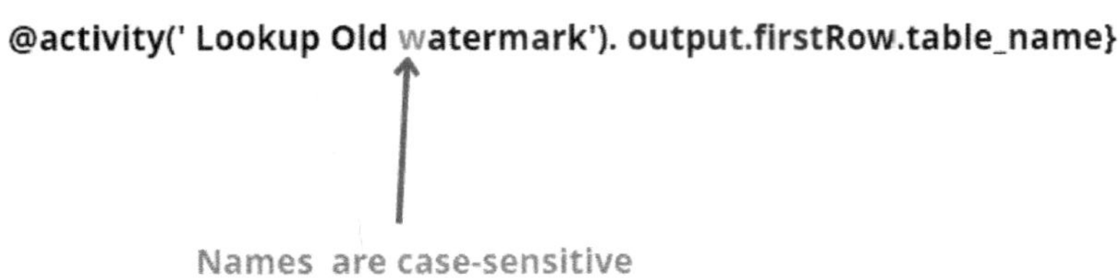

Figure 8.58: Respect the case sensitivity of activity names

Troubleshooting problems early helps validate your logic, strengthen error-handling, and ensure the pipeline behaves reliably under real-world conditions.

The first run

Our assumption is that Electroniz has been operating for several years and therefore their database contains a substantial amount of historical data. Consequently, the initial ingestion run will need to process all this historical information, which may take significantly longer depending on the total volume accumulated over time. Since we are starting with a clean slate, the `electronizlanding` bucket is currently empty, and this first run will populate it from scratch. Let's start by triggering the pipeline manually.

1. Paste the commands below into Azure Cloud Shell. You can execute them one at a time or run the whole block together.

```
DATAFACTORYNAME="electronizlakehouse-df"
PIPELINENAME="electroniz_batch_ingestion_pipeline"
RESOURCEGROUPNAME="training_rg"
az datafactory pipeline create-run \
--factory-name $DATAFACTORYNAME \
--name $PIPELINENAME \
--resource-group $RESOURCEGROUPNAME
```

The command requires the `datafactory` extension. Type `Y` and press enter.

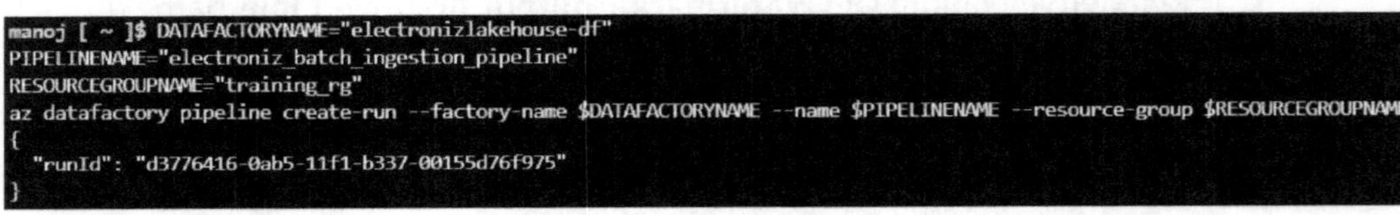

Figure 8.59: Manually triggering the pipeline

2. Navigate to the Azure Data Factory portal and click on the **Monitor** button in the left menu. You should see the pipeline running like this.

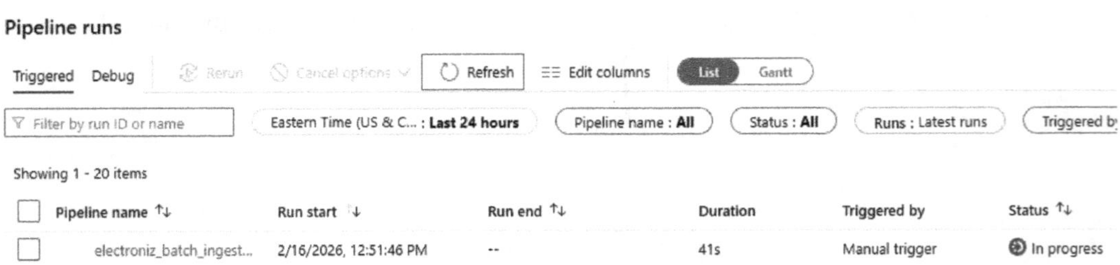

Figure 8.60: Invocation of electroniz_batch_ingestion_pipeline

3. In Azure Data Factory, click on `electroniz_batch_ingestion_pipeline`. If everything has run successfully, you should see green check marks throughout the interface. Scroll through the list of activities in the panel below; each one should display a green check mark indicating successful completion.

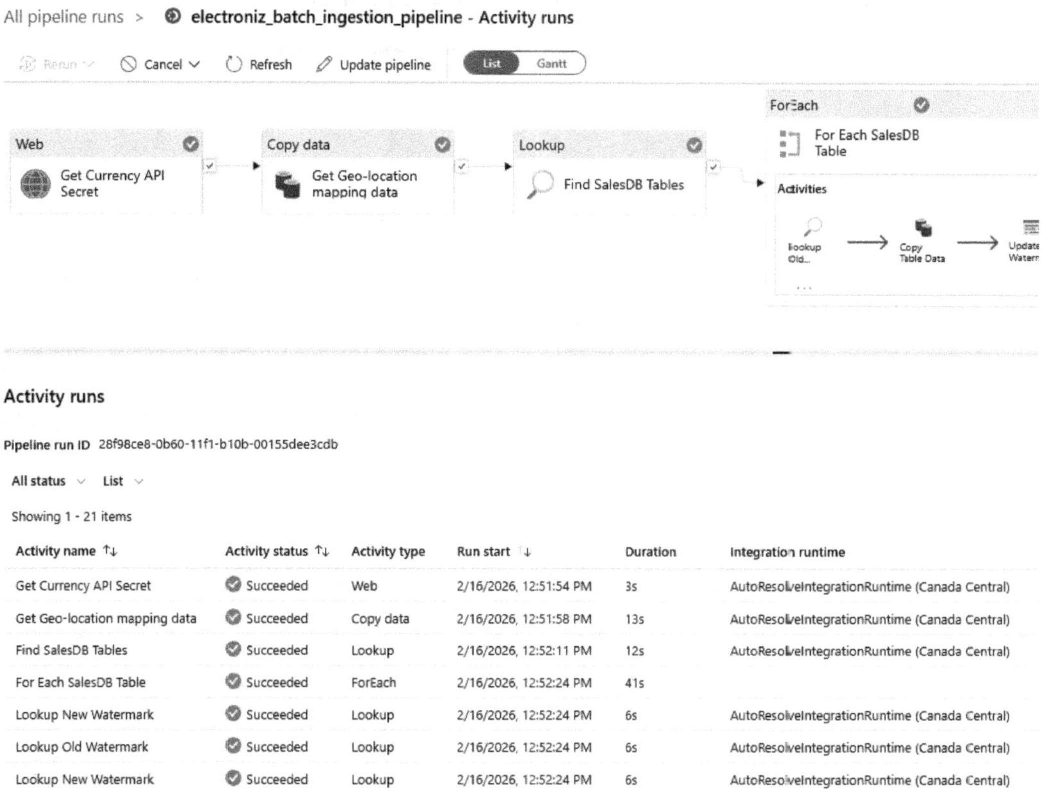

Figure 8.61: Successful completion of electroniz_batch_ingestion_pipeline

4. In the panel below, if you hover your cursor over an activity name, you can view both the input and output logs associated with that activity. Take some time to familiarize yourself with these details—they are extremely helpful for understanding how each step of the pipeline operates. If the pipeline encounters an issue, the error will be displayed in the error column beneath the corresponding activity.

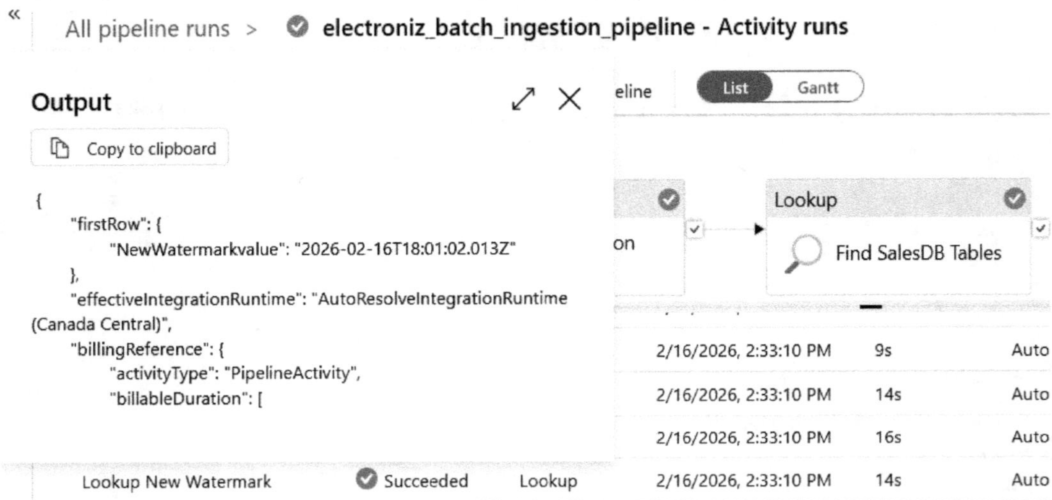

Figure 8.62: Checking input and output logs of activities

5. Note activities such as **Lookup Old Watermark**, **Lookup New Watermark**, **Copy Table Data,** and **Update Watermark**. Can you guess why their names appear more than once in the list?

Lookup New Watermark	Succeeded	Lookup	2/16/2026, 12:52:24 PM	6s
Lookup Old Watermark	Succeeded	Lookup	2/16/2026, 12:52:24 PM	6s
Lookup New Watermark	Succeeded	Lookup	2/16/2026, 12:52:24 PM	5s
Lookup Old Watermark	Succeeded	Lookup	2/16/2026, 12:52:24 PM	5s
Lookup New Watermark	Succeeded	Lookup	2/16/2026, 12:52:24 PM	18s
Lookup Old Watermark	Succeeded	Lookup	2/16/2026, 12:52:24 PM	7s
Copy Table Data	Succeeded	Copy data	2/16/2026, 12:52:31 PM	15s
Copy Table Data	Succeeded	Copy data	2/16/2026, 12:52:31 PM	14s
Copy Table Data	Succeeded	Copy data	2/16/2026, 12:52:31 PM	14s
Copy Table Data	Succeeded	Copy data	2/16/2026, 12:52:43 PM	14s
Update Watermark	Succeeded	Stored procedur	2/16/2026, 12:52:46 PM	4s
Update Watermark	Succeeded	Stored procedur	2/16/2026, 12:52:46 PM	4s
Update Watermark	Succeeded	Stored procedur	2/16/2026, 12:52:46 PM	4s
Update Watermark	Succeeded	Stored procedur	2/16/2026, 12:52:57 PM	4s

Figure 8.63: Multiple executions of the same activity

Each of these activities executes exactly once for every table ingested from the sales database.

6. Let's verify that the data has been ingested correctly. In the Azure portal, go to **Home** > **All resources** > **electronizlanding**. Using the Storage browser, click on **raw**. You should see these four folders:

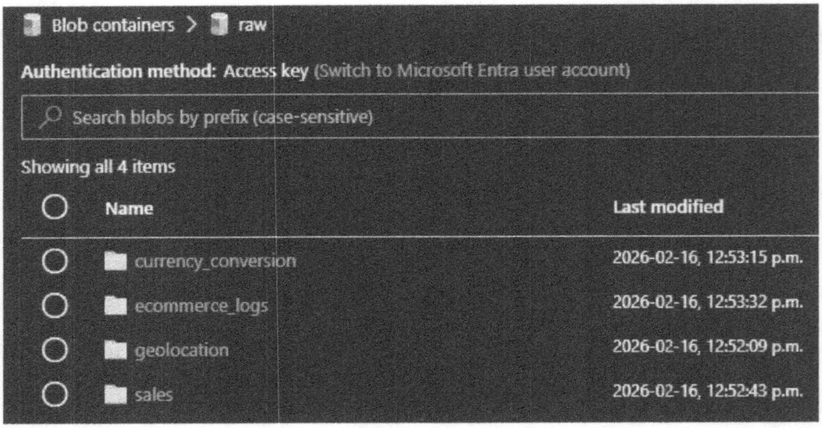

Figure 8.64: Verifying the data ingested in the landing bucket

7. Click on **sales**. Notice that there is one folder for each ingested table.

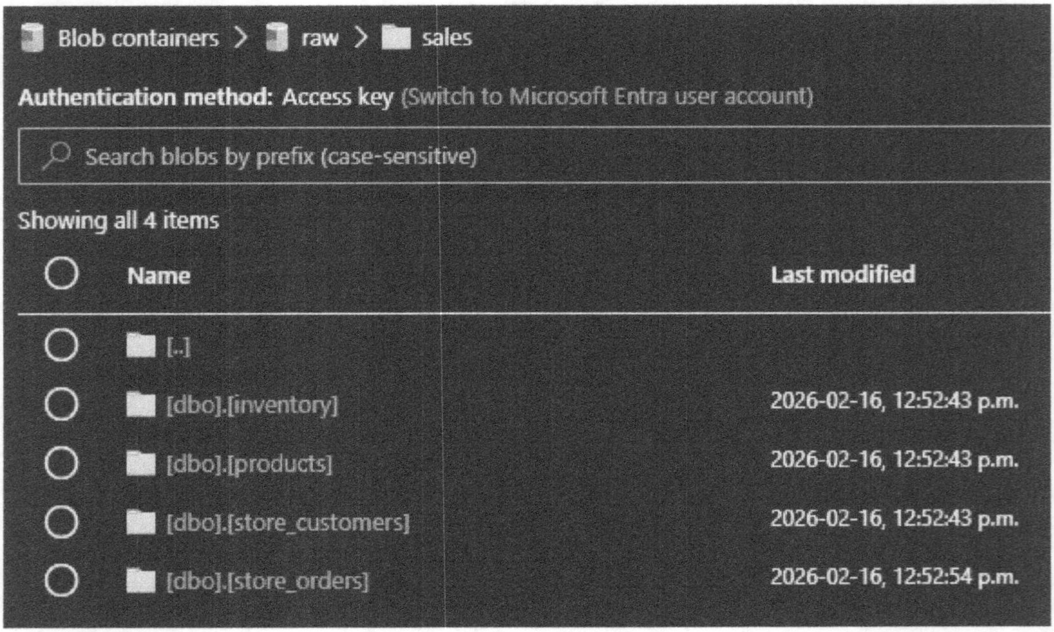

Figure 8.65: One folder is created in landing for each table ingested

8. Starting from *[dbo].[store_orders]*, keep clicking on the folders until you reach a data file. Notice how data has been ingested in partitioned date columns.

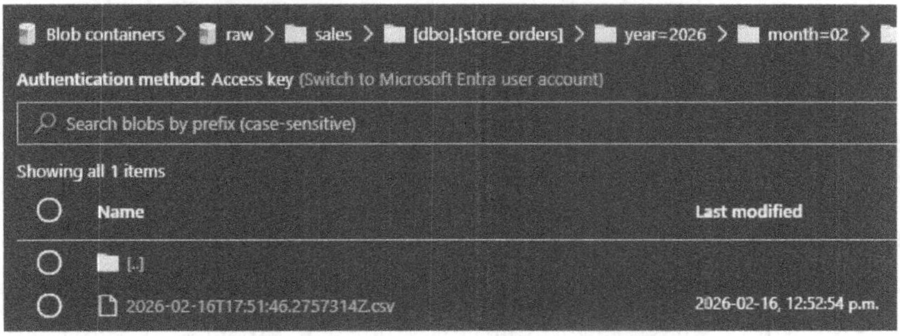

Figure 8.66: Data-partitioned folders

9. Click on the file and click on **Edit**. Notice how the contents of the table have been ingested as CSV format of data. The record count of 2500 records match the source.

Figure 8.67: Contents of the [dbo].[store_orders] file

10. Spend some time browsing through the remaining folders and confirm that the data appears as expected. Keep in mind that since you are running this pipeline on a different date than when the screenshots were captured, the folder names—particularly those containing dates and hours—may not match the examples shown above.

A successful first run indicates that the initial set of tests has passed and the core logic is functioning as expected, allowing you to confidently proceed to the next stage of validation.

The second run

We will now evaluate how the pipeline handles incremental changes in the `salesdb` database. To do this, we will simulate modifications by adding `new (inserts)` records to the source data. After applying these changes, we will manually trigger the `electroniz_batch_ingestion_pipeline` and verify that the newly modified data flows correctly into the lakehouse.

1. Before we trigger the next run, let us verify the state of the watermark table. Navigate to the Query editor of the *salesdb* and execute the following SQL.

```
SELECT TOP (1000) * FROM [dbo].[watermarktable]
```

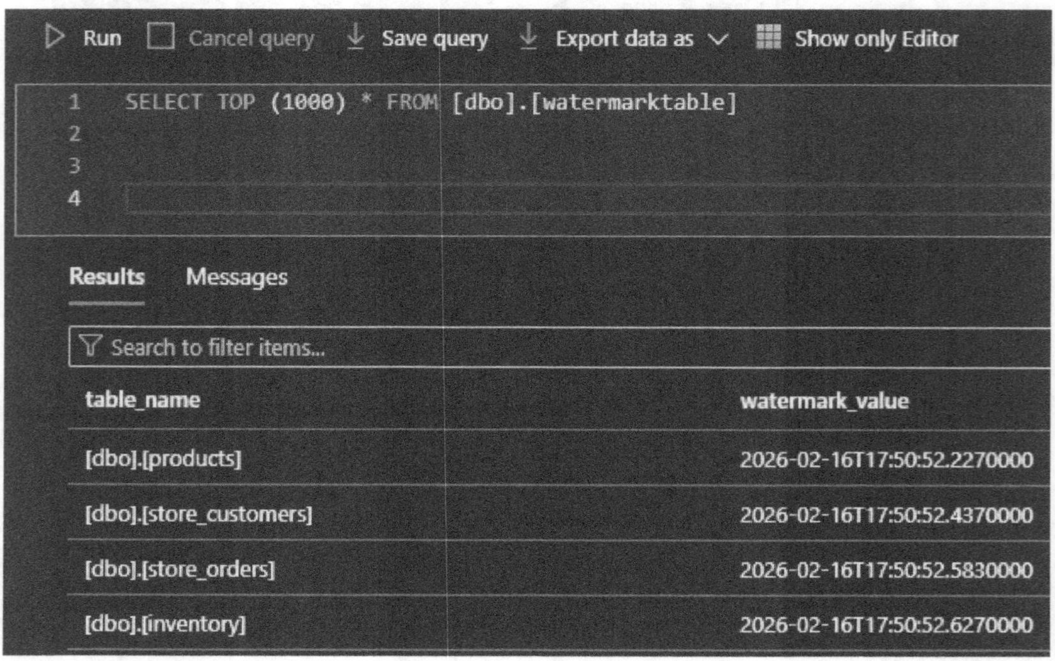

Figure 8.68: Watermark values have shifted since the last run

Notice the watermark value for each table. This timestamp represents the last time data was ingested by `electroniz_batch_ingestion_pipeline`.

2. Copy the contents of the following file from the course Git repository: `https://github.com/PacktPublishing/Data-Engineering-with-Apache-Spark-Databricks-and-Lakehouse-Second-Edition/blob/main/chapter8/sql/storedb_incremental_1.sql`.
3. Paste the contents into the **Query Editor** window. Select Run. This SQL will insert 100 new rows in the *store_customers* table and 200 new rows in the *store_orders* table.

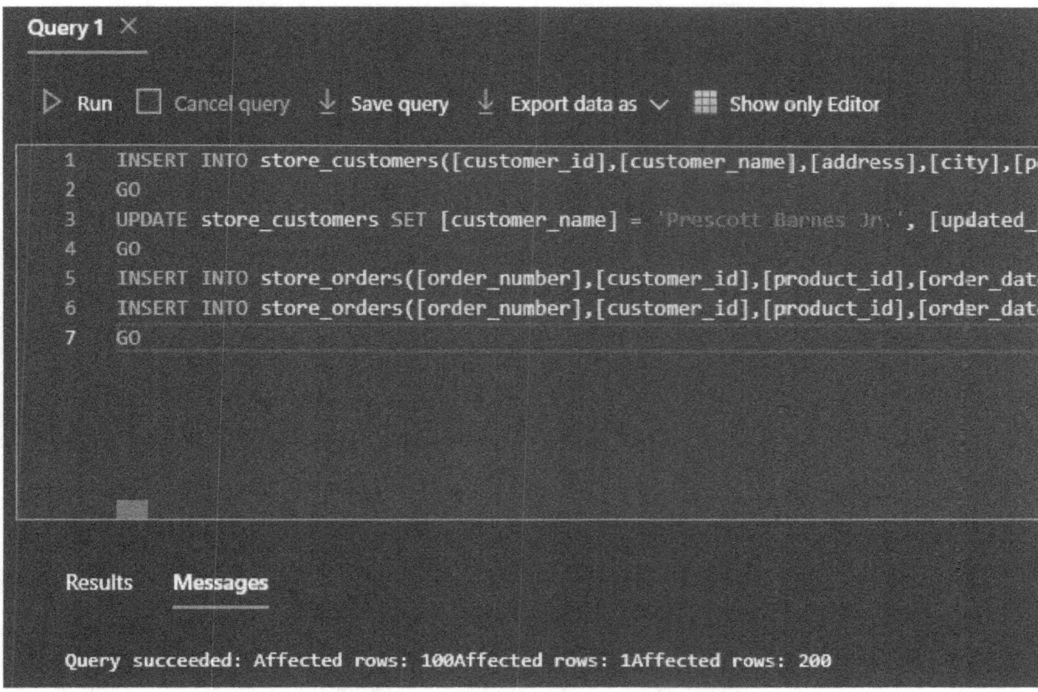

Figure 8.69: Emulating additions to records in salesdb

4. Since the last run, we have received a new website tracking log that needs to be ingested. Copy each of the following commands, line by line, and paste them into the Cloud Shell window. Paste the commands below into Azure Cloud Shell. You can execute them one at a time or run the whole block together.

```
LOGSTORAGEACCOUNTNAME="websitetracking"
LOGSCONTAINER="tracking-logs"
RESOURCEGROUPNAME="training_rg"
LOCATION="canadacentral"
```

```
KEY=`az storage account keys list -g $RESOURCEGROUPNAME -n
$LOGSTORAGEACCOUNTNAME | jq .[0].value`
az storage blob upload \
--container-name $LOGSCONTAINER \
--account-name $LOGSTORAGEACCOUNTNAME \
--name electroniz_access_log_2.json \
--file ~/Data-Engineering-with-Apache-Spark-Databricks-and-Lakehouse-
Second-Edition/chapter8/data/electroniz_access_log_2.log \
--account-key $KEY
```

5. Ensure that at least one minute has passed since the last run of the `electroniz_batch_ingestion_pipeline`.
6. Paste the commands below into Azure Cloud Shell. You can execute them one at a time or run the whole block together.

```
DATAFACTORYNAME="electronizlakehouse-df"
PIPELINENAME="electroniz_batch_ingestion_pipeline"
RESOURCEGROUPNAME="training_rg"
az datafactory pipeline create-run \
--factory-name $DATAFACTORYNAME \
--name $PIPELINENAME \
--resource-group $RESOURCEGROUPNAME
```

7. In Azure Data Factory, click on `electroniz_batch_ingestion_pipeline`. Make sure everything has run successfully; you should see green check marks throughout the interface. Scroll through the list of activities in the panel below; each one should display a green check mark indicating successful completion.
8. In the panel below, if you hover your cursor over an activity name, you can view both the input and output logs associated with that activity. Take some time to check the values of the old and the new watermarks.
9. Let's verify that the incremental data has been ingested correctly. In the Azure portal, go to **Home** > **All resources** > **electronizlanding**.
10. Start at **[dbo].[store_orders]** and continue expanding the folders until you reach the most recent data file. Depending on when the process ran, the latest file may be in the same hour as the previous run or in a new hour.

11. Click on the data file and click on **Edit**. Notice that this file only has 200 records, the ones that were inserted since the last run.

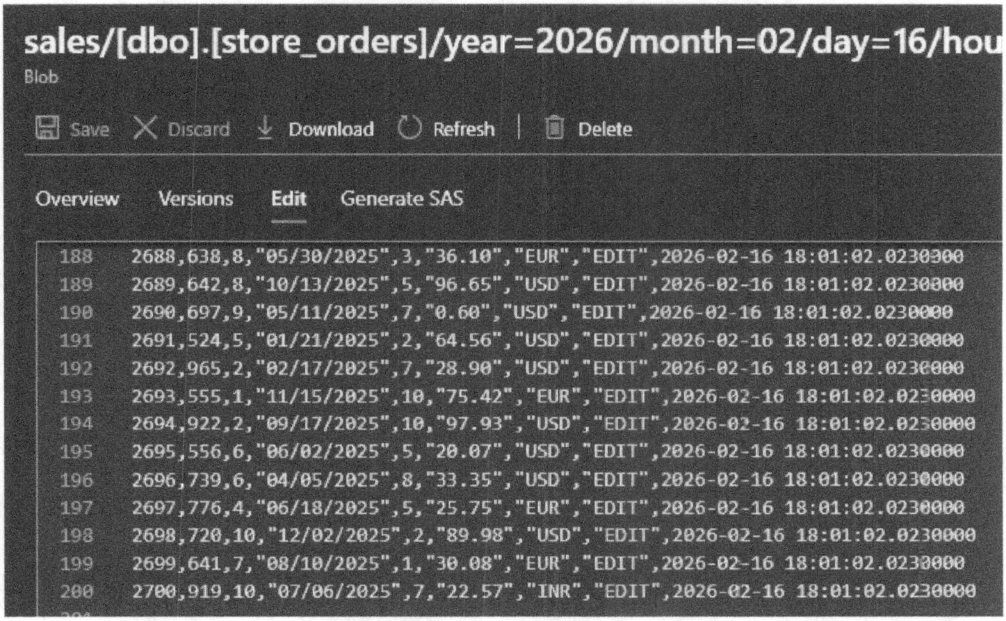

Figure 8.70: Contents of the [dbo].[store_orders] file

12. Now repeat the same verification steps for `store_customers`. You should see that only 100 new customers were ingested.

A successful second run indicates that the incremental ingestion logic is functioning as expected, allowing you to confidently proceed to the next stage of validation.

The third run

The previous run of the pipeline handled newly inserted records well. We will now evaluate how the pipeline handles incremental changes in the `salesdb` database. To do this, we will simulate modifications by changing (updating) records in the source data. After applying these changes, we will manually trigger the `electroniz_batch_ingestion_pipeline` and verify that the newly modified data flows correctly into the lakehouse.

1. Before we trigger the next run, let's verify the state of the watermark table. Navigate to the Query editor of the `salesdb` and execute the following SQL.

```
SELECT TOP (1000) * FROM [dbo].[watermarktable]
```

Figure 8.71: Watermark values have shifted since the last run

Notice that the watermark value has changed only for `store_customers` and `store_orders`. This is because these were the only two tables affected by data changes during the most recent run of the `electroniz_batch_ingestion_pipeline`.

2. Copy the contents of the following file from the course Git repository: `https://github.com/PacktPublishing/Data-Engineering-with-Apache-Spark-Databricks-and-Lakehouse-Second-Edition/blob/main/chapter8/sql/storedb_incremental_2.sql`.

3. Paste the contents into the Query Editor window. Select **Run**. This SQL will update 5 rows in the in the `store_orders` table. This could be due to price adjustments at the source.

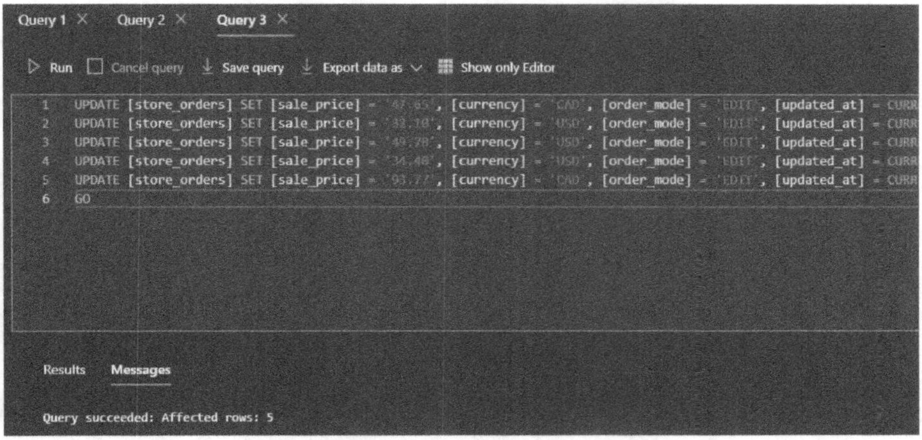

Figure 8.72: Contents of storedb_incremental_2.sql

4. Ensure that at least one minute has passed since the last run of the `electroniz_batch_ingestion_pipeline`.

5. Paste the commands below into Azure Cloud Shell. You can execute them one at a time or run the whole block together.

```
DATAFACTORYNAME="electronizlakehouse-df"
PIPELINENAME="electroniz_batch_ingestion_pipeline"
RESOURCEGROUPNAME="training_rg"
az datafactory pipeline create-run \
--factory-name $DATAFACTORYNAME \
--name $PIPELINENAME \
--resource-group $RESOURCEGROUPNAME
```

6. In Azure Data Factory, click on `electroniz_batch_ingestion_pipeline`. Make sure everything has run successfully; you should see green check marks throughout the interface. Scroll through the list of activities in the panel below; each one should display a green check mark indicating successful completion.

7. In the panel below, if you hover your cursor over an activity name, you can view both the input and output logs associated with that activity. Take some time to check the values of the old and the new watermarks.

8. Let's verify that the incremental data has been ingested correctly. In the Azure portal, go to **Home** > **All resources** > **electronizlanding**.
9. Start at `[dbo].[store_orders]` and continue expanding the folders until you reach the most recent data file. Depending on when the process ran, the latest file may be in the same hour as the previous run or in a new hour.
10. Click on the data file and click on **Edit**. Notice that this file only has 5 records, ones that have been updated since the last run.

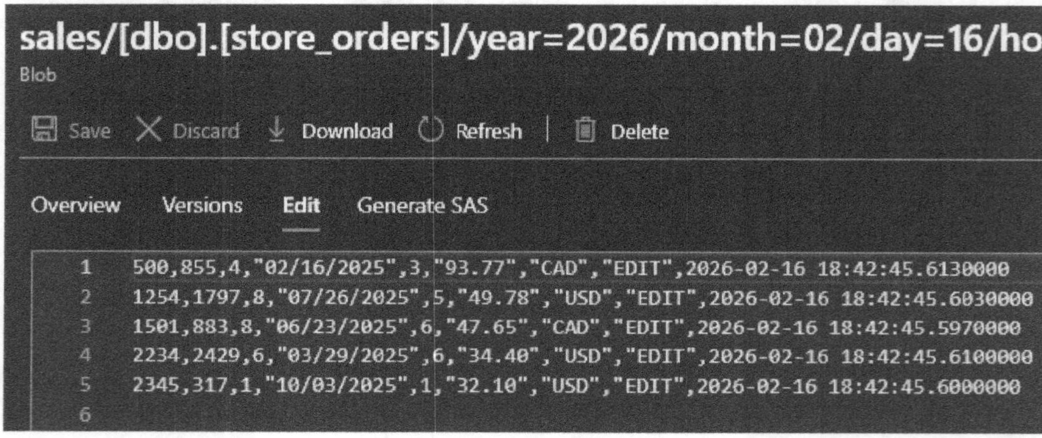

Figure 8.73: Contents of the [dbo].[store_orders] file

A successful third run indicates that the incremental ingestion logic for updates is functioning as desired, allowing you to confidently proceed to the next stage of validation.

The fourth run

The previous run of the pipeline handled newly updated records well. We will now evaluate how the pipeline handles incremental changes in the `salesdb` database. To do this, we will simulate modifications by soft-deleting records from the source data. After applying these changes, we will manually trigger the `electroniz_batch_ingestion_pipeline` and verify that the newly modified data flows correctly into the lakehouse.

1. Before we trigger the next run, let's verify the state of the watermark table. Navigate to the Query editor of the `salesdb` and execute the following SQL.

```
SELECT TOP (1000) * FROM [dbo].[watermarktable]
```

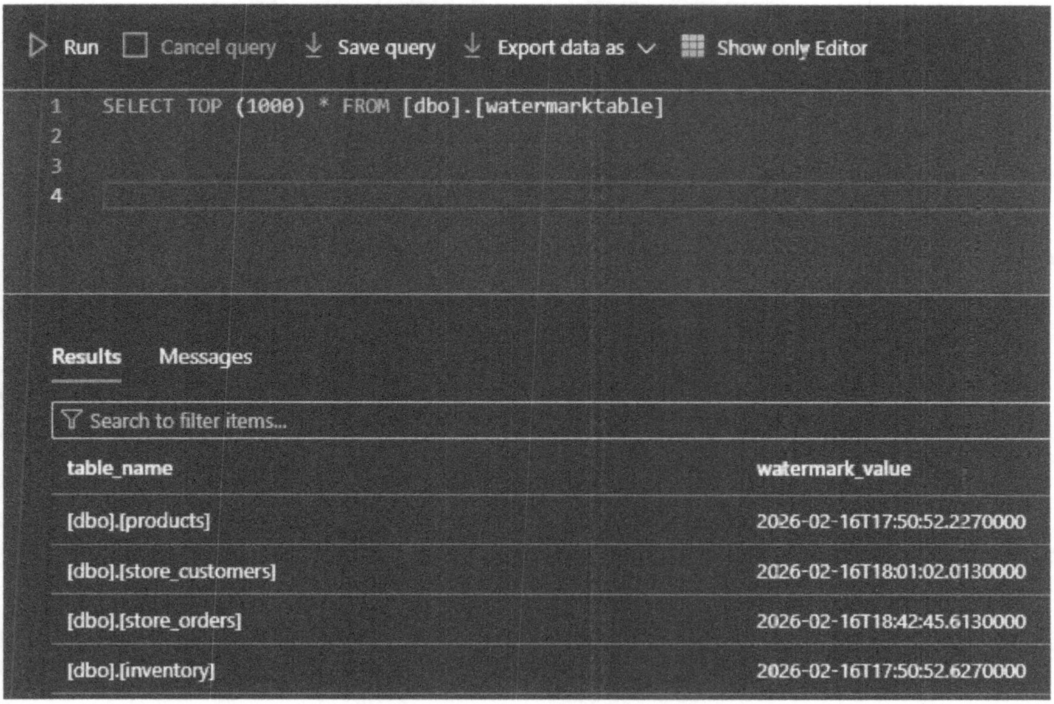

Figure 8.74: Watermark values have shifted since the last run

Notice that the watermark value has changed only for `store_orders`. This is because only one table was affected by data changes during the most recent run of the `electroniz_batch_ingestion_pipeline`.

2. Copy the contents of the following file from the course Git repository: `https://github.com/PacktPublishing/Data-Engineering-with-Apache-Spark-Databricks-and-Lakehouse-Second-Edition/blob/main/chapter8/sql/storedb_incremental_3.sql`.
3. Paste the contents into the Query Editor window. Select **Run**. This SQL will update 5 rows in the in the `store_orders` table. This could be due to price adjustments at the source.

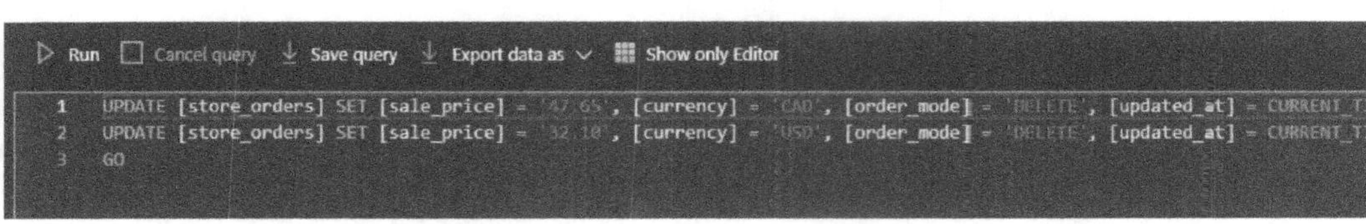

Figure 8.75: Contents of storedb_incremental_3.sql

4. Ensure that at least one minute has passed since the last run of the `electroniz_batch_ingestion_pipeline`.
5. Paste the commands below into Azure Cloud Shell. You can execute them one at a time or run the whole block together.

```
DATAFACTORYNAME="electronizlakehouse-df"
PIPELINENAME="electroniz_batch_ingestion_pipeline"
RESOURCEGROUPNAME="training_rg"
az datafactory pipeline create-run \
--factory-name $DATAFACTORYNAME \
--name $PIPELINENAME \
--resource-group $RESOURCEGROUPNAME
```

6. In Azure Data Factory, click on **electroniz_batch_ingestion_pipeline**. Make sure everything has run successfully; you should see green check marks throughout the interface. Scroll through the list of activities in the panel below—each one should display a green check mark indicating successful completion.
7. In the panel below, if you hover your cursor over an activity name, you can view both the input and output logs associated with that activity. Take some time to check the values of the old and the new watermarks.
8. Let's verify that the incremental data has been ingested correctly. In the Azure portal, go to **Home** > **All resources** > **electronizlanding**.
9. Start at `[dbo].[store_orders]` and continue expanding the folders until you reach the most recent data file. Depending on when the process ran, the latest file may be in the same hour as the previous run or in a new hour.

10. Click on the data file and click on **Edit**. Notice that this file only has the 2 records, only the ones that were deleted since the last run.

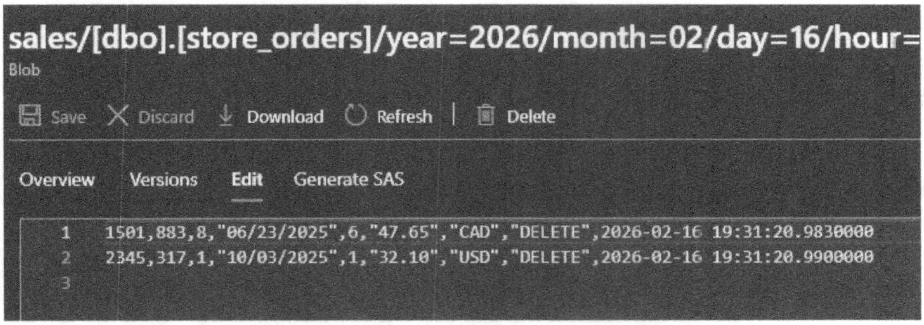

Figure 8.76: Contents of the [dbo].[store_orders] file

We have completed the unit testing of the `electroniz_batch_ingestion_pipeline`. To sum up, we were able to test the following scenarios:

- **The first run**: We ingested historical data from the `salesdb` database. Being the first run, it ingested all rows from all tables.
- **The second run**: We simulated modifications to `salesdb` by adding new (inserts) records to the source data. We inserted 100 new rows into the `store_customers` table and 200 into the `store_orders` table. Our unit test results showed that only newly inserted records were ingested in the second run.
- **The third run**: We simulated modifications to `salesdb` by changing (updates) records to the source data. We updated 5 rows in the `store_orders` table. Our unit test results showed that only updated records were ingested in the third run.
- **The fourth run**: We simulated modifications to `salesdb` by soft-deleting records to the source data. We soft-deleted 2 rows in the `store_orders` table. Our unit test results showed that only the soft-deleted records were ingested in the fourth run.

At this point, we can agree that the `electroniz_batch_ingestion_pipeline` unit testing has been completed successfully. We now move on to unit testing the streaming ingestion pipeline.

Streaming ingestion pipeline

Now we will move on to the streaming ingestion pipeline for Electroniz. In contrast to the batch workflow, this pipeline is designed to handle real-time data as it arrives. During our discovery sessions, we learned that the Electroniz e-commerce platform continuously publishes new sales transactions to Azure Event Hubs. This event stream includes e-commerce order transactions and customer reviews.

With this understanding, we can now focus on how to structure, configure, and implement the streaming pipeline to capture these continuous events from Event Hubs and deliver them reliably to the broader data platform.

Referring to the Electroniz pipeline architecture discussed, the section we will focus on here corresponds to the highlighted component shown in the following figure.

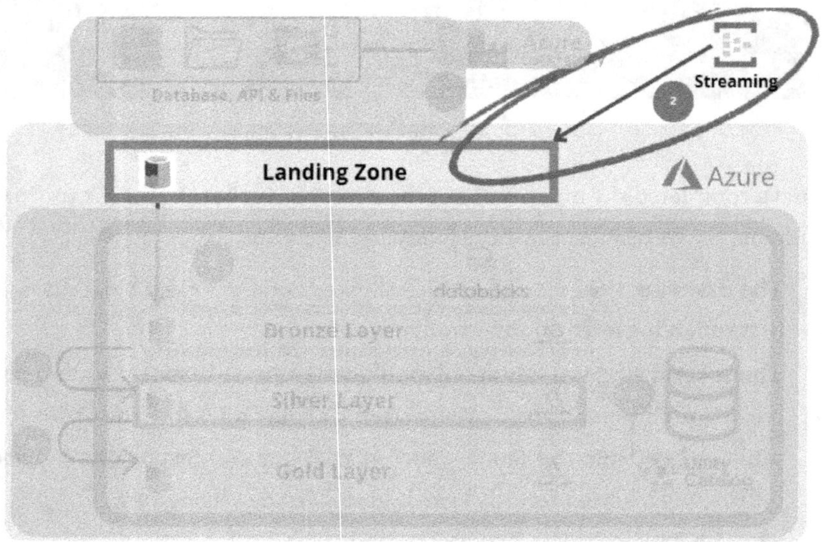

Figure 8.77: Electroniz streaming ingestion pipeline

In the production environment, Azure Event Hubs will receive live transactions and product reviews from the Electroniz e-commerce website.

In the production environment, Azure Event Hubs will serve as the primary entry point for all real-time data generated by the Electroniz e-commerce platform. This includes a continuous stream of live sales transactions—capturing customer purchases the moment they occur—as well as incoming product reviews submitted directly on the website. By funneling both transactional and user-generated content through Event Hubs, Electroniz can ensure that its downstream analytics, monitoring, and processing systems always have immediate access to fresh, high-quality data. This setup also supports real-time reporting, faster operational insights, and improved responsiveness across the entire data ecosystem.

Creating the streaming ingestion pipeline

It's time to create the streaming ingestion pipeline to capture and process real-time events. To do that, we'll start by simulating transactions and reviews to Azure Event Hubs.

1. First, we'll configure the *Event Hubs capture* feature to push the events into the landing zone on Azure Data Lake Storage.
2. You may recall that we had previously created two Event Hubs – **transactions** and **reviews**.

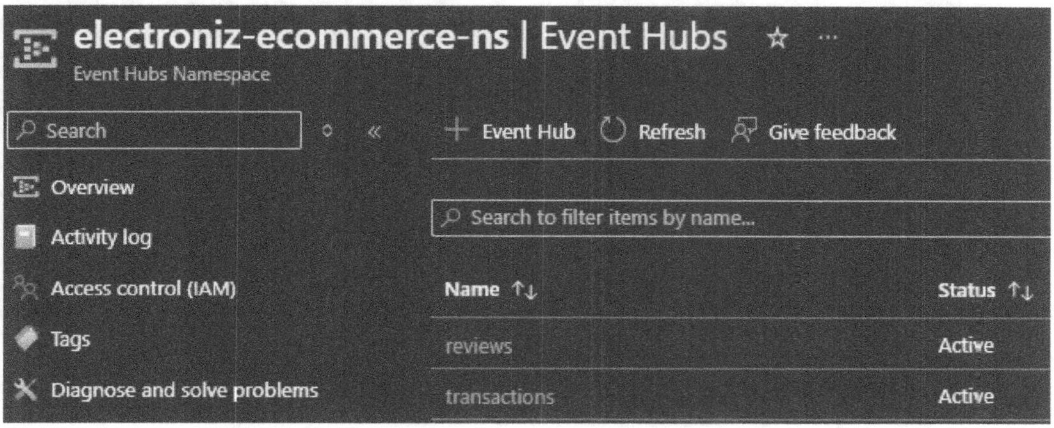

Figure 8.78: Electroniz Event Hubs

3. On the Azure portal, navigate to **Home** > **All resources** > **electroniz-ecommerce-ns**, click on **Entities** > **Event Hubs** > **transactions**.
4. From the left-hand menu, select **Features** > **Capture**.
5. Click on the **Avro** tab. Check the box **Enable capture**.
6. For Azure storage container, select **electronizlanding** > **raw**. Click on **Select**.
7. Change **Time window (minutes)** to **5 minutes** and **Size window (MB)** to **10 MB**. Check the box **Do not emit empty file when no events occur during the capture time window**.

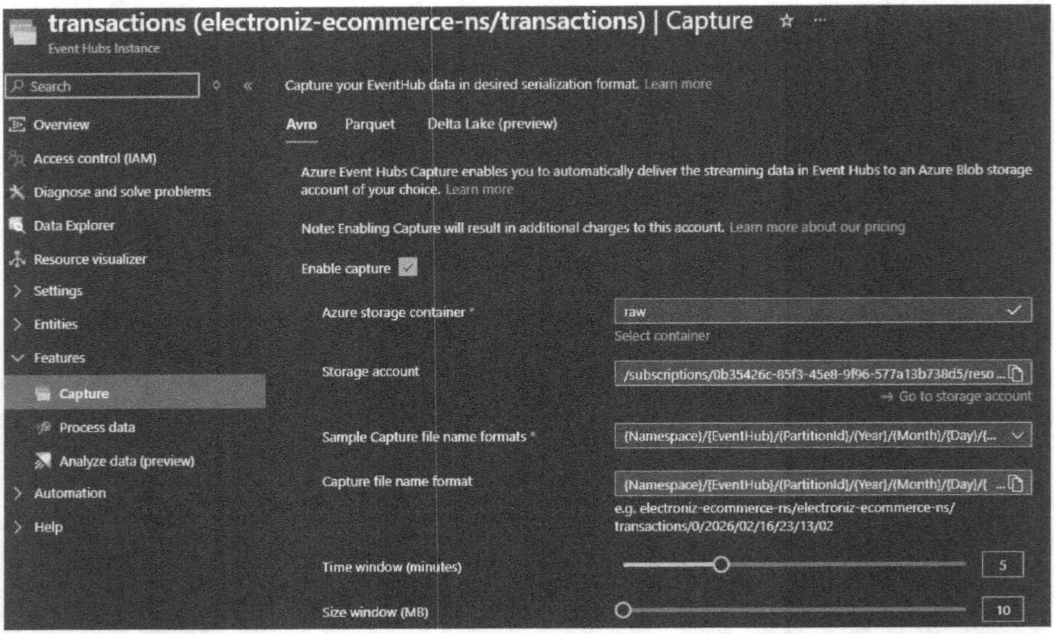

Figure 8.79: Configuration for Event Hubs capture

8. Like how we configured the Capture feature for the transactions Event Hub, we will now do the same for the reviews Event Hub.
9. On the Azure portal, navigate to **Home** > **All resources** > **electroniz-ecommerce-ns**, click on **Entities** > **Event Hubs** > **reviews**. From the left-hand menu, select **Features** > **Capture**.
10. Click on the **Avro** tab. Check the box **Enable capture**.
11. For Azure storage container, select the storage container **electronizlanding** > **raw**. Click on **Select**.
12. Change Time window (minutes) to 5 minutes and Size window (MB) to 10 MB. Check the box *Do not emit empty file when no events occur during the capture time* window.
13. Click on **Apply**.

Unit testing the streaming ingestion pipeline

We will now simulate sending events to each of these Event Hubs. In a real-world scenario, you would typically build an application that sends events using the Azure Event Hubs producer library. To streamline this exercise, a prebuilt script named `send_event.py` is available in the Packt Git repository.

The first run

The following steps will simulate sending a small batch of events to Azure Event Hubs, allowing you to generate controlled test records for unit-testing the streaming pipeline.

1. `send_event.py` requires the Azure Event Hubs Python library. Let's start by installing it. Paste the commands below into Azure Cloud Shell.

```
pip install --user azure-eventhub
```

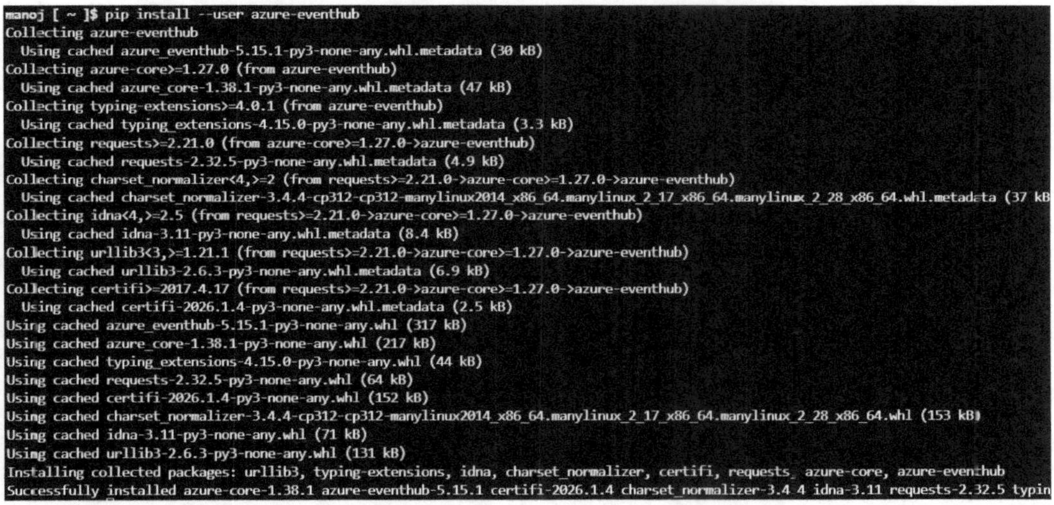

Figure 8.80: Installing the azure-eventhub Python library

2. Start by sending 10 e-commerce transactions to the transactions Event Hub. Paste the commands below into Azure Cloud Shell. You can execute them one at a time or run the whole block together.

```
RESOURCEGROUPNAME="training_rg"
LOCATION="canadacentral"
EVENTHUB_NAMESPACE="electroniz-ecommerce-ns"
EH_CONNECT_STRING=$(az eventhubs namespace authorization-rule keys list --
resource-group $RESOURCEGROUPNAME --namespace-name $EVENTHUB_NAMESPACE --
name RootManageSharedAccessKey --query primaryConnectionString --output
tsv)
EVENTHUB_NAME_TRANSACTIONS="transactions"
python ~/Data-Engineering-with-Apache-Spark-Databricks-and-Lakehouse-
Second-Edition/chapter8/scripts/send_event.py \
$EH_CONNECT_STRING \
```

```
$EVENTHUB_NAME_TRANSACTIONS \
~/Data-Engineering-with-Apache-Spark-Databricks-and-Lakehouse-Second-
Edition/chapter8/data/ecomm_orders_1.json
```

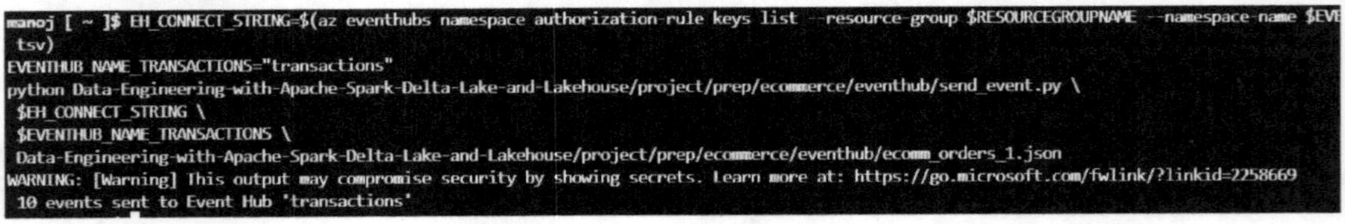

Figure 8.81: Send ecommerce transactions to Event Hub

3. Go back to the Azure portal and click on **Data Explorer** on the left menu. Click on **View events**.

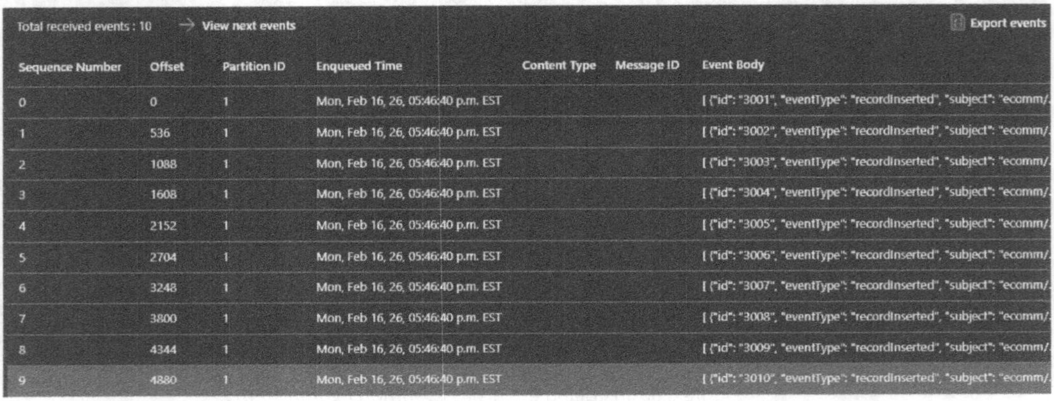

Figure 8.82: Viewing ecommerce transactions on the Event Hub

Notice that each transaction is delivered as a JSON event in the Event Hub.

4. Wait for a few minutes, then navigate to **Home** > **All resources** > **electronizlanding**.
5. Click on **raw**. You should see a new folder named **electroniz-ecommerce-ns**.

6. This folder will store all e-commerce-related streaming events in the landing area.

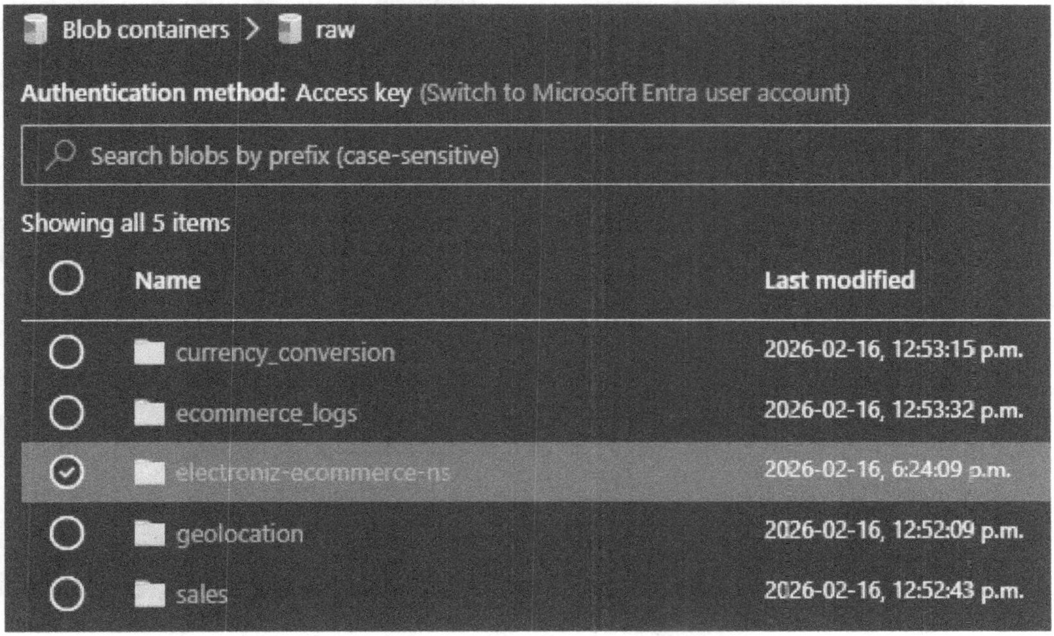

Figure 8.83: New folder in the landing area for e-commerce-related streaming events

7. Click on **electroniz-ecommerce-ns** and keep clicking until you reach the AVRO file.

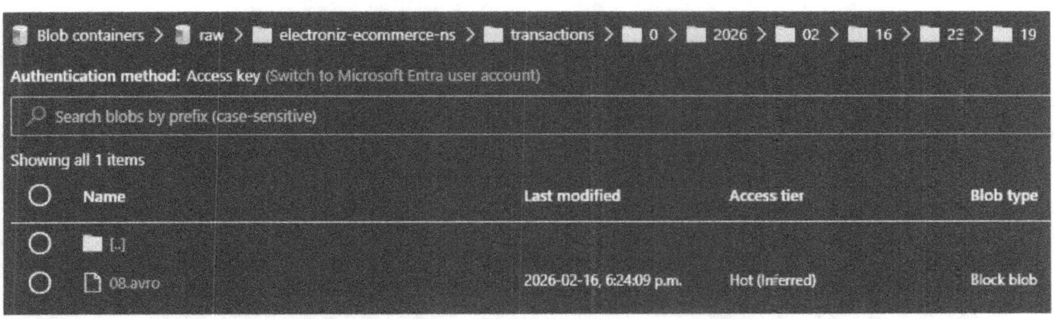

Figure 8.84: Contents of the e-commerce-related streaming events folder

8. We will now send a few customer reviews to Event Hubs. Paste the commands below into Azure Cloud Shell. You can execute them one at a time or run the whole block together.

```
RESOURCEGROUPNAME="training_rg"
LOCATION="canadacentral"
EVENTHUB_NAMESPACE="electroniz-ecommerce-ns"
```

```
EH_CONNECT_STRING=$(az eventhubs namespace authorization-rule keys list --
resource-group $RESOURCEGROUPNAME --namespace-name $EVENTHUB_NAMESPACE --
name RootManageSharedAccessKey --query primaryConnectionString --output
tsv)
EVENTHUB_NAME_REVIEWS="reviews"
python ~/Data-Engineering-with-Apache-Spark-Databricks-and-Lakehouse-
Second-Edition/chapter8/scripts/send_event.py \
$EH_CONNECT_STRING \
$EVENTHUB_NAME_REVIEWS \
~/Data-Engineering-with-Apache-Spark-Databricks-and-Lakehouse-Second-
Edition/chapter8/data/product_reviews_1.json
```

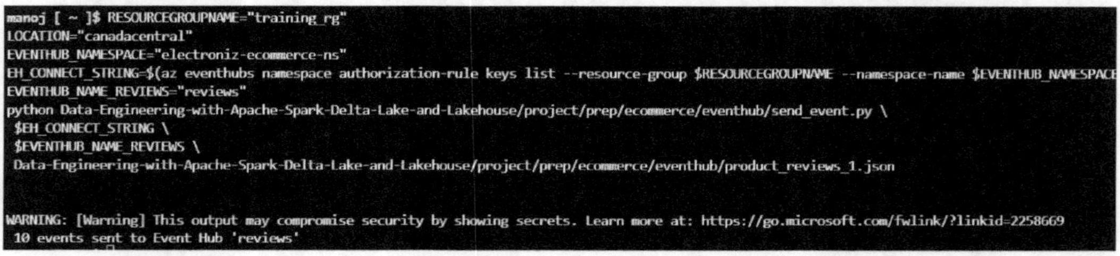

Figure 8.85: Sending customer reviews to Event Hubs

9. Go back to the Azure portal and click on **Data Explorer** on the left menu. Click on **View events**.

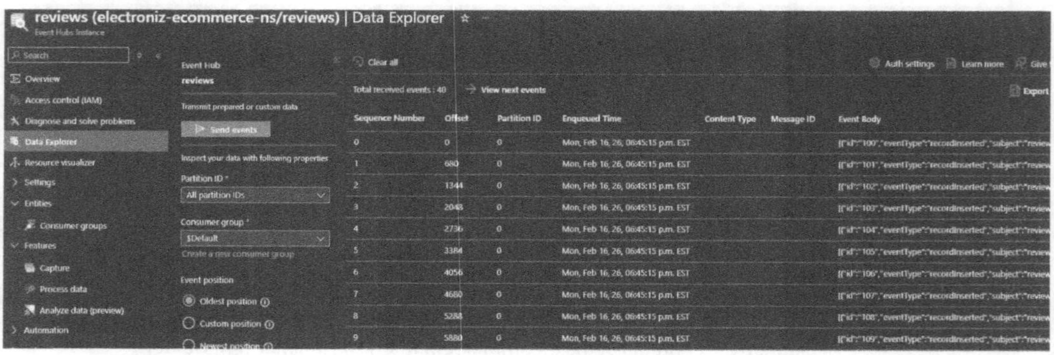

Figure 8.86: Viewing customer reviews on the Event Hub

10. Wait for a few minutes, then navigate to **Home** > **All resources** > **electronizlanding** > **raw** > **electroniz-ecommerce-ns** > **reviews**.

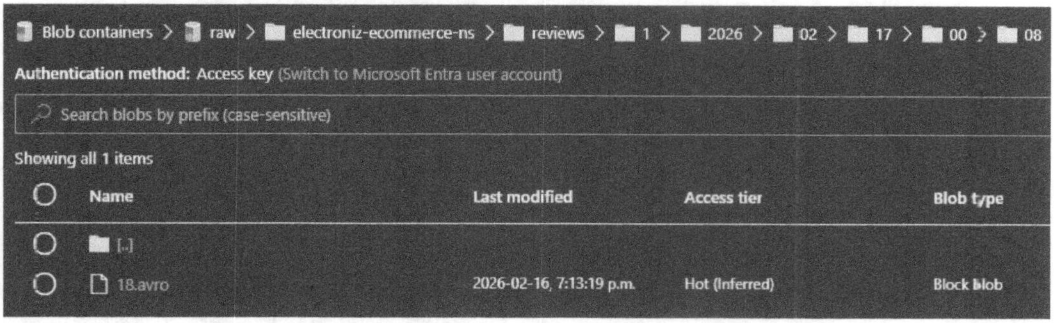

Figure 8.87: Contents of the customer reviews streaming events folder

If you observe streaming reviews being written to Azure Blob Storage, you can conclude that the initial unit-test run has succeeded. This confirms that the core logic is operating correctly and that you can confidently advance to the next stage of validation.

> **Note**
>
> Avro is widely used in modern streaming platforms—such as Kafka, Event Hubs, Spark, and Flink—because its compact, schema-based design makes it exceptionally well-suited for high-volume event ingestion.

The second run

1. Start by sending 10 e-commerce transactions to the transactions Event Hub. Paste the commands below into Azure Cloud Shell. You can execute them one at a time or run the whole block together.

```
RESOURCEGROUPNAME="training_rg"
LOCATION="canadacentral"
EVENTHUB_NAMESPACE="electroniz-ecommerce-ns"
EH_CONNECT_STRING=$(az eventhubs namespace authorization-rule keys list --
resource-group $RESOURCEGROUPNAME --namespace-name $EVENTHUB_NAMESPACE --
name RootManageSharedAccessKey --query primaryConnectionString --output
tsv)
EVENTHUB_NAME_TRANSACTIONS="transactions"
python ~/Data-Engineering-with-Apache-Spark-Databricks-and-Lakehouse-
Second-Edition/chapter8/scripts/send_event.py \
$EH_CONNECT_STRING \
```

```
$EVENTHUB_NAME_TRANSACTIONS \
~/Data-Engineering-with-Apache-Spark-Databricks-and-Lakehouse-Second-
Edition/chapter8/data/ecomm_orders_2.json
```

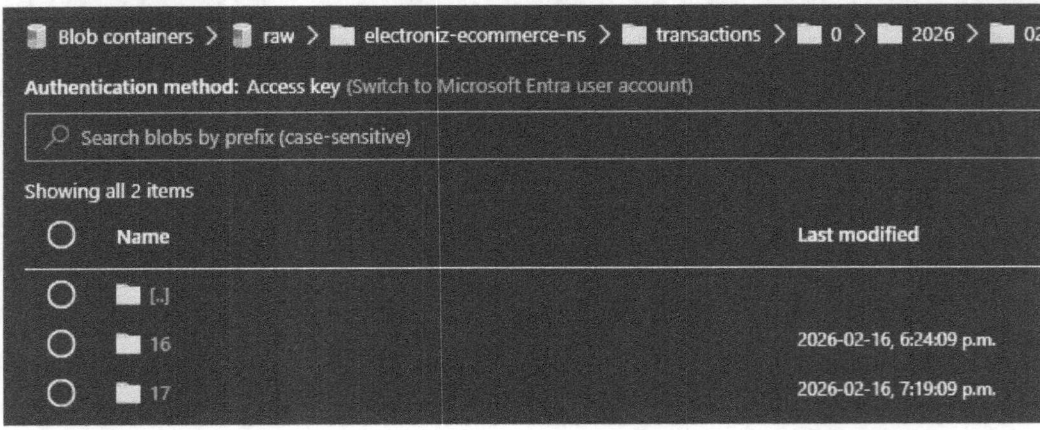

Figure 8.88: Contents of the streaming transactions folder for the second run

2. We will now send a few more customer reviews to the Event Hubs. Paste the commands below into Azure Cloud Shell. You can execute them one at a time or run the whole block together.

```
RESOURCEGROUPNAME="training_rg"
LOCATION="canadacentral"
EVENTHUB_NAMESPACE="electroniz-ecommerce-ns"
EH_CONNECT_STRING=$(az eventhubs namespace authorization-rule keys list --
resource-group $RESOURCEGROUPNAME --namespace-name $EVENTHUB_NAMESPACE --
name RootManageSharedAccessKey --query primaryConnectionString --output
tsv)
EVENTHUB_NAME_REVIEWS="reviews"
python ~/Data-Engineering-with-Apache-Spark-Databricks-and-Lakehouse-
Second-Edition/chapter8/scripts/send_event.py \
$EH_CONNECT_STRING \
$EVENTHUB_NAME_REVIEWS \
~/Data-Engineering-with-Apache-Spark-Databricks-and-Lakehouse-Second-
Edition/chapter8/data/product_reviews_2.json
```

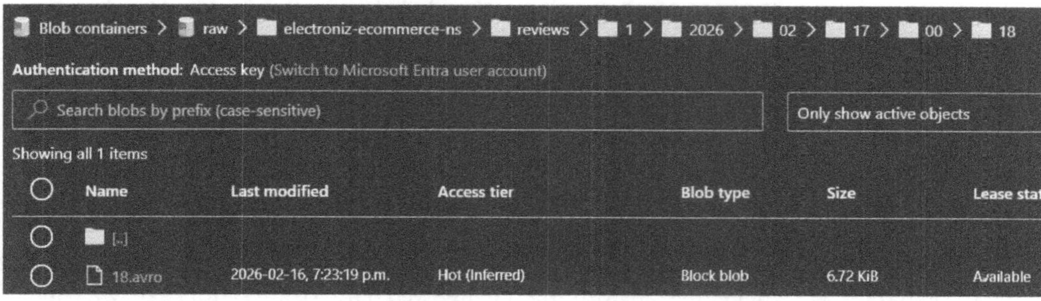

Figure 8.89: Contents of the customer reviews streaming events folder for the second run

We have now completed unit testing for the streaming ingestion pipeline, marking an important milestone in validating the reliability of our real-time data processing flow. In this round of testing, we successfully ingested streaming events from both the transactions and reviews Event Hubs into the landing zone. These tests confirmed that events were captured in the correct format and written to the appropriate storage location in the landing zone. Overall, the streaming ingestion pipeline functioned exactly as expected, with no failures or unexpected behaviors. This gives us confidence that the system is ready to support real-time data ingestion in a production setting and provides a solid foundation for downstream components that will rely on this continuous data flow.

This early assurance of successful unit testing reduces downstream failures, strengthens data quality, and ensures that subsequent layers—such as transformation, enrichment, governance, and analytics—operate on trustworthy inputs. In effect, passing these unit tests not only verifies pipeline correctness but also enhances the overall stability and resilience of the data platform.

Summary

In this chapter, we began the transition from theory to practice—shifting from simply understanding how a lakehouse operates to building one. This step is important because hands-on implementation is where conceptual knowledge transforms into real-world data engineering capability.

We started by setting up the landing zone, the foundational layer of the lakehouse where raw data is ingested and preserved in its original form. This involved identifying and configuring the various data sources—such as operational databases, APIs, files, and streaming systems—that supply data to the lakehouse. We then defined how and where the data would be stored, establishing the necessary structures, formats, and schemas to support scalability, governance, and decision-making.

With sources and destinations in place, the chapter guided you through building the batch and streaming ingestion pipelines that move data into the landing zone. We concluded by validating these pipelines through unit testing to ensure they functioned as designed.

Successfully validating both the batch and streaming ingestion pipelines through unit testing provides a strong foundation for the reliability of the entire data platform. When each pipeline consistently ingests, processes, and lands data as expected, it confirms that the core logic, error handling, and integration points are functioning correctly.

In the next chapter, we will begin transforming the ingested data. Using Delta Lake, we will build the bronze layer of the Electroniz Lakehouse, turning raw data into structured, reliable, and analytics-ready datasets.

Get this book's PDF version and more

Scan the QR code (or go to `packtpub.com/unlock`). Search for this book by name, confirm the edition, and then follow the steps on the page.

UNLOCK NOW

Note: Keep your invoice handy. Purchases made directly from Packt don't require an invoice.

9

Building the Bronze Layer of the Medallion Architecture using Gen AI

In the previous chapters, we laid the groundwork for the Electroniz Lakehouse by constructing the landing zone, the entry point for all data flowing into the platform. This zone captures information in its raw, unprocessed, and unfiltered form—exactly as it is generated by operational systems, devices, and external sources. The landing zone serves as the immutable system of record, preserving original data for compliance, traceability, and future reprocessing needs. Its role cannot be overstated: everything that follows in the data pipeline relies on this uncompromised foundation.

In this chapter, we take the next major step in our lakehouse journey. Building on the raw data stored in the landing zone, we begin shaping it into meaningful, structured layers that the silver layer can consume. Our focus is on constructing the bronze layer of the Electroniz Lakehouse—the stage of the Medallion Architecture that reads raw, chaotic data into structured Delta tables. We start with an in-depth look at the **bronze layer**, the first structured layer in the pipeline. Here, we ingest the data from the landing zone and convert it into the Delta format.

By the end of this chapter, you will have a deeper understanding not only of how the bronze layer is constructed but also of why it is essential in designing a scalable, maintainable, and trustworthy modern data platform. These concepts will form the backbone of every advanced data engineering pattern we explore in the rest of the book.

In this chapter, we will explore the following topics:

- Understanding the bronze layer
- Preparing resources for the Electroniz data pipelines
- Developing the Electroniz bronze pipelines using Claude Code
- Gen AI hallucinations and variations

Technical requirements

This chapter assumes the following technical prerequisites:

- An active Azure free account. You may recall that we created this account in *Chapter 3, Data Engineering on Microsoft Azure.*
- Access to the Packt Publishing GitHub repository to download the code samples and datasets used throughout this chapter. To access the repository, follow the steps in the "*Download the example code files*" section of the *Preface*.
- An active Claude Code subscription, configured according to the instructions provided later in this chapter.

Understanding the bronze layer

In *Chapter 6*, we took an in-depth look at the Medallion Architecture—focusing on how the bronze layer functions within a lakehouse environment.

The bronze layer serves as the first structured stage after raw ingestion, organizing data into a more accessible, queryable form while preserving it as closely as possible to its original state to maintain accuracy, traceability, and data lineage. At this stage, the focus is on reliability and completeness rather than quality or business readiness. Minimal transformations are applied—typically limited to basic schema enforcement, metadata enrichment, and ingestion timestamps—to ensure the data can be consistently processed downstream. Because bronze data has not yet been cleansed, validated, or standardized, it is not suitable for analytical or reporting use. Instead, it serves as a durable, auditable foundation that captures the full history of incoming data, including late-arriving or malformed records. This layer enables reproducibility, supports reprocessing when business logic changes, and provides the raw material required for subsequent silver and gold layers, where data quality, normalization, and business rules are applied.

> **Note**
>
> The primary goal of the bronze layer is to faithfully preserve raw data by keeping it as close to the source as possible, avoiding aggressive transformations, and ensuring that fields are not unnecessarily overwritten or dropped.

Let's start by outlining a high-level plan for implementing the bronze layer.

High-level plan for building the bronze layer

Before we begin preparing the data sources, let's review the section of the Electroniz architecture diagram that we'll be building in this chapter. The red-outlined area in the image below shows the components we will be building in this chapter.

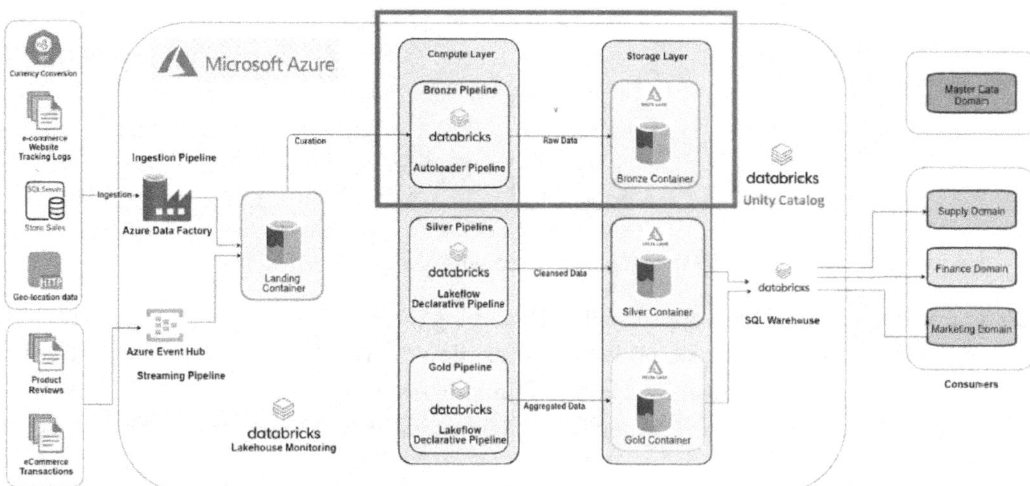

Figure 9.1: Portion of the Electroniz architecture that will be built in this chapter

Before we begin, let's take a moment to understand the structure of the pipelines that will be built in this chapter.

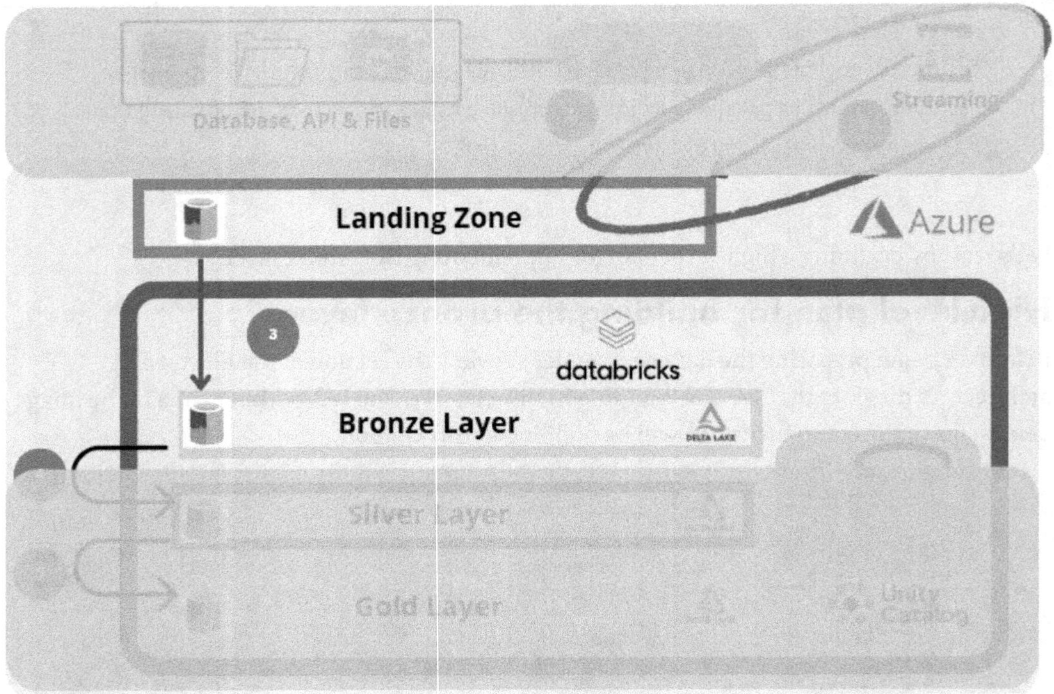

Figure 9.2: Electroniz bronze pipelines

Table 9.1 outlines the high-level approach for developing the bronze data pipelines. These pipelines will be implemented using Databricks Lakeflow Spark Declarative Pipelines and will process data as continuous streaming tables originating from the landing zone. The processed data will then be persisted to their respective containers within the Electroniz Lakehouse ADLS account.

Pipeline	Pipeline Type	Pipeline Mechanism	Data Destination
Bronze Pipelines	Databricks Lakeflow Spark Declarative Pipelines using Streaming tables	Continuous Streaming tables from landing zone	Bronze container in *Electroniz Lakehouse* ADLS account

Table 9.1: High-level approach for developing the bronze pipelines

With this high-level understanding in place, we now turn our attention to the typical approach for developing the bronze layer.

Typical method of data pipeline development

The typical method of pipeline development is a largely manual, engineer-driven process that follows a sequential lifecycle. Historically, data engineers would begin building ETL pipelines by manually writing Python, Spark, or SQL code. Their responsibilities typically included:

- **Mapping schemas:** Defining source-to-target mappings, profiling datasets to understand data types, and determining appropriate destination data types and structures.
- **Coding pipelines:** Developing custom logic for data extraction, transformation, and loading, often handling performance optimizations manually.
- **Unit testing and error handling:** Creating unit tests, implementing graceful error-handling routines, building retry logic with limited context, and manually diagnosing issues using job logs. Applying data quality checks and corrective transformations directly within pipeline code.
- **Managing orchestration:** Designing and scheduling pipeline workflows, configuring time-based or event-based triggers, and managing upstream/downstream dependencies.

> **Note**
>
> Traditional pipeline development is slow and labor-intensive, relying heavily on manual coding, testing, and deployment steps. It often leads to inconsistencies, higher error rates, and limited test and governance coverage across teams. As systems scale, this approach becomes harder to maintain, more costly, and less adaptable to change.

The traditional process is largely effective but time-intensive, highly dependent on individual expertise, and prone to variability across teams and projects.

Changing landscape of data pipeline development

The landscape of pipeline development is undergoing a significant transformation. We learned earlier that the traditional approach typically consumes 60–80% of a data engineer's time, mostly on coding, bug-fixing, and maintenance rather than on innovation. What used to be a manual, code-heavy, error-prone process is rapidly shifting toward AI-generated low-code/no-code pipelines that are self-healing and schema-adaptive. Although chapter 11 of this book is dedicated to *Building the Next-Gen Data Analytics Gold Layer*, this is an ideal point to begin introducing the concept of AI-generated pipelines. In the modern era, AI-powered ETL systems automatically:

- Detect schemas and perform source-to-target mapping
- Generate transformation logic
- Debug and repair broken pipelines

Organizations are increasingly replacing brittle, hand-coded pipelines with dynamic, machine-generated alternatives that evolve as data changes. As discussed in *Chapter 7*, declarative processing emphasizes defining *what* outcome is needed rather than *how* to implement it. Generative AI takes this a step further by enabling pipelines to be created declaratively through plain-language prompts. A user can simply describe the data flow they require, and an AI system can automatically generate the ETL logic, orchestration, dependencies, and validation rules.

AI models trained on languages such as SQL, Python, and Spark can now generate ingestion scripts for structured, semi-structured, and unstructured data, automatically infer schemas, and adapt seamlessly to schema drift. The resulting AI-generated ETL code is modular, consistent, and, by default, aligned with best practices. This dramatically reduces technical debt and compresses development cycles from days or weeks down to minutes. Let's explore one such AI coding system that has taken the development world by storm.

Introducing Claude Code

Claude Code is Anthropic's agent-driven coding platform. It can produce PySpark or SQL notebooks as well as Delta Lake ingestion and transformation pipelines directly from natural-language instructions. Built on Claude's most advanced models (such as Sonnet and Opus), it supports both hands-on and fully automated software development workflows. Rather than functioning as a simple text assistant, Claude Code operates as an AI capable of taking real actions, making it comparable to an autonomous developer rather than a conventional chatbot.

Typical Claude Code workflow

A Claude workflow represents the complete end-to-end process for producing Databricks-ready PySpark, SQL, Delta Lake, or job configuration code. It includes code generation, automated validation, packaging, and deployment into Databricks. A typical Claude Code workflow generally follows this pattern:

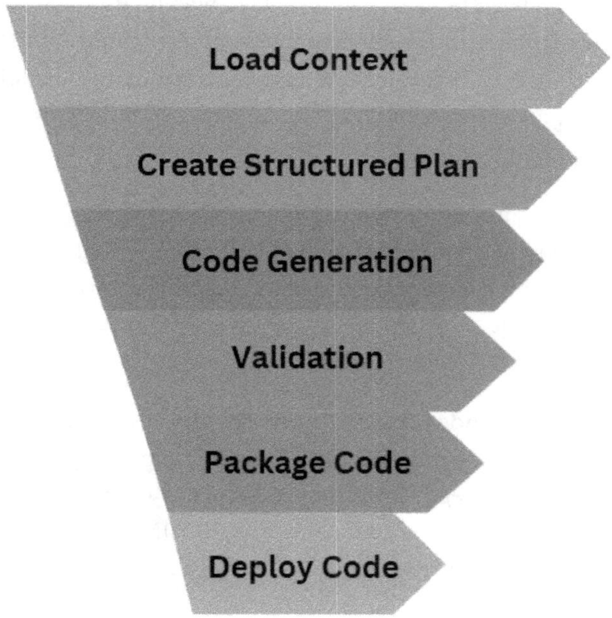

Figure 9.3: A typical Claude Code workflow

Let's take a closer look at each component of the workflow in the sections that follow.

Load context

During this phase, Claude Code retrieves all relevant metadata from your Databricks environment to produce the required code. This typically includes existing notebooks, scripts, Delta tables, Unity Catalog objects, and job definitions. With this context gathered, Claude Code builds an internal understanding of your current Lakehouse landscape and the requirements for the new solution.

Create a structured plan

Claude Code generates a detailed, structured plan that outlines the ingestion steps, file formats, approaches to handling schema drift, and the required cleaning and transformation logic. It also defines the Delta Lake merge or update strategy, job boundaries, and any interdependencies across components. Claude Code is designed specifically for complex, multi-step workflow reasoning and is optimized to handle long-running, end-to-end coding tasks.

Code generation

Claude Code then generates Databricks-ready code—typically delivered as PySpark and Delta Lake notebooks—that includes ingestion logic, write operations to ADLS Gen2, and Delta Lake maintenance commands such as `OPTIMIZE` and `VACUUM`. Beyond notebooks, Claude Code can also produce DLT pipeline definitions, expectations blocks, streaming read/write logic, and CDC merge patterns. Using established job-orchestration templates, it additionally creates full job configurations that specify notebooks, task sequences, dependencies, and cluster settings.

Validation

Once the code and job structures are generated, Claude Code triggers validation through the Agent SDK, running checks such as reading a small Delta sample, validating schemas, verifying row counts and deduplication behavior, and executing quality-control rules to ensure correctness before deployment.

Package code

After validation is complete, Claude Code can automatically assemble all required deployment assets, including the full notebook directory structure, DLT pipeline JSON, Databricks job configurations, and any wheel or egg libraries needed for custom UDFs. It can also generate a project layout and supporting documentation, such as README files and lineage diagrams, ensuring the entire package is ready for seamless deployment to Databricks.

Deploy code

Finally, Claude Code can perform operational tasks using the Databricks CLI, such as uploading notebooks, creating or updating Databricks jobs, and triggering job runs. Claude Code can seamlessly invoke your CLI wrappers to execute actions, enabling automated deployment and orchestration across your Databricks environment.

Using a standard Claude Code workflow as a reference, we can examine how Electroniz bronze pipelines are generated and deployed through a structured, end-to-end process that transforms raw landing-zone data into governed, query-ready tables within Databricks.

Understanding Claude Code workflow for Electroniz bronze pipelines

With reference to the *Electroniz* project, the following illustrates how Claude Code develops a clear, structured narrative that defines both technical objectives and organizational standards to be upheld throughout the entire pipeline lifecycle. By reasoning holistically across ingestion, transformation, validation, packaging, and deployment, Claude Code treats the workflow as a single, cohesive process. This approach ensures that the resulting pipelines conform to Electroniz data standards while consistently delivering governed, query-ready Delta tables that support downstream analytics and reporting.

1. **Load Context**: Claude Code begins by connecting to the *electronizlakehouse-dbx* Databricks environment to gather the full operational context. It first analyzes the raw data stored in the landing zone within the *electronizlanding* Azure Data Lake Storage

Gen2 account. It then identifies the *electronizlakehouse* bronze container as the target location where this raw data should be ingested and structured as Delta Lake bronze tables. In addition, Claude Code loads the relevant Unity Catalog objects and interprets your organization's medallion-architecture standards to build an accurate understanding of the expected data flow and governance model.

2. **Create structured plan**: With full context loaded, Claude Code constructs a detailed plan that maps the data flow from the landing zone to the bronze layer. This plan outlines key design decisions—such as whether to use Auto Loader, Streaming tables, or Lakeflow Declarative pipelines—and defines the approach for schema inference, data persistence, and partitioning. The result is a clear, end-to-end blueprint for how raw data will be ingested and organized within the Lakehouse.
3. **Generate Code**: Claude Code generates Databricks-ready PySpark notebooks for bronze ingestion and silver transforms (Delta reads/writes, merges, UTC normalization, dedupe, expectations), optional DLT specs if requested, and a Databricks Jobs JSON that wires tasks, clusters, schedules, and retries; modern Claude models are optimized for multi-file agentic coding, so they can scaffold utils/ helpers (I/O, data-quality, logging) and thread consistent parameters across notebooks and configs in one session.
4. **Generate validation scripts**: After code generation, Claude Code validates schemas against expected structures, checks for required system columns, and ensures schema drift is handled correctly. Claude Code then verifies data completeness through row-count and deduplication checks, inspects small data samples for correctness, and runs data-quality rules or DLT expectations where defined. In addition, it confirms operational correctness by validating storage paths, Delta properties, Unity Catalog registration, and successful execution of maintenance commands.
5. **Package code**: Claude Code will package code by assembling all validated Databricks assets into a standardized, deployable delivery bundle that aligns with Electroniz Lakehouse and CI/CD conventions. Claude Code organizes generated PySpark and SQL notebooks into a consistent directory structure, includes DLT pipeline definitions (JSON) where applicable, and adds Databricks job configurations that define tasks, dependencies, clusters, and schedules. This packaging step ensures Electroniz receives a complete, versionable, and production-ready bundle that can move cleanly through testing, promotion, and deployment.
6. **Deploy code**: Finally, Claude Code will deploy Electroniz pipelines by acting as an orchestration agent that uses Databricks-approved CLI wrappers and APIs to automate deployment steps. After validation and packaging, it uploads notebooks to the Databricks workspace, registers or updates DLT pipelines and Unity Catalog objects,

and creates or modifies Databricks jobs with the correct tasks, dependencies, clusters, and schedules. Claude Code ensures all configurations point to the appropriate ADLS Gen2 paths and environment-specific settings, then triggers job or pipeline runs to confirm successful deployment.

With the workflow above, let's start building the bronze pipelines using Claude Code.

Preparing resources for the Electroniz data pipelines

To implement the bronze layer of the Electroniz Lakehouse, we will provision and configure the following Azure resources as seen in *Table 9.2*. These components will establish the foundational storage and compute capabilities required to ingest data from the landing layer into the lakehouse environment.

Azure Resource	**Resource Name**
Azure Data Lake Storage Gen 2 Storage Account	`Electronizlakehouse`
Azure Data Lake Storage Gen 2 Container	Bronze
Azure Databricks	`electronizlakehouse-dbx`

Table 9.2: Azure resources required for the bronze pipeline

Let's start by provisioning these resources in Azure.

Provision Azure Databricks

In this section, we will provision Azure Databricks to support the development of our bronze layer data pipelines.

1. Run the commands below to spin up a new Azure Databricks account. Feel free to edit the *LOCATION* to the nearest region you prefer. You may need to change the *SKU* to **Premium** if you have exhausted your free-tier limits. Paste the commands below into Azure Cloud Shell. You can execute them one at a time or run the whole block together.

```
RESOURCEGROUPNAME="training_rg"
LOCATION="canadacentral"
DBX_WORKSPACE="electronizlakehouse-dbx"
DBX_SKU="Premium"
az databricks workspace create \
  --resource-group $RESOURCEGROUPNAME \
```

```
    --name $DBX_WORKSPACE \
    --location $LOCATION \
    --compute-mode Serverless \
    --sku $DBX_SKU \
    --tags owner="electroniz" project=lakehouse environment=development
```

2. Create an Azure Databricks connector to securely access Azure services such as ADLS.

```
RESOURCEGROUPNAME="training_rg"
LOCATION="canadacentral"
DBX_CONNECTOR="electronizlakehouse-dbx-connector"
az databricks access-connector create \
--resource-group $RESOURCEGROUPNAME \
--name $DBX_CONNECTOR \
--identity-type SystemAssigned \
--location $LOCATION
```

3. While running the command, you may be asked to install the Databricks extension. Click **Y**. Press **Enter**.

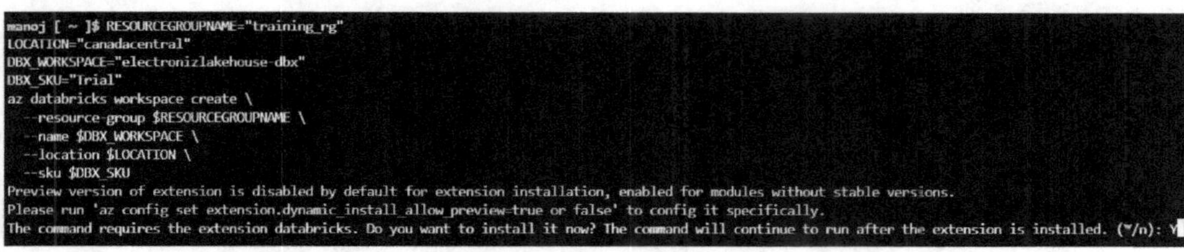

Figure 9.4: Installing the Databricks extension

4. Log in to your Azure account using the URL `https://portal.azure.com/`

5. In the Azure portal, navigate to the **Home** screen, then use the search bar at the top to search for *Databricks*.

6. Click on **Azure Databricks**. You should see the newly created Databricks accounts.

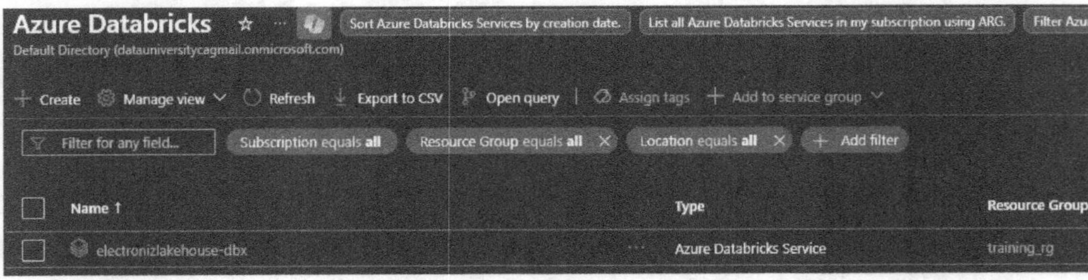

Figure 9.5: Newly created Databricks account

7. Click on **electronizlakehouse-dbx**.

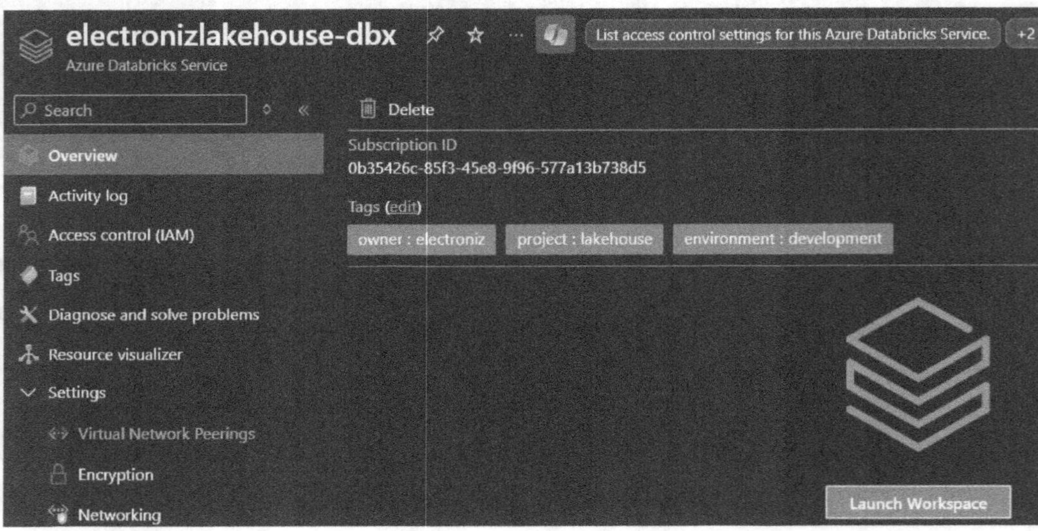

Figure 9.6: Databricks account launchpad

8. Click on **Launch Workspace**. The Azure Databricks account will look like this.

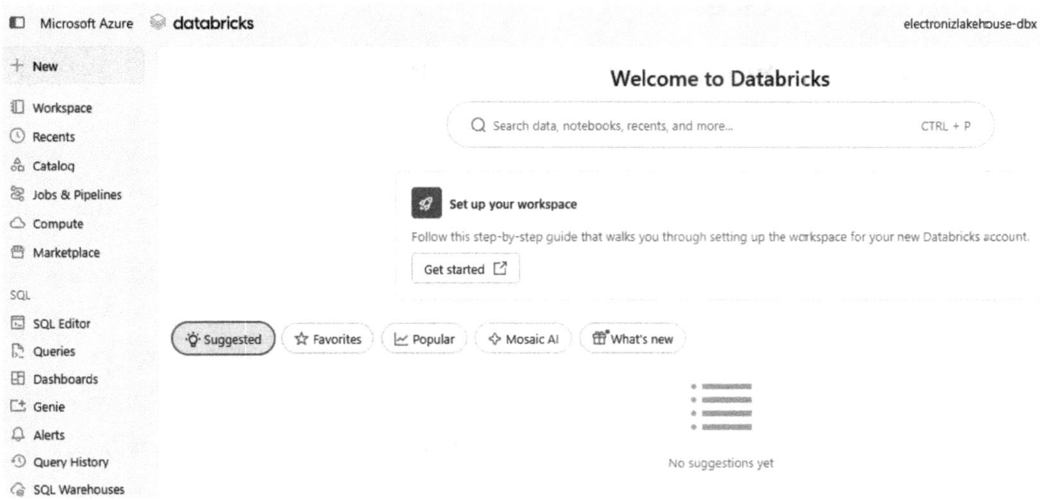

Figure 9.7: electronizlakehouse-dbx Workspace

9. Using the menu on the left, click on **Compute**. Click on **Create SQL Warehouse**.

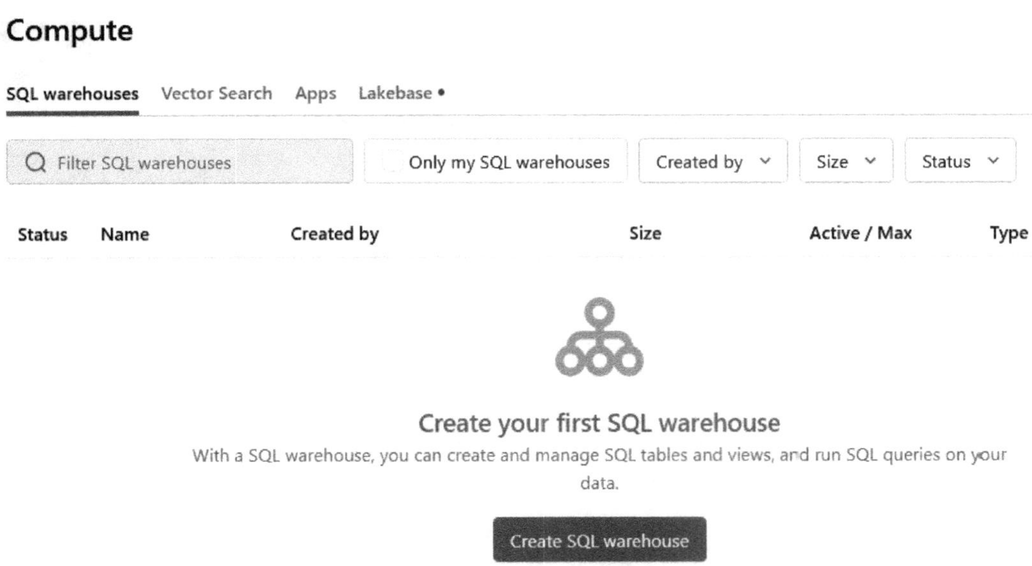

Figure 9.8: Create a new SQL Warehouse in electronizlakehouse-dbx Workspace

10. For Name, enter *electroniz_sql_warehouse*. Keep the rest of the parameters at their defaults. Click on **Create**.

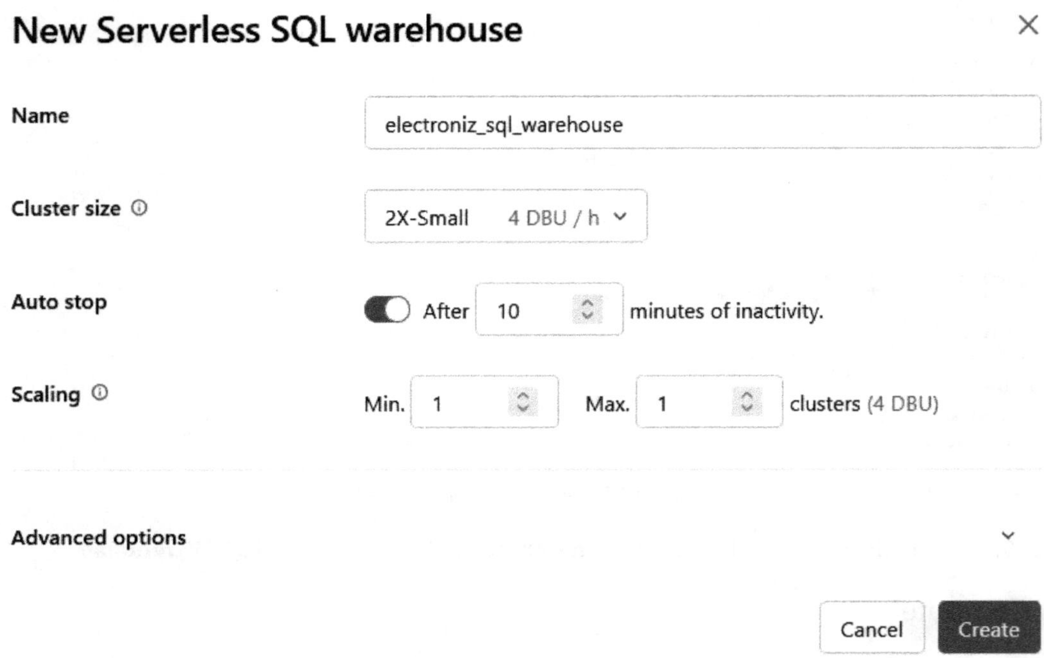

Figure 9.9: Setup parameters for the SQL Warehouse in electronizlakehouse-dbx

11. Simply close the **Manage Permissions** screen. You will now have a new SQL Warehouse as seen in *Figure 9.10*.

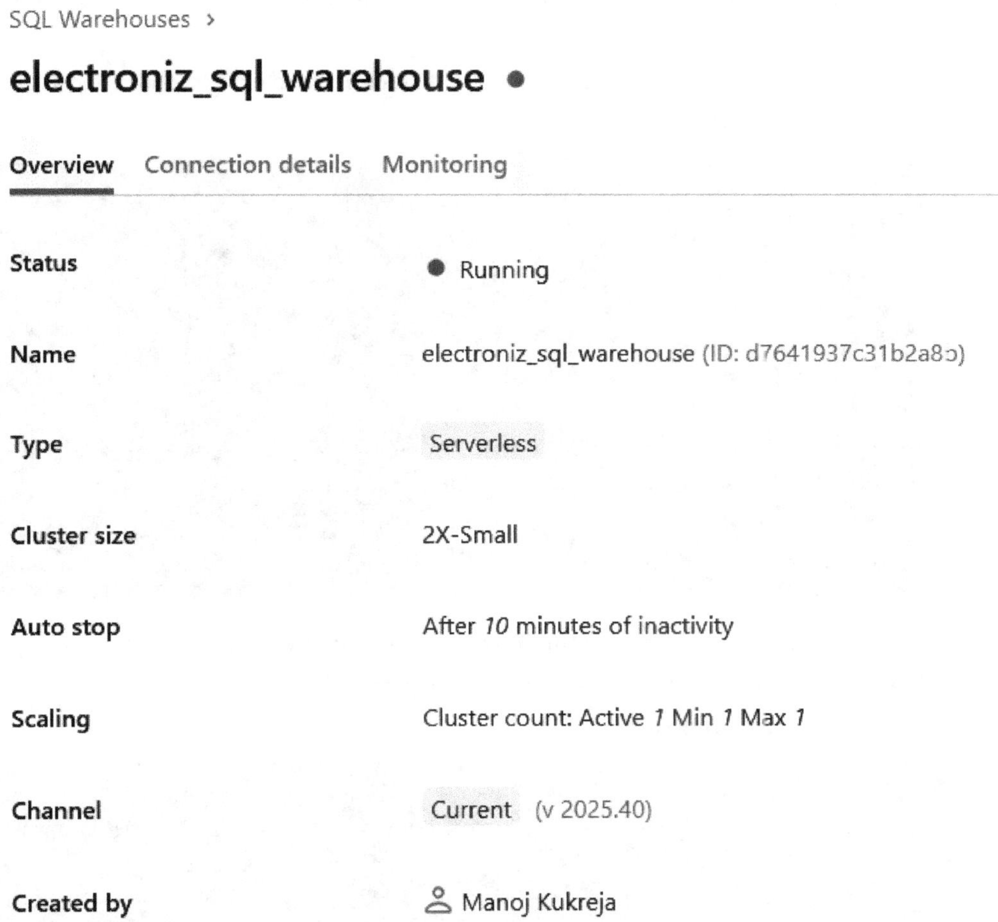

Figure 9.10: New SQL Warehouse in electronizlakehouse-dbx

Now that the Azure Databricks account has been provisioned, we can proceed to create an Azure Data Lake Storage account to serve as the storage location for all bronze-layer data.

Provision Azure Data Lake Storage (ADLS)

To save data in the bronze layer, we will spin up an Azure Data Lake Storage Gen 2 (ADLS) account.

1. Note that Azure Data Lake Storage Gen 2 accounts have globally unique names, so in the next set of commands choose a **STORAGEACCOUNTNAME** that is not already in

use across the Azure ecosystem. Adjust the **STORAGEACCOUNTNAME** and **LOCATION** before running the commands below. After creation, be sure to reference the selected Azure Data Lake Storage Gen 2 account name consistently throughout the remaining instructions.

2. Paste the commands below into Azure Cloud Shell. You can execute them one at a time or run the whole block together.

```
STORAGEACCOUNTNAME="electronizlakehouse"
RESOURCEGROUPNAME="training_rg"
LOCATION="canadacentral"

az storage account create \
--name $STORAGEACCOUNTNAME \
--resource-group $RESOURCEGROUPNAME \
--kind StorageV2 \
--location $LOCATION \
--hns true \
--sku Standard_LRS \
--tags owner=electroniz project=lakehouse environment=development
```

3. In the Azure portal, navigate to the **Home** screen, then use the search bar at the top to search for *"storage accounts"*. Click on **Storage accounts**.
4. Click on **electronizlakehouse**.

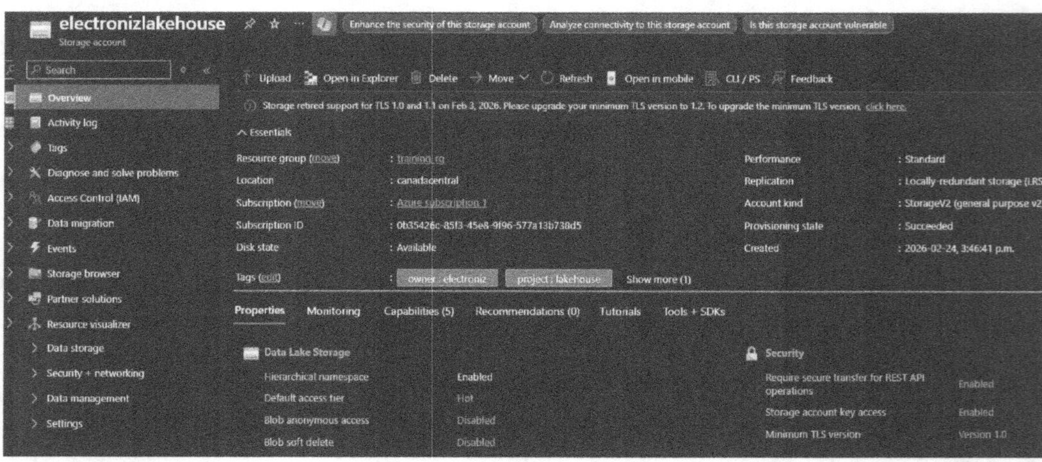

Figure 9.11: Newly created storage account

5. Now let's create a container that will store the bronze layer data. Paste the commands below into Azure Cloud Shell. You can execute them one at a time or run the whole block together.

```
STORAGEACCOUNTNAME="electronizlakehouse"
NAMESPACE="bronze"
az storage fs create \
-n $NAMESPACE \
--account-name $STORAGEACCOUNTNAME \
--metadata project=lakehouse environment=development layer=bronze \
--only-show-errors
```

6. On the Azure portal, click on **electronizlakehouse** > **Storage browser** > **Blob containers**.

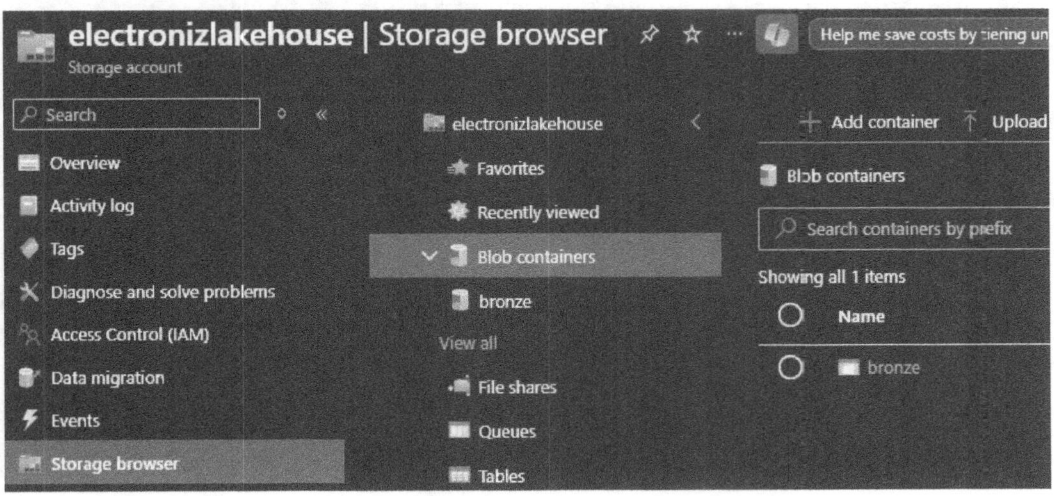

Figure 9.12: Newly created blob container

7. Azure Databricks must have access to `electronizlakehouse` Azure Blob Storage at runtime. It requires grants to the following roles:
    - Storage Blob Data Contributor
    - Storage Account Contributor
    - `EventGridEventSubscription` Contributor
    - Storage Queue Data Contributor

If you need a refresher, we followed the same configuration steps in *Chapter 6*.

8. Assign the first role to your user by clicking on the **Access control (IAM)** menu on the left. Click on **Add role assignment**. Under Job function roles, search for *"Storage blob data contributor"*.
9. Click on **Storage Blob Data Contributor**. Click **Next**.
10. Click on **Managed Identity**, followed by **Select members**.
11. In the **Select managed identities** window for Managed Identity, choose **Access Connector for Databricks**.
12. Now choose **electronizlakehouse-dbx-connector**. Click on **Select**.

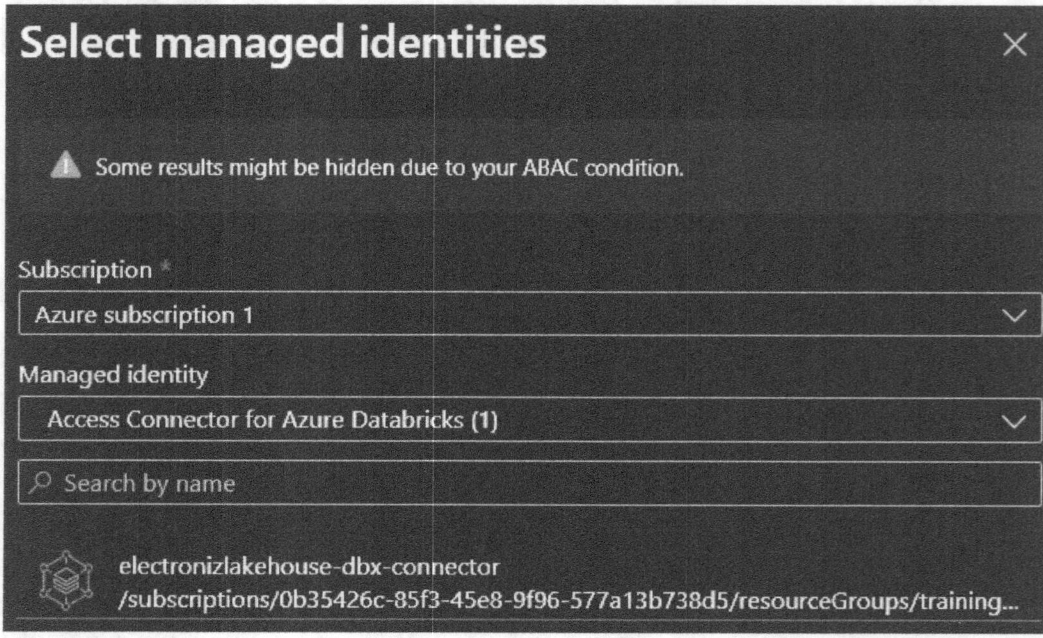

Figure 9.13: Add Databricks role to ADLS

13. Click on **Review + assign**.
14. Using the method above, grant the other three roles to *electronizlakehouse-dbx-connector*.

15. To check the access for managed identity, click on **Check access**. The newly assigned role assignment should be visible for Access Connector for Databricks.

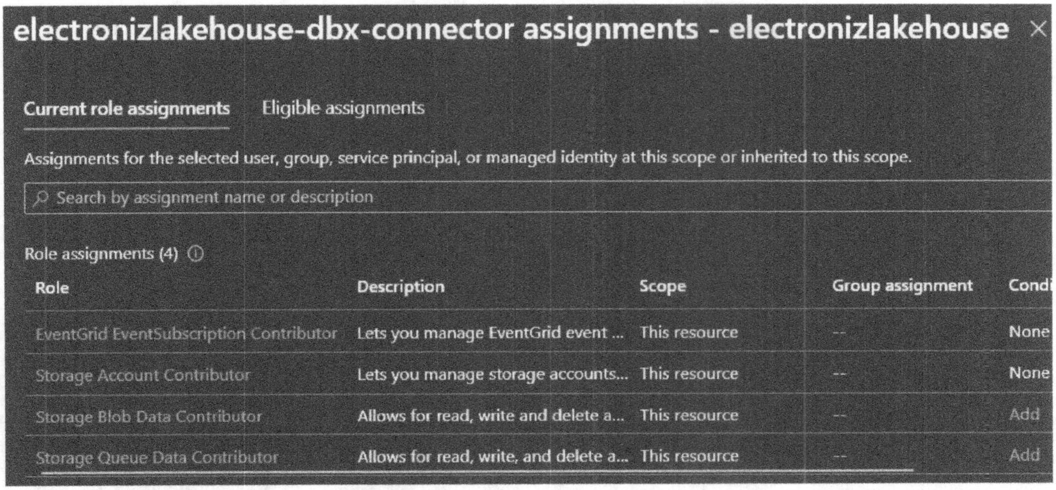

Figure 9.14: Roles required for Databricks access to electronizlakehouse ADLS

16. Navigate to Home on your Azure portal. Then click on **Subscriptions** > **Your Subscription** > **Resource Providers**.
17. Search for *EventGrid* and click **Register**.

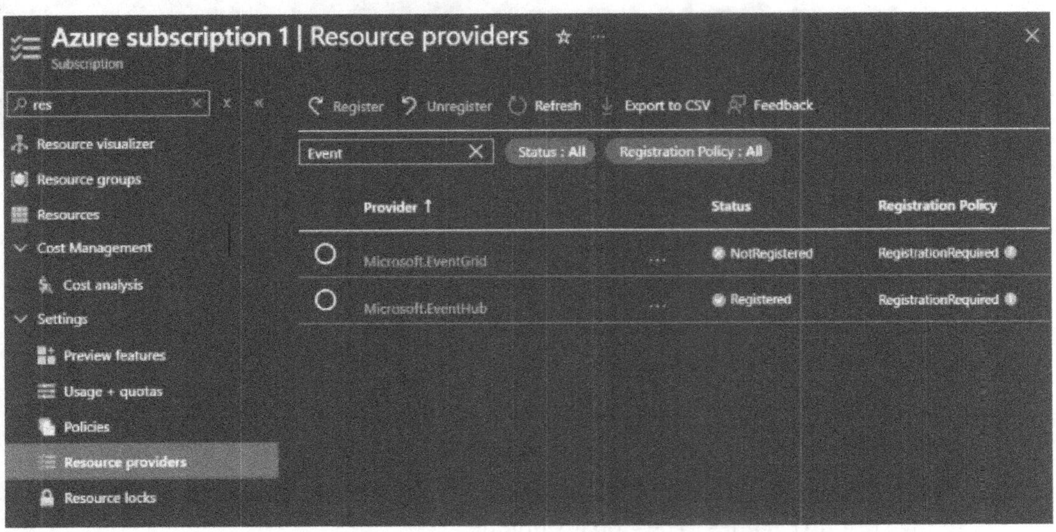

Figure 9.15: Registering EventGrid on the Resource Providers page

18. Azure Databricks must also have access to `electronizlanding`. Note that the name of your landing container may differ, as Azure requires globally unique names for all storage resources. It requires grants for the following roles:
    - Storage Blob Data Contributor
    - Storage Account Contributor
    - `EventGridEventSubscription` Contributor
    - Storage Queue Data Contributor
19. Repeat the steps to grant these roles to `electronizlanding` ADLS account. If you need a refresher, we followed the same configuration steps in *Chapter 6*.

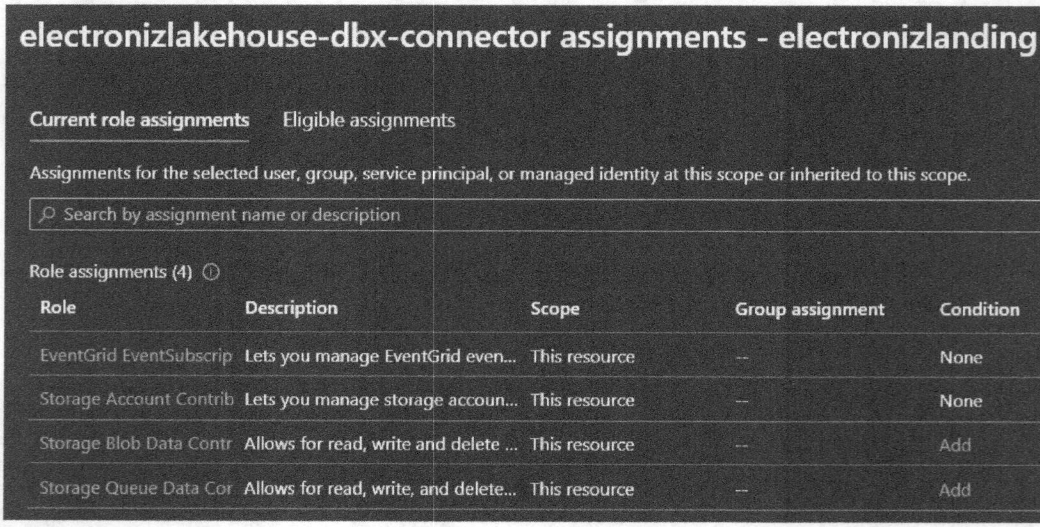

Figure 9.16: Roles required for Databricks access to electronizlanding ADLS

20. Navigate back to the Databricks **electronizlakehouse-dbx** workspace and create the following storage credentials and external location. If you need a refresher, we followed the same configuration steps in *Chapter 6*, using the section "*Creating storage credentials and external location in Databricks*".
21. For creating the storage credential, make sure you use the **Resource ID** of the *electronizlakehouse-dbx-connector*. Make sure to update the names of your landing and bronze storage accounts in the external locations as needed, since Azure requires all storage resource names to be globally unique.
22. Storage credential named `electroniz_landing_storage_credential`

23. External location named `electroniz_landing_storage_location` pointing to `abfss://raw@electronizlanding.dfs.core.windows.net`.
24. Storage credential named `electroniz_lakehouse_storage_credential`
25. External location named `electroniz_lakehouse_bronze_storage_location` pointing to `abfss://bronze@electronizlakehouse.dfs.core.windows.net`.

    These storage locations will be used to fetch data from the landing zone and create bronze tables in the Electroniz lakehouse.

With the Azure resources in place, we can now prepare Claude Code for use.

Preparing Claude Code

While Claude Code can be used in multiple ways, in this setup we will use it as a locally installed client application running on a PC or laptop. After installation, it runs directly on the machine as either a command-line tool or a desktop application.

Install prerequisites

To function, Claude Code requires Python 3.10+ and Node.js LTS installed on your PC or laptop.

Install Python 3.10+

Download and install the latest version of Python from `https://www.python.org/downloads/`, selecting the installer that matches your operating system. Once installed, open the command line to verify the installation as shown below:

Figure 9.17: Verifying the correct version of Python

Please note that the screen shown above is from the Windows command line. The appearance and Python version may differ depending on your operating system and the installed Python version.

Install Node.js

Node.js is the runtime environment required to run the Claude Code agent on a local machine. Download and install the latest version of Node.js from `https://nodejs.org/en/download/`, choosing the installer appropriate for your operating system. For Windows, the MSI installer is recommended. Installing Node.js typically takes longer than installing Python. This behavior is common, as the installer may be installing additional build tools such as Visual Studio Build Tools and Windows updates. Although it may seem unresponsive, the process typically continues running in the background. Please allow the installer to complete the process. After installation, open a new command-line interface to verify the installation as shown below:

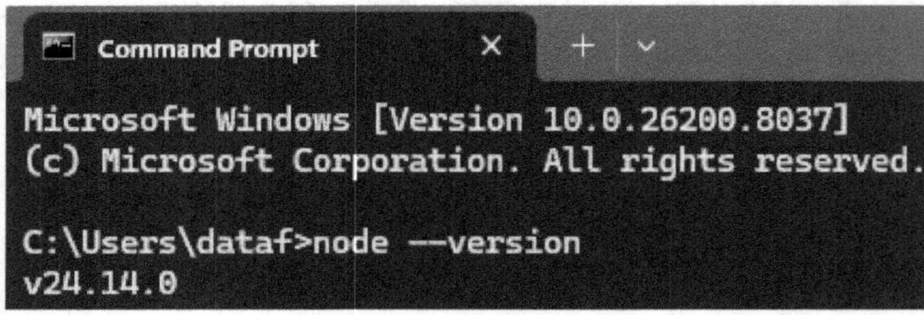

Figure 9.18: Verifying the correct version of Node.js

Now that we have installed Node.js, we can proceed with installing Claude Code.

Install Claude Code

Only after a successful installation of Node.js, install Claude Code by typing the following command on the command line: `npm install -g @anthropic-ai/claude-code`

After installation, verify the installation as shown below:

Figure 9.19: Verifying the correct version of Claude Code

We can now move on to installing the Databricks AI developer toolkit.

Install Databricks AI Dev Kit

The Databricks AI Dev Kit is a developer toolkit that enables AI coding assistants to work effectively and accurately on Databricks. Although AI coding assistants are proficient at generating code, they often struggle with platform-specific challenges—such as lacking up-to-date Databricks knowledge, missing recommended best practices, being unable to directly execute Databricks operations like creating jobs or tables, and occasionally hallucinating outdated APIs or patterns. The Databricks AI Dev Kit addresses these limitations by closing two critical gaps:

- **Bridging the knowledge gap**: Teaches the AI coding assistant how Databricks works
- **Bridging the action gap**: Enables AI coding assistant to execute approved Databricks operations.

> **Note**
>
> In a nutshell, the Databricks AI Dev Kit makes your AI assistant Databricks-aware so it can understand platform-specific concepts in the Databricks environment.

Before we use the Databricks AI Dev Kit, let's focus on its core components:

- **MCP server**: The **Model Context Protocol (MCP)** server enables the code assistant to perform Databricks operations, including running SQL queries, creating schemas and tables, and deploying jobs and pipelines.
- **Skills**: **Skills** are markdown files that serve as instructional guides for the code generation agent, teaching the AI assistant about Databricks architecture, best practices, and recommended actions.
- **Python library**: The shared Python library wraps around the Databricks APIs for simplified integration.
- **Builder App**: In addition to using the AI Dev Kit from the command line, you can optionally use a web-based UI that provides a chat interface for Databricks development.

The following is a typical code generation workflow of the Databricks AI Dev Kit:

1. The code generation workflow begins when a user submits a natural-language request to the AI assistant, referred to as a prompt. In a nutshell, a prompt is a brief piece of text provided as input to a large language model to guide and influence its output in various ways.

   > **Note**
   >
   > Prompt engineering is the process of creating targeted, domain-specific prompts to improve a model's accuracy and performance. It is widely applied in tasks such as code generation, data analysis as well as content creation. From a productivity standpoint, well-crafted prompts reduce rework and limit hallucinations by grounding the model in accurate assumptions.

2. The AI assistant reads the prompt from step 1 and consults the Databricks skills files, which instruct it on Databricks architecture and recommended design patterns.

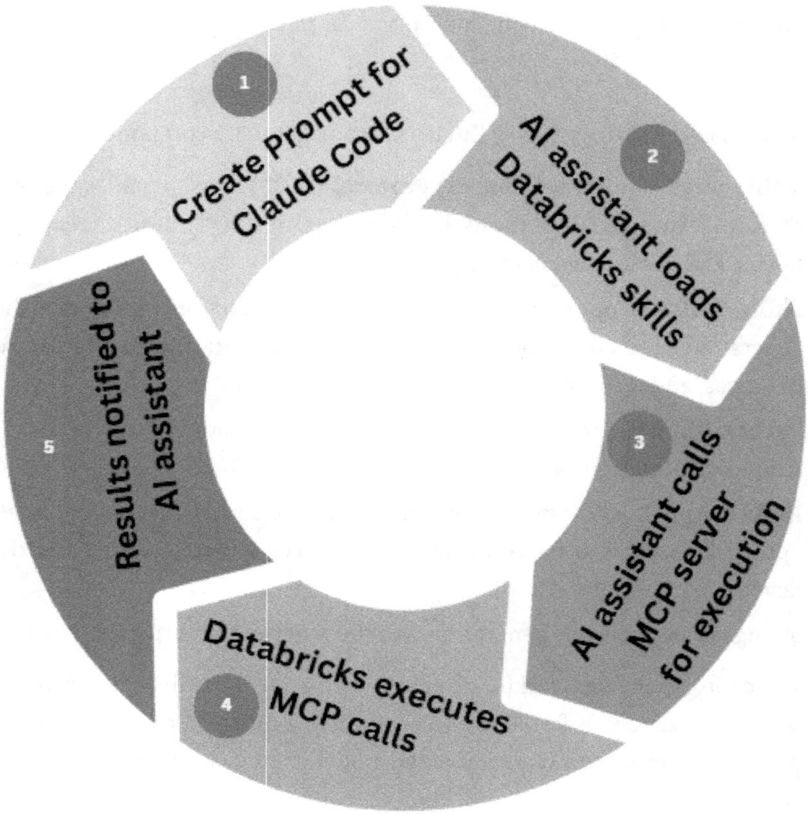

Figure 9.20: Typical workflow of the Databricks AI Dev Kit

3. Using the loaded skills, the AI assistant generates the required code and submits it to the MCP server to execute any actions defined in the generated code.
4. Databricks processes the MCP server requests while enforcing the permissions of the Databricks identity used for the connection. As a result, all actions are constrained by RBAC permissions, cluster policies, and workspace restrictions.
5. After Databricks completes the requested actions, the results are returned to the AI assistant through the MCP server.

With this foundational understanding of the Databricks AI Dev Kit, we can now move forward to the next configuration steps:

1. Databricks AI Dev Kit can be installed by cloning the git repository. Type the following instruction in the command line interface:

```
git clone https://github.com/databricks-solutions/ai-dev-kit.git
```

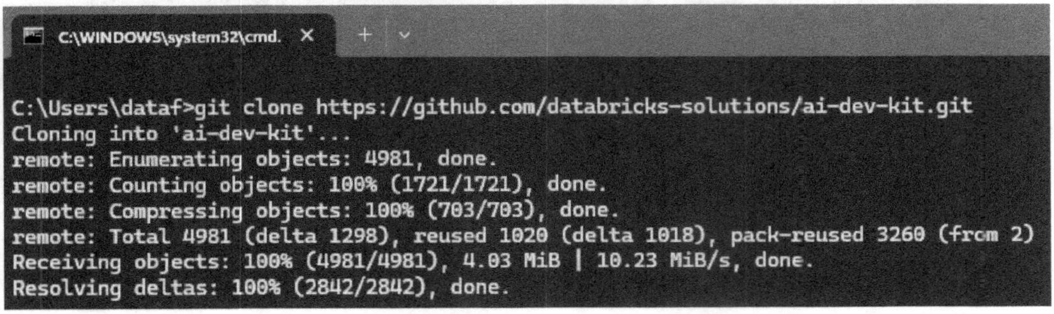

Figure 9.21: Cloning the Databricks AI Dev Kit git repo

   Carefully note the directory where the Databricks AI Dev Kit is cloned. In my case, the folder is `C:\Users\<user-name>\ai-dev-kit`.

2. Next, create a Python virtual environment (.venv) for the project. Using a virtual environment isolates project specific dependencies, preventing them from affecting the global Python installation or conflicting with other projects. Navigate to the same directory where the Git repository was cloned in the previous step and run the following commands in your command line shell. You may need to adjust the commands based on your operating system.
   For Windows users:

```
cd C:\Users\<user-name>\ai-dev-kit\databricks-mcp-server
python -m venv .venv
.venv\Scripts\activate
cd..
pip install databricks-sdk
pip install databricks-mcp
pip install -e databricks-tools-core
cd databricks-mcp-server
pip install -e .
```

For Mac users:

```
cd /users/<user-name>/ai-dev-kit/databricks-mcp-server
python3 -m venv .venv
. .venv/bin/activate
cd ..
pip install fastmcp
pip install databricks-sdk
pip install databricks-mcp
pip install "git+https://github.com/databricks-solutions/ai-dev-
kit.git#subdirectory=databricks-tools-core"
cd databricks-mcp-server
pip install -e .
```

3. Create a working directory for Claude Code on your local machine. This is where all the generated code will be stored.
For Windows users:

```
mkdir C:\Users\<user-name>\databricks-projects
cd C:\Users\<user-name>\databricks-projects
```

For Mac users:

```
mkdir /users/<user-name>/databricks-projects
cd /users/<user-name>/databricks-projects
```

4. Next, we will register the MCP server with Claude Code.
For Windows users:

```
claude mcp add-json databricks "{\"command\":\"C:\\Users\\<user-name>\\ai-
dev-kit\\databricks-mcp-server\\.venv\\Scripts\\python.exe\",\"args\":[\"C:
\\Users\\<user-name>\\ai-dev-kit\\databricks-mcp-server\\run_server.py\"]}"
```

For Mac users:

```
claude mcp add-json databricks '{"command":"/users/<user-name>/ai-dev-kit/
databricks-mcp-server/.venv/bin/python", "args":["/users/<user-name>/
databricks-mcp-server/run_server.py"]}'
```

5. Once the MCP server is registered, you should receive a success message as follows:

```
(.venv) C:\Users\dataf\databricks-projects>claude mcp add-json databricks "{\"command\"
:\"C:\\Users\\dataf\\ai-dev-kit\\databricks-mcp-server\\.venv\\Scripts\\python.exe\",\"
args\":[\"C:\\Users\\ dataf\\ai-dev-kit\\databricks-mcp-server\\run_server.py\"]}"
Added stdio MCP server databricks to local config
```

Figure 9.22: Register the MCP server

> **Note**
>
> The `.claude.json` file is a client-side configuration file that tells Claude Code which MCP servers exist and how to connect to or start them.

6. Verify the details of the newly registered MCP server configuration by opening the file below:

   For Windows users:

```
C:\Users\<user-name>\.claude.json
```

   For Mac users:

```
/users/<user-name>/.claude.json
```

   Make sure all file paths are valid and free of unwanted characters, such as spaces.

7. Copy Databricks skills into the working directory for Claude Code on your local machine.

   For Windows users:

```
mkdir C:\Users\<user-name>\databricks-projects\.claude\skills
xcopy /E /I C:\Users\<user-name>\ai-dev-kit\databricks-skills
C:\Users\<user-name>\databricks-projects\.claude\skills
```

   For Mac users:

```
cd /users/<user-name>/databricks-projects
mkdir .claude
cd .claude
mkdir skills
cp -R /users/<user-name>/ai-dev-kit/databricks-skills/ /users/<user-name>/
databricks-projects/.claude/skills
```

8. Once the skills files have been copied, you should see the directory populated as follows:

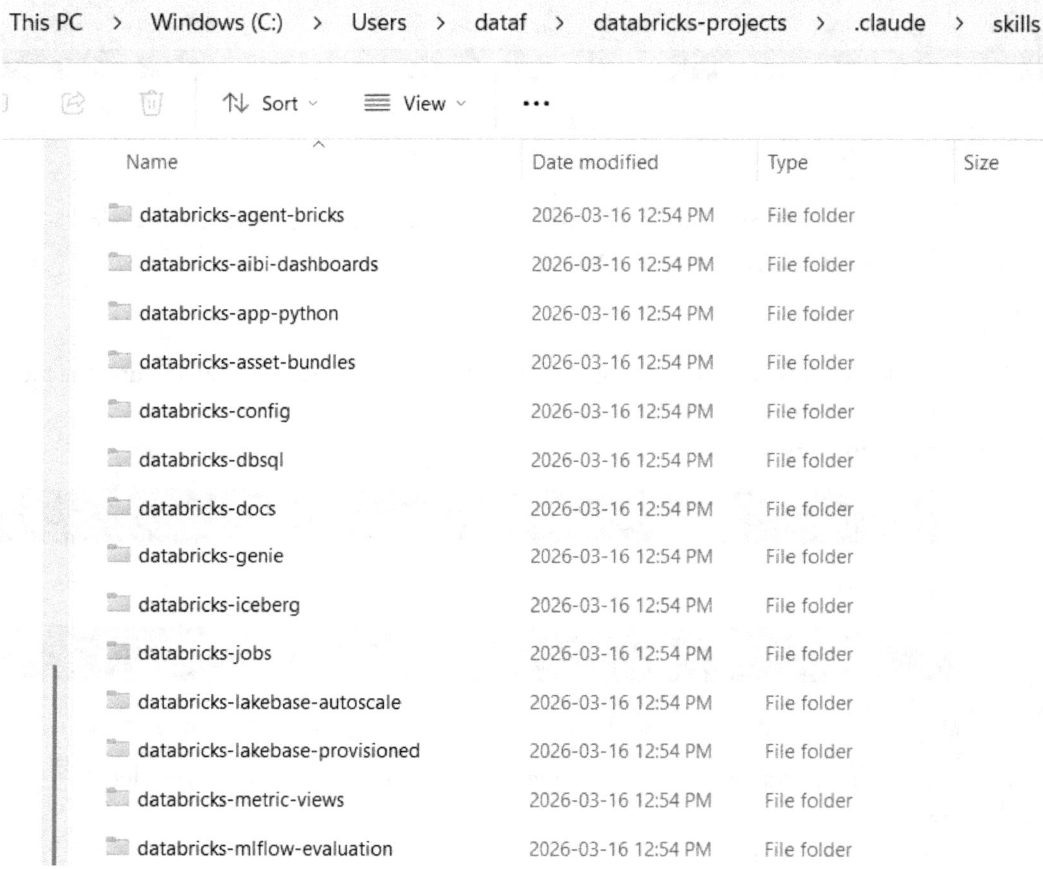

Figure 9.23: Verifying the Databricks skills in the Claude Code project folder

For Mac users:

Since the `.skills` folder is a hidden folder on Mac, you may view the contents of the folder in the terminal using the command below:

```
ls /users/<user-name>/databricks-projects/.claude/skills
```

9. Now we have set up the Databricks credentials. You will need to retrieve a few details from your previously created Databricks workspace.
10. Note down the details of your Databricks host.
    - `DATABRICKS_HOST`: This is your workspace host URL, such as `https://adb-XXXXXXXXXXXX.5.azuredatabricks.net`
    - This can be retrieved from the URL of your Databricks workspace.
11. You need a `DATABRICKS_TOKEN` for Claude Code to authenticate the MCP server with the Databricks REST APIs on your behalf. To fetch the `DATABRICKS_TOKEN`, navigate to **Settings** on your Databricks workspace. Click your name icon in the top-right corner of the workspace screen.
12. Now click on **Developer**.
13. Beside *Access Token,* click on **Manage**. Add details as under and click on **Generate**.

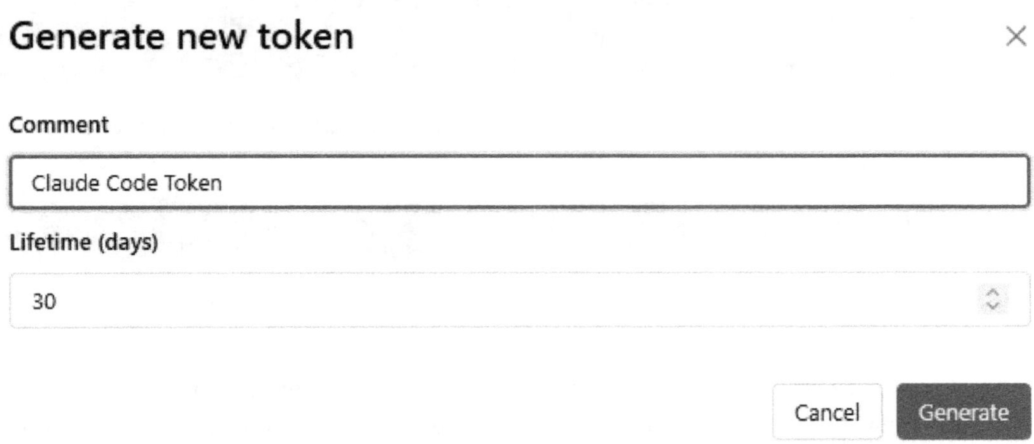

Figure 9.24: Generating a new token for Databricks access

14. Copy the value of the token and save it securely.
15. Navigate back to the terminal on your local machine and set the Databricks variables as follows. You will need the values of `DATABRICKS_HOST` and `DATABRICKS_TOKEN` from the previous step.

For Windows users:

```
setx DATABRICKS_HOST "DATABRICKS_HOST"
setx DATABRICKS_TOKEN "DATABRICKS_TOKEN"
```

For Mac users:

```
export DATABRICKS_HOST "DATABRICKS_HOST"
export DATABRICKS_TOKEN "DATABRICKS_TOKEN"
```

16. To verify Python can successfully connect to your Databricks account, execute the following command on the terminal:
For Windows and Mac users:

```
python -c "from databricks.sdk import WorkspaceClient; w =
WorkspaceClient(host='%DATABRICKS_HOST%', token='%DATABRICKS_TOKEN%');
print('Handshake complete! Connected as:', w.current_user.me().user_name)"
```

17. Now we are ready to launch Claude Code. Simple issue the following command on the terminal:

```
claude
```

18. In the next step pick the desired color style using the Up/Down arrows on your keyboard and press **Enter**.
19. Claude Code uses a prepaid, pay-as-you-go pricing model through the Anthropic Console, where credits must be purchased in advance and charges are based on token usage.

20. For the scope of our work, expected usage is approximately $10–$20. Choose the second option and press **Enter**.

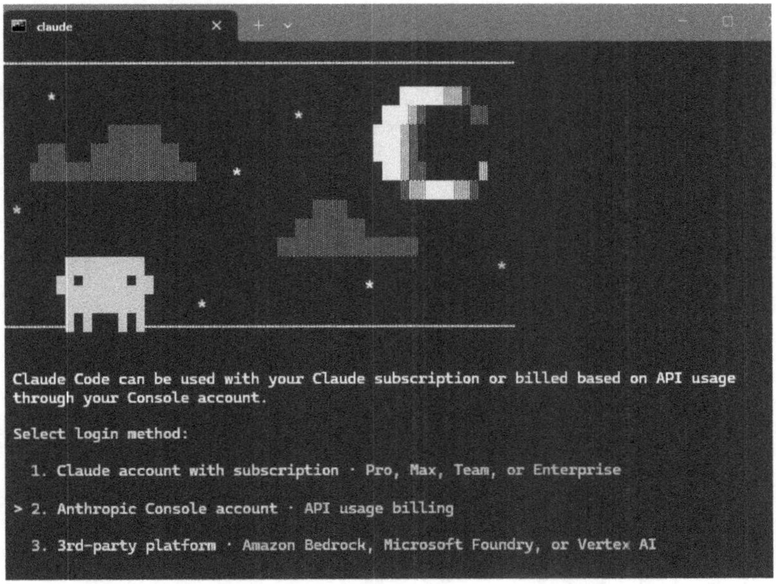

Figure 9.25: Use Claude Code API usage billing

21. Claude Code will open a new browser window like this:

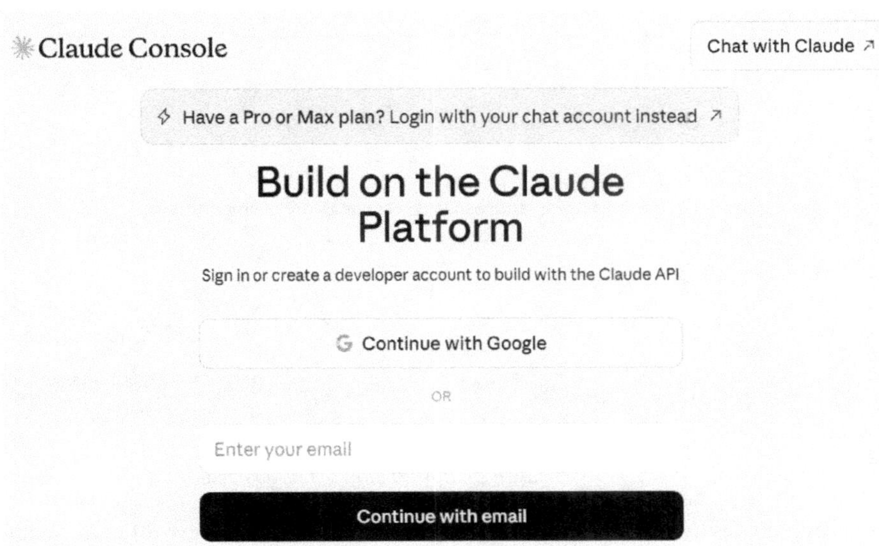

Figure 9.26: Register for Claude Code account

22. Register for the Claude Code account. After registration you should see a screen to buy API credits as follows

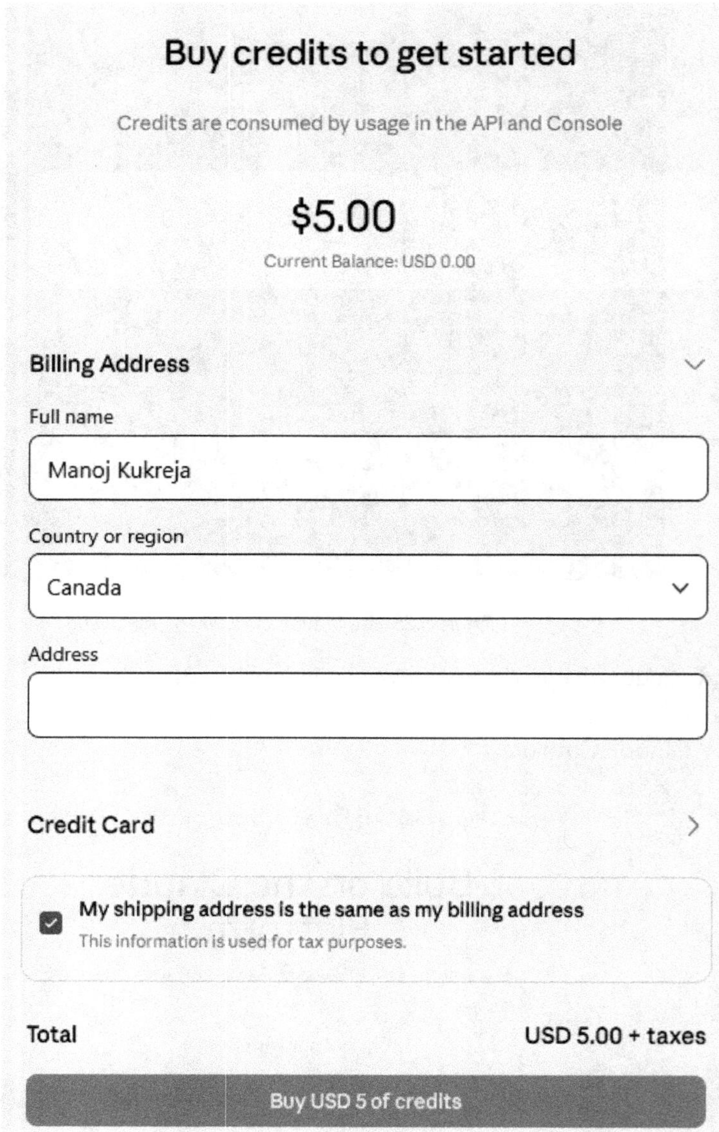

Figure 9.27: Buying Claude Code API credits

23. Purchase Claude Code API credits in $5 increments and renew them as needed when the balance is exhausted.

24. After procuring the credits navigate back to your Claude Code terminal.

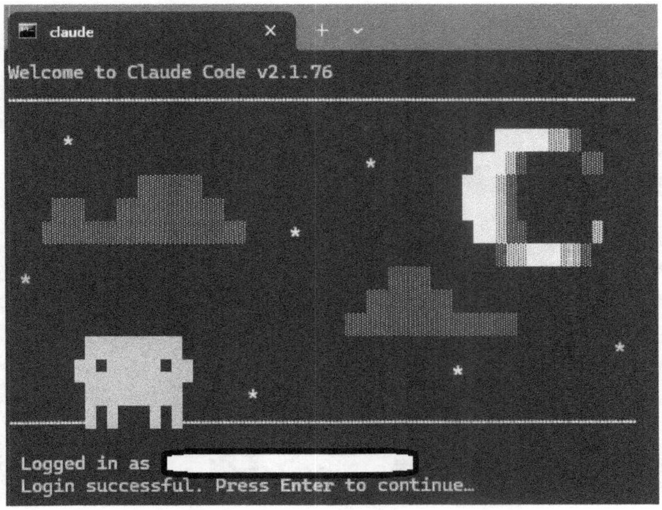

Figure 9.28: Setup Claude Code

25. Press **Enter**.

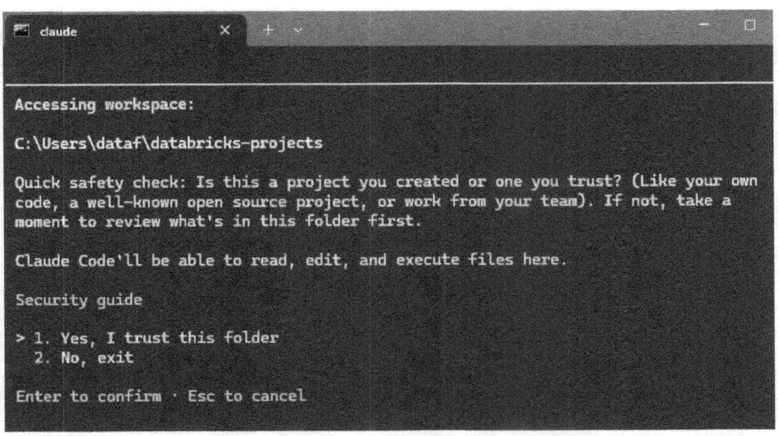

Figure 9.29: Trust the project folder for Claude Code

26. Press **Enter** to trust the project folder. You should now be at the Claude Code control panel:

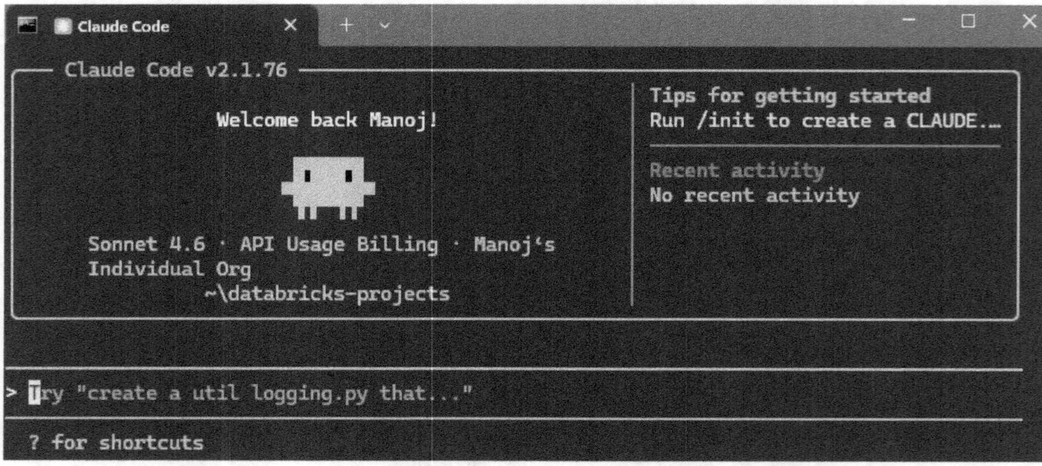

Figure 9.30: Claude Code control panel

27. On the Claude Code control panel, type the following command:

```
/mcp
```

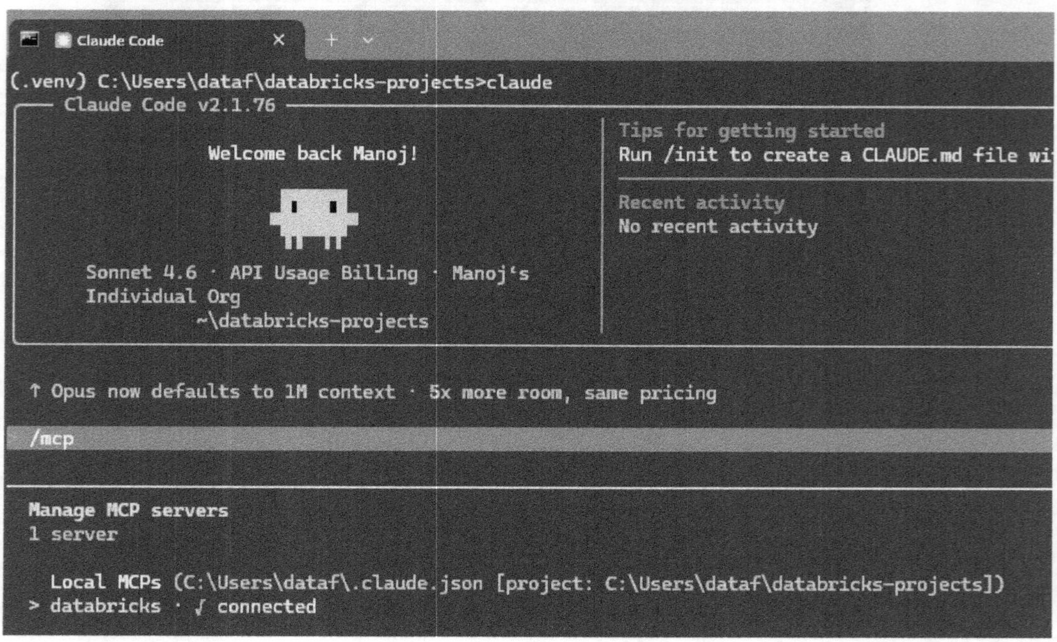

Figure 9.31: Claude Code connected to Databricks

If everything works well, you should see the "Databricks connected" message as shown above. Press **Esc** to come back to Claude Code.

28. To validate the connection to Databricks, let's issue a simple SQL on Claude Code:

```
Run this SQL: SELECT current_user(), current_timestamp()
```

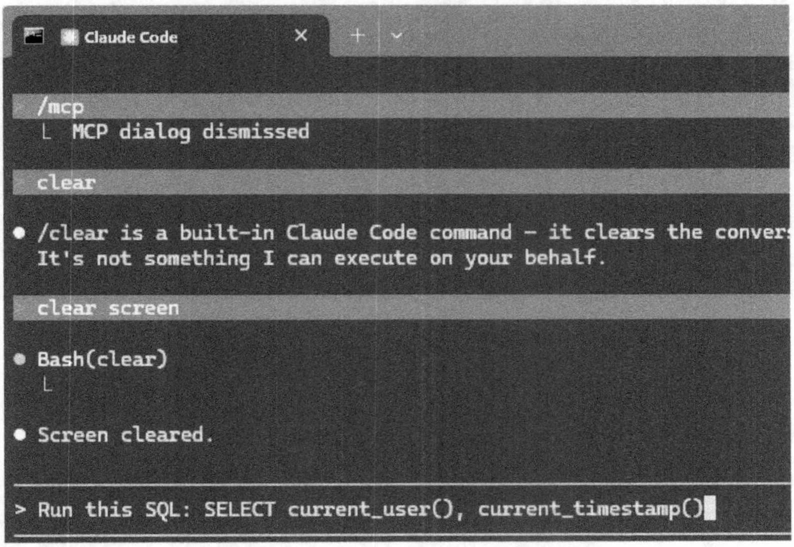

Figure 9.32: Execute SQL on Databricks

29. Expect to get back the results as follows:

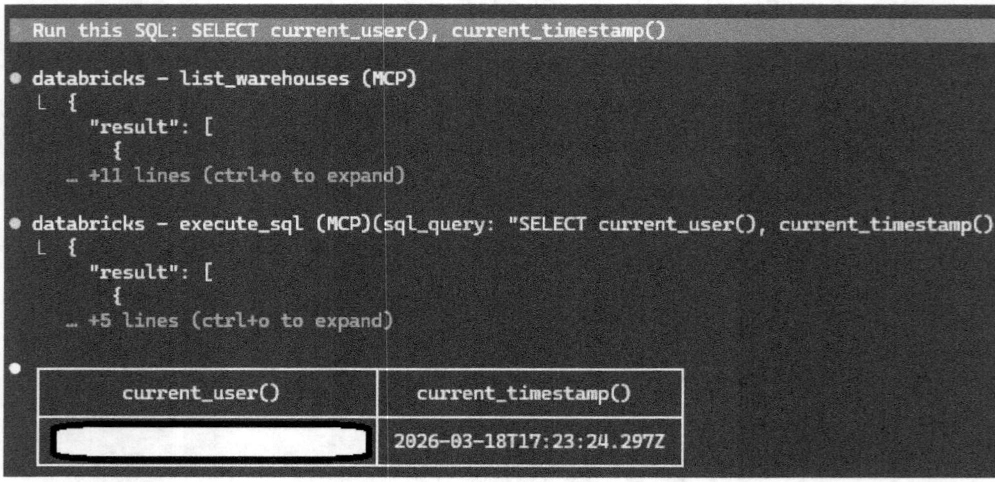

Figure 9.33: Result from the SQL

30. Type `/cost` to keep track of your API credits. You may also keep track of your API credits using `https://platform.claude.com/settings/billing`

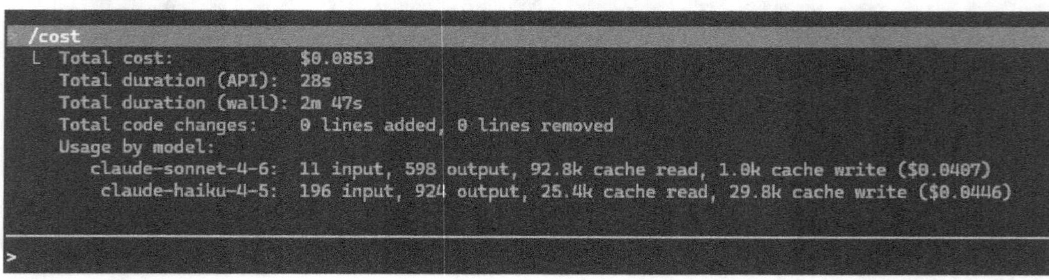

Figure 9.34: Claude Code track usage

This completes the Claude Code setup. It's high time we start building the Electroniz bronze pipeline.

Developing the Electroniz bronze pipelines using Claude Code

You may recall from previous sections that the code generation workflow begins when a user submits a natural-language request to the AI assistant, referred to as a **prompt.** Carefully designing and structuring prompts is key to producing accurate, relevant, and high-quality responses. A clear prompt should accurately define the task, provide sufficient context, set constraints, and specify the desired output format.

> **Note**
>
> It is important to understand that even powerful AI GenAI models can produce poor or inconsistent results if prompts are unclear or vague. Well-engineered prompts improve efficiency, reduce errors, save time, and make AI outputs more reliable and repeatable.

To recap, the landing zone contains data from various source systems, each arriving in its original format. *Table 9.3* summarizes their formats and the names of the pipelines that will be used to build the bronze layer.

Data Source	**Data Format**	**Pipeline Name**	**Bronze Tables**

Store Sales Database
 	
Inventory
 	
Products
 	
Store Customers
 	
Store Orders
	CSV	`electroniz_bronze_inventory_pipeline`
		
		`electroniz_bronze_product_pipeline`
		
		`electroniz_bronze_store_customers_pipeline`
		
		`electroniz_bronze_store_orders_pipeline`
			Catalog: `electroniz_catalog`
			
			Schema: `electroniz_bronze_schema`
			
			Tables:
			
			`electroniz_bronze_inventory`
			
			`electroniz_bronze_products`
			
			`electroniz_bronze_store_customers`
			
			`electroniz_bronze_store_orders`

Data Source	Data Format	Pipeline Name	Bronze Tables
Currency Conversion Data	JSON	electroniz_bronze_currency_pipeline	Catalog: electroniz_catalog Schema: electroniz_bronze_schema Tables: electroniz_bronze_currency
e-commerce Website Tracking Logs	JSON	electroniz_bronze_website_logs_pipeline	Catalog: electroniz_catalog Schema: electroniz_bronze_schema Tables: electroniz_bronze_website_logs
Geo-location data	CSV	electroniz_bronze_geolocation_pipeline	Catalog: electroniz_catalog Schema: electroniz_bronze_schema Tables: electroniz_bronze_geolocation

Data Source	Data Format	Pipeline Name	Bronze Tables
Product Reviews	AVRO	electroniz_bronze_product_reviews_pipeline	Catalog: electroniz_catalog Schema: electroniz_bronze_schema Tables: electroniz_bronze_product_reviews
e-commerce Transactions	AVRO	electroniz_bronze_ecommerce_pipeline	Catalog: electroniz_catalog Schema: electroniz_bronze_schema Tables: electroniz_bronze_ecomm_transactions

Table 9.3: Data format and table details created by the bronze layer pipelines

Having reviewed the various bronze-layer pipelines to be built, we can now move on to creating the Electroniz data catalog and its associated schemas.

Creating the Electroniz catalog

Let's begin by creating a Databricks catalog, which serves as the top-level organizational entity in Unity Catalog for centrally managing and governing data assets, including schemas, tables, views, functions, and volumes.

1. Issue the following prompt on Claude Code to create a new catalog:

```
Create a unity catalog with details as follows:
Name: electroniz_catalog
```

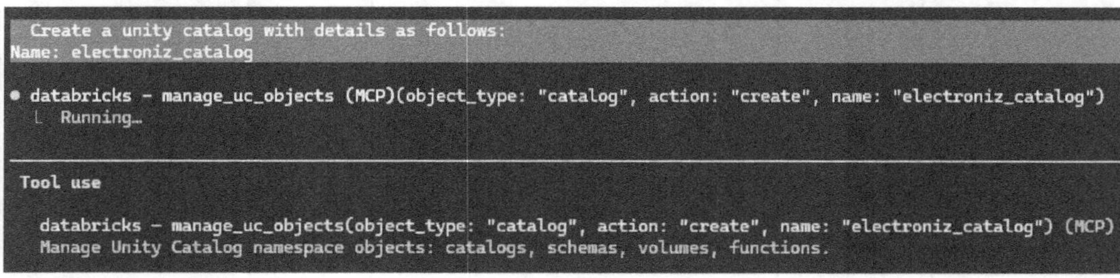

Figure 9.35: Create a new catalog

2. Click **Yes** when asked to proceed.
3. Once created, you will receive confirmation as follows:

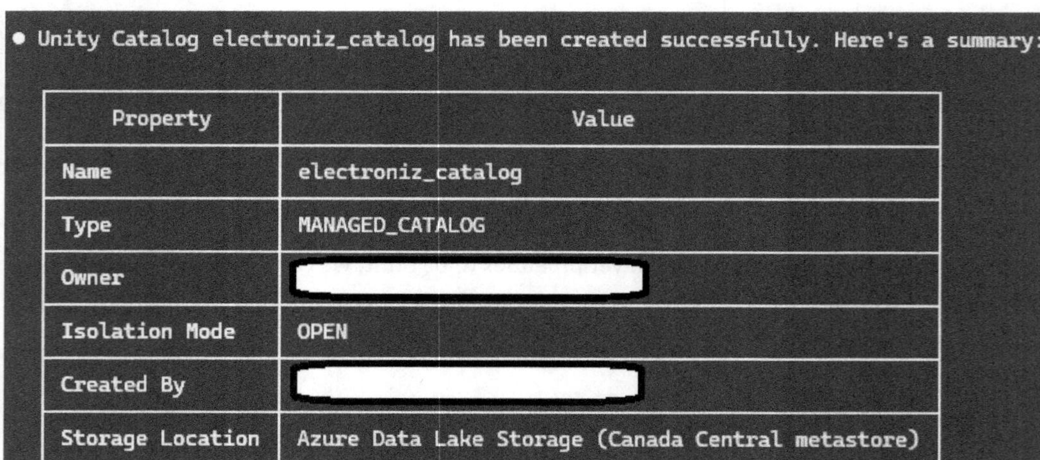

Figure 9.36: Confirmation of new catalog creation

4. If you navigate to the Databricks workspace, you should see the newly created catalog.

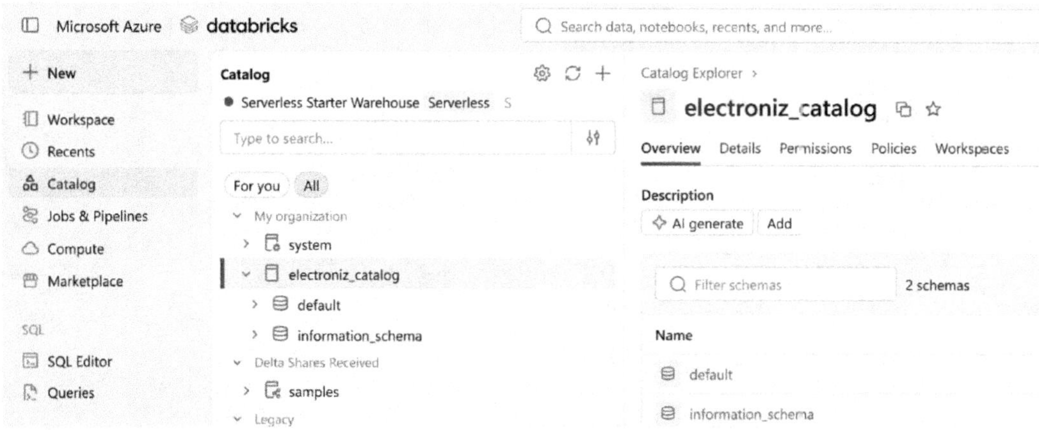

Figure 9.37: Newly created catalog in Databricks.

5. Issue the following prompt on Claude Code to create a new schema under the newly created catalog. Make sure you adjust the name of the Azure Data Lake Storage account as per your settings.

```
Run SQL
CREATE SCHEMA electroniz_catalog.electroniz_bronze_schema
MANAGED LOCATION 'abfss://bronze@electronizlakehouse.dfs.core.windows.net';
```

6. Click **Yes** when asked to proceed.

7. You should see the newly created schema as below.

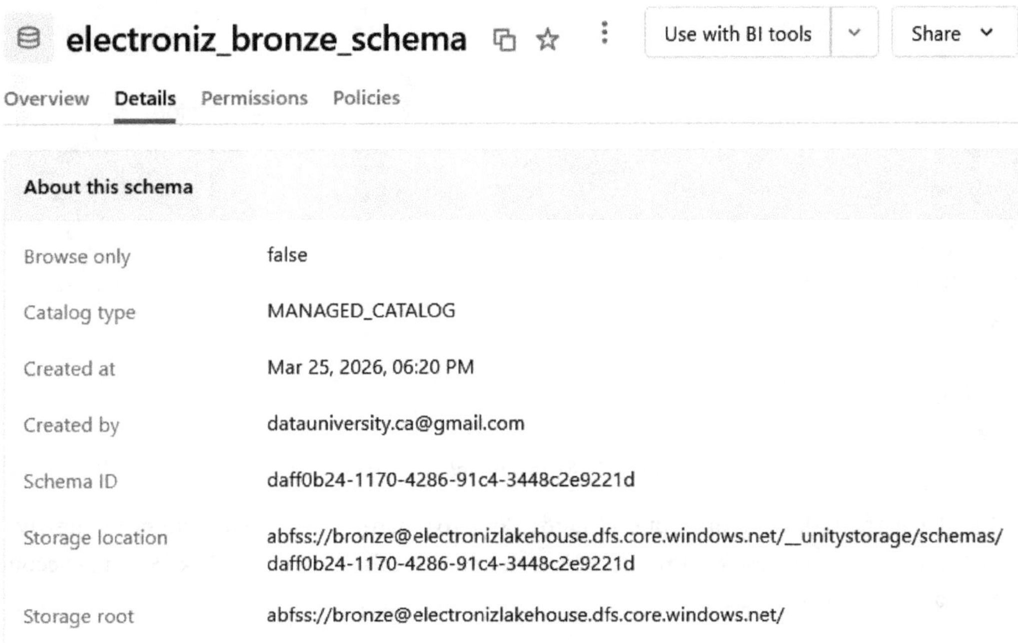

Figure 9.38: Newly created schema in Databricks

Now that the Electroniz catalog and schema have been created, we can begin creating the bronze-layer pipelines.

Creating the Electroniz bronze pipelines

We're starting to get the hang of code generation using Claude Code, so we'll move forward by creating our first pipeline, beginning with a simple example.

Creating the Electroniz bronze pipeline for store sales database

In the Electroniz store sales database, data represents transactional activity generated by customers purchasing products at physical store locations. The database is designed to support operational processing, reporting, and downstream analytics, and typically contains the following categories of information.

Creating the Electroniz bronze pipeline for the inventory table

The store sales inventory table stores information about the current quantities of the Electroniz products. Its main purpose is to provide visibility into what stock is available.

1. Issue the following prompt on Claude Code to create the bronze inventory pipeline. Make sure to update the name of your Azure Data Lake Storage account to match your environment settings.

```
Create a new pipeline using SQL with details as follows
Pipeline Name: electroniz_bronze_inventory_pipeline
Data location: abfss://raw@electronizlanding.dfs.core.windows.net/sales/
[dbo].[inventory]/
You will need to double escape the square brackets in data location.
Table:
electroniz_catalog.electroniz_bronze_schema.electroniz_bronze_inventory
Make sure to reference the complete table as suggested including catalog
and schema
Continuously stream data from the source location using Auto Loader
The Schema of the file is "inventory_date string, product string, inventory
integer, updated_at timestamp"
Use schema option (not schemaHints) and map these columns by position since
there is no header row.
Format: CSV, append mode
Files are stored in deeply nested subfolders make sure to search all
subfolders for csv files
Show code before deployment
```

2. Claude Code will go into thinking mode for a few seconds.

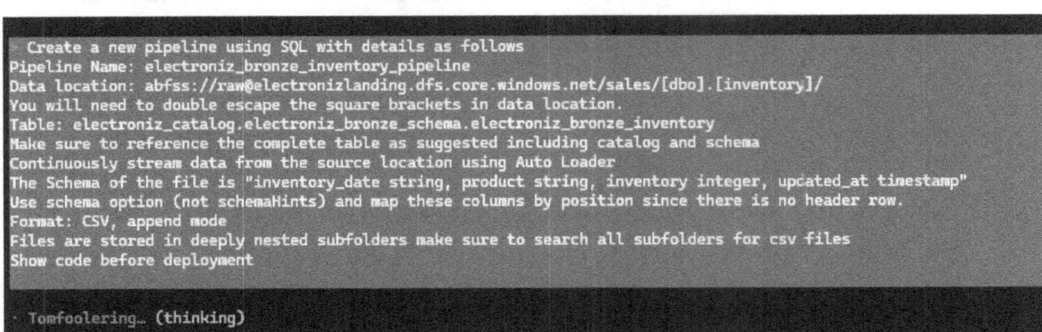

Figure 9.39: Claude Code inferring the provided prompt

At this stage, Claude Code is not generating executable code yet. Instead, it is focusing on reasoning and design, breaking down the requirements and constructing a structured plan for the implementation logic. This planning step helps ensure that the final code aligns with the intended behavior, handles edge cases, and follows best practices before any code is produced.

3. Since we previously provided explicit instructions in the prompt to display the code prior to deployment, Claude returned the generated code along with the key design decisions it made during the code creation process.

```
● Here is the SQL code for the pipeline before deployment:

  ---
  electroniz_bronze_inventory.sql
  CREATE OR REFRESH STREAMING TABLE electroniz_catalog.electroniz_bronze_schema.electroniz_bronze_inventory
  AS SELECT *
  FROM STREAM read_files(
    'abfss://ram@electronizlanding.dfs.core.windows.net/sales/\\[dbo\\].\\[inventory\\]/',
    format => 'csv',
    schema => 'inventory_date string, product string, inventory integer, updated_at timestamp',
    header => false,
    recursiveFileLookup => true
  )

  ---
  Key decisions:
```

Setting	Value	Reason
FROM STREAM read_files(...)	Streaming	Required for streaming tables with Auto Loader
schema =>	Explicit schema	Per your instruction - not schemaHints
header => false	No header	Columns mapped by position
recursiveFileLookup => true	Enabled	Searches all nested subfolders
\\[dbo\\].\\[inventory\\]	Double-escaped	Treats [ ] as literals, not glob patterns
Pipeline mode	Continuous	For real-time streaming

Figure 9.40: Claude Code generated code

A streaming table is a Delta table designed to support streaming and incremental data processing. It can act as the target for one or more flows within a pipeline. Claude Code correctly configured the required parameters—such as format, schema, and header—according to the instructions provided in the prompt. The `recursiveFileLookup` option instructs Spark to recursively scan subdirectories when discovering input files.

4. When prompted with the question "*Shall I deploy this pipeline now?*", select **Yes** and press **Enter**. You may be asked to confirm several additional steps; for each prompt, choose Option 1 and press **Enter**. Pay close attention to the sequence of actions to better understand what is occurring behind the scenes during deployment.

5. Finally, Claude Code will prompt you for a last confirmation to deploy the code to Databricks. Once confirmed, it will proceed with the deployment and display a confirmation message like shown below.

```
● Pipeline deployed successfully. Here's a summary:
```

Property	Value
Pipeline Name	electroniz_bronze_inventory_pipeline
Pipeline ID	57e500c3-85c3-4842-a31c-21b1eb026b4b
Target Table	electroniz_catalog.electroniz_bronze_schema.electroniz_bronze_inventory
Mode	Continuous (streaming)
Compute	Serverless

Figure 9.41: Claude Code pipeline deployment

6. Return to the Databricks workspace. Using the menu on the left, click **Jobs & Pipelines**. You should see the newly deployed pipeline created by Claude Code listed there.

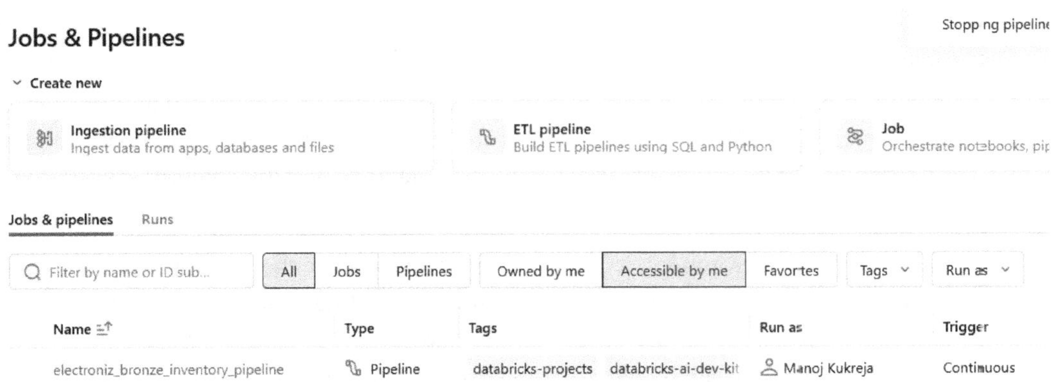

Figure 9.42: New streaming pipeline created in Databricks

7. Click the newly created Lakeflow Declarative Pipeline and review the number of records processed. These values should match the inventory data ingested from the landing zone.

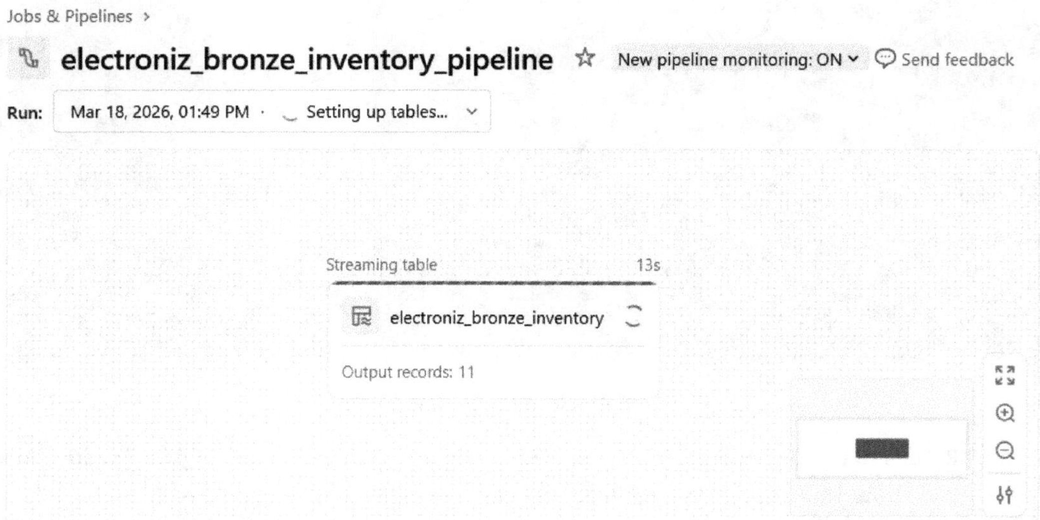

Figure 9.43: Streaming pipeline details

Once all records have been ingested from the landing zone, the Delta streaming table transitions to a **WAITING** state. This indicates that the streaming pipeline is running and ready, but there is currently no new data available to process. This behavior is expected and does not represent an error.

In a production environment, it is common practice to leave the streaming table in the **WAITING** state so it can continuously monitor the landing zone and incrementally ingest new records as they arrive. However, since this is a development or testing scenario, the pipeline can be safely stopped at this point. Stopping the pipeline releases compute resources, helping ensure efficient use of the available Azure free credits.

8. Click on **Jobs & Pipelines** and stop the **electroniz_bronze_inventory_pipeline**.

9. Next, inspect the contents of the streaming table. Click **Catalog**, then navigate to **electroniz_catalog** > **electroniz_bronze_schema** > **electroniz_bronze_inventory**. Click on **Sample Data**.

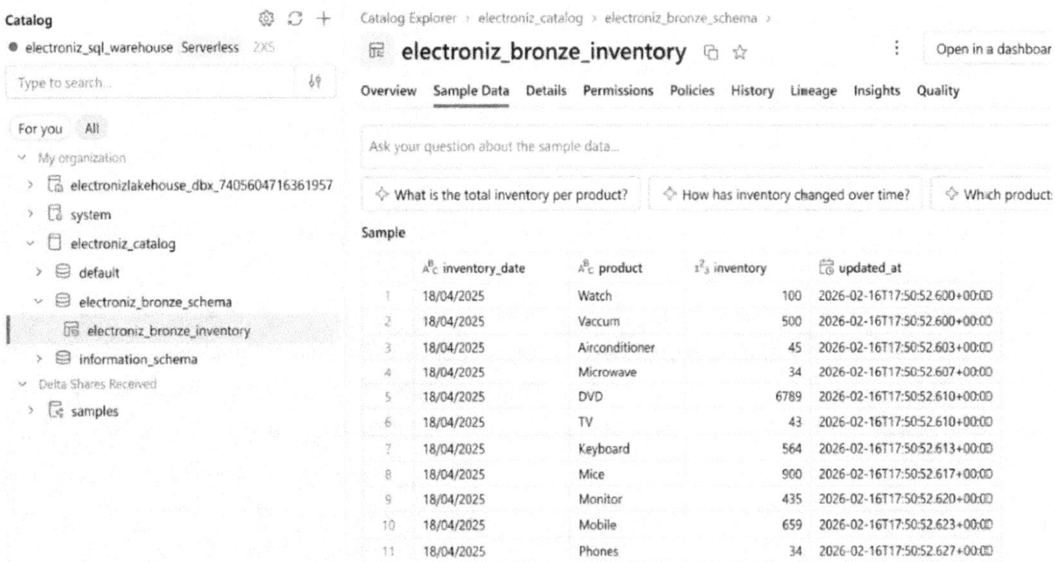

Figure 9.44: Data of electroniz_bronze_inventory table

Now we will move on to creating the bronze products pipeline.

Creating the Electroniz bronze pipeline for the products table

The store sales product table stores information about Electroniz products sold in its stores and ecommerce website.

1. Issue the following prompt on Claude Code to create the bronze products pipeline. Make sure to update the name of your Azure Data Lake Storage account to match your environment settings.

```
Create a new pipeline using SQL with details as follows
Pipeline Name: electroniz_bronze_product_pipeline
Data location: abfss://raw@electronizlanding.dfs.core.windows.net/sales/
[dbo].[products]/
You will need to double escape the square brackets in data location.
Table:
electroniz_catalog.electroniz_bronze_schema.electroniz_bronze_products
Make sure to reference the complete table as suggested including catalog
and schema
```

```
Continuously stream data from the source location using Auto Loader
The Schema of the file is "product_code string, product_name string,
product_category string, updated_at timestamp"
Use schema option (not schemaHints) and map these columns by position since
there is no header row.
Format: CSV, append mode
Files are stored in deeply nested subfolders make sure to search all
subfolders for csv files
Show code before deployment
```

2. Claude Code will generate the code for the **electroniz_bronze_product_pipeline** as under.

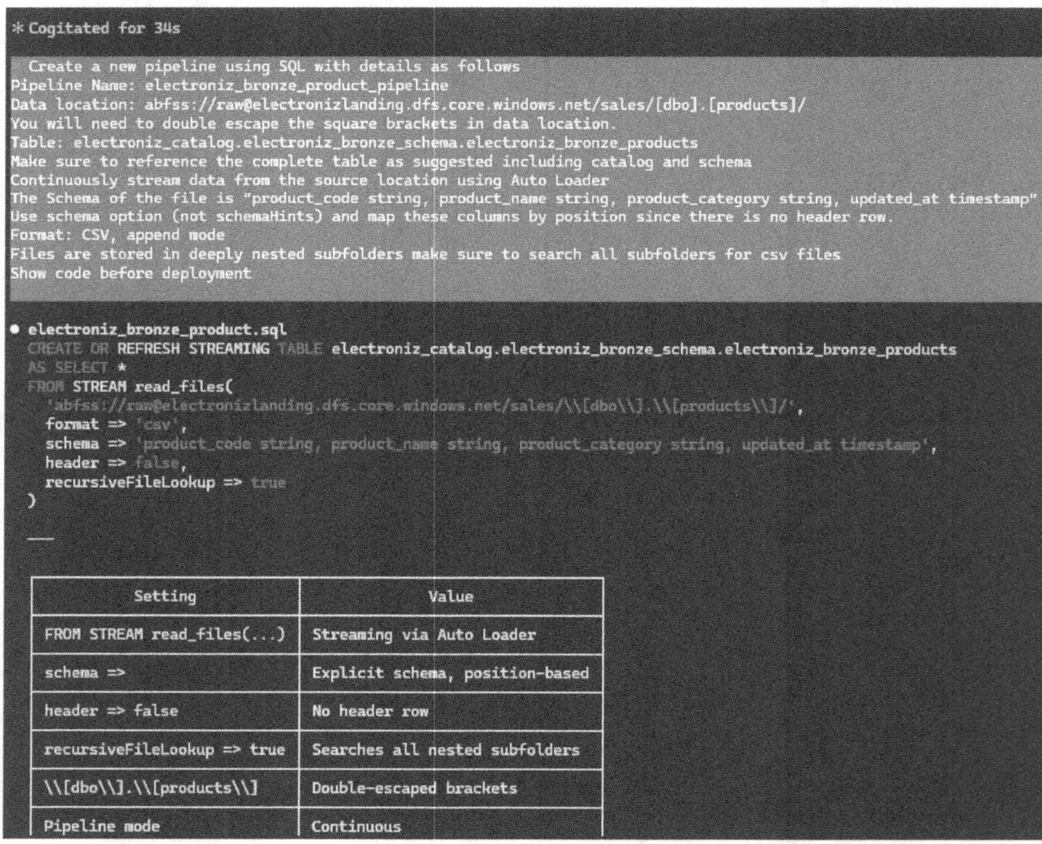

Figure 9.45: Claude Code for the electroniz_bronze_product_pipeline

3. Return to the Databricks workspace. Using the menu on the left, click **Jobs & Pipelines**. You should see the newly deployed pipeline created by Claude Code listed there.

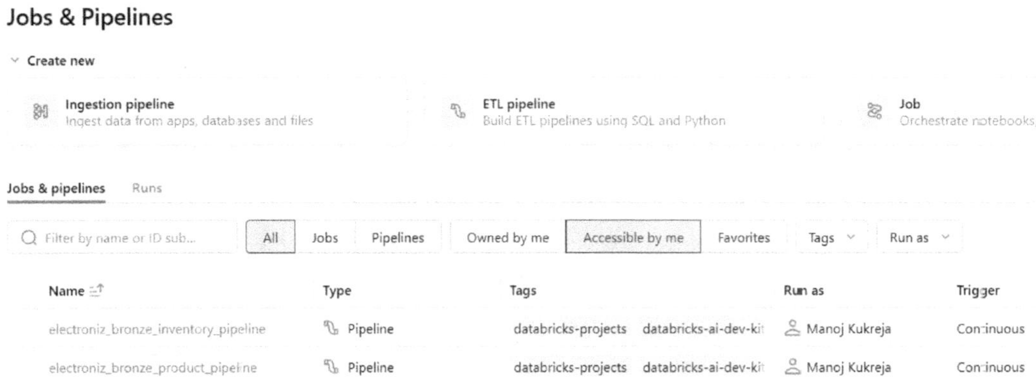

Figure 9.46: New streaming pipeline electroniz_bronze_product_pipeline

4. Next, inspect the contents of the streaming table. Click **Catalog**, then navigate to **electroniz_catalog** > **electroniz_bronze_schema** > **electroniz_bronze_products**. Click on **Sample Data**.

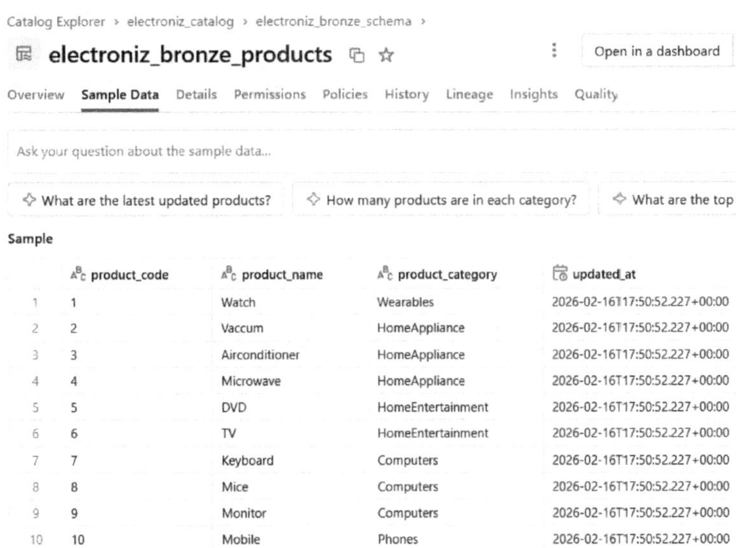

Figure 9.47: Data of electroniz_bronze_products table

5. Click on **Jobs & Pipelines** and stop the **electroniz_bronze_product_pipeline**.

Next, we can move on to creating the bronze customer pipeline.

Creating the Electroniz bronze pipeline for the customers table

The store customer table contains information about Electroniz customers who purchase products in physical stores.

1. Issue the following prompt on Claude Code to create the bronze store customers pipeline. Make sure to update the name of your Azure Data Lake Storage account to match your environment settings.

```
Create a new pipeline using SQL with details as follows
Pipeline Name: electroniz_bronze_store_customers_pipeline
Data location: abfss://raw@electronizlanding.dfs.core.windows.net/sales/
[dbo].[store_customers]/
You will need to double escape the square brackets in data location.
Table:
electroniz_catalog.electroniz_bronze_schema.electroniz_bronze_store_custome
rs
Make sure to reference the complete table as suggested including catalog
and schema
Continuously stream data from the source location using Auto Loader
The Schema of the file is "customer_id integer, customer_name string,
address string, city string, postalcode string, country string, phone
string, email string, credit_card string, updated_at timestamp"
Map these columns by position since there is no header row.
Use schema option (not schemaHints) and map these columns by position since
there is no header row.
Format: CSV, append mode
Files are stored in deeply nested subfolders make sure to search all
subfolders for csv files
Show code before deployment
```

2. Claude Code will generate the code for the **electroniz_bronze_store_customers_pipeline** as under.

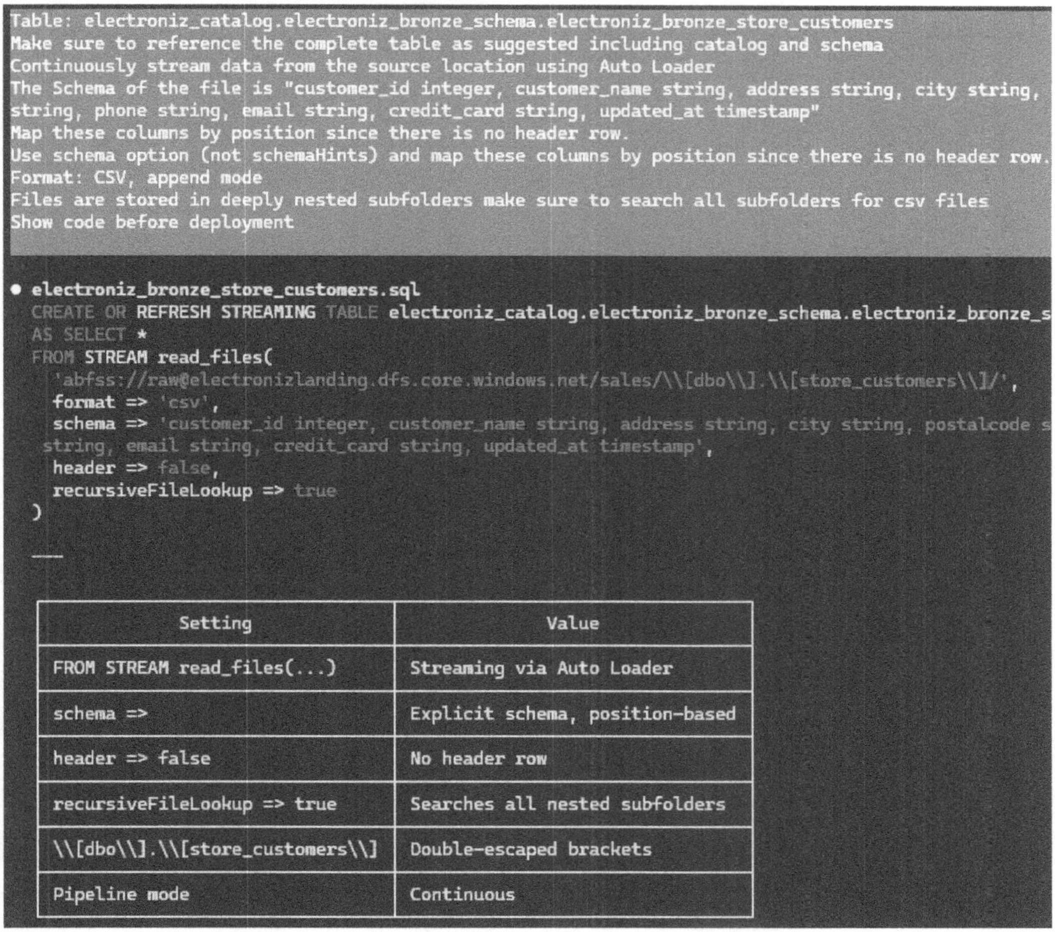

Figure 9.48: Claude Code for the electroniz_bronze_store_customers_pipeline

3. Return to the Databricks workspace. Using the menu on the left, click **Jobs & Pipelines**. You should see the newly deployed pipeline created by Claude Code listed there.

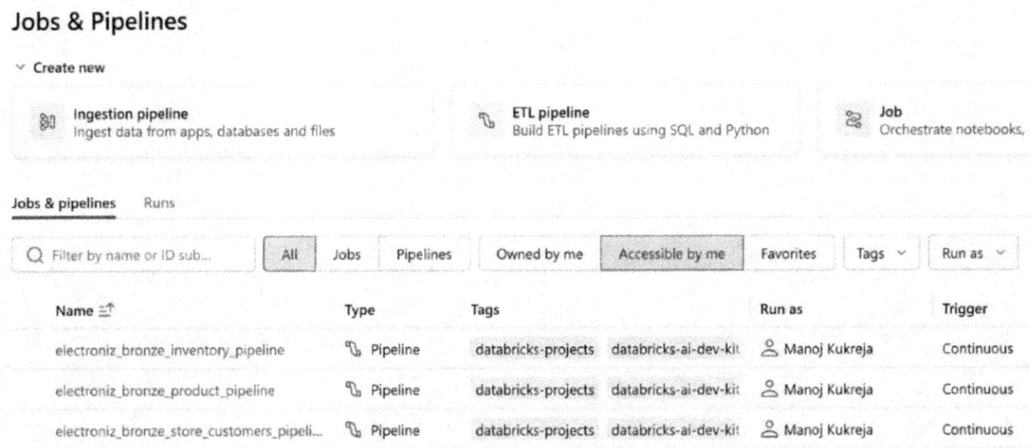

Figure 9.49: New streaming pipeline electroniz_bronze_store_customers_pipeline

4. Next, inspect the contents of the streaming table. Click **Catalog**, then navigate to **electroniz_catalog** > **electroniz_bronze_schema** > **electroniz_bronze_store_customers**. Click on **Sample Data**.

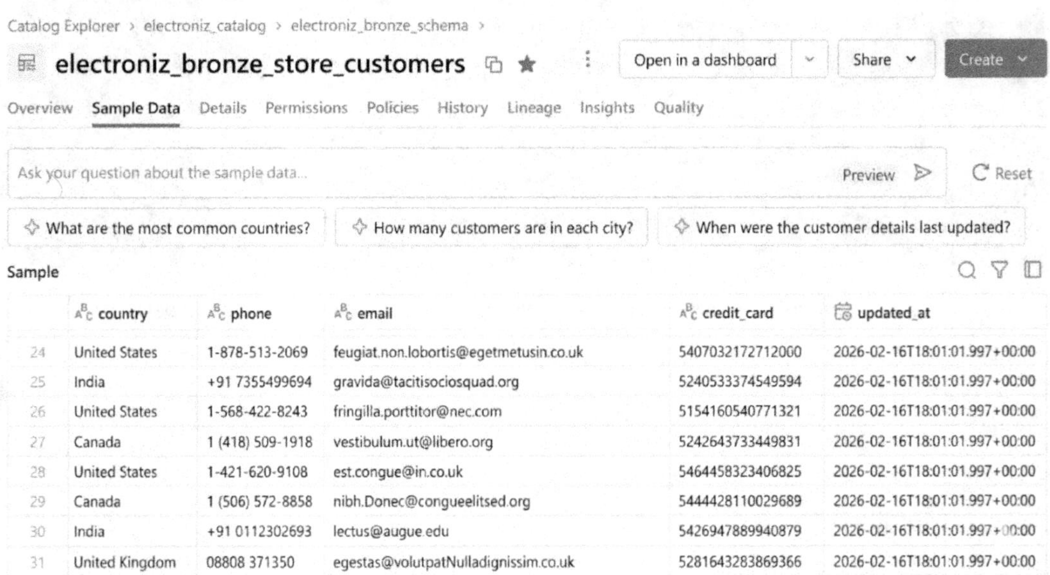

Figure 9.50: Data of electroniz_bronze_store_customers table

5. Click on **Jobs & Pipelines** and stop the **electroniz_bronze_store_customers_pipeline**.

We can now move on to the creation of the bronze orders pipeline.

Creating the Electroniz bronze pipeline for the orders table

The store orders table contains information about customer transactions made in physical stores.

1. Issue the following prompt on Claude Code to create the bronze store orders pipeline. Make sure to update the name of your Azure Data Lake Storage account to match your environment settings.

```
Create a new pipeline using SQL with details as follows
Pipeline Name: electroniz_bronze_store_orders_pipeline
Data location: abfss://raw@electronizlanding.dfs.core.windows.net/sales/
[dbo].[store_orders]/
You will need to double escape the square brackets in data location.
Table:
electroniz_catalog.electroniz_bronze_schema.electroniz_bronze_store_orders
Make sure to reference the complete table as suggested including catalog
and schema
Continuously stream data from the source location using Auto Loader
The Schema of the file is "order_number integer, customer_id integer,
product_id integer, order_date string, units integer, sale_price string,
currency string, order_mode string, updated_at timestamp".
Map these columns by position since there is no header row.
Use schema option (not schemaHints) and map these columns by position since
there is no header row.
Format: CSV, append mode
Files are stored in deeply nested subfolders make sure to search all
subfolders for csv files
Show code before deployment
```

2. Claude Code will generate the code for the **electroniz_bronze_store_orders_pipeline** as below.

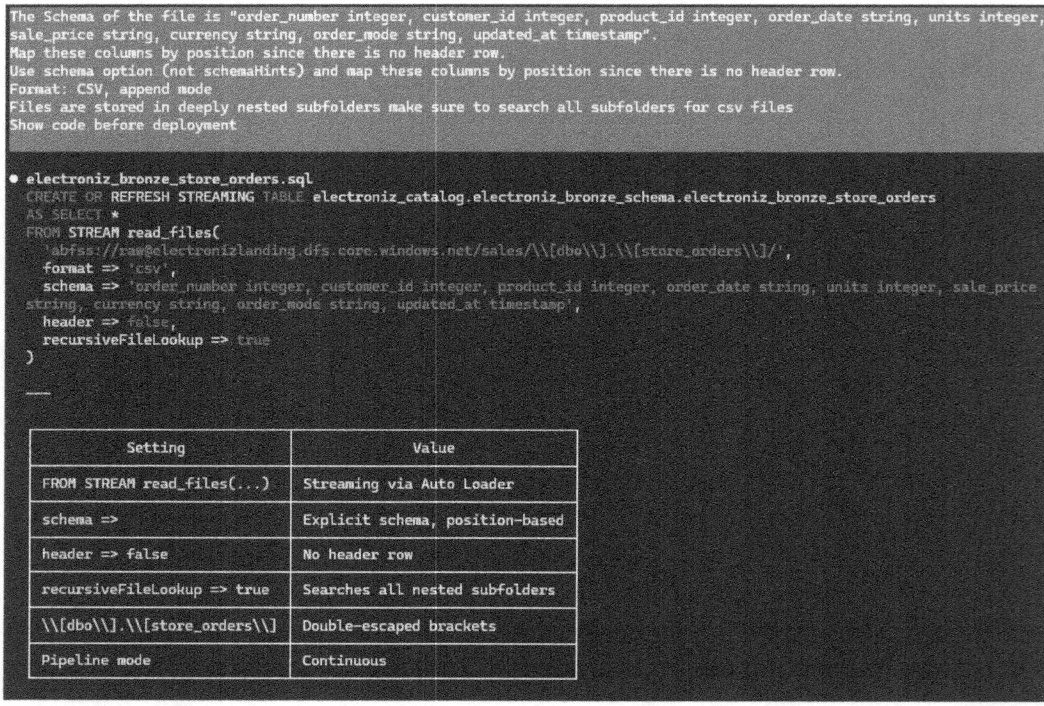

Figure 9.51: Claude Code for the electroniz_bronze_store_orders_pipeline

3. Return to the Databricks workspace. Using the menu on the left, click **Jobs & Pipelines**.

You should see the newly deployed pipeline created by Claude Code listed there.

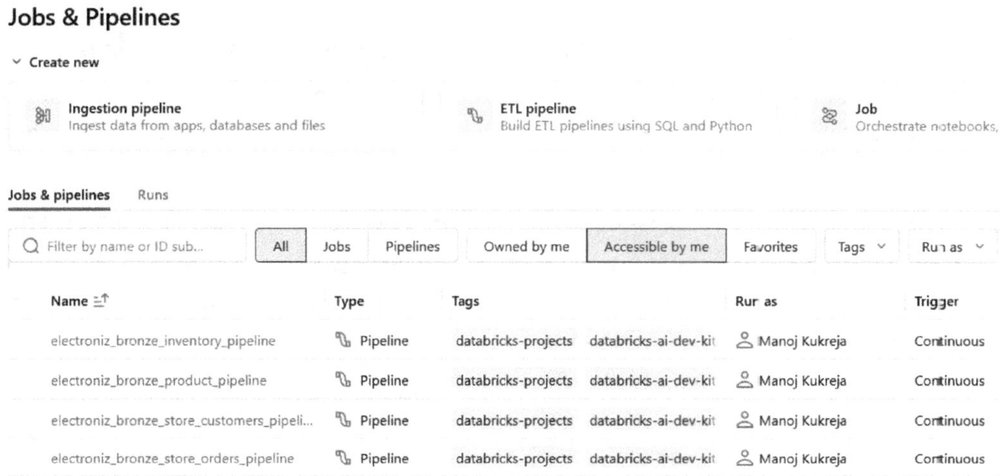

Figure 9.52: New streaming pipeline electroniz_bronze_store_orders_pipeline

4. Next, inspect the contents of the streaming table. Click **Catalog**, then navigate to **electroniz_catalog** > **electroniz_bronze_schema** > **electroniz_bronze_store_orders**. Click on **Sample Data**.

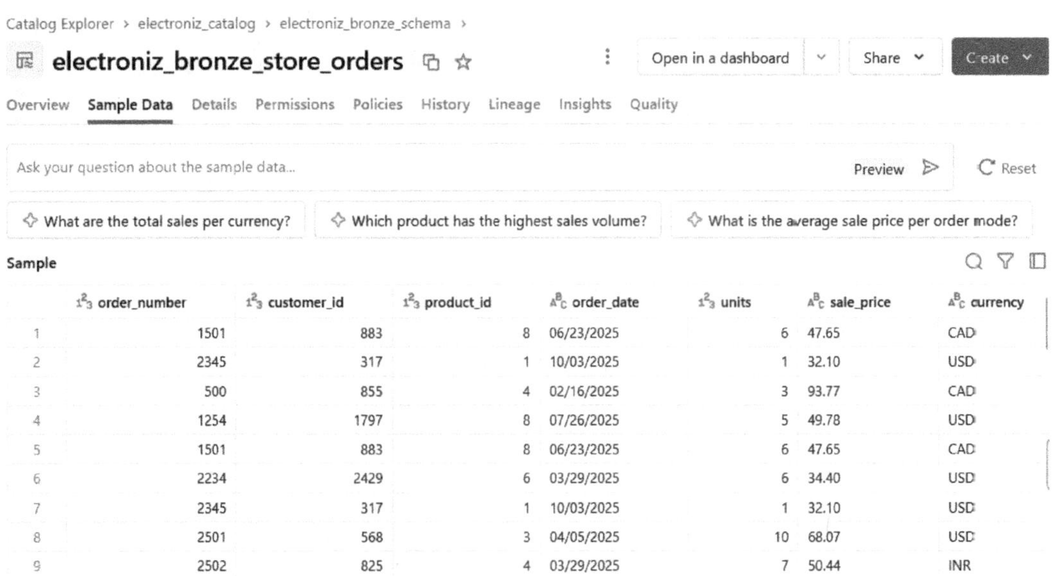

Figure 9.53: Data of electroniz_bronze_store_orders table

5. Click on **Jobs & Pipelines** and stop the **electroniz_bronze_store_orders_pipeline**.

Now that we have generated and deployed code for the Electroniz bronze pipeline for the store sales database, let's move on to the ecommerce data sources.

Creating the Electroniz bronze pipeline for streaming data

Electroniz streaming data represents transactional activity generated by customers through online purchases, capturing order details, purchased items, pricing, payments, and customer reviews.

Creating the Electroniz bronze pipeline for ecommerce transactions

Electroniz commerce data represents transactional activity generated by customers through online purchases, capturing order details, purchased items, pricing, payments, and related customer information.

The store orders table contains information about customer transactions made in physical stores.

1. Issue the following prompt on Claude Code to create the bronze store orders pipeline. Make sure to update the name of your Azure Data Lake Storage account to match your environment settings.

```
Create a new pipeline using SQL with details as follows
Pipeline Name: electroniz_bronze_ecommerce_pipeline
Data location: abfss://raw@electronizlanding.dfs.core.windows.net/
electroniz-ecommerce-ns/transactions/
Table:
electroniz_catalog.electroniz_bronze_schema.electroniz_bronze_ecomm_transac
tions
Continuously stream data from the source location using Auto Loader
Infer the schema automatically
Format: Avro, append mode
Files are stored in deeply nested subfolders make sure to search all
subfolders for avro files
The Avro files come from Azure Event Hub
Each message has a "Body" column containing a JSON array
Extract fields from the first element of the array
The first element has a nested "data" field with actual review content
Extract all fields from inside "data" as individual table columns
Must work without enabling any Delta Lake preview features
Show code before deployment
```

2. Claude Code will generate the code for the **electroniz_bronze_ecommerce_pipeline** as under.

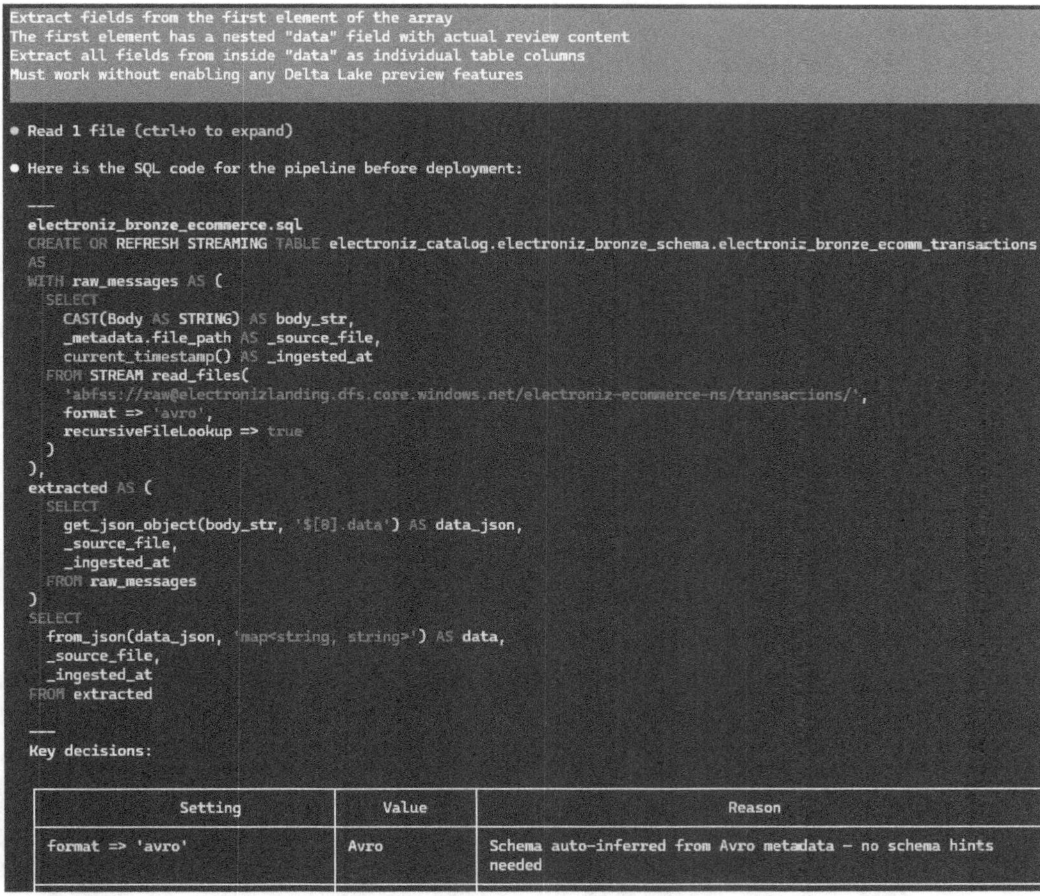

Figure 9.54: Claude Code for the electroniz_bronze_ecommerce_pipeline

3. This **electroniz_bronze_ecommerce_pipeline** differs from the stores sales database files. This pipeline reads Avro files that originate from Azure Event Hubs, which serves as the streaming ingestion layer for Electroniz transaction data. The Avro file consists of:

   - **Header**: Stores the embedded Avro schema along with file metadata and synchronization markers
   - **Data blocks**: Contain collections of serialized event records, with each block holding multiple events

The following is the schema of the record - one event captured from Event Hubs

```
{
  "type": "record",
  "name": "EventRecord",
  "fields": [
    {"name": "eventBody", "type": "bytes"},
    {"name": "enqueuedTime", "type": "string"},
    {"name": "partitionId", "type": "string"},
    {"name": "offset", "type": "string"},
    {"name": "sequenceNumber", "type": "long"}
  ]
}
```

Each Avro event record represents a single Event Hubs event and includes the:

- **Event payload**: Contains the business or application data (often JSON serialized as bytes
- **Event metadata**: Metadata such as enqueued time, partition ID, sequence number, offset, and system properties.

4. Notice the key decisions that Claude Code made to generate code for this pipeline.

Key decisions:

Setting	Value	Reason
format => 'avro'	Avro	Schema auto-inferred from Avro metadata - no schema hints needed
recursiveFileLookup => true	Enabled	Searches all nested subfolders
CAST(Body AS STRING)	Decodes binary	Event Hub Avro stores payload as bytes
get_json_object(body_str, '$[0].data')	Extracts data	Navigates to element [0] then into the data field
from_json(..., 'map<string, string>')	Dynamic fields	Captures all fields inside data without needing a fixed schema
Pipeline mode	Continuous	Real-time streaming

| *Note on individual columns: from_json with map<string, string> captures all fields from data dynamically as a single data map column (accessible as data['field_name']). Expanding to individual typed columns (e.g. data.*) requires a fixed struct schema - which would require using the variant type (a preview feature). This approach avoids that while still capturing all content. Once the actual field names are known from the data, the schema can be made explicit.*

Figure 9.55: Key decisions for the electroniz_bronze_ecommerce_pipeline

5. Go ahead and deploy this pipeline. Notice that Claude Code provided a recap of all the pipelines deployed so far.

● Pipeline deployed successfully. Here's a summary:

Property	Value
Pipeline Name	electroniz_bronze_ecommerce_pipeline
Pipeline ID	a13f87f5-1107-4f53-8ddf-d10259e0b2c8
Target Table	electroniz_catalog.electroniz_bronze_schema.electroniz_bronze_ecomm_transactions
Mode	Continuous (streaming)
Compute	Serverless

Here's a recap of all 5 pipelines created today:

Pipeline	Target Table	Status
electroniz_bronze_inventory_pipeline	electroniz_bronze_inventory	Created
electroniz_bronze_product_pipeline	electroniz_bronze_products	Created
electroniz_bronze_store_customers_pipeline	electroniz_bronze_store_customers	Created
electroniz_bronze_store_orders_pipeline	electroniz_bronze_store_orders	Created
electroniz_bronze_ecommerce_pipeline	electroniz_bronze_ecomm_transactions	Created

Figure 9.56: Recap of pipelines deployed by Claude Code so far

6. Return to the Databricks workspace. Using the menu on the left, click **Jobs & Pipelines**. You should see the newly deployed pipeline created by Claude Code listed there.

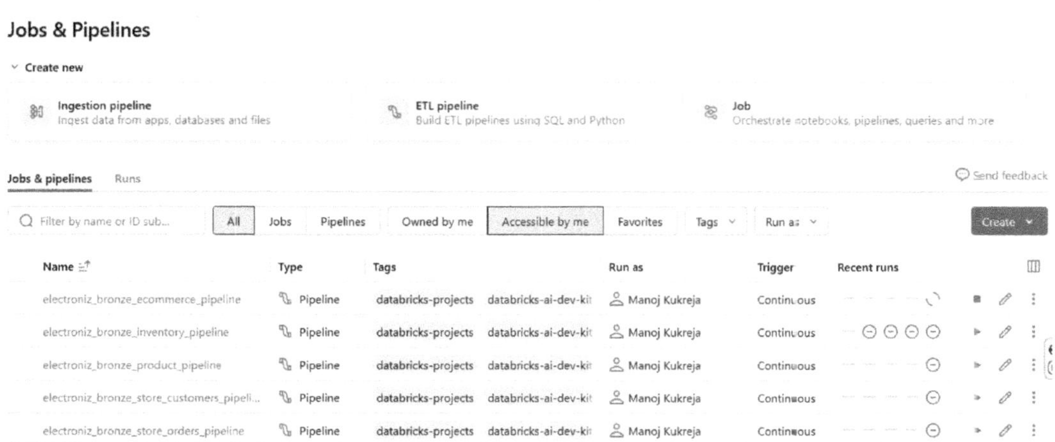

Figure 9.57: New streaming pipeline electroniz_bronze_ecommerce_pipeline

7. Next, inspect the contents of the streaming table. Click **Catalog**, then navigate to **electroniz_catalog** > **electroniz_bronze_schema** > **electroniz_bronze_ecomm_transactions**. Click on **Sample Data**.

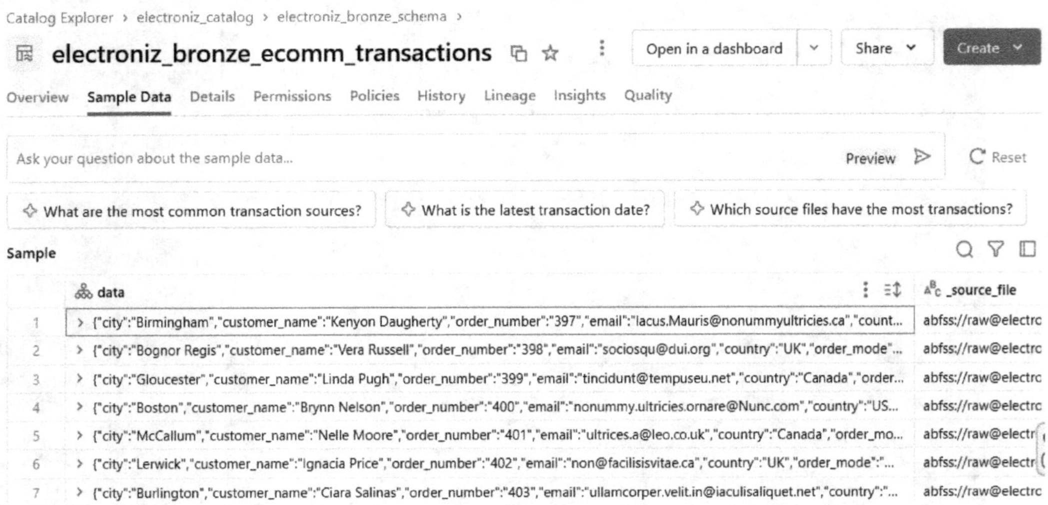

Figure 9.58: Data of electroniz_bronze_ecomm_transactions table

8. Click on **Jobs & Pipelines** and stop the **electroniz_bronze_ecommerce_pipeline**.

> **Note**
>
> The data column in the `electroniz_bronze_ecomm_transactions` table is defined as a MAP type. A Delta MAP column stores dynamic key–value pairs within a single column, making it well-suited for flexible or semi-structured data such as event properties or metadata.

Having completed the first bronze streaming pipeline for ecommerce transactions, we can now proceed to develop the bronze pipeline for product reviews.

Creating the Electroniz bronze pipeline for product reviews

Product reviews data consists of customer feedback collected across Electroniz's digital channels.

1. Issue the following prompt on Claude Code to create the bronze store orders pipeline:

```
Create a new pipeline using SQL with details as follows
Pipeline Name: electroniz_bronze_product_reviews_pipeline
Data location: abfss://raw@electronizlanding.dfs.core.windows.net/
electroniz-ecommerce-ns/reviews/
Table:
electroniz_catalog.electroniz_bronze_schema.electroniz_bronze_product_revie
ws
Continuously stream data from the source location using Auto Loader
Infer the schema automatically
Format: Avro, append mode
Files are stored in deeply nested subfolders make sure to search all
subfolders for avro files
The Avro files come from Azure Event Hub
Each message has a "Body" column containing a JSON array
Extract fields from the first element of the array
The first element has a nested "data" field with actual review content
Extract all fields from inside "data" as individual table columns
Must work without enabling any Delta Lake preview features
Show code before deployment
```

2. Claude Code will generate the code for the **electroniz_bronze_product_reviews_pipeline** as under.

```
CREATE OR REFRESH STREAMING TABLE electroniz_catalog.electroniz_bronze_schema.electroniz_bronze_product_reviews
AS
WITH raw_messages AS (
  SELECT
    CAST(Body AS STRING) AS body_str,
    _metadata.file_path AS _source_file,
    current_timestamp() AS _ingested_at
  FROM STREAM read_files(
    'abfss://raw@electronizlanding.dfs.core.windows.net/electroniz-ecommerce-ns/reviews/',
    format => 'avro',
    recursiveFileLookup => true
  )
),
extracted AS (
  SELECT
    get_json_object(body_str, '$[0].data') AS data_json,
    _source_file,
    _ingested_at
  FROM raw_messages
)
SELECT
  from_json(data_json, 'map<string, string>') AS data,
  _source_file,
  _ingested_at
FROM extracted

---
```

Setting	Value	Reason
format => 'avro'	Avro	Schema auto-inferred from Avro metadata
recursiveFileLookup => true	Enabled	Searches all nested subfolders
CAST(Body AS STRING)	Decodes binary	Event Hub Avro stores payload as bytes
get_json_object(body_str, '$[0].data')	Extracts data	Navigates to element [0] then into the data field
from_json(..., 'map<string, string>')	Dynamic fields	Captures all fields inside data without a fixed schema
Pipeline mode	Continuous	Real-time streaming

| *Note: Same approach as the ecommerce pipeline – data is stored as a map<string, string> column, accessible via data['field_name']. Individual typed columns require a fixed schema, which would need the variant type (preview feature).*

Figure 9.59: Claude Code for the electroniz_bronze_product_reviews_pipeline

3. Return to the Databricks workspace. Using the menu on the left, click **Jobs & Pipelines**. You should see the newly deployed pipeline created by Claude Code listed there.

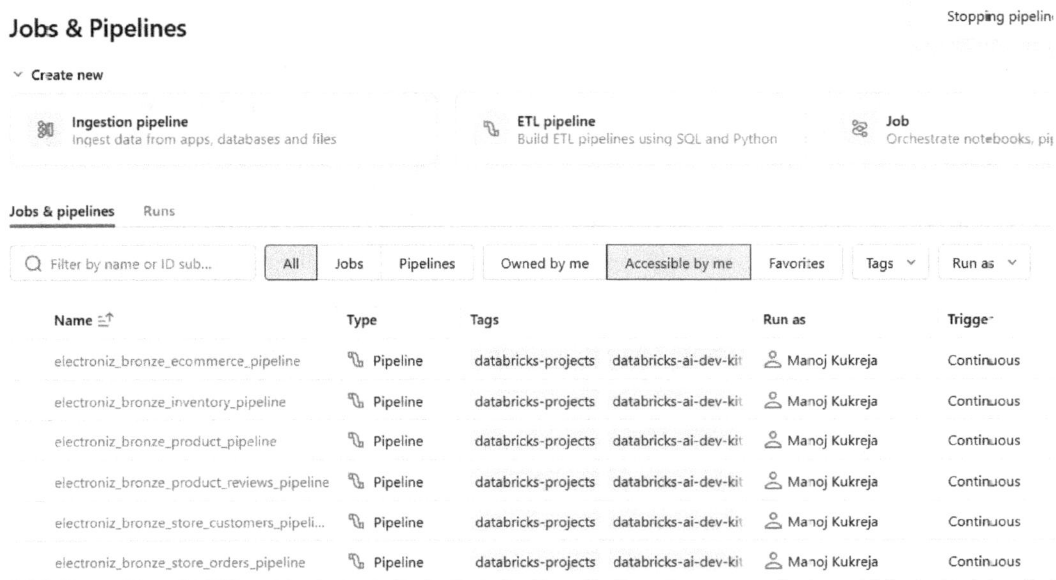

Figure 9.60: New streaming pipeline electroniz_bronze_product_reviews_pipeline

4. Next, inspect the contents of the streaming table. Click **Catalog**, then navigate to **electroniz_catalog** > **electroniz_bronze_schema** > **electroniz_bronze_product_reviews**. Click on **Sample Data**.

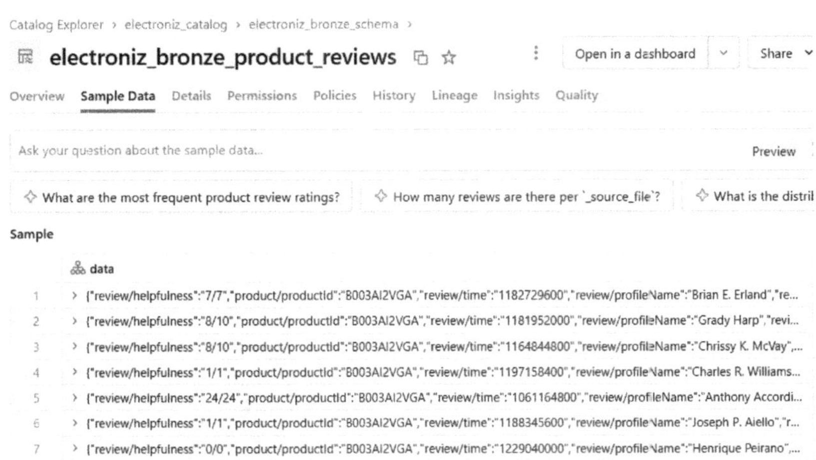

Figure 9.61: Data of electroniz_bronze_product_reviews table

5. Click on **Jobs & Pipelines** and stop the **electroniz_bronze_product_reviews_pipeline**.

The bronze pipeline for product reviews is now complete, so we can proceed to the bronze pipeline for ecommerce website logs.

Creating the Electroniz bronze pipeline for ecommerce website logs

The e-commerce website logs are web server-generated records that capture detailed information about user activity, system behavior, and transactions as visitors interact with the website. These logs are automatically produced by web servers, applications, and supporting services and are primarily used for monitoring, analytics, security, and troubleshooting.

1. Issue the following prompt on Claude Code to create the e-commerce website logs pipeline:

```
Create a new pipeline using SQL with details as follows
Pipeline Name: electroniz_bronze_website_logs_pipeline
Data location: abfss://raw@electronizlanding.dfs.core.windows.net/
ecommerce_logs/
Table:
electroniz_catalog.electroniz_bronze_schema.electroniz_bronze_website_logs
Make sure to reference the complete table as suggested including catalog
and schema
Continuously stream data from the source location using Auto Loader
Infer the schema automatically
Format: JSON, append mode
Files are stored in deeply nested subfolders make sure to search all
subfolders for json files
Show code before deployment
```

2. Claude Code will generate the code for the **electroniz_bronze_website_logs_pipeline** as under.

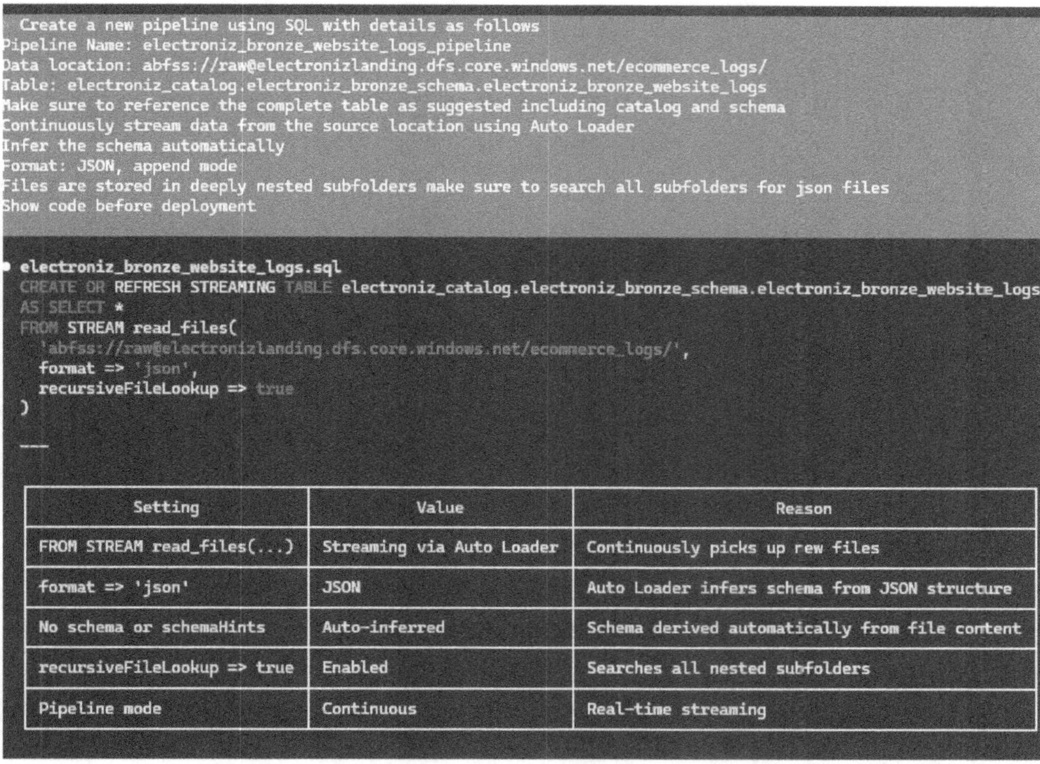

Figure 9.62: Claude Code for the electroniz_bronze_website_lcgs_pipeline

3. Return to the Databricks workspace. Using the menu on the left, click **Jobs & Pipelines**. You should see the newly deployed pipeline created by Claude Code listed there.

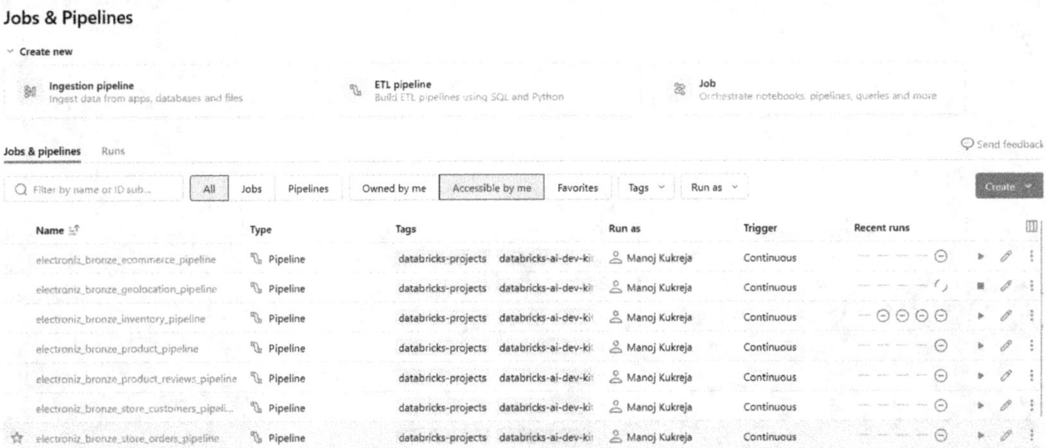

Figure 9.63: New streaming pipeline electroniz_bronze_website_logs_pipeline

4. Next, inspect the contents of the streaming table. Click **Catalog**, then navigate to **electroniz_catalog** > **electroniz_bronze_schema** > **electroniz_bronze_website_logs**. Click on **Sample Data**.

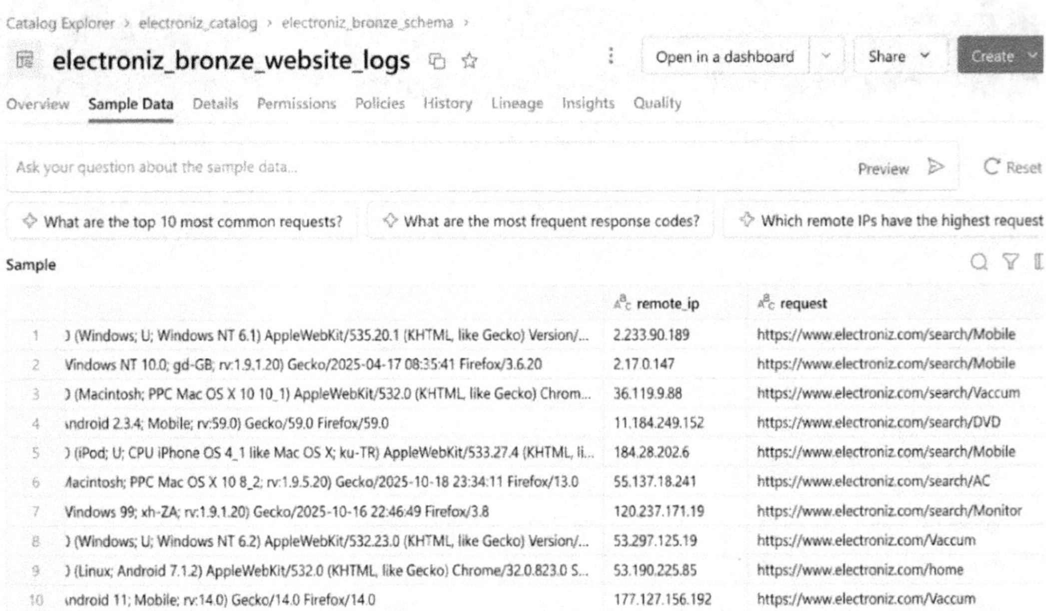

Figure 9.64: Data of electroniz_bronze_website_logs table

5. Click on **Jobs & Pipelines** and stop the **electroniz_bronze_website_logs_pipeline**.

The bronze streaming pipelines are now complete, and we can move on to creating the pipeline for bronze geolocation data.

Creating the Electroniz bronze pipeline for geolocation data

The geolocation data maps IP addresses to their corresponding countries, enabling IP-to-country conversions for geographic identification. The geolocation pipeline processes IP-to-country reference data consisting of `ip1`, `ip2`, and `country_code` fields. The `ip1` and `ip2` columns define the start and end of an IP address range, while `country_code` identifies the country associated with that range. This pipeline ingests and maintains geolocation mappings that enable downstream datasets to enrich transactional or event data with geographic context based on IP addresses.

1. Issue the following prompt on Claude Code to create the bronze geolocation pipeline:

```
Create a new pipeline using SQL with details as follows
Pipeline Name: electroniz_bronze_geolocation_pipeline
Data location: abfss://raw@electronizlanding.dfs.core.windows.net/
geolocation/
Table:
electroniz_catalog.electroniz_bronze_schema.electroniz_bronze_geolocation
Make sure to reference the complete table as suggested including catalog
and schema
Continuously stream data from the source location using Auto Loader
The Schema of the file is " ip1 string, ip2 string, country_code string,
country_name string"
Use schema option (not schemaHints) and map these columns by position since
there is no header row.
Format: CSV, append mode
Files are stored in deeply nested subfolders make sure to search all
subfolders for csv files
Show code before deployment
```

2. Claude Code will generate the code for the **electroniz_bronze_geolocation_pipeline** as under.

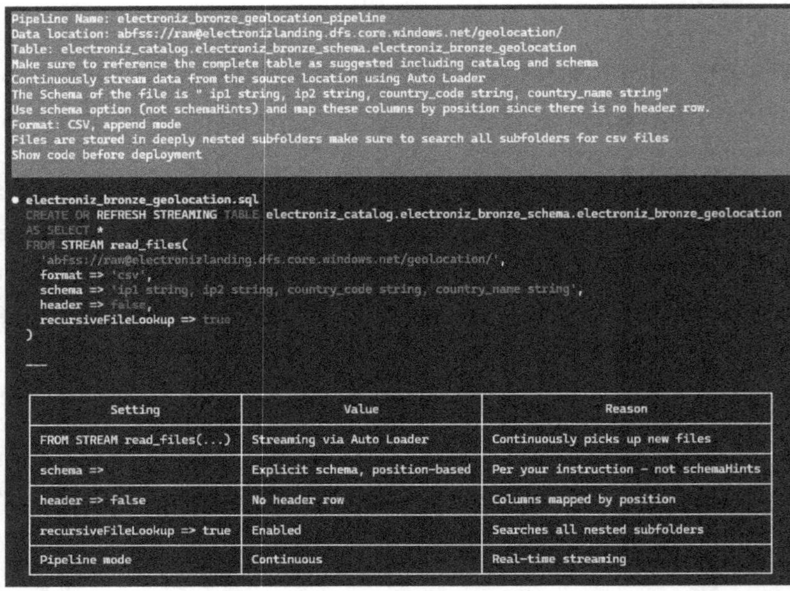

Figure 9.65: Claude Code for the electroniz_bronze_geolocation_pipeline

3. Return to the Databricks workspace. Using the menu on the left, click **Jobs & Pipelines**. You should see the newly deployed pipeline created by Claude Code listed there.

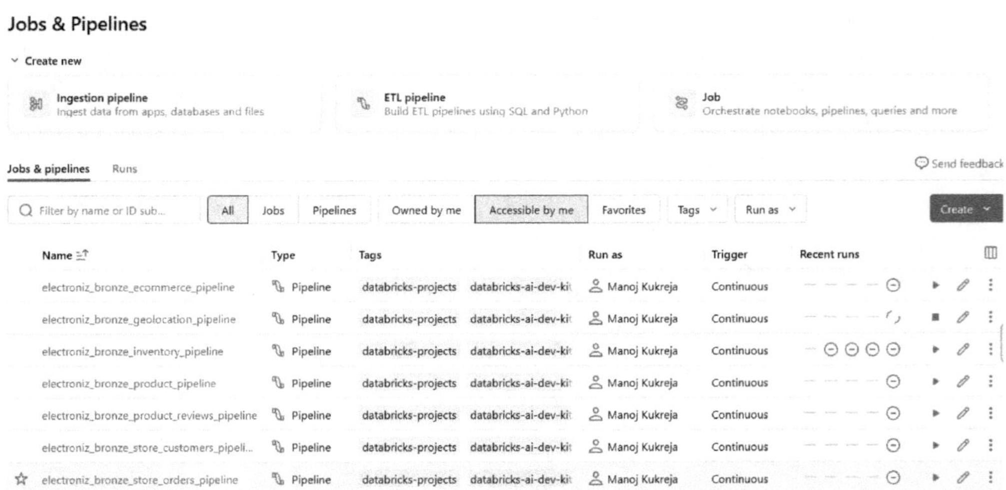

Figure 9.66: New streaming pipeline electroniz_bronze_geolocation_pipeline

4. Next, inspect the contents of the streaming table. Click **Catalog**, then navigate to **electroniz_catalog** > **electroniz_bronze_schema** > **electroniz_bronze_geolocation**. Click on **Sample Data**.

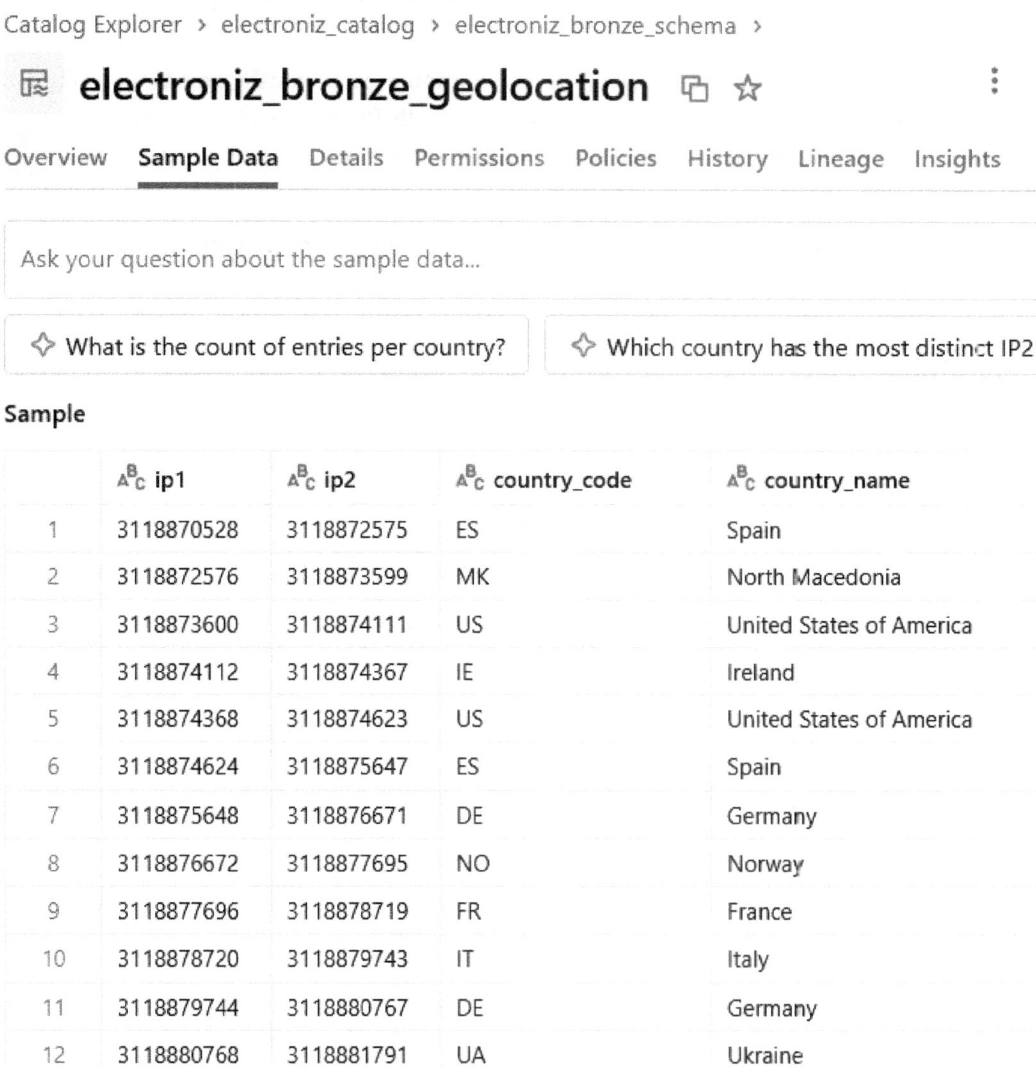

	ip1	ip2	country_code	country_name
1	3118870528	3118872575	ES	Spain
2	3118872576	3118873599	MK	North Macedonia
3	3118873600	3118874111	US	United States of America
4	3118874112	3118874367	IE	Ireland
5	3118874368	3118874623	US	United States of America
6	3118874624	3118875647	ES	Spain
7	3118875648	3118876671	DE	Germany
8	3118876672	3118877695	NO	Norway
9	3118877696	3118878719	FR	France
10	3118878720	3118879743	IT	Italy
11	3118879744	3118880767	DE	Germany
12	3118880768	3118881791	UA	Ukraine

Figure 9.67: Data of electroniz_bronze_geolocation table

5. Click on **Jobs & Pipelines** and stop the **electroniz_bronze_geolocation_pipeline**.

Next, we move on to developing the Bronze pipeline for currency conversion data.

Creating the Electroniz bronze pipeline for currency conversion data

Currency conversion data contains reference information used to translate monetary values between currencies consistently and accurately. It typically includes exchange rates between currency pairs, along with the context needed to apply those rates correctly in transactions and analytics.

1. Issue the following prompt on Claude Code to create the bronze currency conversion pipeline:

```
Create a new pipeline using SQL with details as follows
Pipeline Name: electroniz_bronze_currency_pipeline
Data location: abfss://raw@electronizlanding.dfs.core.windows.net/
currency_conversion/
Table:
electroniz_catalog.electroniz_bronze_schema.electroniz_bronze_currency
Make sure to reference the complete table as suggested including catalog
and schema
Continuously stream data from the source location using Auto Loader
Infer the schema automatically
Format: JSON, append mode
Files are stored in deeply nested subfolders make sure to search all
subfolders for json files
Show code before deployment
```

2. Claude Code will generate the code for the **electroniz_bronze_currency_pipeline** as under.

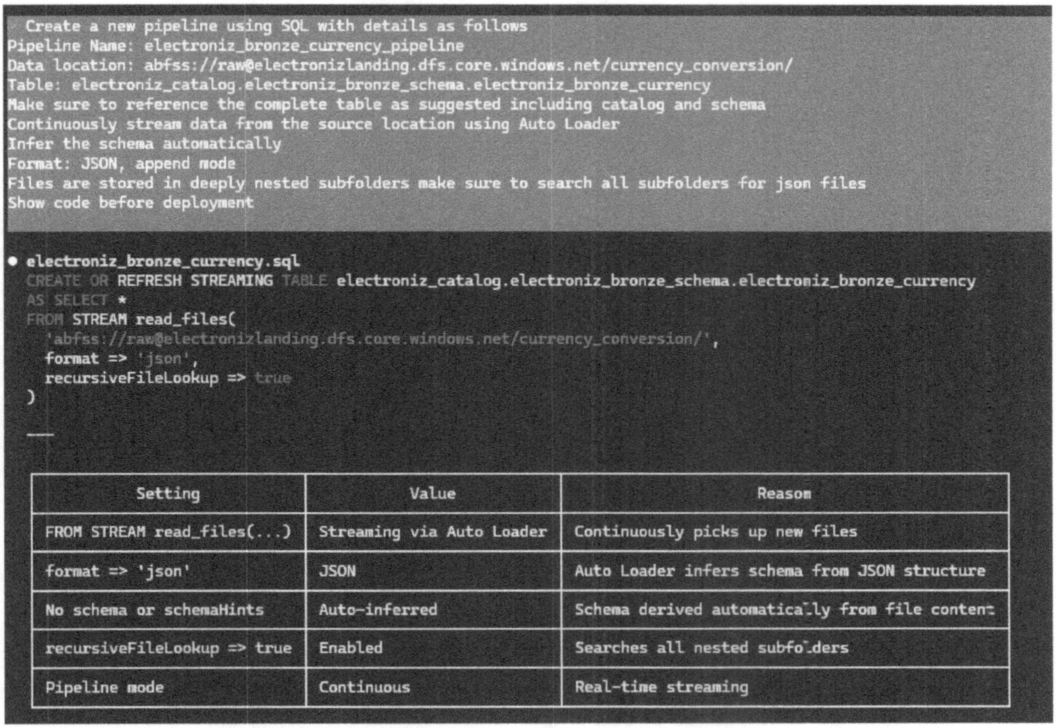

Figure 9.68: Claude Code for the electroniz_bronze_currency_pipeline

3. Return to the Databricks workspace. Using the menu on the left, click **Jobs & Pipelines**. You should see the newly deployed pipeline created by Claude Code listed there.

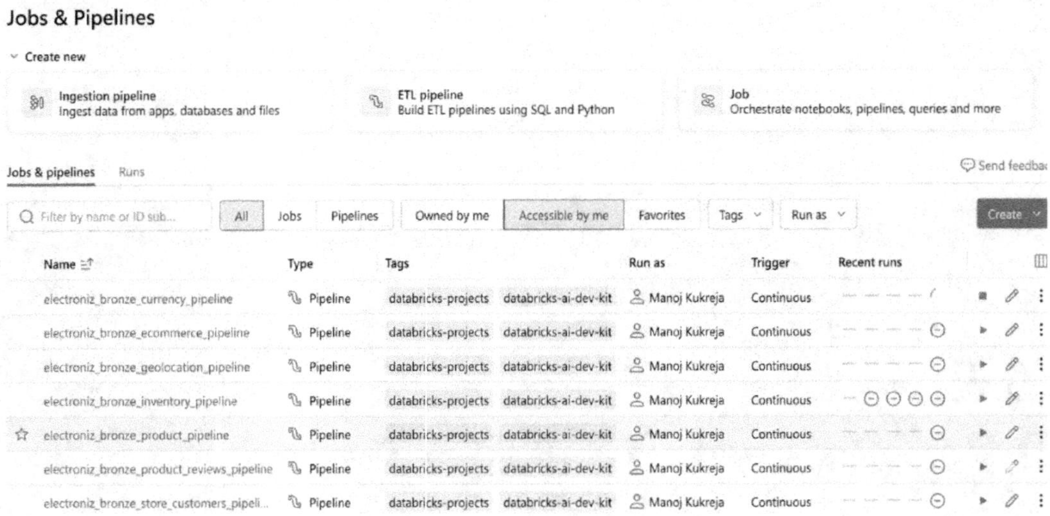

Figure 9.69: New streaming pipeline electroniz_bronze_currency_pipeline

4. Next, inspect the contents of the streaming table. Click **Catalog**, then navigate to **electroniz_catalog** > **electroniz_bronze_schema** > **electroniz_bronze_currency**. Click on **Sample Data**.

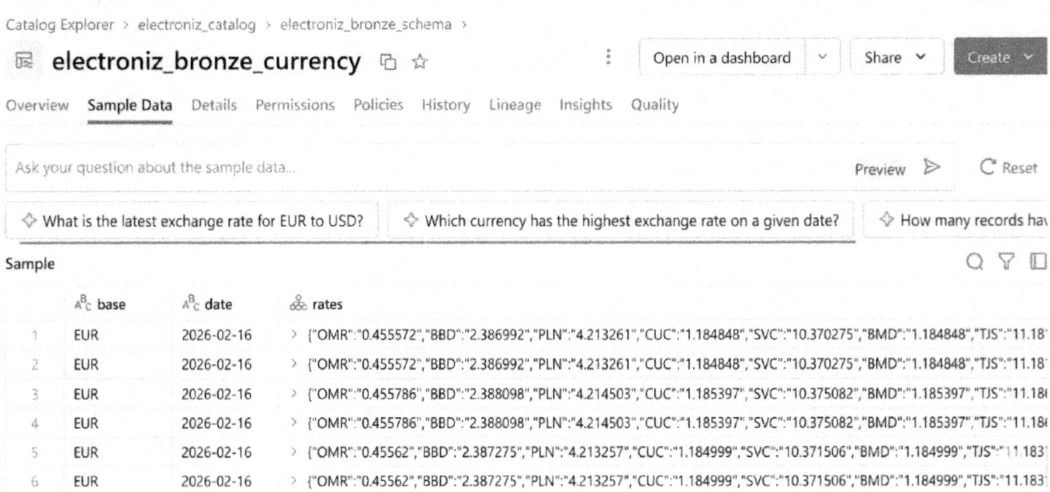

Figure 9.70: Data of electroniz_bronze_currency table

5. Click on **Jobs & Pipelines** and stop the **electroniz_bronze_currency_pipeline**.

To recap, we used Claude Code to generate multiple bronze-layer pipelines for the Electroniz data platform. These pipelines form the first structured layer after raw ingestion and are designed to preserve data fidelity while supporting scalable, reliable downstream processing.

In addition to improving consistency and design quality, using Claude Code resulted in significant time savings during pipeline development. Tasks that would typically require extensive manual effort—such as defining ingestion logic, configuring schemas, setting up Delta streaming tables, and preparing deployment workflows—were completed in a fraction of the time.

Below is the list of nine bronze data pipelines that were generated and deployed using Claude Code.

● Here are all 9 deployed Lakeflow pipelines:

#	Pipeline Name	Pipeline ID	Created
1	electroniz_bronze_inventory_pipeline	57e500c3	2026-03-18 17:37
2	electroniz_bronze_product_pipeline	085217e2	2026-03-18 17:55
3	electroniz_bronze_store_customers_pipeline	025c58ea	2026-03-18 20:34
4	electroniz_bronze_store_orders_pipeline	34bd3c1d	2026-03-18 21:00
5	electroniz_bronze_ecommerce_pipeline	a13f87f5	2026-03-18 22:22
6	electroniz_bronze_product_reviews_pipeline	850a6278	2026-03-19 00:38
7	electroniz_bronze_geolocation_pipeline	0c56240c	2026-03-19 01:00
8	electroniz_bronze_website_logs_pipeline	7b3e761d	2026-03-19 01:09
9	electroniz_bronze_currency_pipeline	4d0b6ccc	2026-03-19 01:15

All pipelines target electroniz_catalog.electroniz_bronze_schema and are configured for continuous serverless streaming.

Figure 9.71: List of all bronze layer pipelines deployed by Claude Code

You should see the same list of pipelines in the Jobs & Pipelines section of the Databricks workspace. To remain cost-efficient, we have intentionally paused the pipelines to free up compute resources. These pipelines can be restarted at any time and will be brought back online when we are ready to proceed with integration testing.

Additionally, you should be able to see the list of nine bronze data tables in the `electroniz_bronze_schema`.

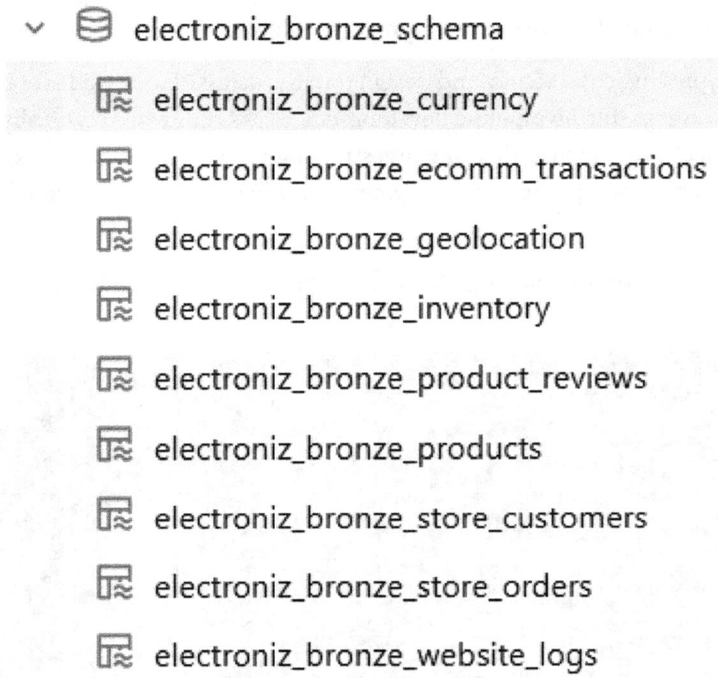

Figure 9.72: List of all bronze layer tables

At this point, our work on the Electroniz bronze layer creation is complete. The bronze tables serve as the authoritative, immutable foundation for silver-layer generation, capturing ingested data in its original form. By deliberately postponing cleansing, deduplication, and business logic, these tables enable silver pipelines to consistently standardize, validate, and enrich the data. This clear separation of responsibilities strengthens pipeline resilience, supports reprocessing as rules evolve, and ensures reliable downstream analytics.

We saw earlier how Claude Code reduced development cycles, minimized iteration overhead, and allowed the team to focus more on validation and architecture rather than boilerplate implementation. This efficiency gain becomes especially valuable when building multiple pipelines with similar patterns at scale. However, GenAI systems can also introduce risks, most notably hallucinations, where the model produces outputs that appear coherent but are factually incorrect or unsupported by the underlying data. Let's explore this phenomenon in greater depth and understand how to manage it effectively.

GenAI hallucinations and variations

Generative AI is still an emerging technology, and as such, it can sometimes produce **hallucinated code**—outputs that look syntactically valid and logically sound but are ultimately inaccurate, incomplete, or incompatible with real-world systems. In software development, relying on such outputs without scrutiny can introduce hidden defects, security risks, operational issues, or unnecessary rework. To reduce these risks, any code generated by GenAI should be thoroughly reviewed, tested, and validated against official documentation, and used to accelerate development rather than to replace sound engineering judgment.

Accordingly, outputs produced by Claude Code should be viewed as suggested implementations rather than definitive solutions. They must be carefully reviewed, tested, and cross-checked before deployment to avoid the risk of introducing incorrect or misleading behavior into production systems.

In addition to hallucinations, Claude Code produces different code in every session because generative AI systems are probabilistic rather than deterministic. Even when given exactly the same prompt, Claude may produce variations in structure, naming, ordering, or implementation details as it balances multiple valid ways to satisfy the request. These differences do not necessarily indicate errors; instead, they reflect the model's ability to adapt, reason, and generate contextually appropriate solutions rather than replaying a fixed response. This means that Claude Code outputs should be treated as representative implementations, not exact templates. While the overall logic and architectural intent are usually consistent, minor differences are expected across sessions.

For this reason, it is important to carefully review generated code for consistency and correctness. Because Claude Code can produce different implementations across sessions, the Electroniz bronze pipeline code you generate may vary from what is shown here. To address this, the exact versions of the generated pipelines are available in the Packt course Git repository link below:

`https://github.com/PacktPublishing/Data-Engineering-with-Apache-Spark-Databricks-and-Lakehouse-Second-Edition/tree/main/chapter9/sql.`

Figure 9.73 shows the SQL files available in the Packt course Git repository, which you can use as a reference point when comparing them with the versions generated by GenAI. In certain cases, the generated pipeline code may deviate from the intended logic, and you may need to override it with the Git repository version as the authoritative source.

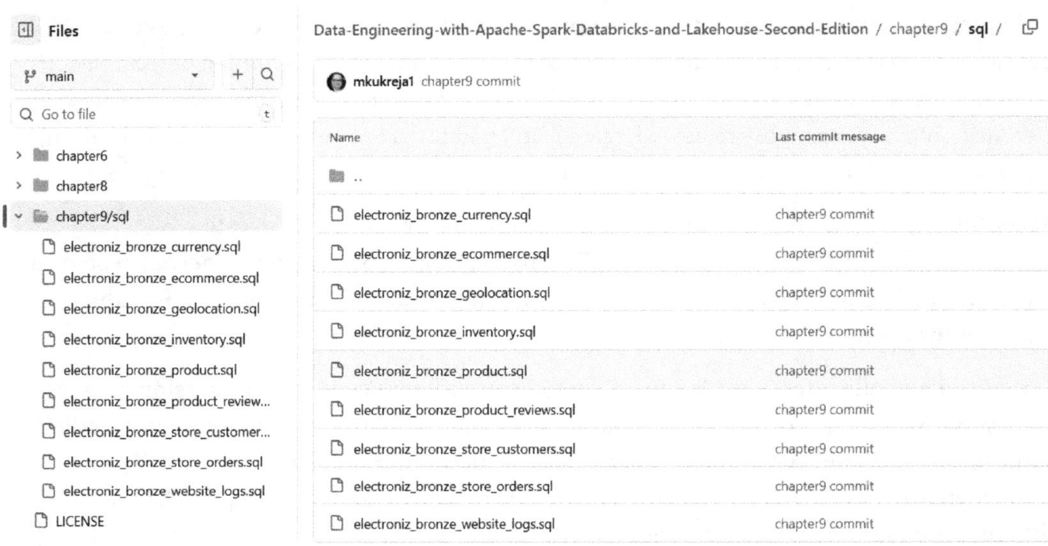

Figure 9.73: Master copy of bronze layer pipelines

Now that we can safely infer that GenAI is probabilistic rather than deterministic, developers should remain cautious and consistently validate generated code against authoritative sources to ensure correctness and reliability. This brings us to the end of the chapter, where we built multiple bronze pipelines for Electroniz; let's conclude by summarizing the key concepts and learnings covered throughout this section.

Summary

In this chapter, we take a decisive step forward in the lakehouse journey by transforming raw data from the landing zone into the bronze layer of the Electroniz Lakehouse. We introduced the bronze layer as the first structured stage in the Medallion Architecture, where raw, often messy source data is ingested and stored in structured Delta tables with minimal transformation.

Through an in-depth exploration of its purpose, design principles, and implementation, the chapter explains how the bronze layer preserves data fidelity while enabling scalable and reliable downstream processing. This chapter also introduced the practical use of Claude Code as an accelerator for building bronze-layer pipelines. By leveraging generative AI, we demonstrated how repetitive, boilerplate-driven ingestion logic can be rapidly generated while still adhering to lakehouse best practices. Claude Code is used to propose pipeline structures, ingestion patterns, and deployment configurations, helping reduce development time and improve consistency across pipelines. At the same time, the chapter emphasizes the importance of reviewing, validating, and testing all generated code, positioning Claude Code as a productivity aid rather than a replacement for sound data engineering judgment.

By the end of the chapter, readers gained both a practical understanding of how to build bronze pipelines and a conceptual appreciation of why this layer is essential for creating a maintainable, resilient, and trustworthy modern data platform—foundational ideas that underpin the advanced data engineering patterns explored throughout the book.

In *Chapter 10,* we will learn how to design and build the silver layer of the Electroniz Lakehouse data platform by transforming bronze-layer data into clean, standardized, and analytics-ready datasets. Once again, we will apply GenAI-assisted techniques to accelerate development while focusing on data quality, validation, deduplication, and enrichment—laying the foundation for reliable downstream analytics and business insights.

Get this book's PDF version and more

10

Building the Silver Layer of the Medallion Architecture using Gen AI

In the previous chapters, we traversed the lakehouse journey by ingesting raw data from the landing zone into the bronze layer of the Electroniz Lakehouse. In this chapter, we take the next major step forward in our lakehouse journey. Building on the bronze layer data, we begin shaping it into meaningful data that end-users can trust and consume. Our focus will be on constructing the **silver** layer of the Electroniz Lakehouse—a critical stage of the Medallion Architecture that transforms raw, chaotic data into clean, curated datasets that power analytics, reporting, and machine learning.

By the end of this chapter, you will have a deeper understanding of how the silver layer is constructed and why it is extremely essential in designing a scalable, maintainable, and trustworthy modern data platform. These concepts will form the backbone of every advanced data engineering pattern we explore in the rest of the book.

In this chapter, we will explore:

- Understanding the silver layer
- High-level plan for building the silver layer
- Preparing resources for the Electroniz silver pipeline
- Developing the Electroniz silver layer pipelines using Genie code
- Validating data quality
- Handling Gen AI inconsistencies

Technical requirements

This chapter assumes the following technical prerequisites:

- An active Azure free account. You may recall that we created this account in *Chapter 3, Data Engineering on Microsoft Azure*.
- Access to the Packt Publishing GitHub repository to download the code samples and datasets used throughout this chapter. You can download the example project and code for this book by following the instructions in the *Download the example code files* section in the *Preface* of this book. This chapter's code files are included in the downloadable code bundle.

Understanding the silver layer

In *Chapter 4*, we explored the Lakehouse architecture as a defining characteristic of next-generation data platforms. One of its greatest strengths is adherence to no-copy data principles, which reinforce a **single source of truth** across all analytical use cases. In *Chapter 9*, we introduced the bronze layer as the Medallion Architecture's initial structured zone, where raw, messy source data is ingested and stored in minimally processed Delta tables.

In *Chapter 6*, we highlighted several key activities performed in the silver layer. Let's take a moment to revisit and reinforce those core responsibilities:

- **Deduplication**: Identify and remove duplicate records, which commonly arise from **Change Data Capture** (**CDC**) processes that generate multiple versions of the same record.
- **Type Casting**: Correct data types for fields that are ingested with incorrect or inconsistent data formats.
- **Data Consistency**: Resolve inconsistencies that occur when the same information is represented differently across multiple datasets.
- **Data Standardization**: Standardize data to address interoperability challenges, particularly those caused by geographic, regional, or source-system differences.
- **Data Uniformity**: Harmonize variations in data representation across datasets to ensure a consistent analytical view.
- **Orphans and Missing Values**: Address records that fail lookup validations, contain null or missing values, or violate referential integrity constraints.
- **PII Redaction**: Anonymize or pseudonymize **Personally Identifiable Information** (**PII**) to meet privacy and compliance requirements.

Beyond deduplication, validation, and standardization, the silver layer extends this foundation by managing **slowly changing dimensions** (**SCDs**). It is also the stage where relationships across datasets are modeled, and more complex **Master Data Management** (**MDM**) challenges are addressed. As a result, the silver layer becomes the organization's **trusted, analytics-ready source of truth**—consistent, reliable, and optimized for broad consumption across the enterprise. In the sections that follow, we will explore each of these key activities in greater depth, except for PII redaction, which is covered separately in *Chapter 12*.

Handling slowly changing dimensions

For decades, the Kimball methodology has served as a foundational approach to dimensional data modeling. As Ralph Kimball famously observed, "*The notion of time pervades every corner of the data warehouse.*" In the context of data analytics, this underscores that analytical systems are inherently temporal. At a high level, modern analytics involves aggregating data that continuously evolves over time. The challenge, however, is that this evolution is not limited to the ingestion of new data. It also encompasses revisions, corrections, and transformations of historical data, making time a critical and complex dimension in analytical design.

The Kimball methodology addresses this challenge by defining a set of well-established strategies—commonly referred to as SCD types—for capturing and managing dimensional change over time. In practice, once an SCD strategy is selected, its implementation within a data warehouse is relatively straightforward. Mature SQL capabilities and reliable ACID-compliant transaction support provide the foundation for enforcing data integrity, tracking historical states, and applying changes in a controlled and predictable manner.

Handling slowly changing dimensions has long been a fundamental challenge in data warehousing. Data practitioners must balance the need to preserve historical changes with the requirement to maintain accurate and consistent relationships to fact tables. While the Kimball methodology defines up to seven distinct approaches for managing SCDs, this discussion will focus on the three most used methods.

SCD Type 1

This approach is commonly known as the *overwrite* method. Under this strategy, any change to a dimension record replaces the existing value associated with the same key. While this method is straightforward to implement, it has a significant limitation: the overwrite operation eliminates all prior history. As a result, not only is the historical evolution of the dimension lost, but past factual records are also implicitly reinterpreted based on the updated state of the dimension, compromising historical analytical accuracy.

Figure 10.1 illustrates the customer dimension before and after an address change for a given customer.

ID	name	address	Phone
1	Julie Rich	Ap #255-3031 Dui Avenue, Billings, USA	1-528-884-4331
2	Eden Byrd	Ap #476-7527 Aenean Road, Harrisburg, USA	1-375-910-8385
3	Magee Cash	**P.O. Box 333, 5820 Vel Avenue, New Haven, USA**	1-853-137-7417

Change of Address

ID	name	address	phone
1	Julie Rich	Ap #255-3031 Dui Avenue, Billings, USA	1-528-884-4331
2	Eden Byrd	Ap #476-7527 Aenean Road, Harrisburg, USA	1-375-910-8385
3	Magee Cash	**687 Magnis Rd., New Haven, USA**	1-853-137-7417

Figure 10.1: SCD Type 1 implementation for an address change record

Losing the historical information can have serious consequences, especially when fact table aggregations are influenced by changes in dimensional attributes. Without a preserved history, it becomes extremely difficult—if not impossible—to trace and explain why an aggregated value changed over time.

Organizations typically choose SCD Type 1 when only the *current* value of an attribute matters and historical changes add no analytical or regulatory value—such as correcting bad data, updating non-critical master attributes, or supporting operational dashboards where the latest truth is all that's required. However, in most situations it becomes essential to retain the full history of changes to support accurate decision-making, regulatory compliance, and reproducible analytics. In such cases, SCD Type 2 is the preferred approach, and we will explore it in detail in the next section.

SCD Type 2

This approach is commonly referred to as the "*add a new record*" method. Under this strategy, any change to the dimension results in the insertion of a **new** row, which is flagged as *current* or *active*, while the previous version of the record is marked as *expired* or *inactive*. Both the current and historical versions are linked through a **surrogate key**. The following image demonstrates the customer dimension before and after applying the SCD Type 2 method.

ID	name	address	phone	startdate	enddate	status
1	Julie Rich	Ap #255-3031 Dui Avenue, Billings, USA	1-528-884-4331	2017-05-12		Current
2	Eden Byrd	Ap #476-7527 Aenean Road, Harrisburg, USA	1-375-910-8385	2020-04-19		Current
3	Magee Cash	**P.O. Box 333, 5820 Vel Avenue, New Haven, USA**	1-853-137-7417	**2019-02-22**		**Current**

Change of Address

ID	name	address	phone	startdate	enddate	status
1	Julie Rich	Ap #255-3031 Dui Avenue, Billings, USA	1-528-884-4331	2017-05-12		Current
2	Eden Byrd	Ap #476-7527 Aenean Road, Harrisburg, USA	1-375-910-8385	2020-04-19		Current
3	Magee Cash	P.O. Box 333, 5820 Vel Avenue, New Haven, USA	1-853-137-7417	2019-02-22	**2022-03-24**	**Expired**
3	Magee Cash	**687 Magnis Rd., New Haven, USA**	1-853-137-7417	**2022-03-24**		**Current**

Figure 10.2: SCD Type 2 implementation for an address change record

At the table level, SCD Type 2 is typically implemented by adding **StartDate** and **EndDate** timestamp columns to track each row's validity period, along with a Status indicator to distinguish active from expired records. Observe that the previous record has been marked as *expired* and its **EndDate** has been updated. A new record reflecting the latest address is then **inserted**, with its **StartDate** set to match the **EndDate** of the prior record.

The SCD Type 2 approach enables **chronological** tracking of changes over time while preserving accurate, time-aligned relationships to fact tables. Although this method provides significantly greater analytical value than SCD Type 1, its implementation is more complex and requires careful handling of versioning and effective dates.

SCD Type 3

This approach is commonly referred to as the *"add a new field"* method. With each change, both the current and the immediately preceding values are stored as separate columns within the same dimension record. Compared to SCD Type 2, SCD Type 3 is simpler to implement; however, it provides only **limited** historical tracking, retaining visibility into the current state and a single prior version.

The following image demonstrates the customer dimension before and after applying the SCD Type 3 method.

ID	name	address	previous_address	Phone
1	Julie Rich	Ap #255-3031 Dui Avenue, Billings, USA		1-528-884-4331
2	Eden Byrd	Ap #476-7527 Aenean Road, Harrisburg, USA		1-375-910-8385
3	Magee Cash	**P.O. Box 333, 5820 Vel Avenue, New Haven, USA**		1-853-137-7417

Change of Address

ID	name	address	previous_address	Phone
1	Julie Rich	Ap #255-3031 Dui Avenue, Billings, USA		1-528-884-4331
2	Eden Byrd	Ap #476-7527 Aenean Road, Harrisburg, USA		1-375-910-8385
3	Magee Cash	**687 Magnis Rd., New Haven, USA**	**P.O. Box 333, 5820 Vel Avenue, New Haven, USA**	1-853-137-7417

Figure 10.3: SCD Type 3 implementation for an address change record

Each attribute in the dimension table maintains both a current and a previous state. When the dimension is initially created, the current state is populated with the latest available data, while the previous state remains empty until a change occurs.

In many respects, SCD Type 2 is regarded as the primary technique for managing slowly changing dimensions. It is important to note that the fundamental goal of SCD is not merely to preserve historical records, but to ensure an accurate and time-appropriate association between dimension data and fact tables. Traditionally, this requirement to update dimension records appears to conflict with the principle of immutability commonly associated with data lakes and modern warehouses. However, recent advancements in storage and processing frameworks—such as Delta Lake—have significantly simplified implementing SCD patterns, enabling efficient change management while maintaining data integrity.

> **Note**
>
> Choosing the right SCD method is driven by business needs and analytical requirements. Use Type 1 when history is not important, Type 2 when full historical accuracy is required, and Type 3 or hybrids when only limited or mixed historical views are needed.

As we develop the Electroniz silver layer pipelines, we will explore the various SCD types and their roles in effectively managing dimensional changes. For now, we will focus on how data quality is handled in Databricks.

Handling data quality in Lakeflow Declarative Pipelines

In *Chapter 4*, we emphasized that data quality and reliability are a foundational requirement for building trust among end users. If not properly handled, poor data quality doesn't stay isolated—it propagates and compounds downstream. Once trust is lost, even high-quality data may be questioned, and the value of the data platform drops sharply.

In data engineering, data quality is managed through a coordinated mix of clearly defined rules, governance standards, engineered controls, and automated validation processes. The following describes a practical, end-to-end approach commonly implemented in modern analytics and data platforms.

In Databricks, the Lakeflow Declarative Expectations are the built-in mechanism for enforcing data quality rules. They allow you to *declare* what valid data looks like and automatically apply those checks as data flows through your pipelines. Expectations are defined as part of streaming tables or materialized views and are evaluated automatically during pipeline execution. Rather than handling data validation through custom imperative code, expectations let you describe data quality rules declaratively, such as:

- Column cannot have null values
- The value of the column must fall within a valid range
- Email address should be in valid format

Expectations consist of three key elements:

1. **Name**: A unique identifier for the expectation that is referenced in monitoring

```
expect_all_or_drop({
    "valid_customer_name": "customer_name IS NOT NULL",
    "valid_address": "address IS NOT NULL",
    "valid_email_not_null": "email IS NOT NULL",
    "valid_order_number": "order_number IS NOT NULL",
    "valid_email_format": "email RLIKE '^[a-zA-Z0-9._%+\\-]+@[a-zA-Z0-9.-]+[.][a-zA-Z]{2,}$'",
    "valid_currency": "currency IN ('USD', 'INR', 'CAD', 'EUR')"
```

Figure 10.4: Key elements of an Expectation

2. **Rule**: A constraint or expression that must be evaluated to **TRUE** for validity.
3. **Action**: Defines what happens when data does not meet expectations. There are three types of actions:
    - **expect**: The pipeline will *keep* the invalid record but log the violation, for example, checking if the address record is populated.
    - **expect_or_drop**: The pipeline will *drop* the invalid record and log the violation, for example, discarding malformed email addresses.
    - **expect_or_fail**: The pipeline fails immediately when an invalid record is encountered, for example, stopping execution if multiple records contain missing or malformed values.

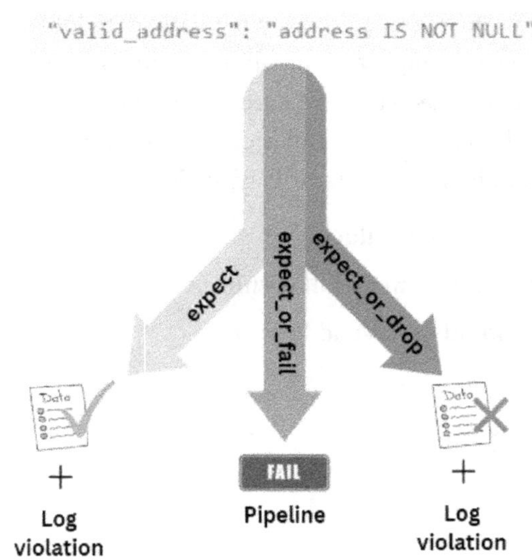

Figure 10.5: Configurable actions for Expectations

In simple terms, expectations allow you to define *what good data looks like* using SQL rules and let Databricks automatically enforce, monitor, and act on those rules as data moves through your pipelines.

We are now well-positioned to deliver data to end users by enabling a streamlined, efficient flow from producers to consumers. Let us now focus on the high-level plan for achieving this success.

High-level plan for building the silver layer

Before we begin preparing the data sources, let's review the section of the Electroniz architecture diagram that we'll be building in this chapter. The red-outlined area in the image below shows the components we will be building in this chapter.

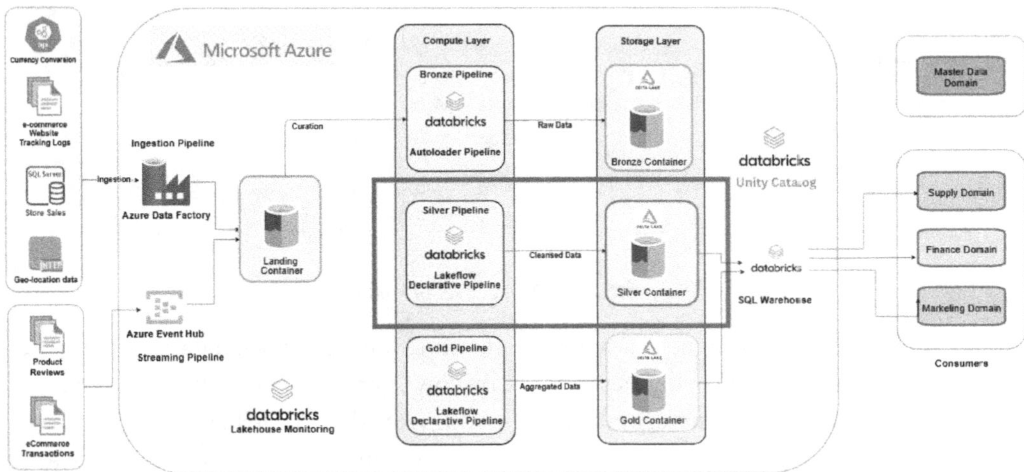

Figure 10.6: Portion of the Electroniz architecture that will be built in this chapter

Before we begin, let's take a moment to understand the structure of the pipelines that will be built in this chapter.

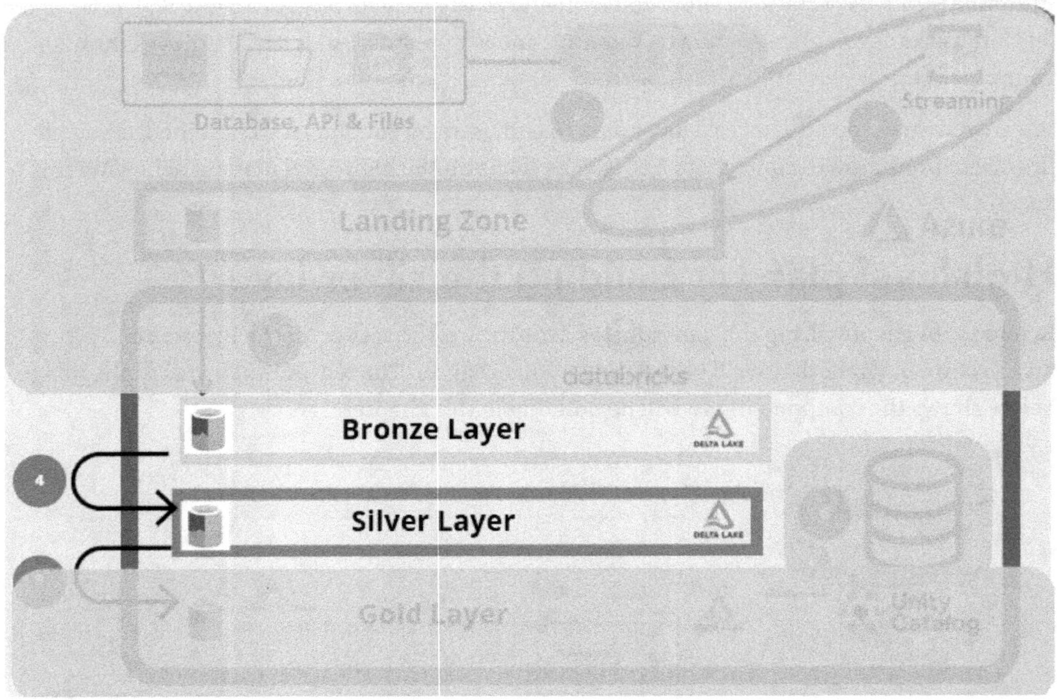

Figure 10.7: Electroniz silver pipeline

The table below outlines the high-level approach for developing the silver data pipelines. The pipelines will be implemented using Databricks Lakeflow Spark Declarative Pipelines and will process data as continuous streaming tables originating from the bronze layer. The processed data will then be persisted to their respective containers within the Electroniz Lakehouse ADLS account.

Pipeline	Pipeline Type	Pipeline Mechanism	Data Destination
Silver Pipeline	Databricks Lakeflow Spark Declarative Pipelines	Continuous Streaming tables from the bronze layer	Silver container in *Electroniz Lakehouse* ADLS account

Table 10.1: High-level approach for developing the silver pipelines

With this high-level plan for building the Silver layer established, we now turn our attention to the typical approach for developing it.

Process of creating the silver pipeline

By this stage, it should be clear that **data curation is not optional—it is essential**. Creating the Silver pipeline is inherently a **collaborative effort**. It requires close partnership between **data engineers**, who bring technical expertise and platform knowledge, and **business stakeholders**, who understand the semantics, rules, and expectations of the data. Business input is critical for defining key decisions such as:

- Which business rules must be applied to validate and enrich the data
- How entities should be standardized, deduplicated, and modeled
- What constitutes valid relationships across datasets
- Which records are considered authoritative when conflicts arise

The Silver pipeline is therefore not just a technical transformation layer—it is where business logic is formalized, embedded, and operationalized. When built correctly, it produces high-quality, governed, and trustworthy datasets that serve as the foundation for analytics, reporting, machine learning, and downstream applications.

Let's focus on the process for making this collaboration effective. The following is the process to drive the data curation process.

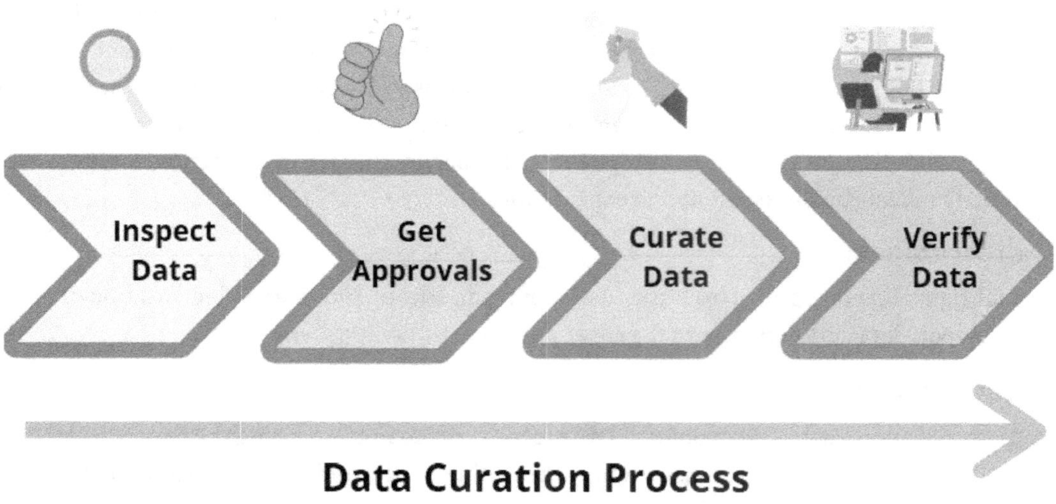

Figure 10.8: Data curation process

With this high-level understanding of the data curation plan, we will explore the process in greater detail in the sections that follow.

Inspecting data

The data curation process begins with inspecting representative samples of the data. This step is typically a collaborative effort between data engineers and members of the customer or business team. Together, they review data from a variety of source systems to build a shared understanding of its structure, quality, and semantics. Initial inspection often involves visual exploration—reviewing sample records, distributions, and key attributes. However, visual analysis alone is rarely sufficient. In many cases, programmatic profiling and validation logic must be implemented to uncover data that is unstandardized, invalid, inconsistent, non-uniform, duplicated, or insecure. This inspection phase lays the groundwork for all downstream transformations by clearly identifying where and why data curation is required.

Deliverables

A comprehensive report that documents:

- All identified data quality rules and conformance issues requiring curation
- The business impact of each issue
- A proposed remediation approach for each case

Getting approvals

The report produced during the data inspection phase should be formally submitted to the customer business team for review. This step ensures alignment and confirms that all stakeholders agree on the identified data quality issues, as well as the business rules and transformation logic to be applied during curation. Formal review and approval are essential to avoid misunderstandings later in the pipeline and to ensure that the implemented logic accurately reflects business intent and expectations.

Deliverables

Formal sign-off and approval from the customer team, authorizing the implementation of the agreed-upon data curation logic in the silver pipeline.

Cleaning data

Once formal approval has been obtained, the focus shifts to implementing the data curation logic. This phase represents the execution of the business rules and transformations defined and agreed upon during the earlier inspection and approval steps. As a data engineer, you may choose from a variety of frameworks, languages, and tools to implement this logic. While multiple options are available, it is generally best to use technologies that are already familiar and supported within the customer's ecosystem. In most enterprise data platforms, Apache Spark and SQL are the predominant choices for implementing scalable, maintainable data curation logic.

After development, the curation logic is integrated into the silver pipeline, where it is applied consistently and repeatably to incoming data. This ensures that curated datasets remain reliable, governed, and ready for downstream consumption.

Deliverables

Production-ready transformation logic that implements the approved data curation rules within the silver pipeline.

Verifying data

The final step in the data curation process is verifying that the implemented logic produces the intended results. This phase focuses on validating that data quality issues identified earlier have been correctly resolved and that the curated data aligns with business expectations.

Although data engineers may support this activity, verification is typically best performed by customer or business team members. Their closer familiarity with the data, domain context, and business semantics makes them uniquely qualified to confirm accuracy, completeness, and correctness.

Verification may include record sampling, reconciliation against source systems, and validation of business rules applied within the silver pipeline. Successful completion of this step ensures confidence in the curated datasets before they are promoted for broader consumption.

Deliverables

Formal validation and approval from the customer team, confirming that the data curation logic has been implemented correctly and meets agreed-upon business requirements. An example data curation approval entry may look like the one below:

```
Table: electroniz_catalog.electroniz_bronze_schema.electroniz_brorze_currency
Column: timestamp
Data Quality Rule:
1. rename timestamp to event_time
2. Cast to timestamp column to TimestampType for example
2026-02-16T19:25:04.000+00:00

Approved: Yes
```

Now that we have a solid understanding of why data curation is necessary and a clear view of the process involved, we can move on to building a real silver-layer pipeline. For the sake of simplicity, we'll assume that we followed the curation process diligently and submitted a detailed report to Electroniz, outlining our findings as described earlier.

After reviewing the report, the Electroniz team has provided formal approval, authorizing us to proceed with the next steps. With alignment established and expectations clearly defined, we are now ready to implement the silver-layer curation pipeline.

Introducing Genie Code

In *Chapter 9*, we explored the evolving landscape of data pipeline development. By leveraging **Claude Code** to develop and deploy bronze-layer pipelines, we demonstrated how Gen AI can significantly streamline engineering workflows. Through practical examples, we showed that tasks that traditionally required substantial manual effort—such as pipeline design, ingestion logic, and deployment orchestration—can now be accelerated dramatically. By offloading much of this boilerplate and repetitive work to Claude Code, data engineers can save a significant portion of their time, allowing them to focus more on data quality and high-value problem-solving.

Databricks introduced **Genie Code** in March 2026 as the newest addition to the Databricks Genie family. Genie Code is now a fully available and supported capability across the Databricks workspaces with no additional licensing cost. Earlier Genie capabilities focused primarily on conversational analytics and natural-language querying for business users.

Both Claude Code and Genie Code leverage Generative AI to accelerate development; they differ significantly in scope and context.

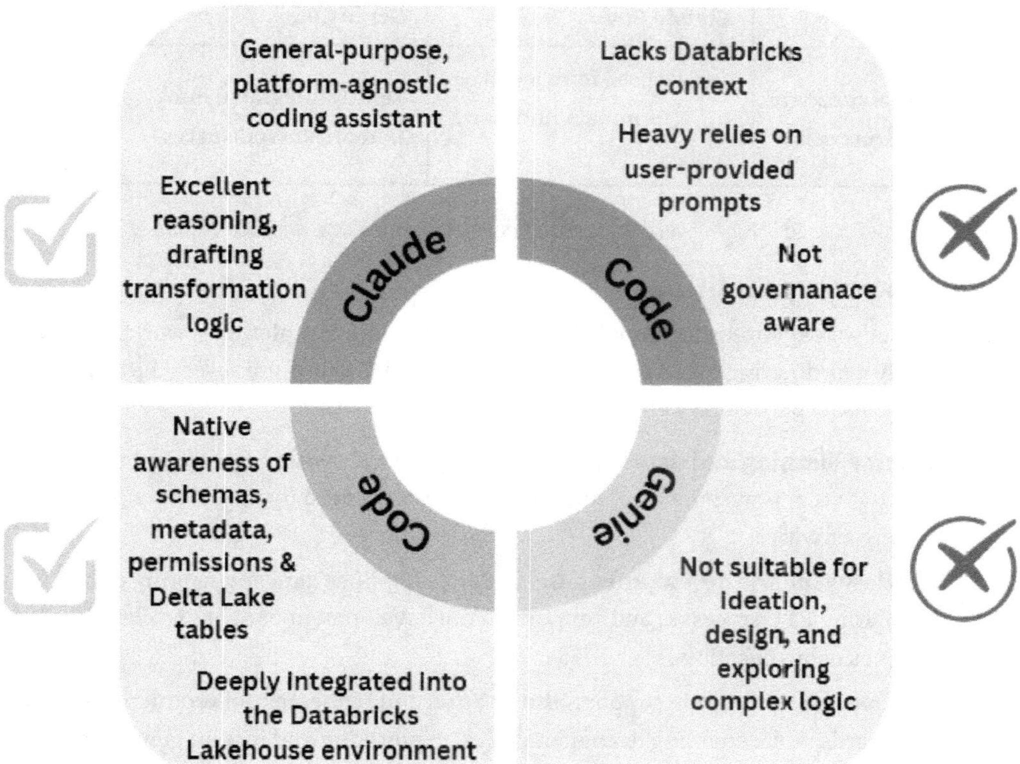

Figure 10.9: Claude Code vs Genie Code

Genie Code was purpose-built to support autonomous data engineering, enabling the planning, development, deployment, and ongoing maintenance of production-grade data workflows. Genie Code supports the full lifecycle of data work, enabling data teams to move seamlessly from experimentation and model development to production pipelines and business intelligence dashboards. The following table compares Claude Code and Genie Code.

	Claude Code	**Genie Code**
Usability	General-purpose AI coding agent	Databricks-native autonomous agent
Scope	Offers broader scope, flexible coding support across ecosystems.	Platform-aware, end-to-end automation tailored specifically for Databricks

	Claude Code	Genie Code
Development environment	Can be used from local IDEs, terminals, and cloud tools	Tightly integrated into Databricks workspaces

Table 10.2: High-level comparison between Claude Code and Genie Code

Genie Code capabilities

Genie Code delivers **agent-based capabilities** that streamline complex data workflows by autonomously coordinating and executing multi-stage tasks. Below are several key use cases where Genie Code is particularly effective:

- **Machine learning and data science**: Working natively within Databricks notebooks, it helps data teams automate exploratory analysis and speed up model development and training activities.
- **Lakeflow pipeline development**: Genie Code simplifies data engineering efforts by automating ETL processes and supporting the development of Spark Declarative Pipelines using Lakeflow.
- **Dashboards:** Genie Code supports the creation and refinement of production-ready dashboards while enabling deeper analytical exploration and insight generation.
- **MLflow:** Genie Code assists with monitoring, diagnosing, and improving GenAI applications by leveraging MLflow's observability and evaluation capabilities.

Using Genie Code modes

Genie Code is embedded within Databricks and provides the following features to assist users with data work.

Genie Code chatbot mode

Genie Code chatbot is the conversational interface for Databricks Genie Code that allows data engineers, data scientists, and analysts to interact with the Databricks platform using natural-language instructions to perform technical data work. Because it is deeply integrated with the Databricks workspace, it is context–aware– this means the chatbot understands schemas, permissions, and lineage, enabling it to deliver precise, platform-aware guidance.

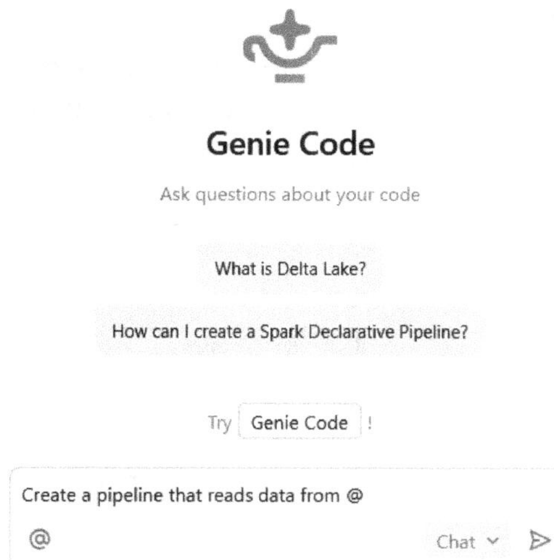

Figure 10.10: Genie Code chatbot

Through the chatbot, users can ask Genie Code to query data, generate, modify, explain, or troubleshoot Spark and SQL code and pipeline logic, and plan and execute multi-step data engineering tasks.

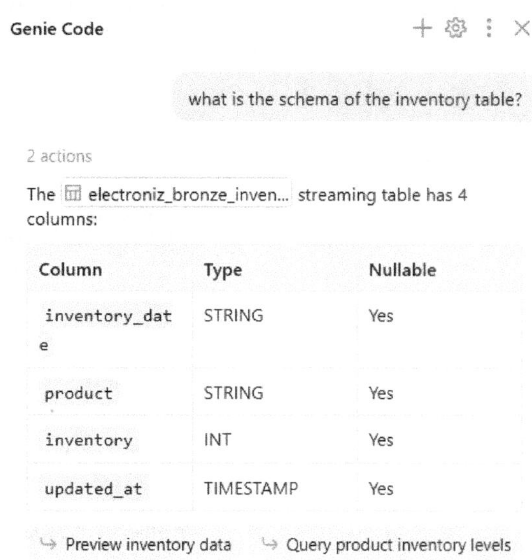

Figure 10.11: Genie Code chatbot mode

Genie Code chatbot is context-aware, leveraging metadata, schemas, governance policies, and lineage to produce environment-validated, executable results rather than generic code snippets.

Genie Code agent mode

Genie Code agent coordinates and executes multi-stage workflows by planning solutions, locating relevant assets, running code, iterating based on cell outputs, and resolving errors automatically.

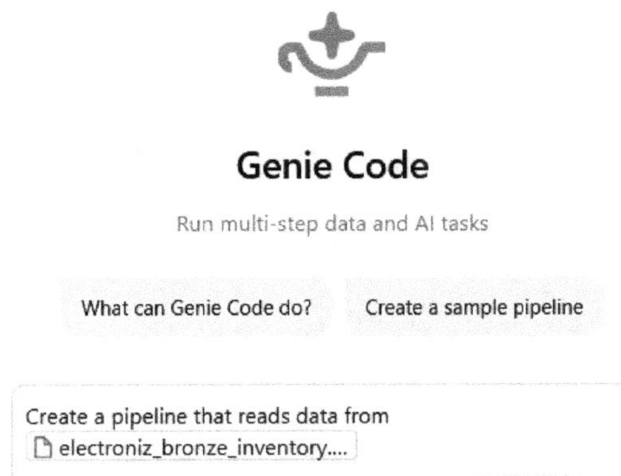

Figure 10.12: Genie Code agent mode

In agent mode, Genie Code does more than generate code—it can reason through a problem, determine the required steps, retrieve relevant assets, execute transformations, evaluate intermediate results, and iteratively refine the solution.

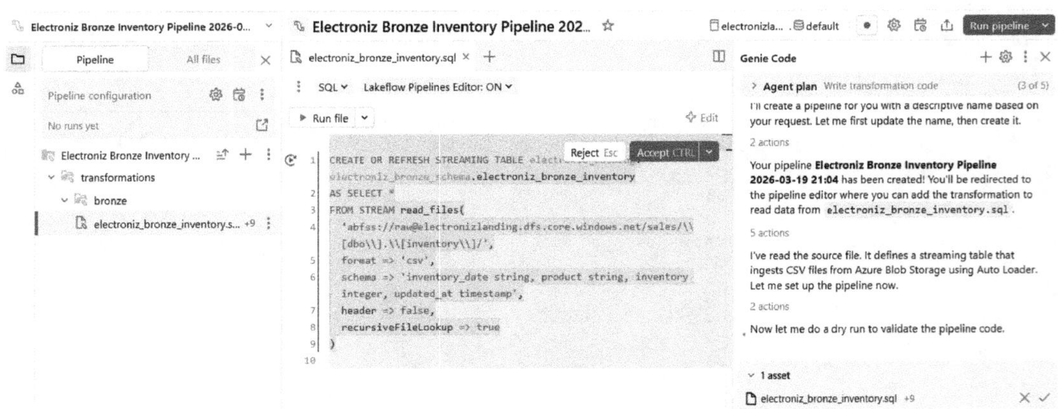

Figure 10.13: Genie Code agent mode pipeline creation

Genie Code agent can automatically run code, interpret outputs, handle errors, and make corrective adjustments, all while operating within Databricks governance, metadata, and security boundaries. However, to generate accurate responses, Genie Code depends on well-formed instructions. Let's take a closer look at what that means.

Using Genie Code custom instructions

Genie Code Custom Instructions enable users to influence how Genie Code operates by supplying persistent guidance at the workspace or user level. This guidance is applied consistently across interactions, allowing Genie Code to generate responses that align with organizational standards, preferred technologies, coding conventions, governance policies, and architectural practices.

In practice, custom instructions can be used to:

- Apply organization-specific naming conventions and development standards
- Define preferred languages or tools, such as SQL or PySpark
- Ensure outputs conform to Medallion Architecture or Lakehouse best practices
- Incorporate data privacy, security, and governance requirements

Here is an example of how custom instructions can help data engineers:

```
Always follow these guidelines when creating a pipeline:
- Use Spark SQL by default.
- Apply Medallion Architecture standards
- Use snake_case for column names and lowercase for table names
- Mask or anonymize PII fields such as email, phone_number, and ssn when working
with customer data.
```

The introduction of **Genie Code** comes at an ideal moment in our journey. In much the same way that we previously leveraged **Claude Code** to accelerate the generation of Bronze-layer pipelines for Electroniz, we will now extend this GenAI-assisted approach to the silver layer using Genie Code. While Claude Code proved invaluable for rapidly designing and deploying ingestion logic, Genie Code's native integration with the Databricks platform makes it particularly well-suited for implementing, deploying, and operating curated silver-layer pipelines.

By using Genie Code, we will translate approved business logic into production-ready transformations more efficiently, while ensuring alignment with Lakehouse best practices, governance standards, and the Medallion Architecture. This approach allows us to reduce manual effort, accelerate delivery, and focus our engineering energy on higher-value data curation and modeling challenges rather than boilerplate implementation details. It's time to move forward and begin the implementation.

Preparing resources for the Electroniz silver pipeline

To implement the silver layer of the Electroniz Lakehouse, we will provision and configure the following Azure resources. These components will establish the foundational storage and compute capabilities required to ingest data from the landing layer into the lakehouse environment.

Azure Resource	Resource Name
Azure Data Lake Storage Gen 2 Storage Account	`electronizlakehouse`
Azure Data Lake Storage Gen 2 Container	`silver`
Azure Databricks	`electronizlakehouse-dbx`

Table 10.3: Azure resource configuration for the Electroniz silver layer

Since the `electronizlakehouse` ADLS account and `electronizlakehouse-dbx` Databricks workspace already exist, the only remaining step is to create a new container. Let's begin by provisioning this resource in Azure.

1. Create a container that will store the silver layer data. Paste the commands below into Azure Cloud Shell. You can execute them one at a time or run the whole block together.

```
STORAGEACCOUNTNAME="electronizlakehouse"
NAMESPACE="silver"
az storage fs create \
-n $NAMESPACE \
--account-name $STORAGEACCOUNTNAME \
--metadata project=lakehouse environment=development layer=silver \
--only-show-errors
```

2. On the Azure portal, click on **electronizlakehouse** > **Storage browser** > **Blob containers**.

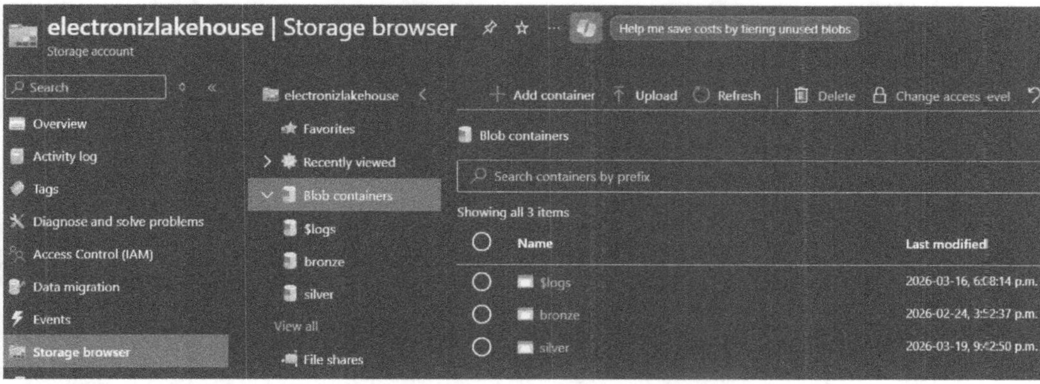

Figure 10.14: Newly created blob container for silver layer data

Now that we have successfully prepared the Azure resources required for the silver layer's foundational storage, we can proceed to develop the silver layer pipeline.

Developing the Electroniz silver layer pipelines using Genie Code

The code-generation workflow begins when a user submits a natural-language prompt to the Genie Code chatbot. As a brief recap, the bronze layer consists of nine streaming Delta tables, each continuously updated with data arriving from the landing zone. The table below summarizes these source tables and the corresponding pipelines used to construct the silver layer.

Data Source	Pipeline Name	Source and Destination Tables
Store Sales Database Inventory Products Store Customers Store Orders	electroniz_silver_inventory_pipeline electroniz_silver_product_pipeline electroniz_silver_store_customers_pipeline electroniz_silver_store_orders_pipeline	Catalog: electroniz_catalog Schema: electroniz_silver_schema Tables: electroniz_bronze_inventory → electroniz_silver_inventory electroniz_bronze_products → electroniz_silver_products electroniz_bronze_store_customers → electroniz_silver_store_customers electroniz_bronze_store_orders → electroniz_silver_store_orders

Data Source	Pipeline Name	Source and Destination Tables
e-commerce Transactions	electroniz_silver_ecommerce_pipeline	Catalog: electroniz_catalog Schema: electroniz_silver_schema Tables: electroniz_bronze_ecomm_transactions → electroniz_silver_ecomm_transactions
Product Reviews	electroniz_silver_product_reviews_pipeline	Catalog: electroniz_catalog Schema: electroniz_silver_schema Tables: electroniz_bronze_product_reviews → electroniz_silver_product_reviews
Currency Conversion Data	electroniz_silver_currency_pipeline	Catalog: electroniz_catalog Schema: electroniz_silver_schema Tables: electroniz_bronze_currency→ electroniz_silver_currency

Data Source	Pipeline Name	Source and Destination Tables

e-commerce Website Tracking Logs
 	
JOIN
 	
Geo-location data
	`electroniz_silver_geolocation_pipeline`	Catalog: `electroniz_catalog`
		
		Schema: `electroniz_silver_schema`
		
		Tables:
		
		`electroniz_bronze_website_logs`
		
		`JOIN`
		
		`electroniz_bronze_geolocation`
		→
		
		`electroniz_silver_logs_geolocation`

Table 10.4: Source and target table details created by the silver layer pipelines

With a clear understanding of the source and target tables for the silver layer pipelines, we now begin our journey into code generation.

Creating the Electroniz silver layer schema

Let's begin by creating the Electroniz silver layer schema in the Electroniz pre-existing catalog.

1. Issue the following prompt on Genie Code to create a new schema:

```
Create a new external location as follows:
Credential: electroniz_lakehouse_storage_credential
Name: electroniz_lakehouse_silver_storage_location pointing to abfss://
silver@electronizlakehouse.dfs.core.windows.net
```

2. Click on **Allow** followed by **Run**.

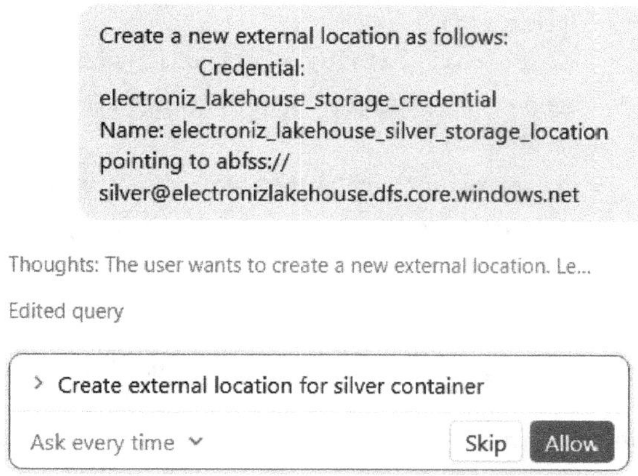

Figure 10.15: Prompt to create a new external location

3. Issue the following prompt on Genie Code to create a new schema:

```
Run SQL
CREATE SCHEMA electroniz_catalog.electroniz_silver_schema
MANAGED LOCATION 'abfss://silver@electronizlakehouse.dfs.core.windows.net';
```

4. Click on **Always activate** on the Code assistance pane. Now click on **Allow.**

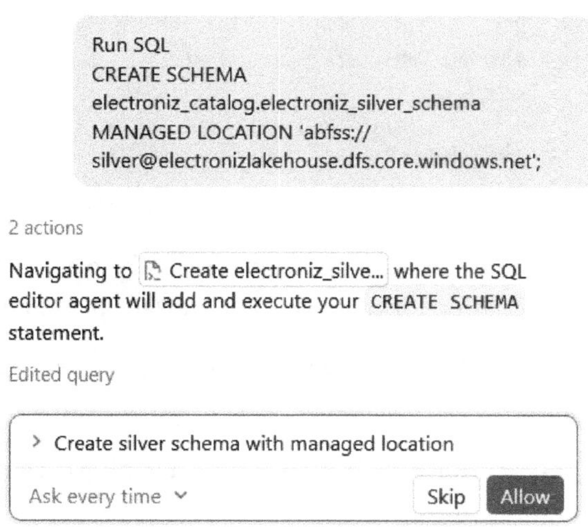

Figure 10.16: Prompt to create the silver layer schema

5. Verify the generated SQL and click **Run suggested**.

The schema `electroniz_catalog.electroniz_silver_schema` has been created successfully with its managed location pointing to `abfss://silver@electronizlakehouse.dfs.core.windows.net`. It's been added as statement 5 in the query.

Figure 10.17: Confirmation of silver layer schema creation

6. The **electroniz_catalog** should now have the silver layer schema created.

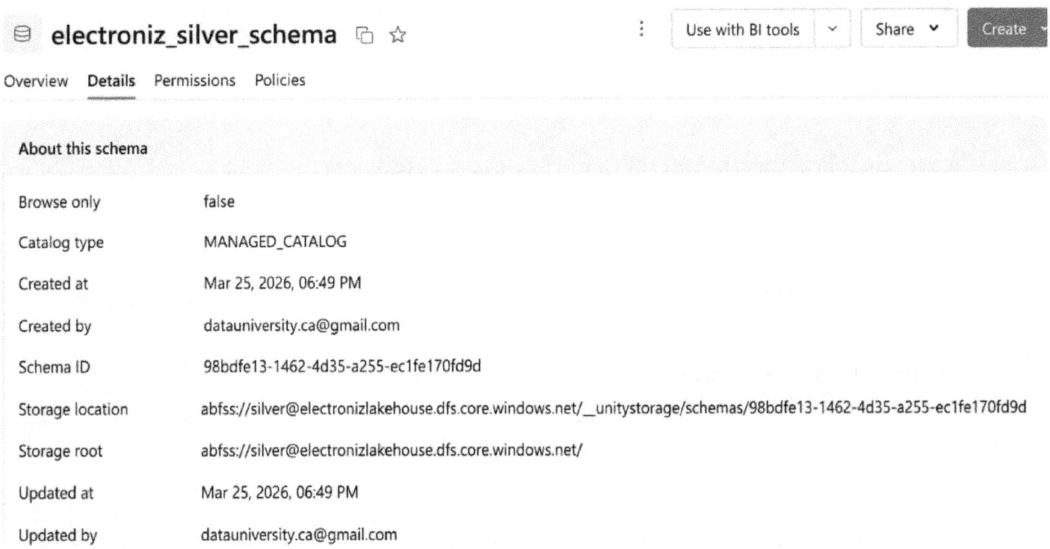

Figure 10.18: Newly created silver layer schema

Now that the necessary resources are in place, we are ready to begin building the **silver layer pipelines**, laying the foundation for curated, standardized, and analytics-ready data.

Creating the Electroniz silver pipeline for currency conversion data

The bronze layer contains currency conversion data, including exchange rates for nearly all global currency pairs.

The following is a list of key transformations to be performed when creating the silver table:

- Although the `electroniz_bronze_currency` table stores currency conversion data for all historical dates and times, only the most recent record will be propagated to the silver layer.
- The `electroniz_bronze_currency` table stores the timestamp as a `BIGINT`. This column will be converted to the `TIMESTAMP` data type and renamed to `event_time`.
- As Electroniz conducts most of its sales in USD, INR, CAD, and EUR, and the finance department aims to standardize all sales reporting in EUR, only the currency conversion rates for these currencies will be retained.
- The `electroniz_bronze_currency` table stores conversion rates in a `rates` column defined as a `STRUCT`. Conversion values for USD, INR, and CAD will be extracted from this `STRUCT` column.

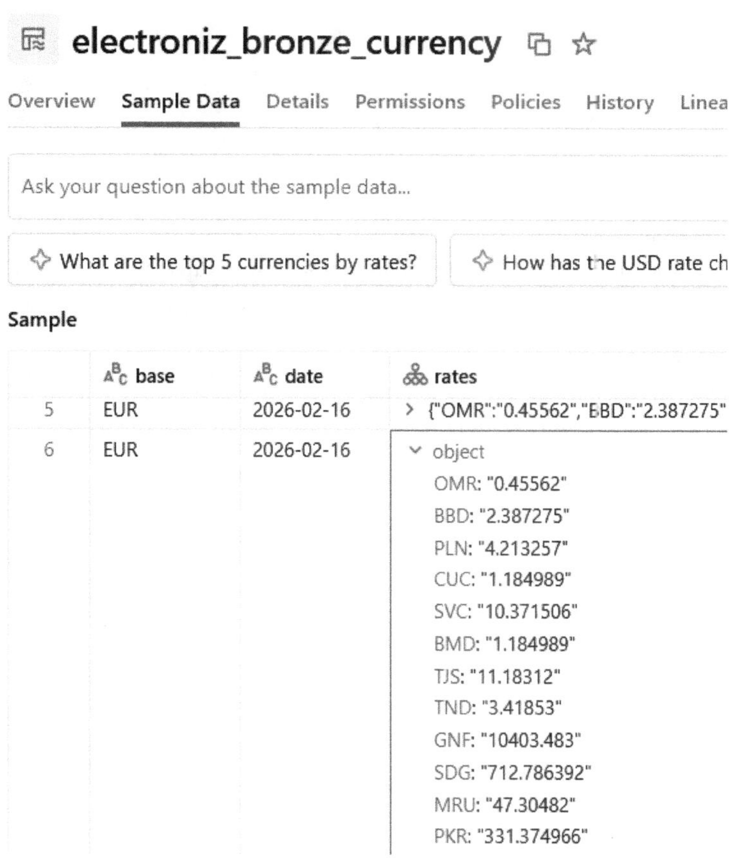

Figure 10.19: Currency conversion rates in STRUCT type column

Follow the steps below to generate the code for the currency conversion data pipeline.

1. Navigate to the Databricks workspace, click on the Genie Code icon on the top right of your screen.
2. Issue the following prompt on Genie Code to create the silver currency conversion pipeline:

```
Create a new streaming pipeline with details as follows
Pipeline Name: electroniz_silver_currency_pipeline
Source Table:
electroniz_catalog.electroniz_bronze_schema.electroniz_bronze_currency
Target table:
electroniz_catalog.electroniz_silver_schema.electroniz_silver_currency
Catalog: electroniz_catalog
Mode: Continuous streaming
Operation: Merge
Transformations:
1. Extract only these currency rate columns from the rates column: EUR,
USD, CAD, INR
2. Cast timestamp column to TimestampType and rename to event_time
```

> **Note**
>
> `STRUCT` is a complex (nested) data type that groups multiple related fields together under a single column. Each field inside a `STRUCT` has its own name and data type.

3. Navigate to the Databricks workspace, click on the Genie Code icon on the top right of your screen. Paste the prompt and run it.

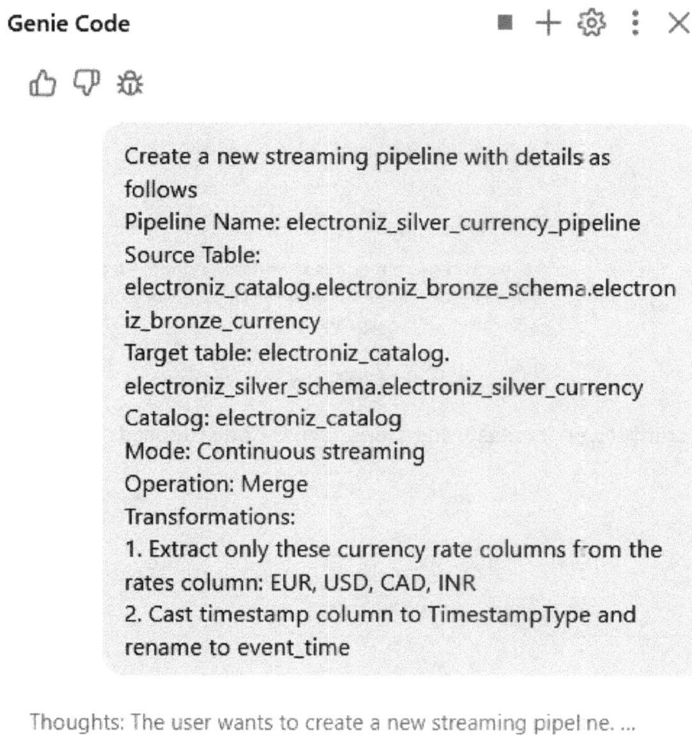

Figure 10.20: Genie Code Prompt for creating the electroniz_silver_currency_pipeline

4. Genie Code will perform extensive reasoning at each step of execution, explicitly articulating its logic and decision-making process using a "think-out-loud" approach. This makes the transformation steps more transparent, easier to understand, and simpler to debug, while also helping reviewers and stakeholders clearly follow how inputs are evaluated and how outputs are derived.

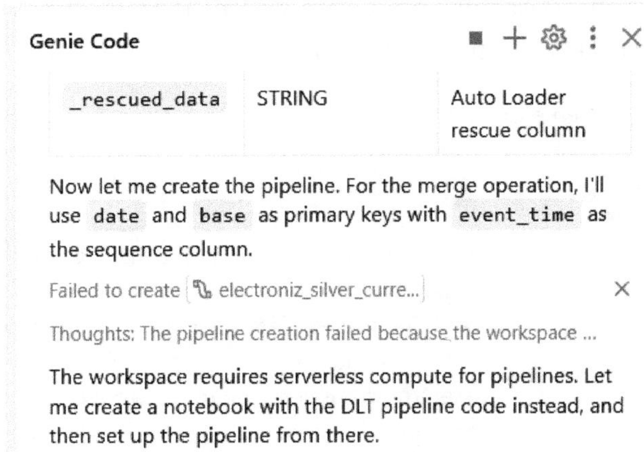

Figure 10.21: Genie Code reasoning process

5. After completing its reasoning steps, Genie Code proceeds to generate a new pipeline.

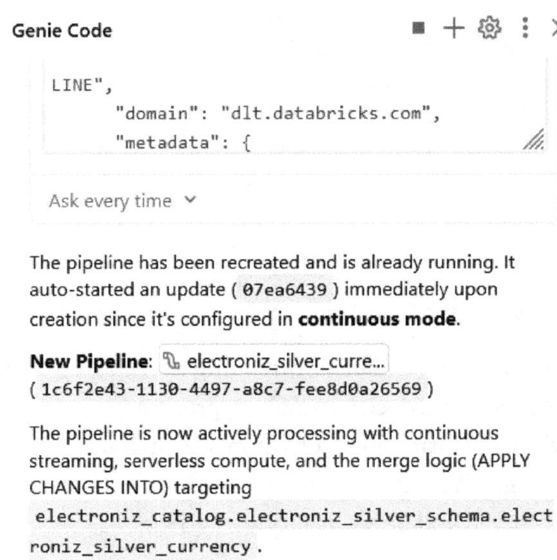

Figure 10.22: Genie Code confirmation regarding the creation of the new pipeline.

6. Return to the Databricks workspace. Using the menu on the left, click **Jobs & Pipelines**.

You should see the newly deployed pipeline listed there. Click on **electroniz_silver_currency_pipeline**.

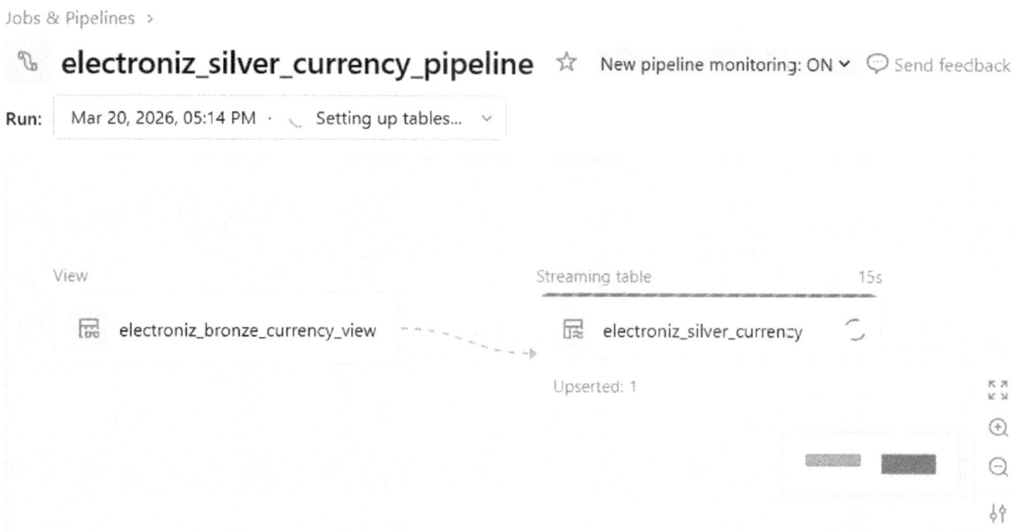

Figure 10.23: electroniz_silver_currency_pipeline created

7. Notice in the image above that only 1 record has been `upserted`. This means that only the most recent record was propagated from the bronze table to the silver layer.

> **Note**
>
> A Delta `UPSERT` operation, also known as a `MERGE`, allows Delta Lake to update existing records and insert new records within a single atomic transaction.

8. Next, inspect the contents of the streaming table. Click Catalog, then navigate to **electroniz_catalog** > **electroniz_silver_schema** > **electroniz_silver_currency**. Notice that the schema of the silver table differs from the bronze table, and the type casting and renaming of the `event_time` were successful.

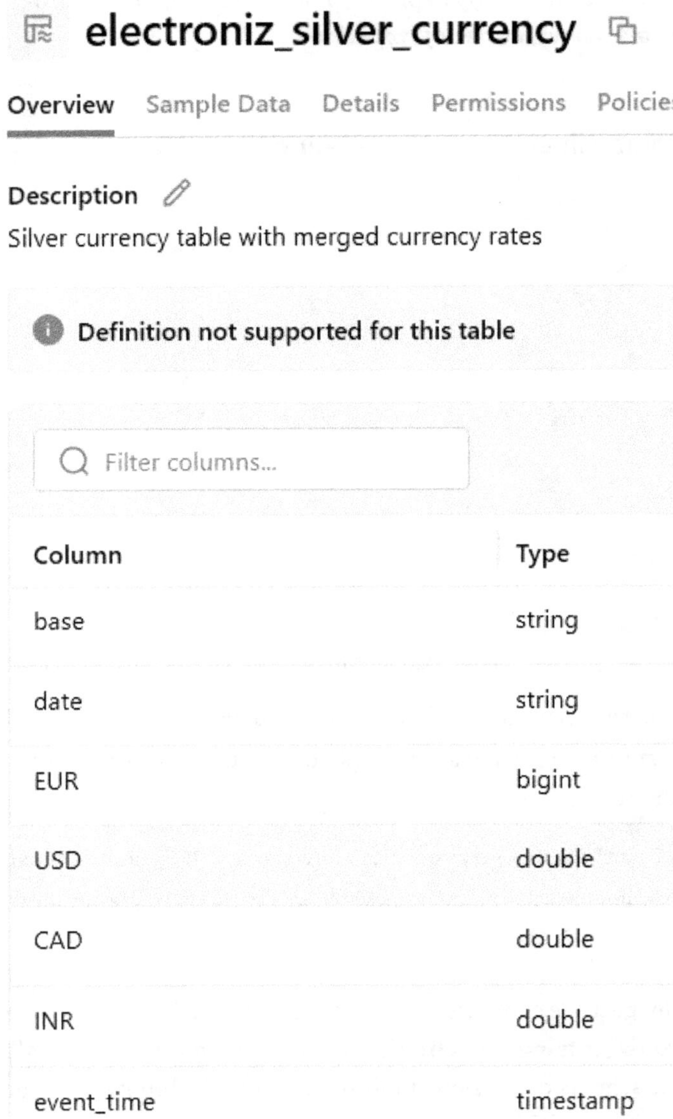

Figure 10.24: Structure of electroniz_silver_currency table

In the Medallion architecture, bronze and silver tables often have different schemas because data is progressively transformed, cleansed, and refined as it moves between layers.

9. Click on **Sample Data**.

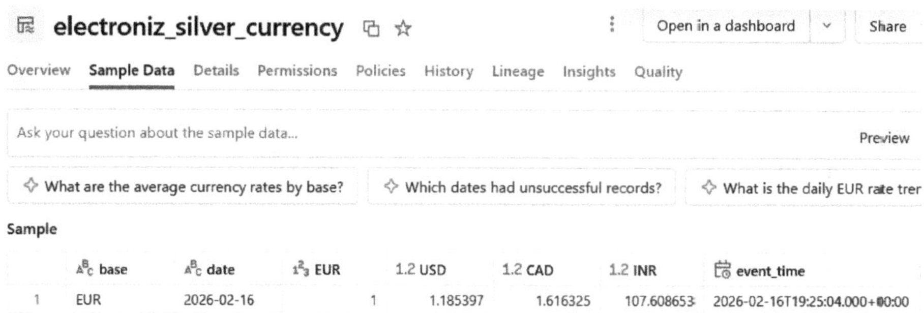

Figure 10.25: Data of electroniz_silver_currency table

10. Click on **Jobs & Pipelines** and stop the **electroniz_silver_currency_pipeline**.

> **Note**
>
> A reminder that in a production environment, it is common practice to leave the streaming table in the WAITING state so it can continuously monitor the landing zone and incrementally ingest new records as they arrive. However, since this is a development or testing scenario, the pipeline can be safely stopped at this point. Stopping the pipeline releases compute resources, helping ensure efficient use of the available Azure free credits.

Now let's move on to creating the silver layer pipeline for e-commerce transactions.

Creating the Electroniz silver pipelines for e-commerce

Electroniz e-commerce data represents transactional activity generated by customers through the online portal.

Creating the Electroniz silver pipeline for e-commerce transactions

The bronze layer contains ecommerce transaction data as ingested from Azure Event Hubs.

Following is the list of some key transformations that will be performed when creating the silver table:

- The `electroniz_bronze_ecomm_transactions` table stores ecommerce transactions in the `data` column with type `MAP`. We want to extract attribute values, such as the customer name, address, and order number, from this field.

Figure 10.26: ecommerce transaction data in MAP type column

- Attributes should be correctly type casted – `sale_price` to `DOUBLE`, `order_number` to `integer`, `order_date` to `DATE`.
- The `country` column contains inconsistent country representations, including abbreviations and full names. These values will be standardized to ensure uniformity.
- The **electroniz_bronze_ecomm_transactions** table will be joined to the **electroniz_bronze_products** dimension table to make sure the product relational integrity is maintained in the silver table.

Following is the list of some key data quality rules that will be performed when creating the silver table:

- Check the values of the following columns is `NOT NULL`: `customer_name`, `address`, `email`, `order_number`
   a. Email addresses must be in a valid format.
   b. The `currency` should fall in the range: (`USD`, `INR`, `CAD`, `EUR`)

Follow the steps below to create the pipeline for e-commerce transactions:

1. Navigate to the Databricks workspace, click on the Genie Code icon on the top right of your screen.
2. Issue the following prompt on Genie Code to create the silver e-commerce conversion pipeline:

```
Create a new streaming pipeline with details as follows
Pipeline Name: electroniz_silver_ecommerce_pipeline
Source tables:
electroniz_catalog.electroniz_bronze_schema.electroniz_bronze_ecomm_transac
tions
electroniz_catalog.electroniz_bronze_schema.electroniz_bronze_products
(dimension table)

Target table:
electroniz_catalog.electroniz_silver_schema.electroniz_silver_ecomm_transac
tions
Mode: Continuous streaming
Operation: Merge
Merge key: order_number
Infer the schema of all source tables.

Transformations:
1. Add a sequential ID column called ecomm_customer_id
2. The source table has a column called data which is a MAP type
   (not JSON string). Extract the following fields:
   customer_name, address, city, postalcode, country, phore, email,
   product_name, order_date, currency, order_mode, sale_price, order_number
2. Cast sale_price to double
3. Cast order_number to integer
4. Cast order_date (format DD/MM/YYYY) to date type using to_date()
5. Standardize country to abbreviation:
    - 'United States', 'US', 'U.S.', 'America' → 'US'
   - 'United Kingdom','U.K' → 'UK'
   - 'India', 'IN' → 'IND'
   - 'Canada', 'CA' → 'CAN'
6. INNER JOIN with electroniz_bronze_products (dimension table, static)
   on LOWER(product_name) == LOWER(products.product_name) to ensure
   case-insensitive matching. This automatically drops records where
   product_name does not match any product in the dimension table.
```

```
   After join, explicitly select ALL transaction columns including
   product_name using df["column"] syntax to avoid ambiguity.

Data Quality Rules:
- NOT NULL: customer_name, address, email, order_number (drop rows that
fail)
- Valid email: email must be valid using strict REGEX pattern (drop invalid
records)
- CHECK CONSTRAINT: currency IN ('USD', 'INR', 'CAD', 'EUR') (drop rows
that fail)
```

> **Note**
>
> MAP is a complex data type used to store key-value pairs within a single column. All values of the keys or values should be of the same type.

The use of `INNER JOIN` in the prompt was specifically chosen to enforce referential integrity by dropping unmatched records.

3. Once again, Genie Code will perform extensive reasoning at each step of execution. After completing its reasoning steps, Genie Code generates a new pipeline.
4. On some occasions, you may receive the message as below:

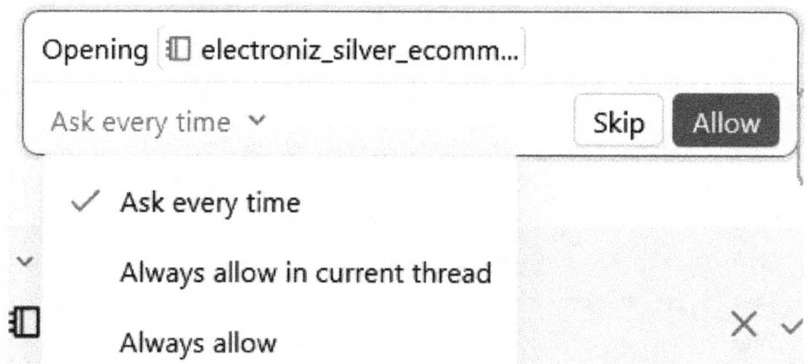

Figure 10.27: Genie Code confirmations to proceed

You may choose to provide confirmations at each step or choose **Always Allow**.

5. Return to the Databricks workspace. Using the menu on the left, click **Jobs & Pipelines**. You should see the newly deployed pipeline listed there. Click on **electroniz_silver_ecommerce_pipeline**.

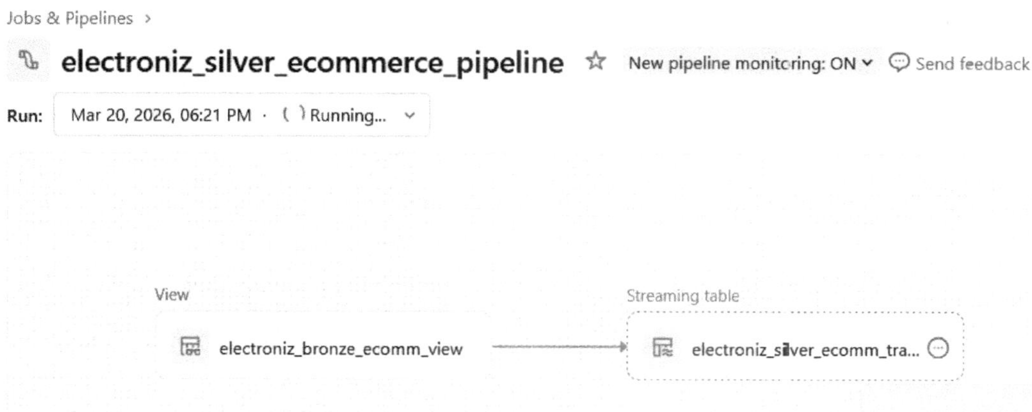

Figure 10.28: electroniz_silver_ecommerce_pipeline created

6. Next, inspect the contents of the streaming table. Click **Catalog**, then navigate to **electroniz_catalog** > **electroniz_silver_schema** > **electroniz_silver_ecomm_transactions**. Click on **Sample Data**.

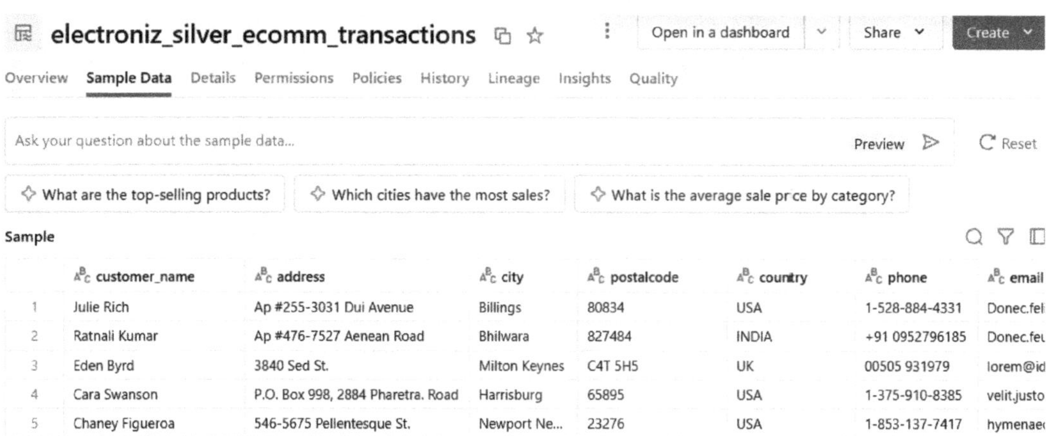

Figure 10.29: Data in electroniz_silver_ecomm_transactions table

7. Let's inspect the code produced for this pipeline by Genie Code. In the pipeline **electroniz_silver_ecommerce_pipeline**, click on **Open in Editor**.

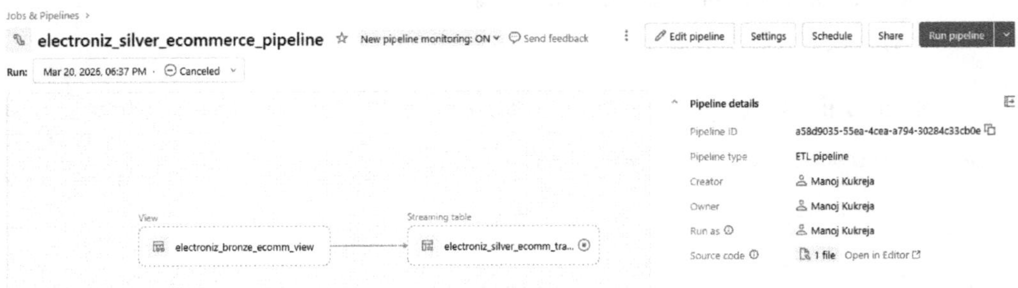

Figure 10.30: Opening the code editor of the electroniz_silver_ecommerce_pipeline

8. Conduct a line-by-line review of the code and map each part back to the original GenAI prompt provided to Genie Code earlier.
9. We can review two sections below in greater detail:

```
dlt.create_streaming_table(
    name="electroniz_silver_ecomm_transactions",
    comment="Silver ecommerce transactions with quality rules",
    expect_all_or_drop={
        "valid_customer_name": "customer_name IS NOT NULL",
        "valid_address": "address IS NOT NULL",
        "valid_email_not_null": "email IS NOT NULL",
        "valid_order_number": "order_number IS NOT NULL",
        "valid_email_format": "email RLIKE '^[a-zA-Z0-9._%+\\-]+@[a-zA-Z0-9.-]+[.][a-zA-Z]{2,}$'",
        "valid_currency": "currency IN ('USD', 'INR', 'CAD', 'EUR')"
    },
    table_properties={
        "quality": "silver"
    }
)

dlt.apply_changes(
    target="electroniz_silver_ecomm_transactions",
    source="electroniz_bronze_ecomm_view",
    keys=["order_number"],
    sequence_by=col("_ingested_at"),
    stored_as_scd_type=1
)
```

Figure 10.31: Data Quality and SCD sections of the code

Observe how Genie Code interpreted the data-quality instructions in the prompt. Also note that the pipelines implement **SCD Type 1** for the final silver-layer table, meaning records with the same key (in this case `order_number`) are overwritten, and existing values are replaced. SCD Type 1 is well-suited for this table because each `order_number` represents a unique, immutable event. When corrections are required, the record is simply overwritten rather than versioned, making historical tracking unnecessary for this use case.

10. Click on Jobs & Pipelines and stop the **electroniz_silver_ecommerce_pipeline**.

Next, we move on to creating the product reviews pipeline.

Creating the Electroniz silver pipeline for product reviews

Product reviews data captures customer feedback gathered across Electroniz's digital channels. The following is the list of some key transformations that will be performed when creating the silver table:

- Several attributes should be correctly renamed and type-cast.
- The **electroniz_bronze_product_reviews** table stores product reviews in the `data` column with type `MAP`. We want to extract values of attributes such as `product_name`, `userId`, `profileName`, and `score` from this field.

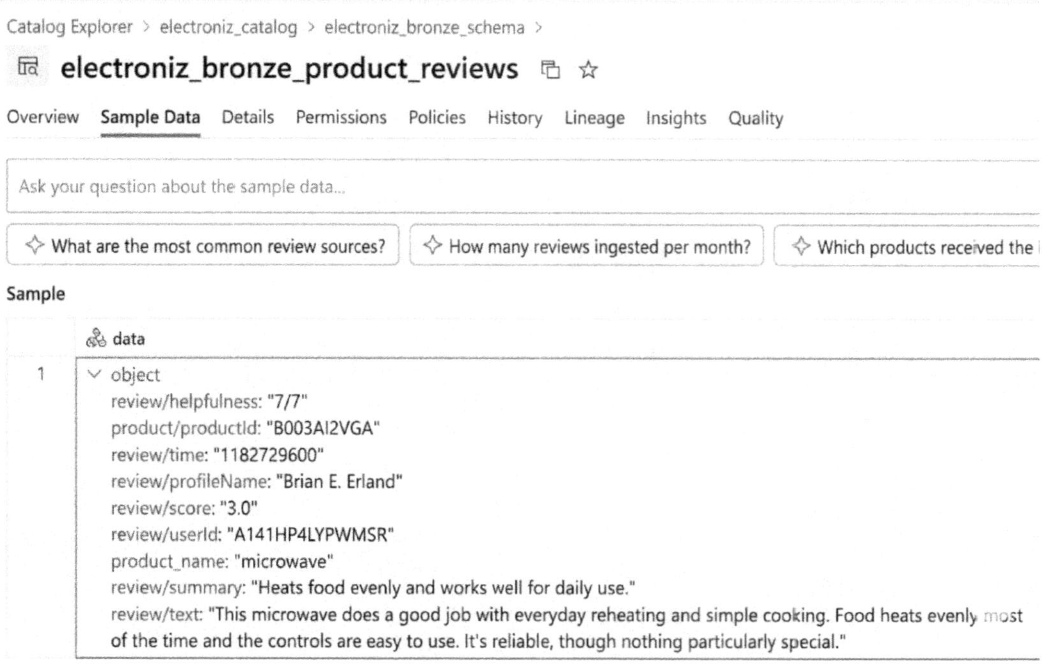

Figure 10.32: Product review data in MAP type column

The following **data quality rule** will be performed when creating the silver table:

- Product reviews are joined with the `electroniz_bronze_products` table as a referential integrity check to ensure that products sold online align with the official Electroniz product catalog.

Follow the steps below to create the pipeline for product reviews.

1. Navigate to the Databricks workspace, and click on the Genie Code icon on the top right of your screen.
2. Issue the following prompt on Genie Code to create the silver product reviews pipeline:

```
Create a new streaming pipeline with details as follows
Pipeline Name: electroniz_silver_product_reviews_pipeline

Source tables:
electroniz_catalog.electroniz_bronze_schema.electroniz_bronze_product_revie
ws
electroniz_catalog.electroniz_bronze_schema.electroniz_bronze_products
(dimension table)

Target table:
electroniz_catalog.electroniz_silver_schema.electroniz_silver_product_revie
ws
Mode: Continuous streaming
Operation: Merge
Merge key: productId + userId

Transformations:
1. Parse data as JSON
2. Extract and rename all fields:
   - product/productId  → product_Id (string)
   - product_name       → product_name (string)
   - review/userId      → userId (string)
   - review/profileName → profileName (string)
   - review/helpfulness → helpfulness (string)
   - review/score       → score (double)
   - review/time        → review_time (cast bigint to timestamp)
   - review/summary     → summary (string)
   - review/text        → review_text (string)
3. Keep ingested_at column
```

```
Data Quality Rules:
Referential check: INNER JOIN with electroniz_bronze_products (dimension
table, static) on LOWER(product_name) == LOWER(products.product_name) to
ensure case-insensitive matching. This automatically drops records where
product_name does not match any product in the dimension table. After join,
explicitly select ALL transaction columns including product_name using
df["column"] syntax to avoid ambiguity.
```

3. Once again, Genie Code will perform extensive reasoning at each step of execution. After completing its reasoning steps, Genie Code generates a new pipeline.
4. Return to the Databricks workspace. Using the menu on the left, click **Jobs & Pipelines**. You should see the newly deployed pipeline listed there. Click on **electroniz_silver_product_reviews_pipeline**.

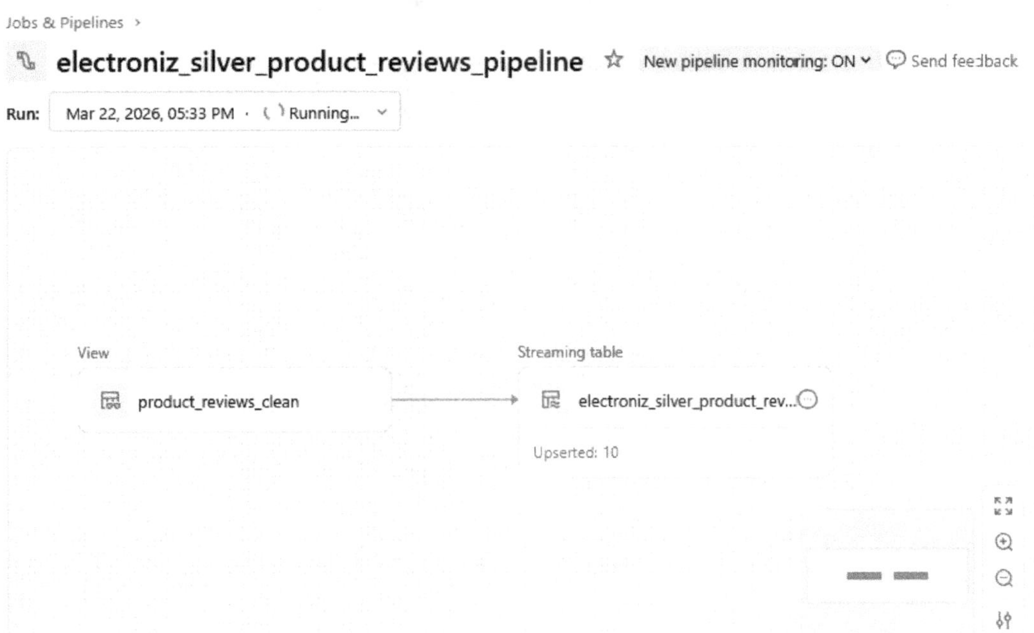

Figure 10.33: electroniz_silver_product_reviews_pipeline created

5. Navigate to the code of the newly created pipeline. Observe how Genie Code interpreted the data-quality instructions in the prompt.

```
# Data Quality: INNER JOIN with products on case-insensitive product_name match
# This automatically drops reviews where product_name doesn't match any product
result = parsed.join(
    products,
    lower(parsed["product_name"]) == lower(products["product_name"]),
    "inner"
```

Figure 10.34: Data Quality section of the code

6. Next, inspect the contents of the streaming table. Click **Catalog**, then navigate to **electroniz_catalog** > **electroniz_silver_schema** > **electroniz_silver_product_reviews**. Click on **Sample Data**.

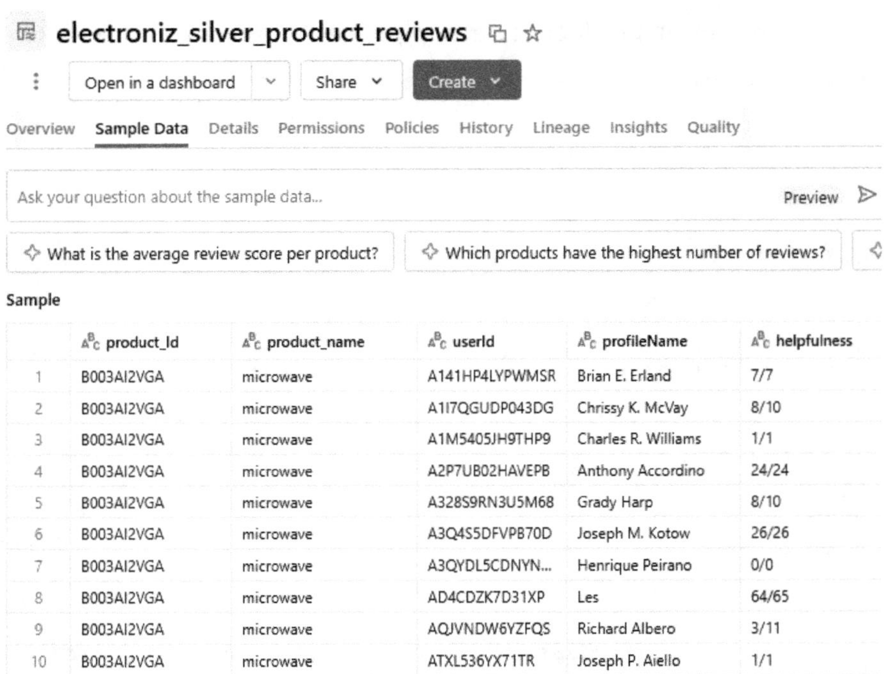

	product_Id	product_name	userId	profileName	helpfulness
1	B003AI2VGA	microwave	A141HP4LYPWMSR	Brian E. Erland	7/7
2	B003AI2VGA	microwave	A1I7QGUDP043DG	Chrissy K. McVay	8/10
3	B003AI2VGA	microwave	A1M5405JH9THP9	Charles R. Williams	1/1
4	B003AI2VGA	microwave	A2P7UB02HAVEPB	Anthony Accordino	24/24
5	B003AI2VGA	microwave	A328S9RN3U5M68	Grady Harp	8/10
6	B003AI2VGA	microwave	A3Q4S5DFVPB70D	Joseph M. Kotow	26/26
7	B003AI2VGA	microwave	A3QYDL5CDNYN...	Henrique Peirano	0/0
8	B003AI2VGA	microwave	AD4CDZK7D31XP	Les	64/65
9	B003AI2VGA	microwave	AQJVNDW6YZFQS	Richard Albero	3/11
10	B003AI2VGA	microwave	ATXL536YX71TR	Joseph P. Aiello	1/1

Figure 10.35: Data in electroniz_silver_product_reviews table

7. Click on Jobs & Pipelines and stop the **electroniz_silver_product_reviews_pipeline**.

With the product reviews pipeline now complete, we can shift our focus to developing the silver layer pipeline for website logs.

Creating the Electroniz silver pipeline for website logs

User activity on the e-commerce site is captured through web server logs, which record granular details about how visitors browse the site, how the system responds, and how transactions are executed during their interactions. The following is a list of key transformations to be performed when creating the silver table.

- This pipeline is complex. It treats `electroniz_bronze_geolocation` as a dimension table and derives the country from IP addresses. To enable a correct and efficient range join, the pipeline must reliably convert `ip1`, `ip2`, and `remote_ip` into numeric `LONG` values using a robust IPv4-to-long UDF.
- Several attributes should be correctly renamed and type-cast.
- Users' browser type must be extracted from the `agent` column using a `REGEX` pattern.

The following data quality rule will be performed when creating the silver table:

- Add robust error handling for `IP` and timestamp parsing as well as join failures, gracefully defaulting to `NULL` or a category such as `'Other'` when parsing or joins fail.

Follow the steps below to create the pipeline for website logs.

1. Navigate to the Databricks workspace, click on the Genie Code icon on the top right of your screen.
2. Issue the following prompt on Genie Code to create the silver logs geolocation pipeline:

```
Create a new streaming pipeline with details as follows
Pipeline Name: electroniz_silver_logs_geolocation_pipeline

Source tables:
electroniz_catalog.electroniz_bronze_schema.electroniz_bronze_website_logs
electroniz_catalog.electroniz_bronze_schema.electroniz_bronze_geolocation
(dimension table)

Target table:
electroniz_catalog.electroniz_silver_schema.electroniz_silver_logs_geolocat
ion
Mode: Continuous streaming
Operation: Merge
Merge key: remote_ip, event_time
Schema Inference: Infer schemas from both bronze tables
```

```
Transformations:
1. Treat electroniz_bronze_geolocation as a dimension, ensuring ip1 and ip2
(and website log remote_ip) are converted to numeric LONG values, using a
reliable IPv4-to-long UDF for a successful range join.
2. Parse time from website logs to event_time (timestamp) using the
accurate format (e.g. 'dd/MM/yyyy:HH:mm:ss').
3. Stream/process logs and perform a range join: remote_ip_long BETWEEN
ip1_long AND ip2_long.
4. Select only: agent, remote_ip, request, response, event_time,
country_code, country_name.
5. Add a new column extracting browser type from the agent string via
regex.
6. Implement robust error handling for IP/timestamp parsing and join
failures (e.g., default to NULL or 'Other' when parsing fails)
```

3. Once again, Genie Code will perform extensive reasoning at each step of execution. After completing its reasoning steps, Genie Code generates a new pipeline.
4. Return to the Databricks workspace. Using the menu on the left, click **Jobs & Pipelines**. You should see the newly deployed pipeline listed there. Click on **electroniz_silver_logs_geolocation_pipeline**.

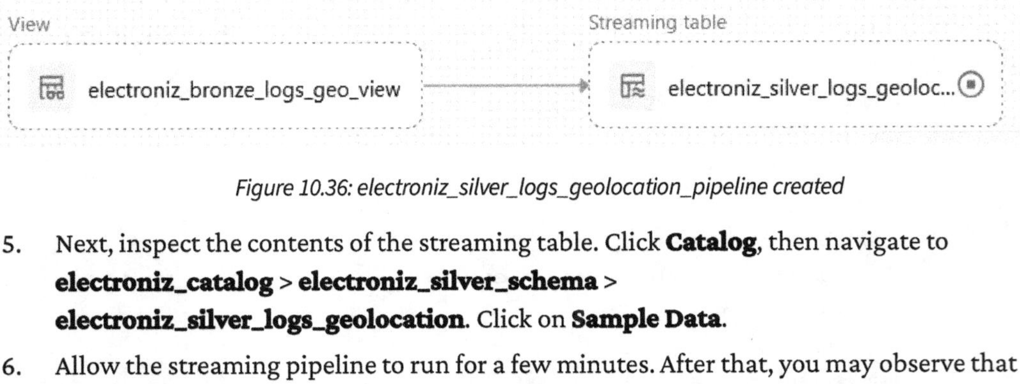

Figure 10.36: electroniz_silver_logs_geolocation_pipeline created

5. Next, inspect the contents of the streaming table. Click **Catalog**, then navigate to **electroniz_catalog** > **electroniz_silver_schema** > **electroniz_silver_logs_geolocation**. Click on **Sample Data**.
6. Allow the streaming pipeline to run for a few minutes. After that, you may observe that the **electroniz_silver_logs_geolocation** table remains empty. Because this is a complex pipeline, Genie-generated code may not be correct on the first attempt.
7. This highlights that AI-assisted development is still evolving and improves iteratively as it learns from earlier mistakes. When issues arise, review the Databricks pipeline event log, which captures operational events, data-quality checks, progress metrics, lineage details, warnings, and errors, all in a format that can be easily queried via both

the UI and SQL. Once you identify the root cause, refine your prompt and provide additional instructions to guide GenAI toward a more accurate solution.

8. Stop the **electroniz_silver_logs_geolocation_pipeline**.
9. Go back to Genie Code and issue the prompt:

```
electroniz_silver_logs_geolocation is empty. Can you fix the code.
```

10. Genie will again carry out extensive reasoning. After working through this reasoning process, Genie will revise and update the pipeline code accordingly.
11. Once the code is corrected, Genie Code will initiate a full pipeline refresh.

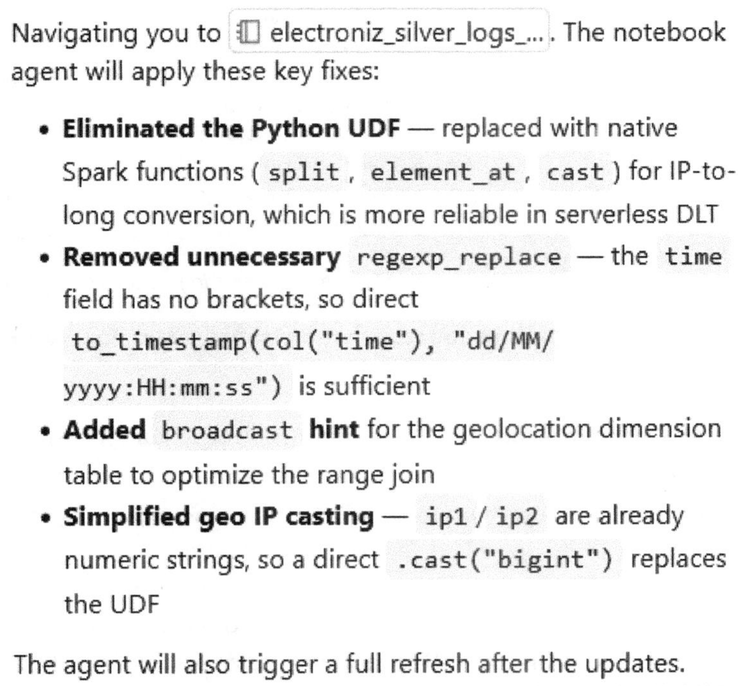

Figure 10.37: electroniz_silver_logs_geolocation_pipeline code regenerated

12. Next, inspect the contents of the streaming table. Click **Catalog**, then navigate to **electroniz_catalog** > **electroniz_silver_schema** > **electroniz_silver_logs_geolocation**. Click on **Sample Data**.

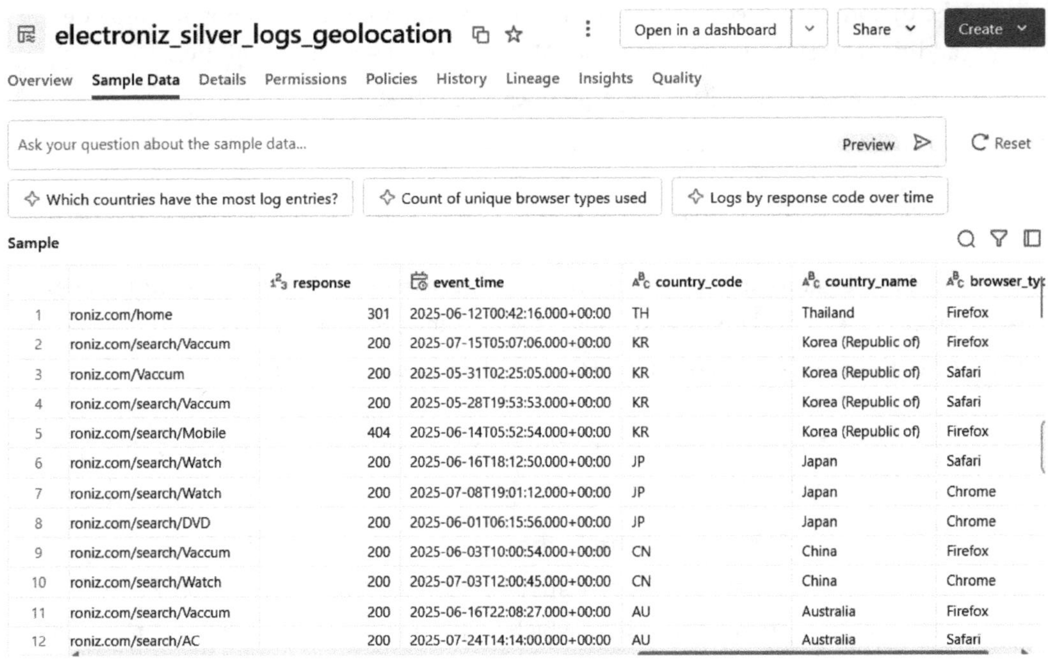

Figure 10.38: Data in electroniz_silver_logs_geolocation table

13. Click on **Jobs & Pipelines** and stop the **electroniz_silver_logs_geolocation_pipeline**.

> **Note**
>
> Even if the second run is successful, it's quite possible that multiple iterations will be required before Genie Code fully resolves all issues. That's simply the nature of working with generative AI—an iterative process of refinement and improvement.

If Genie Code is unable to resolve the issue after two or three iterations, refer to the authoritative pipeline code in the GitHub repository and compare it with the generated output to identify the discrepancy. Once the pipeline is successful, you can move on to create the silver pipeline for the store sale database.

Creating the Electroniz silver pipeline for store sales database

The Electroniz store sales database captures in-store purchase transactions and is structured to support day-to-day operations, reporting, and downstream analytical use cases.

Creating the Electroniz silver pipeline for the inventory table

The store sales inventory table tracks current product stock levels, providing visibility into available Electroniz inventory. The following is the list of some **key transformations** that will be performed when creating the silver table:

1. Attributes should be correctly type-cast – `inventory_date` from string (`DD/MM/YYYY`) to `DATE` type.
2. Rename the column product to `product_name`
3. Keep only these columns in the silver table: `inventory_date`, `product`, `inventory`, `updated_at`

Follow the steps below to create the silver pipeline for the inventory table.

1. Navigate to the Databricks workspace, click on the Genie Code icon on the top right of your screen.
2. Issue the following prompt on Genie Code to create the silver inventory pipeline:

```
Create a new streaming pipeline with details as follows
Pipeline Name: electroniz_silver_inventory_pipeline

Source table:
electroniz_catalog.electroniz_bronze_schema.electroniz_bronze_inventory
Target table:
electroniz_catalog.electroniz_silver_schema.electroniz_silver_inventory
Mode: Continuous streaming
Operation: Merge
Merge key: product_name

Transformations:
1. Rename fields:
   - product → product_name (string)
2. Cast inventory_date from string (DD/MM/YYYY) to date type
3. Keep the columns : inventory_date, product, inventory, updated_at
```

3. Once again, Genie Code will perform extensive reasoning at each step of execution. After completing its reasoning steps, Genie Code generates a new pipeline.
4. Return to the Databricks workspace. Using the menu on the left, click **Jobs & Pipelines**. You should see the newly deployed pipeline listed there.

5. Click on **electroniz_silver_inventory_pipeline**.

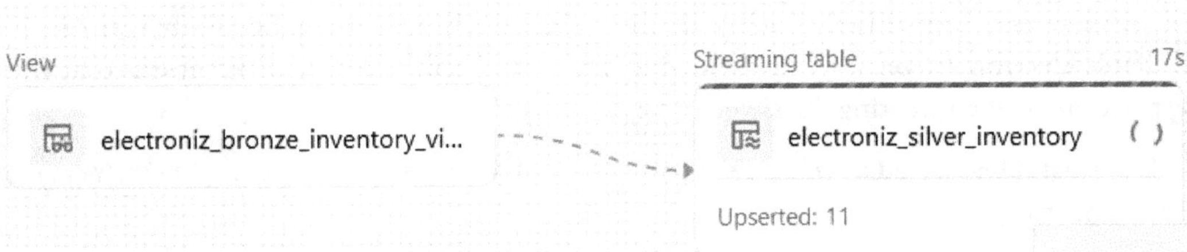

Figure 10.39: electroniz_silver_inventory_pipeline created

6. Next, inspect the contents of the streaming table. Click **Catalog**, then navigate to **electroniz_catalog** > **electroniz_silver_schema** > **electroniz_silver_inventory**. Click on **Sample Data**.

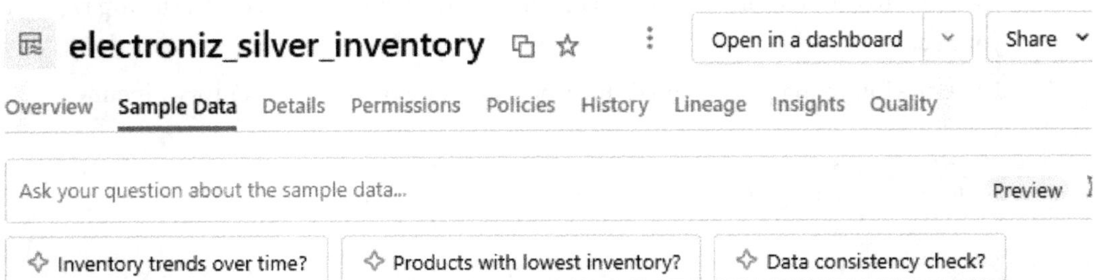

Sample

	inventory_date	product_name	inventory	updated_at
1	2025-04-18	Airconditioner	45	2026-02-16T17:50:52.603+00:00
2	2025-04-18	DVD	6789	2026-02-16T17:50:52.610+00:00
3	2025-04-18	Keyboard	564	2026-02-16T17:50:52.613+00:00
4	2025-04-18	Mice	900	2026-02-16T17:50:52.617+00:00
5	2025-04-18	Microwave	34	2026-02-16T17:50:52.607+00:00
6	2025-04-18	Mobile	659	2026-02-16T17:50:52.623+00:00
7	2025-04-18	Monitor	435	2026-02-16T17:50:52.620+00:00
8	2025-04-18	Phones	34	2026-02-16T17:50:52.627+00:00
9	2025-04-18	TV	43	2026-02-16T17:50:52.610+00:00
10	2025-04-18	Vaccum	500	2026-02-16T17:50:52.600+00:00
11	2025-04-18	Watch	100	2026-02-16T17:50:52.600+00:00

Figure 10.40: Data in electroniz_silver_inventory table

7. Click on **Jobs & Pipelines** and stop the **electroniz_silver_inventory_pipeline**.

Now we can move on to creating the silver pipeline for the products table.

Creating the Electroniz silver pipeline for the products table

The store sales product table contains details about Electroniz products available for sale across both its physical stores and ecommerce platform. The following transformations will be performed when creating the silver table.

1. Keep only these columns in the silver table: `product_code`, `product_name`, `product_category`, `updated_at`

Follow the steps below to create the silver pipeline for the inventory table.

1. Navigate to the Databricks workspace, click on the Genie Code icon on the top right of your screen.
2. Issue the following prompt on Genie Code to create the silver products pipeline:

```
Create a new streaming pipeline with details as follows
Pipeline Name: electroniz_silver_products_pipeline
Source table:
electroniz_catalog.electroniz_bronze_schema.electroniz_bronze_products
Target table:
electroniz_catalog.electroniz_silver_schema.electroniz_silver_products
Mode: Continuous streaming
Operation: Merge
Merge key: product_code, product_name
Transformations:
1. Keep the columns: product_code, product_name, product_category,
updated_at
```

3. Once again, Genie Code will perform extensive reasoning at each step of execution. After completing its reasoning steps, Genie Code generates a new pipeline.
4. Return to the Databricks workspace. Using the menu on the left, click **Jobs & Pipelines**. You should see the newly deployed pipeline listed there. Click on **electroniz_silver_products_pipeline**.

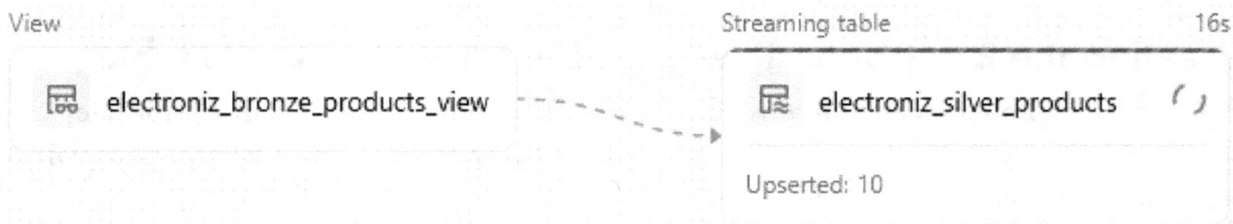

Figure 10.41: electroniz_silver_products_pipeline created

5. Next, inspect the contents of the streaming table. Click **Catalog**, then navigate to **electroniz_catalog** > **electroniz_silver_schema** > **electroniz_silver_products**.
6. Click on **Sample Data**.

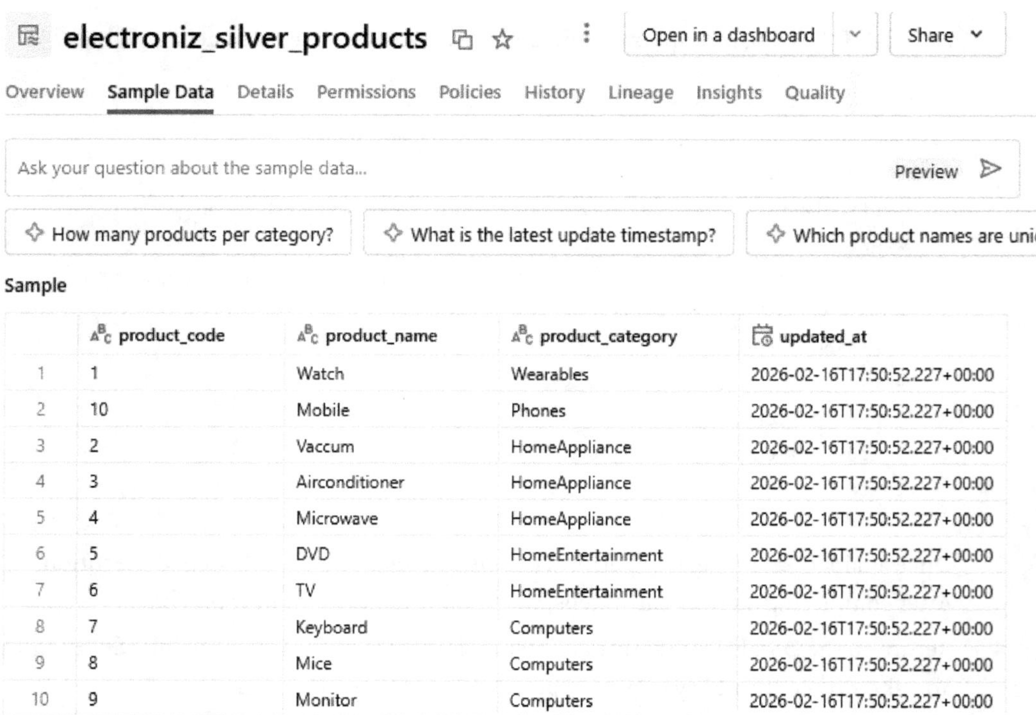

	product_code	product_name	product_category	updated_at
1	1	Watch	Wearables	2026-02-16T17:50:52.227+00:00
2	10	Mobile	Phones	2026-02-16T17:50:52.227+00:00
3	2	Vaccum	HomeAppliance	2026-02-16T17:50:52.227+00:00
4	3	Airconditioner	HomeAppliance	2026-02-16T17:50:52.227+00:00
5	4	Microwave	HomeAppliance	2026-02-16T17:50:52.227+00:00
6	5	DVD	HomeEntertainment	2026-02-16T17:50:52.227+00:00
7	6	TV	HomeEntertainment	2026-02-16T17:50:52.227+00:00
8	7	Keyboard	Computers	2026-02-16T17:50:52.227+00:00
9	8	Mice	Computers	2026-02-16T17:50:52.227+00:00
10	9	Monitor	Computers	2026-02-16T17:50:52.227+00:00

Figure 10.42: Data in electroniz_silver_products table

7. Click on **Jobs & Pipelines** and stop the **electroniz_silver_products_pipeline**.

With the silver layer product pipeline now complete, we can confidently proceed to developing the silver layer orders pipeline.

Creating the Electroniz silver pipeline for the orders table

The orders table contains information about customer transactions made in physical stores. The following is a list of key transformations to be performed when creating the silver table.

- Attributes should be correctly type casted – `sale_price` to `DOUBLE`, `order_date` to `DATE`.
- Drop columns `_ingested_at`, `_source_file`
- Convert the `sale_price` to `EUR` using the latest exchange rates in the `electroniz_silver_currency` table

The following is a list of key data-quality rules to be applied when creating the silver table.

- `order_mode` should fall in range `('NEW', 'DELETE', 'EDIT')`
- `currency` should fall in range `('USD', 'INR', 'EUR', 'CAD')`

Follow the steps below to create the silver pipeline for the orders table.

1. Navigate to the Databricks workspace, click on the Genie Code icon on the top right of your screen.
2. Issue the following prompt on Genie Code to create the silver sales orders pipeline:

```
Create a Lakeflow Declarative pipeline with details as follows
Pipeline Name: electroniz_silver_store_orders_pipeline

Source tables:
electroniz_catalog.electroniz_bronze_schema.electroniz_bronze_store_orders
electroniz_catalog.electroniz_silver_schema.electroniz_silver_currency
(dimension table)

Target table:
electroniz_catalog.electroniz_silver_schema.electroniz_silver_store_orders
Mode: Continuous streaming
Operation: Merge
Sequence by: updated_at
SCD Type 2 on order_number + customer_id sequenced by updated_at
Infer the schema of all source tables.

Transformations:
1. From bronze_store_orders:
   - Cast order_date to date using coalesce of multiple formats:
     DD/MM/YYYY, YYYY-MM-DD, MM/DD/YYYY
   - Cast sale_price to double
```

```
    - Drop columns: _ingested_at, _source_file

  2. Currency Conversion to EUR:
    - Use the latest exchange rates from the currency table
      (based on most recent date)
    - Convert sale_price to EUR using the appropriate exchange
      rate for each order's currency
    - Store the converted amount as sale_price_eur (float)
    - Do not include any currency table columns in the final output

  3. Final table must contain only these columns:
    order_number, customer_id, product_id, order_date, units,
    sale_price, currency, order_mode, updated_at, sale_price_eur

  Data Quality Rules:
  1. Data Quality Checks (drop invalid records):
    - order_mode must be IN ('NEW', 'DELETE', 'EDIT')
    - currency must be IN ('USD', 'INR', 'EUR', 'CAD')
```

Notice the use of **SCD Type 2** in the prompt above. Note that store orders may be edited or deleted over time, and the `order_mode` field captures these transitions using `NEW`, `EDIT`, and `DELETE` states. SCD Type 2 preserves the complete history of these state changes, enabling accurate point-in-time analysis of the order lifecycle.

3. Once again, Genie Code will perform extensive reasoning at each step of execution. After completing its reasoning steps, Genie Code generates a new pipeline.
4. Return to the Databricks workspace. Using the menu on the left, click **Jobs & Pipelines**. You should see the newly deployed pipeline listed there.
5. Click on **electroniz_silver_store_orders_pipeline**.

Figure 10.43: electroniz_silver_store_orders_pipeline created

6. Next, inspect the contents of the streaming table. Click Catalog, then navigate to **electroniz_catalog** > **electroniz_silver_schema** > **electroniz_silver_store_orders**. Click on **Sample Data**.

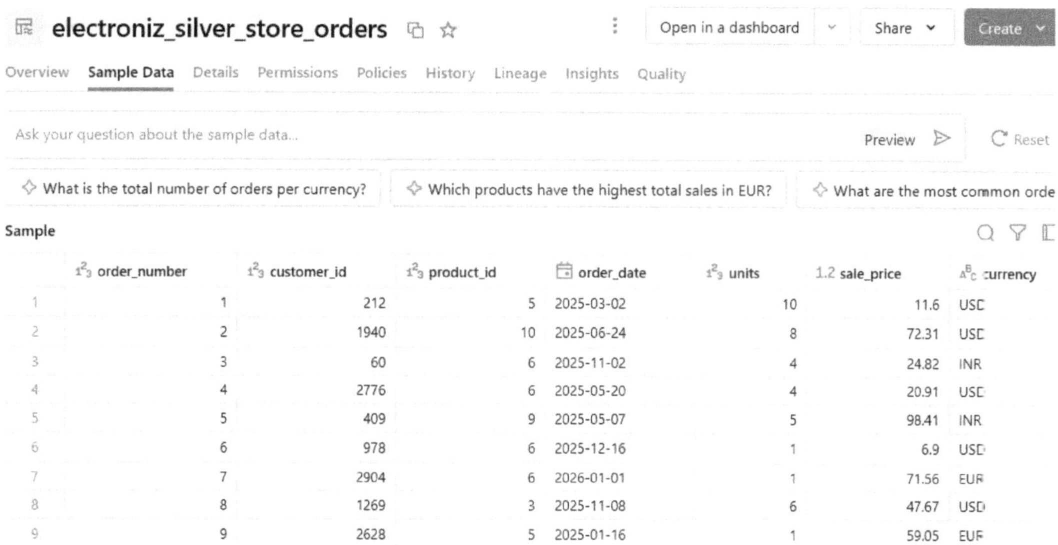

	order_number	customer_id	product_id	order_date	units	sale_price	currency
1	1	212	5	2025-03-02	10	11.6	USD
2	2	1940	10	2025-06-24	8	72.31	USD
3	3	60	6	2025-11-02	4	24.82	INR
4	4	2776	6	2025-05-20	4	20.91	USD
5	5	409	9	2025-05-07	5	98.41	INR
6	6	978	6	2025-12-16	1	6.9	USD
7	7	2904	6	2026-01-01	1	71.56	EUR
8	8	1269	3	2025-11-08	6	47.67	USD
9	9	2628	5	2025-01-16	1	59.05	EUR

Figure 10.44: Data in electroniz_silver_store_orders table

7. Click on **Jobs & Pipelines** and stop the **electroniz_silver_store_orders_pipeline**.

With the silver layer orders pipeline now complete, we can proceed to developing the silver layer customers pipeline.

Creating the Electroniz silver pipeline for the customers table

The store customer table contains information about Electroniz customers who purchase products in physical stores. The following transformations will be performed when creating the silver table:

- The `country` column contains inconsistent country representations, including abbreviations and full names. These values will be standardized to ensure uniformity.

The following is a list of key data-quality rules to be applied when creating the silver table.

- `credit_card` must not be `NULL`
- `email` must be validated using a strict `REGEX` pattern

Follow the steps below to create the silver pipeline for the customers table.

1. Navigate to the Databricks workspace, click on the Genie Code icon on the top right of your screen.
2. Issue the following prompt on Genie Code to create the silver sales customer pipeline:

```
Create a Lakeflow Declarative pipeline with details as follows
Pipeline Name: electroniz_silver_customers_pipeline

Source table:
electroniz_catalog.electroniz_bronze_schema.electroniz_bronze_store_custome
rs
Target table:
electroniz_catalog.electroniz_silver_schema.electroniz_silver_customers
Mode: Continuous streaming
SCD Type 2 on customer_id sequenced by updated_at
Transformations:
1. Standardize country to abbreviation:
    - 'United States', 'US', 'U.S.', 'America' → 'US'
   - 'United Kingdom','U.K' → 'UK'
   - 'India', 'IN' → 'IND'
   - 'Canada', 'CA' → 'CAN'
Data Quality Rules:
1. Data Quality Checks (drop invalid records):
   - credit_card must not be NULL
   - email must be valid using strict REGEX pattern
```

3. Once again, Genie Code will perform extensive reasoning at each step of execution. After completing its reasoning steps, Genie Code generates a new pipeline.

4. Return to the Databricks workspace. Using the menu on the left, click **Jobs & Pipelines**. You should see the newly deployed pipeline listed there. Click on **electroniz_silver_customers_pipeline**.

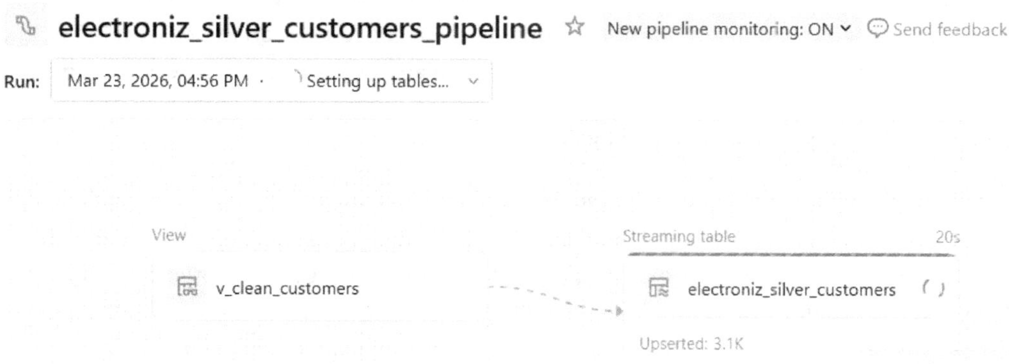

Figure 10.45: electroniz_silver_customers_pipeline created

5. Next, inspect the contents of the streaming table. Click **Catalog**, then navigate to **electroniz_catalog** > **electroniz_silver_schema** > **electroniz_silver_customers**.

6. Click on **Sample Data**.

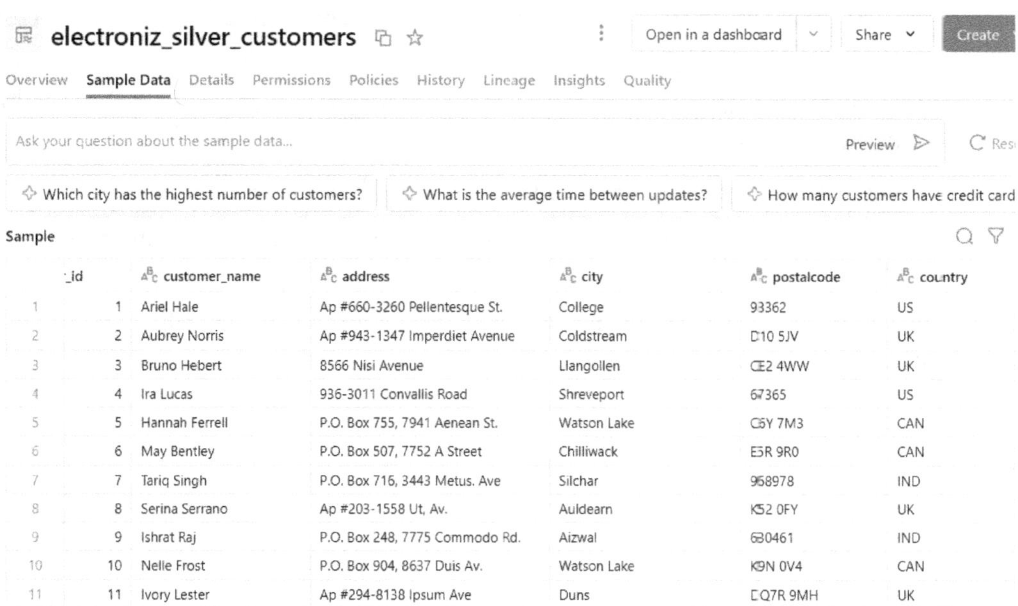

Figure 10.46: Data in electroniz_silver_customers table

7. Click on **Jobs & Pipelines** and stop the **electroniz_silver_customers_pipeline**.

This concludes the generation of the silver-layer pipelines, marking the successful transformation of curated bronze-layer data into more refined, structured, and analytics-ready datasets. At this stage, key business logic, data enrichment, standardization, and quality checks have been applied to ensure the data's consistency, reliability, and usability. The silver layer now serves as a stable foundation for downstream consumers, analytics workloads, and the subsequent gold-layer pipelines that will focus on aggregation and business-level insights.

Validating Data Quality

Did we meet Electroniz's data quality requirements? Validating data quality is a crucial step in ensuring that downstream analytics and business decisions are grounded in reliable and trustworthy data. This involves systematically evaluating the data for accuracy, completeness, consistency, and validity as it flows through the pipeline. By enforcing data quality rules, monitoring for anomalies, and addressing invalid or missing values early, issues can be identified and resolved before they cascade into downstream layers.

Strong data quality validation not only increases confidence in the data but also reduces rework, improves system reliability, and ensures the data remains fit for reporting, analytics, and operational use cases.

Following is a recommended data quality validation pattern aligned to the medallion architecture, ensuring issues are detected as early as possible and refined progressively across layers:

- **Bronze**: Validate schema conformity, perform raw ingestion checks, and detect nulls or malformed records at ingest time.
- **Silver**: Validate business logic, deduplication, type casting, and standardizations.
- **Gold**: Validate metrics to ensure analytical outputs are accurate, consistent, and business-ready.

This layered approach helps contain data quality issues, improves observability, and builds trust as data moves toward consumption.

> **Note**
>
> When building data pipelines, ensure transformations are dedicated to shaping and enriching data, while data quality checks are handled separately for validation and reporting—this clear separation improves maintainability and enables data quality rules to be reused across pipelines.

We can request **Genie Code** to help validate whether the transformation logic is correct and if the data quality requirements have been successfully met in the silver layer.

1. Navigate to the Databricks workspace and click on the Genie Code icon on the top right of your screen.
2. Issue the following prompt on Genie Code to validate data quality:

```
Can you generate a SQL to prove that all data quality expectations and
transformations in the silver pipelines were met?
```

3. Genie Code will perform extensive reasoning at each step of execution. It starts by shortlisting the silver layer tables.

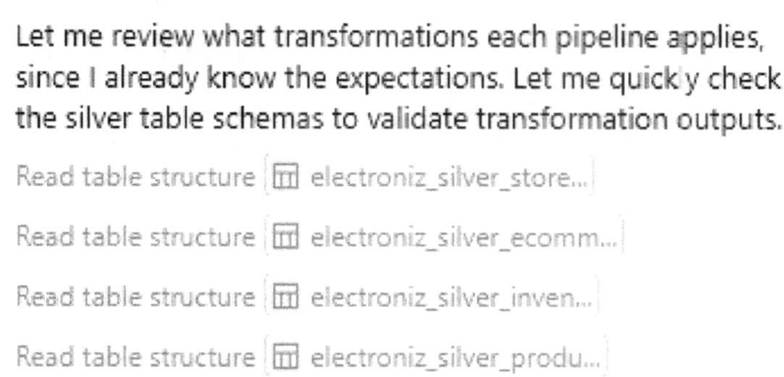

Figure 10.47: Genie Code shortlisting the silver layer tables

4. Once the silver tables have been shortlisted, Genie Code automatically extracts the data quality code from the silver layer pipeline code.

I've analyzed all 8 silver pipeline notebooks and identified **10 data quality expectations** across 3 pipelines that use `expect_or_drop` / `expect_all_or_drop` :

Pipeline	Expectations
`electroniz_silver_customers`	`valid_credit_card` , `valid_email`
`electroniz_silver_store_orders`	`valid_order_mode` , `valid_currency`
`electroniz_silver_ecomm_transactions`	`valid_customer_name` , `valid_address` , `valid_email_not_null` , `valid_order_number` , `valid_email_format` , `valid_currency`

Figure 10.48: Genie Code extracting data quality rules from code

5. Genie Code generates code for data quality validation and runs it. In this case, all data quality checks passed.

All **10 data quality expectations** across 3 silver tables returned **PASSED** — `total_rows` equals `passed_rows` for every check:

Silver Table	Expectations	Rows
`electroniz_silver_customers`	`valid_credit_card`, `valid_email`	3,100
`electroniz_silver_store_orders`	`valid_order_mode`, `valid_currency`	2,707
`electroniz_silver_ecomm_transactions`	6 expectations (name, address, email, order_number, email format, currency)	20

Figure 10.49: Genie Code validating expectations logic

6. Genie Code executed data quality validations and verified that the transformation logic was applied correctly.

Section 1 — DLT Expectations (10 checks): Validates the explicit `expect_or_drop / expect_all_or_drop` rules on customers, store orders, and ecomm transactions.

Section 2 — Transformation Validations (18 checks): Verifies the key transformation logic, including:

Pipeline	Checks
`electroniz_silver_customers`	Country standardization
`electroniz_silver_store_orders`	Date parsing, sale_price cast, EUR conversion
`electroniz_silver_ecomm_transactions`	Product join integrity, date parsing, country standardization
`electroniz_silver_products`	Core columns populated

Figure 10.50: Genie Code validating transformation logic

7. Genie Code generated detailed SQL queries for these checks, producing a comprehensive data quality validation report.

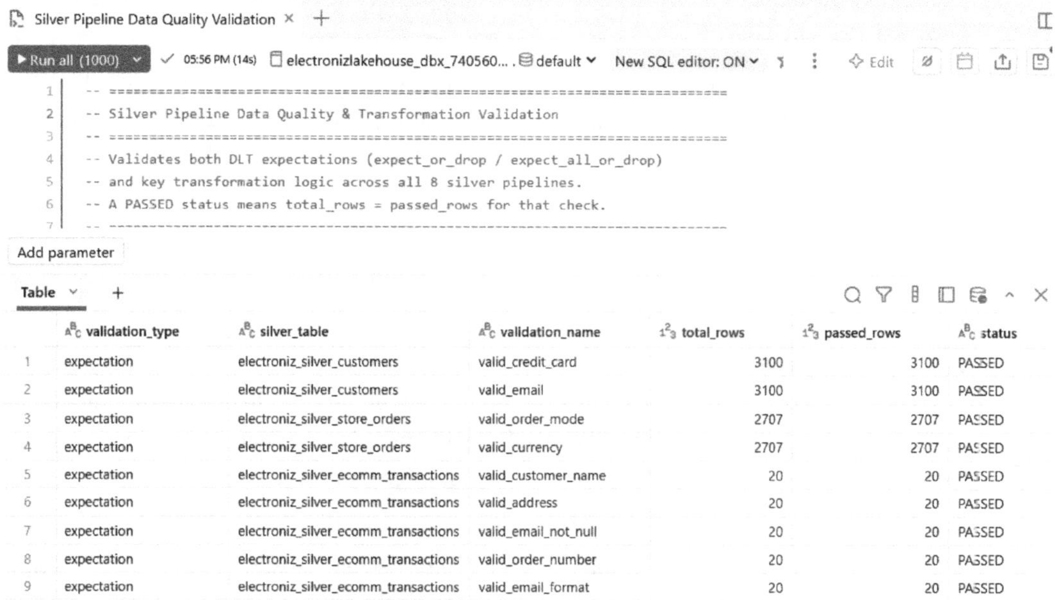

Figure 10.51: Data quality validation report

Strong data quality validation isn't about perfection—it's about predictability, transparency, and trust.

The goal is to know *when* data is good, *when* it's not, and *what to do about it*—before it impacts decisions. In *Chapter 12*, we will explore how organizations approach data observability—how they monitor and ensure the health, reliability, and trustworthiness of data as it moves through modern data pipelines and ultimately powers data products. We will also examine how alerting fits into this ecosystem, enabling teams to proactively detect anomalies, surface data-quality issues, and respond to problems before they impact downstream consumers.

Handling Gen AI inconsistencies

We have observed that, at times, generative AI systems such as Genie Code and Claude Code can behave inconsistently. It's important to recognize that generative AI is not an exact science; it operates on a probabilistic basis. As a result, it commonly adopts an iterative approach to problem-solving, refining its output over multiple cycles rather than delivering a perfect solution on the first attempt.

The following are some of the key reasons why generative AI can fall short in certain scenarios:

- **Inadequate prompt engineering**: When prompts are loosely defined or lack sufficient detail, Gen AI may interpret them differently than intended. Humans naturally rely on domain knowledge to fill in gaps, whereas AI depends entirely on what is explicitly stated in the prompt.

- **Limited runtime awareness:** In some cases, Gen AI may generate code without executing it. As a result, issues may only surface at runtime due to edge cases, data dependencies, or platform-specific behaviors.
- **Complexity**: As pipelines grow more complex—with multiple joins, UDFs, streaming semantics, schema evolution, and error handling—the likelihood of errors increases. In such cases, Gen AI often requires several iterations before arriving at a correct and reliable solution.
- **Predictive approach**: Gen AI does not "understand" systems the way humans do. Instead, it predicts the most likely next steps based on patterns learned from data. As such, these outputs are inherently **probabilistic**, meaning predictions may not always be accurate or optimal, especially in complex or edge-case scenarios.
- **Feedback**: Gen AI improves through continuous user feedback. Each failure, correction, or adjustment helps refine subsequent outputs, much like a junior engineer learning and improving through code reviews and iterative guidance.

Generative AI will continue to improve in areas like reasoning, context handling, and integration. However, it will remain fundamentally probabilistic, meaning it predicts likely outcomes rather than producing guaranteed results. As a result, iteration will remain a natural part of working with Gen AI—especially for complex systems. The key shift in the future will not be the elimination of iteration, but a significant reduction in effort and time per iteration, with Gen AI acting as an increasingly capable collaborator alongside human expertise.

Data engineers can adapt to Gen AI–related challenges by shifting from expecting **perfection** to designing for iteration, validation, and collaboration. Here are a few ways they can easily adapt:

- Instead of treating Gen AI–generated code as production-ready, engineers should view it as a high-quality first draft that accelerates development but still requires careful review.
- Strengthen the fundamentals by clearly defining requirements, applying solid data modeling principles, implementing explicit error handling, and ensuring thorough, robust testing.
- Write precise prompts, providing detailed context, and iteratively refining instructions become core skills, much like code reviews or design discussions.

- Embed safeguards such as data quality checks, runtime validations, and observability to catch issues Gen AI may miss.
- Ultimately, the most successful data engineers will use Gen AI as a force multiplier, pairing automation and speed with human judgment, domain expertise, and accountability.

Because Genie Code can generate different implementations across sessions, the Electroniz silver pipeline code you produce may not exactly match the examples shown here. To mitigate this variability, the definitive versions of the generated pipelines are provided in the Packt course GitHub repository linked below:

`https://github.com/PacktPublishing/Data-Engineering-with-Apache-Spark-Databricks-and-Lakehouse-Second-Edition/tree/main/chapter10/notebooks`.

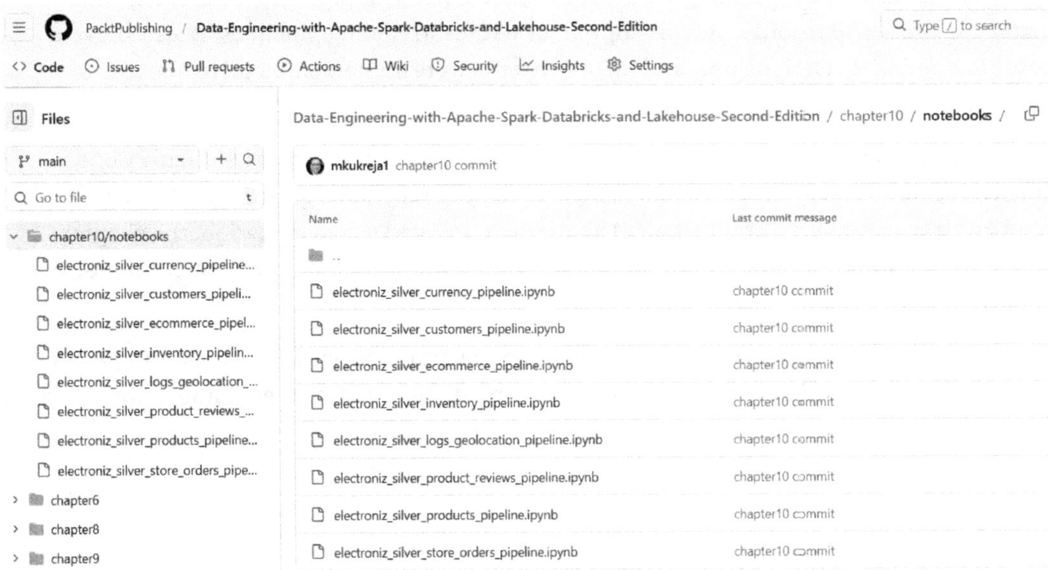

Figure 10.52: Master copy of silver layer pipelines

The notebooks in this repository can be used as a reliable reference for comparison. In some cases, you may need to replace your locally generated pipeline code with the version from the Git repository, which should be treated as the authoritative master copy. Successful data engineers will embrace Gen AI as a collaborator, applying experience and rigor to transform fast drafts into dependable systems.

Summary

In this chapter, we focused on building the silver layer of the Electroniz Lakehouse, which stored cleansed, conformed, and analytics-ready data. The silver layer served as the single source of truth, delivering curated data to end users in a consistent, readily consumable form. We explored why data curation was essential, walked through the end-to-end curation process, and demonstrated how common data-quality scenarios were addressed through practical, code-driven examples.

The silver layer was positioned as the core transformation zone, where streaming data was processed in real time as it arrived. Key activities included deduplication, type casting, standardization, validation, and enrichment. The chapter paid particular attention to handling CDC-driven duplicates, enforcing cross-dataset consistency, applying PII redaction, and managing orphaned records and missing values within streaming pipelines. It also showed how SCDs, dataset relationships, and MDM patterns were implemented incrementally to preserve trusted master data.

A major emphasis was placed on accelerating development using Databricks Genie Code, illustrating how GenAI generated and refined streaming pipeline logic for the silver layer. By combining structured streaming, Delta Lake, and AI-assisted code generation, the chapter demonstrated how teams could rapidly deliver reliable, scalable pipelines that continuously produced trusted silver datasets.

In *Chapter 11*, we build on this foundation by using Electroniz silver data to create aggregated datasets that support descriptive, diagnostic, and predictive analytics, enabling more informed decision-making across the organization.

Get this book's PDF version and more

Scan the QR code (or go to `packtpub.com/unlock`). Search for this book by name, confirm the edition, and then follow the steps on the page.

UNLOCK NOW

Note: Keep your invoice handy. Purchases made directly from Packt don't require an invoice.

11

Building the Next-Gen Data Analytics Gold Layer

Well done on making it this far. Your journey is now entering its final and most impactful stage. I'm pleased to share that our skilled driver (the data engineer) has successfully navigated the vehicle (the data pipeline) to this critical milestone. We have now arrived at the destination where value is fully realized. In this last leg of the journey, all previously curated data is refined and purpose-built to support descriptive, diagnostic, predictive, and prescriptive analytics.

In this chapter, we will explore:

- Understanding the gold layer of the medallion architecture
- Process of transforming curated data into high-value analytical assets
- Walk through the end-to-end process of aggregating data, highlighting key design and modeling considerations
- Validating the aggregation pipeline, ensuring the resulting datasets are analytics-ready and aligned with business requirements.

Understanding the gold layer

The gold is the consumption-ready, business-optimized, and analytics-grade representation of data in the Medallion Architecture. At this stage, data is fully refined, enriched, and modeled to support downstream operational analytics needs such as BI dashboards, ML/AI, and data products. Before diving into the mechanics and the construction of the gold layer in the Electroniz lakehouse, it is important to revisit the original motivation behind building the lakehouse itself. During the discovery phase, Electroniz identified several critical business requirements that continue to guide this effort as follows:

- A need for a near-real-time sales analytics platform to serve customer demands more effectively
- A desire to optimize and streamline the advertising spend through intelligent analysis of user traffic on their e-commerce website
- A goal to reduce customer dissatisfaction by minimizing order fulfillment disruptions caused by inventory shortages.

These objectives directly shape how data is modeled, aggregated, and consumed in the gold layer. Thus far, we have successfully identified, ingested, and curated data from a wide range of sources to support intelligent decision-making through modern analytics. At this stage, the silver layer contains data that has been standardized, validated, duplicated, and secured, providing a trusted and consistent foundation. However, while this curated data is robust and reliable, it does not yet fully answer the business questions Electroniz set out to address. Simply put, the silver layer prepares the data, but it does not deliver the insights. So how do we bridge this gap and uncover the answers that the business truly needs?

The primary objective of the gold layer is to aggregate and summarize data in a way that makes it meaningful and actionable for analytics and decision-making. **Data aggregation** is a technique used to uncover patterns and trends across large sets of observations by grouping data based on selected variables. Common examples include calculating total sales for a given quarter, measuring the number of unique users who visit a website each month, or determining the average employee salary by department. These aggregated views transform detailed data into concise metrics that directly support business insights.

By design, the data structure (or schema) in the silver layer closely mirrors that of the original source systems from which the data was ingested, preserving much of its original shape and granularity. In contrast, aggregated data in the gold layer is purposefully reshaped to support analytics and reporting, typically taking on a two-dimensional structure, such as a relational table, or a multi-dimensional structure, such as a cube optimized for slicing and dicing across multiple analytical dimensions. A cube is a data structure that enables analysis across multiple hierarchies at once, for example, examining sales by product, country, and time period within a single query.

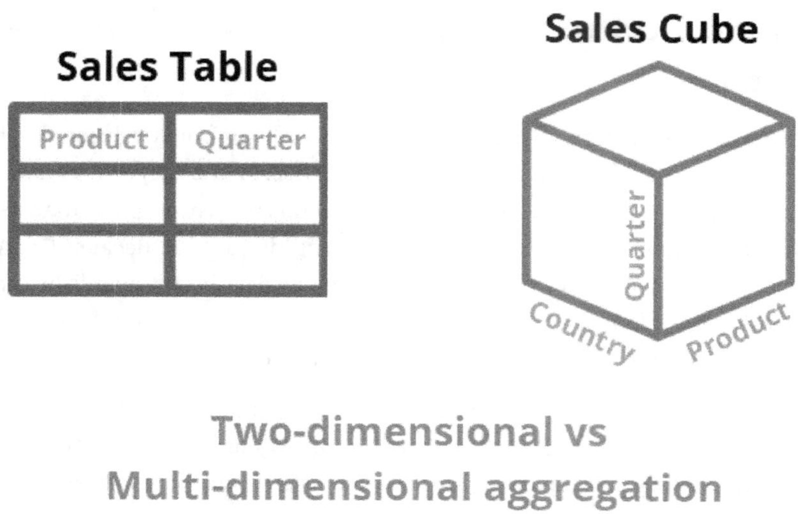

Figure 11.1: Two-dimensional vs. multi-dimensional data

Let's explore this distinction in a bit more detail:

- **Two-dimensional aggregations** summarize data across two variables, typically forming a simple tabular view. For example, you might calculate total sales per quarter for a specific product, where time and product are the two dimensions of analysis.
- **Multi-dimensional aggregations** extend this concept by summarizing data across multiple variables organized into hierarchies. For instance, you could analyze total quarterly sales for a product while further breaking the results down by country or region, enabling richer, multi-angle analysis of the data.

> **Note**
>
> In data terminology, each record in the silver layer represents an individual observation, capturing a single measured data point. A dataset is made up of many such observations, each described by a consistent set of variables that define the attributes or fields associated with each record.

Now that we understand the value of data and the role aggregation plays in extracting meaningful insights, we can turn our attention to how data is aggregated and walk through the key steps involved.

Understanding the role of data stewards in the GenAI era

In the era of **Generative AI** (**GenAI**), data stewards are evolving from traditional data custodians into guardians of trust and responsible data use. While they still oversee data quality, definitions, and governance, their role now extends to ensuring that data used by GenAI systems is accurate, ethical, representative, and fit for purpose. Because GenAI systems generate narratives and recommendations rather than metrics, data stewards help prevent bias, misinformation, and misuse by validating data sources, tracking provenance, and determining whether certain data should be used for AI at all.

At the same time, data stewards are increasingly becoming enablers of AI-ready data and responsible self-service. With modern GenAI tools such as Claude Code and Genie Code, they can now curate datasets, generate insights, and refine data assets more independently, thereby reducing reliance on data engineers for routine preparation and exploration tasks. This shift allows stewards to move faster while staying closely aligned with business context. Rather than acting primarily as gatekeepers, today's data stewards embed governance directly into platforms and workflows. By doing so, they help organizations scale GenAI initiatives safely, ensuring transparency, regulatory compliance, and sustained confidence in AI-generated outcomes.

We can now move forward with kick-starting the creation of the Electroniz gold pipelines, establishing a solid foundation for trusted, analytics- and AI-ready data.

Creating the gold pipeline

While the goal of data aggregation may appear straightforward, achieving it effectively requires a well-defined and disciplined process. Data aggregation is a shared responsibility between the customer and the data engineer, where success depends on their close collaboration. Each party contributes unique expertise: customers bring business context, requirements, and analytical intent, while data engineers apply technical skills to design, implement, and optimize the aggregation logic. Together, these complementary perspectives ensure that aggregated data is both technically sound and aligned with business needs.

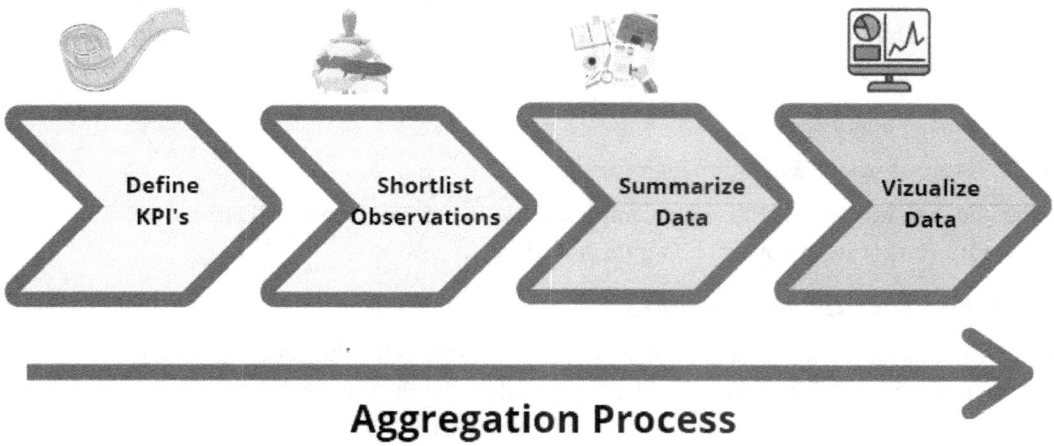

Figure 11.2: Data aggregation process

Defining KPIs

The data aggregation process begins with clearly defining the **key performance indicators (KPIs)**, measurable metrics used to evaluate an organization's progress toward its goals and assess success or failure against defined objectives. Translating a business gold-layer dataset into KPIs entails translating refined, business-aligned data into measurable outcomes that reflect organizational performance. By mapping business questions to specific fields, applying appropriate aggregations, and layering in relevant dimensions like time, region, or product category, organizations can derive clear, consistent metrics that drive decision-making.

Because KPIs are inherently business-focused and closely tied to organizational goals, this responsibility should not rest solely with data engineers. Instead, it is essential to collaborate with customers and business stakeholders, who possess deeper domain-level knowledge and a clearer understanding of what success looks like. Their input ensures that the aggregated data aligns with real business priorities and delivers meaningful, actionable insights.

As selecting the right KPIs requires a deep understanding of business strategy, operations, and success criteria, they are best defined by individuals with strong domain expertise who can accurately judge whether a given indicator truly reflects business performance. Data owners and data stewards are best positioned to perform this role, as they possess both a deep understanding of the data and a direct connection to the business processes it represents. Their involvement ensures that KPIs are not only meaningful and measurable but also aligned with organizational goals and capable of driving informed decision-making.

Once the KPIs have been defined and aligned with business stakeholders, the following deliverables should be documented and officially submitted to business stakeholders before proceeding to the next step.

- List of defined KPIs
- Agreed-upon calculation logic for the KPIs

With the definition of the KPIs now completed, we can move on to shortlisting the observations that will support their interpretation.

Shortlisting observations

After the KPIs have been clearly established, the next step is for the data engineer, in collaboration with the customer, to identify and shortlist the relevant observations (datasets) to be included in the aggregation process. This requires conducting a detailed assessment of the datasets to fully understand their relationships, dependencies, grouping logic, and filtering criteria. Such analysis ensures that the selected datasets align with the defined KPIs and support accurate, meaningful aggregations.

Once the observations have been shortlisted and assessed, the following deliverables should be documented and submitted to business stakeholders for approval before proceeding:

- Curated list of observations
- Defined relationships between datasets
- Defined groupings and filters
- Defined validation rules

After successfully shortlisting the key observations, the next step is to aggregate the data so those insights can be quantified, validated, and transformed into meaningful business metrics.

Aggregating the data

At this stage, the data engineer designs and implements the logic required to perform the defined data aggregations. This aggregation logic can be authored using several technologies, with SQL and Spark being the most used in modern data platforms. Once developed and validated, the aggregation logic is incorporated into the broader data pipeline, which is then executed on a scheduled basis to consistently produce refreshed, analytics-ready datasets in the gold layer.

Once the aggregation logic has been developed and validated, the following deliverable should be in place:

- A comprehensive code and data artifact covering the aggregation logic
- Analytics-ready gold layer datasets

With the gold layer data now prepared, we arrive at the final stage where the data's story is brought to life.

Visualizing the data

Humans naturally connect with visual information, making data visualization a powerful tool for insight and decision-making. Presenting aggregated data through charts, maps, and interactive dashboards allows modern decision-makers to quickly understand trends, patterns, and anomalies. As discussed in *Chapter 1, The Story of Data Engineering and Analytics*, effective data storytelling plays a crucial role in conveying meaning beyond raw numbers. Visualizing aggregated data transforms metrics into a compelling narrative, one that clearly reflects an organization's overall health, performance, and direction. Once the data has been visualized, the following deliverable should be in place:

- Published business intelligence dashboard code
- Data stories and insights in a visual format

We began this book with the statement, "*Every byte of data has a story to tell. The real question is whether that story is being narrated accurately, securely, and efficiently*". Having laid the foundation and built each layer of the lakehouse, we are now at the point where that story can be told with clarity and purpose. We are ready to narrate the story of Electroniz.

Planning the Electroniz gold layer

Before we begin preparing the data sources, it's important to understand the specific portion of the Electroniz architecture we will be implementing in this chapter. Taking a moment to ground ourselves in the overall design helps clarify both the scope of work ahead and how each component fits into the broader data platform.

In the architecture diagram showcased in *Figure 11.3*, the red-outlined section highlights the exact set of components we will focus on building.

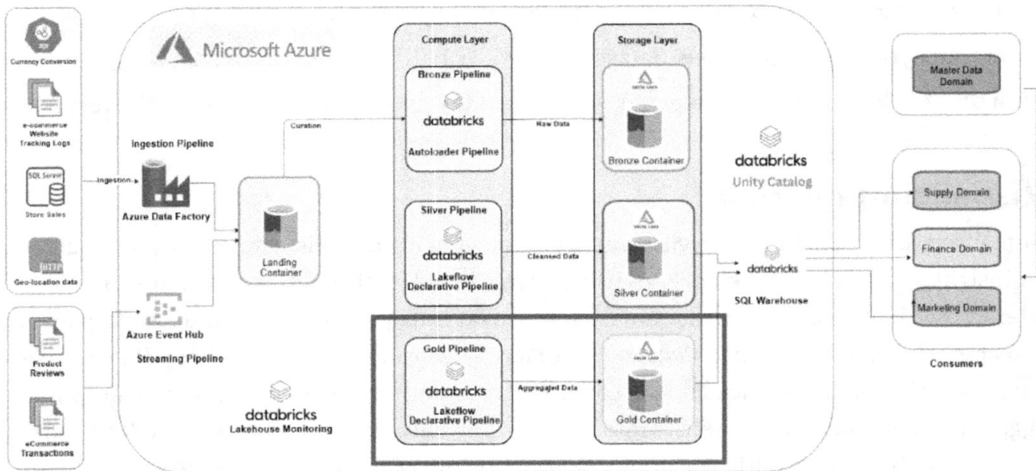

Figure 11.3: Portion of the Electroniz architecture that will be built in this chapter

This section represents the data products and supporting layers that translate curated data into trusted, business-ready outputs. Throughout this chapter, we will incrementally construct these components, explaining the design choices, governance considerations, and technical patterns that underpin them.

> **Note**
>
> A well-designed gold layer encodes trust, intent, and accountability, going beyond aggregation. It reflects agreed business definitions, ownership, and usage contracts, turning data into a dependable product.

Before we begin, let's take a moment to understand the structure of the pipelines that will be built in this chapter.

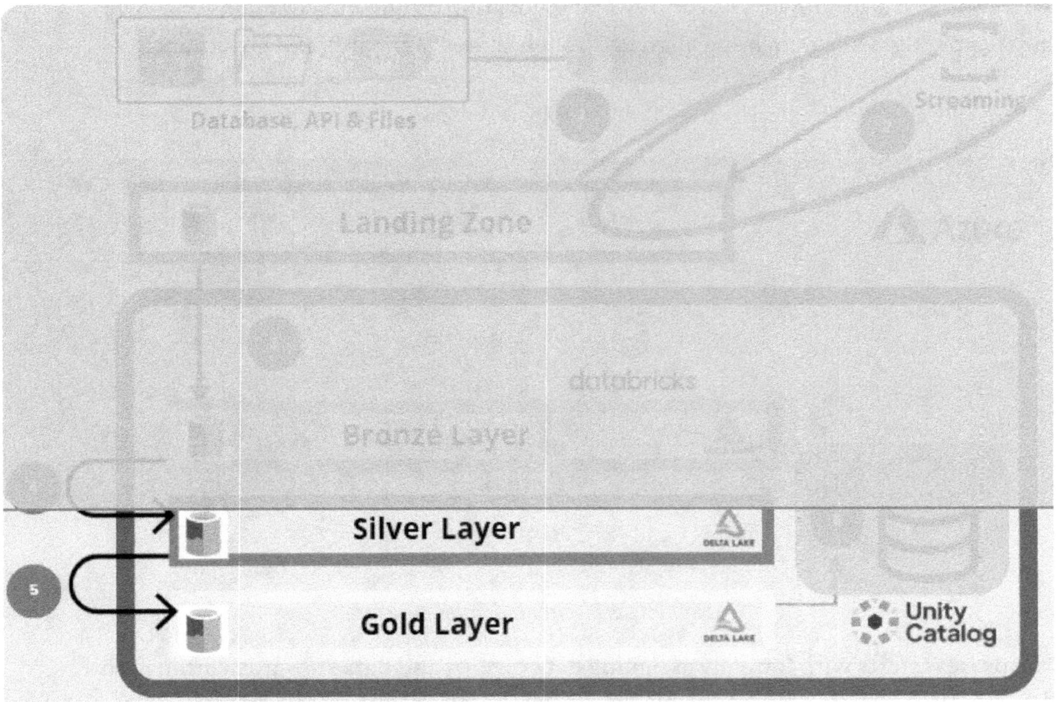

Figure 11.4: Electroniz gold pipeline

Before we start building the gold-layer pipelines, we should first take the time to understand Electroniz's domain structure.

Defining domains

We are going to organize Electroniz into four domains: one general (master) domain and three domains aligned to specific business areas, each accountable for its own set of data products. The master domain will own and manage shared data products used across all business domains, such as the master customer golden record, core dimensions, and enterprise-wide metrics. This ensures consistency, reuse, and a single source of truth for data that spans multiple business areas.

The three business-aligned domains, covering supply, finance, and marketing, will be responsible for developing, maintaining, and evolving data products that support their respective operational and analytical needs. By adopting this domain-oriented structure, Electroniz establishes clear ownership and accountability through designated data owners and data stewards, enables faster decision-making by reducing cross-domain dependencies, and strengthens alignment between data products and business outcomes.

This approach also supports scalability and innovation by allowing domains to evolve independently while remaining aligned through shared standards and governance.

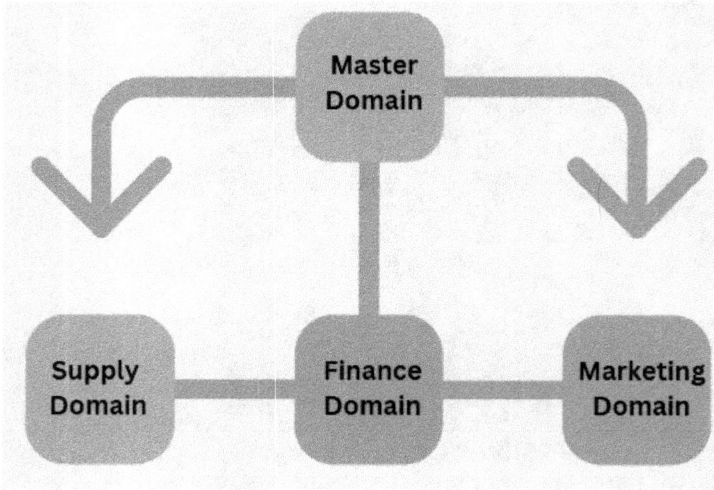

Figure 11.5: Electroniz domain structure

The process starts with formally assigning data owners and data stewards within each domain. Data owners are responsible for setting the vision, priorities, and intended use of the data products within their domains. Data stewards are accountable for day-to-day governance activities, including data quality, consistency, documentation, metadata management, and adherence to security and privacy standards. Together, they will ensure that domain data products are trusted, well-governed, and AI-ready. With the gold schema structure now agreed upon and aligned to the defined domains, we can move forward with spinning up the required resources for the Electroniz gold pipeline.

With the Gold-layer schema now defined and aligned with the established domains, we can proceed to provision the resources required for the Electroniz Gold pipeline.

Preparing resources for the Electroniz gold layer

To implement the gold layer of the Electroniz lakehouse, we will provision and configure the following Azure resources. These components will establish the foundational storage and compute capabilities necessary for ingesting data from the landing layer into the lakehouse environment:

Azure Resource	Resource Name
Azure Data Lake Storage Gen 2 Storage Account	`electronizlakehouse`
Azure Data Lake Storage Gen 2 Container	`gold`
Azure Databricks	`electronizlakehouse-dbx`

Table 11.1: Azure resources for the Electroniz gold layer

Since the **electronizlakehouse Azure Data Lake Storage** (**ADLS**) account and `electronizlakehouse-dbx` Databricks workspace already exist, the only remaining step is to create a new container. Let's begin by provisioning this resource in Azure:

1. Create a container that will store the gold layer data. Paste the following commands into Azure Cloud Shell. You can execute them one at a time or run the whole block together:

```
STORAGEACCOUNTNAME="electronizlakehouse"
NAMESPACE="gold"
az storage fs create \
-n $NAMESPACE \
--account-name $STORAGEACCOUNTNAME \
--metadata project=lakehouse environment=development layer=gold \
--only-show-errors
```

2. On the Azure portal, click on **electronizlakehouse** > **Storage browser** > **Blob containers**

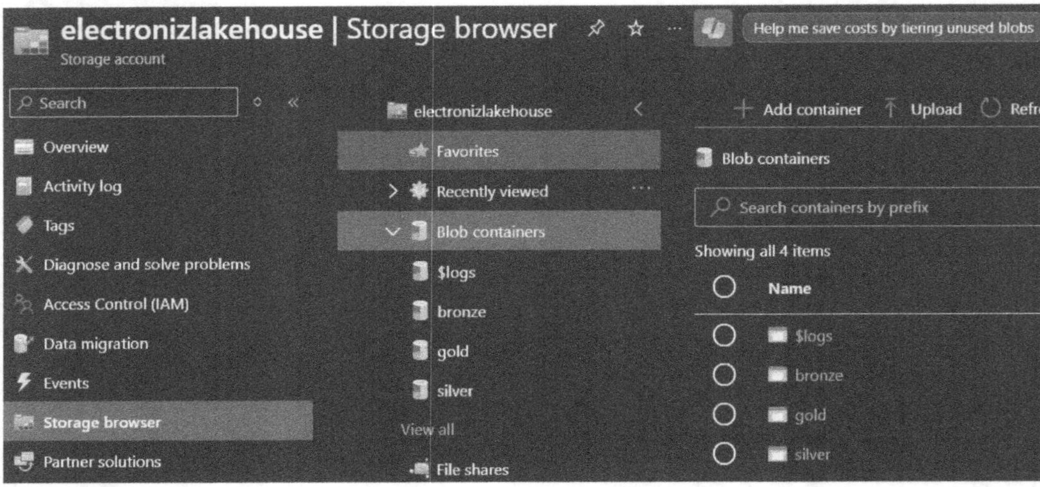

Figure 11.6: Newly created blob container for gold layer data

With the Azure storage resource in place, we can officially start building the Electroniz gold pipeline.

Developing the Electroniz gold layer pipelines

Table 11.2 summarizes the high-level strategy for developing the gold layer pipelines. Using Databricks Lakeflow, Spark Declarative Pipelines, and materialized views, the pipelines will continuously process streaming data originating from the silver layer.

Domain	**Pipeline Type**	**Data Product Dashboards**	**Gold Schema and Views**
Master	Databricks Lakeflow Spark Declarative Pipelines and Materialized View	Master Customer Data	Catalog: `electroniz_catalog` Schema: `electroniz_gold_master_schema` Materialized View: `mvw_electroniz_gold_golden_record_customers`

Domain	Pipeline Type	Data Product Dashboards	Gold Schema and Views
Supply	Databricks Lakeflow Spark Declarative Pipelines and Materialized View	Supply Analytics – Inventory Projections	Catalog: `electroniz_catalog` Schema: `electroniz_gold_supply_schema` Materialized View: `electroniz_product_inventory_projections`
Finance	Databricks Lakeflow Spark Declarative Pipelines and Materialized View	Finance Analytics – Total Sales by Quarter and Year Finance Analytics – Highest Grossing Products	Catalog: `electroniz_catalog` Schema: `electroniz_gold_finance_schema` Materialized View: `electroniz_product_sales_quarter_year`
Marketing	Databricks Lakeflow Spark Declarative Pipelines and Materialized View	Marketing Analytics - Customer Browsing Behavior Marketing Analytics - Web Hits by Country	Catalog: `electroniz_catalog` Schema: `electroniz_gold_marketing_schema` Materialized View: `electroniz_product_web_hits_by_country`

Table 11.2: High-level approach for developing gold pipelines

Figure 11.7 illustrates how the resulting datasets are stored in schemas that align with the Electroniz domain structure described in the previous section. Each gold domain reads its data from a common silver layer that serves as the *single source of truth*.

Figure 11.7: Electroniz gold schemas in line with domains

In *Table 11.2*, we showed that the resulting gold layer outputs will be stored as materialized views. Let's now focus on how these materialized views are organized and leveraged within the Electroniz domain model.

Understanding materialized views

In *Chapter 5, Understanding Databricks*, we briefly touched on materialized views. This is an opportunity to explore them in more depth. Materialized views store precomputed results of a query instead of recomputing them on every execution. They refresh automatically when the underlying data changes and are commonly used to enhance query performance, particularly for frequently queried, aggregated datasets. To fully understand materialized views, it is first important to understand how standard views work.

Consider the scenario in *Figure 11.8*, in which a standard view is created by joining two tables. A standard view does not store data itself; instead, it stores only the SQL definition. The database query optimizer expands the view definition at runtime and executes the underlying query as though it were written directly in the calling SQL statement. Each time the view is queried, the underlying SQL is re-executed for each session. This behavior can be highly undesirable, particularly in complex scenarios involving multiple joins, aggregations, or intricate grouping logic. As data volume and query complexity increase, repeated re-computation can lead to significant performance overhead, increased CPU and I/O usage, and longer query response times, especially in high-concurrency environments.

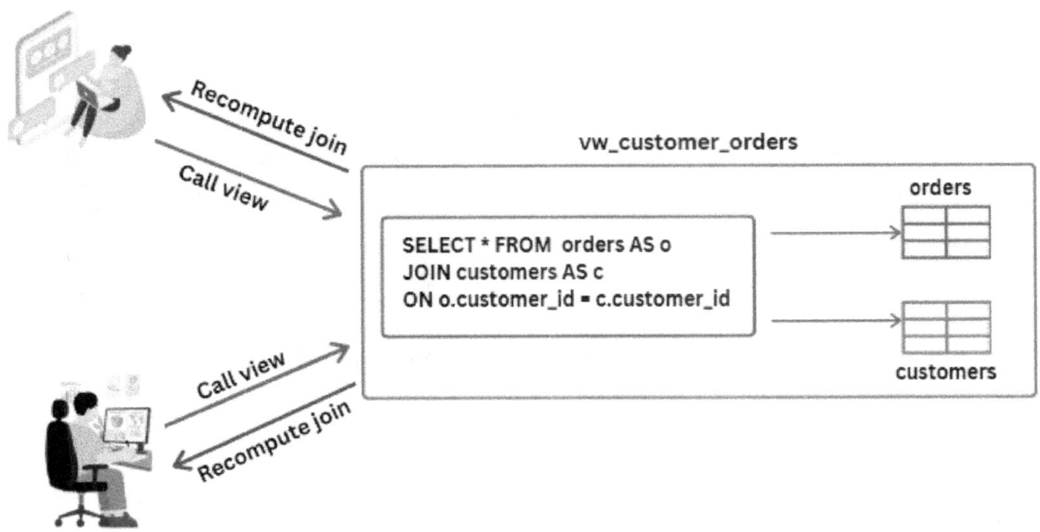

Figure 11.8: Standard views recompute the query at every call

In contrast, a materialized view, as shown in *Figure 11.9*, caches the query result set on disk. Rather than recomputing the joins and aggregations each time the view is accessed, the database can return the precomputed results, significantly improving query performance. Materialized views are particularly beneficial for complex joins, large fact tables, and expensive aggregations, which are common in reporting and analytics workloads.

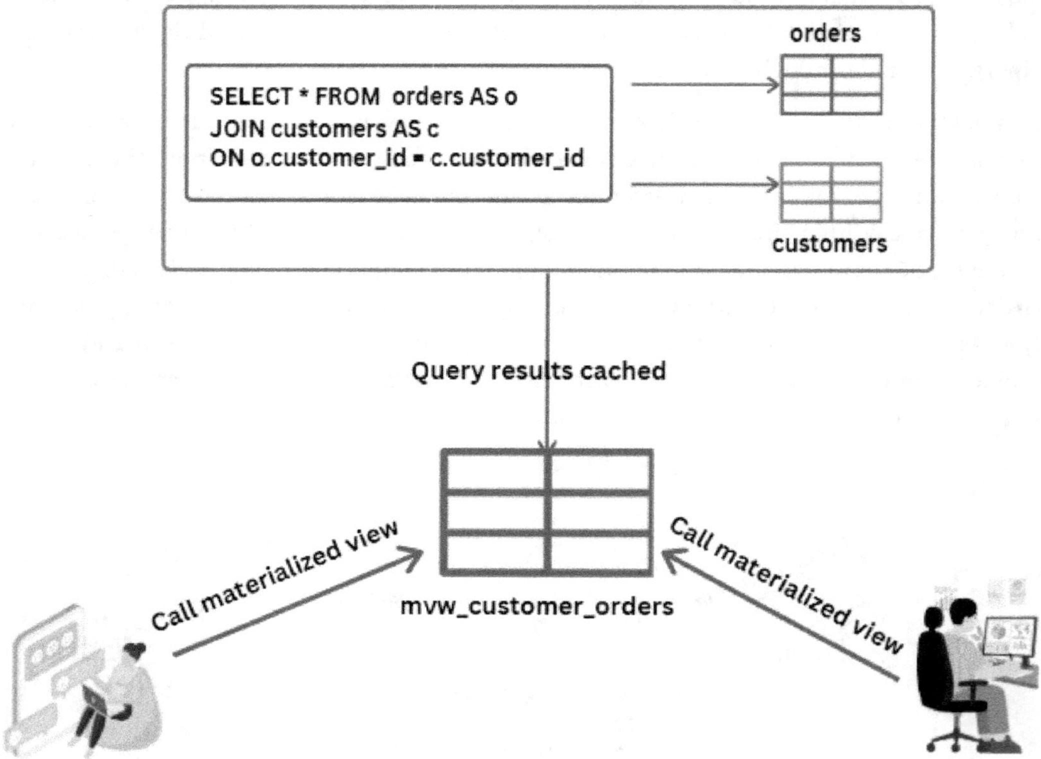

Figure 11.9: Materialized views cache query results

However, these performance gains come with important trade-offs. Unlike standard views, materialized views require storage space and maintenance. They must be refreshed periodically, either on demand, on a schedule, or automatically, to remain synchronized with the underlying base tables. Depending on the refresh strategy, the data exposed through a materialized view may be slightly stale, which may or may not be acceptable depending on business requirements. Also, materialized views may be unsuitable for use when sub-second data freshness is required, when minimizing storage footprint is important, or when the underlying data changes so frequently that cached results lose their value.

> **Note**
>
> Materialized views favor performance and scalability, making them a better choice for complex, read-heavy, or analytical queries where controlled data latency is acceptable.

In summary, standard views favor data freshness and simplicity, making them suitable for lightweight transformations and transactional workloads. Materialized views in Databricks are Unity Catalog–managed objects that physically persist the results of a defined query. Unity Catalog manages their metadata, access controls, lineage, and dependencies, ensuring consistent governance and security. Databricks materialized views automatically manage refresh logic and dependency tracking and are optimized for BI and SQL workloads, effectively functioning as a continuously maintained aggregation or transformation layer.

With this understanding, we can now begin creating the Electroniz gold layer schemas.

Creating the Electroniz gold layer schemas

Let's begin by creating the Electroniz gold layer schemas in the Electroniz pre-existing catalog:

1. Connect to the Databricks workspace and run the following SQL query in SQL Editor:

```
CREATE EXTERNAL LOCATION IF NOT EXISTS
electroniz_lakehouse_gold_storage_location
URL 'abfss://gold@electronizlakehouse.dfs.core.windows.net'
WITH (STORAGE CREDENTIAL electroniz_lakehouse_storage_credential);
```

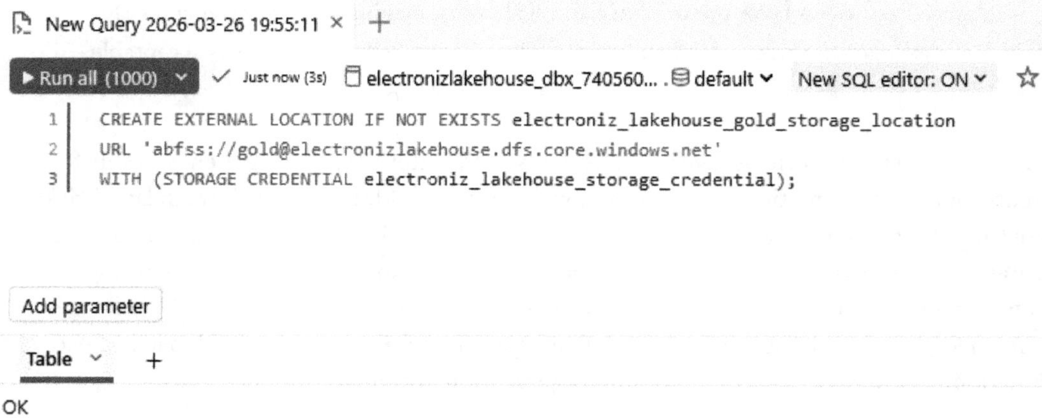

Figure 11.10: Create a new external location for storing the gold schemas.

2. Create four new schemas, one for each domain as follows:

```
CREATE SCHEMA electroniz_catalog.electroniz_gold_master_schema
MANAGED LOCATION 'abfss://gold@electronizlakehouse.dfs.core.windows.net';

CREATE SCHEMA electroniz_catalog.electroniz_gold_supply_schema
MANAGED LOCATION 'abfss://gold@electronizlakehouse.dfs.core.windows.net';

CREATE SCHEMA electroniz_catalog.electroniz_gold_finance_schema
MANAGED LOCATION 'abfss://gold@electronizlakehouse.dfs.core.windows.net';

CREATE SCHEMA electroniz_catalog.electroniz_gold_marketing_schema
MANAGED LOCATION 'abfss://gold@electronizlakehouse.dfs.core.windows.net';
```

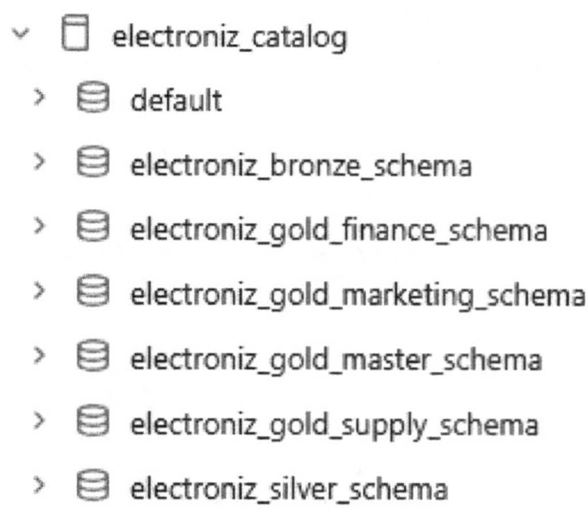

Figure 11.11: Creation of four new gold schemas in Electroniz catalog.

With all the gold schemas in place, we can start creating the Electroniz data products.

Creating the Electroniz gold pipeline for the master domain

At this stage, the Electroniz silver tables have been created, and their data quality has been validated; this is the appropriate time to begin building the Electroniz master data management pipeline. As discussed in *Chapter 4*, the objective of master data management is to consolidate, deduplicate, and refine data to establish a **single source of truth** (**SSOT**), commonly referred to as the **golden record.**

Understanding why the single source of truth matters

A **SSOT** is essential because it ensures everyone across an organization relies on the same, consistent, and validated data when making decisions. When data definitions, calculations, and transformations are centralized, teams avoid conflicting metrics and reports, build confidence in analytics, and reduce time spent reconciling discrepancies. This consistency allows stakeholders to focus on insights and outcomes rather than questioning which numbers are correct. Beyond decision-making, an SSOT improves efficiency, governance, and scalability. It minimizes duplicated logic and errors, strengthens data security and compliance through centralized controls, and provides a stable foundation as data volumes and users grow. Achieving a single SSOT for customer data requires a structured and disciplined approach to managing master data across source systems. This is where **master data management** (**MDM**) plays a critical role.

Understanding master data management

Master data management (MDM) is built on several core components that enable the establishment of an SSOT and maintenance of a trusted golden record. At its core, MDM relies on data integration and consolidation to bring together master data from multiple source systems, resolving duplicates and inconsistencies.

At a high level, *Figure 11.12* depicts the end-to-end process for creating and maintaining the golden record.

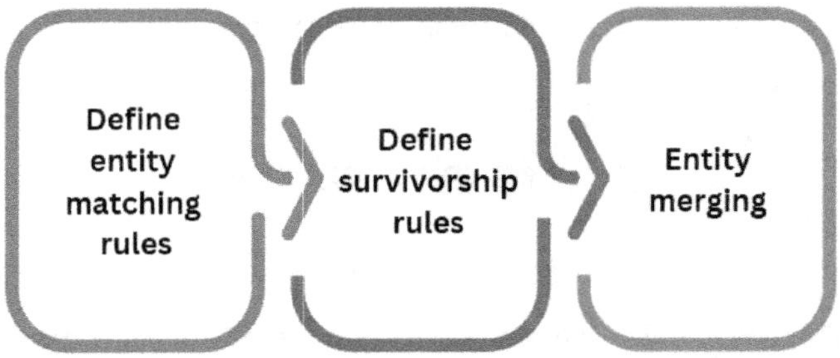

Figure 11.12: Process of creating the golden record

Defining entity matching rules

The process of building a golden record begins with defining entity-matching rules. This initial phase establishes how records that describe the same real-world entity are identified and evaluated across multiple source systems. Matching rules determine which attributes are compared, the techniques used to perform those comparisons (e.g., exact or fuzzy matching), and the confidence thresholds required to confirm a match. Matching logic may be deterministic, relying on unique identifiers such as system-assigned IDs, or probabilistic, enabling the resolution of inconsistencies caused by typographical errors, format variations, and incomplete data. Having well-defined matching rules is essential for minimizing duplicate records, improving data quality, and enabling the accurate and reliable creation of the golden record. When match confidence does not meet predefined thresholds, candidate matches are routed to data stewards for review, ensuring appropriate oversight and sustained trust in master data.

Defining survivorship rules

Following entity matching, survivorship rules define how records identified as matches are combined to create or update a single authoritative record. These rules determine how attribute-level conflicts are resolved by applying business-defined logic, such as preferred source systems, data quality indicators, update recency, or established precedence rules. Survivorship rules also specify how to handle null values, missing or incomplete attributes, and multi-valued attributes such as addresses or contact details. By enforcing consistent, repeatable data consolidation logic, survivorship rules help ensure the accuracy, reliability, and long-term trustworthiness of the golden record, with ambiguous scenarios escalated to data stewards for review as needed.

Merging entities

The final step is entity merging, where records that have already been identified as matches are systematically consolidated to create the golden record. This process is typically automated and guided by predefined rules, but it is integrated with stewardship workflows to enable review of exceptions or low-confidence scenarios. By combining automation with human oversight, entity merging ensures that the golden record remains accurate, consistent, and trustworthy as master data evolves over time.

By aligning business and technical teams around a shared definition of the golden record, organizations ensure consistent data standards, trusted outputs, and confident decision-making.

Exploring MDM styles

Choosing an MDM style is a strategic decision that reflects data maturity, governance readiness, and business ambition. The following are some well-known MDM styles:

- **Registry MDM:** Links records across systems using a master identifier without creating a golden record. This style has low impact and is suitable only for early MDM adoption.
- **Consolidation MDM:** Creates a centralized golden record for analytics and reporting but does not write data back to source systems.
- **Coexistence MDM:** Shares master data ownership between MDM and source systems with bi-directional data synchronization; supports gradual standardization.
- **Centralized MDM:** Establishes MDM as the system of record for master data creation and maintenance; offers the highest consistency but requires significant organizational change.

There is no single "best" style; each MDM approach aligns differently with organizational maturity, integration complexity, and business objectives. The key is choosing a style that best supports how master data is created, governed, and consumed.

Creating the customer golden record MDM data product

Creating the customer golden record MDM data product for the master domain involves consolidating customer information from multiple source systems into a single, trusted, and governed representation of each customer. This data product serves as the authoritative **SSOT** for customer data across the enterprise and is designed to support both operational and analytical use cases. Before building the pipeline, the following data product details were defined and agreed upon with business stakeholders:

- Data product name: **Electroniz Gold Customer MDM Pipeline**
- Domain: **Master**
- KPIs: **Customer golden record**

Manually deploying the customer golden record pipeline

The Electroniz Gold Customer MDM pipeline is a highly complex solution that includes extensive custom logic to implement entity matching and survivorship rules. Because of this level of sophistication, generating the entire pipeline using auto-generated code is often impractical. Entity-matching thresholds require careful, domain-specific tuning, and survivorship rules encode nuanced business decisions that cannot be reliably inferred from a natural-language prompt. Instead, it is more effective to design and build the pipeline using pre-written, well-tested Python code. This approach provides greater control, readability, and maintainability, while allowing fine-grained customization of matching logic and survivorship rules as business requirements evolve. Follow these steps to manually deploy the pipeline:

1. Navigate to the Databricks workspace. Click on **Workspace** on the left menu.
2. Towards the right, click on **Create** > **Folder**.

3. For the new folder, enter **electroniz_gold_customer_mdm**. Click on **Create**.

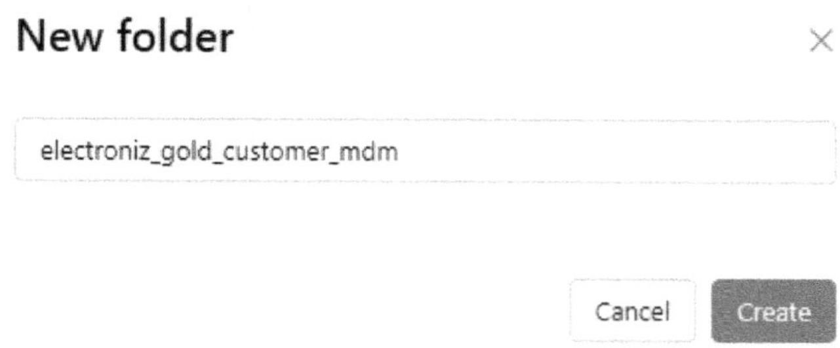

Figure 11.13: Create a new folder for the electroniz_gold_customer_mdm pipeline

4. Now upload the Python file to the new folder. Using the three-dot menu, click **Import**.

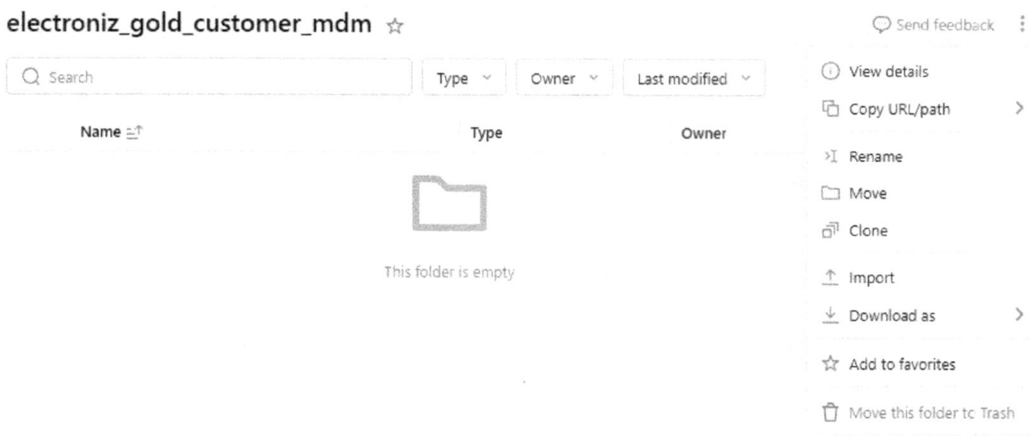

Figure 11.14: Importing the Python code for the electroniz_gold_customer_mdm pipeline

5. Click on the URL radio button and enter the following for the URL:`https://github.com/PacktPublishing/Data-Engineering-with-Apache-Spark-Databricks-and-Lakehouse-Second-Edition/blob/main/chapter11/notebooks/electroniz_gold_customer_mdm.py`.

6. Click on **Import**. After importing, the screen should look like this:

Figure 11.15: Imported Python code for electroniz_gold_customer_mdm pipeline

7. Now navigate to **Jobs & Pipelines** and click on **ETL Pipeline**.

8. Name the pipeline as **electroniz_gold_customer_mdm_pipeline**.
9. Click on **Add existing assets**.

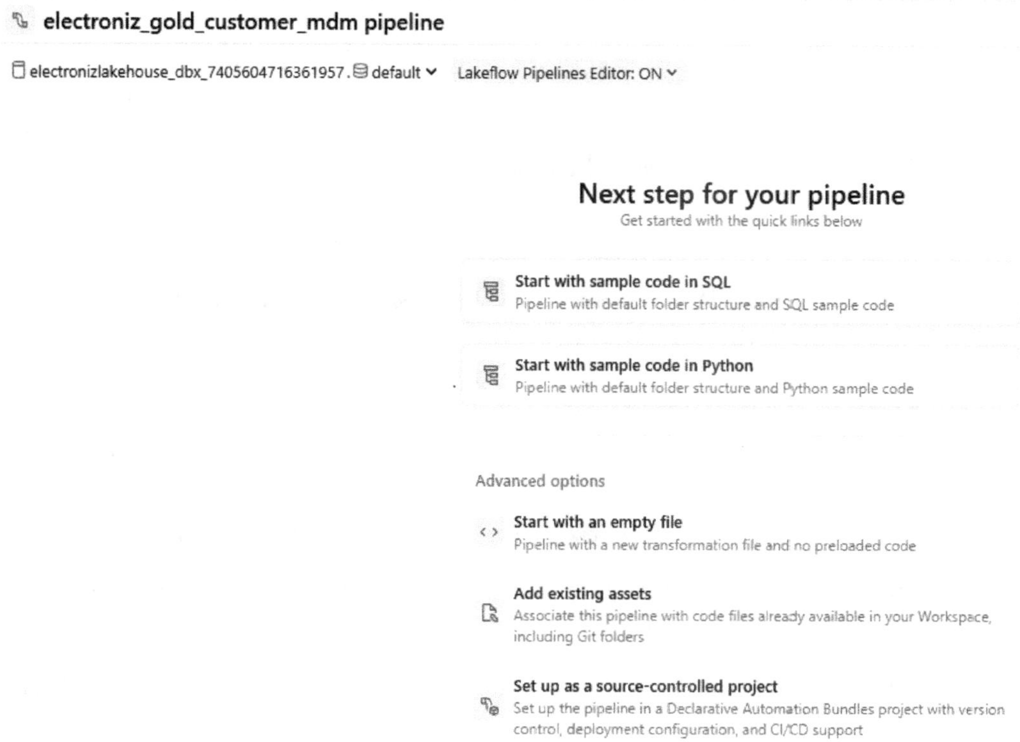

Figure 11.16: Creating a new ETL pipeline for electroniz_gold_customer_mdm_pipeline

10. For Pipeline root folder, choose the newly created folder created earlier. For Source code paths, choose `electroniz_gold_customer_mdm.py`. Click on **Add**.

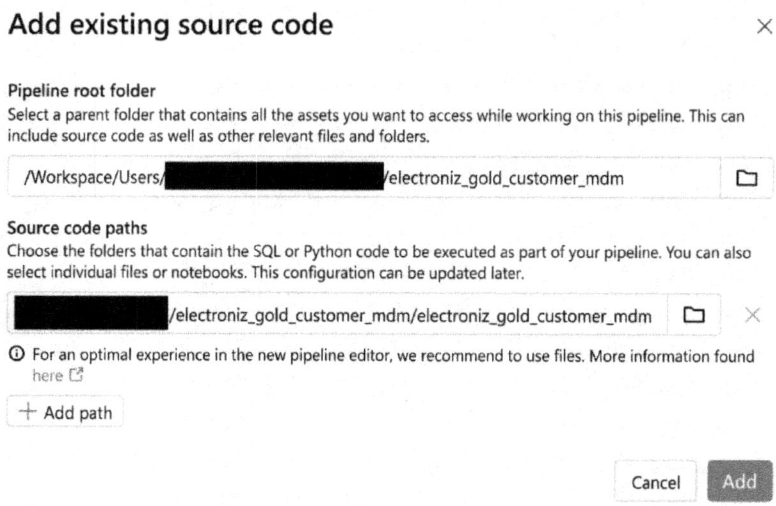

Figure 11.17: Creating a new ETL pipeline for electroniz_gold_customer_mdm

11. The new pipeline has been created; however, one final configuration step must be completed before it can be used.

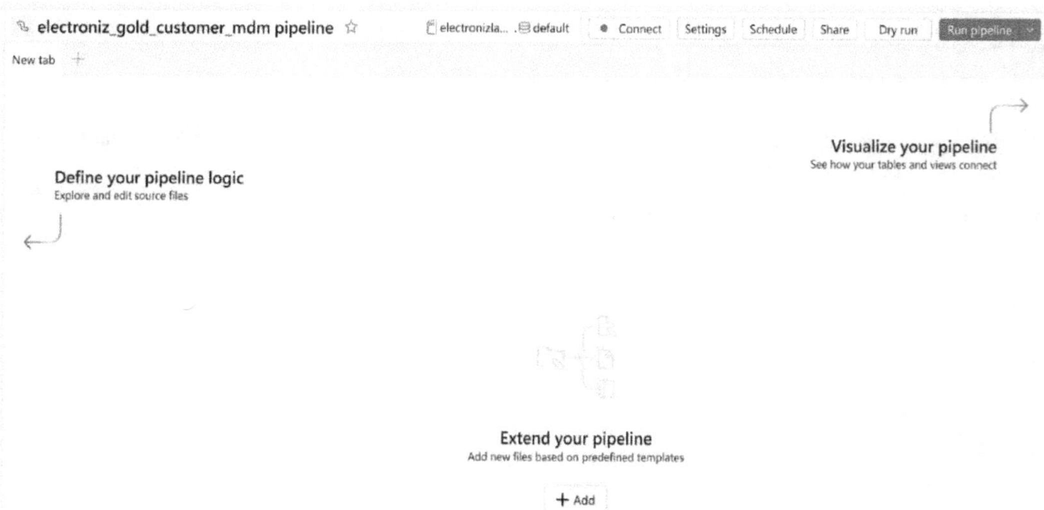

Figure 11.18: New ETL pipeline for electroniz_gold_customer_mdm_pipeline

12. Click on **Settings**. In the Pipeline settings pane, click on **Edit catalog and schema**.

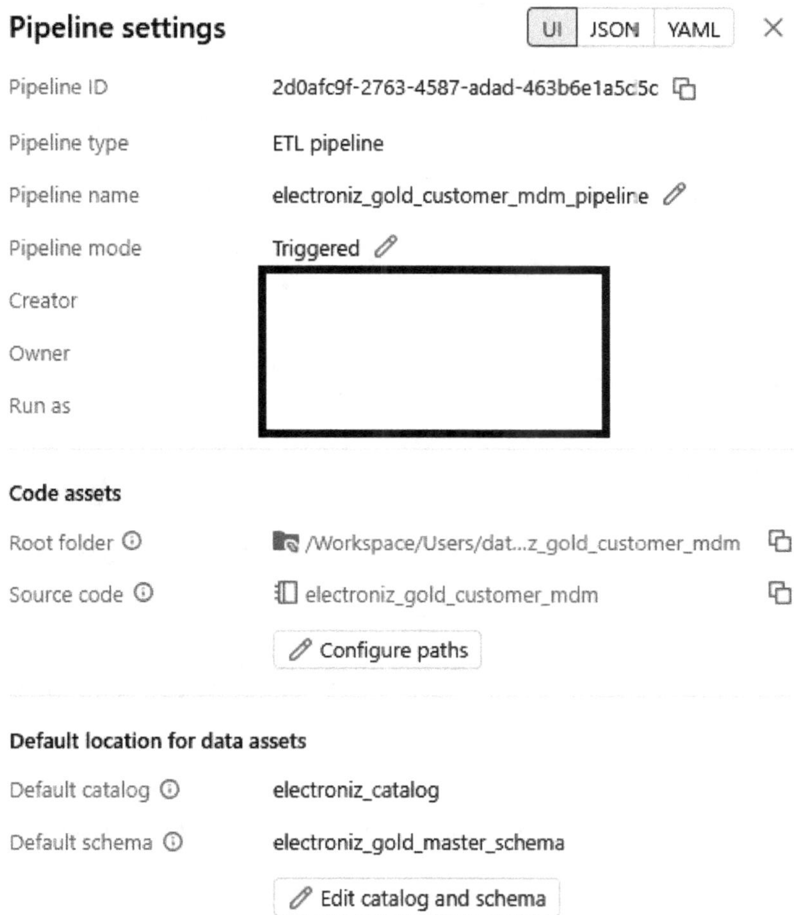

Figure 11.19: Changing the catalog and schema details of the pipeline

13. For Default catalog choose **electroniz_catalog**, and for Default schema choose **electroniz_gold_master_schema**. Click on **Save**.

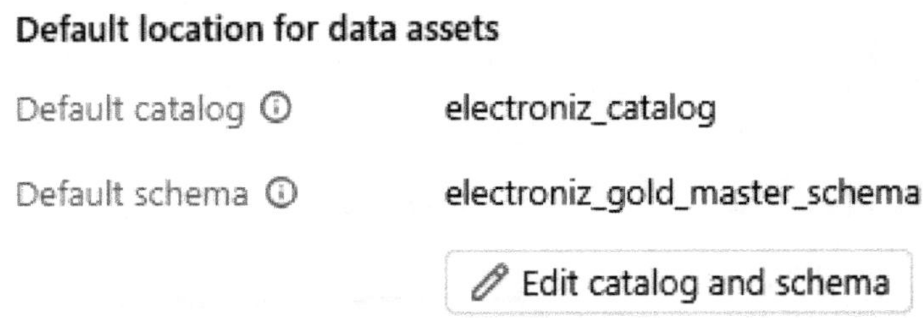

Figure 11.20: Default catalog and schema settings for the pipeline

14. Now change the Pipeline mode to **Continuous**.

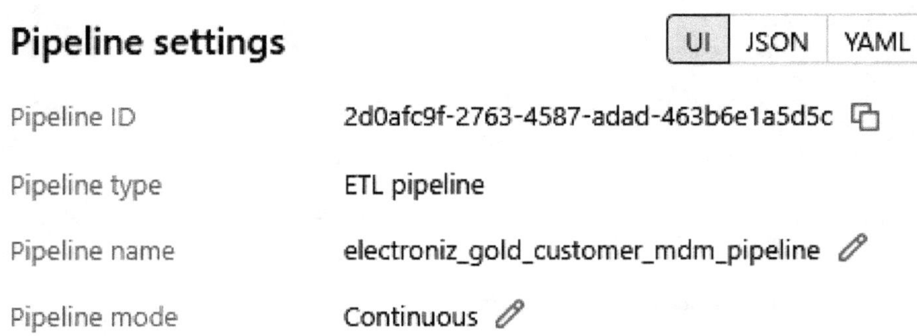

Figure 11.21: Changing the pipeline mode to continuous

15. The pipeline will self-invoke after making the change. Once all the steps have completed successfully, stop the pipeline.

Figure 11.22: The first run of the electroniz_gold_customer_mdm_pipeline

Let us pause briefly to examine and understand the outcomes of the current pipeline execution.

Understanding the pipeline execution steps

The golden record is derived by consolidating data from two key source systems: customers who purchased Electroniz products at retail locations (`electroniz_silver_customers`) and customers who purchased Electroniz products through the website (`electroniz_silver_ecomm_transactions`).

To understand how the customer golden record is constructed, we will trace a single customer record through the various stages of the MDM pipeline.

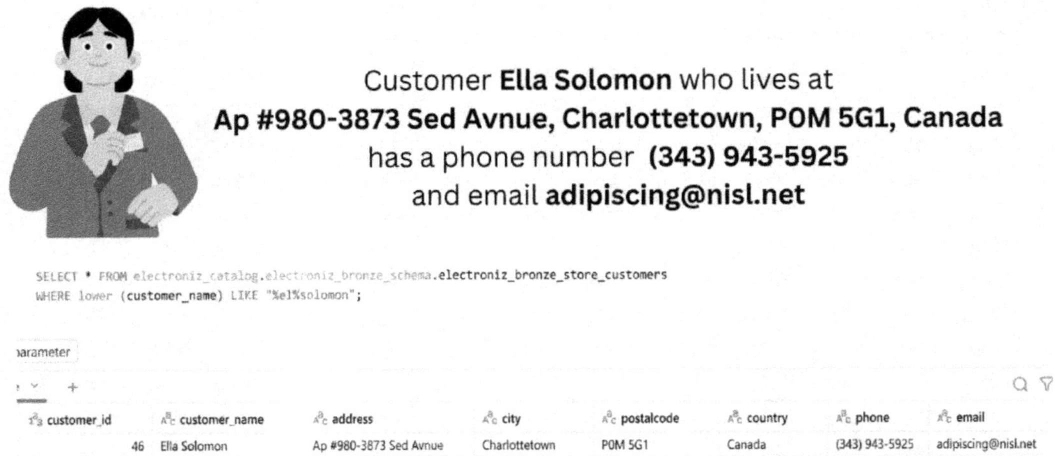

Figure 11.23: Tracing the customer through the customer golden record build process

The following points are important to note about this customer:

- Ella Solomon's relationship with Electroniz began with an in-store purchase at one of their retail locations.
- During this visit, she misspelled her address while providing her details, entering "Avnue" instead of "Avenue."
- Ella Solomon has never made a purchase through the Electroniz web store.

We will now trace Ella Solomon's record through the entire MDM pipeline to see how entity matching, survivorship rules, and golden-record creation operate in practice. As discussed earlier, the process of building a customer golden record begins with defining entity-matching rules. Once matching entities are identified, compared, and evaluated, they are systematically merged using a predefined set of survivorship rules. In the `electroniz_gold_customer_mdm` execution workflow, note how data from the two source systems is combined and analyzed to identify potential matching record pairs.

During the execution of the workflow, records are read from `electroniz_silver_customers` and `electroniz_silver_ecomm_transactions`, then normalized across key attributes such as customer name, address, phone number, and email address. The normalized records are evaluated using the following similarity-based matching rules:

- Name trigram similarity ≥ 0.55 and address trigram similarity ≥ 0.40

- Exact match on normalized phone number
- Exact match on normalized email address

The trigram-similarity thresholds must be determined through empirical testing on representative samples of customer records. It is often best to begin with higher thresholds to maximize precision, then gradually lower them while closely monitoring the resulting false-positive rates and overall match quality.

> **Note**
>
> A trigram is formed by breaking a string into overlapping groups of three consecutive characters. These trigrams are used to compare strings by measuring how much they overlap, enabling fuzzy or similarity-based matching.

At runtime, each record is assigned a `record_id` and a `cluster_id` for identification and grouping. The normalized records get persisted in the **mvw_mdm_combined_staging** materialized view, while entities identified as matching are captured in the **mvw_mdm_match_pairs** materialized view.

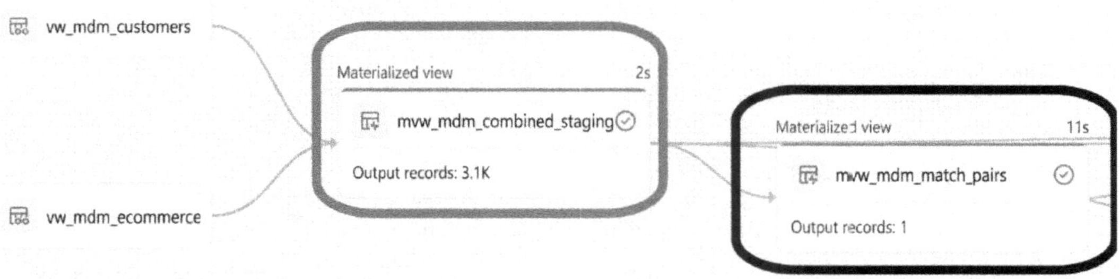

Figure 11.24: Entity matching rules in the electroniz_gold_customer_mdm workflow

Notice that one record has been matched in the **mvw_mdm_match_pairs.** The **mvw_mdm_match_pairs** materialized view was created by the MDM pipeline and contains the *candidate record pairs* that an MDM matching algorithm has evaluated (or will evaluate) to determine whether two records represent the same real-world entity. The matching pairs refer to two records that a matching process has identified as representing the same real-world entity (or likely representing the same entity).

Execute the following SQL query to find out the matching entity pairs.

```
SELECT * FROM
electroniz_catalog.electroniz_gold_master_schema.mvw_mdm_match_pairs;
```

Here's how it works:

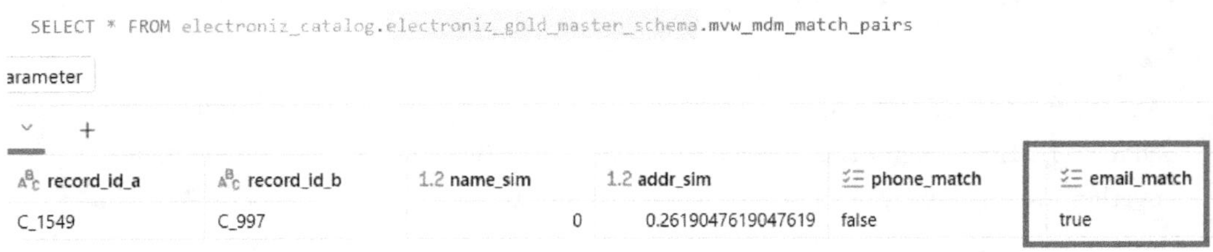

record_id_a	record_id_b	name_sim	addr_sim	phone_match	email_match
C_1549	C_997	0	0.2619047619047619	false	true

Figure 11.25: Matching entity pairs with similarity scores

The **mvw_mdm_combined_staging** materialized view is an intermediate, consolidated staging table used in an MDM pipeline to bring together all customer (or entity) records from multiple upstream systems *before* any matching, deduplication, or survivorship logic is applied. Execute the following SQL query to check the detailed results of the matched pairs above.

```
SELECT record_id, cluster_id, *
FROM electroniz_catalog.electroniz_gold_master_schema.mvw_mdm_combined_staging
WHERE record_id IN ('C_1549', 'C_997');
```

Here's how it looks like:

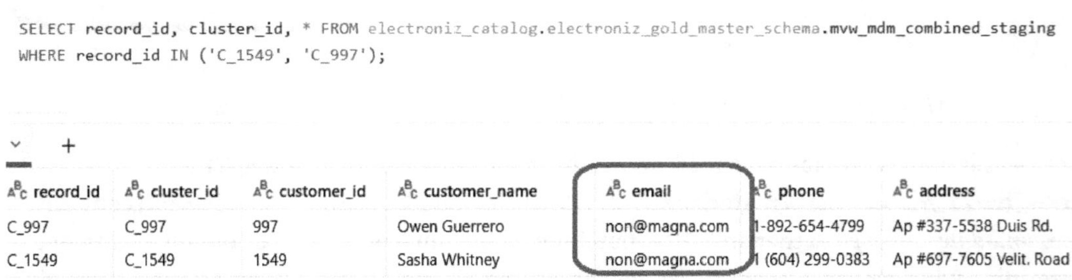

record_id	cluster_id	customer_id	customer_name	email	phone	address
C_997	C_997	997	Owen Guerrero	non@magna.com	1-892-654-4799	Ap #337-5538 Duis Rd.
C_1549	C_1549	1549	Sasha Whitney	non@magna.com	1 (604) 299-0383	Ap #697-7605 Velit. Road

Figure 11.26: Matching records in the electroniz_gold_customer_mdm workflow

Surprisingly, the matched records in **mvw_mdm_match_pairs** do not correspond to Ella Solomon. Based on the comparison of name, phone number, and address attributes, it is evident that these records likely represent two distinct entities. However, the records were identified as a match due to an exact email address match. This type of incorrect match is commonly referred to as a **false positive**. This scenario illustrates a common challenge in entity matching, where strong signals from one attribute, such as email, can override discrepancies in other identifying fields. Identifying and analyzing false positives is critical for refining matching rules, adjusting thresholds, and improving overall master data quality.

Now let's check if Ella Solomon's record matched with any other entity. Execute the steps below to find out:

1. Execute the following SQL to find Ella Solomon's `record_id` and a `cluster_id`:

```
SELECT record_id, cluster_id, * FROM
electroniz_catalog.electroniz_gold_master_schema.mvw_mdm_combined_staging
WHERE lower (customer_name) LIKE "%el%solomon";
```

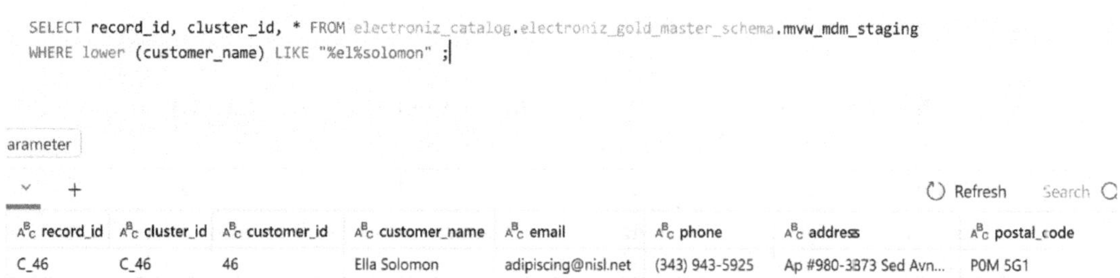

Figure 11.27: record_id and cluster_id of Ella Solomon in mvw_mdm_combined_staging

2. Did Ella Solomon match with any other entities based on the matching rules defined above? Execute the following SQL query to find out. Be sure to replace the `record_id` and `record_id_b` in the query below with the value obtained from the results of the query executed in the previous step:

```
SELECT * FROM
electroniz_catalog.electroniz_gold_master_schema.mvw_mdm_match_pairs
WHERE record_id_a='C_46' OR record_id_b='C_46';
```

3. Apparently, it's not a match at this point. No rows were returned by the query, meaning that Ella Solomon did not match any existing customer (entity).

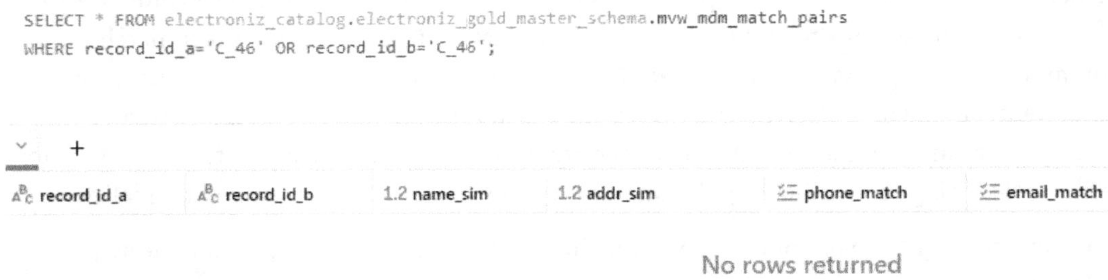

Figure 11.28: Ella Solomon not matching with existing customers

4. Now we can check the golden record for **Ella Solomon.** Execute the following SQL.

```
SELECT * FROM
electroniz_catalog.electroniz_gold_master_schema.mvw_electroniz_gold_golden
_record_customers
WHERE lower (resolved_full_name) LIKE "%el%solomon";
```

5. Although **Ella Solomon** did not match with any other entities, her golden record appears similar, but not identical, to the record stored in `electroniz_silver_customers`. Notably, the address still contains the same misspelling; however, the abbreviation has been standardized, changing from "**Ap**" to "**Apartment.**"

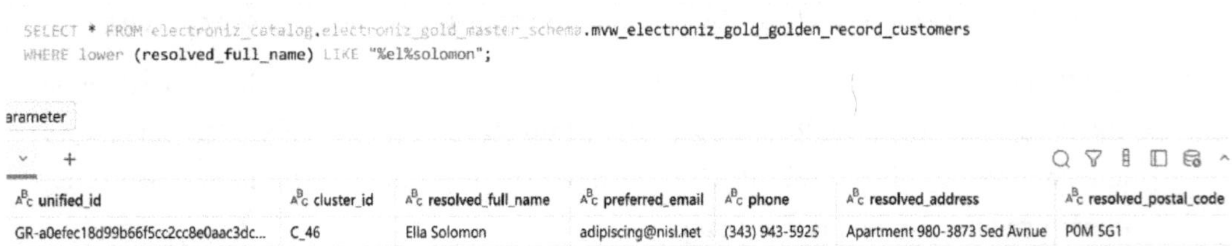

Figure 11.29: Golden record of Ella Solomon after the initial run

If you are wondering how this occurred, the normalization logic in `electroniz_gold_customer_mdm.py` includes the following handling for the address field:

```
# --- 1b. Address normalisation ----------------------------------------
#  Expand abbreviations (whole-word, case-insensitive), collapse whitespace
ABBREV = {
    r"\bst\.?\b":  "Street",
    r"\bav\.?\b":  "Avenue",
    r"\bdr\.?\b":  "Drive",
    r"\brd\.?\b":  "Road",
    r"\bln\.?\b":  "Lane",
    r"\bap\.?\b":  "Apartment",
}
```

Figure 11.30: Address field normalization logic

From an MDM perspective, everything appears to be functioning as expected at this stage. In the upcoming steps, we will ingest additional entities with variations in Ella Solomon's name, address, phone number, and email address. We will then revisit the same materialized views to observe how the data has changed and how the customer golden record has evolved over time. Before proceeding further, let us take a moment to review and understand the testing approach we will be following.

Testing the customer golden record pipeline

Testing the customer golden record pipeline is a critical step to ensure that entity matching, survivorship rules, and entity merging logic are functioning as expected. This testing process validates that customer records from multiple source systems are correctly matched, merged, and resolved into a single, accurate golden record. Test scenarios should include duplicate detection, conflict resolution across attributes, edge cases with partial or inconsistent data, and verification of survivorship outcomes. Successful testing confirms data accuracy, consistency, and reliability before the pipeline is promoted to production.

Integration testing across all pipelines

Until now, we have tested the Electroniz bronze and silver pipelines in tandem. This is an ideal opportunity to perform comprehensive integration testing across the entire data processing chain. The focus of this effort is on end-to-end data lineage, schema and data quality validation, and verification of the correctness of transformations applied at each stage. In addition, this testing ensures that dependencies between pipelines are properly orchestrated, error handling and logging function as expected, and changes in upstream data are accurately propagated downstream. Successful integration testing confirms that all pipelines operate seamlessly to deliver trusted, reliable customer master data.

The following scenario illustrates our approach to integration testing using a representative example. In this case, we assume that Electroniz's marketing team has launched a 20% discount on all cameras purchased through the web store.

Figure 11.31: Electroniz products on sale

However, the offer is limited to one camera per customer. Ella Solomon needs two cameras, one for herself and one for her sister, so she decides to make the purchases using two separate accounts. No judging! I know it's technically cheating, but we've all done it. *Figure 11.32* outlines the details of the one original and two duplicate accounts that were created. Pay close attention to the intentional differences in name, address, postal code, email address, and phone number.

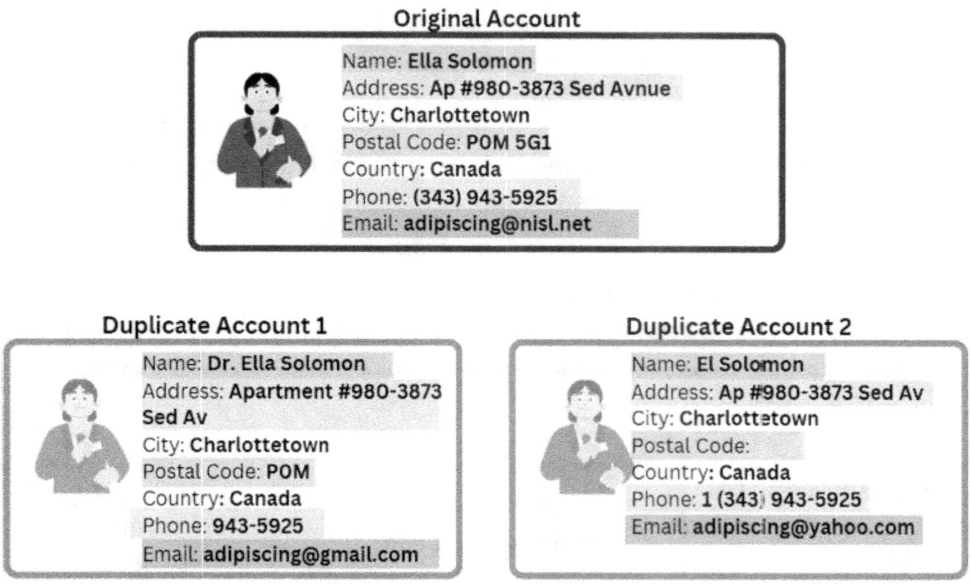

Figure 11.32: The three variations of Ella Solomon's customer records

Effectively handling such duplicates underscores the importance of a well-designed entity matching and merging process. Let's discuss how we will accomplish this while coupling it with integration testing.

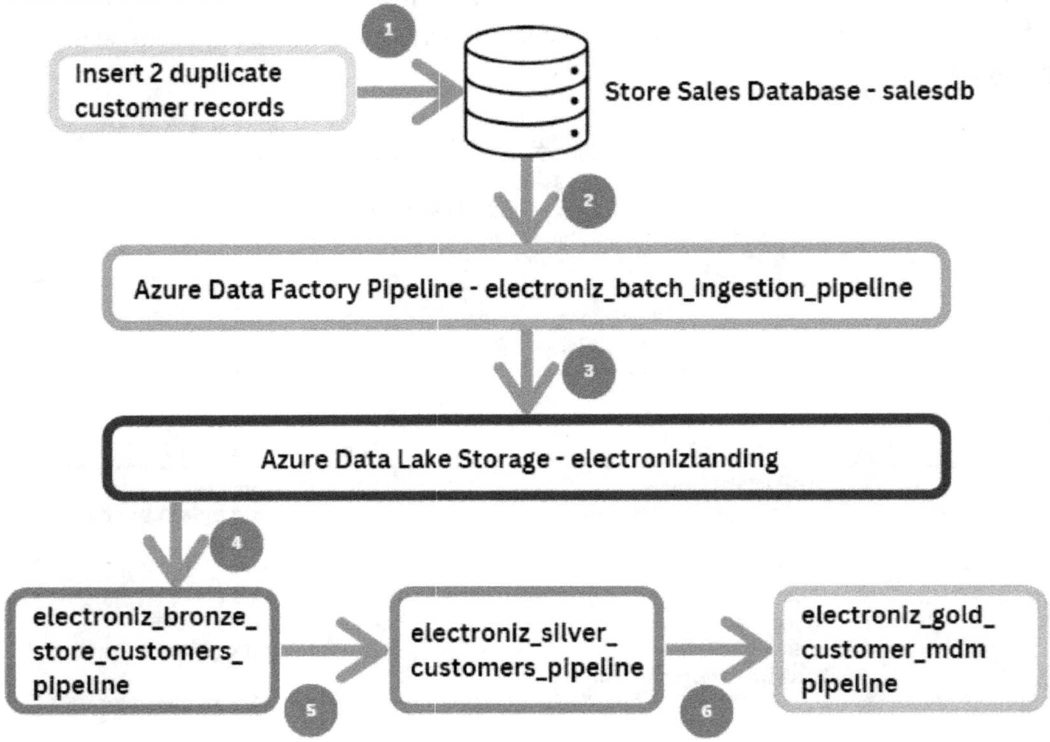

Figure 11.33: Integration testing plan

Figure 11.33 illustrates the progression of data through the various phases of integration testing. The following section explains each step, as indicated by the red-circled markers in the image.

Step 1: Inserting duplicate records in the store sales database

You may recall that in *Chapter 8, Data Ingestion Stage – Building the Landing Zone*, we ingested transactional data from the Electroniz store sales Azure SQL database. That database has been dormant since then; now it's time to reactivate it and begin inserting incremental data. To kick-start our integration testing, we will insert the two duplicate records for Ella Solomon:

1. Connect to your Azure portal. Under your home screen, you should see the **salesdb** Azure SQL database.

2. Click on **salesdb** entry on the home screen to navigate to its control panel.
3. To connect to the newly created Azure SQL database, using the menu on the left, click on the **Query Editor**.
4. Using SQL Server authentication, sign in with the username `salesadmin` and the password you created during setup. If you can't remember the password, select the **Server name** in the control panel and use the **Reset password** option from the top menu.
5. Paste the following SQL statements in the query window and press **Run**:

```
INSERT INTO store_customers([customer_id], [customer_name], [address],
[city], [postalcode], [country], [phone], [email], [credit_card])
VALUES
(4001,'Dr. Ella Solomon','Apartment #980-3873 Sed Av', 'Charlottetown',
'P0M', 'Canada','943-5925', 'adipiscing@gmail.com','5343300510782047'),
(4002,'El Solomon','Ap #980-3873 Sed Av', 'Charlottetown', '', 'Canada',
'1 (343) 943-5925', 'adipiscing@yahoo.com','5154959880757059');
GO
```

6. After successful completion, you should see a message as follows:

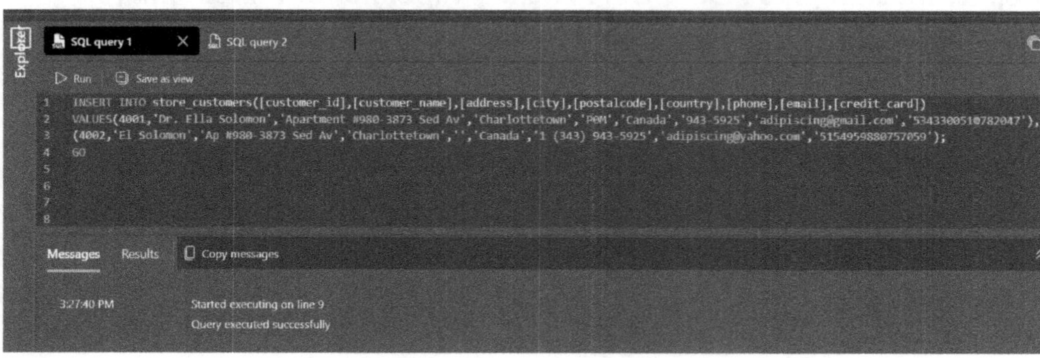

Figure 11.34: Insert two duplicate records for Ella Solomon

7. Just to be sure, we can reconfirm the insertion using the following SQL query:

```
SELECT * FROM store_customers
WHERE customer_id IN (4001, 4002);
```

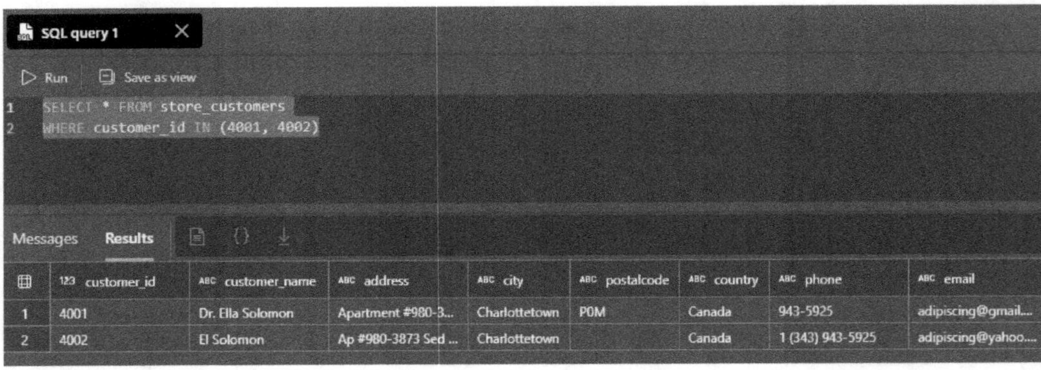

Figure 11.35: Confirmation of the newly inserted records for Ella Solomon

Once duplicate records have been added for testing purposes, we can invoke the Azure Data Factory pipeline.

Step 2: Invoking the Azure Data Factory Pipeline for incremental ingestion

You may also recall from *Chapter 8* that after inserting data into the store sales database, we ingested incremental data into the ADLS account named `electronizlanding`. This was achieved using an Azure Data Factory pipeline called `electronizlakehouse-df`.

1. Connect to your Azure portal. Under your home screen, you should see the `electronizlakehouse-df` Azure Data Factory.
2. On the `electronizlakehouse-df` control panel, click on **electroniz_batch_ingestion_pipeline** entry.

3. Trigger the pipeline using the **Trigger Now** button.

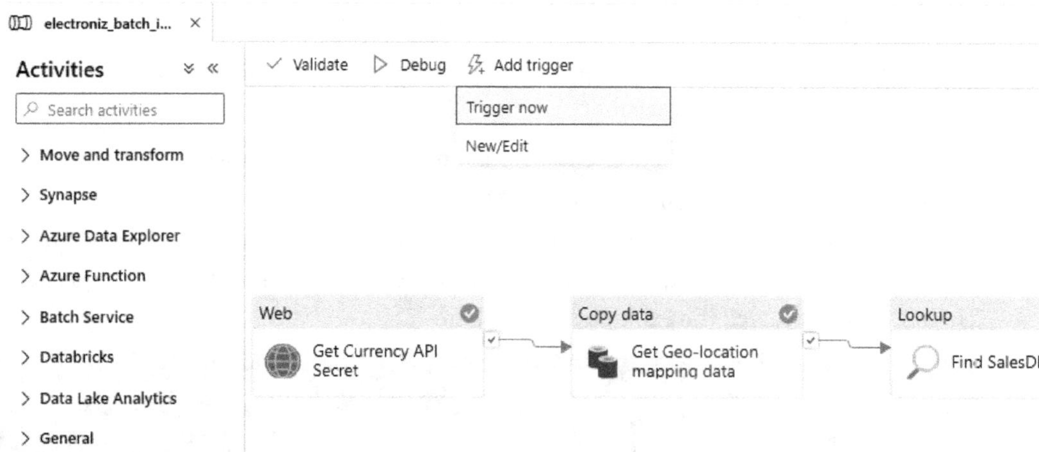

Figure 11.36: Triggering the electroniz_batch_ingestion_pipeline

4. Using the Monitor button on the left menu, carefully monitor the pipeline run to completion.

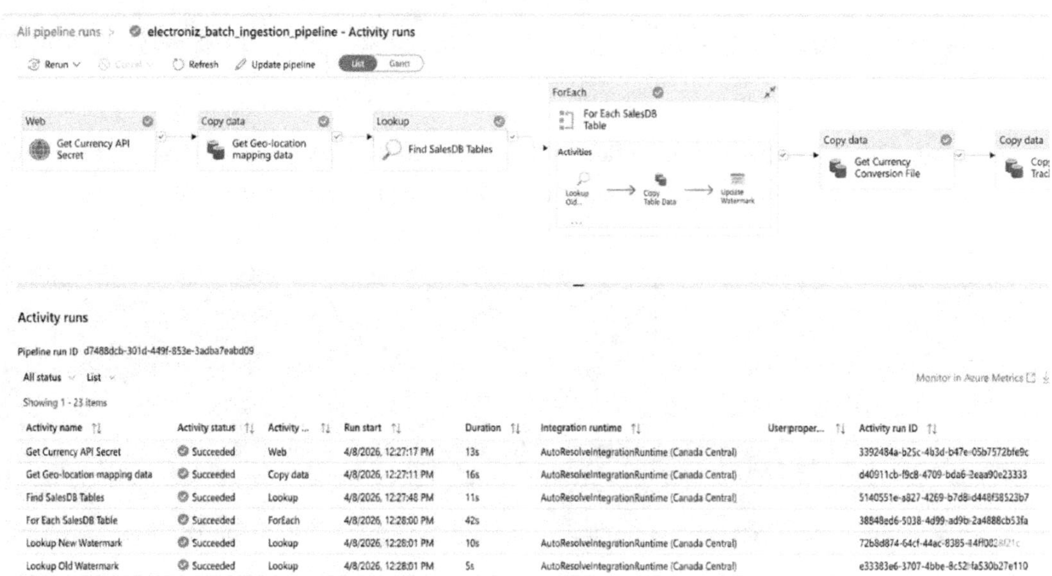

Figure 11.37: Monitoring the electroniz_batch_ingestion_pipeline to completion

We can now move to the next step to assess the results of the pipeline run.

Step 3: Checking the incremental data in the ADLS

Let's verify that the incremental data has been ingested correctly:

1. Connect to your Azure portal. Under your home screen, you should see the `electronizlanding` ADLS account.
2. Using the Storage browser, click on **Raw**. Now navigate to the latest date and time folder under **sales** > **[dbo].[store_customers]**.
3. Keep in mind that since you are running this pipeline on a different date than when the screenshots were captured, the folder names, particularly those containing dates and hours, may not match the examples shown here.

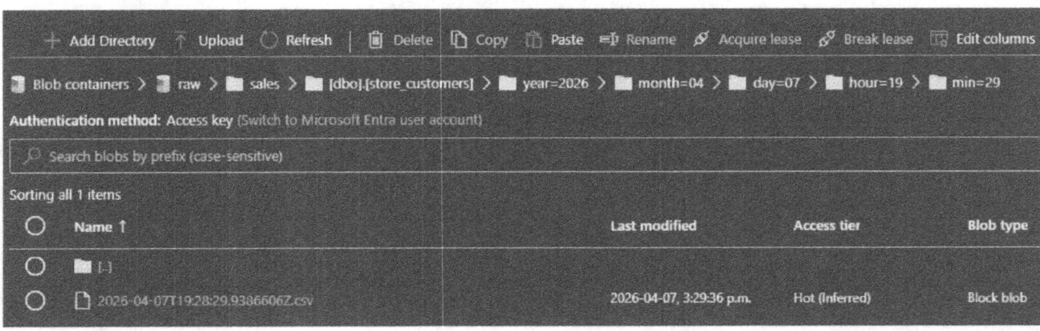

Figure 11.38: Verifying incremental data in electronizlanding bucket

4. Now click on the file and press **Edit**. You should see the newly ingested duplicate records for Ella Solomon**.** Pressing the **preview** button shows a user-friendly view of the data.

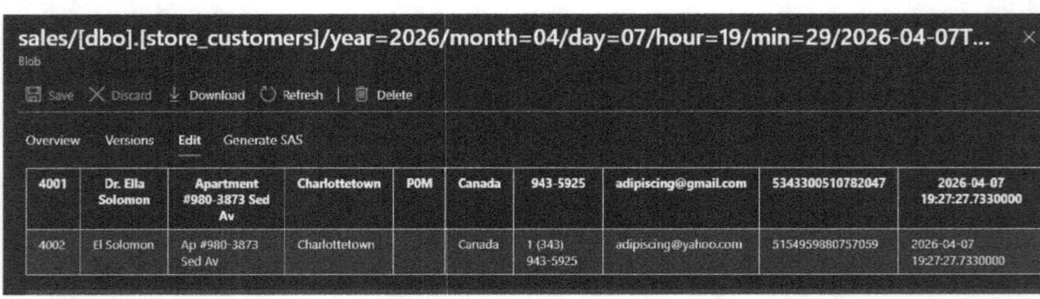

Figure 11.39: Verifying the content of the incremental data in electronizlanding bucket

With incremental record ingestion now complete, we can move on to the more challenging portion: testing the ingestion and transformation pipelines.

Step 4, 5 and 6: Validating the ingestion and transformation pipelines

In *Chapter 9* and *Chapter 10*, we designed and implemented end-to-end data ingestion and transformation pipelines for the bronze and silver layers of the medallion architecture. These pipelines were built using Spark Lakeflow Declarative Pipelines and configured to run in continuous mode, enabling real-time or near–real-time data processing. Although each pipeline was unit tested in isolation, they were never validated collectively as an integrated system. When the bronze, silver, and gold pipelines operate in continuous streaming mode, any incremental change at the source should automatically trigger downstream processing, ensuring that data is refreshed seamlessly across all layers of the medallion architecture.

Refer to *Figure 11.33* above; we will now verify that Steps 3, 4, and 5 work together as intended and correctly process the two newly inserted duplicate records for Ella Solomon.

1. Connect to the Databricks workspace. Navigate to **Jobs & Pipelines** and start the following pipelines:

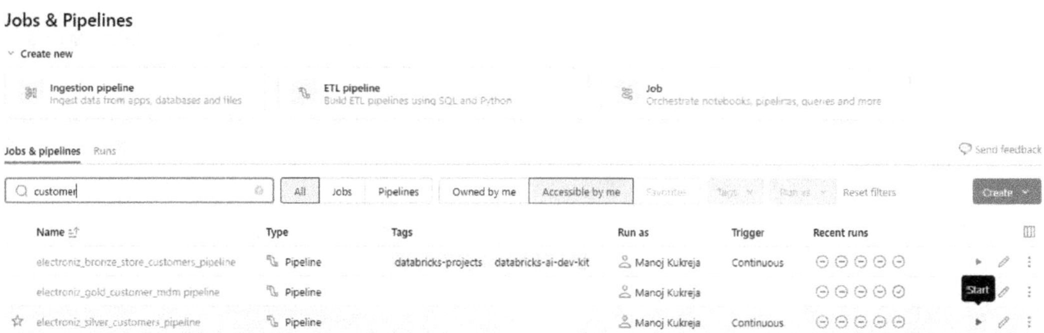

Figure 11.40: Starting the bronze, silver, and gold pipelines for customers

2. Now, click on **electroniz_bronze_store_customers_pipeline**. Notice the output records; the pipeline has automatically processed the two newly inserted records:

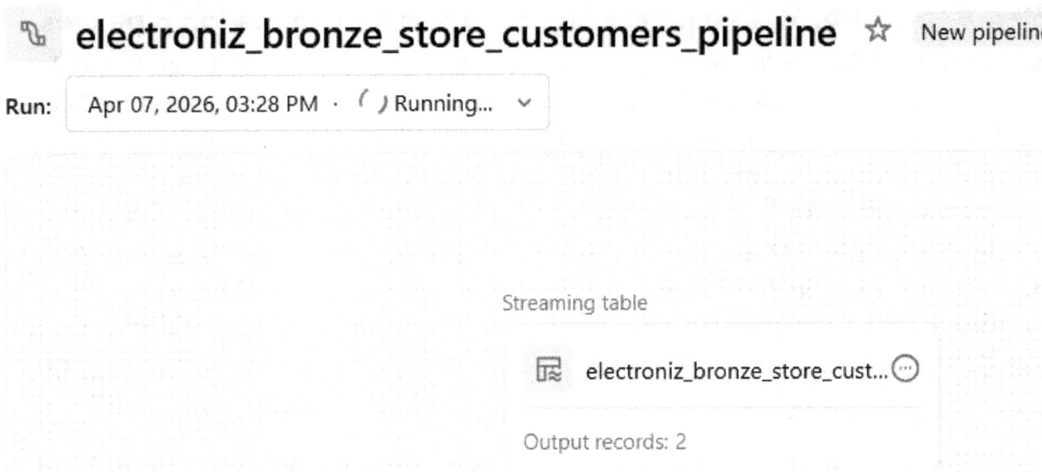

Figure 11.41: Checking the output of the electroniz_bronze_store_customers_pipeline

3. The new records will now be available in the `electroniz_bronze_store_customers` table. Run the following SQL to verify this:

```
SELECT * FROM
electroniz_catalog.electroniz_bronze_schema.electroniz_bronze_store_custome
rs
WHERE customer_id IN (4001, 4002)
```

Figure 11.42: Verifying two new customer records in electroniz_bronze_store_customers

4. Go back to **Jobs & Pipelines** and click on **electroniz_silver_customers_pipeline**.

5. Notice the output records; the pipeline has automatically inserted the two newly inserted records:

Figure 11.43: Checking the output of the electroniz_silver_customers_pipeline

6. The new records will now be available in the `electroniz_silver_customers` table. Run the following SQL to verify this:

```
SELECT * FROM
electroniz_catalog.electroniz_silver_schema.electroniz_silver_customers
WHERE customer_id IN (4001, 4002);
```

```
SELECT * FROM electroniz_catalog.electroniz_silver_schema.electroniz_silver_customers
WHERE customer_id IN (4001, 4002)
```

customer_id	customer_name	address	city	postalcode	country	phone
4001	Dr. Ella Solomon	Apartment #980-3873 Sed Av	Charlotteto...	POM	CAN	943-5925
4002	El Solomon	Ap #980-3873 Sed Av	Charlotteto...	null	CAN	1 (343) 943-5925

Figure 11.44: Verifying two new customer records in electroniz_silver_customers

7. Finally, go back to **Jobs & Pipelines** and click on **electroniz_gold_customer_mdm_pipeline**. Notice the output records for **mvw_mdm_match_pairs**, the pipeline discovered three matching pairs:

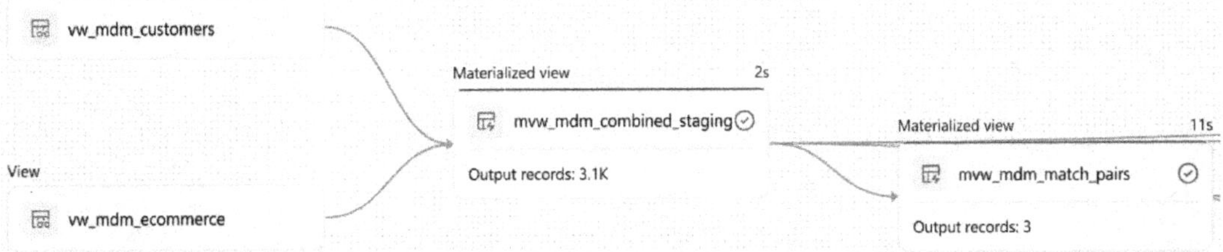

Figure 11.45: Discovering matching pairs in electroniz_gold_customer_mdm_pipeline

8. Ideally, the matching records in **mvw_mdm_match_pairs** should correspond to the duplicated records for Ella Solomon. Let's verify whether this is the case.
9. Run the following SQL to find out which records exist in the staging table for Ella Solomon**:**

```
SELECT record_id, cluster_id, * FROM
electroniz_catalog.electroniz_gold_master_schema.mvw_mdm_combined_staging;
```

10. The staging table now has three records for Ella Solomon - one original and two duplicates.

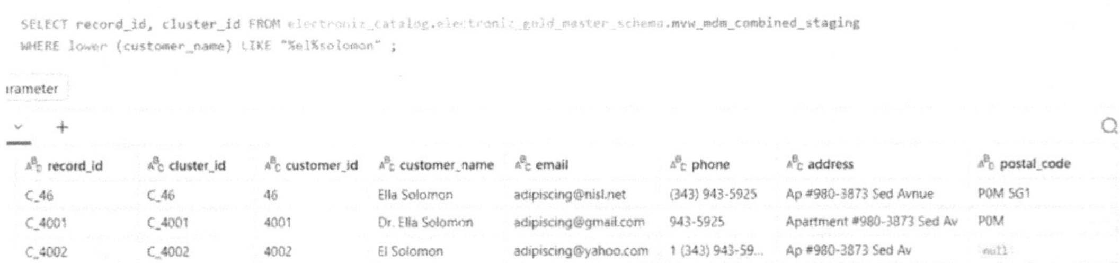

```
SELECT record_id, cluster_id FROM electroniz_catalog.electroniz_gold_master_schema.mvw_mdm_combined_staging
WHERE lower (customer_name) LIKE "%el%solomon" ;
```

record_id	cluster_id	customer_id	customer_name	email	phone	address	postal_code
C_46	C_46	46	Ella Solomon	adipiscing@nisl.net	(343) 943-5925	Ap #980-3873 Sed Avnue	P0M 5G1
C_4001	C_4001	4001	Dr. Ella Solomon	adipiscing@gmail.com	943-5925	Apartment #980-3873 Sed Av	P0M
C_4002	C_4002	4002	El Solomon	adipiscing@yahoo.com	1 (343) 943-59...	Ap #980-3873 Sed Av	null

Figure 11.46: State of the staging table after the insertion of two duplicates

11. For Ella Solomon the original record has **C_46** assigned as the **record_id**. Query the `mvw_mdm_match_pairs` to check for matching pairs**:**

```
SELECT * FROM
electroniz_catalog.electroniz_gold_master_schema.mvw_mdm_match_pairs
WHERE record_id_b='C_46';
```

12. *Figure 11.47* confirms that **record_id C-46** has been matched by the two duplicate records:

```
SELECT * FROM electroniz_catalog.electroniz_gold_master_schema.mvw_mdm_match_pairs
WHERE record_id_b='C_46';
```

record_id_a	record_id_b	name_sim	addr_sim	phone_match	email_match
C_4002	C_46	0.5	1	true	false
C_4001	C_46	1	1	false	false

Figure 11.47: Discovering matched pairs after the insertion of two duplicates

There are a few items to note with regard to the matched pairs as below:

- **C_46** matched **C_4001** due to a perfect similarity score on name and address.
- **C_46** matched **C_4002** due to a partial similarity score on name, perfect similarity score on address, and a perfect phone number match.

13. We will now check `mvw_electroniz_gold_linking_record_customers` that maps each source `record_id` to the cluster,generating a `unified_id`. Execute the following SQL:

```
SELECT * FROM
electroniz_catalog.electroniz_gold_master_schema.mvw_electroniz_gold_linkin
g_record_customers
WHERE lower (source_customer_name) LIKE "%el%solomon";
```

> **Note**
>
> A cluster is a group of source records that refer to the same real-world entity. `cluster_id` is an internal identifier in the MDM table produced by matching and linking logic.

14. The three Ella Solomon records have been grouped into a single cluster identified by **cluster_id = C_4001**. A deterministic UUID, referred to as the **unified_id**, has been generated to serve as the shared key identifier for the resulting golden record.

```
SELECT * FROM electroniz_catalog.electroniz_gold_master_schema.
mvw_electroniz_gold_linking_record_customers
WHERE lower (source_customer_name) LIKE "%el%solomon" ;
```

record_id	customer_id	_source	cluster_id	unified_id
C_46	46	customers	C_4001	GR-28a4a14fea10d8c54da6f598ab06988
C_4001	4001	customers	C_4001	GR-28a4a14fea10d8c54da6f598ab06988
C_4002	4002	customers	C_4001	GR-28a4a14fea10d8c54da6f598ab06988

Figure 11.48: Discovering a deterministic identifier for the golden record

> **Note**
>
> A `unified_id` (UUID) is an authoritative identifier generated through a deterministic, repeatable algorithm, such that the same input consistently results in the same identifier value.

15. Finally, let's query the golden record for Ella Solomon. Execute the following SQL:

```
SELECT * FROM
electroniz_catalog.electroniz_gold_master_schema.mvw_electroniz_gold_golden
_record_customers
WHERE lower (resolved_full_name) LIKE "%el%solomon";
```

16. The golden record generated for Ella Solomon is shown as follows:

```
SELECT * FROM electroniz_catalog.electroniz_gold_master_schema.mvw_electro_golden_record_customers
WHERE lower (resolved_full_name) LIKE "%el%solomon";
```

parameter Refresh Search

unified_id	cluster_id	resolved_full_name	preferred_emai	phone	resolved_address	resolved_postal_code
GR-28a4a14fea10d8c54da6f598ab069885	C_4001	Dr. Ella Solomon	adipiscing@gmail.com	1 (343) 943-5925	Apartment 980-3873 Sed Avenue	P0M 5G1

Figure 11.49: Querying the golden record

As previously noted, following entity matching, survivorship rules govern the consolidation of matched records into a single authoritative record. Attribute-level discrepancies are resolved based on predefined business logic. The following section outlines the survivorship rules applied to the name, address, email, and postal code attributes:

- **Survivorship of the name attribute:** The **resolved_full_name** attribute represents the golden record name selected through defined survivorship rules. After the name field is evaluated across all source systems, the most reliable and authoritative values are resolved and consolidated into a single, standardized full name. For Ella Solomon this authoritative value was chosen as **Dr. Ella Solomon** based on the survivorship logic as follows:

```
# — Rule 1 : FULL NAME (with prefix/suffix preserved) ——————————————
# FILTER nulls FIRST → rank by length DESC → then updated_at DESC
# Use ORIGINAL customer_name to preserve "Dr.", "Jr.", etc. in golden record
```

Figure 11.50: Name attribute survivorship rules

- **Survivorship of the address attribute:** The **resolved_address** attribute represents the golden record address determined through established survivorship rules. For Ella Solomon, the authoritative address was resolved as **Apartment 980-3873 Sed Avenue** based on normalization and survivorship logic that expands address abbreviations using whole-word, case-insensitive matching. In this instance, the abbreviation "*Ap*" was normalized to "*Apartment*" and "*Av*" to "*Avenue*", resulting in a standardized and consistent address value.
- **Survivorship of the phone attribute**: The **phone** attribute represents the golden record phone number determined through established survivorship rules. For Ella Solomon, the authoritative phone number was determined to be **1 (343) 943-5925** based on the applied normalization and survivorship logic. In this case, the value selected was a perfectly formatted, country-specific phone number that met all standardization and data quality criteria.

```
Return phone formatting quality score based on country detection and format:
5 = Perfect country-specific format (e.g., +1 (XXX) XXX-XXXX, +44 XXXX XXXXXX, +91 XXXXX XXXXX)
4 = Has country code prefix (+1, +44, +91, etc.)
3 = Has formatting chars but no country code
2 = Has some formatting (parentheses, hyphens, spaces)
1 = Just digits (unformatted)
0 = Invalid (< 7 digits or null)
```

Figure 11.51: Phone attribute survivorship rules

- **Survivorship of the email attribute**: The **preferred_email** attribute represents the golden record email address determined through established survivorship rules. For Ella Solomon, the authoritative email was resolved as **adipiscing@gmail.com** based on the applied normalization and survivorship logic. As part of this logic, email domains are explicitly ranked, with well-known providers such as **Gmail, Hotmail, and Yahoo** designated as preferred domains. This ranking ensures that standardized, widely trusted email providers are selected when multiple candidate values are available.

```
# --- 1d. Email domain rank  -----------------------------------
@F.udf(LongType())
def email_rank(email: str) -> int:
    if not email:
        return 99
    domain = email.strip().lower().split("@")[-1]
    ranks = {"gmail.com": 1, "hotmail.com": 2, "yahoo.com": 3}
    return ranks.get(domain, 4)
```

Figure 11.52: Email attribute survivorship rules

The Electroniz bronze, silver, and gold pipelines have now been fully validated through end-to-end integration testing, with all tests passing successfully. This confirms that data flows correctly across all layers, with transformations, dependencies, error handling, and survivorship rules all performing as expected.

Creating the Electroniz gold pipeline for the marketing domain

Electroniz would like insights on **web hits by country** to better understand the geographic distribution of users and engagement trends across regions. These insights will support the identification of key markets, reveal regional traffic patterns, and inform decisions related to marketing strategy, localization efforts, and infrastructure optimization.

To support this need, the marketing domain would like to create a couple of data products that deliver standardized, trusted, and regularly refreshed country-level web analytics.

Creating the web hits by country data product

This data product will serve as a reliable foundation for campaign analysis and market expansion planning.

Defining KPIs for the data product

The first step in the data aggregation process is establishing clearly defined KPIs to support analysis and decision-making. The following are the details of the KPIs:

- Data product name: **Marketing Analytics - Web Hits by Country**
- Domain: **Marketing**
- KPI: **Total count of web hits grouped by country**

Shortlisting observations for the data product

Following a detailed assessment, the data stewards and data engineers agreed that the `electroniz_catalog.electroniz_silver_schema.electroniz_silver_logs_geolocation` table is the most suitable source for building this data product. The table records web request events enriched with geolocation data derived from each request's originating IP address. It captures user agent information, detailed HTTP request attributes, response status codes, and event timestamps. In addition, it includes geographic attributes such as country codes and country names, as well as the browser types used by clients.

Aggregating the data for the data product

At this stage, the data engineer is responsible for designing and implementing the aggregation logic defined for the data product. Let's generate a gold layer pipeline for this data product:

1. Navigate to the Databricks workspace, click on the Genie Code icon on the top right of your screen.
2. Issue the following prompt on Genie Code to create the gold products pipeline:

```
Create a new materialized view for the following data product:
Data product name: web hits by country
Domain: marketing
Pipeline Name: electroniz_gold_web_hits_pipeline
Materialized view name: electroniz_product_web hits by country
Source table:
electroniz_catalog.electroniz_silver_schema.electroniz_silver_logs_geolocat
ion
Target table:3
electroniz_catalog.electroniz_gold_marketing_schema.electroniz_product_web_
hits_by_country
            Mode: Continuous streaming
            Add appropriate data product metadata tags such as
domain:marketing
```

```
            Add AI generated descriptions for the materialized view and
its columns
```

3. Genie code performs extensive reasoning at each step of execution. After completing this reasoning, it generates a new pipeline. The initial pipeline run may fail; if that happens, check the Databricks pipeline event logs, the pipeline code, and for any schema discrepancies between the source and target materialized views. Once you identify the root cause, refine your Genie Code prompt and provide additional instructions to guide GenAI toward a more accurate solution. If Genie Code is unable to resolve the issue after two or three iterations, refer to the authoritative pipeline code in the GitHub repository and compare it with the generated output to identify the discrepancy.
4. Genie Code reads the table structure of the table and ascertains which columns can be used to build the data product. After extensive reasoning, Genie Code creates the data product.

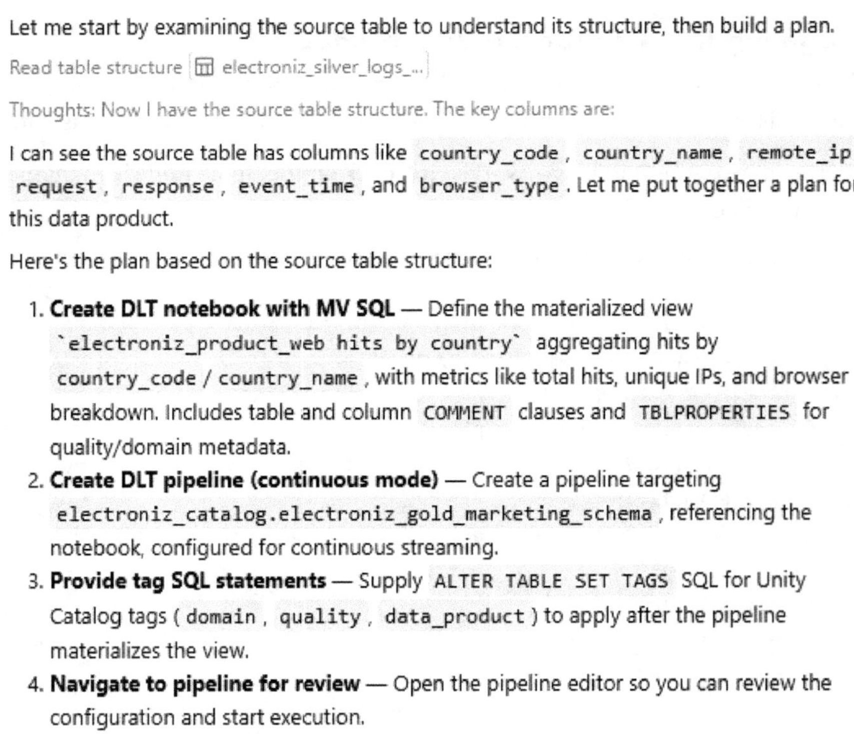

Figure 11.53: Genie Code shortlisting the key columns for building the data product

5. Using the menu on the left, click **Jobs & Pipelines**. You should see the newly deployed pipeline listed there. Click on **electroniz_gold_web_hits_pipeline**.

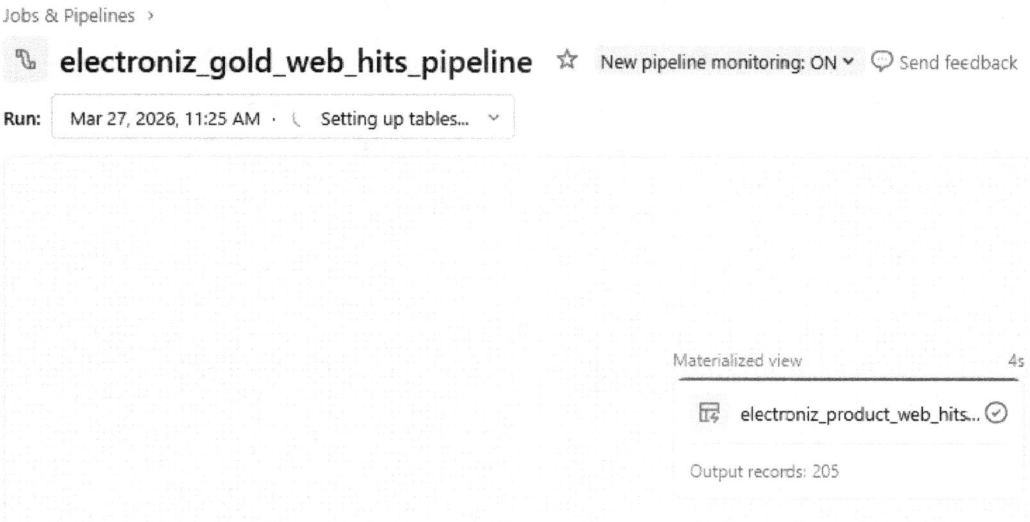

Figure 11.54: electroniz_gold_web_hits_pipeline created

6. Genie Code creates the data product as a materialized view as follows:

Data Product: Web Hits by Country

Domain: Marketing

Target Schema: `electroniz_catalog.electroniz_gold_marketing_schema`

Source: `electroniz_catalog.electroniz_silver_schema.electroniz_silver_logs_geolocation`

Mode: Continuous Streaming

```sql
CREATE OR REFRESH MATERIALIZED VIEW electroniz_product_web_hits_by_country (
  country_code COMMENT 'ISO country code identifying the geographic origin of the web hit',
  country_name COMMENT 'Full country name corresponding to the ISO country code',
  total_hits COMMENT 'Total number of web server hits originating from this country',
  unique_visitors COMMENT 'Count of distinct IP addresses representing unique visitors from
  this country',
  unique_pages_requested COMMENT 'Count of distinct URL paths requested by visitors from
  this country',
  first_hit_time COMMENT 'Timestamp of the earliest recorded web hit from this country',
  last_hit_time COMMENT 'Timestamp of the most recent recorded web hit from this country'
)
COMMENT 'Gold-layer materialized view aggregating web server hits by country for marketing
analytics. Provides geographic traffic distribution, unique visitor counts, and page
engagement metrics per country. Part of the Web Hits by Country data product in the
marketing domain.'
TBLPROPERTIES (
  'quality' = 'gold',
  'domain' = 'marketing',
  'data_product' = 'web hits by country'
)
```

Figure 11.55: Materialized view code for the web hits by country data product

7. Next, inspect the contents of the streaming table. Click **Catalog**, then navigate to **electroniz_catalog** > **electroniz_gold_marketing_schema** > **electroniz_product_web_hits_by_country.** Click on **Sample Data**.

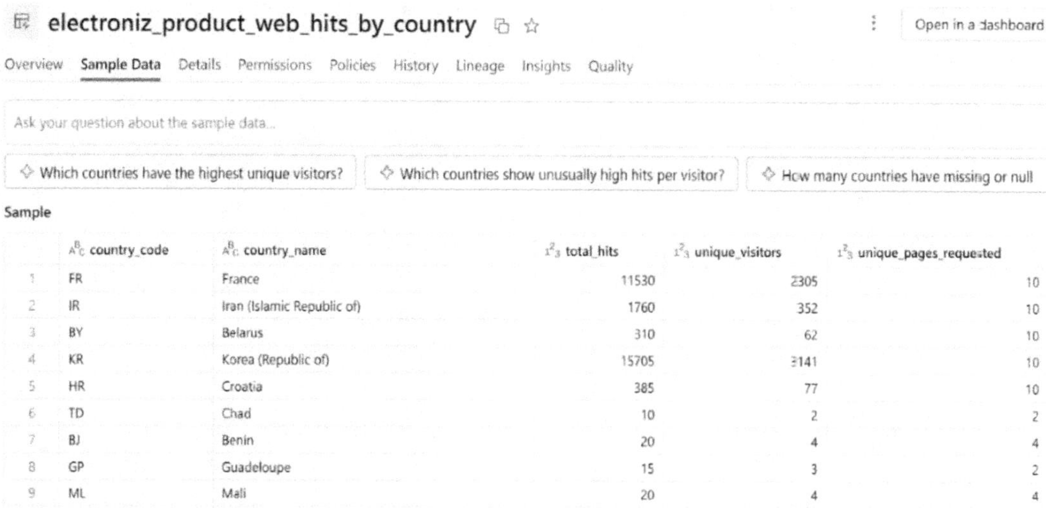

Figure 11.56: Data in electroniz_product_web_hits_by_country

8. Click on **Jobs & Pipelines** and stop the **electroniz_gold_web_hits_pipeline**.

After a successful run of the pipeline, you may add the business metadata describing the newly created data product.

Adding metadata to the data product

In *Chapter 4,* we discussed the role of data stewards in improving data discoverability by capturing metadata for data products, including clear descriptions, source details, schema information, tags, and business glossary terms. At this stage, the data steward should validate the data product for accuracy and completeness and begin enriching it with the appropriate metadata. Follow the steps below to add metadata for the data product.

1. Click on **Catalog**, then navigate to **electroniz_catalog** > **electroniz_gold_marketing_schema** > **electroniz_product_web_hits_by_country**.
2. Note that GenAI has automatically generated a table description. The data steward may review and override this description as needed.

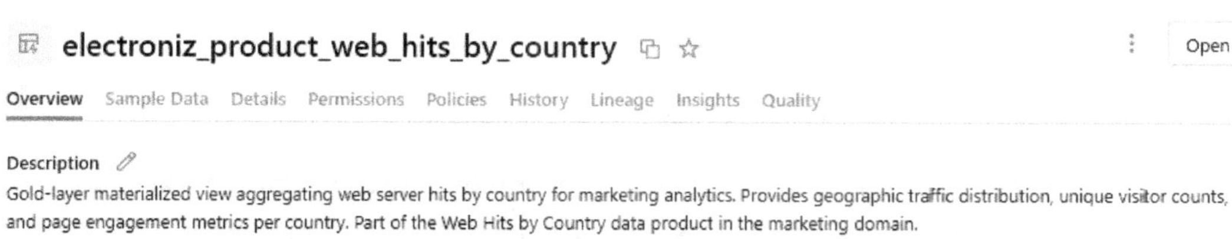

Figure 11.57: AI-generated table-level description

3. The data steward may also generate descriptions for each column in the data product, either using AI assistance or by creating them manually.

Column	Type	Comment
country_code	string	ISO-style two-letter identifier for the country associated with the web hits
country_name	string	Human-readable country label associated with the web hits
total_hits	bigint	Total number of web server hits recorded for the country within the aggregation period
unique_visitors	bigint	Count of distinct visitors generating web hits for the country during the aggregation period
unique_pages_requested	bigint	Number of distinct web pages requested from this country during the aggregation period
first_hit_time	timestamp	Timestamp of the earliest web server hit recorded for the country in the aggregation period
last_hit_time	timestamp	Earliest timestamp a web hit from the country was recorded in the aggregation period

Figure 11.58: AI-generated column-level descriptions

4. Now let's tag a few columns as *key business metric*. In the **Tags** section, click on **Add tags**. Since we do not have a tag named *key business metric* available in the **Key** dropdown, let's create a new one. Click on **Manage governed tags**.

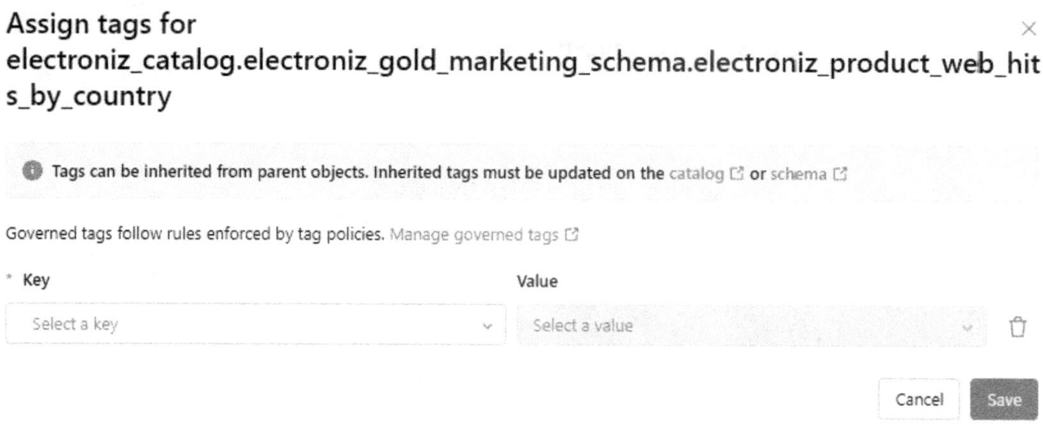

Figure 11.59: Create a new governed tag

5. A new window will open. Click on **Create governed tag** and add the new tag as follows:

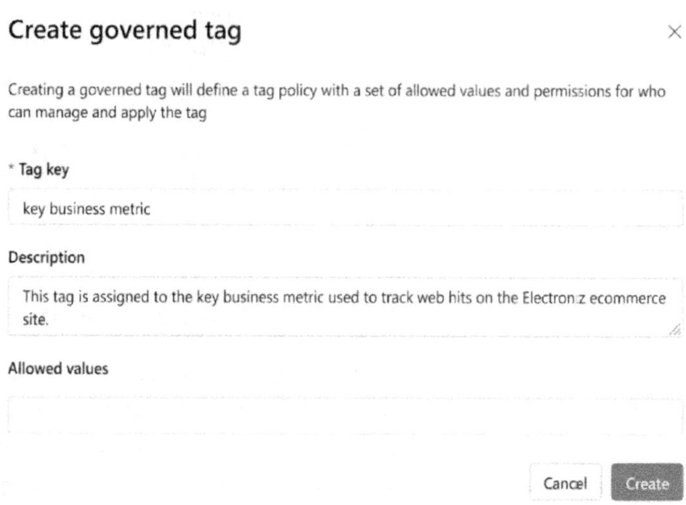

Figure 11.60: New governed tag for the key business metric

6. Navigate back to the previous window and refresh the browser. Add the newly created tag to the **total_hits** and **unique_visitors** columns.

Column	Type	Comment	Tags
country_code	string	ISO-style two-letter identifier for the country associated with the web hits	
country_name	string	Human-readable country label associated with the web hits	
total_hits	bigint	Total number of web server hits recorded for the country within the aggregation period	key business metric
unique_visitors	bigint	Count of distinct visitors generating web hits for the country during the aggregation period	key business metric

Figure 11.61: New governed tags added to the table

In addition to enriching data products with business metadata, data stewards must ensure that each data product complies with broader usability expectations and governance standards. In *Chapter 12*, we will introduce additional elements-such as governance tags, control policies, lineage tracking, and data classification that address these requirements. For now, we will proceed to generate a dashboard for the newly created data product.

Visualizing the data for the data product

Data visualization plays a critical role in driving insight and informed decision-making. By presenting aggregated data through charts, maps, and interactive dashboards, stakeholders can quickly identify trends, patterns, and anomalies, enabling faster and more effective understanding of the data product's value. Follow the steps below to generate a dashboard for the data product.

1. Navigate to the Databricks workspace, and click on the Genie Code icon on the top right of your screen. Issue the following prompt on Genie Code to create the dashboard for `electroniz_product_web_hits_by_country`:

```
can you create a dashboard for
electroniz_catalog.electroniz_gold_marketing_schema.electroniz_product_web_
hits_by_country
```

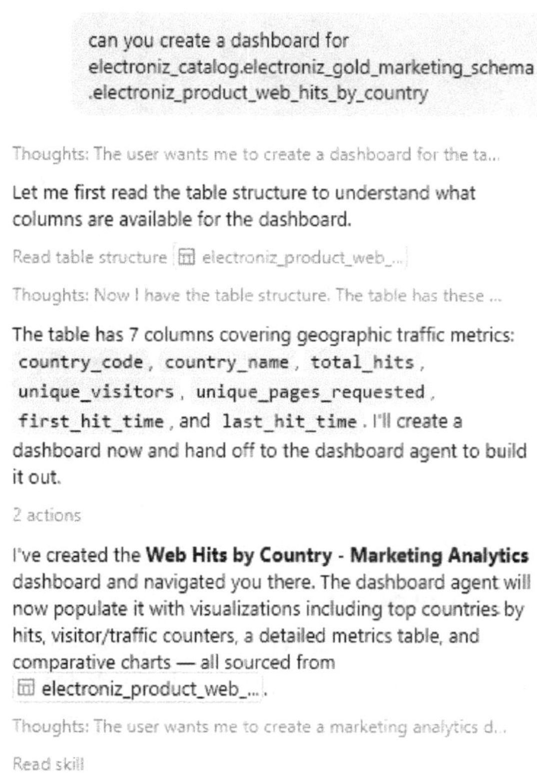

Figure 11.62: New dashboard created for the data product

2. Using the menu on the left, click on **Dashboards**. Then click on the newly generated dashboard **Marketing Analytics - Web Hits by Country**.

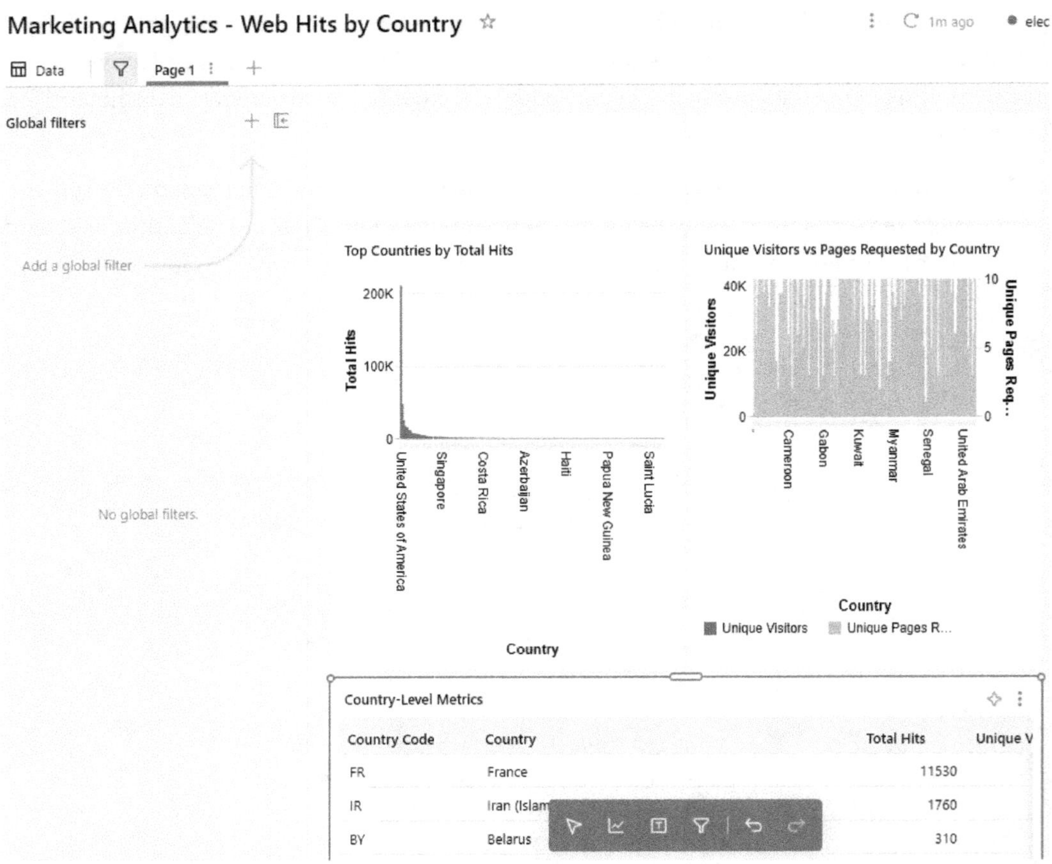

Figure 11.63: Dashboard for Marketing Analytics - Web Hits by Country

Dashboarding helps you interpret the metrics that a data product exposes—but only if the dashboard itself can be easily discovered by end users.

Discovering the data product

As discussed in *Chapter 4*, an effective data product empowers users to independently find, understand, and evaluate it without relying on tribal knowledge or direct support from the data team. In the same chapter, we explored how the FAIR principles of data products promote discoverability and reuse.

In *Chapter 5*, we introduced **Databricks One** as a tool designed for non-technical users to explore data and AI without requiring familiarity with clusters, notebooks, queries, or models.

It is now time to bring these concepts together. Follow the steps below to discover the data product.

1. Navigate to the Databricks workspace using the icon on the top right of the screen that is marked with nine dots; click on **Databricks One**.

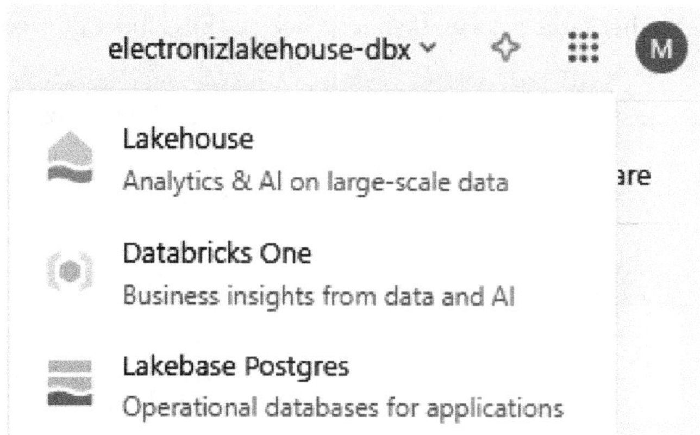

Figure 11.64: Navigate to Databricks One

2. You should now navigate to a screen with a search box. In the search box, type *web hits*. Notice that Databricks One discovers the data product using keywords as follows:

Figure 11.65: Databricks One data product discovery

3. Clicking on the entry will navigate you to the dashboard.

Having delivered the first data product for the marketing domain, we now move on to the second, focused on measuring browsing behavior.

Creating the customer browsing behavior data product

The customer browsing behavior data product exposes customer and prospect browsing behavior as a trusted, consumable, and governed dataset optimized for marketing use cases. The following are the high-level details of the data product:

- Data product name: **Marketing Analytics - Customer Browsing Behavior**

- Domain: **Marketing**
- KPI: **Total count of web hits grouped by browser type, top 10 frequently visited pages**

Using the details outlined above, we can now create the data product as shown below.

1. Navigate to the Databricks workspace, click on the Genie Code icon on the top right of your screen.
2. Issue the following prompt on Genie Code to create the gold products pipeline:

```
Create a data product: Marketing Analytics - Customer Browsing Behavior
Domain: marketing
Source table:
electroniz_catalog.electroniz_silver_schema.electroniz_silver_logs_geolocat
ion
Show the number of hits by the browser type in form of a bar chart
Show the top 10 visited pages
```

3. Genie Code reads the table structure and creates the data product.

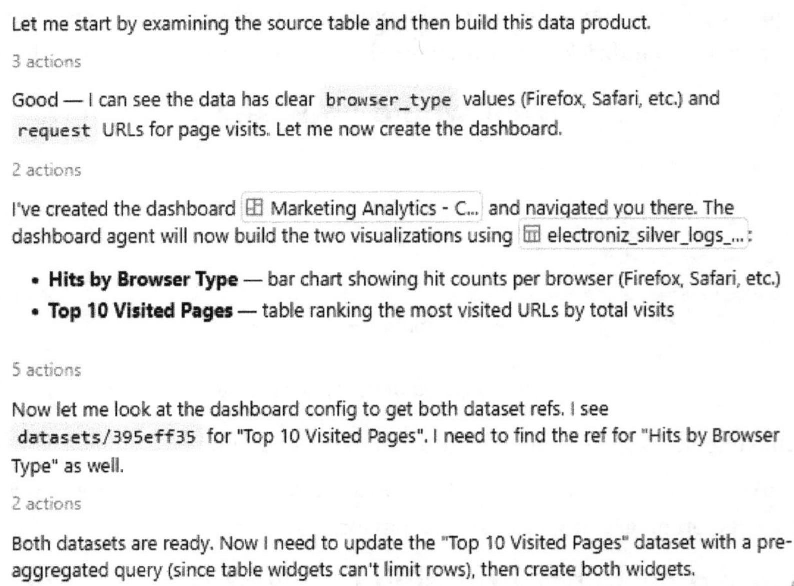

Figure 11.66: Creation of the customer browsing behavior data product

4. Using the menu on the left, click on **Dashboards**. Then click on the newly generated dashboard **Marketing Analytics - Customer Browsing Behavior**.

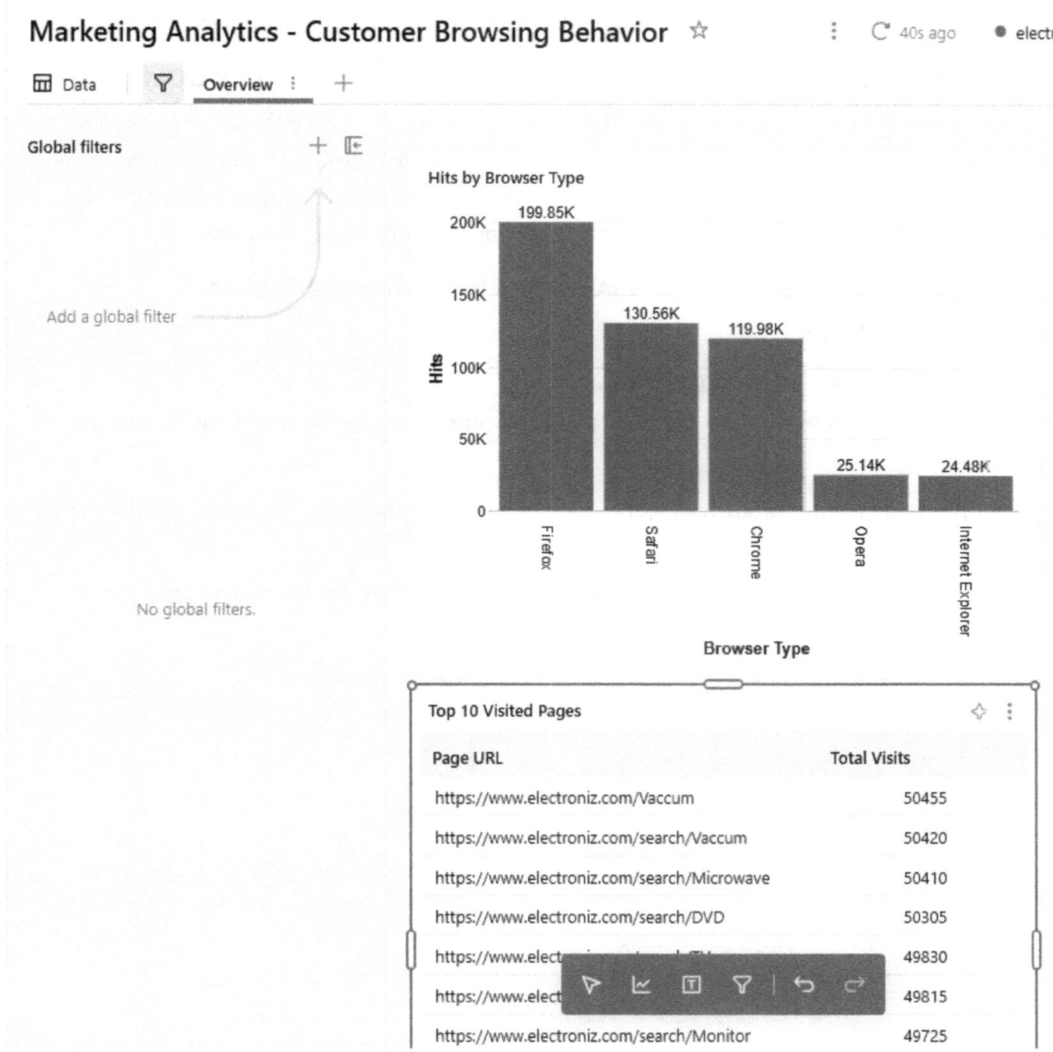

Figure 11.67: Customer Browsing Behavior data product

With the successful delivery of the second marketing domain data product, marketing capabilities are further strengthened through improved audience targeting, enhanced campaign performance measurement, and advanced journey analytics and attribution. Next, let us help the finance domain create data products to enable accurate sales projections and support informed financial planning.

Creating the Electroniz gold pipeline for the finance domain

Data products in the finance domain will improve sales projections, financial visibility, product performance and variance analysis, and enable more robust forecasting and reporting.

Creating the highest-grossing products sold data product

Knowing which products generate the highest total revenue will help the finance team focus resources on their strongest performers, optimize product and pricing strategies, and drive profitability. It also supports more accurate forecasting and better-informed strategic and investment decisions. The following are the high-level details of the data product:

- Data product name: **Finance Analytics – Highest Grossing Products**
- Domain: **finance**
- KPIs: **Total revenue by product**

Follow the steps below to create the gold products pipeline and generate a dashboard for the data product.

1. Navigate to the Databricks workspace and click on the Genie Code icon on the top right of your screen.
2. Issue the following prompt on Genie Code to create the gold products pipeline:

```
Create a new materialized view for the following data product:
Data product name: highest grossing products
Domain: finance
Pipeline Name: electroniz_gold_highest_grossing_products
Materialized view name: electroniz_product_highest_grossing_products
Source tables:
electroniz_catalog.electroniz_silver_schema.electroniz_silver_store_orders
electroniz_catalog.electroniz_silver_schema.electroniz_silver_ecomm_transac
tions
electroniz_catalog.electroniz_silver_schema.electroniz_silver_products
Target table:
electroniz_catalog.electroniz_gold_finance_schema.electroniz_product_highes
t_grossing_products
Required columns in the materialized view are: product_name, total_sales
(combination of sales from electroniz_silver_store_orders and
electroniz_silver_ecomm_transactions)
Mode: Continuous streaming
Add appropriate data product metadata tags such as domain:finance
Add AI generated descriptions for the materialized view and its columns
```

3. Genie Code creates the plan for the new data product as follows:

Here's my plan to create the materialized view and pipeline:

1. **Read source table schemas** — Inspect the 3 silver source tables to understand column names, types, and join keys.
2. **Design materialized view SQL** — Build the query combining sales from `electroniz_silver_store_orders` and `electroniz_silver_ecomm_transactions` , joined with `electroniz_silver_products` for `product_name` .
3. **Create DLT pipeline** — Create pipeline `electroniz_gold_highest_grossing_products` targeting `electroniz_catalog.electroniz_gold_finance_schema` with continuous mode.
4. **Add MV notebook code** — Write the notebook with the materialized view definition, AI-generated descriptions, column comments, and `domain:finance` tags.

Figure 11.68: Genie Code plan for generating the data product

4. Using the menu on the left, click on **Jobs & Pipelines**. Then click on the newly generated pipeline **electroniz_gold_highest_grossing_products**.

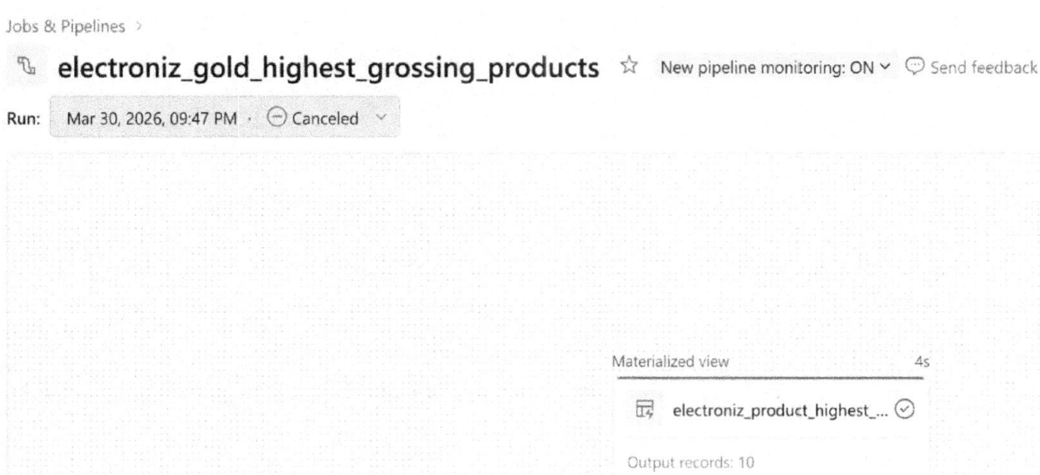

Figure 11.69: electroniz_gold_highest_grossing_products pipeline created

5. Next, inspect the contents of the streaming table. Click **Catalog**, then navigate to **electroniz_catalog** > **electroniz_gold_finance_schema** > **electroniz_product_highest_grossing_products**. Click on **Sample Data**.

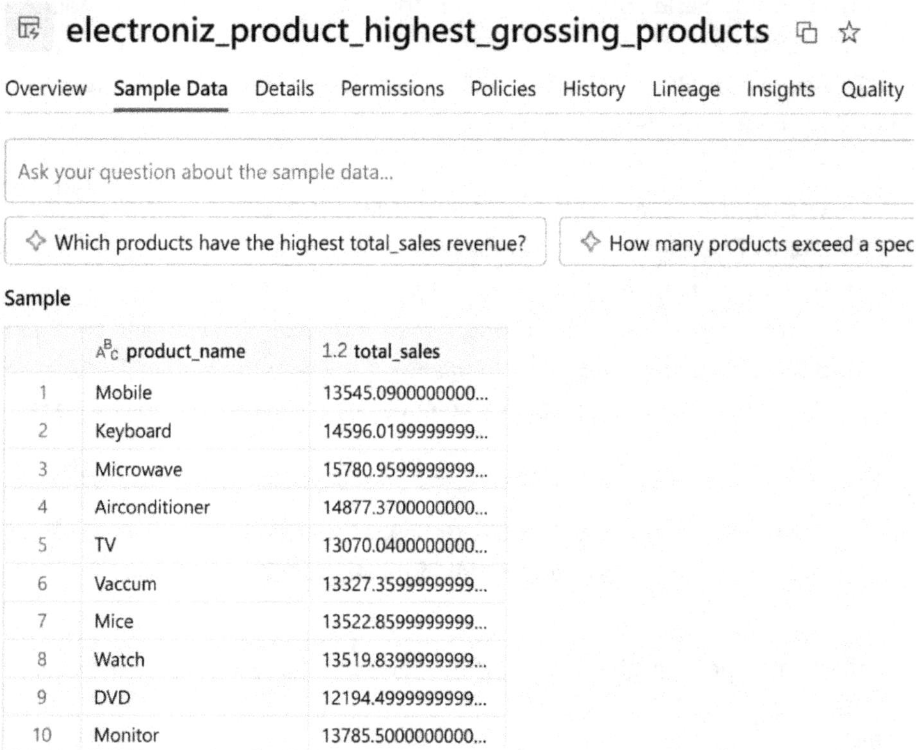

	product_name	total_sales
1	Mobile	13545.0900000000...
2	Keyboard	14596.0199999999...
3	Microwave	15780.9599999999...
4	Airconditioner	14877.3700000000...
5	TV	13070.0400000000...
6	Vaccum	13327.3599999999...
7	Mice	13522.8599999999...
8	Watch	13519.8399999999...
9	DVD	12194.4999999999...
10	Monitor	13785.5000000000...

Figure 11.70: Highest grossing products data product table

6. As part of data stewardship activities, enrich the data product with metadata such as table and column descriptions, along with governed tags to support discovery and governance.
7. Click on **Jobs & Pipelines** and stop the **electroniz_gold_highest_grossing_products**.

8. Next, let us add a dashboard for this data product. Issue the following prompt on Genie Code:

```
Create a new dashboard for
electroniz_catalog.electroniz_gold_finance_schema.electroniz_product_highes
t_grossing_products
Name: Finance Analytics - Highest Grossing Products
Show results as a horizontal bar chart
```

9. Using the menu on the left, click on **Dashboards**. Then click on the newly generated dashboard **Finance Analytics – Highest Grossing Products**.

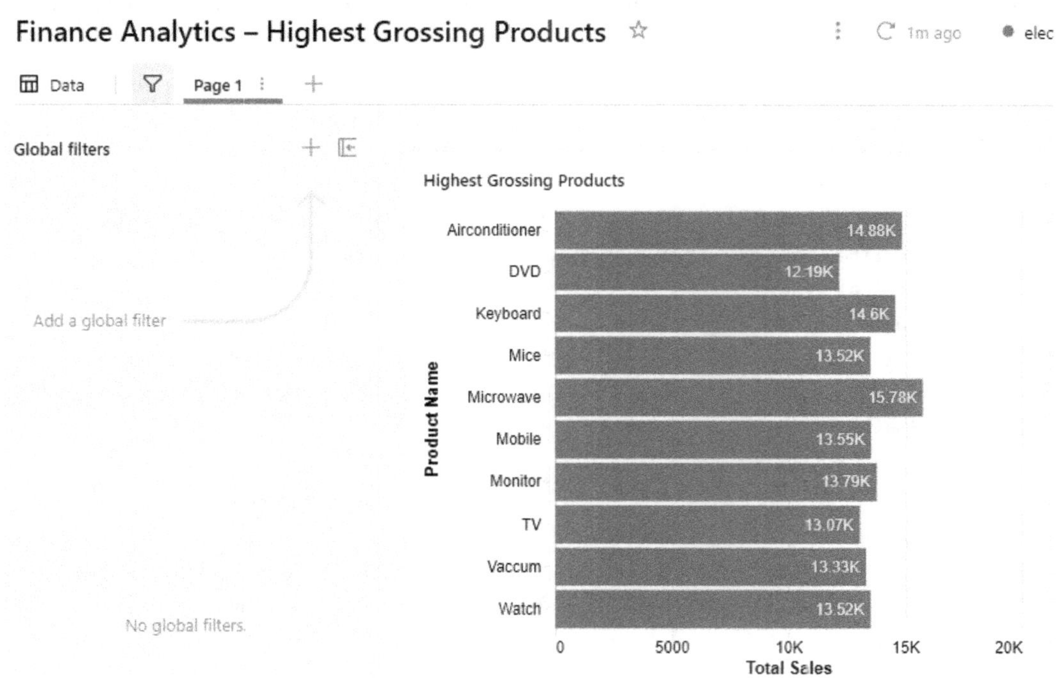

Figure 11.71: Dashboard for Finance Analytics – Highest Grossing Products

The highest-grossing products sold data product for the finance domain will significantly support financial analysis and decision-making. Building on this, we can further assist the finance domain by enabling quarterly sales projections.

Creating the total sales by quarter and year data product

The total sales by quarter and year data product provides a trusted, time-based view of sales performance, aggregated at quarterly and yearly levels. It enables the finance domain to consistently track revenue trends, compare performance across periods, and support forward-looking sales projections. The following are the high-level details of the data product:

- Data product name: **Finance Analytics – Total Sales by Quarter and Year**
- Domain: **Finance**
- KPIs: **Total sales grouped by quarter, total sales grouped by year**

Here's how you can do it:

1. Navigate to the Databricks workspace and click on the Genie Code icon on the top right of your screen.
2. Issue the following prompt on Genie Code to create the gold products pipeline:

```
Create a new materialized view for the following data product:
Data product name: total sales by quarter and year
Domain: finance
Pipeline Name: electroniz_gold_sales_quarter_year
Materialized view name: electroniz_product_sales_quarter_year
Source tables:
electroniz_catalog.electroniz_silver_schema.electroniz_silver_store_orders
electroniz_catalog.electroniz_silver_schema.electroniz_silver_ecomm_transac
tions
Target table:
electroniz_catalog.electroniz_gold_finance_schema.electroniz_product_sales_
quarter_year
Required columns in the materialized view are: year, quarter, total_sales
(combination of sales from electroniz_silver_store_orders and
electroniz_silver_ecomm_transactions)
Mode: Continuous streaming
Add appropriate data product metadata tags such as domain:finance
Add AI generated descriptions for the materialized view and its columns
```

3. Genie Code creates the plan for the new data product:

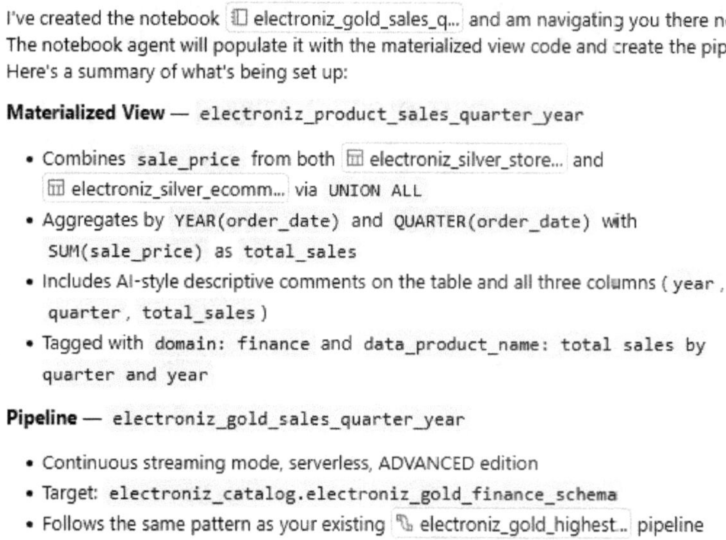

Figure 11.72: Genie code plan for generating the data product

4. Using the menu on the left, click on **Jobs & Pipelines**. Then click on the newly generated pipeline **electroniz_gold_sales_quarter_year**.

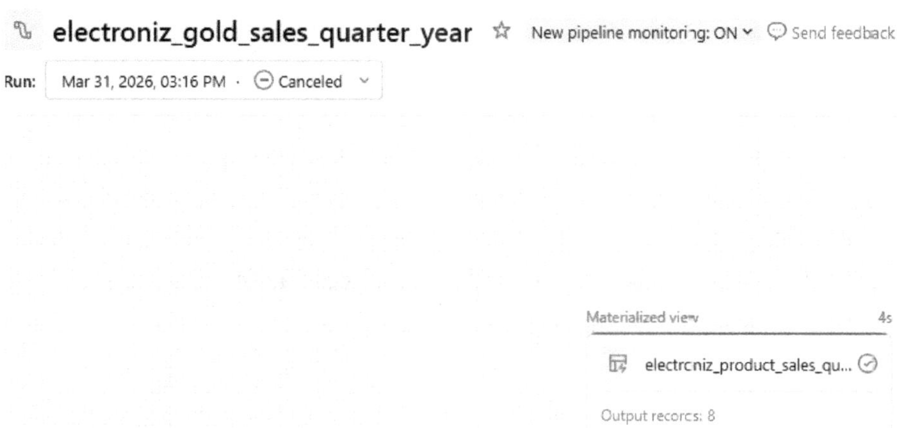

Figure 11.73: electroniz_gold_sales_quarter_year pipeline created

5. Next, inspect the contents of the streaming table. Click **Catalog**, then navigate to **electroniz_catalog** > **electroniz_gold_finance_schema** > **electroniz_product_sales_quarter_year**. Click on **Sample Data**.

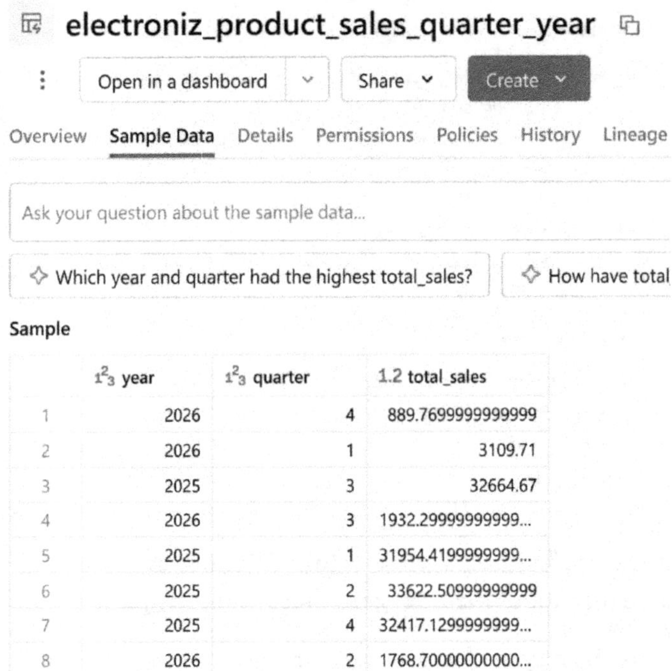

	year	quarter	total_sales
1	2026	4	889.7699999999999
2	2026	1	3109.71
3	2025	3	32664.67
4	2026	3	1932.29999999999...
5	2025	1	31954.4199999999...
6	2025	2	33622.50999999999
7	2025	4	32417.1299999999...
8	2026	2	1768.70000000000...

Figure 11.74: Total sales by quarter and year data product table

6. As part of data stewardship activities, enrich the data product with metadata such as table and column descriptions, along with governed tags to support discovery and governance.
7. Click on **Jobs & Pipelines** and stop the **electroniz_gold_sales_quarter_year**.
8. Next, let us add a dashboard for this data product. Issue the following prompt on Genie Code:

```
Create a new dashboard for
electroniz_catalog.electroniz_gold_finance_schema.electroniz_product_sales_
quarter_year
Name: Finance Analytics - Total Sales by Quarter and Year
```

```
Show total sales by quarter as a line chart
Show total sales by year as a pie chart
```

9. Using the menu on the left, click on **Dashboards**. Then click on the newly generated dashboard **Finance Analytics – Total Sales by Quarter and Year**.

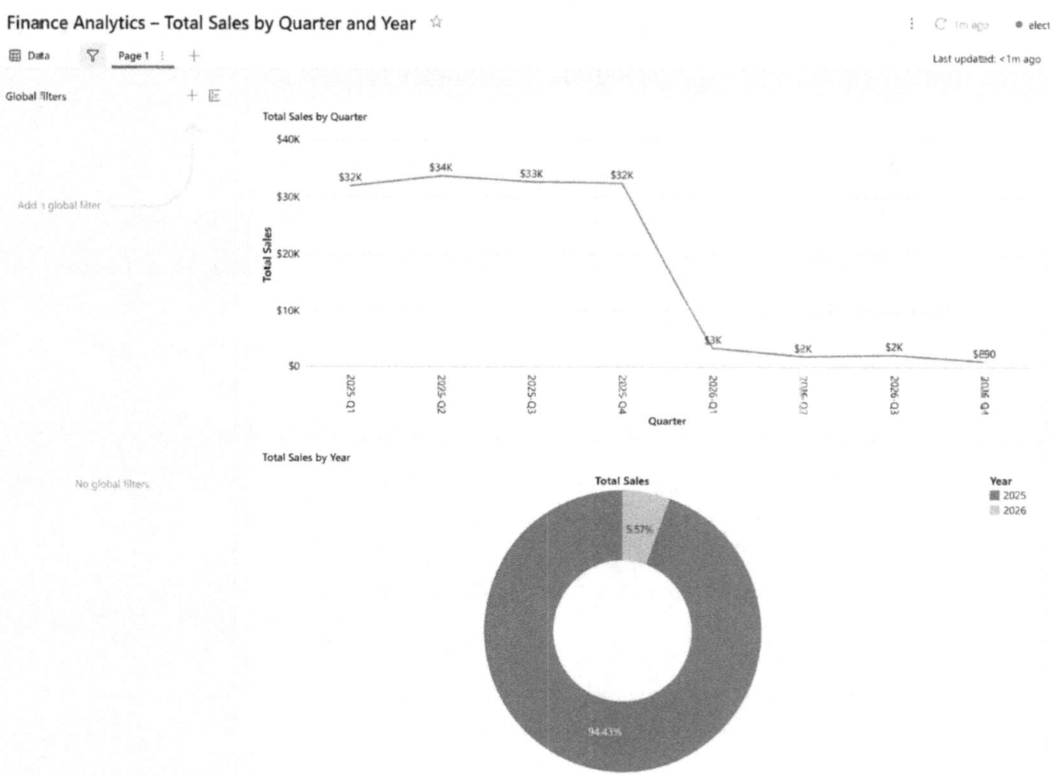

Figure 11.75: Dashboard for Finance Analytics – Total Sales by Quarter and Year

The Finance Analytics – Total Sales by Quarter and Year dashboard provides the finance domain with clear, time-based visibility into sales performance, supporting quarterly forecasting, budgeting, and planning through consistent trend and year-over-year analysis. Similarly, the supply team can be provided with the same level of visibility into product inventory.

Creating the Electroniz gold pipeline for the supply domain

Data products in the supply domain will enable more accurate inventory projections, deeper insights into demand trends, and more reliable sales forecasting.

Creating inventory projections data product

The inventory projections data product enables the supply domain to proactively plan, manage, and optimize inventory levels by combining historical sales, current stock positions, and forecasted demand. It provides forward-looking visibility into inventory needs across products, locations, and time horizons, helping supply teams avoid stock-outs while minimizing excess inventory. The following are the high-level details of the data product:

- Data product name: **Supply Analytics – Inventory Projections**
- Domain: **Supply**
- KPIs: **Predicted inventory needed, stock status by product**

Follow the steps below to create and deploy the Inventory Projections data product.

1. Navigate to the Databricks workspace, and click on the Genie Code icon on the top right of your screen.
2. Issue the following prompt on Genie Code to create the gold products pipeline:

```
Create a new materialized view for the following data product:
Data product name: inventory projections
Data product description: estimate inventory projections for next month and
compare against available inventory
Domain: supply
Pipeline Name: electroniz_gold_inventory_projections
Materialized view name: electroniz_product_inventory_projections
Source tables:
electroniz_catalog.electroniz_silver_schema.electroniz_silver_store_orders
electroniz_catalog.electroniz_silver_schema.electroniz_silver_ecomm_transac
tions
electroniz_catalog.electroniz_silver_schema.electroniz_silver_products
electroniz_catalog.electroniz_silver_schema.electroniz_silver_inventory
Target table:
electroniz_catalog.electroniz_gold_supply_schema.electroniz_product_invento
ry_projections
Mode: Continuous streaming
Add appropriate data product metadata tags such as domain:supply
Add AI generated descriptions for the materialized view and its columns
```

3. Genie Code goes through the usual motions of creating an extensive plan for the new data product.

4. Using the menu on the left, click on **Jobs & Pipelines**. Then click on the newly generated pipeline **electroniz_gold_inventory_projections**.

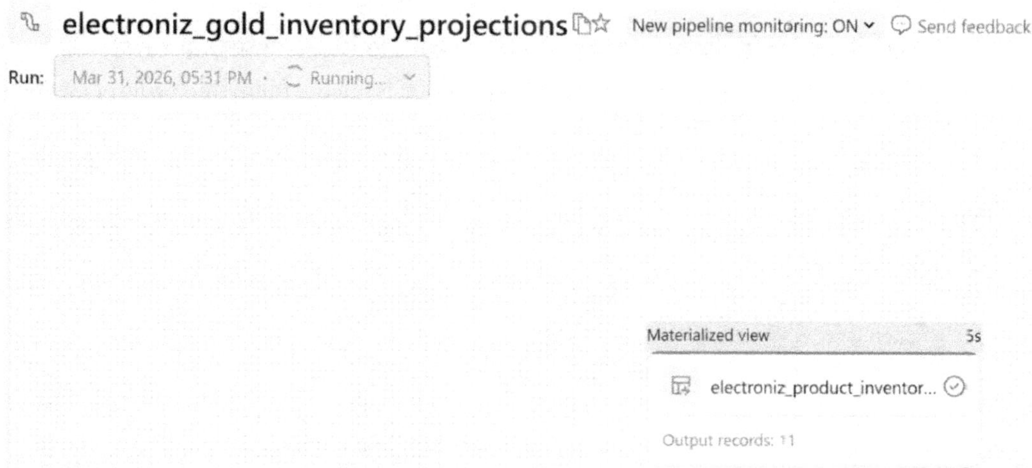

Figure 11.76: electroniz_gold_inventory_projections pipeline created

5. Next, inspect the contents of the streaming table. Click **Catalog**, then navigate to **electroniz_catalog** > **electroniz_gold_supply_schema** > **electroniz_product_inventory_projections**. Click on **Sample Data**.

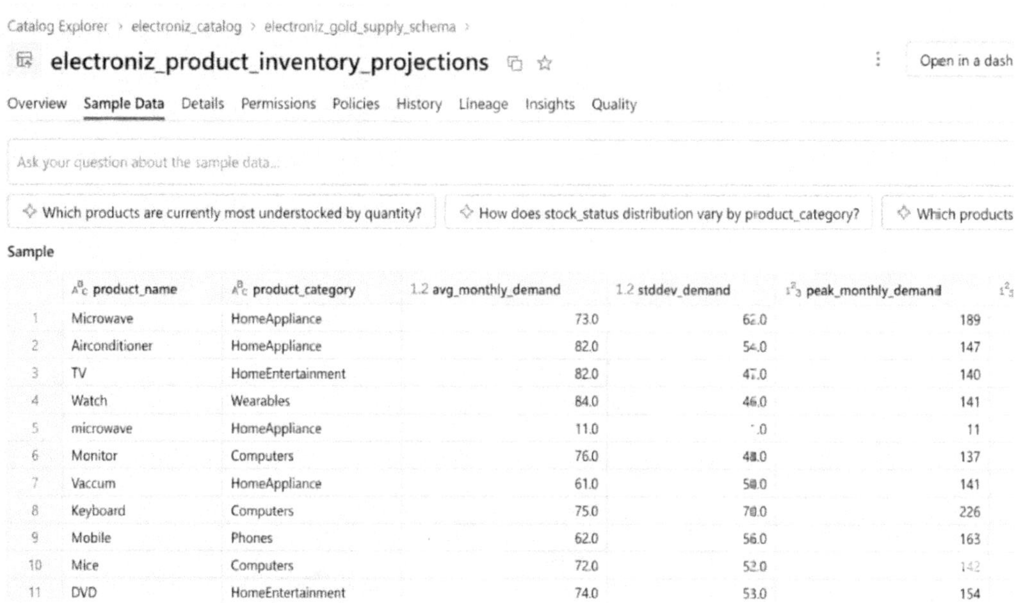

	product_name	product_category	avg_monthly_demand	stddev_demand	peak_monthly_demand
1	Microwave	HomeAppliance	73.0	[illegible]	189
2	Airconditioner	HomeAppliance	82.0	54.0	147
3	TV	HomeEntertainment	82.0	[illegible]	140
4	Watch	Wearables	84.0	46.0	141
5	microwave	HomeAppliance	11.0	[illegible]	11
6	Monitor	Computers	76.0	[illegible]	137
7	Vaccum	HomeAppliance	61.0	[illegible]	141
8	Keyboard	Computers	75.0	[illegible]	226
9	Mobile	Phones	62.0	56.0	163
10	Mice	Computers	72.0	52.0	142
11	DVD	HomeEntertainment	74.0	53.0	154

Figure 11.77: Inventory projections data product table

6. As part of data stewardship activities, enrich the data product with metadata such as table and column descriptions, along with governed tags to support discovery and governance.
7. Click on **Jobs & Pipelines** and stop the **electroniz_gold_inventory_projections**.
8. Next, let us add a dashboard for this data product. Issue the following prompt on Genie Code:

```
Create a new dashboard for
electroniz_catalog.electroniz_gold_supply_schema.electroniz_product_invento
ry_projections
Name: Supply Analytics - Inventory Projections
Show stock_status as a pie chart
Show predicted_inventory_needed as a table
```

9. Using the menu on the left click on **Dashboards**. Then click on the newly generated dashboard **Supply Analytics – Total Sales by Quarter and Year**.

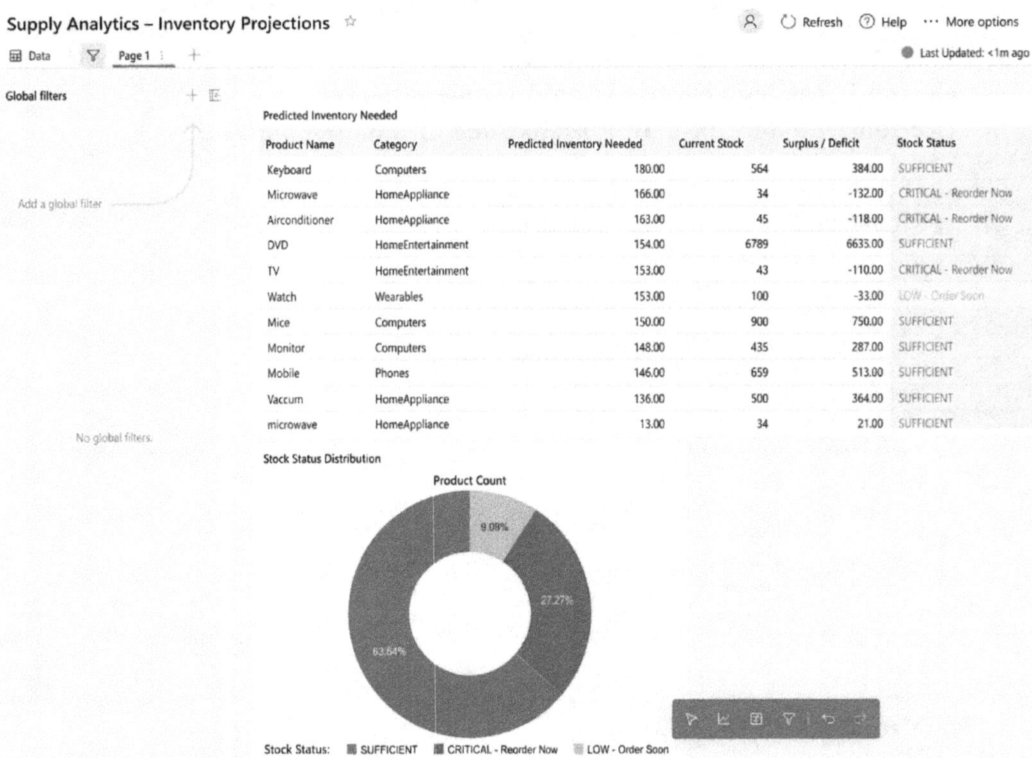

Predicted Inventory Needed

Product Name	Category	Predicted Inventory Needed	Current Stock	Surplus / Deficit	Stock Status
Keyboard	Computers	180.00	564	384.00	SUFFICIENT
Microwave	HomeAppliance	166.00	34	-132.00	CRITICAL - Reorder Now
Airconditioner	HomeAppliance	163.00	45	-118.00	CRITICAL - Reorder Now
DVD	HomeEntertainment	154.00	6789	6635.00	SUFFICIENT
TV	HomeEntertainment	153.00	43	-110.00	CRITICAL - Reorder Now
Watch	Wearables	153.00	100	-33.00	LOW - Order Soon
Mice	Computers	150.00	900	750.00	SUFFICIENT
Monitor	Computers	148.00	435	287.00	SUFFICIENT
Mobile	Phones	146.00	659	513.00	SUFFICIENT
Vaccum	HomeAppliance	136.00	500	364.00	SUFFICIENT
microwave	HomeAppliance	13.00	34	21.00	SUFFICIENT

Figure 11.78: Dashboard for Supply Analytics – Inventory Projections

The Supply Analytics – Inventory Projections data product provides forward-looking inventory visibility by combining demand trends and sales forecasts to project future stock levels, identify overstock or stock-out risks early, and support effective replenishment and procurement planning.

Summary

As we conclude this chapter, we have demonstrated how curated data can be transformed into high-value, analytics-ready assets through thoughtful aggregation in the gold layer. This approach bridges the gap between raw operational data and meaningful business insight, positioning aggregation as a critical step in delivering value from master data.

Throughout this chapter, we emphasized design decisions that reinforce trust and reliability, from selecting the appropriate aggregation grain to preserving alignment with golden record definitions established through master data management. The resulting gold-layer datasets are more than just optimized tables; they are trusted data products, built with clear semantics, governed schemas, and quality expectations that enable confident reuse across reporting, analytics, and decision-making.

By executing and validating the aggregation pipeline, we confirmed that these data products meet both technical and business requirements. The successful validation reinforces that when aggregation is built on a strong MDM foundation, organizations can deliver consistent, governed, and scalable analytical assets. With these trusted data products in place, downstream consumers can focus on generating insights, confident in the accuracy and integrity of the data that supports them.

In the final chapter, *Chapter 12, Governing Data Products,* we extend our understanding of data product validation, security, access control, and delivery at scale. The chapter focuses on how governance principles are applied across the data lifecycle to ensure that data products remain secure, compliant, and trustworthy. We also explore how to implement data observability to continuously monitor data quality, freshness, and reliability, enabling teams to detect issues early and maintain confidence in their analytical and master data assets.

Get this book's PDF version and more

Scan the QR code (or go to `packtpub.com/unlock`). Search for this book by name, confirm the edition, and then follow the steps on the page.

UNLOCK NOW

Note: Keep your invoice handy. Purchases made directly from Packt don't require an invoice.

12

Governing Data Products

The journey of data is now nearing its destination. In the previous chapter, we explored data aggregation and the construction of the gold layer within the Lakehouse, where refined data is shaped into business-ready data products. These gold-layer assets represent the highest level of curation—encapsulating agreed business definitions, trusted metrics, and consumption-oriented models.

With all the foundational components of the Electroniz Lakehouse now designed, implemented, and validated, the focus shifts from *building* data products to *governing* them. Creating a data product is only the first step; sustaining its value requires intentional controls to ensure it remains reliable, secure, up to date, and fit for purpose as it is consumed across teams and use cases.

This transition marks a critical inflection point—from technical enablement to sustained value delivery. At this stage, data products are no longer evaluated solely by how they are built, but by how well they are governed, trusted, and consumed across the organization. To support this shift without sacrificing team autonomy or agility, we begin by exploring how a federated governance model provides the structure and guardrails needed to scale data products with confidence.

In this chapter, we shift our focus to operationalizing governance practices that elevate data products to first-class organizational assets. This step goes beyond technical construction and examines how data products are owned, protected, certified, and sustained over time. Key elements include establishing clear product ownership, enforcing consistent access and security boundaries, managing lifecycle and certification, and ensuring that data products are delivered reliably and consistently at enterprise scale.

This chapter covers the following topics:

- Federated Governance
- Data access policies
- Data privacy and regulatory compliance standards
- Data classification policies
- Data lineage tracking policies
- Data lifecycle management policies
- Data quality and observability standards
- Data stewardship

In the section below, we explore the central role of federated governance within an organization's overall governance strategy.

Federated Governance

Federated governance is the operating model that allows data products to scale without centralizing every decision. It strikes a deliberate balance between autonomy and control—empowering domain teams to own and evolve their data products, while ensuring the enterprise maintains consistent standards for trust, security, and compliance. In *Chapter 4*, we examined the convergence of the data delivery lifecycle and the pursuit of balance among standards, processes, and governance. We focused on identifying the sweet spot where consistency and control coexist with flexibility and speed. In doing so, we highlighted how thoughtfully designed standards and processes reinforce the core principles of a data mesh—most notably decentralized domain ownership and federated governance. Given Electroniz's domain-driven structure (master, supply, finance, marketing), a federated governance model enables each domain to own and manage its data products while still adhering to enterprise-wide standards for trust, quality, and compliance.

Before exploring how federated governance enables this balance at scale, it is important to ground our discussion in a clear understanding of what data governance entails.

Implementing a robust data governance strategy

A well-designed governance strategy not only safeguards organizational data assets but also enables organizations to fully realize the value of analytics by fostering trust among business users and providing assurance to security, risk, and compliance stakeholders. At its core, data governance brings together a set of complementary practices that collectively establish trust, protect sensitive information, and ensure consistent, responsible use of data across the organization. When implemented effectively, these practices form a cohesive framework that balances control with enablement, allowing data products to be shared confidently and consumed at scale.

As shown in *Figure 12.1* below, a comprehensive data governance strategy typically encompasses several key areas, each contributing to the organization's ability to safeguard data while maximizing its analytical value. Together, these governance dimensions define how data is owned, secured, classified, certified, monitored, and evolved over time—ensuring that users can trust not only the data itself, but also the processes and controls that support it.

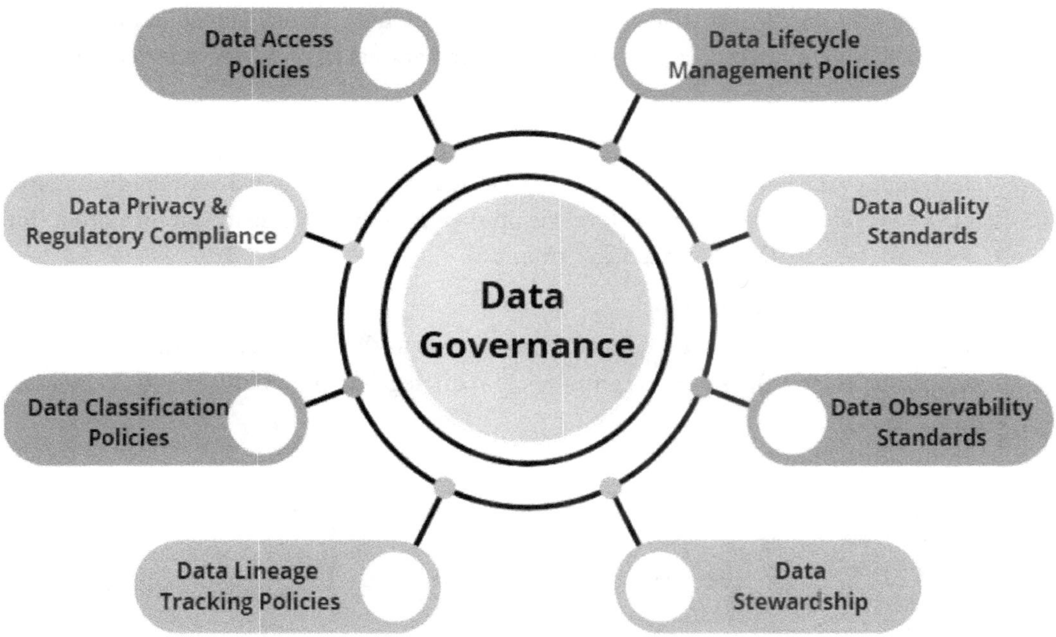

Figure 12.1: Data governance standards and policies

Data governance encompasses a set of principles, policies, processes, and enabling technologies designed to ensure that data is secure, trustworthy, and compliant with regulatory requirements. We will conduct a detailed review of each data governance standard and relate it to the Electroniz data products.

Data access policies

At a high level, access policies define who can access which data, at what level of detail, and under what conditions. These policies ensure that data is used securely and responsibly, in compliance with organizational standards and regulatory requirements. By enforcing the principle of least-privilege access, they help minimize the risk of unauthorized data exposure.

To understand this in more detail:

- **Who**
  Defines the authorized users, groups, roles, or service accounts that are permitted to access data. This is typically aligned with business domains or functions and supports access models such as **role-based access control** (**RBAC**) and **attribute-based access control** (**ABAC**).
- **What data**
  Specifies the data assets that can be accessed, including catalogs, schemas, tables, views, files, or models. Access is granted only to datasets that are relevant to a user's role or business responsibility.
- **Level of detail**
  Determines the granularity of access, such as read-only versus read-write permissions, row-level filtering, and column-level visibility or masking for sensitive information (for example, personally identifiable information).
- **Under which conditions**
  Establishes contextual constraints for access, such as the environment (development, test, or production), as well as compliance, audit, legal, or policy-driven requirements.

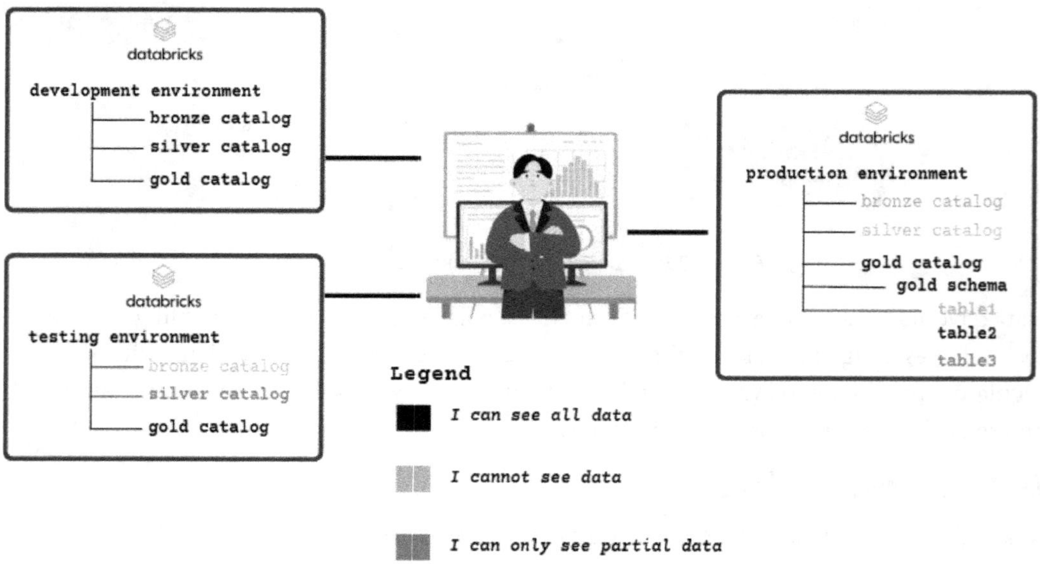

Figure 12.2: Data access levels

As illustrated in the image above, an Electroniz analyst has broad access to data assets in the **development** environment, more restricted access to selected data assets in the **testing** environment, and access to only a limited set of tables in the **production** environment. In addition, certain tables apply row-level and column-level controls, filtering the data returned based on the analyst's classification level.

To illustrate how this works in practice, the following section presents a sample scenario that demonstrates how access controls can be implemented using Electroniz data products.

As per best practices, the Databricks RBAC security model governs access to data, compute, and workspace resources by assigning permissions to roles (groups) rather than to individual users. RBAC is implemented through the Unity Catalog using **Access Control Lists (ACLs).** RBAC simplifies access management and supports the principle of least privilege across the Databricks platform.

> Note
>
> The principle of least privilege states that users, roles, and systems should be granted only the minimum access necessary to perform their authorized tasks. This reduces security risk by limiting unnecessary exposure to data, systems, and sensitive operations.

Fine-grained access control

Fine-grained access control (**FGAC**) is a security authorization model that governs access to data assets across multiple hierarchical scopes, including the catalog, schema, and individual securable objects such as tables, views, functions, and columns. FGAC enables precise, object-level permission management by explicitly defining and enforcing privileges based on the operation type (e.g., `SELECT`, `INSERT`, `UPDATE`, `DELETE`, `EXECUTE`, `ADMIN`). Under FGAC, access can be progressively constrained. For example, a principal (user, group, or service identity) may be granted read-only access at the catalog level, restricted access to specific schemas within that catalog, and further limited to a subset of tables or columns within a schema. This hierarchical and explicit grant model ensures tight control over data exposure and usage. By enabling authorization at a highly granular level, FGAC supports:

- Enforcement of the principle of least privilege, ensuring identities have only the minimum permissions required
- Protection of sensitive and regulated data such as PII through scoped and explicit access controls
- Regulatory and audit compliance by providing clear, traceable permission boundaries
- Reduced risk of unauthorized data access or leakage through minimized permission sprawl

FGAC is most effective in environments where data structures, access patterns, and ownership models are well defined and relatively stable. It typically serves as the foundational authorization layer in an organization's broader data security and governance architecture. For environments with rapidly evolving schemas or complex multi-group membership scenarios, **attribute-based access control (ABAC)** offers a more flexible and dynamic approach to enforcing access policies. ABAC will be discussed later in this chapter; for now, we focus on a detailed examination of FGAC through the following example implementation. We will create the following users, groups, and permissions to provision the access for the financial analysts.

- **RBAC group:** `electroniz_finance_domain_grp_write`
- **RBAC user:** `finance_analyst_1`
- Limited ACLs:
    a. Read and write on `electroniz_catalog.electroniz_gold_finance_schema`
    b. Read on `electroniz_catalog. electroniz_gold_master_schema.mvw_electroniz_gold_golden_record_customers`
    c. Read on `electroniz_catalog.electroniz_silver_schema.electroniz_silver_store_orders`
- **RBAC group:** `electroniz_finance_domain_grp_read`
- **RBAC user:** `finance_analyst_2`
- Limited ACLs:
    a. Read on `electroniz_catalog.electroniz_gold_finance_schema`
    b. Read on `electroniz_catalog.electroniz_gold_master_schema.mvw_electroniz_gold_golden_record_customers`

Provisioning access in Databricks requires logging into the **Databricks account console**. Up to this point, we have been working primarily within the **Databricks workspace console**; this will be our first time accessing the account console.

Enabling Databricks account console

The Databricks Account Console provides a unified, account-wide administration layer for managing Databricks at an organizational level. Rather than operating within a single workspace, it supports centralized governance, identity management, and configuration across the entire platform.

1. Microsoft Entra ID serves as the identity and access management system for authenticating and authorizing users and applications that access Azure Databricks. As

part of this setup, we will create a few new Entra ID accounts for users in the finance domain.

2. Navigate to the **Azure portal** and go to **Users**.
3. Add a new Azure user for **finance_analyst_1**.

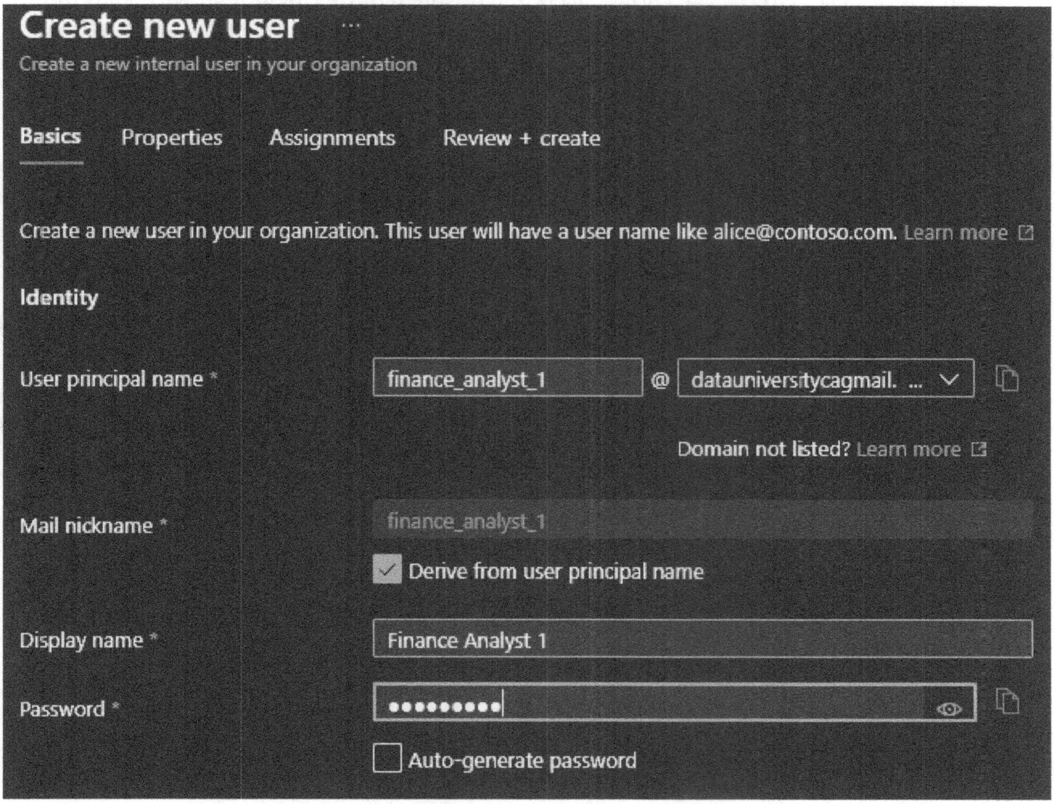

Figure 12.3: Creating a new Azure user

4. Similarly, create a new Azure user for **finance_analyst_2**.

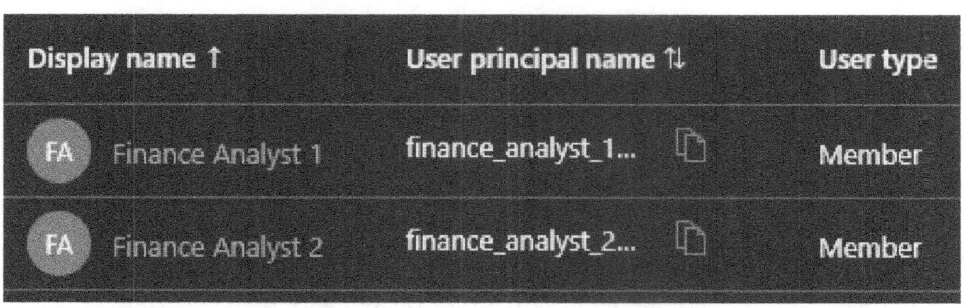

Figure 12.4: Added two new Azure users

5. Open each user entry individually and record the User Principal Name (email address), as you will need these later. Also ensure you note the passwords that were set when the users were created, as these accounts will be used to log in to the Databricks workspace.
6. In Azure, access to the Databricks account console requires logging in with your fully qualified Microsoft Entra ID as the username.
7. Now take note of your own fully qualified Microsoft Entra ID, which includes the `#EXT#` identifier.

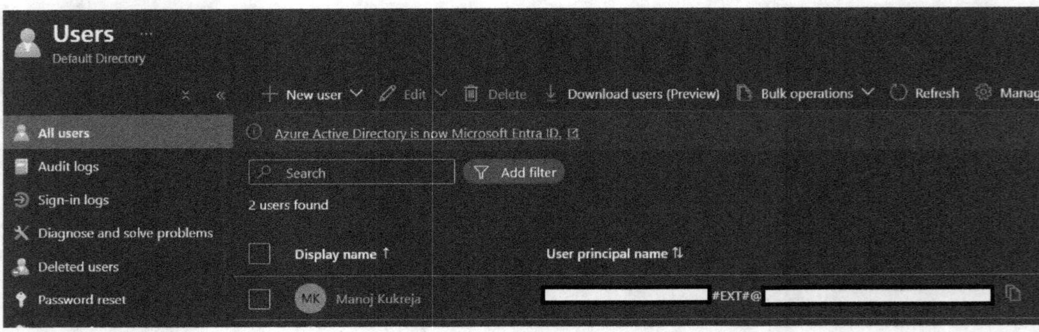

Figure 12.5: Microsoft Entra ID for the Databricks account console

8. Now go to Databricks Account login at `accounts.azuredatabricks.net` and login with the `#EXT#` username. You may need to reset the password to log in as this user.
9. After logging in, you should see a console like the one shown below:

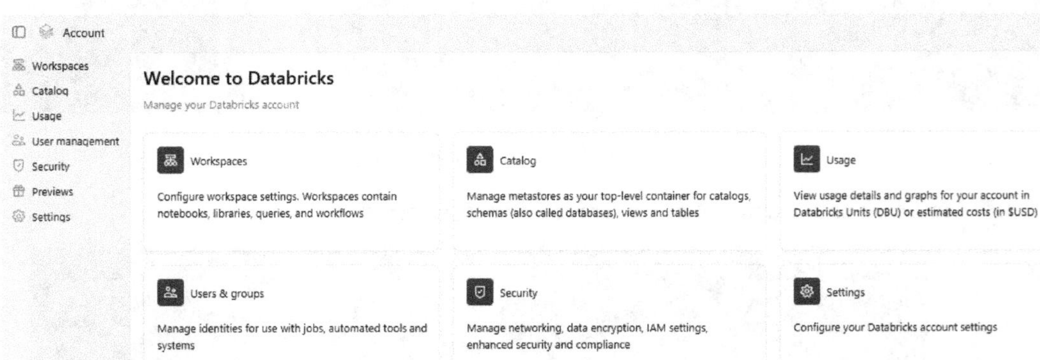

Figure 12.6: Databricks account console

10. Click on **User & Groups**.
11. Under User management, click on your username followed by Roles.

12. Make sure you enable the following roles for your account.

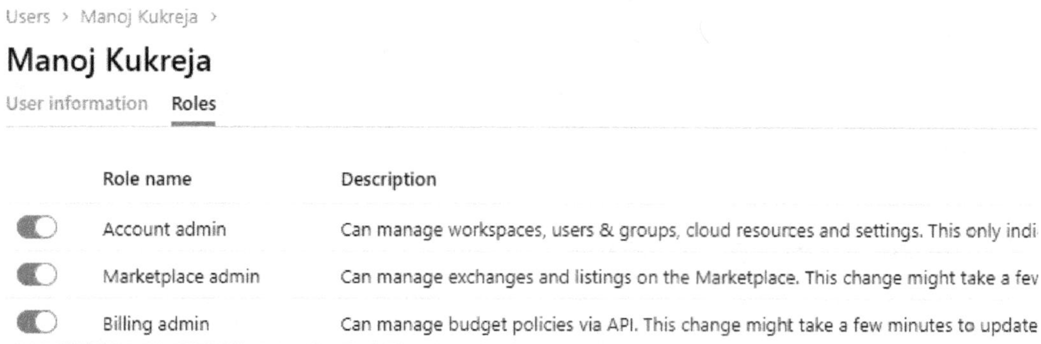

Figure 12.7: Enabling user management roles

Creating Databricks users and groups

Databricks users and groups are defined in the workspace console and are limited in scope to the individual workspace in which they are created.

1. Log in to your Databricks workspace. Click on your name icon on the top right of the screen. Click on **Settings**.
2. Navigate back to **Identity and access**. Click on the **Manage** button beside **Users.**
3. Add two new users, each using the **User principal name** noted earlier.

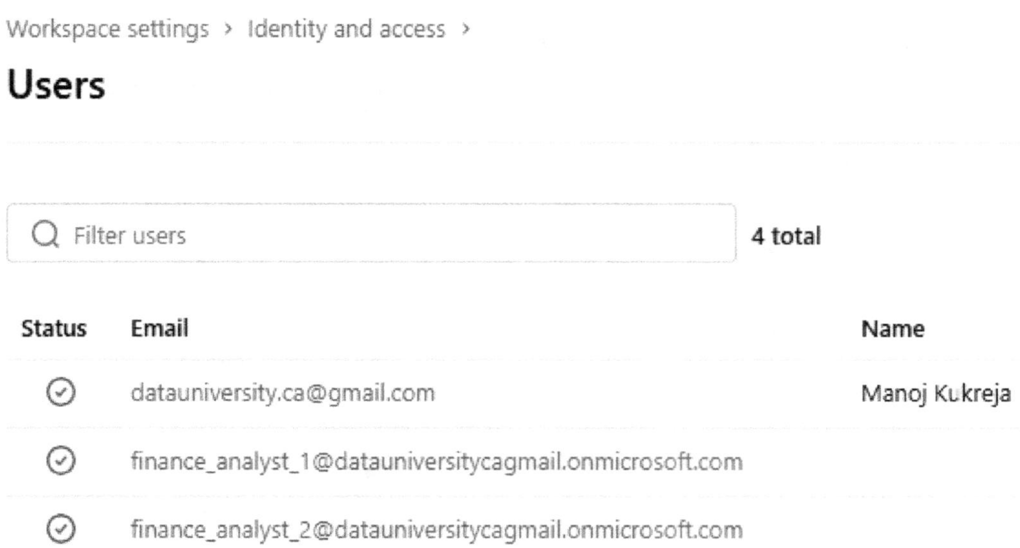

Figure 12.8: Two new users created in the Databricks workspace

4. Click on the user entry for **finance_analyst_1** and change the **Entitlements.** Enable **Workspace access** and **Databricks SQL access** for the user.
5. Do the same for user **finance_analyst_2.**
6. Under Settings, click on **Identity and access**.

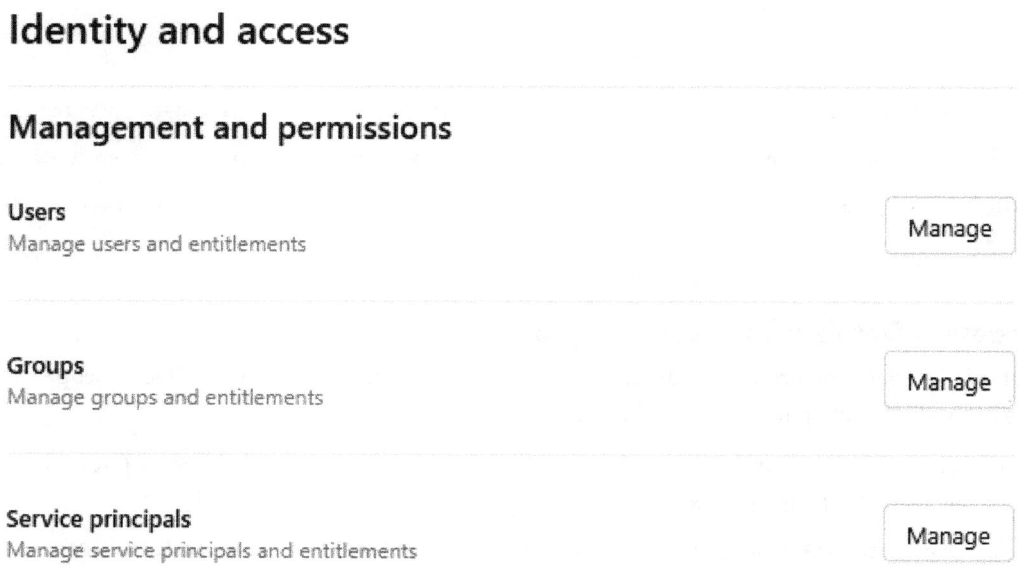

Figure 12.9: Navigating Identity and access

7. Now click on the **Manage** button beside **Groups**.
8. Add a new group name **electroniz_finance_domain_grp_write** as follows:

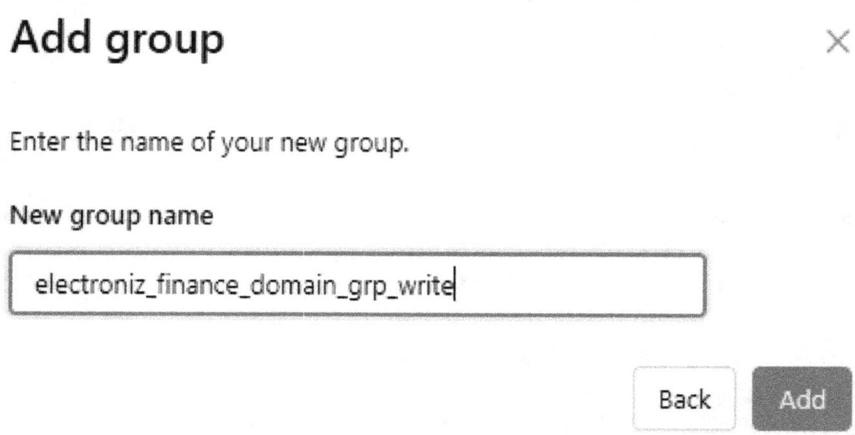

Figure 12.10: Add a new write group

9. Similarly, add a new read group named **electroniz_finance_domain_grp_read**.

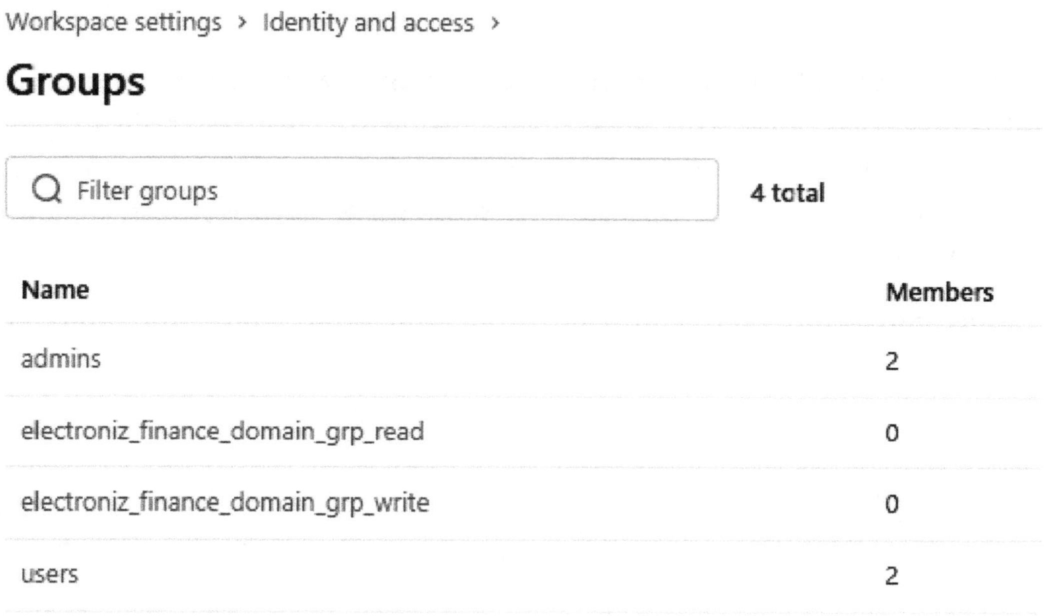

Figure 12.11: Two new groups created for the finance domain

10. Click on **electroniz_finance_domain_grp_write**. On the Group Details screen, click on **Add members**.
11. Search for **finance_analyst_1** and press **Add**.
12. Similarly add **finance_analyst_2** to the **electroniz_finance_domain_grp_read** group.

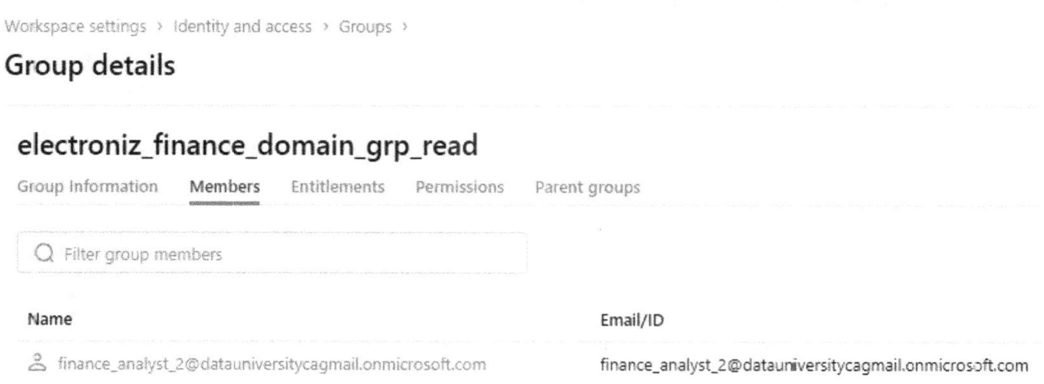

Figure 12.12: Adding users to groups

Now that the users and groups have been created and users have been assigned to their respective groups, let's verify that these users can successfully log in to the Databricks workspace.

Allowing the Databricks groups to use the SQL warehouse

Before logging in as the newly created users, we must ensure they have access to the SQL Warehouse compute, which is required to run queries.

1. Under **Settings**, click on **Compute**. Make the **electroniz_sql_warehouse** as the default warehouse.

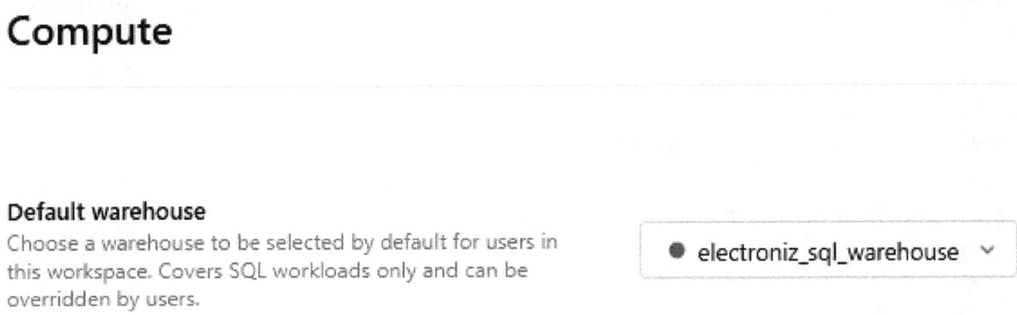

Figure 12.13: Assigning a default warehouse

2. On the Databricks workspace, click on **SQL Warehouses**. Click on **electroniz_sql_warehouse.**
3. Click on **Permissions** and assign both groups **Use** privileges.

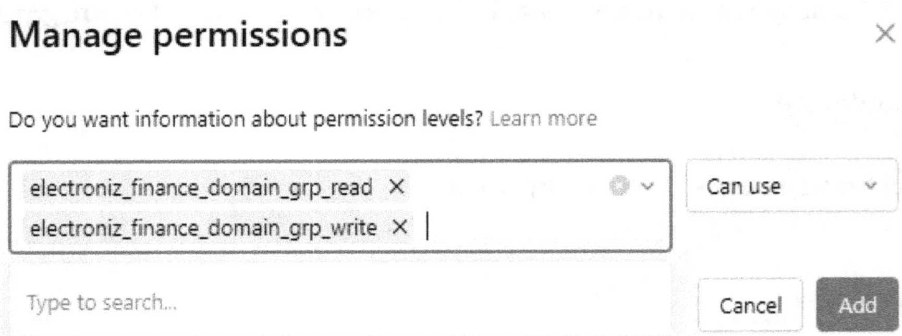

Figure 12.14: Assigning groups use privileges on the SQL warehouse

Assigning group permissions to `electroniz_sql_warehouse` ensures that group members can query data and run workloads using that warehouse.

Accessing Databricks workspace as new users

Domain users authenticate to Databricks like any other users; however, their access may be limited by assigned permissions.

1. Note down the URL of your Databricks workspace; it will look like `https://adb-xxxxxxxxxxx.xx.azuredatabricks.net`.
2. Open the URL above in a new browser window, preferably in incognito mode. Alternatively, you can use a different browser than the one you are using for the Databricks workspace. Use the User principal name **finance_analyst_1** as the username.
3. Since this is the first time logging in, you will be asked to change the password. Once again, make sure you remember the changed password for future use.

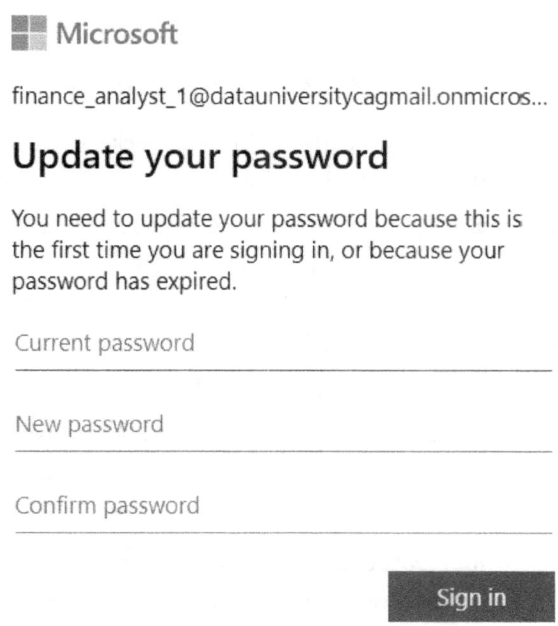

Figure 12.15: Changing the password of the new user

4. You should be able to log in to Databricks as follows:

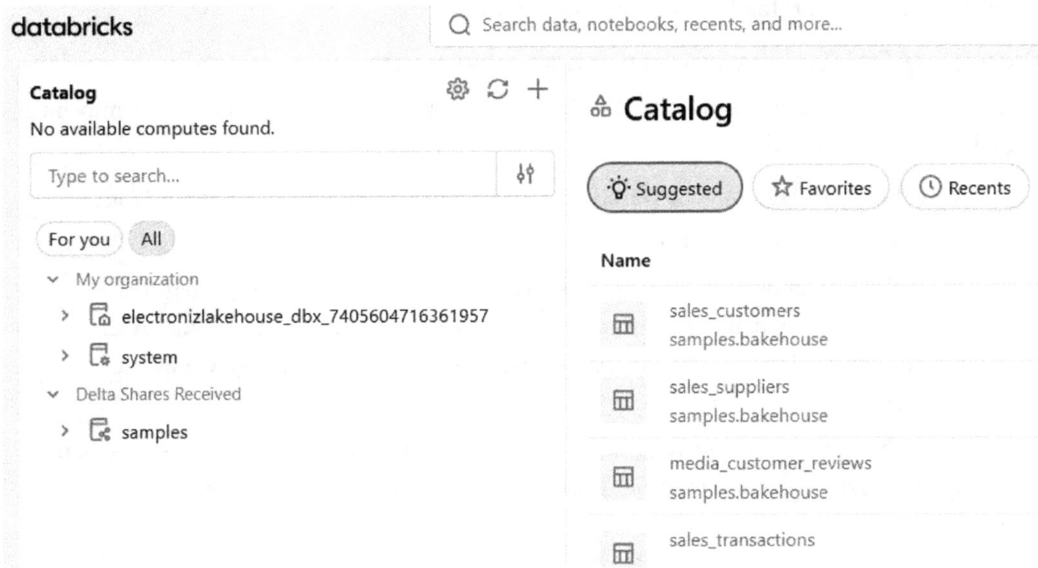

Figure 12.16: Databricks access as a finance domain user

5. Leave this browser window open—we'll come back to it shortly. For clarity, we'll refer to this as the **finance_analyst_1 session**.

At this stage, **finance_analyst_1** does not have access to any objects within the **electroniz_catalog**, as no permissions have been granted at the catalog, schema, or table level. This is exactly how the **principle of least privilege** is intended to work—access is denied by default and granted only when explicitly required.

Granting users access to the data catalog

Granting users access to the data catalog in Databricks involves assigning the appropriate permissions at the catalog, schema, and table levels using Unity Catalog and group-based access controls.

1. Navigate back to your **Databricks workspace**. Run the following SQL that grants the required read and write access to the group **electroniz_finance_domain_grp_write**.

```
GRANT USE CATALOG ON CATALOG electroniz_catalog TO
`electroniz_finance_domain_grp_write`;

GRANT USE SCHEMA ON SCHEMA
electroniz_catalog.electroniz_gold_finance_schema TO
`electroniz_finance_domain_grp_write`;
```

```
GRANT SELECT, MODIFY ON SCHEMA
electroniz_catalog.electroniz_gold_finance_schema TO
`electroniz_finance_domain_grp_write`;

GRANT USE SCHEMA
ON SCHEMA electroniz_catalog.electroniz_gold_master_schema TO
`electroniz_finance_domain_grp_write`;

GRANT SELECT ON
electroniz_catalog.electroniz_gold_master_schema.mvw_electroniz_gold_golden
_record_customers TO `electroniz_finance_domain_grp_write`;

GRANT USE SCHEMA ON SCHEMA electroniz_catalog. electroniz_silver_schema TO
`electroniz_finance_domain_grp_write`;

GRANT SELECT ON
electroniz_catalog.electroniz_silver_schema.electroniz_silver_store_orders
TO `electroniz_finance_domain_grp_write`;
```

2. The SQL statements above should work as expected; however, if you encounter issues, the most common error scenarios include the executing user lacking **ADMIN** privileges, the target group not existing, or the catalog not being accessible from the current workspace.

3. Log back into the **finance_analyst_1** session. Press the **Refresh catalog** icon beside the gear icon. Now you should be able to see all data products that **finance_analyst_1** has access to.

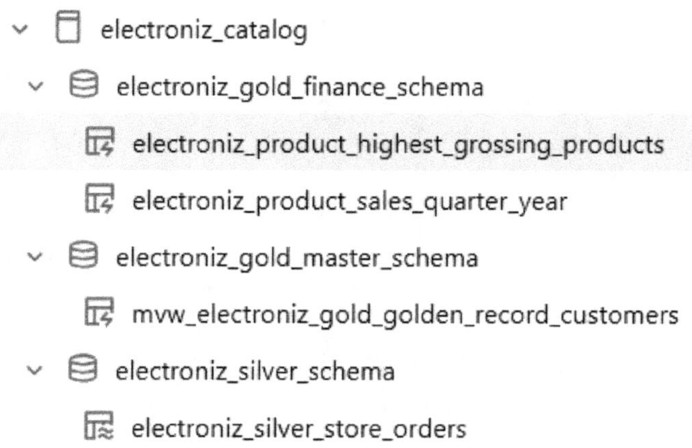

Figure 12.17: Access to data products for the finance_analyst_1 user

4. Navigate back to your **Databricks workspace**. Run the following SQL statements to grant the required read and write access to the group **electroniz_finance_domain_grp_read.**

```
GRANT USE CATALOG ON CATALOG electroniz_catalog TO
`electroniz_finance_domain_grp_read`;

GRANT USE SCHEMA ON SCHEMA
electroniz_catalog.electroniz_gold_finance_schema TO
`electroniz_finance_domain_grp_read`;

GRANT SELECT ON SCHEMA electroniz_catalog.electroniz_gold_finance_schema
TO `electroniz_finance_domain_grp_read`;

GRANT USE SCHEMA
ON SCHEMA electroniz_catalog.electroniz_gold_master_schema TO
`electroniz_finance_domain_grp_read`;

GRANT SELECT ON
electroniz_catalog.electroniz_gold_master_schema.mvw_electroniz_gold_golden
_record_customers TO `electroniz_finance_domain_grp_read`;
```

Following the steps outlined above, sign in to the Databricks workspace as c. While **finance_analyst_2 e** has similar access to **finance_analyst_1**, it is limited to viewing data products; **finance_analyst_1** has permission to modify data products in the Finance domain.

Planning Databricks users, groups, and ACLs should be centered on a group-based, least-privilege security model, with groups preferably aligned to business domains and clearly defined access levels to ensure scalable, auditable, and well-governed access.

Data privacy and regulatory compliance standards

Databricks data privacy and regulatory compliance standards are designed to help organizations use the Databricks Data Intelligence Platform while meeting global data protection, privacy, and security obligations. Databricks aligns its controls with widely recognized international frameworks and regulations, including GDPR and CCPA. These standards emphasize strong governance of customer data, ensuring that personal and sensitive information is processed lawfully and transparently, and for clearly defined purposes. Customers retain ownership and control of their data, while Databricks acts as a data processor under applicable privacy laws.

From a security and operational standpoint, Databricks implements a range of robust technical controls to protect customer data, including:

- Encryption in transit and at rest
- Sensitive data tagging and redaction
- Strict role-based access controls
- Support for regional data residency to meet local regulatory obligations

In addition, Databricks provides contractual safeguards such as data processing agreements and standard contractual clauses to enable compliant cross-border data transfers. Collectively, these measures help customers demonstrate regulatory compliance, minimize risk, and confidently deploy analytics and AI workloads at scale while keeping pace with evolving privacy and regulatory requirements.

In today's data-driven world, the influence of data is undeniable. While this power has enabled many organizations to drive growth and innovation, it has also led some to monetize and market personal data in ways that stretch—or even violate—ethical boundaries. In certain instances, data has been leveraged without sufficient regard for individual privacy or informed consent. At its extremes, such misuse has gone beyond commercial exploitation, shaping opinions and influencing human behavior itself. These realities underscore the growing need for responsible data governance, ethical use of information, and stronger regulatory oversight to ensure data serves society without compromising trust or individual rights.

Earlier regulations, such as the HIPAA, drew attention to the need to protect PII, but enforcement was often limited and inconsistent. This changed significantly in 2018 when the European Union enacted the GDPR, which not only redefined standards for the ethical collection, storage, and use of personal data, but also introduced strict enforcement mechanisms, including substantial fines and penalties, marking a decisive shift toward accountability in data privacy.

In addition to protecting PII under GDPR, individuals are granted strong rights to control how their personal data is collected, used, and shared. These include the right to be informed and to access their data, to correct inaccuracies, to request deletion in certain cases, and to restrict or object to processing, particularly for marketing or profiling. Consumers are primarily empowered through transparency and choice. They have the right to know what personal data businesses collect and how it is used, access and delete their information, and opt out of the sale or sharing of their data.

Personally Identifiable Information (PII)

Before we deep dive into how Databricks handles data privacy, it is important to clearly understand what PII means. PII refers to any information that can be used—on its own or combined with other data—to identify a specific individual. Because PII can be used to identify, contact, or track individuals, it is subject to strict protection requirements under privacy and data protection regulations such as GDPR, HIPAA, and CCPA. Organizations that collect or process PII are expected to handle it responsibly by ensuring secure storage, limiting access, and using it lawfully and transparently.

The PII handling process describes the end-to-end lifecycle of how personal data is discovered and managed securely and ethically, in compliance with privacy regulations such as GDPR, CCPA, and HIPAA. A typical PII process includes the following three key stages:

PII definition

We discussed earlier that PII is any information that can be used to identify an individual. The direct PII identifiers include government-issued ID numbers (e.g., Social Security or passport numbers, driver's license numbers), but they can also include indirect identifiers such as email addresses, phone numbers, IP addresses, precise location data, or financial account details when they can reasonably be linked to an individual. Organizations that collect or process PII are expected to ensure lawful collection, purpose limitation, secure storage, restricted access, and proper disposal throughout the data lifecycle.

The handling of PII begins with a clear and shared understanding of what constitutes direct and indirect identifiers. Within an organization, this definition is typically established through collaboration among the **Data Protection Officer** (**DPO**), Privacy Office, Legal and Compliance teams, and Information Security. Together, these groups define, document, and maintain authoritative PII classifications and related handling policies to ensure alignment with regulatory requirements and organizational risk standards.

In a federated data governance model, these centrally defined PII standards are then propagated to individual business domains. Data owners and data stewards apply the definitions in practice by identifying, classifying, and labeling PII within their domain-specific datasets, considering how the data is used, combined, and accessed. As a result, PII determination becomes a structured, collaborative governance activity—grounded in law, risk management, and business context—rather than an isolated or ad hoc decision.

PII discovery

PII discovery is the process of identifying and locating Personally Identifiable Information across an organization's data landscape. Its goal is to answer three critical questions: *where PII lives, what type of PII it is (direct or indirect), and how it is being used.* This includes scanning structured data such as databases, data warehouses, data lakes, and lakehouses, as well as unstructured data like documents, logs, emails, and files stored in cloud platforms. Effective PII discovery creates visibility into sensitive data that may otherwise be hidden or inconsistently labeled.

PII discovery typically combines automated techniques—such as pattern matching, keyword searches, machine-learning classifiers, and metadata analysis—with human validation by data owners and stewards. Following is a list of some well-known tools and services that can automate the PII discovery process:

- **Microsoft Purview**: Built-in PII discovery and classification across Azure environments
- **AWS Macie**: PII and sensitive data discovery for Amazon S3
- **Google Cloud DLP**: Pattern- and ML-based PII detection across GCP services
- **Databricks Unity Catalog**: Column-level lineage, tagging, and integration with PII detection tools
- **BigID**: ML-driven discovery of PII, sensitive data, and data relationships across on-prem and cloud
- **Collibra Protect**: Integrates governance metadata with sensitive data discovery
- **Informatica Data Privacy Management**: Enterprise-grade PII discovery, classification, and risk scoring

Automated discovery accelerates PII identification; most organizations combine automated scanning tools with human validation by data owners and stewards.

PII handling

To handle PII responsibly, it is important to understand the data protection techniques of anonymization and pseudonymization. These approaches are commonly used to reduce privacy risk while still enabling data analysis, testing, or sharing. The table below summarizes some well-known techniques for handling PII.

Technique	Pros	Cons	Usage
Data Masking	Easy to understand Simple to implement	Masked data cannot be converted back to true values Masked data cannot be used for comparisons and joins	Use where data computations on PII columns are not required
Data Encryption	Relatively easy to implement	Requires proper creation and management of encryption keys	Use where PII data is required for data computations Use where proper security classification/clearance permits reversal of pseudonymization
Table Splits	Little extra code but relatively easy to implement	Need to be cautious about access to the table that contains PII table	Use where encryption of data is not possible Use where PII data is required for data computations Use where proper security classification/clearance permits reversal of pseudonymization

Technique	Pros	Cons	Usage
Tokenization	Complex coding	Need to be cautious about access to table that contains PII tokens in cleartext	Use where PII data is required for data computations Use where proper security classification/clearance permits reversal of tokens

Table 12.1: PII handling techniques

Anonymization using hashing

Anonymization involves transforming personal data so that individuals can no longer be identified, either directly or indirectly, and so that the process cannot be reversed to restore the original identity. Data masking is one of the most widely used anonymization techniques for obscuring PII. It is typically implemented using one-way cryptographic functions, such as hashing, which convert clear-text data into a fixed, non-readable value. While it is easy to generate a hash from the original data, the process is intentionally irreversible, meaning that once the data is de-identified, it cannot be reconstructed in its original form.

However, cryptographic hashes are not entirely immune to attack. Techniques such as brute-force or dictionary attacks can sometimes be used to infer original values, especially when the input data follows predictable patterns. To mitigate this risk, organizations commonly use salted hashes, where a random value (the salt) is added to the input before hashing. Salting significantly increases the difficulty of reverse-engineering masked PII and strengthens the overall effectiveness of data masking. The following image demonstrates how **Social Security Numbers (SSNs)** and credit card data appear after hashing has been applied, showing the original values transformed into non-readable, fixed-length representations that cannot be directly traced back to the original information.

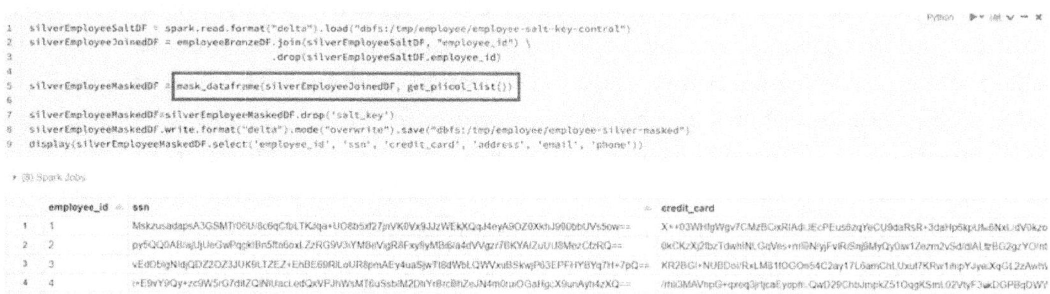

Figure 12.18: Anonymization of sensitive data

Pseudonymization using encryption

Pseudonymization is a data protection technique that replaces identifiable personal data with artificial identifiers—known as pseudonyms—while preserving the ability to re-identify individuals under strictly controlled conditions. Unlike anonymization, pseudonymization is reversible because the original identifiers are stored separately in a secure mapping table, encryption key vault, or tokenization service.

In practice, pseudonymization works by substituting sensitive fields such as names, email addresses, Social Security Numbers, or customer IDs with tokens or encrypted values. Data encryption is a pseudonymization technique that can be used to obscure PII data. Data encryption is a two-way cryptographic function whereby it is not only possible to de-identify PII but also to reverse-engineer it back to its original form. A core requirement for implementing encryption is the creation and safe management of a symmetric/asymmetric key. The following image illustrates how **Social Security Numbers (SSNs)** and credit card data appear after encryption has been applied, with the original values transformed into non-readable representations that can only be restored to their original form by authorized users with access to the appropriate decryption keys.

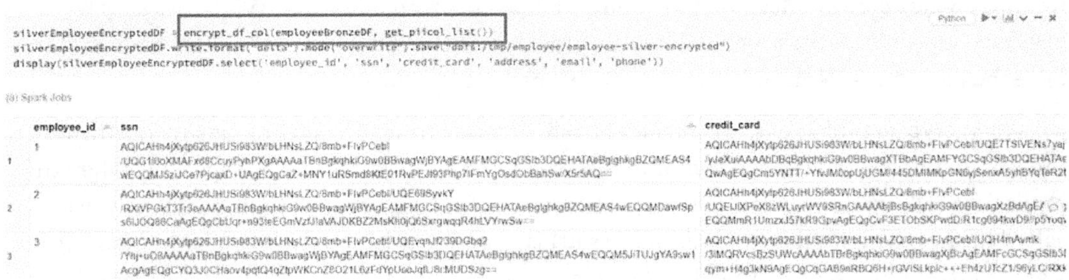

Figure 12.19: Pseudonymization of sensitive data using encryption

Pseudonymization using table splitting

Another widely used pseudonymization technique involves separating PII and non-PII into two distinct tables and linking them through a **pseudonymous** key. In this approach, sensitive identifiers are stored in a secure table, while analytical or operational data resides in a separate table, with the pseudonym serving as the only connection between the two. This design reduces direct exposure of PII while still allowing controlled joins when reidentification is legitimately required. The following image illustrates how PII data is split across two tables, showing sensitive information split from non-PII data and linked through a pseudonymous key to reduce direct exposure while maintaining controlled referential access.

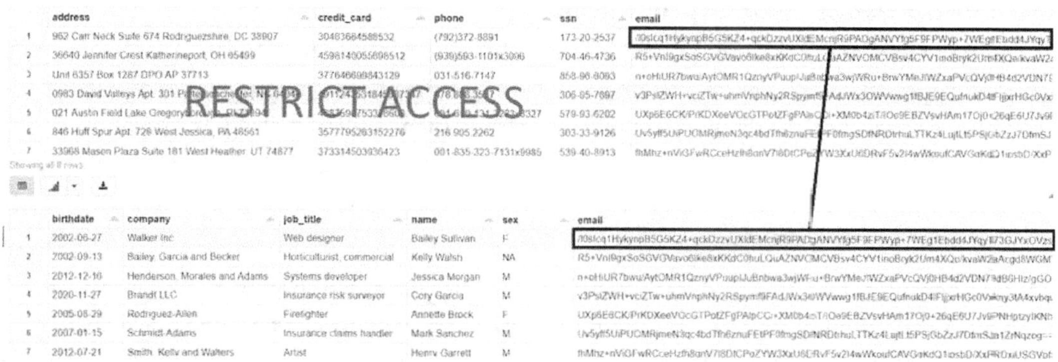

Figure 12.20: Pseudonymization of sensitive data using table splitting

Pseudonymization using Tokenization

The final pseudonymization technique discussed is **tokenization**. Tokenization works by replacing columns containing PII with tokens, typically meaningless placeholders. The original PII values are securely stored in a separate table or vault, and only the tokens are used in downstream systems. This approach effectively obscures sensitive data while allowing controlled re-identification when access to the token mapping is explicitly authorized. The following image illustrates how PII data is tokenized, with original sensitive values replaced by non-meaningful tokens, while the actual data is securely stored and managed separately.

employee_id	token_name	token_value	token
1	phone	(792)372-8891	11
1	address	962 Carr Neck Suite 674 Rodriguezshire, DC 38907	1
1	credit_card	30483664588532	19
1	email	ebutler@example.org	10
1	ssn	173-20-2537	38

employee_id	address_token	phone_token	ssn_token	email_token	credit_card_token
1	1	11	38	10	19
2	16	6	30	8	2
3	14	35	25	20	3
4	12	33	36	15	21
5	24	37	13	31	29
6	9	17	23	22	40
7	32	5	39	18	27

Figure 12.21: Pseudonymization of sensitive data using tokenization

Obscuring using masking functions

In addition to the techniques discussed above, PII obscuring using functions is a widely adopted approach that relies on custom or built-in transformation functions to reduce the exposure of sensitive data while maintaining usability for analytics, testing, or operational purposes. These functions can be applied at ingestion time, during data transformation pipelines, or at query time, enabling organizations to protect PII without physically removing it from the underlying dataset.

Common examples include masking functions, which replace all or part of a sensitive value with fixed or dynamic patterns—for example, displaying only the last four digits of a Social Security Number or credit card number. Function-based PII obscuring is particularly effective when combined with data classification, role-based access controls, and policy enforcement, ensuring that only authorized users can view clear-text values while others see masked, hashed, or tokenized data.

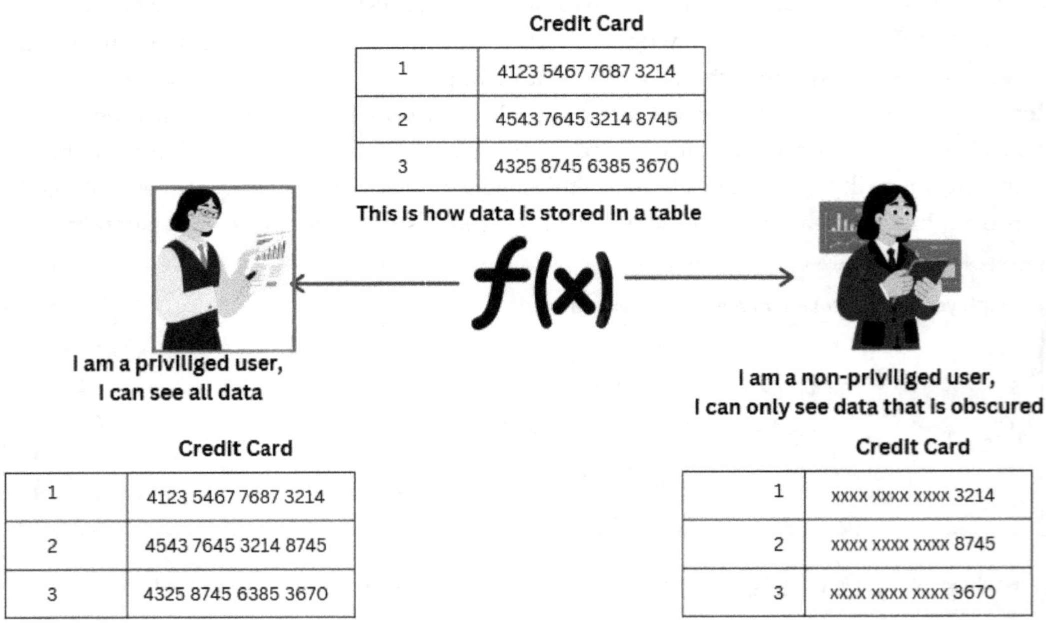

Figure 12.22: Data masking functions

This approach helps organizations meet privacy and compliance requirements, reduce risk, and preserve analytical value, making it a core component of modern data governance and privacy-by-design strategies. Let's see this approach in action. By defining `finance_analyst_1` and `finance_analyst_2` as two users in different access groups, we can implement a data-masking function that dynamically obscures sensitive customer data for `finance_analyst_2` at query time, while allowing `finance_analyst_1` to view the data in clear text. This setup demonstrates how role- and group-based logic can be applied to enforce differentiated data visibility without altering the underlying dataset.

1. Navigate back to your **Databricks workspace**. Run the following SQL to create a data-masking function for email addresses.

```
CREATE OR REPLACE FUNCTION
electroniz_catalog.electroniz_gold_master_schema.mask_email(email STRING)
RETURNS STRING
RETURN
  CASE
    WHEN is_account_group_member('electroniz_finance_domain_grp_write')
THEN email
    WHEN instr(email, '@') = 0
    AND is_account_group_member('electroniz_finance_domain_grp_read') THEN
'***'
    ELSE concat('***', substring(email, instr(email, '@')))
  END;
```

   Notice the email-handling logic in the SQL above. For read-only users, this condition masks the portion of the email address before the "@" symbol, ensuring that sensitive user identifiers are not exposed.

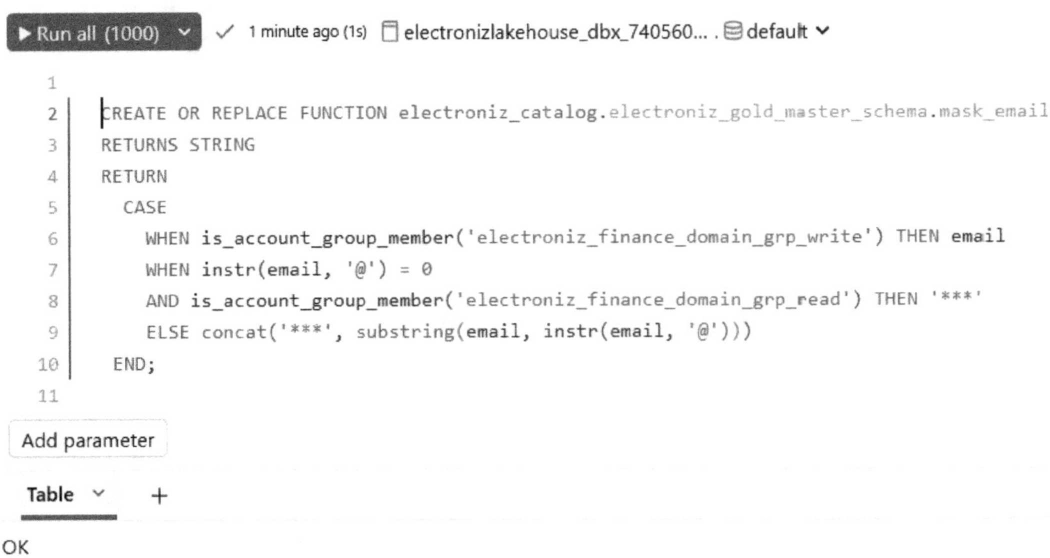

Figure 12.23: Creating the email masking function

2. Now apply the email masking function to the customer golden record materialized view. Under **Catalog,** navigate to **electroniz_catalog > electroniz_gold_master_schema.**
3. Under Tables, click on **mvw_electroniz_gold_golden_record_customers**. In the right pane, hover over **preferred_email** and click **Add column mask**.

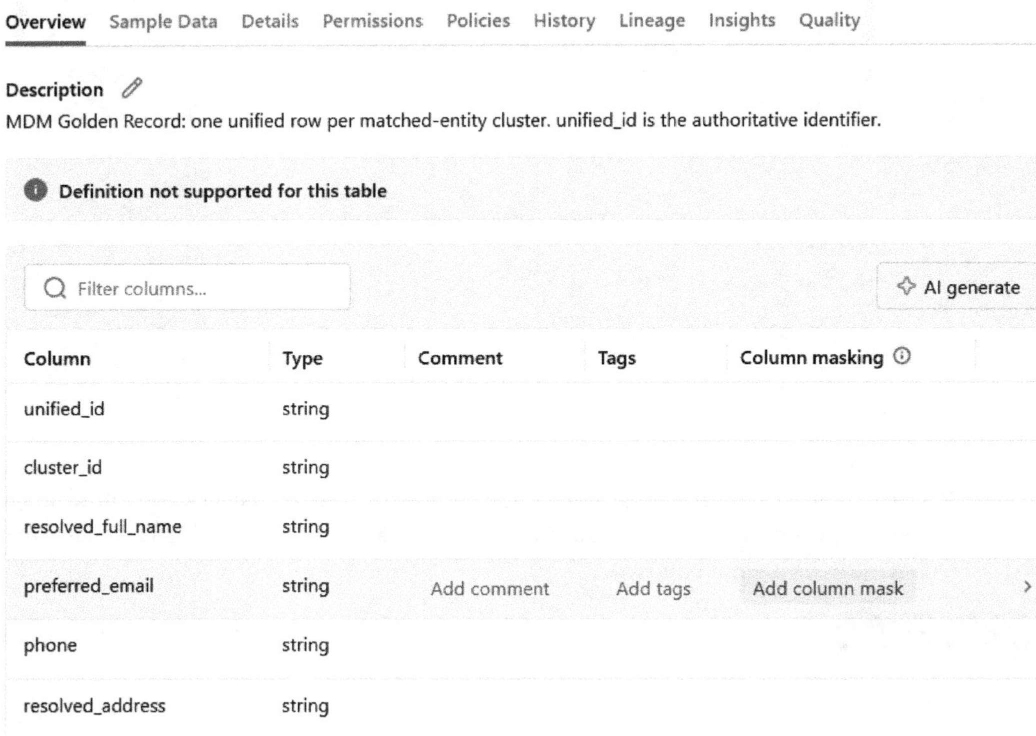

Figure 12.24: Adding a column mask to a column

4. Under **electroniz_gold_master_schema** choose **mask_email**. Click on **Add**.

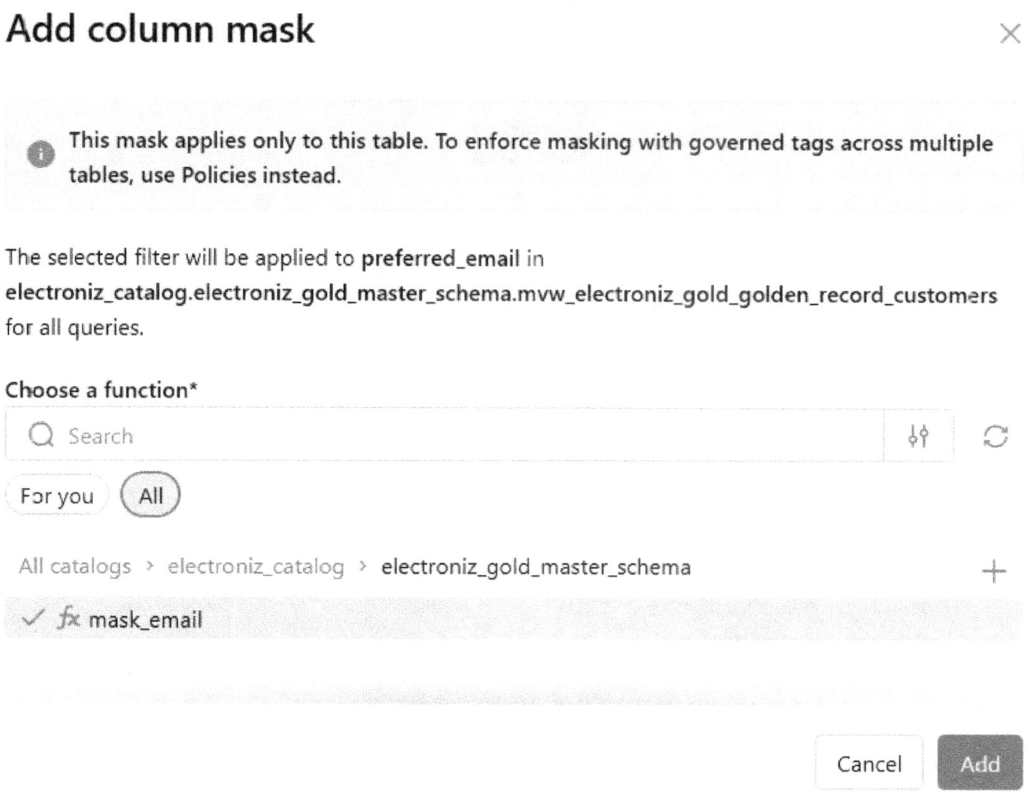

Figure 12.25: Apply the mask_email function to the column

5. To test the working of the function, let's log on to **finance_analyst_1** followed by **finance_analyst_2.**
6. Log in as **finance_analyst_1** and review the sample data in **mvw_electroniz_gold_golden_record_customers**. The email values should appear in clear text, unchanged from their original form. This occurs because the masking function is configured to allow members of the **electroniz_finance_domain_grp_write** group to view unobscured email data.

7. Now Log in as finance_analyst_2 and review the sample data in **mvw_electroniz_gold_golden_record_customers**.

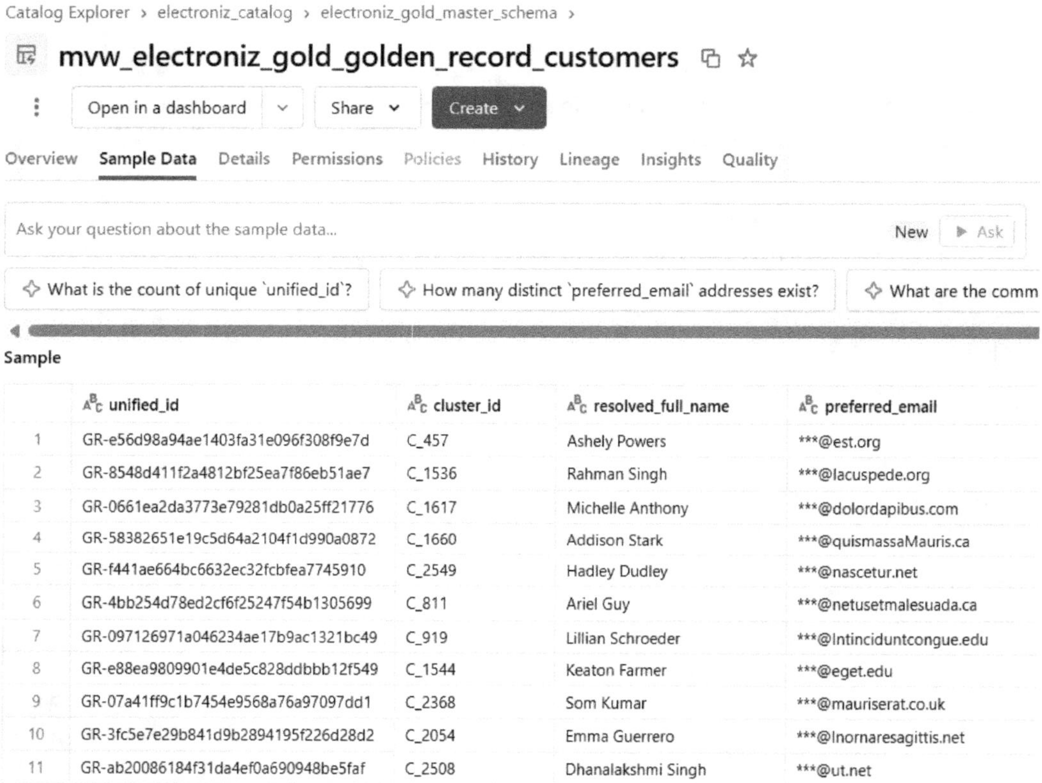

	unified_id	cluster_id	resolved_full_name	preferred_email
1	GR-e56d98a94ae1403fa31e096f308f9e7d	C_457	Ashely Powers	***@est.org
2	GR-8548d411f2a4812bf25ea7f86eb51ae7	C_1536	Rahman Singh	***@lacuspede.org
3	GR-0661ea2da3773e79281db0a25ff21776	C_1617	Michelle Anthony	***@dolordapibus.com
4	GR-58382651e19c5d64a2104f1d990a0872	C_1660	Addison Stark	***@quismassaMauris.ca
5	GR-f441ae664bc6632ec32fcbfea7745910	C_2549	Hadley Dudley	***@nascetur.net
6	GR-4bb254d78ed2cf6f25247f54b1305699	C_811	Ariel Guy	***@netusetmalesuada.ca
7	GR-097126971a046234ae17b9ac1321bc49	C_919	Lillian Schroeder	***@Intinciduntcongue.edu
8	GR-e88ea9809901e4de5c828ddbbb12f549	C_1544	Keaton Farmer	***@eget.edu
9	GR-07a41ff9c1b7454e9568a76a97097dd1	C_2368	Som Kumar	***@mauriserat.co.uk
10	GR-3fc5e7e29b841d9b2894195f226d28d2	C_2054	Emma Guerrero	***@Inornaresagittis.net
11	GR-ab20086184f31da4ef0a690948be5faf	C_2508	Dhanalakshmi Singh	***@ut.net

Figure 12.26: Obscured preferred_email column

8. The email values should appear masked. This is because the masking function is configured to dynamically obscure email addresses at query time for users in the **electroniz_finance_domain_grp_read** group.

Each PII handling technique offers a different balance between data utility and privacy protection, and their suitability depends on factors such as regulatory requirements, intended use, and risk tolerance. Because anonymization irreversibly removes the ability to identify individuals, while pseudonymization retains a controlled link to original identities, each method has distinct advantages and limitations. Rather than prescribing a single approach, this discussion presents both techniques so readers can evaluate and select the one that best aligns with their PII-handling objectives, compliance obligations, and operational needs. In addition to anonymization and pseudonymization, there is another approach to managing sensitive data that offers greater flexibility—enabling organizations to control how much data is exposed, rather than choosing between fully hiding it and exposing it entirely.

Data classification policies

Data classification policies impose a systematic process of organizing data into defined categories based on factors such as its sensitivity, business value, regulatory impact, and risk level. By classifying data, organizations can determine who should have access to it, how it must be protected, and which policies and controls apply. For example, highly sensitive data such as PII or financial records may require encryption, restricted access, and strict retention rules, while public or low-risk data can be more openly shared with minimal controls. Common classification levels include *Public*, *Confidential*, and *Restricted*, though organizations often tailor these to their specific business and regulatory needs. Overall, data classification forms the foundation for scalable data protection, access control, and governance. In Databricks, data classification can be implemented through both manual and automated mechanisms. The following sections examine each approach in detail.

Automated data classification

Databricks automated data classification is a Unity Catalog–enabled capability that automatically discovers, classifies, and tags sensitive data—such as PII, financial data, and regulated attributes—using AI-driven data scanning and detection techniques. The classification process analyzes metadata and data content to identify sensitive elements and applies standardized classification tags directly to supported data assets at scale.

These automatically generated classification tags become first-class governance metadata within Unity Catalog and can be leveraged to enforce downstream data protection and access control policies. By integrating automated classification with policy enforcement, Databricks enables organizations to operationalize data governance, reduce manual effort, and consistently protect sensitive data across large, evolving data estates while maintaining scalability and regulatory compliance. Let's perform an automated data classification:

1. Navigate to your Databricks workspace. Click on **Catalog** > **electroniz_catalog**.
2. In the panel on the right, click on the **Details** tab.
3. In the Advanced section, enable **Data Classification**.

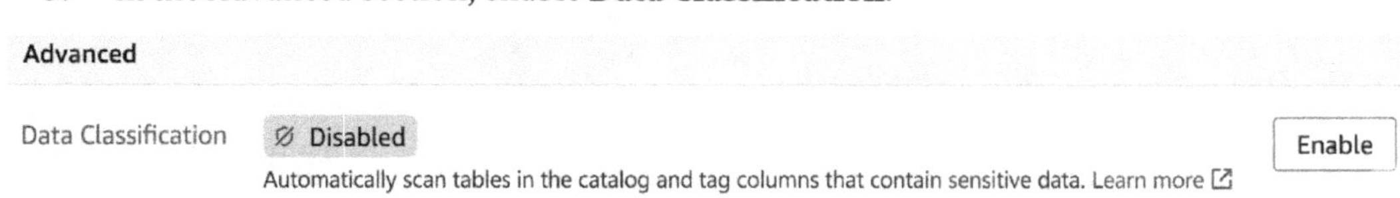

Figure 12.27: Enabling Databricks automated data classification

4. Choose the Schema as **electroniz_gold_master_schema** and press **Save**.

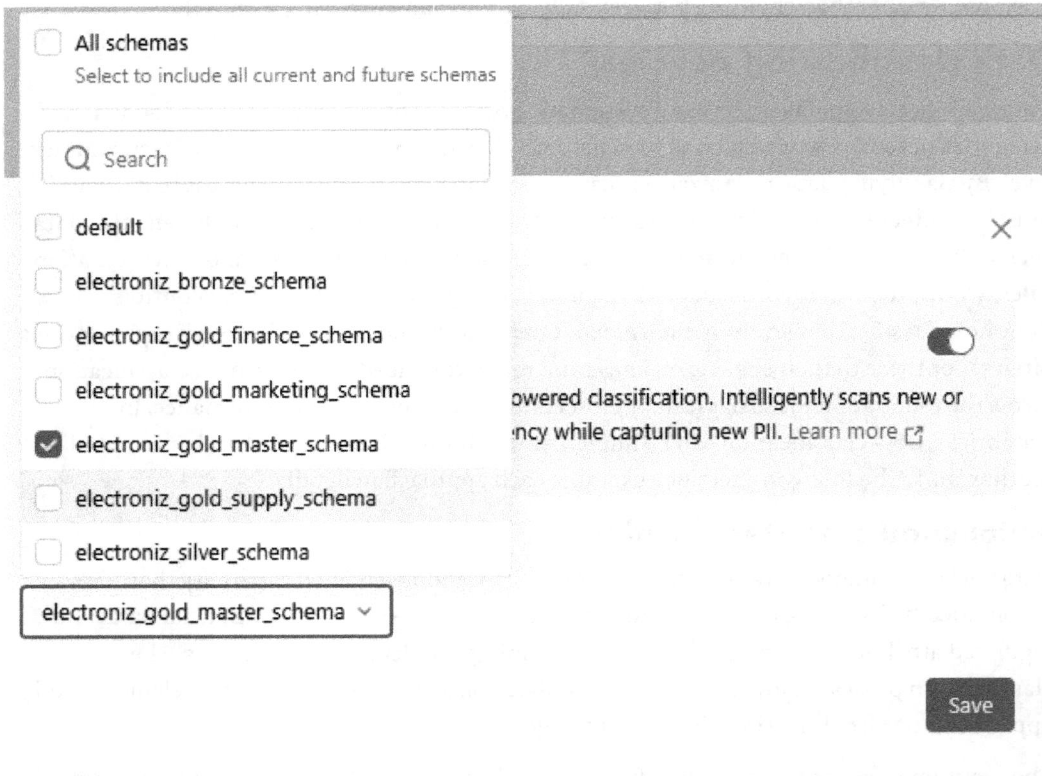

Figure 12.28: Choosing schema for Databricks automated data classification

5. Databricks immediately schedules an initial AI scan. The scan detects sensitive patterns and classifies columns into system classes.

6. Please note that the initial scan may take a few minutes to complete. Once the scan is completed, you can view the results of the scan as follows:

Figure 12.29: Viewing results for Databricks automated data classification

7. The scan results above are for the **mvw_electroniz_gold_golden_record_customers** materialized view. Notice the scan has detected columns with classifications such as `email_address` and `credit_card`.

8. Further, you may choose to enable automatic tagging for the classification tag, allowing Databricks to automatically apply the appropriate governed system tags to detected columns based on the AI classification results. This helps ensure consistent labeling of sensitive data and enables downstream governance controls such as access policies, masking, and auditing without manual intervention.

Manual data classification

Manual data classification in Databricks is a Unity Catalog–based, user-driven approach for identifying, labeling, and managing data sensitivity using explicitly defined metadata, rather than automated AI scanning. In this model, data owners, stewards, or platform administrators intentionally apply classification tags to data assets based on business context, regulatory requirements, or domain knowledge. Manual classification is typically implemented by assigning Unity Catalog governed tags to securable objects such as catalogs, schemas, tables, views, or columns.

Governed tags

Governance tags are **standardized labels** that are applied to resources, data, or content to enable consistent classification, management, and control across an organization. They are commonly used to support policy-based access control, data cataloging and discoverability, cost and risk visibility, and scalable compliance without manual effort. Data classification also plays a critical role in:

- **Security:** enforcing appropriate protection controls aligned to data sensitivity to minimize breach risk.
- **Compliance:** meeting regulatory and legal obligations such as privacy, data protection, and retention mandates.
- **Data governance:** establishing consistent standards for data handling, ownership, and accountability.
- **Chargebacks and cost management:** enabling domain- or classification-based cost allocation and financial controls.

There are two types of governed tags in Databricks:

- **System governed tags**: predefined tags that are managed by Databricks and primarily used by the Databricks data classification AI feature. Some examples of system governed tags include:
    a. `class.email_address`
    b. `class.phone_number`
    c. `class.credit_card`
- **Custom governed tags**: Custom governed tags are defined by the organization and are used to apply business-specific or policy-driven classifications. Common examples include:
    a. `sensitivity = public | confidential | restricted`
    b. `data_domain = finance | marketing | supply`
    c. `data_owner = department_name`

To illustrate how governed tags work, let's apply governance tags to data products.

1. Navigate to your Databricks workspace. Click on **Catalog** > **electroniz_catalog** > **electroniz_gold_master_schema**. Under Tables, click on **mvw_electroniz_gold_golden_record_customers**.

2. In the right pane, hover your mouse over the **credit_card** column. Click on **Add tags**.

Figure 12.30: Adding tags for the credit_card column

3. Clicking on the Key drop-down will display the predefined system-governed tags in Databricks. System-governed tags are marked with a wrench icon and cannot be edited or deleted.

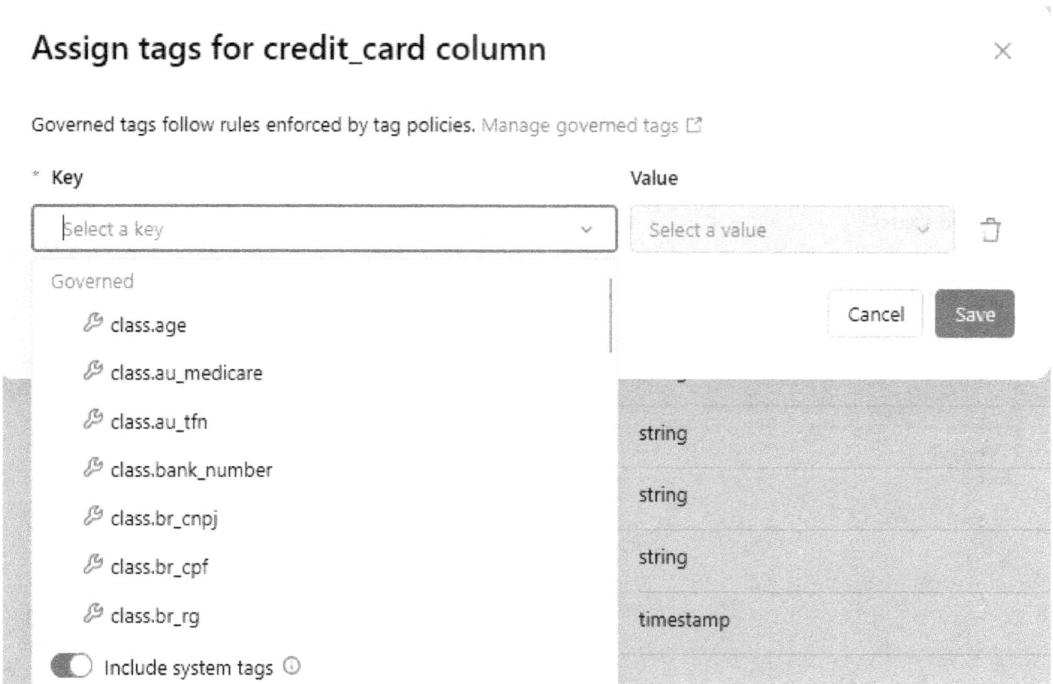

Figure 12.31: List of predefined system governed tags

4. Our intention is to tag the PII columns, so instead of using the system-governed tags, we will create custom governed tags. Click on **Manage governed tags**.
5. This should open a new tab with the title **Governed tags**. Click on **Create governed tag**.

6. Add a new custom tag named **PII** as below. Click on Create.

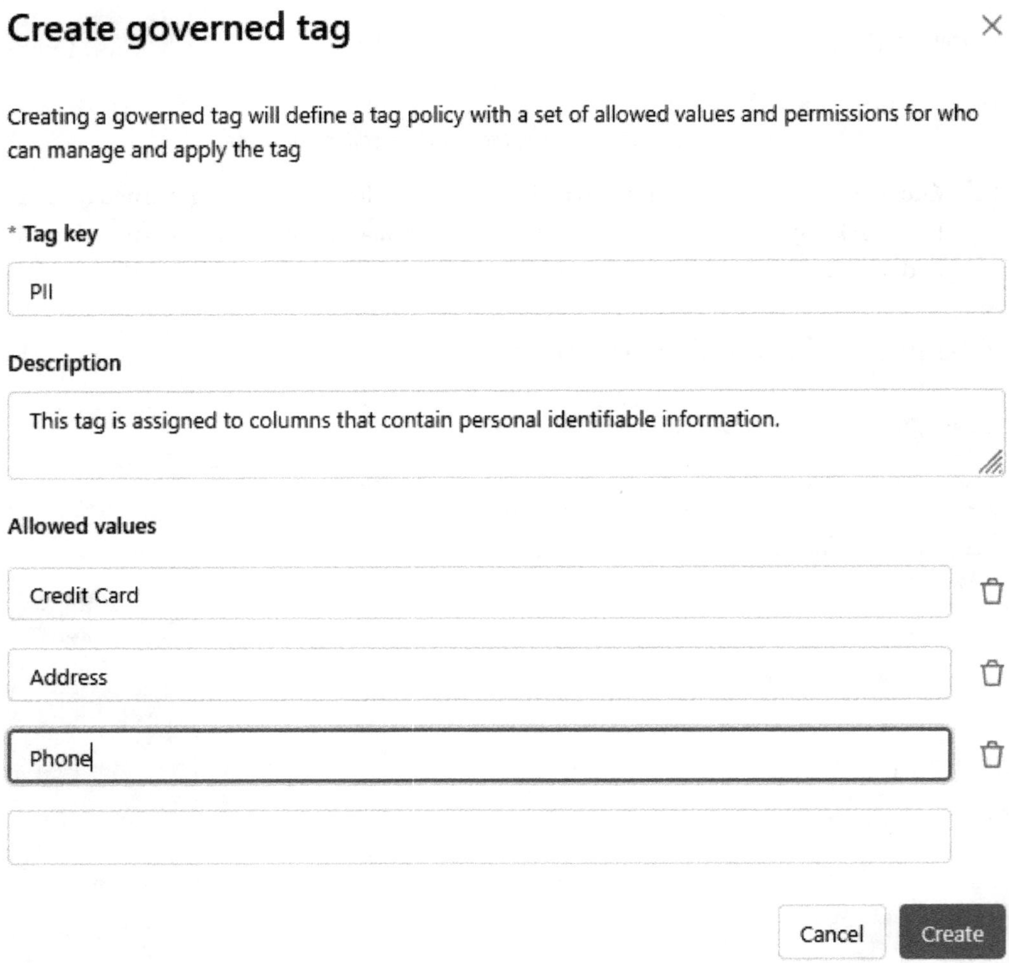

Figure 12.32: Creating a new custom governed tag

7. Navigate back to the previous tab where we were trying to add a new tag for the **credit_card** column. Refresh your window so that the newly added custom governed tag is visible in the drop-down list.
8. Assign the new PII tag to the **credit_card** column as under. Click on **Save**.

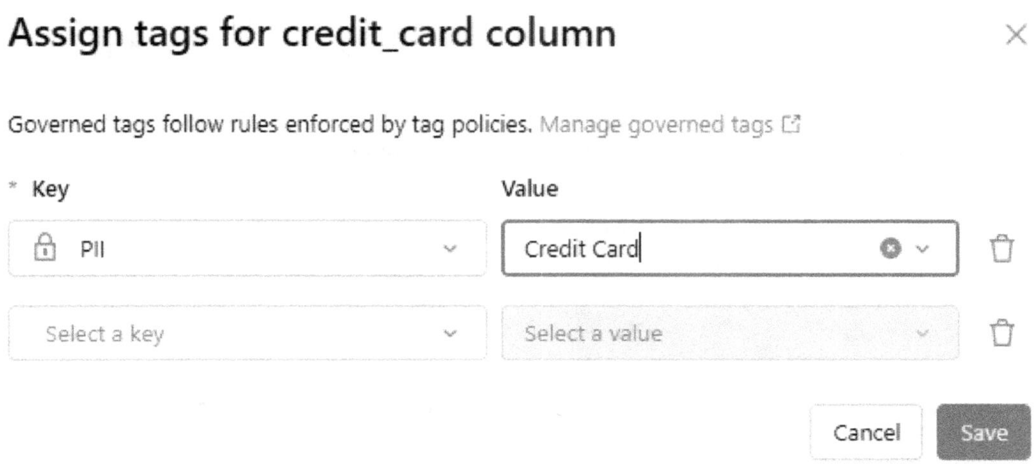

Figure 12.33: Assigning the new custom governed tag to the credit_card column

9. Similarly, add the governed tags for the phone and address columns. Make sure you choose the correct PII value.

Once completed, the **mvw_electroniz_gold_golden_record_customers** overview screen should display like this.

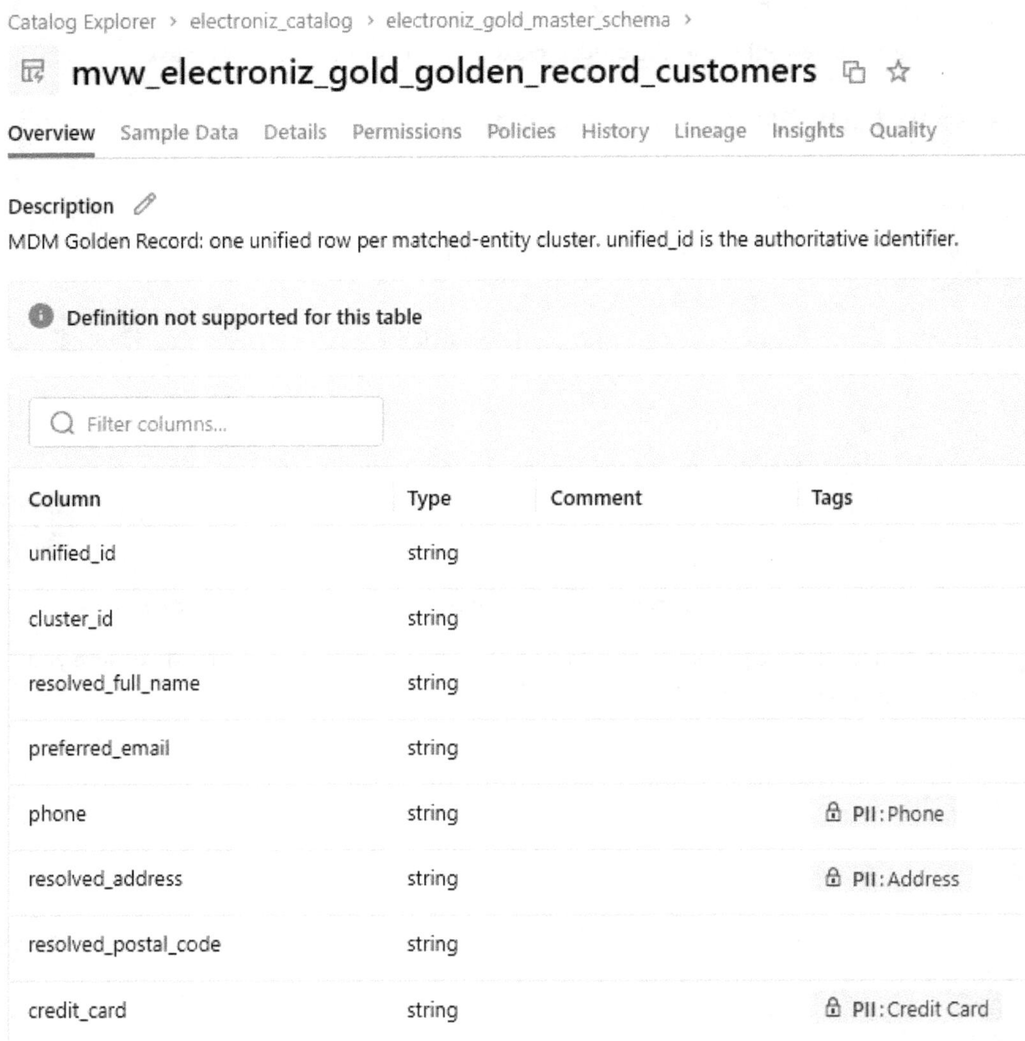

Figure 12.34: Assigning the new custom governed tag to the phone and address columns

10. Observe that all columns containing PII have been correctly tagged.

The key question now is how governed tags help us manage data classification. The next step is to establish policies that enforce these tags at the column or attribute level.

Attribute-based access control

Using governed tags, **Attribute-Based Access Control (ABAC)** evaluates data attributes at query time to determine access. These tags are assessed against defined access policies, allowing the system to dynamically filter, mask, or exclude sensitive information—such as PII—based on the user's attributes, role, and context. This ensures that only authorized data is returned while enforcing consistent data protection without hard-coded rules.

ABAC is a governance model that enforces policies such as row-level filtering to dynamically hide unauthorized rows and column-level masking to obfuscate sensitive fields. These controls are applied at query execution time, ensuring that access responds immediately as governed tags or policies change.

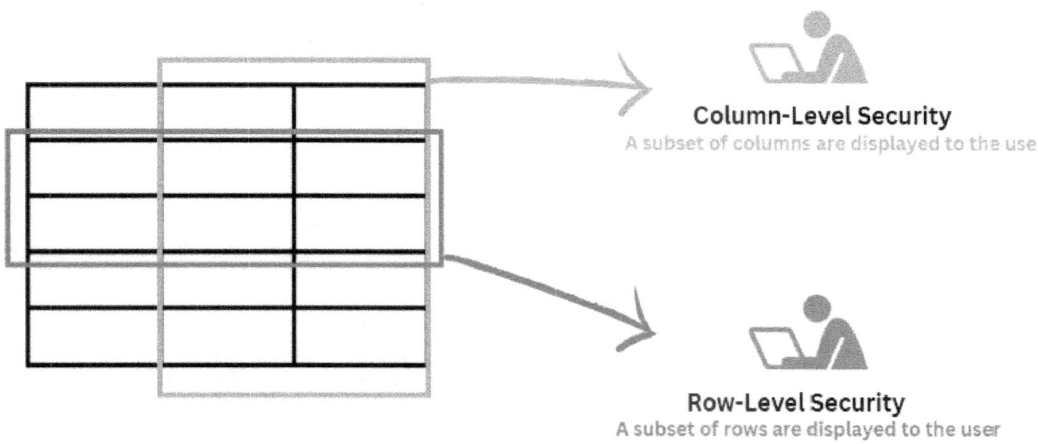

Figure 12.35: ABAC enforcing row and column-level controls

Within ABAC, policies are designed to evaluate governed tags. We will now create a policy that responds to the custom governed tag created previously.

1. Navigate to your Databricks workspace. Click on **Catalog** > **electroniz_catalog** > **electroniz_gold_master_schema**. Under Tables, click on **mvw_electroniz_gold_golden_record_customers**.

2. In the right pane, click on **Policies**. Click on **New policy**.
3. Create a new policy that will mask PII columns for all members in the **electroniz_finance_domain_grp_read** group.

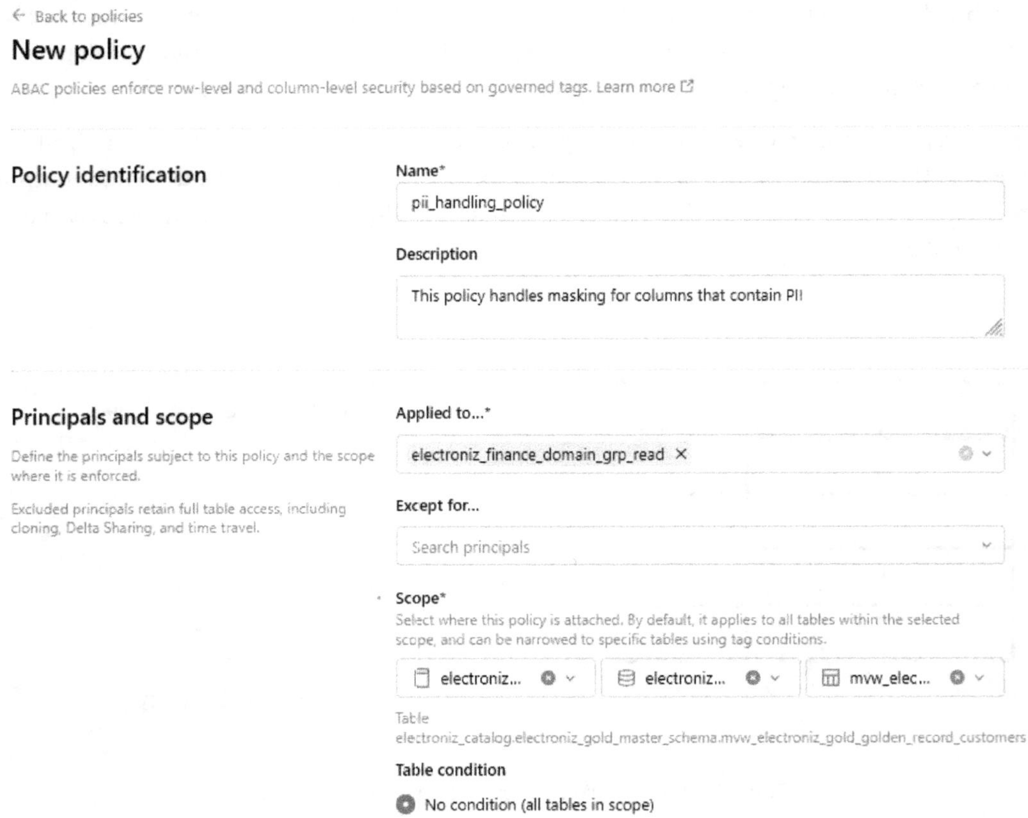

Figure 12.36: Creating a new ABAC policy

4. For Column conditions, choose the following PII governed tags.

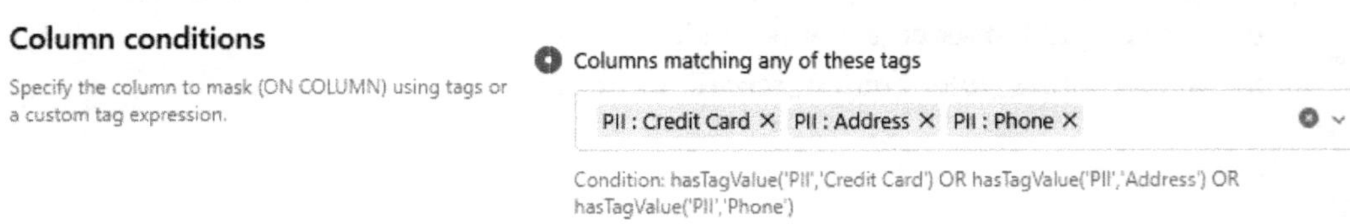

Figure 12.37: Adding column conditions for the ABAC policy

5. Finally, for the Masking function, click on **Create**. Choosing the "**Mask with asterisks**" option will generate code for the masking function. Change the value of '*******' to **REDACTED**.

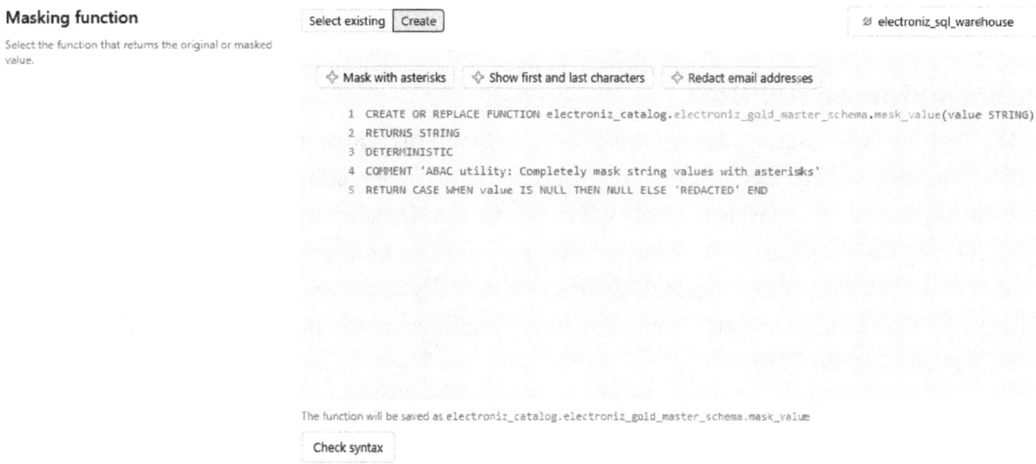

Figure 12.38: Creating the masking function for the ABAC policy

6. Click on the **Check syntax** button**,** followed by **Create policy**.
7. A new policy has now been created, as shown below. This policy is designed to redact PII columns for members of the **electroniz_finance_domain_grp_read** group, while allowing clear-text access for all other users.

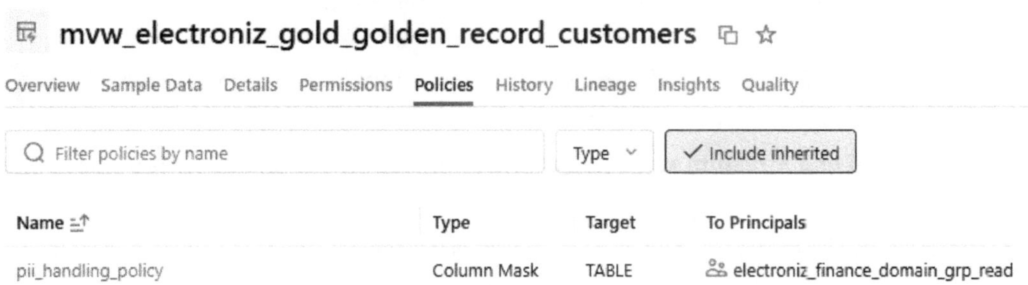

Figure 12.39: New ABAC policy created for PII redaction

It's important to note that the `pii_handling_policy` exists only as a logical definition until it is evaluated and enforced by **Fine-Grained Access Control (FGAC)**. While ABAC defines policies using governed tags, FGAC provides an enforcement engine that evaluates these policies at query time. The policy itself does not alter the data or permissions upfront; instead, FGAC applies it dynamically at query execution time. During query evaluation, the policy is assessed against the user's attributes and the governed tags on the data, and the appropriate controls—such as masking or filtering—are enforced in real time.

FGAC policies can be applied at table, schema, or catalog level. Table-level policies target a single asset, schema-level policies cover all tables within that schema, and catalog-level policies propagate across every schema and table for broad, consistent enforcement.

Policy enforcement flow

In Databricks, Fine-Grained Access Control (FGAC) and Attribute-Based Access Control (ABAC) are closely intertwined and work together to enforce modern data governance at scale. At a conceptual level, ABAC is the policy framework that Databricks uses to implement FGAC within Unity Catalog. Rather than hard-coding permissions on individual objects, ABAC enables Databricks to make access decisions dynamically based on attributes (metadata) associated with data assets and users. The following flow should hopefully clarify the inner workings of FGAC and ABAC.

1. **Governed tags are created and assigned** to data assets (catalogs, schemas, tables, or columns) to describe attributes such as sensitivity, domain, or region.
2. **ABAC policies are defined** at the catalog, schema, or table level, specifying how data with tags should be governed.
3. **A user submits a query** against a data asset.
4. **Unity Catalog identifies the user context**, including user identity and group memberships.
5. Tags associated with the requested data are evaluated against the relevant ABAC policies.
6. **FGAC rules are enforced dynamically**, applying row-level filtering and/or column-level masking as defined by the policies.
7. **The final query results are returned**, reflecting only the data the user is permitted to see under the active policies.

To illustrate how the `pii_handling_policy` operates in practice, consider two users with different levels of access within the finance domain.

- `finance_analyst_2`, who is a member of the `electroniz_finance_domain_grp_read` group, has read-only access to finance data. When this user queries data assets that contain columns tagged as PII, the policy enforces column-level masking, returning `REDACTED` values for all sensitive fields. This ensures that the analyst can work with the data structure and non-sensitive attributes without being exposed to raw PII.

- `finance_analyst_1`, who belongs to the `electroniz_finance_domain_grp_write` group, has elevated privileges aligned with authorized financial operations. For this user, the same PII-tagged columns are returned in cleartext, as the policy recognizes their group membership as meeting the criteria for full PII access.

To test the operation of the ABAC policy, let's log on to `finance_analyst_1`, then `finance_analyst_2`.

1. Log in as `finance_analyst_1` and review the sample data in `mvw_electroniz_gold_golden_record_customers`. The email values should appear in clear text, unchanged from their original form. This occurs because the ABAC policy is configured to allow members of the `electroniz_finance_domain_grp_write` group to view unredacted PII.
2. Now Log in as finance_analyst_2 and review the sample data in **mvw_electroniz_gold_golden_record_customers**.
3. Observe that values in columns containing PII have been dynamically masked and replaced with the placeholder **REDACTED** at query time.

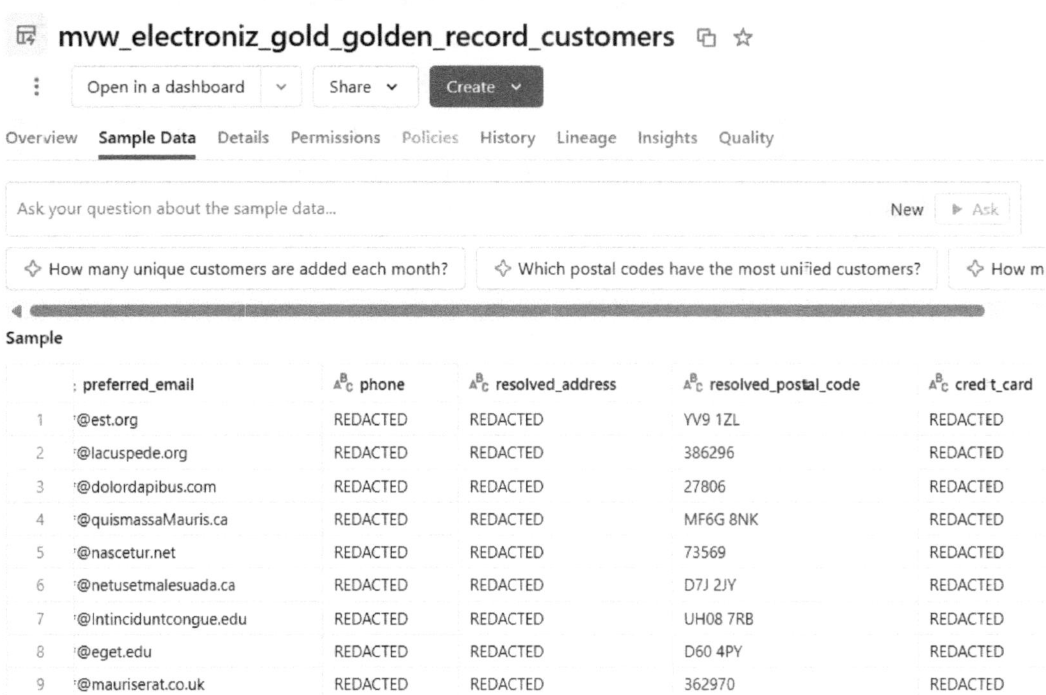

Figure 12.40: PII redaction for finance_analyst_2 user

This example demonstrates how the `pii_handling_policy` dynamically adapts query results based on user context. Both users query the same underlying data, yet Unity Catalog—via ABAC-driven FGAC—ensures each receives only the level of data exposure appropriate to their role. The result is strong PII protection without duplicating datasets or introducing separate access paths for different user types.

Now we shift our focus from controlling data access through RBAC, governed tags, and policies to tracking and understanding how data moves across the platform.

Data lineage tracking policies

Data lineage is the practice of tracking how data is used as it flows through systems—from where it's created to where it's consumed. It involves systematic documentation of data origins, flow, dependencies, transformations, and downstream consumption across systems throughout the data lifecycle. Data lineage policies enable control, trust, and governance over data in complex, distributed data ecosystems.

In modern, distributed data architectures, data lineage policies provide the foundation for control, trust, and effective governance. By making data flows transparent and traceable, lineage enables organizations to manage complexity, reduce risk, and scale analytics with confidence.

> Note
>
> In this context, lineage refers to the ability to trace the full journey of data over time. Many compliance frameworks treat data lineage as concrete evidence of whether an organization has adhered to best practices for data usage.

Benefits of tracking data lineage

From both a technical and organizational standpoint, the value of data lineage policies is realized across several critical areas as below:

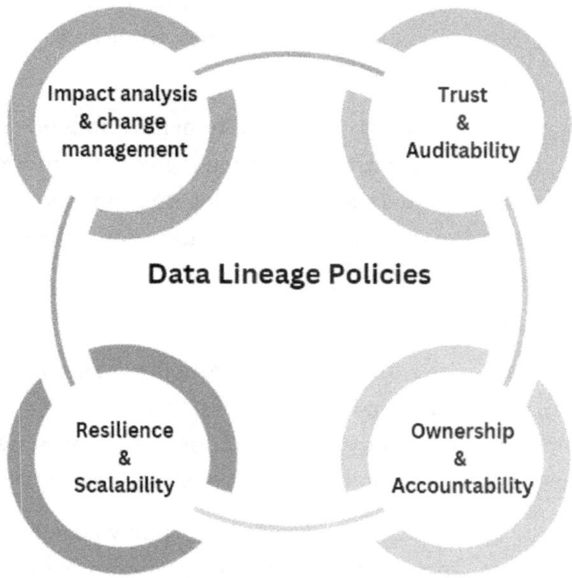

Figure 12.41: Benefits of data lineage policies

Impact analysis and change management

In complex data architectures with tightly coupled and highly interdependent assets, the ability to proactively detect and remediate issues is critical. Data lineage enables:

- **Impact and risk assessment** for pipeline, schema, or transformation changes by identifying all downstream dependencies prior to modification.
- **Prevention of unintended downstream failures** across reports, dashboards, APIs, and machine learning models.
- **Reduced mean time to resolution (MTTR)** by enabling precise upstream and downstream tracing to the originating source, process, or transformation.
- **Accelerated root-cause analysis**, eliminating reliance on blind or manual debugging across multiple systems.

Trust and auditability

Data lineage provides clear visibility into how data is sourced, transformed, and processed throughout its lifecycle. This visibility allows stakeholders to validate calculations, confirm business rules, and evaluate data completeness and accuracy. As a result, it strengthens confidence in dashboards, reports, and analytical outputs, while helping establish a trusted single source of truth for decision-making.

In addition, regulatory and internal governance requirements frequently require well-defined documentation of data provenance and transformation logic. Data lineage supports auditable traceability of sensitive and regulated data by clearly documenting its origins, transformations, and usage, thereby demonstrating compliance with organizational policies, industry standards, and regulatory obligations.

Resilience and scalability

As data platforms scale in both size and architectural complexity, institutional knowledge of data flows, dependencies, and transformations becomes increasingly fragmented and difficult to maintain. Critical understanding of how data is produced and consumed often resides in undocumented pipelines, legacy code, or individual expertise, creating operational risk.

Data lineage systematically captures and externalizes this knowledge by formally documenting end-to-end data flows, transformation logic, and asset dependencies across systems. By reducing reliance on tribal or implicit expertise, lineage improves organizational resilience and continuity. New team members can onboard more quickly, cross-functional teams can collaborate more effectively, and knowledge transfer becomes repeatable and auditable. As teams, technologies, and platforms evolve, data lineage provides a durable, system-level record that supports operational stability, reduces single points of failure, and enables sustainable scaling of data engineering, analytics, and governance capabilities.

Ownership and accountability

Data lineage plays a critical role in establishing and enforcing clear ownership and accountability across the data lifecycle. In complex, distributed data environments, data assets often span multiple systems, teams, and business domains, making it difficult to determine who is responsible for data quality, integrity, and usage without formal mechanisms.

By providing end-to-end visibility into how data originates, is transformed, and is consumed, data lineage creates transparency into the responsibilities associated with each stage of data processing. From an accountability perspective, lineage enables faster and more precise issue resolution. When data quality issues, failures, or inconsistencies arise, lineage allows teams to quickly identify the responsible upstream system, process, or transformation and engage the appropriate owner. This reduces ambiguity, prevents blame diffusion, and supports a culture of measurable responsibility.

Databricks data lineage

In Databricks, data lineage provides end-to-end visibility into where data originates, how it is transformed, and where it is consumed across the Lakehouse platform. Lineage is delivered through Unity Catalog, Databricks' centralized governance and metadata management layer. Lineage metadata is automatically captured at query runtime whenever workloads are executed on Databricks, eliminating the need for manual instrumentation or documentation. This enables near real-time visibility into data dependencies and usage patterns. Databricks captures lineage at multiple levels of granularity, including:

- **Table-level lineage**: Tracks upstream and downstream relationships between tables and views, enabling dependency and impact analysis across data pipelines.
- **Column-level lineage**: Captures source-to-target column mappings, providing fine-grained traceability of data elements—critical for regulatory use cases such as GDPR and sensitive data management.
- **Code-level lineage**: Associates data assets with the jobs, notebooks, queries, and dashboards that produce or consume them, enabling traceability between execution logic and resulting data products.

Viewing data lineage

Databricks provides three ways to view data lineage, enabling both technical and business users to understand how data flows through the lakehouse. Lineage can be viewed interactively in the Catalog Explorer UI, queried using Unity Catalog system tables for programmatic access and auditing, or accessed through REST APIs for custom applications and external metadata integration.

Catalog Explorer (UI)

The most common way to view Databricks lineage is via the Catalog Explorer UI, which provides an interactive visual representation of upstream and downstream data dependencies across tables, columns, jobs, notebooks, and dashboards. This view updates in near real time when an activity is detected. To check the data lineage using the Catalog Explorer:

1. Log on to your Databricks workspace. Click on **Catalog** > **electroniz_catalog** > **electroniz_gold_master_schema**. Under Tables, click on **mvw_electroniz_gold_golden_record_customers**.

2. Open the **Lineage** tab and explore upstream/downstream graphs. You may filter by tables, dashboards, jobs, or notebooks.

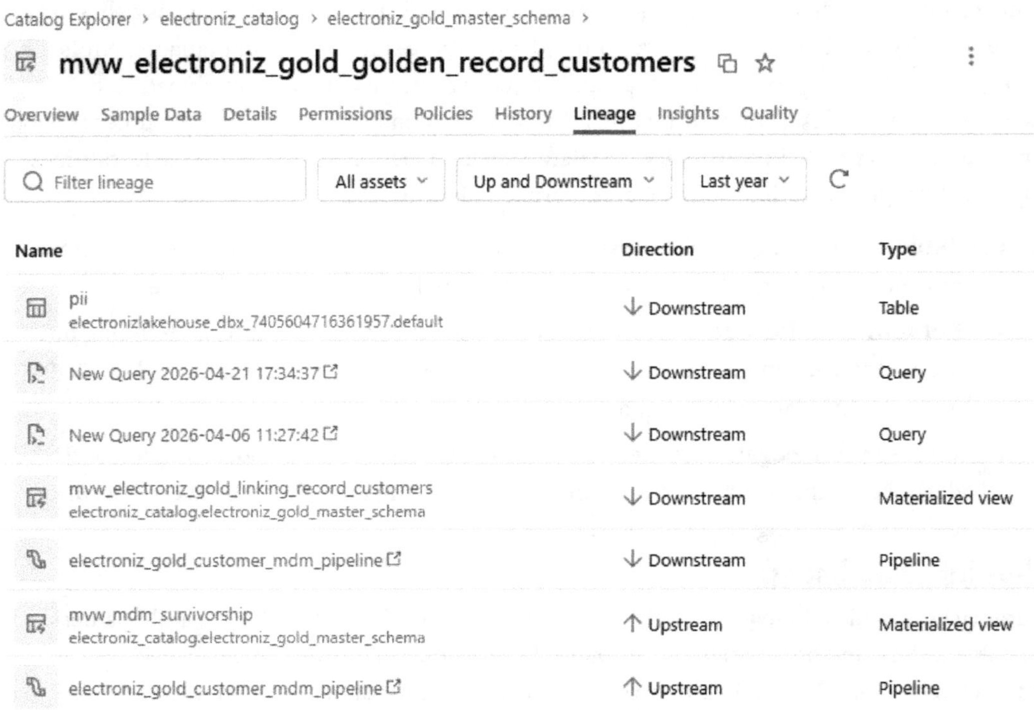

Figure 12.42: Checking data lineage to explore upstream/downstream graphs

The upstream and downstream lineage graphs help answer the following questions:

a. **Upstream lineage:** Where does the data originate? Sources may include tables, files, or upstream processes. Upstream lineage is particularly useful for tracing source system failures and changes in transformation logic.

b. **Downstream lineage:** Who is using the data? Downstream consumers may include processes, views, or dashboards. Downstream lineage is especially valuable for assessing the impact of changes to transformation logic on dashboards, jobs, and notebooks.

> **Note**
>
> In data lineage, upstream and downstream refer to the direction of data flow and dependencies across systems, pipelines, and reports.

3. In Databricks, the Lineage Graph visually maps upstream and downstream data dependencies across tables, views, files, notebooks, jobs, and dashboards. Integrated with Databricks Unity Catalog, it supports governance, impact analysis, and data trust. Click on **See lineage graph**.

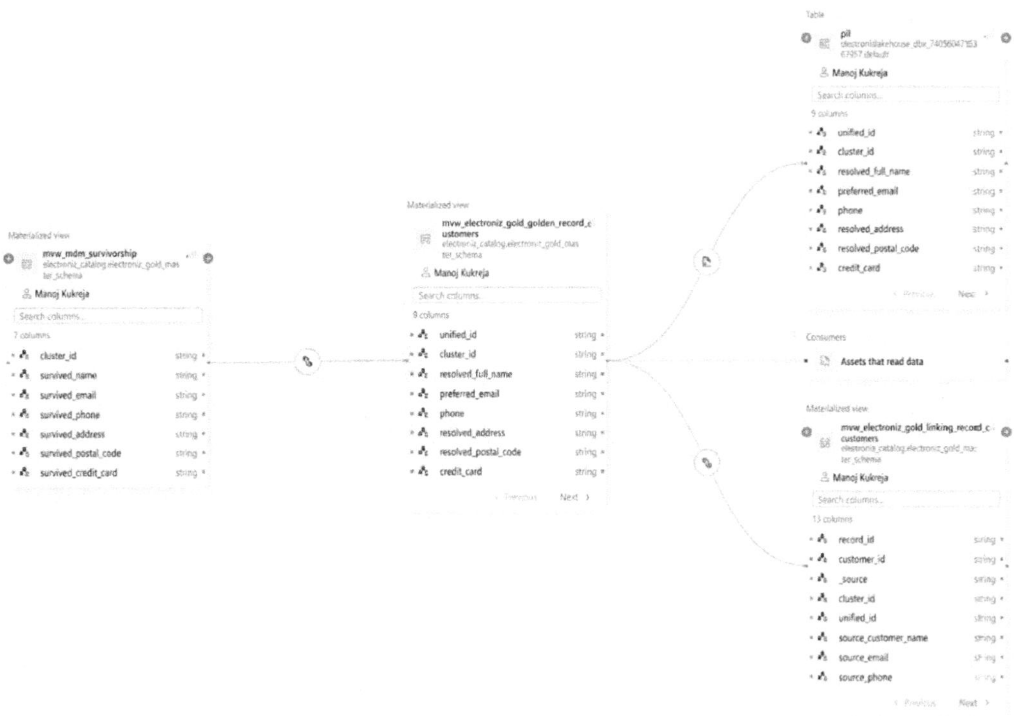

Figure 12.43: Data lineage visual graph

The data lineage graph is a valuable artifact for architectural reviews and audits. While the Catalog Explorer UI is the preferred method for reviewing data lineage, lineage analysis can also be performed using SQL.

System Tables (SQL)

Databricks exposes data lineage through Unity Catalog system tables, primarily **table_lineage** and **column_lineage**, which enable programmatic querying of lineage information, as shown below.

1. Log on to your Databricks workspace and execute the following SQL to check table lineage for **mvw_electroniz_gold_golden_record_customers.**

```
SELECT
  source_table_full_name,
  target_table_full_name,
  entity_type,
  entity_id,
  entity_run_id,
  workspace_id,
  event_time
FROM system.access.table_lineage
WHERE target_table_full_name =
'electroniz_catalog.electroniz_gold_master_schema.mvw_electroniz_gold_golde
n_record_customers'
ORDER BY event_time DESC;
```

2. The **system.access.table_lineage** table in Databricks records **up**stream and downstream dependencies between tables and views based on executed SQL and Spark operations.

Figure 12.44: Checking table-level data lineage using system tables

3. Similarly, the **system.access.column_lineage** table provides column-level data lineage by recording how individual target columns are derived from source columns across tables and views based on executed SQL and Spark operations. Execute the following SQL to check table lineage for **mvw_electroniz_gold_golden_record_customers**.

```
SELECT
*
FROM system.access.column_lineage
WHERE target_table_full_name =
'electroniz_catalog.electroniz_gold_master_schema.mvw_electroniz_gold_golde
n_record_customers'
ORDER BY event_time DESC;
```

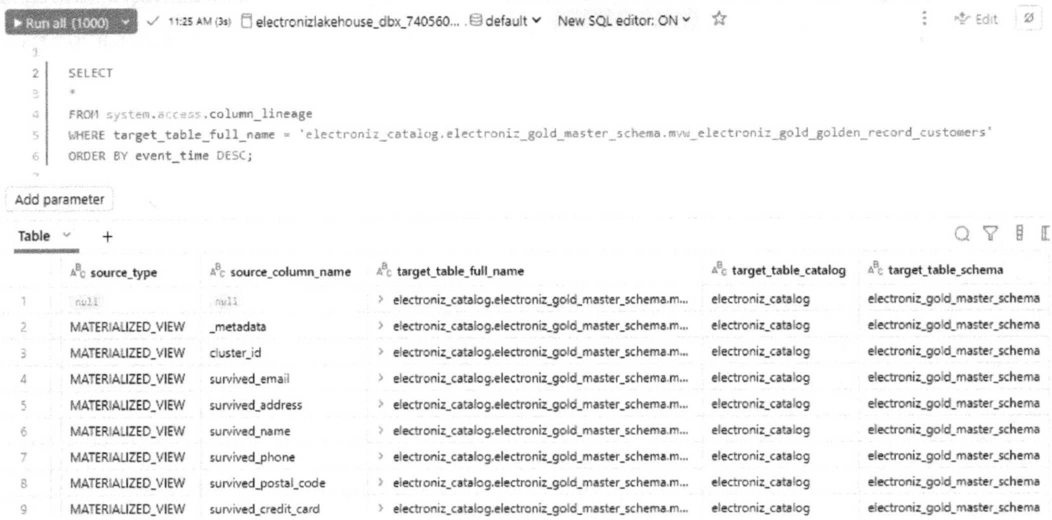

Figure 12.45: Checking column-level data lineage using system tables

Column-level lineage enables tracing how data is derived, understanding metric and transformation logic, diagnosing issues through root cause analysis, meeting audit and compliance requirements, and tracking the flow of sensitive or governed data elements. While it does not replace the Unity Catalog Lineage Graph, SQL-based analysis provides a powerful complementary approach for audits, troubleshooting, and governance workflows.

REST APIs

Finally, you may use Databricks REST APIs to check data lineage captured by Unity Catalog. Databricks provides the following APIs to check data lineage:

- Table lineage API: Accessible using `GET /api/2.0/lineage-tracking/table-lineage`
- Column lineage API: Accessible using `GET /api/2.0/lineage-tracking/column-lineage`

Below is an example command that programmatically checks column lineage using the Databricks REST API.

```
curl -X GET \
  -H "Authorization: Bearer <PAT>" \
  -H "Content-Type: application/json" \
  https://<YOUR_WORKSPACE_URL>/api/2.0/lineage-tracking/column-lineage \
  -d '{
        "table_name":
"electroniz_catalog.electroniz_gold_master_schema.mvw_electroniz_gold_golden_recor
```

```
d_customers",
        "column_name": "resolved_address"
    }'
``
```

The API above uses a **Personal Access Token** (**PAT**) for authentication. You may recall creating a similar token for Claude Code in Chapter 9. You can reuse that token or generate a new one by following the same steps.

While REST APIs provide a fast and lightweight way to check data lineage, they return only direct dependencies. For comprehensive lineage analysis, it is recommended to use the Catalog Explorer UI or Unity Catalog system tables.

Databricks access audit

Databricks records audit logs for access and activity events across the platform in the audit table, which is hosted in the system catalog. This table is primarily used for monitoring security, compliance, and governance. It captures detailed information about who accessed Databricks, when and from where the access occurred, and which resources were accessed. This visibility is essential for auditing user activity, investigating security incidents, and demonstrating compliance. Maintaining a comprehensive and reliable audit log is critical to meeting regulatory and organizational compliance standards.

1. Log on to your Databricks workspace and execute the following SQL to check the audit log.

```
SELECT
event_time ,
action_name ,
user_identity ,
source_ip_address ,
service_name ,
workspace_id ,
request_id
FROM system.access.audit
```

2. The audit table records events related to user and service principal access, interactions with data products, and modifications to permissions and grants for both data objects and workspaces.

```
SELECT
event_time ,
action_name ,
user_identity ,
source_ip_address ,
service_name ,
workspace_id ,
request_id
FROM system.access.audit
```

event_time	action_name	user_identity	source_ip_address	service_name
2026-04-25T01:50:43.577+00:00	listVolumes	{"email":"System-User","subject_name":null}		unityCatalog
2026-04-25T01:50:42.443+00:00	listTables	{"email":"System-User","subject_name":null}		unityCatalog
2026-04-25T01:50:44.926+00:00	listRegisteredModels	{"email":"System-User","subject_name":null}		unityCatalog
2026-04-25T01:50:45.212+00:00	listFunctions	{"email":"System-User","subject_name":null}		unityCatalog
2026-04-25T01:50:44.842+00:00	listRegisteredModels	{"email":"System-User","subject_name":null}		unityCatalog
2026-04-25T01:50:44.758+00:00	listRegisteredModels	{"email":"System-User","subject_name":null}		unityCatalog
2026-04-25T01:50:43.637+00:00	listVolumes	{"email":"System-User","subject_name":null}		unityCatalog
2026-04-25T01:50:40.222+00:00	getPermissions	{"email":"9e9a2522-5460-474d-91f9-075636e7f0db","subject_name"...		unityCatalog
2026-04-25T01:50:44.815+00:00	listRegisteredModels	{"email":"System-User","subject_name":null}		unityCatalog

Figure 12.46: Checking user activity in the audit log

Audit data is primarily used to support security and compliance initiatives by enabling access auditing, tracking privileged actions and permission changes, detecting suspicious or unauthorized behavior, and supporting both internal and external audits. Audit data commonly powers governance and security dashboards by integration with **Security Information and Event Management** (**SIEM**) platforms. This integration provides centralized, near real-time visibility into security-relevant activity across the platform, enabling continuous monitoring, alerting, investigation, and compliance reporting by transforming raw access and activity events into actionable security insights.

Having established how Databricks maintains a strict audit log of user activity, we now turn our attention to its data retention policies.

Data lifecycle management policies

Data lifecycle management policy is a formal framework that establishes how long an organization retains information, the purpose for retaining it, where it is stored, and the conditions and methods for its secure disposal. It applies to both digital and physical records and is a fundamental component of data governance, privacy protection, security, and regulatory compliance. Data retention policies must be understood in conjunction with the retention policies of the underlying object storage (such as Azure Data Lake Storage Gen2, Amazon S3, or Google Cloud Storage).

Data retention policies at Databricks level

In Databricks, data retention extends beyond Delta Lake table data to include associated metadata, lineage information, audit events, and operational telemetry. The retention policies for these artifacts are outlined below.

System tables retention

In Databricks, system tables are stored in the **system** catalog and serve as a centralized source of historical observability, offering detailed visibility into security activities, cost usage, performance metrics, and end-to-end data lineage. The following are the retention policies for system tables.

- As discussed earlier, data lineage in Unity Catalog is primarily stored in two system tables: **table_lineage** and **column_lineage**. Lineage information in these tables is retained for one year, after which it is automatically deleted.
- Audit logs are stored in the audit system table and capture data access, permission modifications, and connection events. These logs are retained for 365 days.
- The **query_history** system table captures information about executed queries, including the initiating user, query text, execution duration, status, and error details. This data is retained for a period of 365 days.

Databricks enforces **fixed retention periods** for lineage, audit, SQL history, and operational metadata, typically retaining this data for approximately one year. If longer retention is required, lineage data should be periodically archived to an external location, such as object storage.

Data quality result retention

The `data_quality_monitoring.table_results` system table captures summarized results of data quality evaluations for tables monitored by Databricks Data Quality Monitoring, including checks based on expectations, constraints, and quality rules. As part of the system catalog, it offers a historical, table-level view of data quality performance, allowing teams to observe how dataset quality changes and improves over time.

These results are leveraged to assess the overall condition of monitored tables, uncover repeating or widespread data quality problems, and reinforce governance and reliability practices. The table also supports confidence in analytical data and provides verifiable evidence for compliance and data stewardship activities. Data stored in `data_quality_monitoring.table_results` is retained indefinitely, enabling long-term review of data quality trends, incident impacts, and root cause analyses across monitored tables.

Delta table retention

You may recall from *Chapter 6* that Delta Lake maintains a complete history of data changes by recording every write operation in a transactional log. This log automatically versions the data, enabling users to query, compare, or restore previous states of a dataset. As a result, teams can easily perform rollbacks, troubleshoot data issues, and satisfy auditing requirements using reliable point-in-time snapshots. By default, Delta Lake retains this history for seven days; however, this retention period is fully configurable. Databricks customers can increase or decrease the retention window to align with their specific compliance and regulatory requirements. Delta table retention is primarily controlled by two variables:

- `delta.logRetentionDuration`: `delta.logRetentionDuration` controls how long Delta Lake keeps transaction log history. Old log files are removed automatically once the retention period has passed and a new checkpoint is created.
- `delta.deletedFileRetentionDuration`: `delta.deletedFileRetentionDuration` determines the retention period for obsolete data files, after which they become eligible for physical deletion during a VACUUM operation.

Let's see how these variables can be configured for a delta table:

1. Execute the following SQL to change the transaction log history to 30 days and the retention period for obsolete data files to 15 days.

```
ALTER TABLE electroniz_catalog.electroniz_silver_schema.event_log_ecommerce
SET TBLPROPERTIES (
  'delta.logRetentionDuration' = '30 days',
  'delta.deletedFileRetentionDuration' = '15 days'
);
```

Delta Lake retention alone does *not* guarantee long-term recoverability if object storage retention policies are more restrictive. While Delta Lake provides logical versioning and time-travel capabilities at the table level, object storage ultimately controls the physical lifecycle of data files.

Data retention policies at object storage level

Object storage lifecycle policies can automatically delete or archive files once they reach a certain age. To ensure reliable time travel, rollback capabilities, auditability, and point-in-time recovery, the object storage retention period should be at least as long as the configured Delta Lake retention period. If object storage retention is shorter than Delta Lake retention, time-travel queries may fail with 'file not found' errors because the underlying Parquet files have been deleted while the Delta log still references them. For this reason, it is strongly recommended that Delta Lake retention and object storage retention be configured in tandem.

With data retention considerations addressed, we now shift our focus to data quality policies and the mechanisms used to ensure accuracy, completeness, and trust in governed data products.

Data quality standards

Among the four Vs of big data, data veracity emphasizes the key dimensions of accuracy, trustworthiness, and reliability. Data quality measures how well data aligns with key business objectives based on these dimensions. Data quality issues are often difficult to identify and resolve; in most cases, they only become evident when the data is actively used and produces skewed results. For this reason, data quality has often been overlooked, leading to significant challenges months or even years after the decision-making process has been put into production.

Figure 12.47: Data quality issues

As the saying goes, "*prevention is better than cure*". Taking a proactive approach rather than a reactive is key to avoiding data quality issues. Here are some practical approaches that can be taken proactively during data platform design:

- Embed data governance early in the design phase.
- Apply data quality checks during ingestion or curation.
- Automate data quality validations wherever possible.
- Enable real-time data monitoring and alerting mechanisms when thresholds are breached.
- Document data quality rules in data contracts with a robust validation process.

Defining data quality standards

During the data quality management process, domain experts should formally document data quality standards for data experts. Data quality standards are guidelines that establish clear rules and detailed instructions for identifying and managing data quality issues effectively. The most common data quality standards include the following checks:

- **Validity**: Ensure data conforms to organizational formats and business constraints.
- **Completeness**: Verify that no critical information is missing.
- **Accuracy**: Confirm data closely represents real-world business events or values.
- **Uniqueness**: Eliminate duplicate records from data.
- **Referential Integrity**: Preserve relationships between related data elements
- **Freshness**: Keep data current and a close representation of its source

Data experts collaborate with domain experts to identify and resolve data quality issues through a combination of coding solutions and monitoring tools. Data quality monitoring and remediation are a continuous process; they demand consistent, ongoing attention.

Implementing data quality standards

Once data quality standards are defined, the corresponding rules, expectations, and controls are communicated back to data experts for implementation. Putting these standards into practice requires a blend of proactive validation, automated monitoring, and strong governance to ensure that bad data is identified early and prevented from entering downstream systems. Databricks uses a tiered strategy for managing data quality, beginning with rule-based validation and extending into automated anomaly detection and continuous monitoring. Although the next section will dive into the anomaly detection and monitoring capabilities, we'll first focus on the foundation of this approach: rule-based validation.

Rule-based validation using pipeline expectations

Within a pipeline, Databricks enforces data quality through a declarative mechanism known as expectations. Expectations are optional clauses that serve as embedded validation rules applied to data as it moves through each stage of the pipeline. As records flow from one transformation to the next, these expectations evaluate whether the data meets defined criteria—such as required fields, valid ranges, or business logic constraints—and then take the appropriate action. The image below demonstrates how expectations are applied to the `credit_card` and email columns. Each expectation must be assigned a unique name, which serves as its identifier for tracking, monitoring, and reporting. The constraint must be written in valid SQL syntax and evaluate to *true* or *false* for every record, ensuring that each row can be validated consistently against the defined rule.

2: Cleaned streaming view with DQ rules — Python

```
@dlt.view
@dlt.expect_or_drop("valid_credit_card", "credit_card IS NOT NULL")
@dlt.expect_or_drop("valid_email", "email RLIKE '^[a-zA-Z0-9._%+\\\\-]+@[a-zA-Z0-9.\\\\-]+\\\\.[a-zA-Z]{2,}$'")
```

Figure 12.48: Data pipeline expectations

You can also group multiple expectations together and apply shared enforcement behavior by using the corresponding expectation functions, allowing you to define collective actions for a set of validation rules.

```
dp.create_streaming_table(
    name="electroniz_catalog.electroniz_silver_schema.electroniz_silver_ecomm_transactions",
    comment="Silver ecommerce transactions with quality rules",
    table_properties={"quality": "silver"},
    expect_all_or_drop={
        "valid_customer_name": "customer_name IS NOT NULL",
        "valid_address": "address IS NOT NULL",
        "valid_email_not_null": "email IS NOT NULL",
        "valid_order_number": "order_number IS NOT NULL",
        "valid_email_format": "email RLIKE '^[a-zA-Z0-9._%+-]+@[a-zA-Z0-9.-]+\\\\.[a-zA-Z]{2,}$'",
        "valid_currency": "currency IN ('USD', 'INR', 'CAD', 'EUR')"
    }
)
```

Figure 12.49: Data pipeline grouped expectations

This approach ensures that data quality is continuously assessed and enforced at the point where it matters most: directly within the data processing workflow. Databricks supports three enforcement actions for expectations, each designed for a different level of data quality control. The choice depends on how strict the rule is and how tolerant the pipeline can be of bad data.

- `expect`: Captures validation failures but **continues** processing.

  Applicable use case: This behaviour is ideal for where you want visibility into data quality issues but do not want to block processing. For example, if you expect most email values to contain an "@" symbol but don't want to stop the pipeline when a few malformed entries appear, `expect` lets you monitor the issue while still loading the data.

- `expect_or_drop`: This enforcement **discards** records that fail the rule, ensuring only valid data moves forward.

  Applicable use case: This behaviour is useful when invalid data should not contaminate downstream tables but shouldn't halt the entire pipeline. For instance, if a `credit_card` field must be 16 digits, any row that doesn't meet this requirement is dropped, allowing the rest of the dataset to continue through the pipeline cleanly.

- `expect_or_fail`: This enforcement **stops the pipeline** immediately when a rule is violated.

  Applicable use case: This behaviour is reserved for strict, business-critical rules where even a single bad record is unacceptable. For example, if a regulatory dataset requires that every record contain a non-null `customer_id`, a violation should halt the pipeline so the issue can be corrected before any further processing occurs.

The implementation of quality rules is typically carried out by data experts, such as data engineers, and followed by a validation process to ensure those rules function correctly and consistently across real datasets.

Validating data quality standards

After implementation, each data quality rule needs to be validated. Each rule must be tested, verified, and continuously evaluated to ensure it behaves as intended across real datasets and evolving pipeline conditions.

Databricks automatically tracks how many records passed, failed, or were dropped, and exposes these metrics in the pipeline UI.

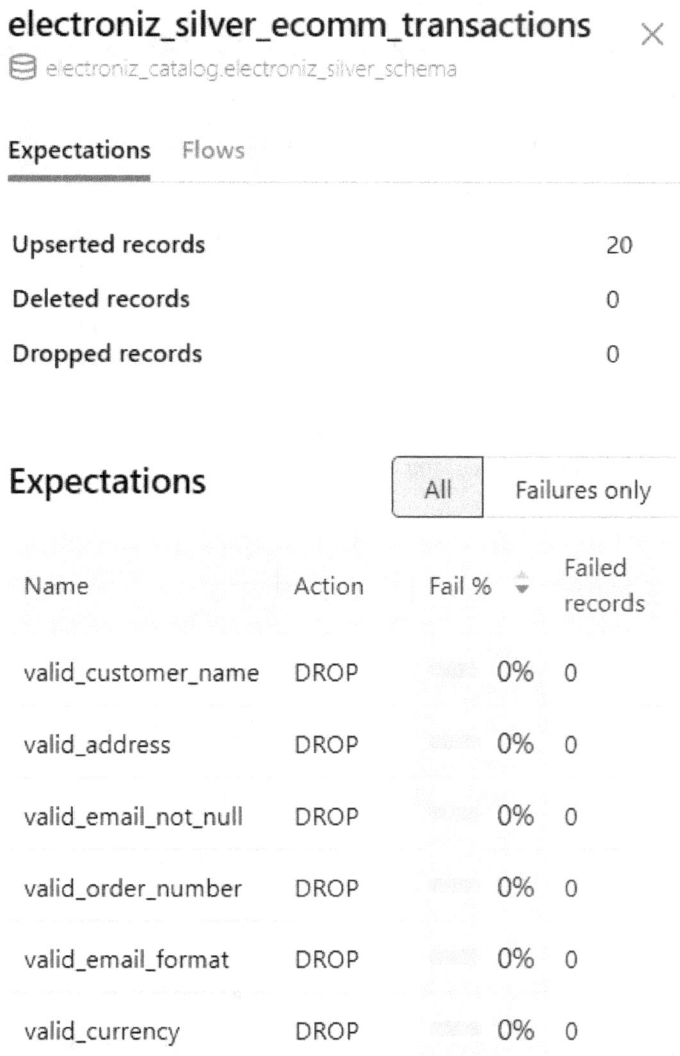

Figure 12.50: Data pipeline UI expectation metrics

Expectation metrics are reflected directly in the Pipeline UI, giving users a clear, real-time view of data quality as records flow through the system. For every expectation defined in the pipeline, the UI displays a set of key indicators:

- **Records Evaluated**: The number of rows checked against the expectation.
- **Name:** The unique identifier of the expectation as specified in the pipeline code.
- **Action**: Enforcement action on rows that failed the rule.
- **Failed Records**: How many rows violated the rule.

These metrics are updated for every pipeline run, making it easy to track quality trends over time.

Alternatively, you may extract expectation metrics using SQL. This approach complements the visual insights provided by the Pipeline UI, giving teams both interactive and programmatic ways to monitor and operationalize data quality. Start by enabling the Event Logs under the Advanced settings of the pipeline settings as shown below. You will need to specify the schema and table name for the intended event log table.

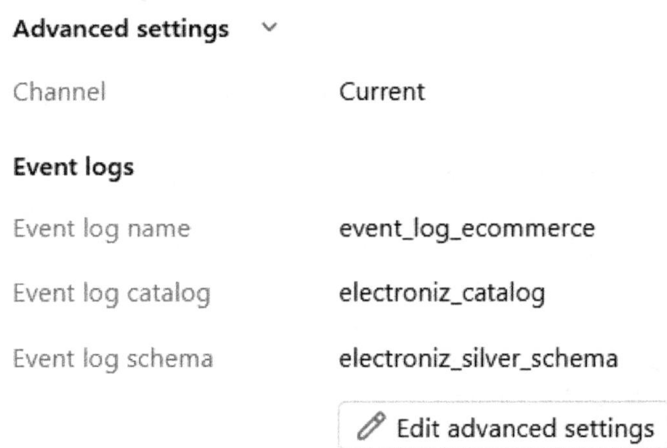

Figure 12.51: Data pipeline event log settings

Once these settings are in place, the event-log table becomes fully configured. To populate it with fresh expectation results, run the pipeline using the full table refresh option. This forces all pipeline activities to re-execute, re-evaluates every expectation, and writes the corresponding metrics and events into the event-log table.

```
-- Extract data quality metrics from Lakeflow Declarative Pipelines event log
expectations
WITH parsed AS (
  SELECT
```

```
    timestamp,
    origin.flow_name,
    origin.dataset_name,
    details:flow_progress.data_quality.expectations AS expectations_json
  FROM electroniz_catalog.electroniz_silver_schema.event_log_ecommerce
  WHERE details LIKE '%expectation%'
),
exploded AS (
  SELECT
    timestamp,
    flow_name,
    dataset_name,
    explode(from_json(
      expectations_json,
      'ARRAY<STRUCT<name: STRING, dataset: STRING, passed_records: BIGINT,
failed_records: BIGINT>>'
    )) AS expectation
  FROM parsed
  WHERE expectations_json IS NOT NULL
)
SELECT
  timestamp,
  flow_name,
  dataset_name,
  expectation.name AS expectation_name,
  expectation.dataset AS expectation_dataset,
  expectation.passed_records,
  expectation.failed_records,
  ROUND(
    expectation.failed_records * 100.0 / NULLIF(expectation.passed_records +
expectation.failed_records, 0),
    2
  ) AS failure_rate_pct
FROM exploded
ORDER BY timestamp DESC
```

This event log table is especially useful when you want to automate governance reporting, integrate quality results into dashboards or enterprise catalogs, or perform deeper historical analysis across multiple pipeline runs.

```
-- Extract data quality metrics from DLT event log expectations
WITH parsed AS (
  SELECT
    timestamp,
    origin.flow_name,
    origin.dataset_name,
    details:flow_progress.data_quality.expectations AS expectations_json
  FROM electroniz_catalog.electroniz_silver_schema.event_log_ecommerce
  WHERE details LIKE '%expectation%'
```

arameter

expectation_name	expectation_dataset	passed_records	failed_records	failure_rate_pct
valid_address	electroniz_catalog.electr...	20	0	
valid_email_not_null	electroniz_catalog.electr...	20	0	
valid_currency	electroniz_catalog.electr...	20	0	
valid_address	electroniz_catalog.electr...	20	0	
valid_email_format	electroniz_catalog.electr...	20	0	
valid_email_not_null	electroniz_catalog.electr...	20	0	
valid_customer_name	electroniz_catalog.electr...	20	0	
valid_order_number	electroniz_catalog.electr...	20	0	

Figure 12.52: Extracting expectation metrics using SQL

The data quality validation process typically involves close collaboration with data stewards, analysts, and domain experts, who verify that the rules accurately reflect business requirements and do not introduce unintended data loss or bias. Together, these roles ensure that data quality controls are both technically robust and aligned with organizational expectations. In a subsequent section, we will expand on the role of Data Stewardship and explain how domain experts help maintain data quality and build trust among end users through data contracts.

Earlier, we noted that Databricks adopts a tiered strategy for managing data quality—starting with rule-based validation and extending into automated anomaly detection and continuous monitoring. We now turn our attention to those next layers in the framework.

Data observability standards

Data observability standards define how organizations monitor and ensure the health, reliability, and trustworthiness of data as it moves through modern data pipelines and ultimately powers data products. While expectation-based rules validate data against predefined conditions, observability focuses on detecting unexpected behaviors—such as anomalies in volume, freshness, schema, or distribution—that signal deeper issues in the pipeline. By continuously monitoring these patterns, observability standards help teams identify problems early, prevent silent data failures, and maintain confidence in the data that drives analytics, AI models, and operational systems.

Core dimensions of data observability

From a data product standpoint, data observability ensures that each product consistently delivers trustworthy, high-quality data to its consumers. Data observability is typically organized around several core dimensions of product health.

- **Freshness**: Data freshness measures whether a data product is updated at the cadence its consumers expect or as defined in its data contract. When freshness slips, the product's usefulness erodes—whether it feeds dashboards, ML features, or operational workflows. Freshness monitoring surfaces delayed ingestion, missed updates, and upstream job failures, enabling product owners to uphold reliable delivery guarantees.
- **Volume:** Volume ensures that a data product contains the expected number of records. Missing rows, duplicate entries, or unexpected spikes can distort analytics and break downstream logic. Observability at the volume level helps data product teams detect ingestion gaps, source-system issues, or unexpected surges that may indicate business anomalies.
- **Distribution:** Distribution tracks the statistical shape of the data product—its ranges, percentiles, categorical frequencies, null rates, and outliers. Shifts in distribution often signal deeper issues such as data drift, incorrect transformations, or changes in business processes. For data products, maintaining stable distributions is essential to preserving semantic meaning and analytical trust.

- **Schema:** Schema observability ensures that the structure of the data product remains consistent with its contract. Unexpected column additions, deletions, or type changes can break downstream consumers. Monitoring schema stability helps data product owners enforce data contracts, prevent breaking changes, and maintain compatibility across dependent systems.
- **Lineage:** Lineage provides visibility into how a data product is created, transformed, and consumed. It shows upstream dependencies, downstream consumers, and the full transformation graph. For data product teams, lineage is essential for impact analysis, debugging, governance, and communicating the product's provenance to stakeholders.

These core dimensions collectively ensure that a data product behaves predictably, evolves safely, and maintains the trust of its consumers. Observability becomes not just an operational concern but a core product capability—one that supports reliability, transparency, and long-term adoption.

Databricks Lakehouse Monitoring delivers automated, ML-driven observability across your entire data platform. By continuously analyzing how datasets evolve over time, it can detect emerging data drifts and trigger alerts whenever it identifies deviations from expected patterns. Databricks approaches data observability through two core capabilities:

- **Anomaly detection:** Focused on identifying data-quality issues related to freshness and completeness. Its purpose is to answer the question, *"Is something wrong with my data quality right now?"*.
- **Data profiling:** Focused on understanding distributions, percentiles, null rates, categorical frequencies, and drift over time. Its purpose is to answer, *"What does my data look like over time?"*.

Although they work together, they serve different purposes. Anomaly detection is primarily used for data operations, where the goal is to catch issues such as delayed updates or unexpected changes in row counts as soon as they occur. Data profiling, on the other hand, is used for understanding the statistical behavior of the data—its distributions, null patterns, categorical frequencies, and drift—so teams can analyze trends, diagnose issues, and design quality rules with deeper context. Let's look at how both capabilities work, starting with how anomaly detection operates in Databricks.

Anomaly detection

Let's configure a few core dimensions in the bronze schema to evaluate the resulting metrics. The process begins by enabling anomaly detection, which applies an ML-based model to identify unusual patterns in the data.

1. To enable data quality monitoring, navigate to the table in Unity Catalog. Under **Catalog** click on **electroniz_catalog** > **electroniz_bronze_schema**.
2. Under the **Details** tab, toggle Data Quality Monitoring to **Enabled**.

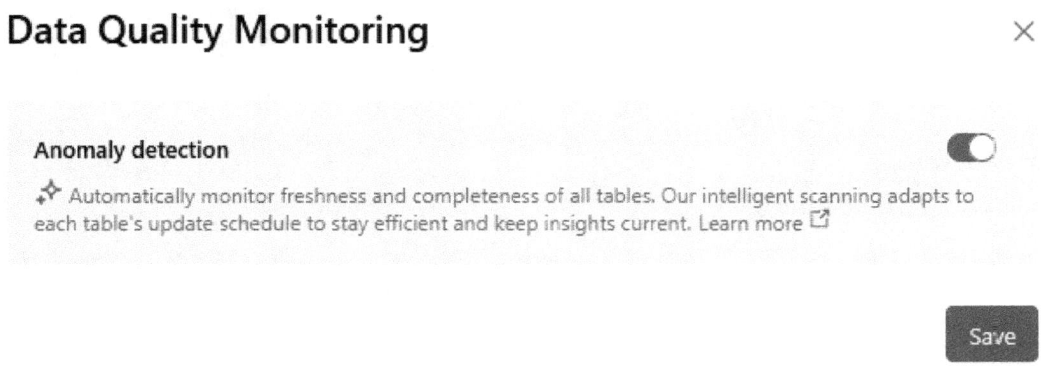

Figure 12.53: Enabling anomaly detection

3. Databricks promptly initiates a scan of all tables in the schema. During the initial setup, it also analyzes the previous two weeks of data to build a historical baseline.
4. After a few minutes have elapsed, click on **View results**.

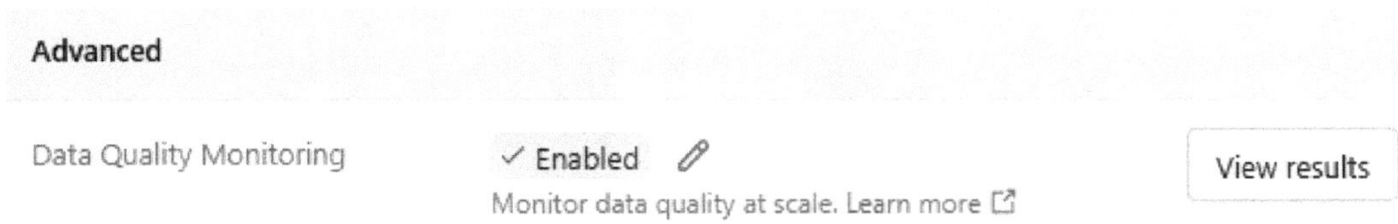

Figure 12.54: Checking the results of anomaly detection

5. The results page summarizes overall data quality for all tables in the **electroniz_bronze_schema**. Each table displays its status—Healthy, Unhealthy, or Error—along with its impact on downstream processes and the frequency with which it is scanned.

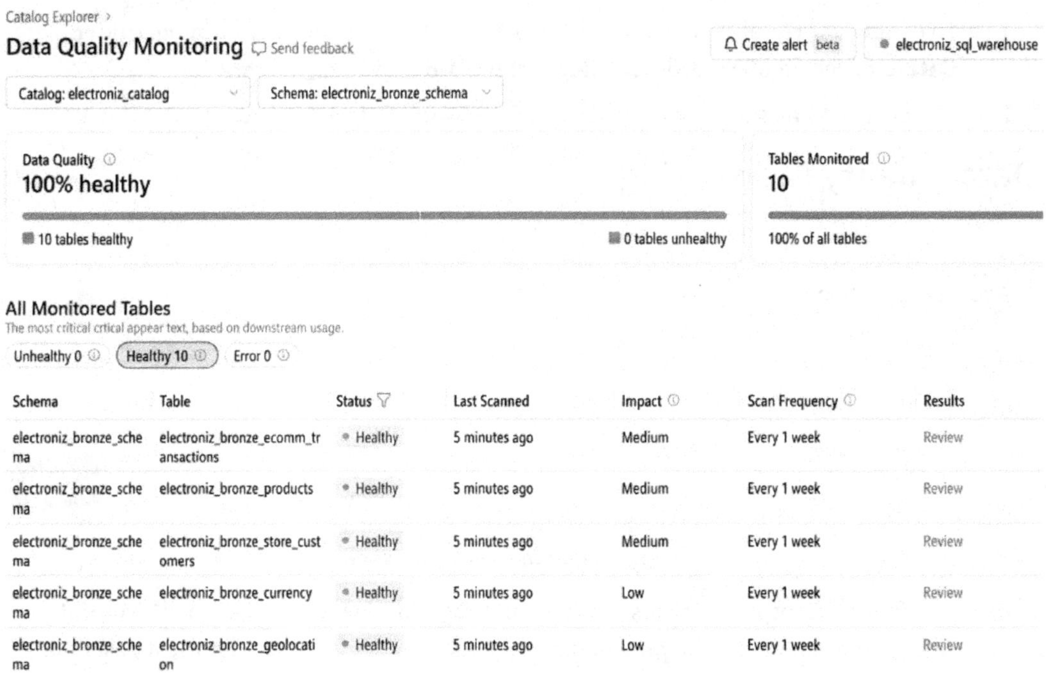

Figure 12.55: Results of anomaly detection

6. You may also configure alerts to inform you when anomaly detection identifies a data quality concern, for example, delayed updates or unusual changes in row volume. Press the Alerts button to create a new one.

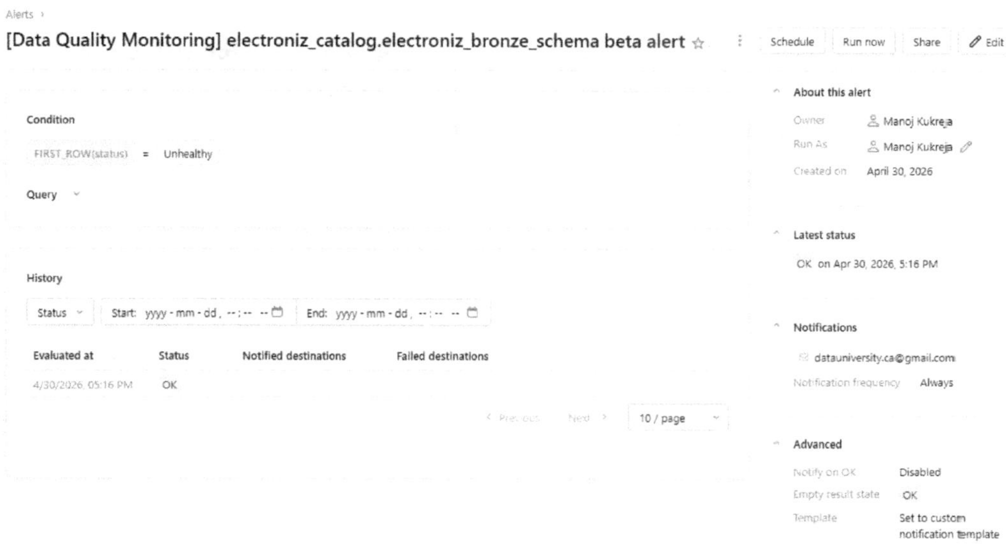

Figure 12.56: Creating anomaly detection alerts

7. Databricks anomaly detection alerts notify you whenever the platform identifies a potential data-quality issue, enabling teams to act quickly. Each alert is evaluated against the conditions you define. You can trigger the alert immediately using **Run Now** or schedule it to run at a recurring interval.
8. To conserve resources and minimize costs during training, it is advisable to remove the alert after it has served its purpose.

While anomaly detection is designed to automatically surface irregular or problematic patterns in your data, data profiling provides a statistical overview that helps you understand how the data behaves and evolves.

Data profiling

As discussed earlier, data observability detects, explains, and helps prevent data issues to maintain the overall health of a data product. Data profiling provides the key metrics that make this possible—capturing distributions, percentiles, null rates, categorical frequencies, and drift patterns. These metrics form the analytical foundation that observability systems use to understand normal behavior, diagnose anomalies, and monitor long-term data quality trends. Data profiling metrics often include row counts, NULL value counts and drifts.

While anomaly detection flags that something is off, data profiling shows the story behind it—what shifted and how the data's behavior evolved. In Databricks, data profiling statistics are stored as time-series metrics, enabling easy analysis of historical trends. Follow these steps to turn data profiling on for a table:

1. Log on to your Databricks workspace. Click on **Catalog** > **electroniz_catalog** > **electroniz_gold_master_schema**. Under Tables, click on **mvw_electroniz_gold_golden_record_customers**.
2. Click on the **Quality** tab. Click on **Enable**.

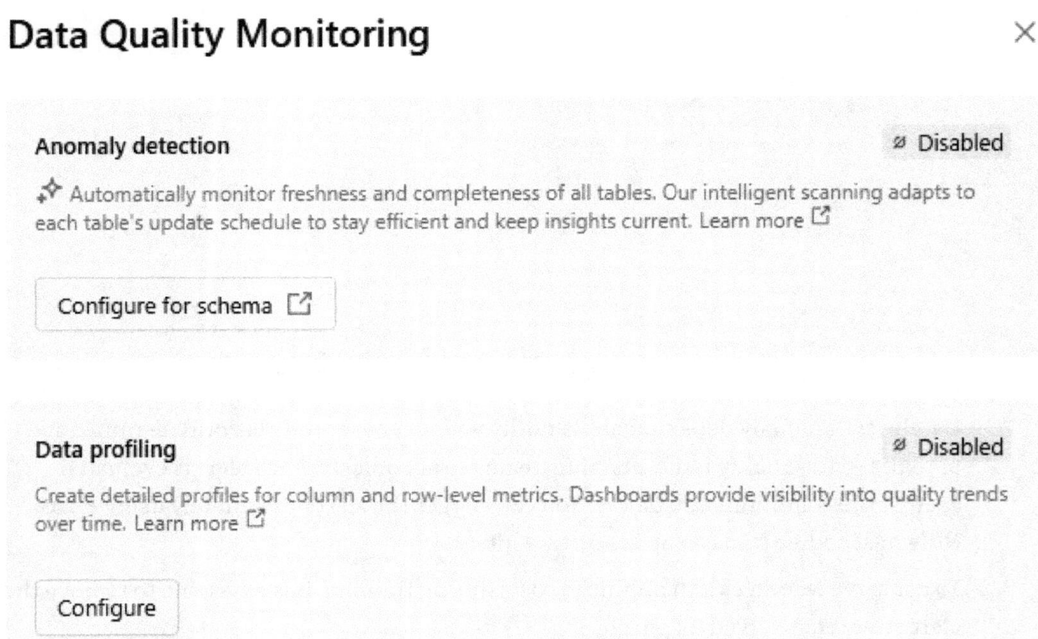

Figure 12.57: Enabling data profiling

3. Under Data profiling, click on **Configure**. You now need to make an important choice for **Profiling type.**

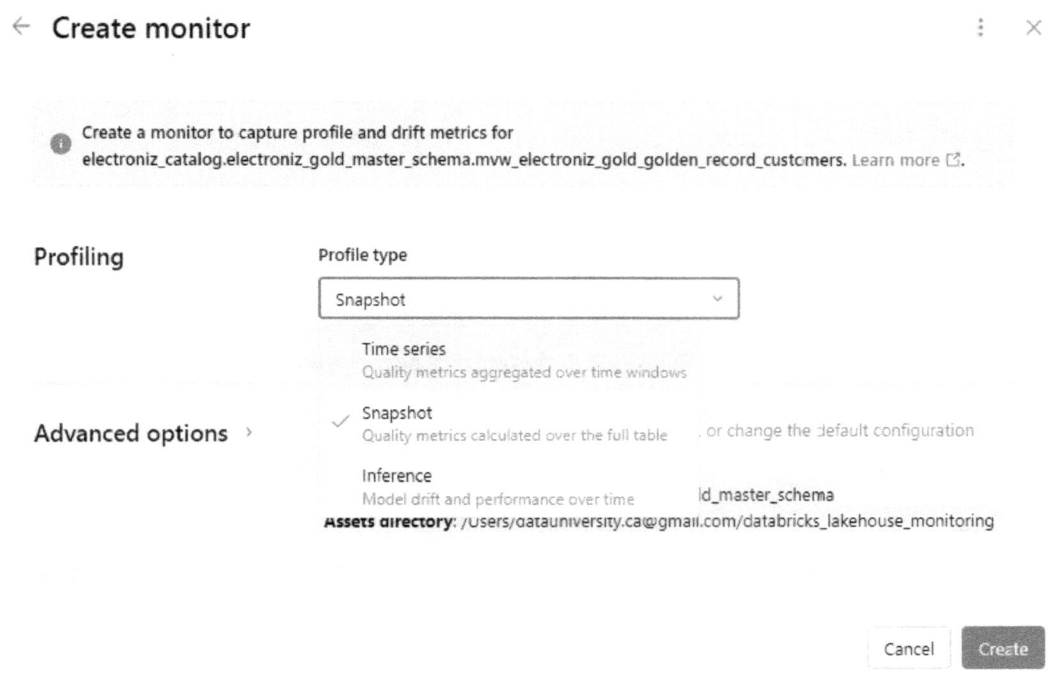

Figure 12.58: Choosing the data profiling type

Databricks supports three core types: snapshot, time-series, or inference profiling.

 a. **Snapshot profiling**: Provides a one-time statistical summary of a table. It captures the data's current state at that moment, and the results are not tracked over time.
 b. **Time-series profiling**: Designed for long-term monitoring where historical visibility is important. Profiling metrics are computed in time-based windows, allowing you to observe how distributions, null rates, and other characteristics evolve over time.
 c. **Inference profiling**: Inference profiling is built to analyze the statistics of ML models and predictions.

4. Choose the Snapshot type and click on **Create**.

5. Now click on **Refresh history**. Wait until the Status changes to **Succeeded**.

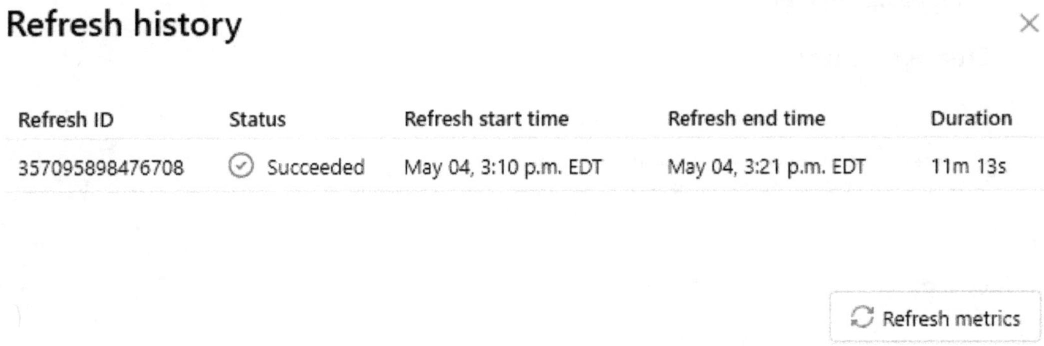

Figure 12.59: Refreshing data profiling metrics

6. Now click on **View dashboard**.

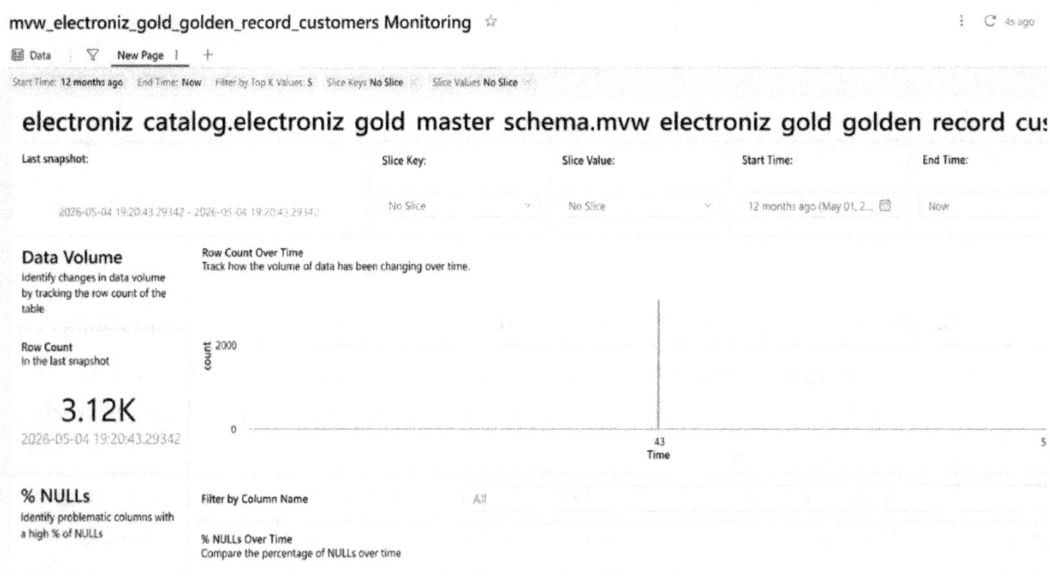

Figure 12.60: Checking data profiling metrics

7. Toward the end of the dashboard, you'll see how data profiling surfaces key row-level statistics—including data types, record counts, and minimum or average value lengths —highlighting important structural characteristics of the table.

Categorical Data Profile Over Time
Inspect categorical metrics across all snapshots

column_name	Window	data_type	count	distinct_count	percent_distinct	min_length	avg_length	max_length
unified_id	2026-05-04 19:20:43.293	string	3118	3118	100.00	35.00	35.00	35.00
phone	2026-05-04 19:20:43.293	string	3118	2992	95.96	12.00	14.02	16.00
resolved_address	2026-05-04 19:20:43.293	string	3118	3064	98.27	10.00	25.12	40.00
cluster_id	2026-05-04 19:20:43.293	string	3118	2995	96.06	3.00	5.85	38.00
resolved_full_name	2026-05-04 19:20:43.293	string	3118	3104	84.70	9.00	12.82	21.00
resolved_postal_code	2026-05-04 19:20:43.293	string	3118	3082	98.85	5.00	6.28	8.00
credit_card	2026-05-04 19:20:43.293	string	3098	3069	99.06	16.00	16.00	16.00
_source	2026-05-04 19:20:43.293	string	3118	2641	84.70	9.00	19.09	38.00

Figure 12.61: Categorical data profiling metrics

Note

Data-profiling statistics change as the underlying data evolves, making it challenging to interpret the results as a fixed snapshot; however, the first iteration should provide sufficient context to convey the intended behavior.

8. Typically, you would keep data profiling enabled to observe how new trends evolve over time. Once it has provided the necessary insights for testing, though, disabling profiling helps minimize resource usage and control training costs.

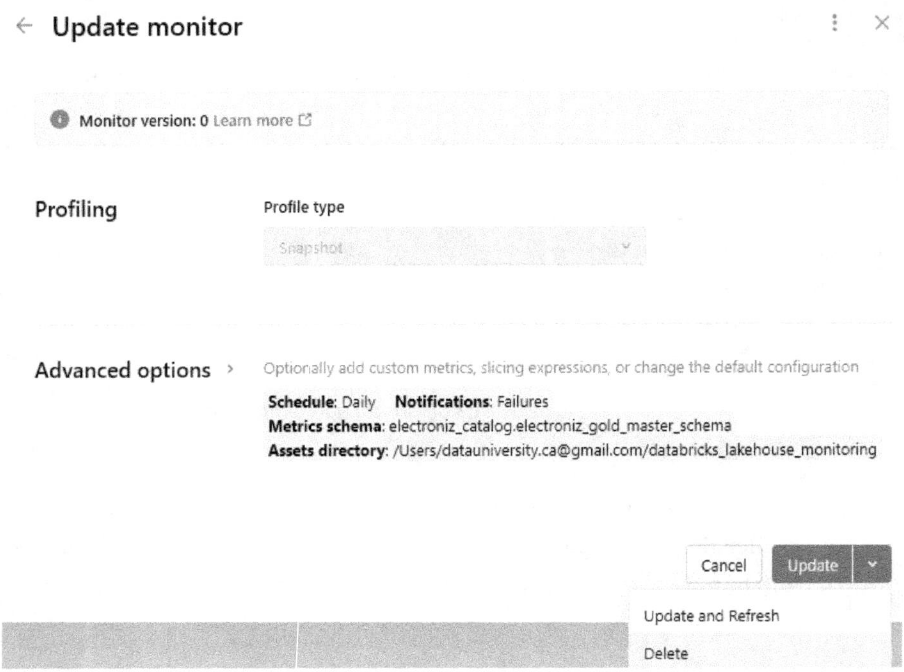

Figure 12.62: Turning data profiling off to conserve resources

As data profiling reveals how your data behaves and how its characteristics evolve over time, the next step is ensuring that someone is accountable for interpreting those insights and acting on them—this is where data stewardship comes in.

Data stewardship

Data stewardship is the human accountability layer of data governance—the set of roles and responsibilities that ensure data is accurate, trusted, well-understood, and used appropriately across an organization. If data governance policies define the rules, data stewards bring those rules to life.

In the last few chapters, we've taken a journey—the journey of data. We followed it through pipelines, transformations, validations, observability checks, and quality checks. We watched it navigate steep bumps, unexpected turns, and operational hazards. And now, that journey has brought us to its **final** destination.

The theme of this book has been the creation of **trusted data products**. We've explored the technical foundations required to make that possible, but we have not yet addressed the final and most essential step: **formulating the data product itself**. This is where data stewardship becomes indispensable. Trusted data products do not emerge from technology alone—they are shaped, validated, and sustained by the people who understand the data, interpret its behavior, and ensure it remains fit for purpose. In this section, we will build a **trusted data product**—the culmination of the entire journey we've taken so far. Everything we've explored up to this point—governance, quality controls, observability, stewardship, contracts, and platform capabilities—has been preparing the ground. Now we bring it all together.

A trusted data product is not simply a dataset with a name; it is a deliberately designed, governed, high-quality asset with a clear purpose, defined consumers, measurable expectations, and human accountability. This is where the technical foundations meet product thinking. This is where stewardship becomes operational. And this is where data finally becomes something people can rely on. In the steps ahead, we will walk through the practical steps required to shape raw, governed data into a product that is discoverable, trustworthy, and ready for real-world use.

> **Note**
>
> The creation of the data product is the moment when the journey of data becomes the value of data.

Before we dive deep into creating the data product, we need to align on the data delivery and consumption process in Databricks, especially how data products are ultimately distributed.

Data distribution and consumption

The journey of a data product doesn't end at the gold layer. The Lakehouse delivery lifecycle—bronze ingestion, silver refinement, gold aggregation—prepares data for consumption, but the actual delivery happens through governed distribution channels. This is where Databricks Marketplace and Delta Sharing come into play.

Traditional method of data distribution

Traditional data distribution services rely on brittle, manual, and inconsistent mechanisms—FTP servers, CSV extracts, custom APIs, and vendor-specific formats—all of which require copying data, managing refresh cycles, and operating without lineage or governance.

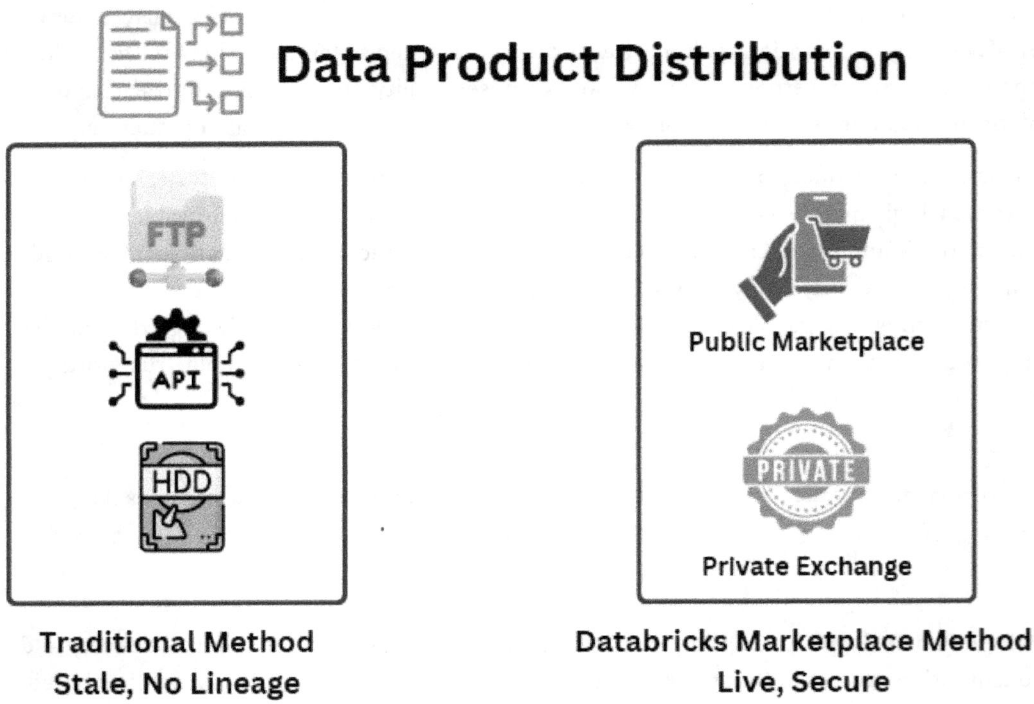

Figure 12.63: Databricks Marketplace

Databricks Marketplace replaces this fragmented approach with live, versioned Delta tables delivered through governed access in Unity Catalog, eliminating data copies and enabling secure, cross-platform consumption.

Databricks Marketplace

Databricks Marketplace provides a commercial and discovery-driven layer on top of the Lakehouse. Databricks Marketplace is a governed, cloud-native exchange where organizations can publish, discover, and consume high-quality data, AI models, and Lakehouse assets. Built on top of the open Delta Sharing protocol, it enables secure, no-copy data access across platforms, making it far more flexible than traditional vendor-locked data exchanges. Marketplace acts as a distribution layer for the Lakehouse, allowing producers to package curated datasets, ML models, notebooks, and dashboards into fully documented, governed data products.

Databricks Marketplace producers

For data product producers such as data stewards, Databricks Marketplace provides a commercial-grade channel for distributing internal or external data products, with built-in governance, usage controls, and monetization options. Listings must meet higher standards of quality, documentation, and trust, as Unity Catalog enforces schema governance, lineage, auditing, and access policies. Producers can offer free, licensed, or paid products, with Databricks handling billing, metering, and subscription management. The following image outlines the key steps that Databricks Marketplace producers follow to publish their data products.

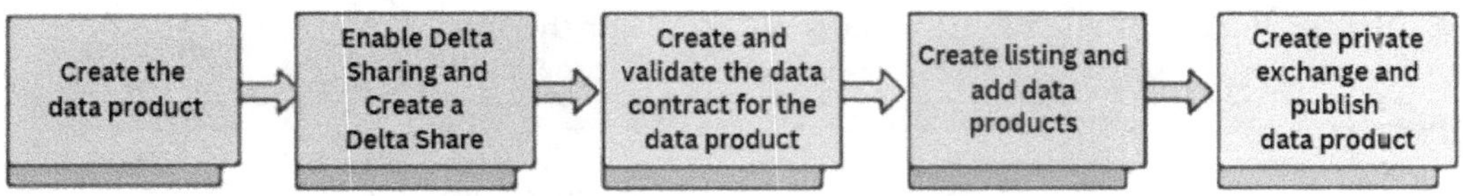

Figure 12.64: Databricks Marketplace producer workflow

Once the data contract has been created, the account administrator enables Delta Sharing at the Databricks account level. From there, the provider selects the tables, dashboards, or notebooks they intend to share. These assets are packaged into a private listing and placed in a private exchange, a controlled environment for governed sharing. Within this exchange, the provider adds members using sharing identifiers and associates the relevant listings with the space. Once this configuration is complete, only the designated members can view and access the shared data or assets, ensuring a secure and fully governed sharing experience.

> **Note**
>
> Organizations can share data through either the public Marketplace or a private, internal exchange. In both cases, Marketplace serves as the final stage of the Databricks data delivery lifecycle—where data products are fully discoverable and ready for consumption.

Databricks Marketplace consumers

For consumers, Databricks Marketplace offers a searchable catalog of ready-to-use data and AI assets that can be evaluated, subscribed to, and used immediately without ETL or data movement. Because access is delivered through Delta Sharing, consumers receive live, versioned data that updates automatically and can be queried directly in Databricks or other compatible platforms. This makes Databricks Marketplace not just a data exchange, but a discovery and operational layer for reusable, trustworthy data products.

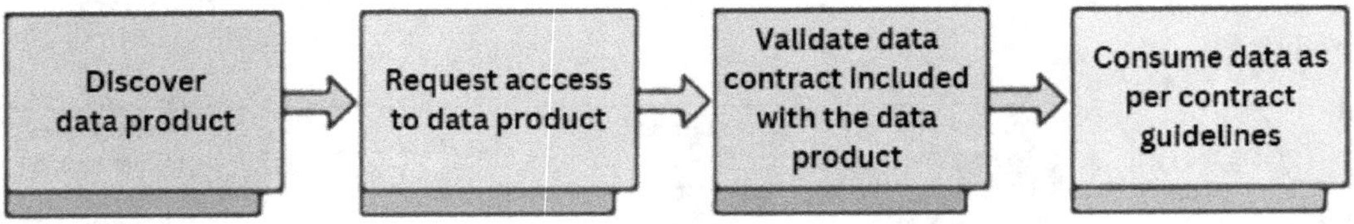

Figure 12.65: Databricks Marketplace consumer workflow

The consumer workflow begins with discovering the data product, followed by requesting access to it. Once access is granted, the consumer reviews the data contract accompanying the product to understand its terms and guarantees. After verifying the contract, the consumer proceeds to use the data in accordance with the agreed-upon guidelines.

Delta Sharing

Delta sharing is the open protocol that powers secure, cross-platform data exchange. It ensures that once a data product is ready for delivery, it can be shared with consumers—inside or outside the organization—without copying data, complex integrations, or locking anyone into a specific platform. Delta Sharing enforces the trust model: governed access, versioned tables, and real-time updates delivered through a standardized interface.

Trusted data products

A trusted data product is not just technically correct; it is **publishable**, **discoverable**, and **shareable** through the Lakehouse's delivery channels. A trusted data product is not simply a dataset with a name; it is a deliberately designed, governed, high-quality asset with a clear purpose, defined consumers, measurable expectations, and human accountability. This is where the technical foundations meet product thinking.

This is where stewardship becomes operational. And this is where data finally becomes something people can rely on. In the role of data producer, the data steward can assign a certification status to a table.

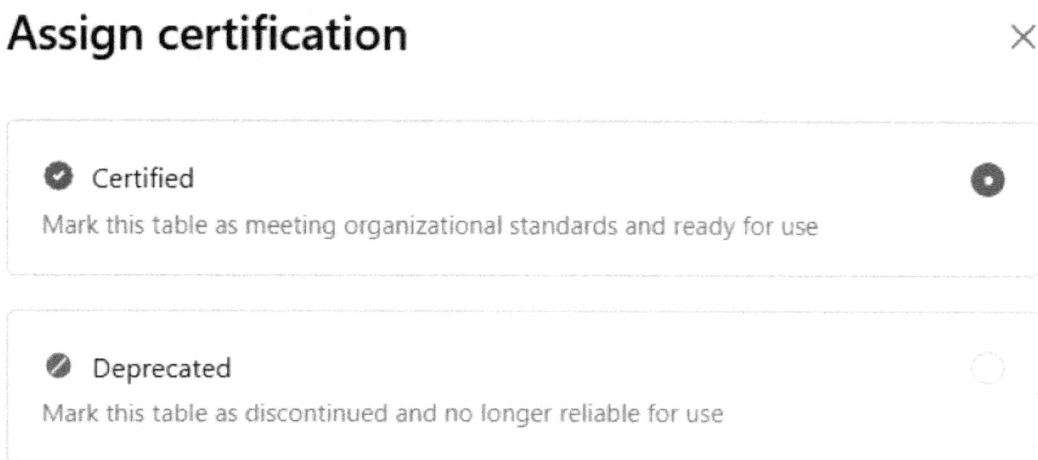

Figure 12.66: Certified data products

They can mark a table as **Certified**, indicating it meets organizational standards and is approved for use, or as Deprecated, signaling it is discontinued and should no longer be relied upon. This certification step helps enforce governance, trust, and clarity across Lakehouse by making the status of each data asset explicit to all consumers.

With this alignment in place, we can now move forward and create a data product that is not only high-quality and well-governed, but also ready for real-world delivery through Databricks Marketplace and Delta Sharing.

Data product creation

In previous steps, we created the customer view **mvw_electroniz_gold_golden_record_customers** as our single source of truth for customer information. We then enriched this materialized view with a set of data quality rules to ensure that every record meets the standards required for downstream analytics, governance, and data product consumption. These rules validate critical attributes, enforce consistency, and provide measurable quality signals that accompany the data as it moves through the Lakehouse delivery lifecycle.

Creating the data product

This **mvw_electroniz_gold_golden_record_customers** materialized view serves as the foundation for building our first Electroniz data product within the master domain. To move from this curated customer record to a fully defined and governed data product, we will follow a series of structured steps executed by the Databricks Marketplace data producers.

1. Connect to the Databricks workspace and run the following SQL in SQL Editor. This SQL will create a new schema under the **electroniz_catalog**.

```
CREATE SCHEMA electroniz_catalog.electroniz_data_products_schema
MANAGED LOCATION 'abfss://gold@electronizlakehouse.dfs.core.windows.net';
```

2. Create the data product table using the SQL below:

```
CREATE or REPLACE TABLE
electroniz_catalog.electroniz_data_products_schema.electroniz_product_golde
n_record_customers
AS
SELECT
unified_id AS customer_id,
resolved_full_name AS customer_name,
CONCAT ('*** ',substring(preferred_email, instr(preferred_email, '@'))) AS
email,
CONCAT ('***-***-', RIGHT (phone, 4)) AS phone,
resolved_postal_code AS postal_code,
CONCAT('*** ', TRIM(REGEXP_EXTRACT(resolved_address, '(Avenue|Road|Street|
Ave)\\.?\\s*$', 1))) AS address,
CONCAT ('****-****-****-', RIGHT(credit_card, 4)) AS credit_card,
'INTERNAL' AS classification,
current_timestamp() AS updated_at
FROM
electroniz_catalog.electroniz_gold_master_schema.mvw_electroniz_gold_golden
_record_customers;
```

You will notice that the data product is a stand-alone table. For an externally shared products, this may sometimes be intentional done to avoid exposing the dynamic-unmask path.

3. The **electroniz_product_golden_record_customers** data product table will appear as shown below. Note that we have applied partial redaction to PII-sensitive columns and assigned an **INTERNAL** classification to reflect the appropriate governance level.

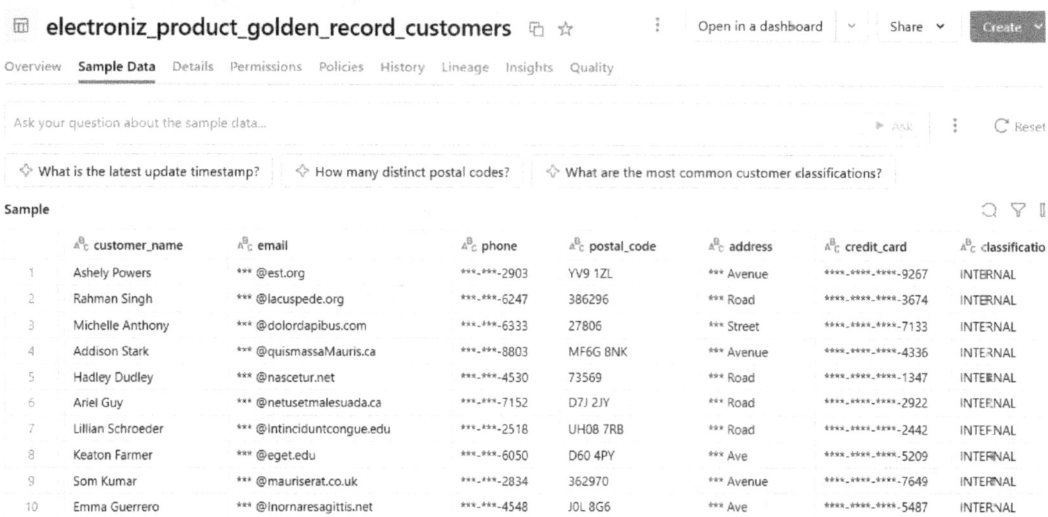

Figure 12.67: Data for the newly created data product

4. Navigate to the **electroniz_product_golden_record_customers** data product table under Catalog. Add a new description using AI Suggested Description. Follow the same steps to generate column descriptions.
5. Now click on the three-dot menu and choose **Assign certification.**

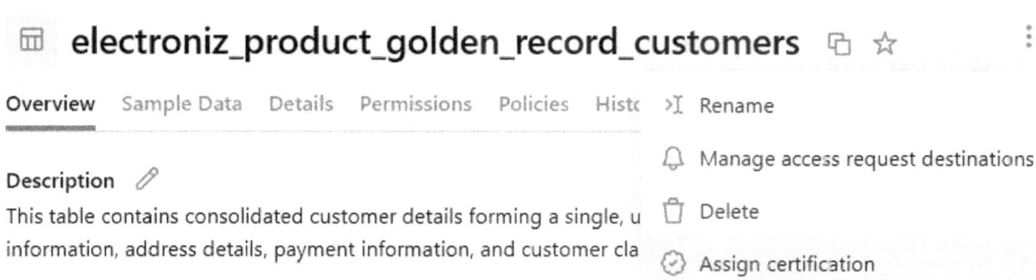

Figure 12.68: Assign certification to the data product

6. Choose **Certified** and press **Save**.

7. Notice the blue check mark next to the data product name. It indicates that this asset meets the criteria for high quality and is now recognized as a trusted data product.

Figure 12.69: Trusted data product

8. We learnt earlier that the Delta Sharing protocol enables secure access to live data. We need to enable delta sharing at the Databricks account level. Click on the Databricks workspace name on the top right and choose **Manage account**. This will open a new window for you.
9. On the new Databricks account window, click on **Catalog**. Choose your metastore entry.
10. Enable the entry Allow Delta Sharing with parties outside your organization. Enter your organization's name as the delta share name, then press Enable.

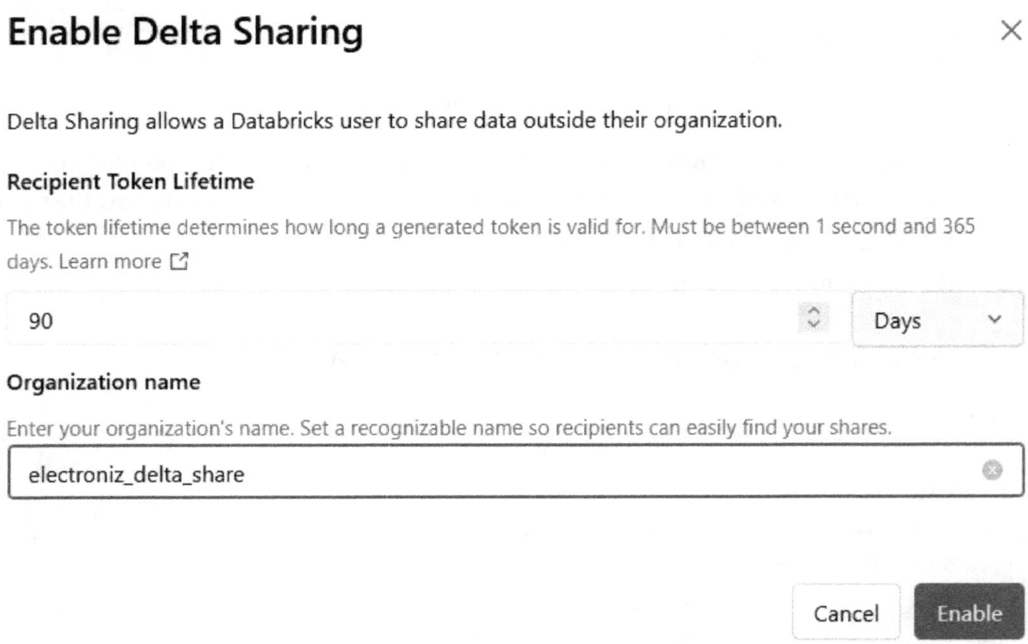

Figure 12.70: Enabling delta sharing at the Databricks account level

11. Navigate back to the Databricks workspace. Navigate to **electroniz_product_golden_record_customers** data product table under **Catalog**.

12. Click on the **Share** button and choose the option of **Share via Delta Sharing**.

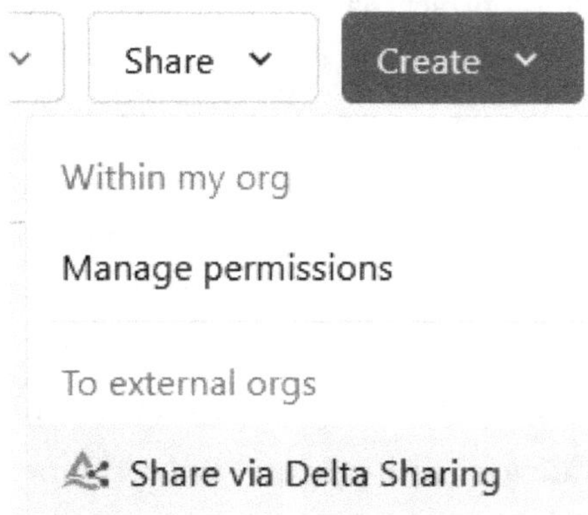

Figure 12.71: Enabling delta sharing for electroniz_product_golden_record_customers

13. This will open a screen where you will fill in some details to proceed. Click on **Create a new share with the table** option. Enter the share name as **electroniz_product_golden_record_customers_ds.**

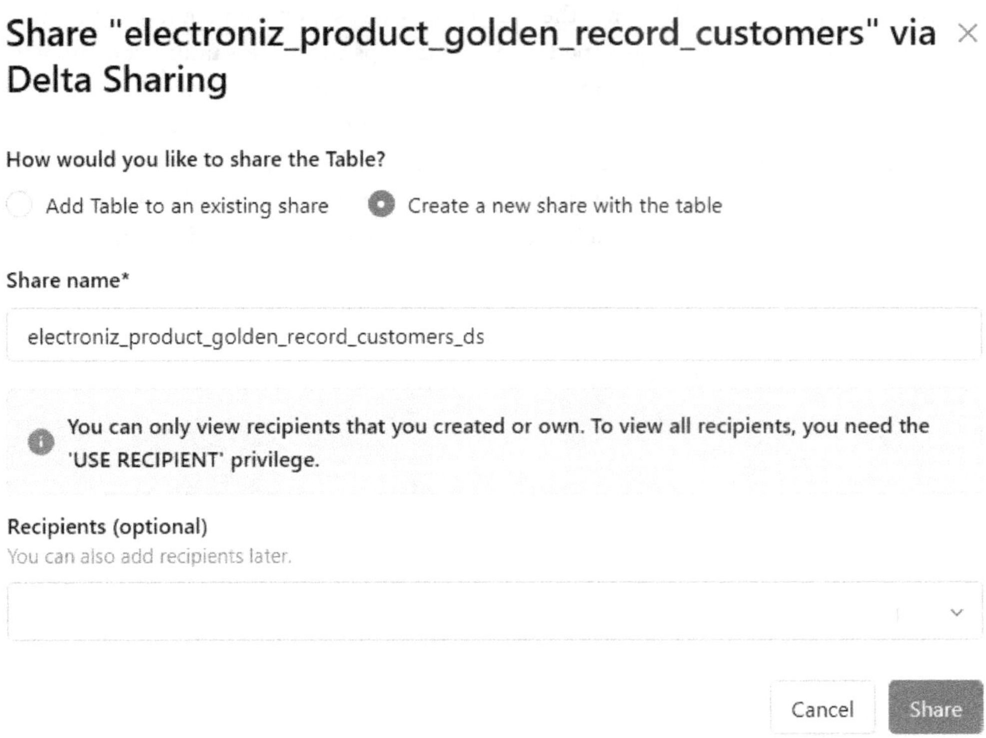

Figure 12.72: Setting up a delta share for electroniz_product_golden_record_customers

The trusted data product is now live and ready for discovery. However, our goal is to publish this asset under a strict data contract that formalizes the agreement between the producer and the consumer.

Creating the data contract

A data contract defines the ownership, structure, semantics, quality expectations, and terms of use for exchanging data between a producer and consumers. It establishes a shared understanding of what the data represents, how it is shaped, and the guarantees that accompany it. A data contract typically includes:

- **Schema definitions** that describe the shape and meaning of the data.
- **Clear responsibilities** for both producer and consumer.
- **Acceptable usage guidelines** that define how the data may be accessed and consumed.
- Documented quality thresholds the data must meet.
- **Change-management expectations** to ensure the data product evolves in a controlled and predictable way.

In practice, the data contract becomes the foundation of trust between domains. It ensures producers deliver reliable, well-governed data, and it helps consumers understand how to use that data safely and consistently within analytical or operational workflows. Data contracts also play a critical role in data discovery by publishing standardized metadata, making it easier for consumers to evaluate whether a data product is fit for their purpose. By exposing structure, semantics, ownership, and guarantees consistently, data contracts accelerate onboarding, reduce ambiguity, and help teams quickly identify the right data assets across the organization.

> Note
>
> Trust is engineered: data contracts define it; data products deliver it.

Every data contract includes the following details:

- **Data product details:** Includes the product name, description, unique identifier, contract version, and status. This metadata also captures governance-related information, including applicable limitations, terms of use, regulatory considerations, and compliance requirements.

```
apiVersion: v3.1.0
kind: DataContract

id: electroniz_product_golden_record_customers
name: Electroniz Golden Record Customers - Data Product Contract
version: 1.0.0
status: active

description:
  purpose: >
    Provides a PII-masked, analyst-safe unified customer data product derived from
    Electroniz's golden record pipeline. All sensitive PII columns (phone, address,
    credit_card, email) are present but masked using standardised redaction patterns,
    making this product safe for sharing across analytics, marketing, and CRM consumers
    who require customer identity data without exposure to raw personal identifiers.

  usage: >
    Used as the primary customer data product for downstream analytics, dashboards,
    and CRM integrations where direct PII access is not required or permitted.
    Consumers should use this data product instead of the upstream golden record
    materialized view.

  limitations: >
    - phone is masked to last 4 digits only (format: ***-***-XXXX)
    - email exposes only the email domain (format: *** @domain.com)
    - credit_card is masked to last 4 digits only (format: ****-****-****-XXXX)
    - address exposes only the street suffix component extracted from the resolved address
    - represents survived (best) attributes per cluster and not raw source records
    - freshness depends on the upstream materialized view refresh cadence
```

Figure 12.73: Data product details in the data contract

- **Data product schema:** Defines the structure and semantics of the data assets included in the product. This covers the table layout, including column definitions, data types, business meaning, and governance attributes such as classification.

```
- name: customer_id
  logicalType: string
  physicalType: STRING
  businessName: Customer ID
  primaryKey: true
  required: true
  unique: true
  classification: internal

  description: >
    Unique identifier assigned to the unified customer entity.
    Deterministically generated from cluster_id in the upstream MDM pipeline.

  examples:
    - "GR-a1b2c3d4e5f6"
    - "GR-f7e8d9c0b1a2"
```

Figure 12.74: Schema details in the data contract

- **Data quality rules:** Defines the rules that ensure the data meets agreed-upon expectations. These include valid-value constraints, row-count thresholds, and custom SQL validation logic.

```
quality:

  - type: sql
    description: customer_id must be unique
    query: >
      SELECT COUNT(*) AS invalid_count
      FROM (
        SELECT customer_id
        FROM electroniz_catalog.electroniz_data_products_schema.electroniz_product_golden_record_customers
        GROUP BY customer_id
        HAVING COUNT(*) > 1
      ) t

    mustBe: 0

  - type: sql
    description: email must remain masked
    query: >
      SELECT COUNT(*) AS invalid_count
      FROM electroniz_catalog.electroniz_data_products_schema.electroniz_product_golden_record_customers
      WHERE email NOT LIKE '*** @%'

    mustBe: 0
```

Figure 12.75: Data quality rules in the data contract

- **Data owners and stewards**: Specifies the individuals and teams responsible for owning and maintaining the data product and the data contract. This includes the team's name, a brief description of their role, identified members and their responsibilities, and the support channels consumers can use to contact them.

```
team:

  - username: data.owner@electroniz.com
    name: Data Owner
    role: dataOwner
    description: >
      Accountable for governance, lifecycle management,
      and approval of contract-level changes.

  - username: data.steward@electroniz.com
    name: Data Steward
    role: dataSteward
    description: >
      Responsible for metadata quality, contract validation,
      and consumer coordination.

  - username: data.engineering@electroniz.com
    name: Data Engineering Team
    role: dataCustodian
    description: >
      Responsible for implementation, deployment,
      storage, operational reliability,
      and refresh management.
```

Figure 12.76: Team details in the data contract

- **SLA**: Service Level Agreements define the non-functional guarantees of the data product, such as freshness, availability, and update frequency. These commitments help consumers determine whether the data meets the requirements of their specific use cases.

```
slaProperties:

  - property: availability
    value: 99.9%
    description: >
      Availability inherited from Databricks platform SLA.

  - property: freshness
    value: "5"
    unit: minutes
    description: >
      Data freshness depends on upstream materialized view refresh cadence.

  - property: retention
    value: "2"
    unit: years
    description: >
      Retention inherited from upstream golden record storage policy.
```

Figure 12.77: Service level agreement details in the data contract

- **Servers**: Provides the connectivity details for where the data resides. This includes the server configuration and the connection information required for each environment.

```
servers:

  - server: production
    environment: prod
    type: databricks

    catalog: electroniz_catalog
    schema: electroniz_data_products_schema

    jdbcUrl: "jdbc:databricks://<DATABRICKS_URL>:443/default;transportMode=http;s
```

Figure 12.78: Server details in the data contract

> **Note**
>
> The leading industry framework for defining data contracts is the Open Data Contract Standard (ODCS). With the release of ODCS 3.1, the ecosystem now has a unified, mature, and widely adopted specification.

The creation of a data contract typically begins with defining an ODCS-compliant specification —a collaborative effort involving data owners, data stewards, and data engineers. Together, these stakeholders establish the structure, semantics, quality expectations, and governance rules that will guide the data product's behavior and reliability.

Validating the data contract

Before a data product can be published, its data contract must be thoroughly validated to ensure it is accurate, complete, and compliant with ODCS standards. The following are some well-known data contract validation patterns:

- **Producer validation:** By validating the data contract upfront, data producers establish a reliable foundation for trust, reduce downstream surprises for consumers, and ensure the data product is ready for governed distribution through platforms like the Databricks Marketplace.
- **Consumer validation:** By validating the data contract downstream, consumers review and confirm that the contract accurately reflects their expectations and usage needs.

- **CI/CD validation:** In mature data environments, data contracts are not only authored and reviewed manually—they are also validated automatically through a **CI/CD pipeline**. This automation ensures that every change to the contract is tested, verified, and governed before it can impact downstream consumers.

For training purposes and for data contract validation purposes, we will use a predefined ODCS data contract available at: `https://github.com/PacktPublishing/Data-Engineering-with-Apache-Spark-Databricks-and-Lakehouse-Second-Edition/blob/main/chapter12/datacontract_valid.yaml`.

It is highly recommended that the reader review the data contract YAML file in detail and familiarize themselves with its structure, fields, and semantics. Understanding the contract firsthand makes it easier to follow the validation steps and appreciate how each component contributes to the overall data product design.

1. Log in to the Databricks workspace and navigate to **Workspace**. Click on **Create** > **Notebook**.
2. On the File menu, click on **Import**. Choose the URL radio button. For URL, enter `https://github.com/PacktPublishing/Data-Engineering-with-Apache-Spark-Databricks-and-Lakehouse-Second-Edition/blob/main/chapter12/electroniz_data-contract_validator.ipynb`.
3. Click **Import**.
4. Let's walk through the logic behind the data contract validation notebook, examining each cell step by step.

```
%pip install 'datacontract-cli'
%pip install soda-core-spark-df
```

Figure 12.79: Importing datacontract-cli library

With reference to importing the first Python library, the datacontract CLI is an open-source (`https://github.com/datacontract/datacontract-cli`) library designed for working with data contracts. It provides native support for the Open Data Contract Standard, allowing you to lint contracts, connect to data sources, run schema and data-quality tests, and export contracts into multiple formats. Built in Python, it can be used as a standalone CLI utility, integrated into CI/CD pipelines, or imported directly as a Python library. **Run** this cell.

5. Also run the next cell to restart Python.
6. The next cell contains instructions for downloading the predefined ODCS data contract and running a lint check on it. Linting performs automated validations to ensure the contract is well-formed, internally consistent, and fully compliant with the ODCS specification.

```python
import requests
from datacontract.data_contract import DataContract

# Step 1: Download YAML from GitHub
url = "https://raw.githubusercontent.com/PacktPublishing/Data-Engineering-with-Apache-Spark-Databricks-and-Lakehouse-Second-Edition/refs/heads/main/chapter12/datacontract_valid.yaml"

response = requests.get(url)
response.raise_for_status()

yaml_path = "/tmp/datacontract_valid.yaml"
with open(yaml_path, "w") as f:
    f.write(response.text)

print("Downloaded successfully!")

# Step 2: Use the /tmp path to create a DataContract object
dc = DataContract(data_contract_file=yaml_path, spark=spark)

# Lint check
lint_result = dc.lint()
print("Lint Result:", lint_result.result)
print("\nValidation checks:")
for check in lint_result.checks:
    print(f"  [{check.result}] {check.name}: {check.reason}")
```

Figure 12.80: Linting the data contract

7. **Run** this cell. You should receive the message below. This confirms that the data contract is well-formed and fully compliant with the ODCS specification, making it ready for use.

```
Downloaded successfully!
Lint Result: ResultEnum.passed

Validation checks:
  [ResultEnum.passed] Data contract is syntactically valid: None
```

Figure 12.81: Linting results

8. **Run** the next cell. The next cell contains instructions to execute the data contract's schema and data-quality tests against the actual data source defined in the contract.

```
test_result = dc.test()

print("Test Result:", test_result.result)
print("\nChecks:")
for check in test_result.checks:
    print(f"  [{check.result}] {check.name}: {check.reason}")
#To display the results in a table

import pandas as pd

rows = []
for check in test_result.checks:
    rows.append({
        "Check": check.name,
        "Result": str(check.result),
        "Reason": check.reason or ""
    })

df = pd.DataFrame(rows)
display(df)
```

Figure 12.82: Testing the data contract

9. The schema and data-quality tests are automatically inferred from the ODCS data contract. Each test is validated against data product assets such as tables.

```
Test Result: ResultEnum.passed

Checks:
  [ResultEnum.passed] Check that field 'customer_id' is present:
  [ResultEnum.passed] Check that field customer_id has type STRING:
  [ResultEnum.passed] Check that field customer_id has no missing values:
  [ResultEnum.passed] Check that unique field customer_id has no duplicate values:
  [ResultEnum.passed] Check that field 'customer_name' is present:
  [ResultEnum.passed] Check that field customer_name has type STRING:
  [ResultEnum.passed] Check that field 'email' is present:
  [ResultEnum.passed] Check that field email has type STRING:
  [ResultEnum.passed] Check that field 'phone' is present:
  [ResultEnum.passed] Check that field phone has type STRING:
  [ResultEnum.passed] Check that field 'postal_code' is present:
  [ResultEnum.passed] Check that field postal_code has type STRING:
  [ResultEnum.passed] Check that field 'address' is present:
  [ResultEnum.passed] Check that field address has type STRING:
  [ResultEnum.passed] Check that field 'credit_card' is present:
  [ResultEnum.passed] Check that field credit_card has type STRING:
  [ResultEnum.passed] Check that field 'classification' is present:
  [ResultEnum.passed] Check that field classification has type STRING:
```

Table +

	Check	Result	Reason
1	Check that field 'customer_id' is present	ResultEnum.passed	
2	Check that field customer_id has type STRING	ResultEnum.passed	
3	Check that field customer_id has no missing values	ResultEnum.passed	
4	Check that unique field customer_id has no duplicate values	ResultEnum.passed	
5	Check that field 'customer_name' is present	ResultEnum.passed	
6	Check that field customer_name has type STRING	ResultEnum.passed	
7	Check that field 'email' is present	ResultEnum.passed	
8	Check that field email has type STRING	ResultEnum.passed	

Figure 12.83: Data contract test results

A successful test run confirms that the data contract is valid, enforceable, and ready to be shared with downstream consumers. Now that the data product is fully prepared and its data contract has been defined and validated, we can proceed with publishing it on the Databricks Marketplace.

Listing the data product

Listing a data product on the Databricks Marketplace involves publishing it to make it discoverable and accessible to consumers across the Databricks ecosystem. The following are the steps to make that happen.

1. Connect to the Databricks workspace; using the menu on the left, click on **Marketplace**.
2. Click on **Provider console**. Access to the provider services requires the **Marketplace admin role.**
3. Click on **Assign Marketplace Admin**. This will take you to a new **User management** window.
4. Toggle the **Marketplace admin role** and return to your Databricks workspace window.
5. Now you will be able to see the **Create provider profile**. If you are still unable to view this option, click on **Refresh page**.

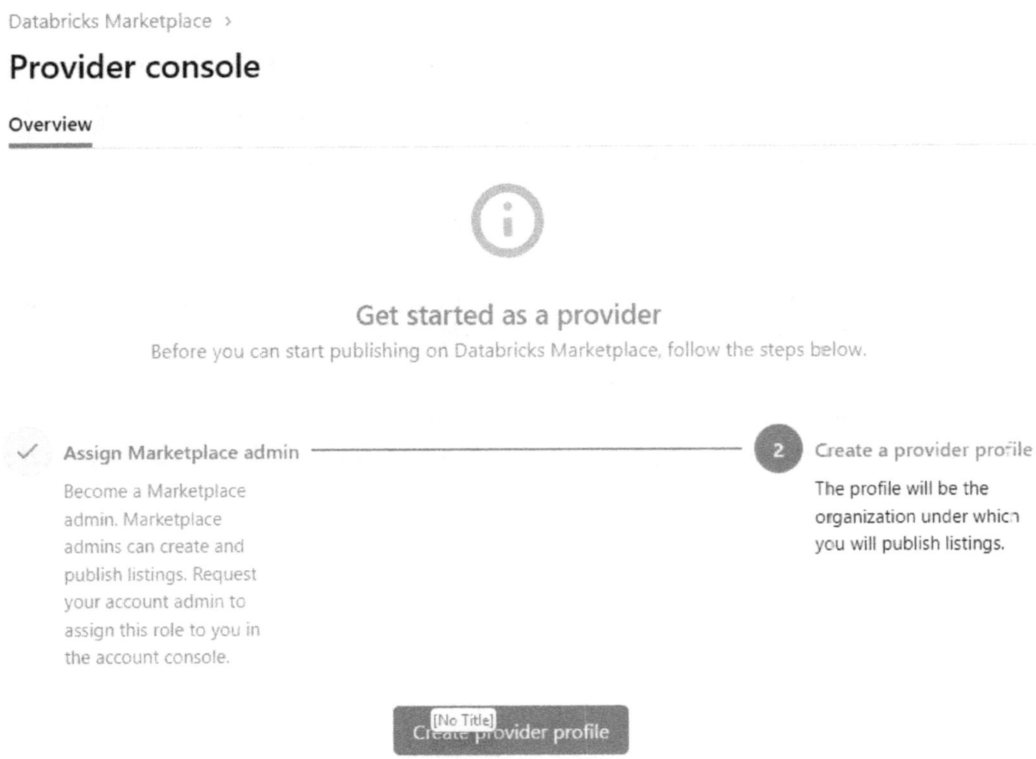

Figure 12.84: Creating the data provider profile

6. Navigate back to the Databricks workspace and click on the round icon with your initial on it. Take note of your Databricks account ID and Delta Sharing ID as marked in the image below. You will need them later.

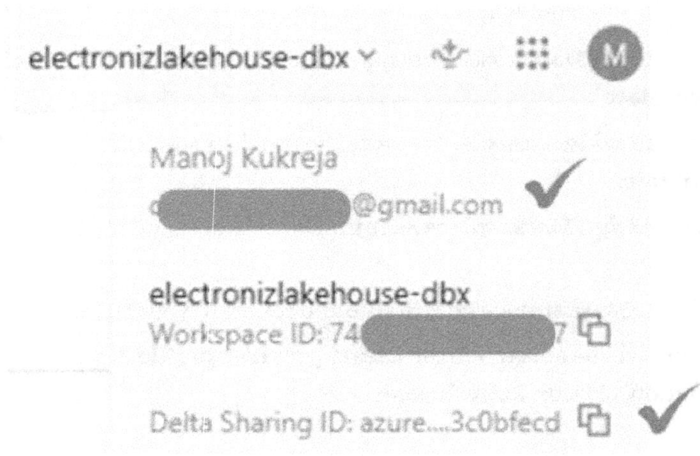

Figure 12.85: Noting down Databricks account ID and Delta Sharing ID

7. Replace the `<DATABRICKS_ACCOUNT_ID>` in the following SQL with your Databricks account ID noted in the previous step and run it on SQL Editor.

```
GRANT USE_RECIPIENT ON METASTORE TO `<DATABRICKS_ACCOUNT_ID>`;
```

8. Navigate back to the Provider Console. Databricks Marketplace requires a profile even when you're only creating private exchanges. This profile represents your organization's identity as a data publisher on the Databricks Marketplace and is used by Databricks to associate your listings and exchanges with your company. It's a one-time setup—once created, you won't need to modify it again. Click on **Create provider profile**.

9. Enter the profile with details as follows:
    a. Enter Provider name: Electroniz
    b. Logo: Download and upload the Electroniz logo from `https://github.com/PacktPublishing/Data-Engineering-with-Apache-Spark-Databricks-and-Lakehouse-Second-Edition/blob/main/chapter12/Electroniz_logo.png`.
    c. Description:

    ```
    Electroniz is a retail and e-commerce provider operating across both
    physical and digital storefronts, specializing in consumer
    electronics and household appliances. The company offers a broad
    product catalog spanning personal electronics (mobile devices,
    watches, keyboards, mice, monitors), home entertainment (TVs, DVDs),
    and home appliance categories (air conditioners, microwaves, vacuum
    cleaners).
    Data assets listed by Electroniz consist of master customer data,
    specifically PII-masked golden record customer profiles derived from
    an MDM survivorship pipeline. These assets provide de-duplicated,
    survivorship-resolved customer entities containing unified
    identifiers, cluster identifiers, resolved customer names, and postal
    codes – curated for safe consumption by trusted private exchange
    partners without exposure to sensitive personal identifiers.
    ```

    d. Organization website: `https://www.electroniz.com`
    e. Business email: `info@electroniz.com`
    f. Support email: `support@electroniz.com`
    g. Terms of service: `https://www.electroniz.com/terms`
    h. Privacy policy: `https://www.electroniz.com/privacy`

10. Click on **Submit profile**.

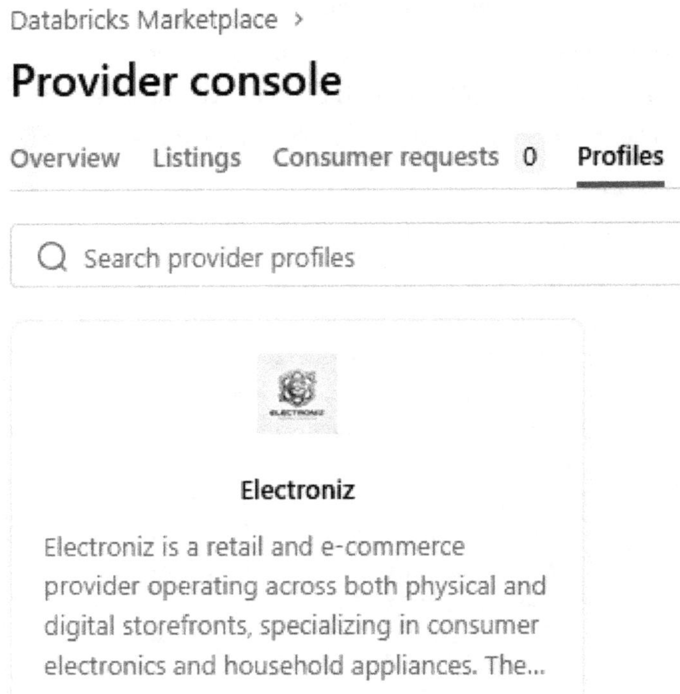

Figure 12.86: Electroniz provider profile

11. Click on the **Listings** tab to create a new listing.
12. Click on **Create listing** and fill in the details as under:
    a. Listing name: Electroniz Master Customer List
    b. Provider profile: Electroniz
    c. How can consumers access the assets listed?: Customers must request access to the listing
    d. Publish to*: Private Exchange
    e. Click on **Continue**.
13. Under **Assets**, choose **Tables** and **Notebooks**.
14. Click on **Continue**.
15. Under Attributes, for Categories choose Commerce. For Update Frequency, choose 5 minutes.
16. Click on **Continue**.

17. Under Details, or Short Description:

```
Electroniz masked MDM golden customer records with deduplicated profiles,
customer IDs, and PII-safe attributes for analytics consumption.
```

18. For Description, remove the existing text and replace it with the updated version below. This enhanced description provides richer detail, offering greater visibility and clarity during the discovery process.

```
Electroniz Master Customer Data – PII-Masked Golden Customer Records

Electroniz Master Customer Data provides a trusted, analytics-ready
customer dataset designed for secure consumption across reporting, CRM,
customer intelligence, and downstream analytical workloads. The product
delivers de-duplicated customer profiles consolidated across Electroniz
retail and e-commerce operations, enabling consumers to work with a single
authoritative customer representation instead of fragmented source-system
records.

This data product is curated for private exchange consumers who require
reliable customer intelligence while maintaining strict protection of
personally identifiable information (PII). All sensitive customer
attributes are masked using standardized redaction patterns, making the
dataset suitable for broader internal analytics and approved partner use
cases without exposing raw personal identifiers.

**Key Use Cases**

**Customer Analytics & Segmentation** Build customer cohorts, behavioural
analysis models, customer lifetime value calculations, and segmentation
strategies using unified customer entities across physical and online
channels.

**CRM & Customer Intelligence** Improve customer visibility and downstream
operational consistency by integrating standardized customer records into
CRM, reporting, and customer intelligence platforms.

**BI Reporting & Operational Dashboards** Use as a trusted customer
dimension dataset for reporting unique customer counts, regional trends,
postal-code analysis, and operational metrics.
```

```
**Safe Data Sharing & Governance** Enable secure analytics consumption
using masked customer attributes aligned with internal governance and data-
sharing standards.

**Dataset Features**
- De-duplicated customer profiles
- Deterministic customer identifiers
- PII-masked customer attributes
- Standardized customer schema - Analytics-ready tabular structure
- Governed through a published data contract
- Compatible with Databricks SQL, notebooks, dashboards, and downstream BI
tools

**Included Fields**
***customer_id*** – Deterministic customer identifier for each resolved
customer entity
***customer_name*** – Unified customer name selected using survivorship
logic ***postal_code*** – Resolved postal or ZIP code associated with the
customer ***email*** – Masked email exposing domain information only
***phone*** – Masked phone number exposing last four digits only
***address*** – Partially masked address exposing only street suffix
information
***credit_card*** – Masked payment card exposing last four digits only
***classification*** – Internal data classification indicator
***updated_at*** – Timestamp representing the latest dataset refresh
execution

***Masking Standards** -
***email*** → *** @domain.com -
***phone*** → ***-***-1234 -
***credit_card*** → ****-****-****-5678 -
***address*** → *** Avenue

**Quality & Governance**

This product is governed through a published data contract with schema,
masking, uniqueness, and quality validations enforced during refresh
operations. Customer identifiers are guaranteed to be unique, and the
dataset maintains row-level parity with the upstream golden customer
dataset because only masking and projection transformations are applied.
```

*A notebook validating this data asset against its published data contract is attached below for reference. *

19. For notebook choose the `electroniz_data-contract_validator.ipynb`
    a. Documentation: `https://www.electroniz.com/documentation`
    b. Privacy policy: `https://www.electroniz.com/privacy`
    c. License: https: `http://www.electroniz.com/license`
    d. Terms of service: `https://www.electroniz.com/terms`
20. Click on **Publish**. Once published, the listing should look like this.

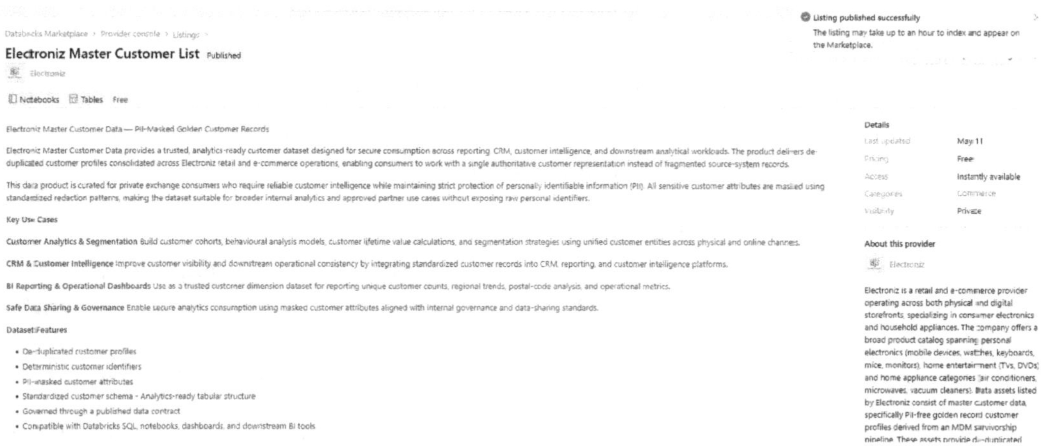

Figure 12.87: Electroniz marketplace published listing

21. So far so good. Next, we navigate back to the Provider console and click the **Exchanges** tab.
22. Click on Create exchange.
23. For Exchange name, enter Electroniz Private Exchange.
24. Click on **Create**. Now click on the newly created exchange **Electroniz Private Exchange**.
25. Click on Add Listing. Choose Electroniz Master Customer List.
26. Click on Add listing.
27. Now click on **Members**.

28. Click on **Add member**.
29. For Member Name, add Electroniz Members List.
30. For Sharing identifier, add the Delta Sharing ID noted in step 6.
31. Click on **Add member**.

At this point, the Databricks listing is fully configured, published, and live—ready for users to discover and subscribe to. Allow Databricks approximately 15–20 minutes after creating the listing for it to propagate and become visible to consumers during discovery. The propagation delay results from the asynchronous indexing process used across the Databricks Marketplace discovery infrastructure. If the listing has not surfaced after 20 minutes, verify that:

- Your provider profile is active
- Delta Share configuration is valid
- The listing status shows **Published** in the provider console.

After the data product appears in Databricks Marketplace, you may continue with the discovery process described in the following section.

Discovering the data product

Discovering the data product is the first step a consumer takes when engaging with the published content. Through the Databricks Marketplace or your private exchange, consumers can browse, search, and evaluate available listings, review their descriptions and metadata, and understand the value the product provides before requesting access or subscribing.

For the following steps, we will log in using a different user account with limited permissions. Earlier, during the **Fine-Grained Access Control** (**FGAC**) testing, we created two such users—`finance_analyst_1` and `finance_analyst_2`. You can use either of these accounts to simulate the data-product discovery experience.

1. Using a different browser than the one you normally use for Databricks, sign in to the Databricks workspace as `finance_analyst_2`.

2. Navigate to **Marketplace**. Type *master customer* in the search box. The data product should show up first in the list.

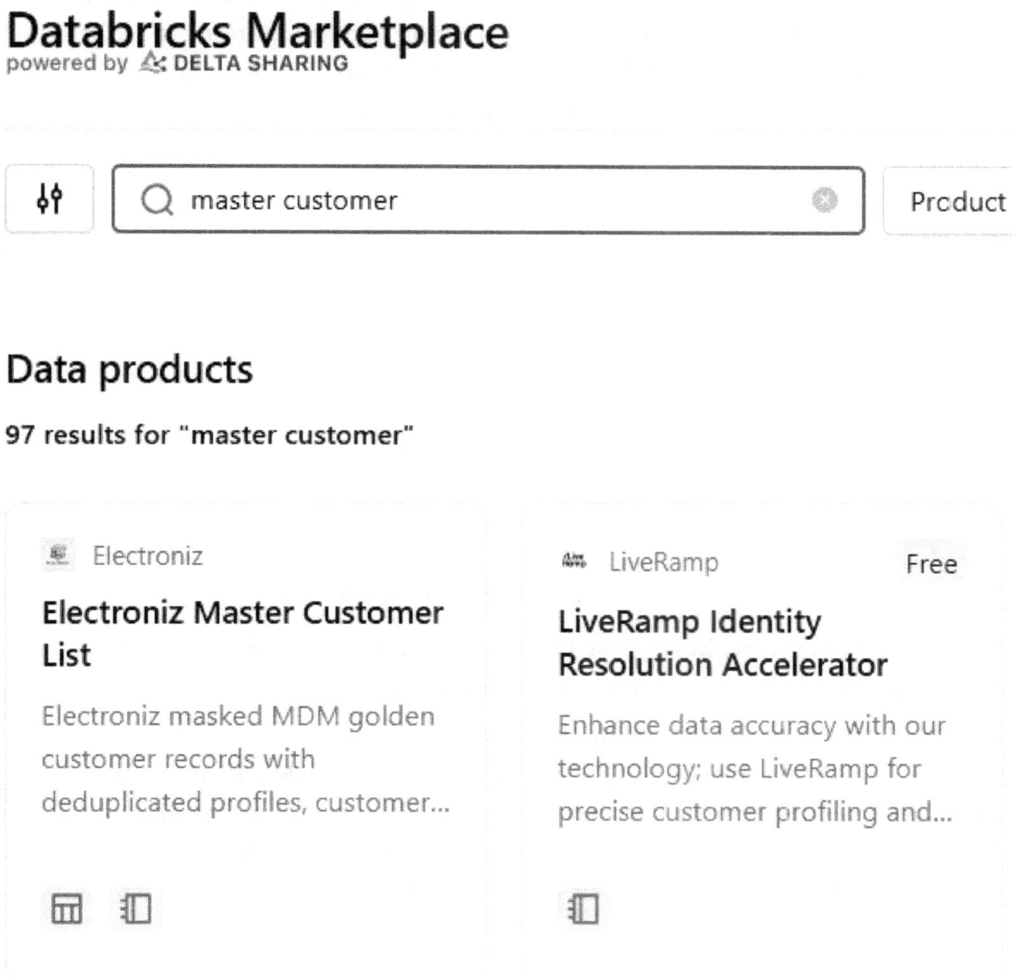

Figure 12.88: Searching for the data product

3. Click on the **Electroniz Master Customer List**. Notice the rich metadata included in the data product—such as its description, intended use cases, and provider information. This metadata plays a critical role in helping consumers quickly understand what the product offers, how to use it, and who is responsible for maintaining it. Well-crafted metadata not only improves discoverability but also builds trust by giving consumers the context they need to evaluate the product before subscribing.

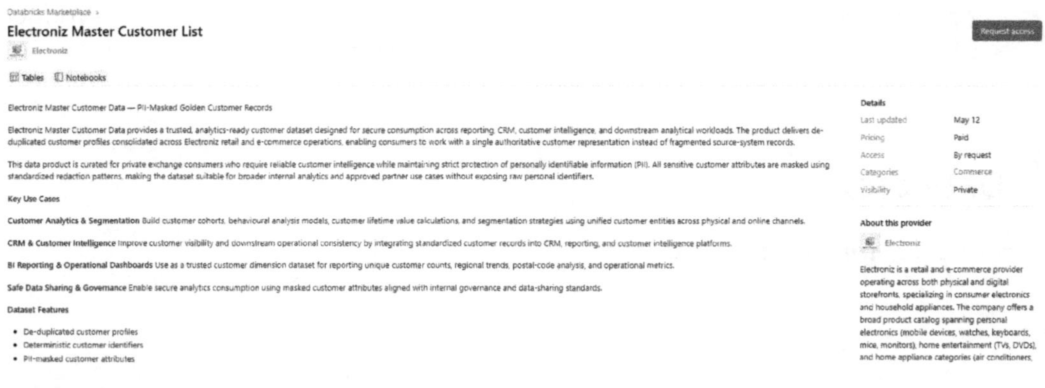

Figure 12.89: Data product metadata

4. Once the consumer has reviewed the listing and finds the offering valuable, the next step is to submit a request for access to the data product.

Requesting access to the data product

Requesting access is the step where a consumer formally signals their intent to use the data product. After reviewing the listing details, metadata, and usage terms, the consumer submits an access request, which is then routed to the product owner for approval. Once approved, the consumer can begin interacting with the data product in accordance with the permissions and policies defined by the provider.

1. Click on **Request access**. Enter the details as shown below, accept the usage terms, and click on **Request access**.

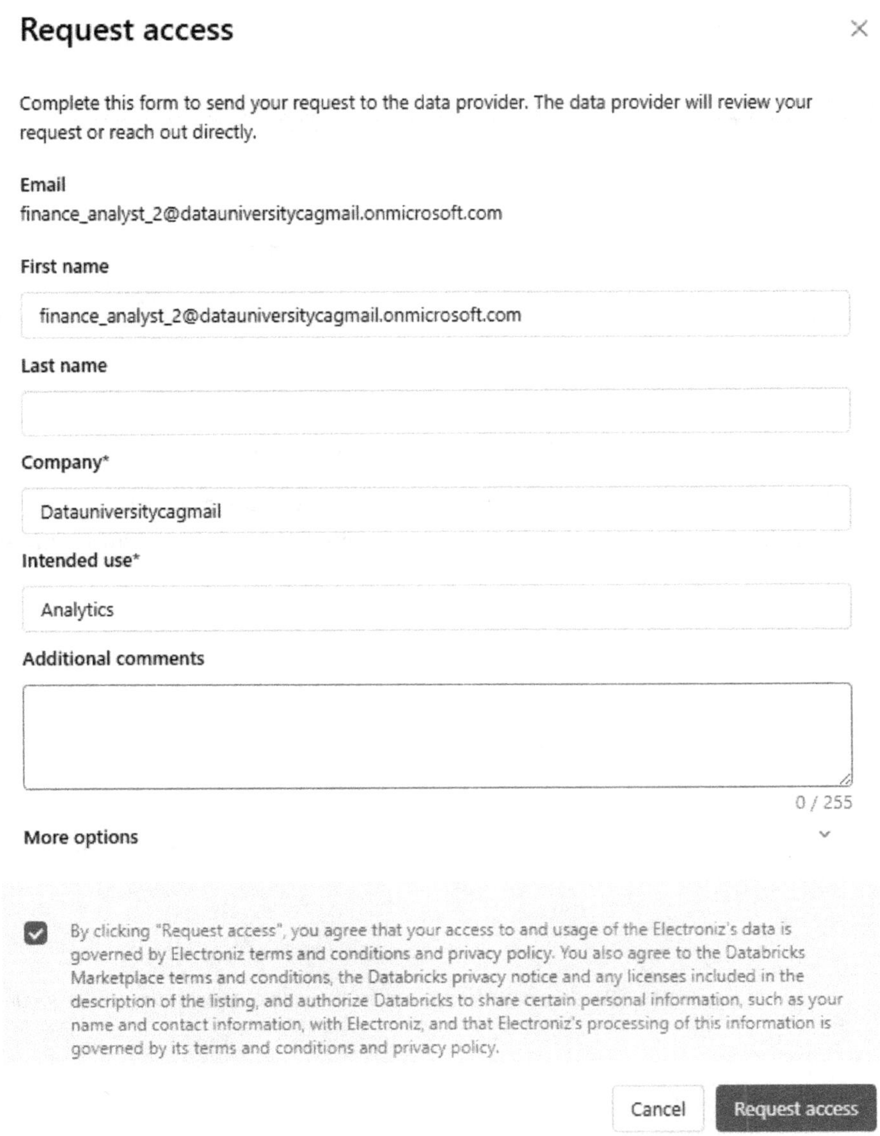

Figure 12.90: Requesting access to the data product

2. At this point, an access request is submitted to the data product owner, who must review and approve it before you can begin using the data product. Until access is granted, your request will remain pending. Go back to the Marketplace screen and click on **My requests** on the top right.

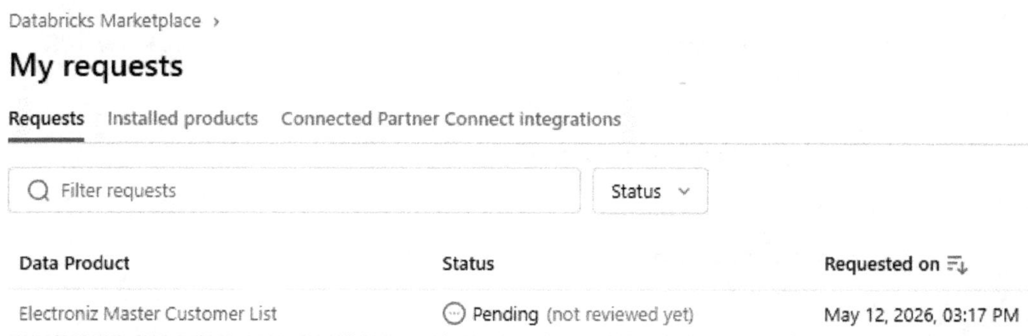

Figure 12.91: Pending consumer request for the data product in the consumer queue

3. We now need to switch back to the provider's role to approve this request. Log in to the Provider Console again and review the pending access request. You should see a new request

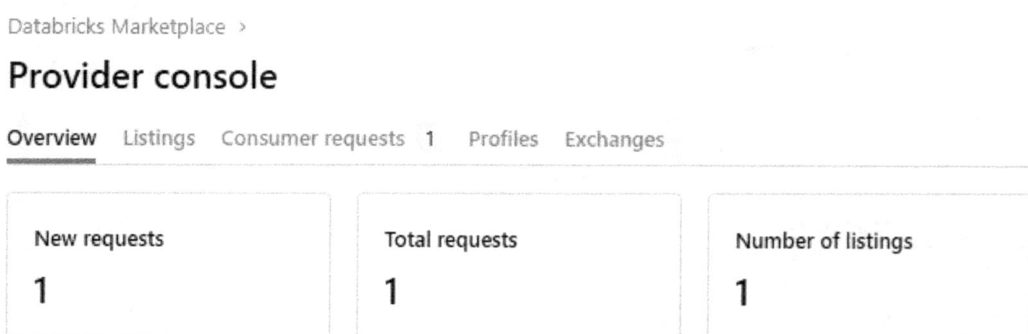

Figure 12.92: Pending provider request for the data product in the producer queue

4. Click on **Consumer requests**. You should see the new request as below:

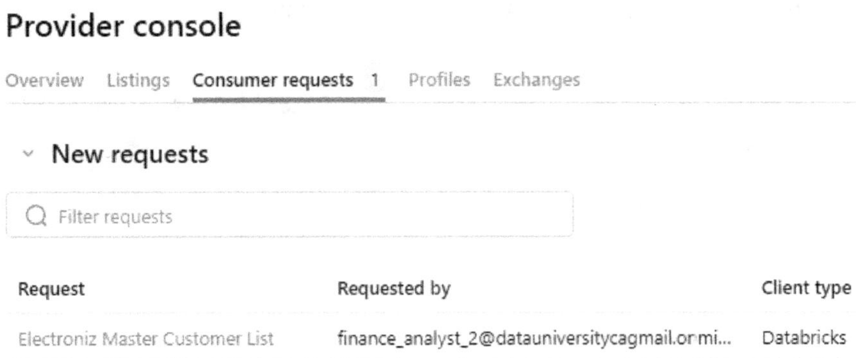

Figure 12.93: List of pending requests in the provider queue

5. Click on **Electroniz Master Customer List**. This will open a **Review request** window as under:

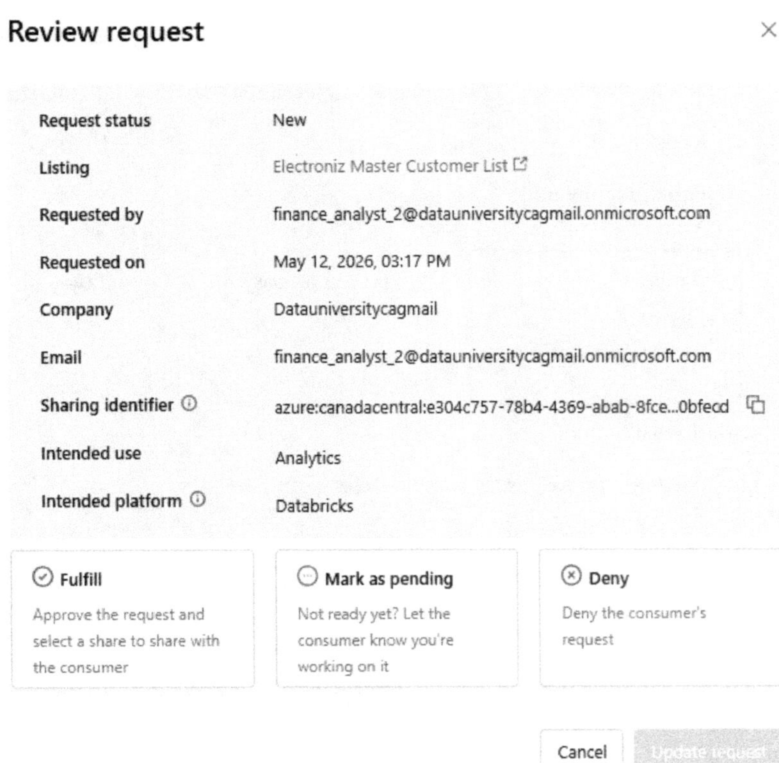

Figure 12.94: Review the pending request

6. At this stage, the provider can choose to fulfill the request, deny it, or leave it marked as pending. We will proceed with approving the request.
7. Click on **Fulfill**.
8. For Select a share, choose `electroniz_product_golden_record_customers_ds`. Click on **Update request**.

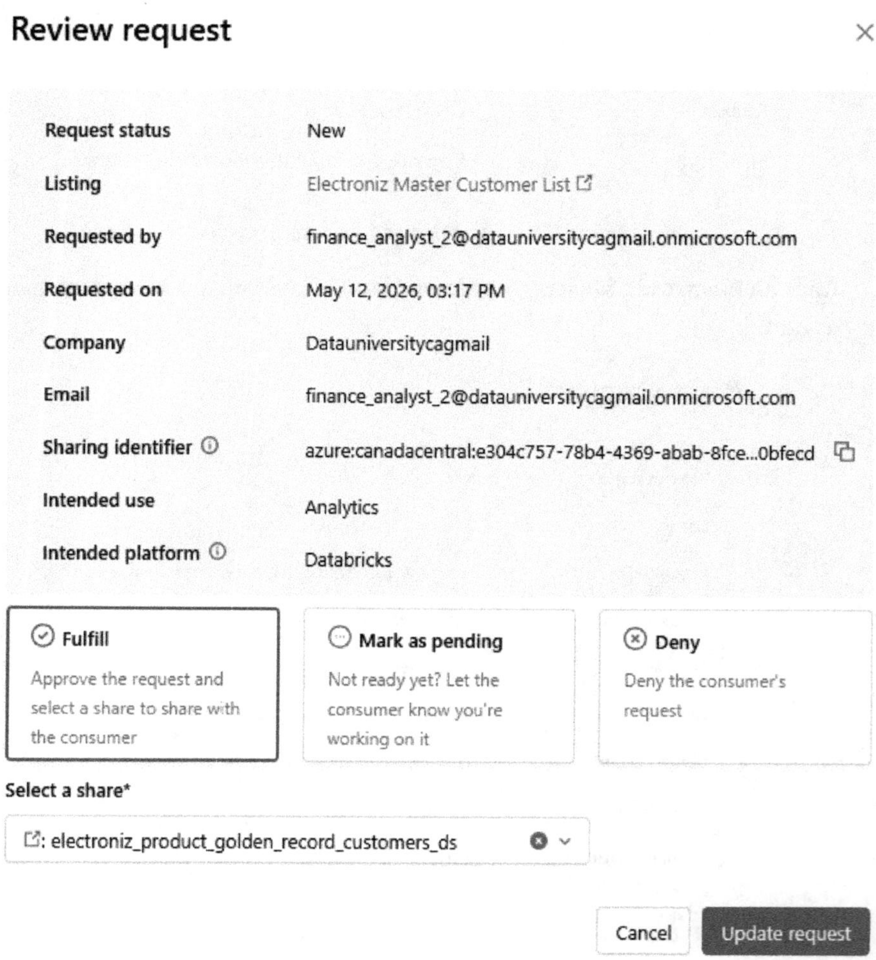

Figure 12.95: Fulfilling the pending request

Fulfilling data product access requests is a core responsibility of the data steward, ensuring that only the right consumers receive the appropriate level of access in alignment with governance policies and usage terms. As a data steward, you can deny the request if it does not meet policy, quality, or compliance requirements, or you may mark it as *Pending* when further investigation or input from other stakeholders is needed. Depending on usage conditions, once the request has been granted, the data steward may revoke access if the consumer no longer requires the data.

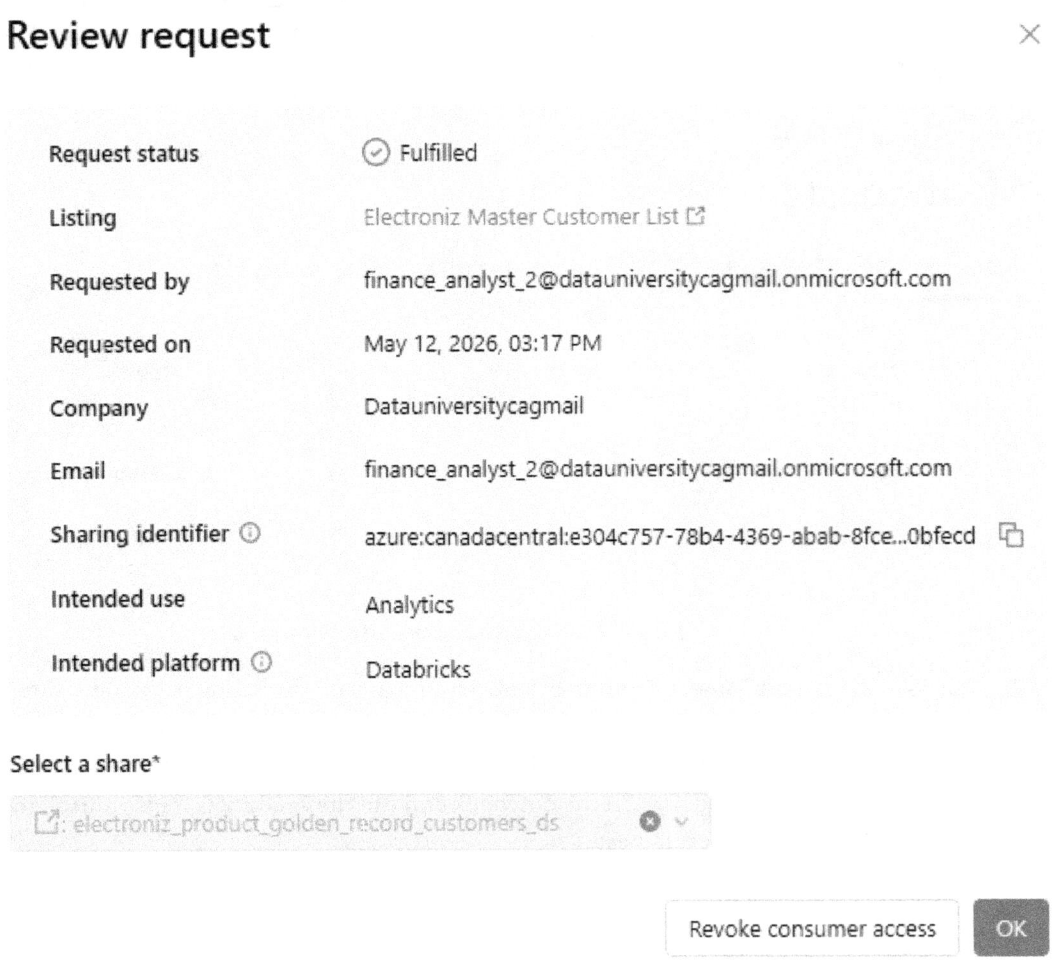

Figure 12.96: Revoking data product access request

Validating the data contract (Consumer)

Validating the data contract from the consumer's perspective ensures that the published contract accurately reflects the structure, semantics, and quality expectations of the data they intend to use. This step allows consumers to independently confirm that the contract aligns with their analytical or operational needs before subscribing to or integrating the data product.

1. Sign back in to the Databricks workspace as `finance_analyst_2`. Refresh the My requests page—your previously pending request should now appear with a status of **Fulfilled**.

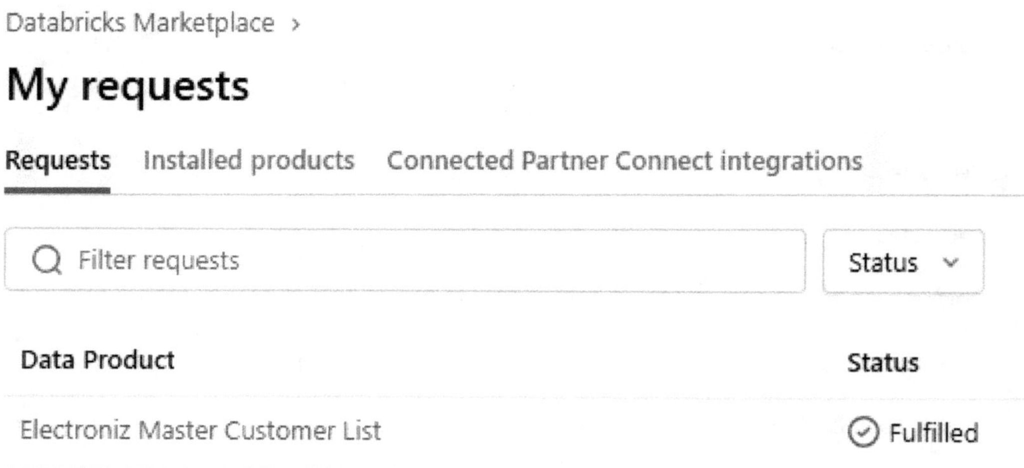

Figure 12.97: Data product request fulfilled

2. Click on **Electroniz Master Customer List.** Scroll down on the listing page and locate the Data Contract Validator notebook. This notebook allows consumers to independently verify that the published contract is accurate and aligns with the actual data. You are encouraged to open the notebook and run the validation steps yourself to confirm the contract's correctness.

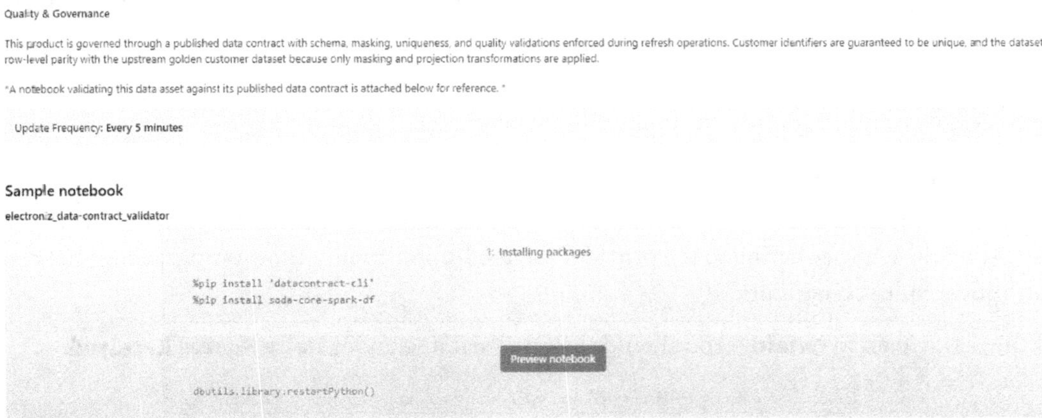

Figure 12.98: Running the data contract validator as a consumer

3. For now, let's click the **Get instance access** button on the top right.

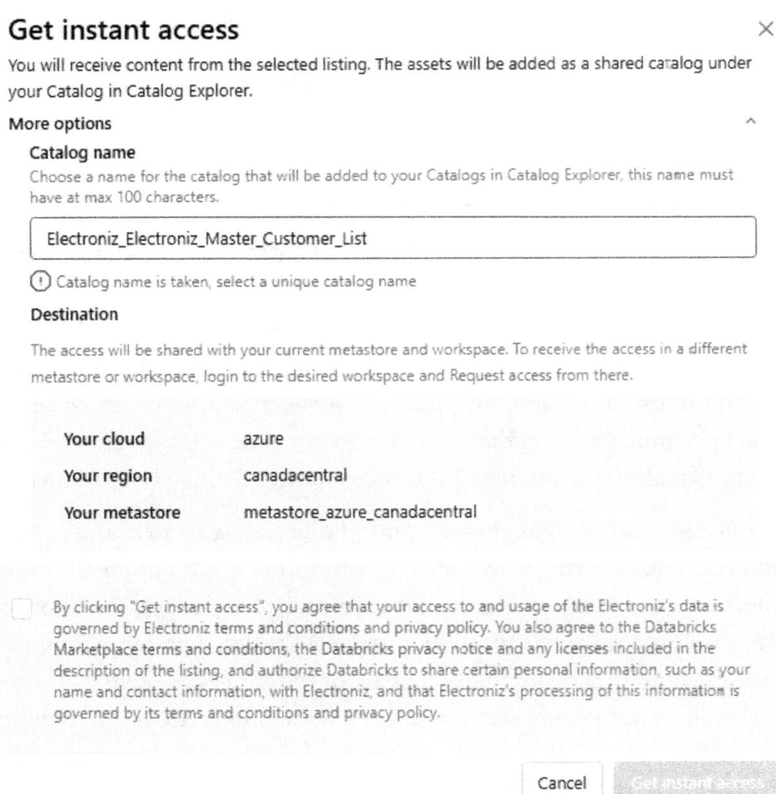

Figure 12.99: Getting instant access to the data product

4. Agree to the terms and conditions set by Electroniz for the fair use of the data product and click on the **Get instance access** button.

At this stage, the consumer may use the data product in accordance with the rules, expectations, and guarantees set out in the data contract.

Consume data as per contract guidelines

Once access is granted, the consumer can query, analyze, and integrate the data into their workflows—while adhering to the provider's agreed-upon quality expectations, usage policies, and governance constraints.

1. Navigate to **Catalog**. You should see a new catalog under **Delta Shares Received**.

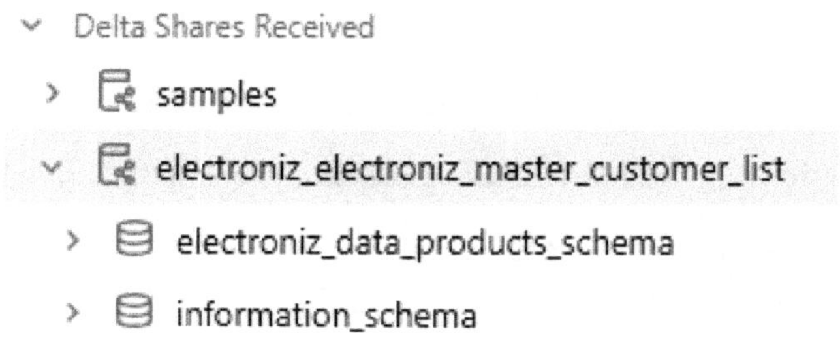

Figure 12.100: Accessing the new catalog for the data product

2. Click on **electroniz_data_products_schema** > **electroniz_product_golden_record_customers**. Click on **Sample Data**. You should now be able to view the table details and sample data.

At this stage, the consumer can begin using the data product within their analytical workflows, dashboards, or downstream processes—so long as all usage complies with the agreed-upon terms and conditions. This marks the point where the data product transitions from evaluation to active consumption, enabling the consumer to integrate it into their work while respecting the governance, quality expectations, and usage policies defined in the data contract.

This end-to-end workflow highlights the central role of data owners and data stewards in governing access and ensuring responsible consumption of data products. From publishing accurate metadata and maintaining the data contract, to reviewing and approving access requests, to enabling consumers to validate and use the data in a compliant manner, these roles provide the human accountability that keeps the data ecosystem trustworthy and well-managed. Their oversight ensures that every consumer interaction—from discovery to validation to active use—aligns with organizational policies, quality expectations, and the agreed-upon terms of the data contract.

Data governance maturity roadmap

Organizations typically evolve their data governance capabilities through a structured maturity roadmap, gradually layering more advanced controls as their data estate and regulatory obligations grow. Figure 12.100 below provides a recommended roadmap for achieving maturity in data governance.

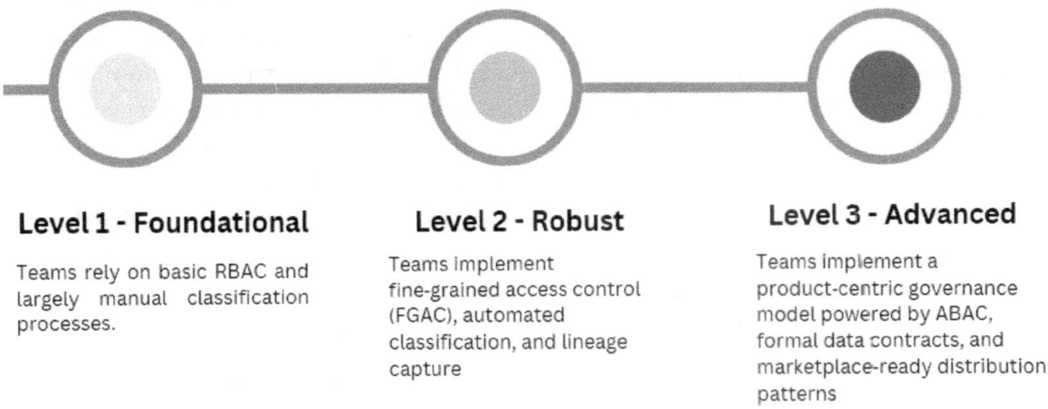

Figure 12.101: Recommended data governance maturity roadmap

- At **Level 1**, teams rely on basic RBAC and largely manual classification processes—sufficient for foundational access control but limited in scalability and consistency.
- At **Level 2**, organizations introduce a more robust governance posture with FGAC, automated classification, and lineage capture, enabling policy enforcement at a more granular level and improving auditability across domains.
- At **Level 3**, organizations reach an advanced, product-centric governance model powered by ABAC, formal data contracts, and Marketplace-ready distribution patterns, allowing them to operationalize trust, automate entitlement decisions, and confidently share governed data products internally and externally.

As organizations advance and their data environment becomes more sophisticated, this roadmap provides a structured path for adopting each level in alignment with their evolving governance requirements.

Summary

This chapter presents a comprehensive framework for governing data products, emphasizing the policies, controls, and human roles required to ensure data is trustworthy, compliant, and used responsibly across the enterprise. It explores how data access policies define who can use which data and under what conditions, while data privacy and regulatory compliance standards safeguard sensitive information and ensure adherence to laws such as GDPR and HIPAA. Data classification policies establish consistent rules for labeling and handling data based on sensitivity, and data lineage tracking policies provide transparency into how data flows, transforms, and is consumed. The chapter also covers data lifecycle management policies governing how data is created, maintained, archived, and retired, as well as data quality standards that ensure accuracy, completeness, and reliability. Underpinning all these controls is the discipline of data stewardship, where data owners and stewards provide the human accountability needed to enforce policies, maintain metadata, oversee access, and uphold the integrity of every data product throughout its lifecycle.

As we reach the end of this book, it's remarkable to look back on how far we've traveled together. Over the past twelve chapters, we followed the journey of data—one filled with twists, challenges, and moments of discovery. We began with the fundamentals of collecting and storing data, then progressed through curating, refining, and aggregating it across the layers of the Lakehouse. Along the way, we explored how to design, build, monitor, and automate robust data pipelines, and we confronted the real-world obstacles data engineers face, offering practical guidance for overcoming them. It has been a demanding journey at times, but ultimately a rewarding one—because by the end, we not only mastered the technical steps, but also gained a deeper appreciation for the craft and discipline required to turn raw data into reliable, governed, high-value data products.

Every byte of data carries its own story, and I'm confident that we've told that story with accuracy, security, and purpose.

Get this book's PDF version and more

Scan the QR code (or go to `packtpub.com/unlock`). Search for this book by name, confirm the edition, and then follow the steps on the page.

UNLOCK NOW

Note: Keep your invoice handy. Purchases made directly from Packt don't require an invoice.

13

Unlock Access to the Code Bundle and the PDF Version

Your copy of this book includes the following exclusive benefits:

Complete Code Bundle

Download the full source code for this book's examples and projects.

DRM-Free PDF Version

Download DRM-free PDF and ePub copies of this book.

7-Day Packt Library Access

Get 7-day unlimited access to 8,000+ books and videos. No credit card required.

Available for first-time Packt+ trial users only.

Next-Gen Reader Access

Read this book on Packt Reader with progress sync, dark mode and note-taking.

Follow this guide to unlock them. The process takes only a few minutes and only needs to be completed once.

Unlock this book's free benefits in three easy steps

Step 1

Have your purchase invoice ready for *step 3*. If you have a physical copy, scan it using your phone and save it as a PDF, JPG, or PNG.

For more help on finding your invoice, visit `https://www.packtpub.com/unlock-benefits/help`.

> Note
>
> **Note**: If you bought this book directly from the Packt website, no invoice is required. After *step 2*, you can access your exclusive content right away.

Step 2

Scan the QR code or go to `packtpub.com/unlock`.

On the page that opens (similar to *Figure 13.1* on desktop), search for this book by name and select the correct edition.

Figure 13.1: Packt unlock landing page on desktop

Step 3

After selecting the book, sign in to your Packt account or create one for free. Then, upload your invoice (PDF, PNG, or JPG, up to 10 MB). Follow the on-screen instructions to finish the process.

Need help?

If you get stuck and need help, visit `https://www.packtpub.com/unlock-benefits/help` for a detailed FAQ on how to find your invoice and more. This QR code will take you to the help page.

> Note
>
> **Note**: If you are still facing issues, reach out to `customercare@packt.com`.

Other Books You May Enjoy

If you enjoyed this book, you may be interested in these other books by Packt:

Engineering Lakehouses with Open Table Formats

Dipankar Mazumdar, Vinoth Govindarajan

ISBN: 978-1-83620-723-8

- Explore lakehouse fundamentals, such as table formats, file formats, compute engines, and catalogs
- Gain a complete understanding of data lifecycle management in lakehouses
- Learn how to systematically evaluate and choose the right lakehouse table format
- Optimize performance with sorting, clustering, and indexing techniques
- Use the open table format data with ML frameworks like TensorFlow and MLflow
- Interoperate across different table formats with Apache XTable and UniForm
- Secure your lakehouse with access controls and ensure regulatory compliance

Data Engineering with Azure Databricks

Dmitry Foshin, Dmitry Anoshin, Tonya Chernyshova, Sergii Volodarskyi

ISBN: 978-1-80610-637-0

- Set up a full-featured Azure Databricks environment
- Implement batch and streaming ingestion using Auto Loader
- Optimize Spark jobs with partitioning and caching
- Build real-time pipelines with structured streaming and DLT
- Manage data governance using Unity Catalog
- Orchestrate production workflows with jobs and ADF
- Apply CI/CD best practices with Azure DevOps and Git
- Secure data with RBAC, encryption, and compliance standards
- Use MLflow and Feature Store for ML pipelines
- Build generative AI applications in Databricks

Packt is searching for authors like you

If you're interested in becoming an author for Packt, please visit `authors.packt.com` and apply today. We have worked with thousands of developers and tech professionals, just like you, to help them share their insight with the global tech community. You can make a general application, apply for a specific hot topic that we are recruiting an author for, or submit your own idea.

Share your thoughts

Now you've finished *Building Trusted Data Platforms with Azure Databricks and GenAI*, we'd love to hear your thoughts! Scan the QR code below to go straight to the Amazon review page for this book and share your feedback or leave a review on the site that you purchased it from.

`https://packt.link/r/1806679779`

Your review is important to us and the tech community and will help us make sure we're delivering excellent quality content.

Index

E

L

M

N

O

P

R

V

W

Y

Z

www.ingramcontent.com/pod-product-compliance
Lightning Source LLC
LaVergne TN
LVHW060008210926
848481LV00013B/3671
9781806679775